DATE DUE

APR 5 2000			
APR	5 2000		
GAYLORD			PRINTED IN U.S.A.

DEVELOPMENTAL PSYCHOLOGY:
AN ADVANCED TEXTBOOK

DEVELOPMENTAL PSYCHOLOGY:
AN ADVANCED TEXTBOOK

Edited by

Marc H. Bornstein
New York University

Michael E. Lamb
University of Utah

LEA LAWRENCE ERLBAUM ASSOCIATES, PUBLISHERS
1984 Hillsdale, New Jersey London

Copyright © 1984 by Lawrence Erlbaum Associates, Inc.
    All rights reserved. No part of this book may be reproduced in
    any form, by photostat, microform, retrieval system, or any other
    means, without the prior written permission of the publisher.

Lawrence Erlbaum Associates, Inc., Publishers
365 Broadway
Hillsdale, New Jersey 07642

Library of Congress Cataloging in Publication Data
Main entry under title:

Developmental psychology.

   Bibliography: p.
   Includes indexes.
   1. Developmental psychology—Addresses, essays,
lectures.   I. Bornstein, Marc H.   II. Lamb, Michael E.

BF713.5.D48   1984   155   84-10214
ISBN 0-89859-376-X

Printed in the United States of America
10   9   8   7   6   5   4   3

Contents

v

List of Contributors

Thomas M. Achenbach
Research Coordinator
Child, Adolescent, Family and
    Community Psychiatry
University of Vermont
    College of Medicine
1 South Prospect
Burlington, VT 05405

Paul B. Baltes
Max Planck Institute for
    Human Development and Education
94 Lentzeallee
D 1000 Berlin 33
WEST GERMANY

Marc H. Bornstein
Department of Psychology
New York University
6 Washington Place—Room 1065
New York, New York 10003

Roger A. Dixon
Max Planck Institute for
    Human Development and Education
94 Lentzeallee
1000 Berlin 33
WEST GERMANY

Shari Ellis
Department of Psychology
University of Utah
Salt Lake City, UT 84112

Matia Finn
Department of Psychology
Yale University
Box 11A Yale Station
New Haven, CT 06520

Mary Gauvin
Department of Psychology
University of Utah
Salt Lake City, UT 84112

Lila R. Gleitman
Department of Psychology
University of Pennsylvania
3815 Wallnut St.
Philadelphia, PA 19104

Martin L. Hoffman
Department of Psychology
3433 Mason Hall
University of Michigan
Ann Arbor, MI 48109

Deanna Kuhn
Department of Psychology
Box 119
Teachers College
Columbia University
New York, NY 10027

Michael E. Lamb
Department of Psychology
University of Utah
Salt Lake City, UT 84112

Richard M. Lerner
Department of Individual and
    Family Studies
S-110 Human Development
    Building
Pennsylvania State University
University Park, PA 16802

Charlotte J. Patterson
Department of Psychology
University of Virginia
Charlottesville, VA 22901

Hayne W. Reese
Department of Psychology
West Virginia University
P.O. Box 6040
Morgantown, WV 26506-6040

Barbara Rogoff
Department of Psychology
University of Utah
Salt Lake City, UT 84112

Diane N. Ruble
Department of Psychology
New York University
6 Washington Place, Room 769
New York, NY 10003

Victoria Seitz
Department of Psychology
Yale University
P.O. Box 11A Yale Station
New Haven, CT 06520

Eric Wanner
The Sloan Foundation
630 Fifth Ave.
New York City, NY 10111

Edward F. Zigler
Department of Psychology
Yale University
Box 11A Yale Station
New Haven, CT 06520

Preface

Developmental psychology is a unique, comprehensive, and important aspect of psychology for at least three reasons. First, developmental psychologists adopt a vital perspective on psychological theory and research. When psychologists conduct experiments in perception, investigate language, or study personality, they usually concentrate on perception, language, or personality in individuals of a particular age, be they children, college students, or the elderly, and in so doing may gain important knowledge about perception, language, or personality. To study psychological phenomena at only one point in the life cycle, however, is to limit knowledge about those phenomena by failing to consider the continuity or change in psychological phenomena that are the province of developmental psychology. Indeed, it could be arqued that when we undertake the psychological study of any phenomenon, we must — wittingly or unwittingly — do so in a developmental context. The chapters in this volume on substantive areas of psychology, like perception, cognition, and language, by Bornstein, Kuhn, and Gleitman and Wanner, and those on personality and social psychology by Lamb, Hoffman, Ruble, Patterson, and Achenbach, all demonstrate that the developmental perspective transcends and enriches any focus on particular points in the life span. One purpose of this volume, then, is to provide the inescapable and valuable developmental perspective on all substantive areas in psychology.

Second, developmental psychology is also a major sub-discipline in its own right. It has its own history and systems, as Dixon and Lerner point out, its own methodologies, as Seitz shows, and its own perspectives, as both Baltes and Reese and Rogoff, Gauvain, and Ellis demonstrate. If studying psychology comprehensively involves attending to developmental psychology, then there are systems, methodologies, and perspectives to be learned, and a second purpose of this volume is to clarify those systems, methodologies, and perspectives for the would-be student of psychology.

Third, the many aspects of developmental psychology have obvious and immediate relevance in applied issues and problems. Each of the chapters in this book illustrates the relevance of developmental psychology through reviews of the history, theory, and substance of the subdiscipline. In addition, questions about application and universality are specifically emphasized in chapters by Zigler and Finn and by Rogoff, Gauvain, and Ellis.

In summary, developmental psychology provides a perspective that bears on all substantive phenomena in psychology, that applies across the life span, that has its own internal value, and that has manifest relevance to everyday life. It is for these reasons that we, the editors, have taken up the study of developmental psychology and have organized this introduction to developmental psychology for the advanced student of psychology.

This volume meets a need for texts in this area that can be used at the advanced undergraduate and introductory graduate levels. To our knowledge, there is currently no other work available to the instructors of such courses. Sadly, it is not possible today for any one or two individuals to convey, with proper sensitivity, the breadth of contemporary developmental psychology at this level. For that reason we invited several experts to prepare original, comprehensive, and topical treatments of the major areas of developmental psychology. We then organized and edited these chapters, with their cooperation and good-will, into a single coherent volume.

Developmental Psychology has many purposes. We hope that readers will obtain a new perspective on psychology, a greater appreciation of the varied phenomena that constitute psychology, and a fundamental grounding in developmental psychology itself.

January 1984

Marc H. Bornstein
New York City

Michael E. Lamb
Salt Lake City

1 A History of Systems in Developmental Psychology

Roger A. Dixon
Max Planck Institute for
Human Development and Education

Richard M. Lerner
The Pennsylvania State University

INTRODUCTION

A student beginning the advanced study of developmental psychology is probably all too aware of the vast array of theories, methods, and ideas present in the field. Such an array may suggest a picture of formidable complexity, or even anarchy. Closer inspection, however, reveals that there are some identifiable clusters of these theories, methods, and ideas and that, although these clusters differ in important ways, they also share certain foci, themes, and—most important for the purposes of this chapter—their historical roots. Accordingly, we examine some of the key historical bases of the major modern systems of developmental psychology. In considering this history we trace early connections among what have evolved into major theoretical orientations toward development; in addition, we specify some major similarities and differences in these approaches to understanding development. By referring to the field's history, we are able to understand much of the contemporary scene in developmental psychology.

Today there are two major conceptual features in developmental psychology that can be identified by an analysis of the field's history. First, more than ever (Lerner, 1983), developmental psychologists are now concerned with the explanation of developmental change (i.e., with the specification of the causes or antecedents of development) as opposed to just the description of development (i.e., the depiction or representation of change). Second, and based on the recognition that one's explanation of development derives from one's theory of development, developmental psychologists have recently begun to attend to one

1

or more of the several viable theories or systems of interpretation available (e.g., Baldwin, 1980; Lerner, 1976). Much current, exemplary developmental research is aimed at theory or model testing as opposed to the mere generation of developmental norms.

What led to these current emphases? To begin with, we trace some of the recent events that have led to today's emphasis on theory and explanation. Next, we find that, although the current emphasis on theory has been associated with the recognition of the range of systems that may be used to account for development, there has also been a concern with explaining the presence of several viable theories of development. In other words, why is there more than one theory of development? Are these mutually compatible or do they compete in some way with one another? Although we shall see that the answers to such questions depend on philosophical differences among psychologists, we shall also see that another answer exists. Distinct in many important ways, today's major theoretical systems can be linked historically to a common intellectual "source": Nineteenth century evolutionary thinking and, in particular, the ideas of Charles Darwin. Thus, one explanation for the presence of distinct theories of development is that different scientists devised their accounts of development by emphasizing different aspects of such prominent accounts of historical change as Darwin's theory of evolution (White, 1968; Wohlwill, 1973). We return to this point later in the chapter.

In this chapter we discuss the historical bases of two key conceptual features of contemporary developmental psychology—the emphasis on explanation and the presence of, and concern with, several different theories of development. Let us turn to the bases of the first feature.

Some Bases of the Contemporary Concern with the Explanation of Development

In the early decades of this century, and continuing through at least the beginning years of the 1940s, developmental psychology was primarily a descriptive, normative discipline. Prototypic of this descriptive emphasis was the research associated with the work of Arnold Gesell (1880–1961). Gesell's (1929, 1931, 1934, 1946, 1954) work was based on the theory that maturationally-based changes unfolded independent of learning, and his research stressed the need for the careful and systematic cataloging of growth norms. His work provided the field with useful information about the expected sequence for, and normative times of, the emergence of numerous physical and mental developments in infants and children. Conceptually, Gesell's work is related to one side of what has been a continuing debate in the history of developmental psychology: the nature–nurture controversy. This controversy pertains to a debate about where the sources of development lie, e.g., in inborn (or hereditary) mechanisms or in acquired (or learned) processes. By stressing that maturation rather than learning was the prime impetus for developmental change, Gesell (1929) was taking a nature, as opposed to a nurture, stance. Historically, other terms associated with the nature position are preformationism, nativism, and innateness, and terms associated with the nurture position are learning, conditioning, experience, and socialization.

It is important to recognize that differences in views of the source of development are associated with differences regarding the nature–nurture issue because, although Gesell's (1929, 1931, 1934) work was doing much to forge the character of this period's developmental psychology as a descriptive and normative field, there was work occurring in other areas of psychology that began to counter Gesell's emphasis (White, 1970). Some experimental psychologists began stressing the applicability of learning principles to the study of child functioning (e.g., Dollard, Doob, Miller, Mowrer, & Sears, 1939; Miller & Dollard, 1941). One consequence of this activity was to provide evidence that nurture-based learning phenomena, as opposed to nature-based maturation phenomena, could account for some features of children's behavior and development. Thus, by offering a different and viable interpretation of children's behavior these learning psychologists began to move the focus in developmental psychology away from a concern with the facts of development per se (e.g., ''What is the age at which an infant sits, stands, walks, or has a two word vocabulary?'') to a concern with the interpretation of those facts (e.g., ''What mechanisms—nature or nurture ones—need to be referred to in order to explain these facts?'').

The movement away from an emphasis on description to one on explanation was furthered in the 1940s by events leading up to and including World War II (Lerner, 1983). Nazi persecution led many Jewish intellectuals to flee Europe, and many sought refuge and a new start for their careers in the United States. Many of these refugees were able to secure positions in American universities and associated institutions, despite the fact that they often brought with them ideas counter to those predominant in the American academic scene (i.e., behaviorism and learning theory). For instance, although Freud himself settled in London (and died there in 1939), many psychoanalytically oriented people, some trained by Freud or his daughter Anna, did come to this country (e.g., Peter Blos and Erik Erikson).

Once America entered the war, and numerous soldiers needed to be tested for psychological as well as physical fitness, the federal government gave universities large amounts of money to train clinical psychologists. This program opened the door for many professionals with psychoanalytic orientations to become faculty members in universities previously dominated by behaviorists (Misiak & Sexton, 1966), because they were the people with backgrounds appropriate for teaching clinical skills. Therefore, one impact of World War II was to encourage such alternative forms of thinking as psychoanalysis in many psychology departments. This resulted in the introduction of a nature-based perspective into some departments where behaviorists were previously in control of the intellectual domain (Gengerelli, 1976). Nevertheless, this orientation represented just one of many different theoretical accounts of human functioning—accounts that stressed either nature or nurture or both nature and nurture as sources of behavior and development—that were now making inroads into American thinking.

Similarly, nativistic ideas about perception and learning, introduced by psychologists who believed in the holistic aspects of behavior, were juxtaposed with behaviorist learning ideas. The gestalt (meaning "totality") views represented by these Europeans (people like Max Wertheimer, Kurt Koffka, Wolfgang Kohler, Kurt Goldstein, and Kurt Lewin, all of whom were active during the first four or five decades of this century) were shown to be pertinent also to areas of concern such as brain functioning, group dynamics, and social problems (Sears, 1975). Ideas explicitly relevant to development were also introduced. For example, Heinz Werner (1948) presented to Americans a view of development that involved continual nature–nurture interactions. Furthermore, the work of the Swiss, Jean Piaget, who proposed a view of cognitive development emphasizing its naturational (nature) components (Piaget, 1923), and who used "clinical," nonexperimental methods, became increasingly accepted in American circles.

The outcome of these changes in ideas about development, fostered by events relating to the importation of European perspectives, was to provide a pluralism of ideas about development. Although there had always been some cross-fertilization, now there were more numerous interpretations of behavior and development, interpretations that were based on substantially different conceptions of the source of human behavior and development. Any given behavior, then, could be explained by a number of different theories, and these various theories were advanced by respected advocates often working in the same academic contexts (Gengerelli, 1976). Thus, at least in American departments of psychology, developmentalists were confronted with alternative perspectives. We suggest that such fundamental differences in approaches to and interpretations of behavior may have led to more serious efforts to articulate one position over another. In this way, the pluralistic situation in American academia may have fostered or strengthened interest in issues surrounding the explanation of human development. That is, the simultaneous presentation of diverse interpretations further promoted a move away from a mere focus on description and toward a more serious concern with theoretical interpretations of development. This focus on explanation continued in the post-World War II era, in the late 1950s and 1960s.

In a review of the history of developmental science, Bronfenbrenner (1963) notes that from the 1930s to the early 1960s there was a continuing shift away from studies involving the mere collection of data toward research concerned with abstract processes and constructs. Some books and essays published during this period epitomized this trend by calling for the study of developmental processes and mechanisms (e.g., Harris, 1956, 1957; McCandless & Spiker, 1956; Spiker & McCandless, 1954). Accordingly, describing the status of the field in 1963, Bronfenbrenner said that "first and foremost, the gathering of data for data's sake seems to have lost in favor. The major concern in today's developmental research is clearly with inferred processes and constructs'' (p. 527).

Similarly, in a review almost a decade later, Looft (1972) found a continuation of the trends noted by Bronfenbrenner. Looft's review, like Bronfenbrenner's, was based on an analysis of major handbooks of developmental psychology published from the 1930s to the time of the review (1972). Each handbook represented a reflection of the current content, emphasis, and concerns of the field. Looft found that in the first handbook (Murchison, 1931) developmental psychology was largely descriptive. Consistent with our analysis and with Bronfenbrenner's conclusion, Looft saw workers devoting their time essentially to the collection of norms. However, a shift toward more general, integrative concerns was seen by 1946 (after World War II), and the trend continued through 1963 (Bronfenbrenner, 1963) to 1972 (Looft, 1972). As a case in point we may note that the editor of a 1970 handbook (Mussen, 1970) points out: ''The major contemporary empirical and theoretical emphases in the field of developmental psychology, however, seem to be on *explanations* of the psychological changes that occur, the mechanisms and processes accounting for growth and development'' (p. vii).

It may be seen, then, that interest came to be focused on a variety of theories, on explanations, and on processes of development. Such concerns led to the recognition that there is not just one way (one theory) to follow in attempting to put the facts (the descriptions) of development together. Rather, a pluralistic approach is needed. When followed, it may indicate that more descriptions are necessary. Thus, theoretical concerns guide descriptive endeavors. One gathers facts because one knows they will have a meaning within a particular theory. Moreover, since theory-guided research can proceed from any theoretical base, the data generated must be evaluated in terms of their use in advancing an understanding of change processes.

In the 1970s this trend toward the explication of developmental processes continued in a rather more abstract way. In particular, the theoretical and metatheoretical bases upon which individual development is studied and interpreted itself became a focus of investigation (e.g., Overton & Reese, 1973; Reese & Overton, 1970). Following the work of such philosophers as Kuhn (1970) and Pepper (1942), Reese and Overton (1970; Overton & Reese, 1973, 1981) identified two major philosophical models that provide the basis for many extant assumptions about human development. These models provided a set of assumptions, or metatheoretical ideas, about human nature and so influenced lower order, theoretical and methodological statements.

The two models discussed by Reese and Overton (1970) were termed ''organicism'' and ''mechanism.'' Although we discuss these two metatheories in greater detail later, suffice it to say here that the organismic position stresses the qualitative features of developmental change and the active contribution of the organism's processes in these changes. The theories of Piaget (e.g., 1970) and to some extent of Freud (e.g., 1954) are examples of such organismically oriented ideas. In contrast, the mechanistic position stresses quantitative change and the active contribution of processes lying outside the primary control of the organism (e.g., in the external stimulus environment) as the major source of development. The behavioral, functional analysis theories of Bijou (1976) and of Bijou and Baer (1961) are major examples of such mechanistically oriented ideas.

Again, on the basis of some well-known philosophical ideas, discussions occurred concerning the "family of theories" associated with each model (Reese & Overton, 1970). For instance, as we noted above, there are at least two types of organismically oriented theories, those of Freud and those of Piaget. Although there are differences among family members (Freud emphasizes emotional development, and Piaget emphasizes cognitive development), there is greater similarity among the theories within a family (e.g., the common stress on the qualitative, stage-like nature of development) than there is between theories associated with different families (e.g., mechanistically oriented theories would deny the importance, indeed the reality, of qualitatively different stages). Due to the philosophically-based differences between families of theories derived from the organismic and the mechanistic models, the period since the early 1970s has involved several discussions about the different stances regarding an array of key conceptual issues of development; for example, the nature and nurture bases of development (Lehrman, 1970; Lerner, 1976, 1978; Overton, 1973), the quality, openness, and continuity of change (Brim & Kagan, 1980; Looft, 1973), appropriate methods for studying development (Baltes, Reese, & Nesselroade, 1977; Nesselroade & Baltes, 1979), and ultimately, the alternative truth criteria for establishing the "facts" of development (Overton & Reese, 1973; Reese and Overton, 1970).

This awareness of the philosophical bases of developmental theory, method, and data contributed to the consideration of still other models appropriate to the study of psychological development. In part, this consideration developed as a consequence of interest in integrating assumptions associated with theories derived from organismic and mechanistic models (Looft, 1973). For instance, Riegel (1973, 1975, 1976) attempted to apply an historical model of development that seemed to include some features of organicism (e.g., active organism) and some features of mechanism (e.g., active environment). However, interest in continual, reciprocal relations between an active organism and its active context (and not in either element per se) and the concern with these relations as they existed on all phenomenal levels of analysis also formed a basis for proposing so-called dialectical (Riegel, 1975, 1976), transactional (Sameroff, 1975), relational (Looft, 1973), or dynamic interactional (Lerner, 1976, 1978, 1979) conceptions of human development.

By the end of the 1970s, then, developmental psychology had become a field marked not by one, but by several explanatory theories of human development.

This theoretical pluralism, or multiplicity of reasonable theoretical alternatives, continues to exist today (Dixon & Nesselroade, 1983). An interesting paradox exists, however, that leads us to see both similarities and differences among the major theoretical systems existing in developmental psychology today. Although these systems differ in the superordinate philosophical models to which they adhere, as well as in their respective definitions of development, variables and problems of interest, and methods of research, to a great extent all share a common intellectual heritage: All have been influenced by Charles Darwin's theory of evolution.

In this chapter, we argue that Darwinism provided an intellectual basis for five different theoretical systems in developmental psychology. First, the influence of Darwinian evolutionary thought on the *organismic model* may be traced from the work of (early) G. Stanley Hall, James Mark Baldwin, and Pierre Janet, to the continuously influential work of Jean Piaget and Heinz Werner. Second, the related *psychoanalytic model* developed in a less direct fashion from the work of Sigmund Freud and Carl Jung to that of Erik Erikson. Third, Wilhelm Preyer, Sir Francis Galton, as well as (later) G. S. Hall and John B. Watson were the early contributors to the development of the *mechanistic model.* Two less thoroughly developed models will also be described. *Contextualism* derived from the turn-of-the-century American pragmatic philosophers, most notably William James, Charles Sanders Peirce, John Dewey, and G. H. Mead. Finally, the *dialectical model,* influenced by G. W. F. Hegel and Karl Marx, was later developed more specifically by Lev S. Vygotsky and Klaus F. Riegel. Thus, one way in which we can understand the present meaning of each of the different theoretical systems in developmental psychology is to appreciate their relatively common intellectual heritage and the historical trajectories they followed in developing away from one another. To understand Darwin's influence on developmental psychology it is useful first to consider the historical setting within which Darwin developed his theory.

DARWINISM AND THE EMERGENCE OF DEVELOPMENTAL PSYCHOLOGY

Early Work in the Concept of Development

It is impossible to understand either the genesis or the eventual impact of Darwin's theory without understanding the interest among eighteenth and nineteenth century intellectuals in the topic of *history,* and the consequent historical nature of Darwinism (Vidal, Buscaglia, & Vonèche, 1983). In his intellectual history of the nineteenth century, Mandelbaum (1971) observes:

> It is generally agreed that one of the most distinctive features of nineteenth-century thought was the widespread interest evinced in history. The manifestations of this interest are not only to be found in the growth and diversification of professional

historical scholarship, but in the tendency to view all of reality, and all of man's achievements, in terms of the category of development. (p. 41)

The category of development implies the method of *historicism;* that is, an adequate understanding of any phenomenon (biological or philosophical) requires that it be considered in terms of its position in the present situation and its role in a continuous developmental or historical process. As Mandelbaum (1971) describes it, the concern is not with the "nature of the event itself, [but] . . . with its place in some process of change" (p. 46). Events have no autonomous existence (and, especially, no independent meaning) outside of the role they play in the stream of history. In the human sciences, where the events of concern are sociohistorical in nature (e.g., wars and plagues), the province of general human history is indicated; where the events are of an individual nature (e.g., the onset of logical thinking, puberty, or marriage), the province of individual human history, or developmental psychology, is implied.

In general, during the late eighteenth and early nineteenth centuries, the concept of development received attention on two fronts, both of which helped to influence the emergence of developmental psychology. The thrust of the interest in the idea of development (and individual development in particular) was an ongoing attempt by researchers in a variety of disciplines to understand humankind in a temporal and historical context. On the philosophical front, this involved a dynamic, dialectical theory of history, such as the ideal philosophy of G. W. F. Hegel (1770–1831) and the material philosophy of Karl Marx (1818–1883). On the scientific front, the interest in development was manifested in two mutually influential areas of investigation. On the one hand, there were the notions of natural history informed by research in geology; of particular note in this regard was the gradual and developmental method of Sir Charles Lyell (1797–1875). On the other hand, there were various biological theories of evolution, especially those of Jean Baptiste de Lamarck (1744–1829), Charles Darwin (1809–1882), and Herbert Spencer (1820–1903).

Many early efforts to understand human development did not result in sustained developmental psychologies. Many such efforts derived primarily from philosophical, literary, or theological domains: From Aristotle (384 B.C.–322 B.C.) through St. Augustine (354–430) to William Shakespeare (1564–1616) and Jean-Jacques Rousseau (1712–1778), many important thinkers wrote about the ages or stages of human life, often speculating on their unique needs and purposes (Dennis, 1972). It was not until the eighteenth and the early nineteenth century, however, that these theoretical perspectives were attached to empirical investigations.

Reinert (1979; see also Groffmann, 1970) views the nineteenth century as the formative period in the emergence of developmental psychology. In support of this argument, three major advances are noted: (1) the appearance of the first psychological diary of the growth of a young child by Dietrich Tiedemann

(1748–1803); (2) Friedrich August Carus' (1770–1808) efforts to develop a comprehensive, general age-oriented science; and (3) Adolphe Quetelet's (1796–1874) highly advanced methods to disentangle the multiple influences on the course of human development. Johann Nikolas Tetens (1736–1807), who argued that only through natural science could one arrive at general laws regarding human development from birth to death, is also worthy of note. In the same vein, Cairns and Ornstein (1979) call the subsequent period 1880–1912 the "era of discovery" in developmental psychology. Darwin's (1877) "Biographical Sketch of an Infant" was one of the earliest attempts at careful, observational ontogenetic study. Many other baby biographies appeared around the turn of the century (e.g., Braunshvig & Braunshvig, 1913; Champneys, 1881; Hall, 1891; Moore, 1896; Perez, 1878; Prior, 1895; Shinn, 1893–1899, 1900; Simpson, 1893; Sully, 1903). Shinn's (1893–1899, 1900) work with her niece was perhaps especially well known, for comparisons with other, similar research were made. This biographically oriented activity continued through the 1930s (Bühler, 1930; Dennis, 1949, 1951).

Peters (1965) refers to two general categories of influence in the emergence of developmental psychology in the nineteenth century. The first, a quite practical social influence, consisted of pressure applied by educational administrators and social planners concerned with the large-scale education of a growing population of children. Such a development served to focus institutional attention on the practical issues of ontogenesis (Sears, 1975). The second category of influence was the theory of evolution, insofar as it focused some attention on the scientific analysis of progress and suggested a certain measure of continuity, both between human and animal, and (significantly for developmental psychology) between adult and child.

Darwin and the Theory of Evolution

Charles Darwin was perhaps the exemplary component of the emergence of historicism in the nineteenth century, but even he was not without intellectual antecedents (Eiseley, 1958). Although it is certainly difficult to disentangle his multiple intellectual influences, for the sake of clarity they may be portrayed as deriving from two interrelated strands. On the one hand, it has been shown that Darwin gathered from his own family, his life history, and his early cultural context much of the intellectual disposition that is apparently necessary to effect a massive scientific revolution and to effect the precise kind of revolution with which he was associated (Gillespie, 1979; Gruber, 1974; Manier, 1978). On the other hand, it is quite clear that Darwin possessed an identifiable intellectual lineage that stemmed from more formal or academic sources. For example, it is well known that Darwin's views about evolution were influenced by the English geologist Sir Charles Lyell (1797–1875), who viewed natural phenomena from a historical and developmental perspective.

Thus, while we argue in this chapter that Darwin's model of nature served as a conceptual impetus from which early and later psychologists derived their models of human development, Vidal et al. (1983) point out that, in turn, Darwin's theorizing was influenced by his knowledge of extant models of human functioning:

> The first impact of Charles Darwin's theory of evolution on culture was to consolidate the idea of the naturalness of man considered as a species among others. In turn, however, human activity served as a model for Darwinian nature . . . Darwin's program of readings outside natural history, which included his rediscovery of Thomas Malthus's *Essay on Population* was equally fundamental: models *of* man provided models *for* nature. (p. 81)

Indeed, Vidal et al. (1983, p. 82) go on to point out that, "From his notebooks, it is clear that Darwin made a conscious and explicit effort to justify his biological thought on philosophical–psychological grounds." Thus, what has occurred historically is a bi-directional relation between Darwin's theory and the philosophical and theoretical issues that have shaped developmental psychology. Darwin developed his theory in the context of, and influenced by, the then extant philosophical models and scientific theories of human activity and development. His theory, once formulated, then "fed back" to this philosophical–scientific arena, shaping then (and through today) the philosophical and theoretical bases of the study of developmental psychology.

The key features of Darwin's theory of evolution deserve specific attention. Darwin proposed a theory of evolution in which species development occurs in gradual, continual, and adaptive steps. In other words, Darwin (1859) believed that new species emerge gradually over long periods of time; thus, there is a continuous chain of being from our now extinct ancestors to us, a chain built on the concepts of natural selection and survival of the fittest. Briefly, let us explain this theory by noting the meaning of these key ideas.

The environment places demands on the members of a given species. In effect, it selects individuals that possess some characteristic contributing, for example, to the successful gathering of available nourishment. If the individual has that characteristic, it will fit in with its environment, obtain nourishment, and survive. If not, it will either move to another ecological setting or die. The weakest, or least adaptable, members of the species are unable to reach maturity and mate (Morgan, 1902). Thus, the natural setting determines which characteristics of the organism will lead to survival and which ones will not. This action of the natural environment, selecting organisms for survival, is termed *natural selection* (Loewenberg, 1957; Mayr, 1977).

Hence, Darwin proposed the idea of *survival of the fittest*. Organisms that possess characteristics that fit the survival requirements for a particular environmental setting will "survive" in the sense of successfully passing on their genes. In other words, certain characteristics in certain settings have fundamental biological significance—they allow the organism to survive. Characteristics that meet the demands of the environment (and so allow survival) are adaptive, or functional, characteristics.

In an evolutionary sense, something is functional if it is adaptive; that is, if it aids survival. Thus, the structure of an organism (its physical makeup, its constitution, its morphological or bodily characteristics) may be functional. However, although Darwin emphasized the function of physical structures of species in 1859, he later (Darwin, 1872) pointed out that behavior, too, had survival value. Showing the emotion of fear when a dangerous bear approaches and being able to learn to avoid certain stimuli (e.g., poisonous snakes) and to approach others (e.g., food) are examples of behaviors that, if shown, would be adaptive; they would further our chances for survival.

Thus, mental activity and behavior also have a function (Stout & Baldwin, 1902). The function of behavior became the focus of much social scientific concern. This concern was reflected not only in the ideas of those interested in the phylogeny of behavior; additionally, the idea was promoted that those behavior changes characterizing ontogeny could be understood on the basis of adaptation. The adaptive role of behavior thus became a concern providing a basis for all American psychology (White, 1968) and has played a major part in the ideas of theorists as diverse as Hall (1904), Freud (1954), Piaget (1950), Erikson (1959), and Skinner (1938, 1950).

Peters (1965) indicates that, prior to Darwin, emphasis was placed on differences between human and animal on the one hand, and adult and child on the other. After Darwin's argument for continuity in the former case, emphasis in human study shifted to the detection and consideration of similarities between adult and child. Peters (1965) summarizes the sentiment of this period: "And if under the influence of theology, men had tended to say before Darwin: 'What a piece of work is man,' they would now tend to say, under the influence of biology: 'How wonderful are children and the beasts of the field' " (p. 732). In his 1871 work, *Descent of Man,* Darwin argued that the predominant social value system of the nineteenth century was in need of significant reorganization. Not only should the social system reflect scientific advance, it should itself advance; that is, it should keep pace with the critical developments in the scientific sector. Thus, an interactional relationship between science and society was proposed. Particularly in the latter half of the nineteenth century, it became clear that science and society were both of a dynamic character and intimately interrelated in their developmental trajectories. Specifically, Darwin argued that since morally and spiritually animals exhibited behavior continuous with that of humans, society should entertain fewer "illusions" about the absolute uniqueness of human beings and that since the relationship between adult and child is also characterized more by similarity than dissimilarity, the absolute, ahistorical view of adults was also called into question (see Richards, 1982).

We now consider how the general impetus provided by Darwin for a developmental psychology led to the theoretical pluralism (i.e., the multiplicity of theories) we find in developmental psychology today.

ROOTS OF CONTEMPORARY THEORIES IN
DEVELOPMENTAL PSYCHOLOGY

To some extent, all extant metatheoretical, and derivative theoretical, views about human development were influenced by, or progressed through, the prism of Darwinian evolutionary thinking. At present there are at least five major models of developmental psychology and, we suggest, these models share this common historical heritage. That is, if an originative figure in developmental psychology exists, one that is historically most common to all modern theories in the discipline, that figure is Charles Darwin (Angell, 1912; Dixon, 1983; Kirkpatrick, 1909; Misiak & Sexton, 1966; White, 1968; Wohlwill, 1973).

However, several important reservations about this proposal should be noted. First, and perhaps foremost, it is apparent that Darwin is by no means the original evolutionist (Ruse, 1979; Toulmin & Goodfield, 1965); it appears, however, that he is the evolutionist with the greatest influence on the emergence of a developmental approach to studying humans. Second, and related to the first reservation, we have seen that there were several "developmental psychologists" antedating Darwin; for the most part, however, these figures were of incidental influence in the emergence of the field of developmental psychology. Third, it is not proposed that Darwin is the single generative figure in developmental psychology; rather, the intellectual climate of historicity—that, as we have seen, both preceded Darwin and gained impetus from him and that, in some ways, was epitomized by him—is the originative intellectual core of developmental psychology. Nor is it proposed that all present versions of developmental psychology embrace a Darwinian evolutionism, for, as we shall see below, this is simply not the case. Nevertheless, in the developmental "tradition" there is a stress on the history of the organism; on the functional, adaptive features of behavioral and mental ontogeny; and on the study of the role of the environment or context in such ontogeny. This is a tradition propagated in part by Darwin, and it is present in all current major systems; as a consequence, their intellectual heritage can, at least indirectly, be traced to Darwin. Indeed, it is this connection between what we see as key features of the developmental tradition—a tradition we believe is identifiable in all the models of development we discuss—and the ideas propagated by Darwin that allows us to argue for his seminal contribution. Finally, we should note that there were, of course, other sources of influence on today's developmental theories and metatheories. These other influences account for many specific features of the different approaches to developmental psychology.

Despite these disclaimers, we should note that other, earlier reviewers have also depicted Darwin as a point of origin for several of the major lines of thought in contemporary developmental psychology (White, 1968; Wohlwill, 1973). However, consistent with our earlier suggestions, White (1968) notes that each of these lines of thought apparently selected something different from the writings of the evolutionist, and it is partly due to this selection that they all developed in different fashions. As White (1968) notes, ''Within 50 years after the publication of Darwin's *The Origin of Species* in 1859, the theory of evolution has crystallized its influence upon developmental psychology not once but several times. As happens with a broad and powerful ideology, different people took different messages from evolutionism and occasionally those messages could come into conflict'' (p. 187). Wohlwill's (1973) views about the originative nature of Darwin's thought are somewhat distinct from those of White (1968), in that Wohlwill stresses not Darwin's influence on developmental theories per se, but the contribution of Darwinian thinking to the development of metatheories.

The first metatheoretical line of thought stimulated by Darwin was the *organismic model*. It developed out of the early work of G. Stanley Hall (1846–1924), and James Mark Baldwin (1861–1934), through Pierre Janet (1859–1947) to Jean Piaget (1896–1980) and Heinz Werner (1890–1964). A second, organismically oriented, line of thought identified by Wohlwill (1973) is the *psychoanalytic;* it stemmed from the work of Sigmund Freud (1856–1939) through Carl Jung (1875–1961) and Erik Erikson (b. 1902). The third metatheoretical line, the *mechanistic model,* developed from Wilhelm Preyer (1841–1897) and Sir Francis Galton (1822–1911) to the works of the later G. Stanley Hall and John B. Watson (1878–1958). In addition, a fourth line of thought, *contextualism,* may also be traced to Darwinism; this line was promoted by William James (1842–1910), Charles Sanders Peirce (1839–1914), John Dewey (1859–1952), and George Herbert Mead (1863–1931), the major figures of pragmatic philosophy. Further, a fifth line will be described that has its principal roots in both the social philosophy (Marx) and the biology (Darwin) of the nineteenth century; it culminates in the *dialectical* model of developmental psychology as it was proposed by Lev S. Vygotsky (1894–1934) and, more recently in America, by Klaus F. Riegel (1925–1977). Although we noted some of the general features of some of these metatheoretical positions earlier, it is useful to treat them in more detail here. The historical lineages presented for each of the models serve only a heuristic purpose; they represent more the flow of ideas since Darwin than the impact of one individual upon another.

Organicism

As described by Pepper (1942; see also Lerner, 1976; Overton & Reese, 1973; Reese and Overton, 1970), the organismic model was patterned after the view of biological growth that prevailed in the preceding century. That is, psychological development was thought to be goal-directed and teleological in character. Developmental change is characterized as qualitative rather than (or, in isolated cases, in addition to) quantitative and is unidirectional and irreversible. Following the emphasis on qualitative changes a stage pattern is often employed, resulting in a conception of development that is discontinuous and universal in sequence and pattern. The organism is seen as relatively active, constructing a relatively passive environment. The major figures in the emergence of this model are thought to be linked as shown in Column A of Figure 1.1.

G. Stanley Hall is the first major figure linking the elaboration of an organismically derived theory with a Darwinian evolutionism. Hall organized the American Psychological Association, became its first president, and started the first American journal of psychology (aptly called *The American Journal of Psychology*), as well as the first scientific journal devoted to human development (first entitled *Pedagogical Seminary,* and then given its present name *The Journal of Genetic Psychology*). Hall (1883) contributed one of the earliest papers on child psychology and also wrote the first text on adolescence (a two volume work, entitled *Adolescence,* 1904), as well as a text on old age (*Senescence,* 1922). The latter is an example of his later mechanistic tendencies (see below).

One of the most prominent and influential psychologists at the turn of the century, Hall had his most specific influence on developmental psychology. Hall saw development from a nativistic (nature, or hereditary) point of view. As such, although not many people (including his students) adopted his specific nature-based theory of development, they did follow his general nature orientation. Consequently, Hall's influence was to direct scientific concern to human development, but to do so from a predominantly nature perspective.

In devising his nature viewpoint, Hall was profoundly influenced by Darwin. In fact, Hall, fancying himself the "Darwin of the mind" (White, 1968), attempted to translate Darwin's phylogenetic evolutionary principles into conceptions relevant to ontogeny. The ideas through which he believed he could connect phylogeny to ontogeny derived from those of the embryologist, Ernst Haeckel (1834–1919). Haeckel believed that an embryo's ontogenetic progression mirrored the phylogenetic history—the evolution—of its species. Thus, when one looks at the changes characterizing an individual member of a species as it progresses across its embryological period, one sees a recapitulation of the evolutionary changes the species went through. In short, Haeckel said that ontogeny recapitulates phylogeny.

Hall applied to postnatal life the recapitulationist idea that Haeckel used for prenatal, embryological development. Arguing that during the years from birth to sexual maturity a person was repeating the history of the species, as had been done prenatally, Hall believed that the postnatal recapitulation was somewhat more limited (Gallatin, 1975). Further, although an ardent evolutionist and a strong proponent of recapitulation theory, and so an exemplar of organismic theories, Hall nevertheless placed considerable emphasis on environmental, especially social, factors in later ontogenesis. That is, at separate points, recapitulation theory and environmental influences were incorporated into Hall's perspective, becoming one that encompassed the life span. In his attempt to extend the work of previous developmentalists beyond childhood, Hall (1904) argued that until adolescence the developing child repeats (through both play and

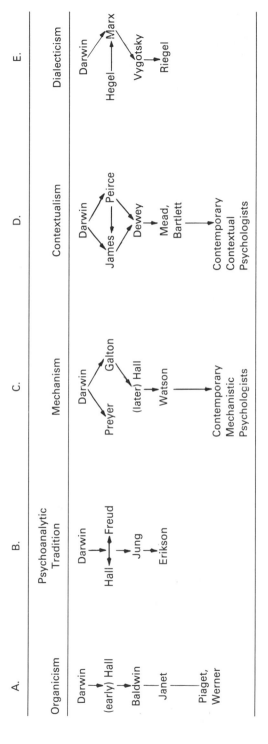

FIG. 1.1. Heuristic scheme representing the Darwinian origins of five metatheoretical traditions in contemporary developmental psychology.

15

fear) the evolution of human society. During adolescence, however, environmental factors increase their developmental significance (McCullers, 1969); this gives the latter part of Hall's ideas a definite mechanistic tone (see below). Indeed, Hall believed that during adolescence genetic changes could be effected by the environment (Charles, 1970).

Like Hall, James Mark Baldwin is difficult to classify in purely organismic terms. There are two major intellectual sources to Baldwin's (1895, 1906) developmental psychology. Fundamentally a Darwinian evolutionist, he was also influenced by British empiricism/associationism (see Baldwin, 1913). The former influence is manifested most positively by Baldwin's devotion to a Darwinian psychology (Baldwin, 1909; Russett, 1976) and, less positively, by his endorsement of recapitulation theory, although some authors suggest that Baldwin managed to avoid a thorough parallelism (Reinert, 1979). The British influence is revealed through his stimulus–response system based on pleasure and pain. Baldwin saw the child as developing from the simple to the more complex, first through an instinctive biological stage and second a plastic or learning stage. The social system, especially the interactions between the child and the system (Cairns & Ornstein, 1979), was a critical feature of ontogenesis.

Although much of Baldwin's work appears to be antithetical to organismic theory, his endorsement of the genetic method (Baldwin, 1930) and leadership, with G. S. Hall, of the genetic psychology movement assures him a place in the history of organicism. (In this period of psychology the term "genetic" was used to refer to the study of origin or genesis; thus, it is roughly synonymous with such terms as developmental and historical.) Moreover, much of his work prefigures the assimilation–accomodation theory of Piaget (Piaget, 1982; Reinert, 1979; Ross & Kerst, 1978) and has been firmly placed in the history of genetic epistemology, the theory of knowledge most appropriate to organismic thinkers (Wozniak, 1982). His speculations on the biological nature of at least early behavioral development often led to criticism from (mechanistic) experimentalists who thought that his questionnaires and experimental studies were not a sufficient basis on which to found a genetic or developmental psychology. In complementary fashion, Baldwin expressed doubt that a mechanistic account would ever succeed.

Rather more isolated from mainstream developmental psychology than either Hall or Baldwin, Pierre Janet developed a historical (i.e., "genetic," again in the developmental, not the hereditary sense) clinical psychology (Mayo, 1952). He viewed the life course as a succession of adaptive moments, each of which could influence the long-range adjustment of the individual (Janet, 1930). An evolutionary concept of psychic tension, together with the genetic method of, for example, Baldwin, informed the study of the development of human action and behavior (Sjövall, 1967). To understand the psychological conditions of adulthood, then, the investigator must also explore the childhood and adolescent history of the individual (Mayo, 1952). The mental life of the organism is seen as both active and passive (reflective). Piaget took courses from Janet, and it has been noted that Janet had an active appreciation of Baldwin (Mueller, 1976). Indeed, it may have been through Janet that Piaget was most influenced by Baldwin (Cairns & Ornstein, 1979; Mueller, 1976; Piaget, 1978).

Although Piaget's early work does not cite Baldwin, his later publications contain ample acknowledgment of Baldwin's influences (Cairns & Ornstein, 1979; Evans, 1973; Langer, 1969; Piaget, 1978, 1982; White, 1977; Wozniak, 1982). Piaget may have taken from Baldwin an interest in such processes as imitation and play. Further, according to McCullers (1969), Piaget's early work contains some endorsement of a modified recapitulation theory (later termed correspondence theory; Gould, 1977). Like Baldwin, Piaget proposed a qualitative stage model of the development of the individual's interpretation of reality. Indeed, Piaget's (1972) genetic psychology was anticipated by Baldwin (Wozniak, 1982). Unlike Baldwin, however, the early Piaget accords less emphasis to the influence of the social environment on individual development.

As noted above, Piaget's theory of the development of cognition was known in America in the 1920s (Piaget, 1923). Yet because of the "clinical," nonexperimental nature of his research methods, this nonstatistical style of data analysis, and the abstract constructs with which he was concerned—all of which ran counter to predominant trends in the United States—his theory and research work were generally ignored until the late 1950s. Perhaps due to the European intellectual influences on American thinking occurring from events related to World War II, greater attention was given by Americans to the intellectual resources coming from and present in Europe. Thus, Piaget was "rediscovered," and in the 1960s achieved prominence in American developmental psychology. Indeed, his influence continues to this writing, both as a result of further substantiation of portions of his theory, and of promoting discussions of alternative (but still organismic) theoretical conceptualizations (Brainerd, 1978; Siegel & Brainerd, 1977).

Due to Piaget's centrality in modern organismic metatheory, most of the introductory comments to this section are directly applicable to his developmental psychology. Piaget produced a massive amount of writings, and these have served as a framework for his many followers in the United States and Europe. His influence has been felt in educational practice (primarily dealing with young children) and research (on cognitive development through adolescence). Although continually criticized, amended, and extended, the Piagetian organismic model has been virtually institutionalized in contemporary developmental psychology (Liben, 1981). Recently, some notable efforts have been made to apply the Piagetian perspective to adult cognitive development as well (Labouvie-Vief, 1982).

Werner's (1948) orthogenetic principle—that development proceeds from a lack of differentiation to increasing differentiation, integration, and hierarchic organization—was anticipated by Baldwin and supported by embryology (Langer, 1969). His early work (*Introduction to Developmental Psychology,* first published in German in 1926) was influenced by the genetic–wholistic psychology of Felix Krueger (Baltes, 1983). In keeping with his conviction that developmental theory was not systemizable, but rather a way of viewing behavior in general, Werner did not generate a methodical scheme of developmental psychology. In his later writing (e.g., 1957), he considered recapitulation theory (in particular, G. S. Hall's version) and rejected it. He was, however, willing to accept a parallel between evolutionary development and ontogenetic development, but not a one-to-one correspondence (see Brent, 1978).

As noted earlier, Freud's (e.g., 1954) theoretical position is, in many ways, an organismic one akin to that of Piaget (1970). Nevertheless it is sufficiently distinct to merit attention as a line of thought independent of organicism per se (Wohlwill, 1973).

The Psychoanalytic Tradition

The organismic, dynamic psychology of Sigmund Freud (1954) did not emerge until the last few years of the nineteenth century. A hydraulic model of man is employed, and developmental change is viewed as qualitative, proceeding through tension resolution from one stage to the next. Generally, a direction of development is implied; i.e., there is an endstate toward which development progresses. Regression is possible and, in some cases, frequent. The focus of attention is on emotional or personality development (especially abnormal personality), with only secondary interest given to cognitive progression (Wolff, 1960). The proposed line of influence is shown in Figure 1.1 (Column B).

According to Groffmann (1970), "The psychoanalysts were usually outsiders [to the developmental tradition]. As physicians they were confronted mainly with the psychological disorders of adult persons. . . . It is doubtful whether [Freud] was influenced by early developmental psychology" (p. 62). Somewhat to the contrary, however, McCullers (1969) argues that Freud may have been influenced by G. S. Hall, especially in light of the former's active endorsement of recapitulation theory in such seminal works as *Totem and Taboo* (first published in 1913), *Introductory Lectures on Psychoanalysis* (first published in 1916), and *Moses and Monotheism* (first published in 1939), and the fact that Freud visited Hall in 1909, at the twentieth anniversary of Clark University (of which Hall was then president). This was the only time that Freud visited the United States, and it resulted in the establishment of a long-term correspondence between Hall and Freud (Freud, 1938). It is certain that Freud was influenced by Darwin, at least in some respects, for he credited Darwin (along with, interestingly, the German poet Goethe) for his decision to enter medical school (Schur, 1972).

Gould (1977) argues that Freud was a devout adherent to Haeckel's recapitulation law, in part because he was trained as a biologist when biology reigned supreme, and in part because of his unremitting Lamarckian perspective on evolution (and Lamarckism, more than Darwinism, justifies recapitulation theory; see Gillispie, 1968; Lovejoy, 1968). In his first year of medical school, Freud took a class on biology and Darwinism taught by Carl Claus, an adherent of Darwin and of Haeckel's recapitulation theory (Schur, 1972). In addition, Groffmann (1970) points out that although it was Quetelet who helped make it clear that behavioral changes were, in part, a result of the interaction between the individual and his or her social and cultural context, it was psychoanalysis that brought this relationship into focus in developmental research. It is worth noting that such a characterization of environment–organism interaction (minus the Lamarckian view of inheritance) is not antithetical to Darwin's evolutionary theory. Certainly Freud adopted a genetic or developmental approach to understanding his preferred domain of psychological phenomena. In addition, psychoanalytic theory delineates two major mechanisms (fixation and regression) through which early events influence or determine later behavior (Cairns & Ornstein, 1979).

Groffmann (1970, p. 61), following C. S. Hall and Lindzey (1957), views Freud's psychosexual theory of development as partly mechanistic and partly Darwinian: "[Freud's] theory of personality development was basically a theory of the development of the libido, which he attempted to explain in terms of both a phylogenetic and ontogenetic process." Significant events in the life course (or significant confrontations) disposed people to particular developmental paths.

Another potential, albeit indirect, Darwinian connection may also exist in that Galton appears to have anticipated Freud in one important way. Galton (1883) describes mental operations and incidents that may appear in childhood and then lie dormant for years, until roused to consciousness. Alternatively, permanent traces of these incidents may continually influence the development of mental operations throughout life. This notion, which appeared prior to Freud, bears a striking resemblance to Freud's theory of the unconscious. One other indirect linkage between Darwin and Freud can be noted. It has been claimed that Darwin influenced Baldwin, who in turn influenced Janet and Piaget. As it happens, Freud is a minor figure in this equation, for he shared a direct intellectual ancestor with Janet. Both Freud and Janet studied under Jean Martin Charcot (1825–1893) in Paris (Flugel, 1933).

One of Freud's early followers, Carl Jung, became one of his most distinguished critics, and one of the most notable contributors to psychoanalytic developmental theory. According to Havighurst (1973), "disciples of Jung generally claim that his personality theory was more 'developmental' than that of Freud" (p. 19). Although Havighurst disputes the developmental claim with regard to Jung—calling Jung's theories more a "philosophy of life than a theory of life-span development" (p. 61)—he does not question the veracity of the comparison. Jung's developmental psychology was more explicit, if not more refined, than Freud's.

Jung, criticizing both Freud's model of psychosexual development (as too reductionistic) and the Christian view of personal transformation (as lacking applicability to rational modern man), proposed an individuation process consisting of four stages. A rather teleological perspective, the goal of such development is the emergence of self. Jung, taking an explicit life-course perspective and also adopting a recapitulation view, is seen by McCullers (1969) as more closely parallel to Hall than Freud.

Like Freud, Jung was a lifelong supporter of recapitulation theory (Gould, 1977; Jung, 1916). For Jung, few psychopathologies were developed during the childhood period recapitulation. As did Freud, Jung had a potential source of Darwinian thinking inculcated through a reliance on the work of Galton. In his early work Jung employed the method of associative word reaction, which had been invented by Galton and Wundt (Flugel, 1933). Whereas the latter two researchers were primarily interested in intellectual factors related to word association, Jung demonstrated that the affective dimension was also influential.

Modern psychoanalytic views of development are represented by Erik Erikson (b. 1902), who developed a life-span theory of personality. His theory, revolving around a set of sequential psychosocial tasks (note again the confrontation between organism and environment), is also a stage theory (see Emmerich, 1968; Erikson, 1950, 1959). His organismically oriented views have begun to influence some conceptions of cognition in later adulthood. His view of wisdom, for example, suggests that wisdom is a virtue emerging after the successful mastery of earlier life tasks (Erikson, 1968). Although it is clearly clothed in developmental terms—i.e., it may appear in earlier stages of life as an expression of the contingencies of that level of development—wisdom, like most concepts in the psychoanalytic model, is largely restricted to the realm of personal and emotional development. Nevertheless, Erikson's perspective has inspired more generalized inquiry into the cognitive aspects of wisdom and other such potentially progressive forms of adult development (e.g., Clayton & Birren, 1980).

Mechanism

The mechanistic model represents the organism as analogous to a machine in that it is composed of discrete parts interrelated by forces in a space–time field (see Overton & Reese, 1973; Pepper, 1942; Reese & Overton, 1970). Development depends on the level of stimulation, the kind of stimulation, and the history of the organism. The organism is seen as relatively passive (or reactive), whereas its environment is considered relatively active. The major figures in the progression of this model are shown in Column C of Fig. 1.1.

It is to Preyer (1882, 1893), Galton (1883), and Watson (1924, 1926) that the origin of the mechanistic view of the science of developmental psychology is usually traced. Preyer's 1882 German publication, later translated as *The Mind of the Child,* was the first book devoted to a systematic consideration of the development of the mental faculties of the child, and the one to which responsibility for the advent of developmental psychology is often assigned (Hardesty, 1976; Reinert, 1979). Although he devoted much attention to patterns of physical development, Preyer also commented on such psychological phenomena as re-flexes, language, spatial knowledge, and memory. Primarily a physiologist, it is difficult to estimate the magnitude of influence of evolutionary thought on Preyer (see Jaeger, 1982). He was, however, well within the scientific biological tradi-tion and was interested in the development of both mind and body. In this way, although in somewhat the same mold as Darwin's (1877) "Biographical sketch of an infant," Preyer's effort is, from a contemporary point of view, more ambitious. Although Preyer (1893) upholds a basically voluntaristic position, the organism must exert some effort to overcome immediate environmental con-tingencies. Thus, development is viewed as a struggle for freedom or emancipa-tion. Dennis (1972) notes that Preyer's method of response management antici-pates much of the reinforcement theory of modern mechanistic psychology.

Darwin's influence on the work of his half cousin Sir Francis Galton is quite apparent. Galton's investigations of individual differences in psychology form an intellectual bridge between Darwinian evolutionism and individual psychology. His well-known work on heredity (e.g., *Hereditary Genius,* first published in 1869) is one of the earliest scientific formulations of one of the basic issues of developmental psychology, the nature–nurture question (Galton, 1978). Gal-ton's consuming interest in this issue, however, was practical as well as theoreti-cal and thus led to the founding of eugenics, the applied science of heredity (Hearnshaw, 1964). In addition, his classic treatise on human development (Gal-ton, 1883) contained an array of essays that anticipated both experimental and correlational developmental psychology (although some of his methods and sta-tistics were apparently influenced by Quetelet). Galton's extreme view on the complete inheritance of mental traits was, according to Buss (1975), partly ascribable to the prevailing political orientation of the time, which, in effect, demanded a genetic (in the hereditary sense) interpretation.

G. S. Hall, who wrote the introduction to the American edition of Preyer's (1888) *The Mind of the Child,* placed considerable emphasis in his later work on environmental, especially social, factors in post-childhood behavioral on-togenesis. Thus, at separate points in the life span, nature *and* nurture compo-nents were incorporated into Hall's perspective. As a developmental psychol-ogist, Hall lacked a systematic program of thought. In this respect he fits neither the mechanistic nor the organismic model perfectly. Hall's somewhat loose eclecticism is revealed by his simultaneous attachment to correlational, experi-mental, and psychoanalytic traditions, in addition to his a priori dedication to recapitulation theory (Cairns & Ornstein, 1979). Regarding the latter, Hall actu-ally represents the peak of the influence of recapitulation theory in psychology; as it was being increasingly discredited in embryology, the foundation of its application to psychology was crumbling (Gould, 1977; Thorndike, 1904).

Although John B. Watson is not normally identified as a developmental psychologist, he had a lasting impact on the emergence of behavioral or mecha-nistic developmental psychology. His atomistic, reductionistic framework (Watson, 1924) continues to influence the contemporary scene, and his subsequent view of development as tantamount to cumulative learning (Watson, 1926) could hardly contrast more with the biological, organismic view of Baldwin and Piaget (Cairns & Ornstein, 1979). Further, Watson modified James' contextual interest in the stream of consciousness to a more empirical interest in stream of behavior (White, 1968).

Today the mechanistic tradition in developmental psychology is best represented by those adopting a functional, behavior-analytic approach to studying change across life (e.g., Bijou, 1976). As noted by Morris (1982), the concepts, methods, and principles of behavior analysis (e.g., Skinner, 1953) were extended to developmental psychology by Bijou and Baer (1961). As with all approaches to development, the behavior-analytic approach has evolved in the more than 20 years since Bijou and Baer's (1961) seminal work. Morris and Hursh (1982) indicate that behavior-analytic developmentalists have become increasingly concerned with metatheoretical issues (e.g., Bijou, 1979; Skinner, 1974), and in this regard they have examined the usefulness of key developmental concepts and issues such as those pertinent to the nature of change and to the usefulness of age as a variable in developmental research (Baer, 1970, 1973, 1976; Baltes & Lerner, 1980).

Despite this interest among behavior analysts in issues of development, there is some consensus (e.g., Baer, 1982; Reese, 1982) that as far as one is concerned with the *current* status of the relationship between the group of psychologists studying phenomena relevant to development from a behavior-analytic perspective, and the group of psychologists studying development from other perspectives, "each of the groups has its own interests and its own conceptions of fact, truth, and so on, and therefore each has its own best research methods. Ideas and methods are often not directly transferable between positions" (Reese, 1982, p. 357). As a consequence, "behavior analysis will continue untroubled by whether it can integrate developmental psychology" (Baer, 1982, p. 361).

The behavior-analytic approach to development is not the only one that can be identified within contemporary developmental psychology as consistent with a mechanistic tradition. Current cognitive social learning approaches to development (e.g., Bandura, 1977; Mischel, 1977) also have features consistent with a mechanistic orientation. These latter positions have also been revised, and they now include ideas pertinent to reciprocal, person-context interaction models of development (cf. Bandura, 1978). As such, these cognitive social learning approaches do share common elements with contextualism.

Contextualism

The contextual model of developmental psychology is perhaps the least refined of the five presented in this chapter. As a philosophical position, however, it is one of the more advanced (Pepper, 1942). Recently revived in psychology (see Lerner et al., in press; Sarbin, 1977), it represents a promising interpretive framework. Its basic metaphor is change or the historic event. The individual and the social environment are viewed as mutually influential, acting upon one another in dynamic interaction. The proposed line of influence is presented in Fig. 1.1 (Column D).

William James, although disenchanted with the deterministic evolutionary psychology of Spencer (as in the latter's *Principles of Psychology*, first published in 1855), was highly influenced by Darwin's natural selection theory of evolution. James' (1890) psychology was nonreductionistic in character; that is, he argued against the Wundtian analysis of mental events into more primitive parts or complexes. Experience consists of a stream of events, each of which possesses a unique quality or meaning. The novelty of each event is assured by the stream metaphor. The implication James developed was that the meaning or significance of a mental event is inseparable from the context of its occurrence, which is itself in flux. Development is continuous, "without breach, crack, or division" (1890, p. 237); it is composed of quantitative differences rather than qualitatively distinct stages. His approach to psychology may be characterized as historical in that "mental reaction on every given thing is really a resultant of our experience of the whole world up to that date" (1890, p. 234).

As had Darwin, James viewed the human mind as both dynamic (active) and functional, continuously involved in the process of adaptation to a changing ecology (Hearnshaw, 1964). Both James and Peirce sought to infuse the developmental stream (at the individual, phyletic, and cosmological levels) with the elements of chance (e.g., Peirce's "tychism") so integral to the Darwinian hypothesis. Eschewing the directional or teleological focus of Lamarckian evolutionists and psychologists, these early contextualists were nonetheless historical in method. According to the Darwinian interpretation, a chance event, while not wholly determined by the past, does reflect the character of preceding events (Russett, 1976). In this way, both novelty and developmental continuity are maintained (James, 1977).

The functional approach to psychology is often dated to John Dewey's (1896) classic paper "The Reflex Arc Concept in Psychology." However, even in his earlier work in psychology, Dewey had already demonstrated a strong dynamic orientation to the study of mental phenomena. In this period, however, Dewey was still casting developmental questions in the framework of a Hegelian telos, or necessary movement to a final end state. But Dewey soon fell under the influence of Darwinism (see Dewey, 1910) and his subsequent psychological writings stressed the genetic (or developmental) method, the continuous model of developmental change, as well as the Darwinian view of the dynamic organism–environment transaction (Russett, 1976). Like James, Dewey offered a relatively active organism (and active environment) model of this transaction. Finally, Dewey (1910) attributed the discovery of the historical (or genetic) method to Darwin.

No modern contextual developmental psychologist has produced a system as complete as that of James or, for that matter, even Dewey and Peirce. Certainly, with the exception of areas pertinent to language development, Peirce and Mead have had little effect on developmental psychology. Indeed, with the exception of the work of F. C. Bartlett (1932) and perhaps Vygotsky (1934/1962), who at least cited James, contextual developmental psychology appears to have lain dormant for much of this century. Recently, however, numerous psychologists have rediscovered contextual thinking and have attempted to articulate its methodological implications (Dixon & Nesselroade, 1983; Hultsch & Pentz, 1980; Jenkins, 1974; Lerner et al., in press; Sarbin, 1977).

At the risk of oversimplification, psychological development for the contextual psychologist is portrayed as a continuing, adaptive life-long process, related to other internal or mental processes, and interacting with external activities and sociohistorical processes. In principle, both the internal and external conditions of behavioral ontogenesis are examined with respect to a given psychological process. A corresponding interest is evident in examining a target dependent measure in conditions approximating those that occur in the natural ecology of the individual. This interest has resulted in a concern for such attendant methodological issues as ecological representativeness and external validity (Bronfenbrenner, 1977; Hultsch & Hickey, 1978). Simply put, in the assessment of psychological development, it is both theoretically and methodologically profitable to use measures that are representative of (or drawn from) the population of related psychological activities that individuals could encounter in their everyday lives. In this respect, performance on experimental tasks may be generalized to cognitive adaptiveness and efficiency in the familiar ecology of the individual.

With a slightly different emphasis, Sarbin (1977) has adapted the dramaturgical model of G. H. Mead (1934), one of the important figures in the development of contextualism. Assuming that individuals carry on their activities and interactions in an episodic, changing way, Sarbin argued for an emplotment methodology. That is, Sarbin suggested that psychologists develop a taxonomy of plots; action is temporal, occurring in historical, concurrent, and future contexts. This is the thrust of Jenkins' (1974) arguments for a contextual approach (reminiscent of both William James and F. C. Bartlett) to memory research. According to this view, a memory is not an item, a thing, or a spot in the cortex (all of which appear in mechanistic accounts); nor is memory separable from other processes, much less the world (as the organismic account often suggests); rather, "what memory is depends on context" (Jenkins, 1974, p. 786). As the context is ever-changing, so is the memory. Of course, these writers acknowledge that not every aspect of the context may be considered in every research project, but they assert that it is the investigator's duty to assimilate as much of the context as possible.

Dialecticism

The dialectical materialism of the nineteenth century has significantly influenced one modern approach to developmental psychology. Under the contemporary dialectical model, the basic metaphor appears to be contradiction or conflict

(Riegel, 1975, 1976). As with the contextual model, the activities of the individual are here viewed as being in dynamic interaction with the activities of the environment. The individual, like the society, develops through a continuous process of thesis, antithesis, and synthesis (Wozniak, 1975a,b). A schematic representation of the line of influence is presented in Column E of Fig. 1.1.

Although neither Hegel nor Marx proposed a specific program of individual development, their views on both ideational and social change have been adapted for the individual psychological level. Hegel was unquestionably an influence on Marx, although in certain respects his ideas were rejected by the much younger revolutionary. The important point of commonality between them is the dialectic itself. The influence of Darwin on Marx is difficult to assess completely, but some writers have suggested that Marx wanted to dedicate *Das Kapital* to the evolutionist (Berlin, 1978; but see also Fay, 1978). Further, it is known that Marx warmly inscribed a copy of the second edition of his magnum opus to Darwin (Huxley & Kettlewell, 1965). And Marx's own intellectual companion, Friedrich Engels (1820–1895), vividly portrayed the intellectual kinship of Darwin and Marx in his notes read at the latter's graveside. Several of Marx's letters to Engels in the years immediately following the 1859 publication of Darwin's *Origins* indicated that he believed evolutionary thinking to be consonant with his own dialectical materialism (see Padover, 1978).

In point of fact, however, Marx's own evolutionism may have more closely resembled Spencer's or Lamarck's than Darwin's, especially with regard to the Marxist view that historical change is directed toward a goal (Dixon, Lerner, & Hultsch, 1982). Nevertheless, both Darwin and Marx shared a concern, emerging on multiple fronts in the nineteenth century, with historicity and with development. It is this shared fundamental concern that forms a critical link between the two.

After the Bolshevik revolution in 1917, dialectical psychology in the Soviet Union burgeoned. The most influential of these dialectical developmentalists was Vygotsky (1929, 1934/1962, 1978). Through his students (e.g., Luria, 1971, 1976; Leontiev & Luria, 1968) a strongly Marxist approach to psychology developed. Among its other features, this psychology can be characterized as teleological–historical, social–cultural, and active–organismic (Dixon et al., 1982; Wozniak, 1975a).

For both intellectual and political reasons, dialectical developmental psychology was not, until recently, a noticeable, much less a prominent, force on the American scene (Riegel, 1972). Thus, there is little explicit linkage between Marx and American developmental psychology until after the mid-twentieth century. The leading figure in contemporary developmental dialectics was the late Klaus Riegel (e.g., 1979). Wozniak (1975a,b) has proposed the following three laws of developmental change based on Marxist dialectics: (1) the unity and opposition of contradictory principles and their resolution through synthesis; (2) the possibility of transforming basic quantitative change into qualitative change; and (3) the negation of a negation, or the continual process of replacing the old by the new. Developmental psychology is viewed dialectically as the study of the changing individual in a changing world (Riegel & Meacham, 1976). As with the historical methods of Marx's dialectical materialism, the utility of the methods involved in a dialectical approach to the empirical study of human development is questionable (Baltes & Cornelius, 1977; Hultsch, 1980).

CONTEMPORARY PERSPECTIVES IN DEVELOPMENTAL PSYCHOLOGY

Earlier, we noted that the developmental "tradition," promoted by the contributions of Darwin, stresses an organism's history, the functional (adaptive) features of ontogeny, and the role of context in ontogeny. While these features of the developmental tradition are present (albeit in different ways) in each of the five models we have discussed, there arose in the 1970s a "life-span perspective" of development that not only emphasized these features but also constituted an attempt to integrate compatible ideas derived from the several models we have discussed (e.g., Baltes, 1979; Baltes & Reese, in this volume). Due to the emphasis on history and on context found in the developmental tradition to which proponents of this perspective subscribed, an attempt was made to integrate ideas from the many disciplines involved in the study of human lives. As a consequence, the life-span perspective was influenced not only by the Darwinian thinking reflected in the theoretical approaches to development we have reviewed, but also by developmental, historical, and evolutionary thinking transmitted from other disciplines.

As Havighurst (1973) and Baltes (1979) have discussed, some isolated historical instances of the life-span perspective can be found in eighteenth and nineteenth century publications by Tetens (1777), Carus (1808), and Quetelet (1835); and in some twentieth century contributions from both Europe and the United States, such as those by Sanford (1902), Hall (1922), Hollingworth (1927), Bühler (1933), Pressey, Janney, and Kuhlen (1939), Havighurst (1948), Erikson (1950), and by Neugarten (1964; Neugarten & Guttman, 1958). In the work of Havighurst, for example, (1948) we find some concern for an active organism changing across life (as a consequence of having to confront new "developmental tasks") and an emphasis on the need to use a multidisciplinary perspective to understand organism-context relations across life.

By the late 1960s and throughout the 1970s, these historical antecedents began to be synthesized, and interest in adult development and aging began to grow rapidly. This interest in adult development and aging provided the recent, major impetus to the current empirical concern with life-span development because, most obviously, it moved scientific investigation beyond the childhood and adolescent years. However, this life-span research interest was also critically concerned with issues of explanation and theory.

Earlier in this chapter we noted that part of the changes in the 1970s in developmental psychology could be ascribed to an explanatory problem that arose when specific research findings could not be adequately integrated with extant developmental theories. That is, it soon became apparent that, as Brim and Kagan (1980) have noted, "humans have a capacity for change across the entire life span . . . there are important growth changes across the life span from birth to death, many individuals retain a great capacity for change, and the consequences of the events of early childhood are continually transformed by later experiences, making the course of human development more open than many have believed" (p. 1).

The nature of the life-span orientation has become somewhat clearer through the publication of several conference proceedings, symposia, and an annual volume, as well as numerous empirical and theoretical papers (e.g., Baltes, Reese, & Lipsitt, 1980). From this perspective, the potential for developmental change is seen to be present across all of life; the human life course is held to be potentially multidirectional and necessarily multidimensional. In addition, the sources of the potentially continual changes across life are seen to involve both inner-biological and outer-ecological levels of the context within which the organism is embedded. Indeed, although it is an orientation *to* the study of development rather than a specific theory *of* development (Baltes, 1979), life-span developmental psychology is disposed to a reciprocal model of organism-context relations (see Baltes & Reese, in this volume).

CONCLUSIONS

The review we have presented indicates that developmental psychology has come to be characterized by an emphasis on explanation and process, and by a concern with several theoretical systems and their philosophical bases. We have emphasized that from a common intellectual source—evolutionism, and more specifically, Darwinism—numerous figures drew sustenance and then turned to face the fresh demands of their own context. These demands were sufficiently varied to propagate views about human development that today appear distinct. Perhaps one of the greatest contributions of Darwinism to the emergence of developmental psychology derives from its accentuation of the underlying general issues pertaining to ontogeny. Among these abiding problems are such classical polarities as nature versus nurture (Lerner, 1978), continuity versus discontinuity of development (Brim & Kagan, 1980), and unidirectionality versus non- or multidirectionality of temporal progression (Dixon et al., 1982), all of which are addressed elsewhere in this volume.

It is reasonable to assert that the structure of these five major contemporary developmental metatheories cut across these salient issues in qualitatively different ways. Thus, contemporary developmental theories may share a certain intellectual lineage, embrace a generalized historical or developmental approach to human phenomena, and at the same time represent relatively distinct meta-theoretical positions, resulting in relatively specific methods and unique interpretations of data.

ACKNOWLEDGMENT

Richard M. Lerner's work on this chapter was supported in part by a grant from the John D. and Catherine T. MacArthur Foundation.

REFERENCES

Angell, J. R. *Chapters from modern psychology.* New York: Longmans, Green, 1912.

Baer, D. M. An age-irrelevant concept of development. *Merrill-Palmer Quarterly,* 1970, *16,* 238–245.

Baer, D. M. The control of developmental process: Why wait? In J. R. Nesselroade & H. W. Reese (Eds.), *Life-span developmental psychology: Methodological issues.* New York: Academic Press, 1973.

Baer, D. M. The organism as host. *Human Development,* 1976, *19,* 87–98.

Baer, D. M. Behavior analysis and developmental psychology: Discussant comments. *Human Development,* 1982, *25,* 357–361.

Baldwin, A. L. *Theories of child development.* (2nd ed.). New York: Wiley, 1980.

Baldwin, J. M. *Mental development in the child and the race.* New York: Macmillan, 1895.

Baldwin, J. M. *Mental development in the child and the race: Methods and processes* (2nd ed.). New York: Macmillan, 1906.

Baldwin, J. M. *Darwin and the humanities.* Baltimore: Review Publishing, 1909.

Baldwin, J. M. *History of psychology: A sketch and interpretation (Vol. 2): From Locke to the present time.* London: Watts, 1913.

Baldwin, J. M. [Autobiography] In C. Murchison (Ed.), *A history of psychology in autobiography* (Vol. 1). Worcester, Mass.: Clark University Press, 1930.

Baltes, M. M., & Lerner, R. M. Roles of the operant model and its methods in the life-span approach to human development. *Human Development,* 1980, *23,* 362–367.

Baltes, P. B. Life-span developmental psychology: Some converging observations on history and theory. In P. B. Baltes & O. G. Brim, Jr. (Eds.), *Life-span development and behavior* (Vol. 2). New York: Academic Press, 1979.

Baltes, P. B. Life-span developmental psychology: Observations on history and theory revisited. In R. M. Lerner (Ed.), *Developmental psychology: Historical and philosophical perspectives.* Hillsdale, N.J.: Lawrence Erlbaum Associates, 1983.

Baltes, P. B., & Cornelius, S. W. The status of dialectics in developmental psychology: Theoretical orientation versus scientific method. In N. Datan & H. W. Reese (Eds.), *Life-span developmental psychology: Dialectical perspectives on experimental research.* New York: Academic Press, 1977.

Baltes, P. B., Reese, H. W., & Lipsitt, L. P. Life-span developmental psychology. *Annual Review of Psychology,* 1980, *31,* 65–110.

Baltes, P. B., Reese, H. W., & Nesselroade, J. R. *Life-span developmental psychology: Introduction to research methods.* Monterey, CA: Brooks/Cole, 1977.

Bandura, A. *Social learning theory.* Englewood Cliffs, N.J.: Prentice-Hall, 1977.

Bandura, A. The self system in reciprocal determinism. *American Psychologist*, 1978, *33*, 344–358.

Bartlett, F. C. *Remembering*. Cambridge: Cambridge University Press, 1932.

Berlin, I. *Karl Marx: His life and his environment* (4th ed.). Oxford: Oxford University Press, 1978.

Bijou, S. W. *Child Development: The basic stage of early childhood*. Englewood Cliffs, N.J.: Prentice-Hall, 1976.

Bijou, S. W. Some clarifications on the meaning of a behavior analysis of child development. *Psychological Record*, 1979, *29*, 3–13.

Bijou, S. W., & Baer, D. M. *Child development. Volume 1: A systematic and empirical theory*. New York: Appleton-Century-Crofts, 1961.

Brainerd, C. J. The stage question in cognitive-developmental theory. *The Behavioral and Brain Sciences*, 1978, *2*, 173–182.

Braunshvig, M., & Braunshvig, G. *Notre enfant: Journal d'un père et d'une mère*. Paris: Hachette, 1913.

Brent, S. B. Individual specialization, collective adaptation and rate of environmental change. *Human Development*, 1978, *21*, 21–33.

Brim, O. G., Jr., & Kagan, J. Constancy and change: A view of the issues. In O. G. Brim, Jr. & J. Kagan (Eds.), *Constancy and change in human development*. Cambridge, Mass.: Harvard University Press, 1980.

Bronfenbrenner, U. Development theory in transition. In H. W. Stevenson (Ed.), *Child psychology. Sixty-second yearbook of the National Society for the Study of Education, part I*. Chicago: University of Chicago Press, 1963.

Bronfenbrenner, U. Toward an experimental ecology of human development. *American Psychologist*, 1977, *32*, 513–531.

Bühler, C. *The first year of life*. New York: John Day, 1930.

Bühler, C. *Der menschliche Lebenslauf als psychologisches Problem*. Leipzig: Hirzel, 1933.

Buss, A. R. The emerging field of the sociology of psychological knowledge. *American Psychologist*, 1975, *30*, 988–1002.

Cairns, R. B., & Ornstein, P. A. Developmental psychology. In E. Hearst (Ed.), *The first century of experimental psychology*. Hillsdale, N.J.: Lawrence Erlbaum Associates, 1979.

Carus, F. A. *Psychologie Zweiter Teil: Specialpsychologie*. Leipzig: Barth & Kummer, 1808.

Champneys, E. H. Notes on an infant. *Mind*, 1881, *6*, 104–107.

Charles, D. C. Historical antecedents of life-span developmental psychology. In L. R. Goulet & P. B. Baltes (Eds.), *Life-span developmental psychology: Research and theory*. New York: Academic Press, 1970.

Clayton, V. P., & Birren, J. E. The development of wisdom across the life-span: A reexamination of an ancient topic. In P. B. Baltes & O. G. Brim, Jr. (Eds.), *Life-span development and behavior* (Vol. 3). New York: Academic Press, 1980.

Darwin, C. *On the origin of species*. London: John Murray, 1859.

Darwin, C. *Descent of man*. London: John Murray, 1871.

Darwin, C. *The expression of emotions in man and animals*. London: John Murray, 1872.

Darwin, C. Biographical sketch of an infant. *Mind*, 1877, *2*, 285–294.

Dennis, W. Historical beginnings of child psychology. *Psychological Bulletin*, 1949, *46*, 224–235.

Dennis, W. (Ed.). *Readings in child psychology*. New York: Prentice-Hall, 1951.

Dennis, W. (Ed.). *Historical readings in developmental psychology*. New York: Appleton-Century-Crofts, 1972.

Dewey, J. The reflex arc concept in psychology. *Psychological Review*, 1896, *3*, 357–370.

Dewey, J. *The influence of Darwin on philosophy*. New York: H. Holt, 1910.

Dixon, R. A. Human development: History of research. In T. Husén & T. N. Postlethwaite (Eds.), *International encyclopedia of education: Research and studies*. Oxford: Pergammon Press, 1983.

Dixon, R. A., Lerner, R. M., & Hultsch, D. F. *Contextual and dialectical models for the study of individual development and behavior: A critical comparison*. Unpublished manuscript, Max Planck Institute for Human Development and Education, Berlin, West Germany, 1982.

Dixon, R. A., & Nesselroade, J. R. Pluralism and correlational analysis in developmental psychology: Historical commonalities. In R. M. Lerner (Ed.), *Developmental psychology: Historical and philosophical perspectives*. Hillsdale, N.J.: Lawrence Erlbaum Associates, 1983.

Dollard, J., Doob, L. W., Miller, N. E., Mowrer, O. H., & Sears, R. R. *Frustration and aggression*. New Haven, CT: Yale University Press, 1939.

Eiseley, L. *Darwin's century*. Garden City, NY: Doubleday, 1958.

Emmerich, W. Personality development and concepts of structure. *Child Development*, 1968, *39*, 671–690.

Erikson, E. H. *Childhood and society*. New York: Norton, 1950.

Erikson, E. H. Identity and the life cycle. *Psychological Issues*, 1959, *1*, whole volume.

Erikson, E. H. *Identity, youth and crisis*. New York: Norton, 1968.

Evans, R. I. *Jean Piaget: The man and his ideas*. New York: Dutton, 1973.

Fay, M. A. Did Marx offer to dedicate *Capital* to Darwin? *Journal of the History of Ideas*, 1978, *39*, 133–146.

Flugel, J. C. *A hundred years of psychology*. New York: Macmillan, 1933.

Freud, S. The history of the psychoanalytic movement. In A. A. Brill (Ed. and trans.), *The basic writings of Sigmund Freud*. New York: Random House, 1938.

Freud. S. *Collected works, standard edition*. London: Hogarth Press, 1954.

Gallatin, J. E. *Adolescence and individuality*. New York: Harper & Row, 1975.

Galton, F. *Inquiries into human faculty and its development*. London: Macmillan, 1883.

Galton, F. *Hereditary Genius: An inquiry into its laws and consequences*. New York: St. Martins, 1978.

Gengerelli, J. A. Graduate school reminiscence: Hull and Koffka. *American Psychologist*, 1976, *31*, 685–688.

Gesell, A. L. Maturation and infant behavior pattern. *Psychological Review*, 1929, *36*, 307–319.

Gesell, A. L. The individual in infancy. In C. Murchison (Ed.), *Handbook of child psychology*. Worcester, MA: Clark University Press, 1931.

Gesell, A. L. *An atlas of infant behavior*. New Haven, CT: Yale University Press, 1934.

Gesell, A. L. The ontogenesis of infant behavior. In L. Carmichael (Ed.), *Manual of child psychology*. New York: Wiley, 1946.

Gesell, A. L. The ontogenesis of infant behavior. In L. Carmichael (Ed.), *Manual of child psychology* (2nd ed.). New York: Wiley, 1954.

Gillespie, N. C. *Charles Darwin and the problem of creation*. Chicago: University of Chicago Press, 1979.

Gillispie, C. C. Lamarck and Darwin in the history of science. In B. Glass, O. Temkin, & W. L. Straus, Jr. (Eds.), *Forerunners of Darwin: 1745–1859*. Baltimore: The Johns Hopkins Press, 1968.

Gould, S. J. *Ontogeny and phylogeny*. Cambridge, MA: Harvard University Press, 1977.

Groffmann, K. J. Life-span developmental psychology in Europe: Past and present. In L. R. Goulet & P. B. Baltes (Eds.), *Life-span developmental psychology: Research and theory*. New York: Academic Press, 1970.

Gruber, H. E. *Darwin on man: A psychological study of scientific creativity*. New York: Dutton, 1974.

Hall, C. S., & Lindzey, G. *Theories of personality*. New York: Wiley, 1957.

Hall, G. S. The contents of children's minds. *Princeton Review*, 1883, *11*, 249–272.

Hall, G. S. Notes on the study of infants. *Pedagogical Seminary*, 1891, *1*, 127–138.

Hall, G. S. *Adolescence: Its psychology and its relations to physiology, anthropology, sociology, sex, crime, religion, and education* (2 vols.). New York: D. Appleton, 1904.

Hall, G. S. *Senescence: The last half of life*. New York: Appleton, 1922.

Hardesty, F. P. Early European contributions to developmental psychology. In K. F. Riegel & J. A. Meacham (Eds.), *The developing individual in a changing world*. Chicago: Aldine, 1976.

Harris, D. B. *Child psychology and the concept of development*. Presidential address to the Division of Developmental Psychology, American Psychological Association, September 3, 1956. Reprinted in D. S. Palermo & L. P. Lipsitt (Eds.), *Research readings in child psychology*. New York: Holt, Rinehart & Winston, 1963.

Harris, D. B. (Ed.). *The concept of development*. Minneapolis, MN: University of Minnesota Press, 1957.

Havighurst, R. J. *Developmental tasks and education*. New York: David McKay, 1948.

Havighurst, R. J. History of developmental psychology: Socialization and personality development through the life span. In P. B. Baltes & K. W. Schaie (Eds.), *Life-span developmental psychology: Personality and socialization*. New York: Academic Press, 1973.

Hearnshaw, L. S. *A short history of British psychology 1840–1940*. New York: Barnes & Noble, 1964.

Hollingworth, H. L. *Mental growth and decline: A survey of developmental psychology*. New York: Appleton, 1927.

Hultsch, D. F. (Ed). Implications of a dialectical perspective for research methodology. *Human Development*, 1980, *23*, 217–267.

Hultsch, D. F., & Hickey, T. External validity in the study of human development: Theoretical and methodological issues. *Human Development*, 1978, *21*, 76–91.

Hultsch, D. F., & Pentz, C. A. Encoding, storage, and retrieval in adult memory: The role of model assumptions. In L. W. Poon, J. L. Fozard, L. S. Cermak, D. Arenberg, & L. W. Thompson (Eds.), *New directions in memory and aging: Proceedings of the George A. Talland Memorial Conference*. Hillsdale, N.J.: Lawrence Erlbaum Associates, 1980.

Huxley, J., & Kettlewell, H. B. D. *Charles Darwin and his world*. New York: Viking, 1965.

Jaeger, S. Origins of child psychology: William Preyer. In W. R. Woodward & M. G. Ash (Eds.), *The problematic science: Psychology in nineteenth-century thought*. New York: Praeger, 1982.

James, W. *The principles of psychology* (Vol. 1). New York: Dover, 1890.

James. W. *A pluralistic universe*. Cambridge, MA: Harvard University Press, 1977.

Janet, P. [Autobiography] In C. Murchison (Ed.), *A history of psychology in autobiography* (Vol. 1). Worcester, MA: Clark University Press, 1930.

Jenkins, J. J. Remember that old theory of memory? Well, forget it! *American Psychologist*, 1974, *29*, 785–795.

Jung, C. G. *Psychology of the unconscious*. London: Kegan Paul, Trench, Trubner, 1916.

Kirkpatrick, E. A. *Genetic psychology: An introduction to an objective and genetic view of intelligence*. New York: Macmillan, 1909.

Kuhn, T. S. *The structure of scientific revolutions* (2nd. ed.). Chicago: University of Chicago Press, 1970.

Labouvie-Vief, G. Dynamic development and mature autonomy: A theoretical prologue. *Human Development*, 1982, *25*, 161–191.

Langer, J. *Theories of development*. New York: Holt, Rinehart, & Winston, 1969.

Lehrman, D. S. Semantic and conceptual issues in the nature–nurture problem. In L. R. Aronson, E. Tobach, D. S. Lehrman, & J. S. Rosenblatt (Eds.), *Development and evolution of behavior: Essays in memory of T. C. Schneirla*. San Francisco: W. H. Freeman, 1970.

Leontiev, A. N., & Luria, A. R. The psychological ideas of L. S. Vygotskii. In B. B. Wolman (Ed.), *Historical roots of contemporary psychology*. New York: Harper & Row, 1968.

Lerner, R. M. *Concepts and theories of human development*. Reading, MA: Addison-Wesley, 1976.

Lerner, R. M. Nature, nurture, and dynamic interactionism. *Human Development*, 1978, *21*, 1–20.

Lerner, R. M. A dynamic interactional concept of individual and social relationship development. In R. L. Burgess & T. L. Huston (Eds.), *Social exchange in developing relationships*. New York: Academic Press, 1979.

Lerner, R. M. (Ed.). *Developmental psychology: Historical and philosophical perspectives.* Hillsdale, N.J.: Lawrence Erlbaum Associates, 1983.

Lerner, R. M., & Busch-Rossnagel, N. A. Individuals as producers of their development: Conceptual and empirical bases. In R. M. Lerner & N. A. Busch-Rossnagel (Eds.), *Individuals as producers of their development: A life-span perspective.* New York: Academic Press, 1981.

Lerner, R. M., Hultsch, D. F., & Dixon, R. A. Contextualism and the character of developmental psychology in the 1970s. *Annals of the New York Academy of Sciences,* in press.

Liben, L. S. Individuals' contributions to their own development during childhood: A Piagetian perspective. In R. M. Lerner & N. A. Busch-Rossnagel (Eds.), *Individuals as producers of their development: A life-span perspective.* New York: Academic Press, 1981.

Loewenberg, B. J. *Darwin, Wallace and the theory of natural selection.* Cambridge, MA: Arlington, 1957.

Looft, W. R. The evolution of developmental psychology: A comparison of handbooks. *Human Development,* 1972, *15,* 187–201.

Looft, W. R. Socialization and personality throughout the life-span: An examination of contemporary psychological approaches. In P. B. Baltes & K. W. Schaie (Eds.), *Life-span developmental psychology: Personality and socialization.* New York: Academic Press, 1973.

Lovejoy, A. O. Recent criticism of the Darwinian theory of recapitulation: Its grounds and its initiator. In B. Glass, O. Temkin, & W. L. Straus, Jr. (Eds.), *Forerunners of Darwin: 1745–1859.* Baltimore: The Johns Hopkins Press, 1968.

Luria, A. R. *Cognitive development: Its cultural and social foundations.* (Trans. by M. Lopez-Morillas & L. Solotaroff; ed. by M. Cole). Cambridge, MA: Harvard University Press, 1976.

Luria, A. R. *Cognitive development: Its cultural and social foundations.* (Trans. by M. Lopez-Morillas & L. Solotaroff; Ed. by M. Cole). Cambridge, MA: Harvard University Press, 1976.

Mandelbaum, M. *History, man, and reason.* Baltimore: The Johns Hopkins Press, 1971.

Manier, E. *The young Darwin and his cultural circle.* Dordrecht, Holland: D. Reidel, 1978.

Mayo, E. *The psychology of Pierre Janet.* Westport, CT: Greenwood, 1952.

Mayr, E. Evolution through natural selection: How Darwin discovered this highly unconventional theory. *American Scientist,* 1977, *65,* 321–328.

McCandless, B. R., & Spiker, C. C. Experimental research in child psychology. *Child Development,* 1956, *27,* 78–80.

McCullers, J. C. G. Stanley Hall's conception of mental development and some indications of its influence on developmental psychology. *American Psychologist,* 1969, *24,* 1109–1114.

Mead, G. H. *Mind, self, and society.* Chicago: University of Chicago Press, 1934.

Miller, N. E., & Dollard, J. *Social learning and imitation.* New Haven: Yale University Press, 1941.

Mischel, W. On the future of personality measurement. *American Psychologist,* 1977, *32,* 246–254.

Misiak, H., & Sexton, V. S. *History of psychology in overview.* New York: Grune & Stratton, 1966.

Moore, K. C. The mental development of a child. *Psychological Review Monograph,* 1896 (Supplement, Vol. 1, No. 3).

Morgan, C. L. Selection. In J. M. Baldwin (Ed.), *Dictionary of philosophy and psychology* (Vol. 2). New York: Peter Smith, 1902.

Morris, E. K. Behavior analysis and developmental psychology. *Human Development,* 1982, *25,* 340–364.

Morris, E. K., & Hursh, D. E. Behavior analysis and developmental psychology: Metatheoretical considerations. *Human Development,* 1982, *25,* 344–349.

Mueller, R. H. A chapter in the history of the relationship between psychology and sociology in America: James Mark Baldwin. *Journal of the History of the Behavioral Sciences,* 1976, *12,* 240–253.

Murchison, C. (Ed.). *Handbook of child psychology.* Worcester, MA: Clark University Press, 1931.

Mussen, P. H. (Ed.). *Carmichael's manual of child psychology* (3rd ed.). New York: Wiley, 1970.

Nesselroade, J. R., & Baltes, P. B. (Eds.). *Longitudinal research in the study of behavior and development*. New York: Academic Press, 1979.

Neugarten, B. L. *Personality in middle and late life*. New York: Atherton Press, 1964.

Neugarten, B. L., & Guttman, D. L. Age–sex roles and personality in middle age: A thematic apperception study. *Psychological Monographs, 1958, 72,* No. 470.

Overton, W. F. On the assumptive base of the nature–nurture controversy: Additive versus interactive conceptions. *Human Development, 1973, 16,* 74–89.

Overton, W. F., & Reese, H. W. Models of development: Methodological implications. In J. R. Nesselroade & H. W. Reese (Eds.), *Life-span developmental psychology: Methodological issues*. New York: Academic Press, 1973.

Overton, W. F., & Reese, H. W. Conceptual prerequisites for an understanding of stability-change and continuity-discontinuity. *International Journal of Behavioral Development, 1981, 4,* 99–123.

Padover, S. K. (Ed.). *The essential Marx: The non-economic writings*. New York: New American Library, 1978.

Pepper, S. C. *World hypotheses*. Berkeley: University of California Press, 1942.

Perez, B. *Les trois premières années de l'enfant*. Paris: Ballieze, 1878.

Peters, R. S. (Ed.). *Brett's history of psychology*. Cambridge, MA: The MIT Press, 1965.

Piaget, J. La pensée symbolique et la pensée l'enfant. *Archives of Psychology,* Geneva, 1923, *18,* 273–304.

Piaget, J. *The psychology of intelligence*. London: Routledge & Kegan Paul, 1950.

Piaget, J. Piaget's theory. In P. H. Mussen (Ed.), *Carmichael's manual of child psychology* (Vol. 1). New York: Wiley, 1970.

Piaget, J. *Problèmes de psychologie génétique*. Paris: Denoel, 1972.

Piaget, J. *Behavior and evolution*. New York: Pantheon, 1978.

Piaget, J. Reflections on Baldwin. In J. M. Broughton & D. J. Freeman-Noir (Eds.), *The cognitive-developmental psychology of James Mark Baldwin: Current theory and research in genetic epistemology*. Norwood, N.J.: Ablex, 1982.

Pressey, S. L., Janney, J. E., & Kuhlen, R. G. *Life: A psychological survey*. New York: Harper & Row, 1939.

Preyer, W. *Die Seele des Kindes*. Leipzig: Fernau, 1882.

Preyer, W. *The mind of the child: Part I: The senses and the will*. (Trans. by H. W. Brown). New York: D. Appleton, 1888.

Preyer, W. *Mental development in the child*. (Trans. by H. W. Brown). New York: D. Appleton, 1893.

Prior, M. D. Notes on the first three years of a child. *Pedagogical Seminary,* 1895, *3,* 339–341.

Quetelet, A. *Sur l'homme et le développement de ses facultés*. Paris: Bachelier, 1835.

Reese, H. W. Behavior analysis and developmental psychology: Discussants comments. *Human Development,* 1982, *25,* 352–357.

Reese, H. W., & Overton, W. F. Models of development and theories of development. In L. R. Goulet & P. B. Baltes (Eds.), *Life-span developmental psychology: Research and theory*. New York: Academic Press, 1970.

Reinert, G. Prolegomena to a history of life-span developmental psychology. In P. B. Baltes & O. G. Brim, Jr. (Eds.), *Life-span development and behavior* (Vol. 2). New York: Academic Press, 1979.

Richards, R. J. Darwin and the biologizing of moral behavior. In W. R. Woodward & M. G. Ash (Eds.), *The problematic science: Psychology in nineteenth-century thought*. New York: Praeger, 1982.

Riegel, K. F. Influence of economic and political ideologies on the development of developmental psychology. *Psychological Bulletin,* 1972, *78,* 129–141.

Riegel, K. F. Developmental psychology and society: Some historical and ethical considerations. In

J. R. Nesselroade & H. W. Reese (Eds.), *Life-span developmental psychology: Methodological issues*. New York: Academic Press, 1973.

Riegel, K. F. Toward a dialectical theory of development. *Human Development,* 1975, *18,* 50–64.

Riegel, K. F. The dialectics of human development. *American Psychologist,* 1976, *31,* 689–700.

Riegel, K. F. *Foundations of dialectical psychology.* New York: Academic Press, 1979.

Riegel, K. F., & Meacham, J. A. (Eds.). *The developing individual in a changing world* (2 vols.). Chicago: Aldine, 1976.

Ross, B. M., & Kerst, S. M. Developmental memory theories: J. M. Baldwin and Piaget. In H. W. Reese (Ed.), *Advances in child development and behavior* (Vol. 12). New York: Academic Press, 1978.

Ruse, M. *The Darwinian revolution.* Chicago: University of Chicago Press, 1979.

Russett, C. E. *Darwin in America: The intellectual response 1865–1912.* San Francisco: W. H. Freeman, 1976.

Sameroff, A. J. Transactional models in early social relations. *Human Development,* 1975, *18,* 65–79.

Sanford, E. C. Mental growth and decay. *American Journal of Psychology,* 1902, *13,* 426–449.

Sarbin, T. R. Contextualism: A world view for modern psychology. In J. K. Cole & A. W. Landfield (Eds.), *Nebraska Symposium on Motivation* (Vol. 24). Lincoln, NE: University of Nebraska Press, 1977.

Schur, M. *Freud: Living and dying.* New York: International Universities Press, 1972.

Sears, R. R. Your ancients revisited: A history of child development. In E. M. Hetherington (Ed.), *Review of child development research* (Vol. 5). Chicago: University of Chicago Press, 1975.

Shinn, M. W. *Notes on the development of a child* (Vol. 1). Berkeley: University of California Press, 1893–1899.

Shinn, M. W. *The biography of a baby.* Boston: Houghton Mifflin, 1900.

Siegel, L. S., & Brainerd, C. J. (Eds.). *Alternatives to Piaget: Critical essays on the theory.* New York: Academic Press, 1977.

Simpson, W. G. A chronicle of infant development. *Journal of Mental Sciences,* 1893, *39,* 378–389, 498–505.

Sjövall, B. *Psychology of tension: An analysis of Pierre Janet's concept of "tension psychologique" together with an historical aspect.* (Trans. by Alan Dixon). Norstedts, Sweden: Scandinavian University Books, 1967.

Skinner, B. F. *The behavior of organisms.* New York: Appleton, 1938.

Skinner, B. F. Are theories of learning necessary? *Psychological Review,* 1950, *57,* 211–220.

Skinner, B. F. *Science and human behavior.* New York: Macmillan, 1953.

Skinner, B. F. *About behaviorism.* New York: Macmillan, 1974.

Spiker, C. C., & McCandless, B. R. The concept of intelligence and the philosophy of science. *Psychological Review,* 1954, *61,* 255–266.

Stout, G. F., & Baldwin, J. M. Adaptive (mental processes). In J. M. Baldwin (Ed.), *Dictionary of philosophy and psychology* (Vol. 1). New York: Peter Smith, 1902.

Sully, J. *Studies of childhood.* New York: D. Appleton, 1903.

Tetens, J. N. *Philosphische Versuche über die menschliche Natur und ihre Entwicklung.* Leipzig: Weidmanns Erben und Reich, 1777.

Thorndike, E. L. The newest psychology. *Educational Review,* 1904, *28,* 217–227.

Toulmin, S., & Goodfield, J. *The discovery of time.* Chicago: University of Chicago Press, 1965.

Vidal, F., Buscaglia, M., & Vonèche, J. J. Darwinism and developmental psychology. *Journal of the History of the Behavioral Sciences,* 1983, *19,* 81–94.

Vygotsky, L. S. The problem of the cultural development of the child. *Journal of Genetic Psychology,* 1929, *36,* 415–434.

Vygotsky, L. S. *Thought and language.* Cambridge, MA: The MIT Press, 1962. (Originally published, 1934.)

Vygotsky, L. S. *Mind in society.* (Ed. by M. Cole, V. John-Steiner, S. Scribner, & E. Souberman.) Cambridge, MA: Harvard University Press, 1978.

Watson, J. B. *Behaviorism.* New York: W. W. Norton, 1924.

Watson, J. B. What the nursery has to say about instincts. In C. Murchison (Ed.), *Psychologies of 1925.* Worcester, MA: Clark University Press, 1926.

Werner, H. *Comparative psychology of mental development.* New York: International Universities Press, 1948.

Werner, H. The concept of development from a comparative and organismic point of view. In D. B. Harris (Ed.), *The concept of development.* Minneapolis: University of Minnesota Press, 1957.

White, S. H. The learning–maturation controversy: Hall to Hull. *Merrill-Palmer Quarterly,* 1968, *14,* 187–196.

White, S. H. The learning theory tradition and child psychology. In P. H. Mussen (Ed.), *Carmichael's manual of child psychology* (3rd ed.). New York: Wiley, 1970.

White, S. H. Social proof structures: The dialectic of method and theory in the work of psychology. In N. Datan & H. W. Reese (Eds.), *Life-span developmental psychology: Dialectical perspetives on experimental research.* New York: Academic Press, 1977.

White, S. H. The idea of development in developmental psychology. In R. M. Lerner (Ed.), *Developmental psychology: Historical and philosophical perspectives.* Hillsdale, N.J.: Lawrence Erlbaum Associates, 1983.

Wohlwill, J. F. *The study of behavioral development.* New York: Academic Press, 1973.

Wolff, P. H. The developmental psychologies of Jean Piaget and psychoanalysis. *Psychological Issues,* 1960, *2* (1, Monograph No. 5).

Wozniak, R. H. A dialectical paradigm for psychological research: Implications drawn from the history of psychology in the Soviet Union. *Human Development,* 1975, *18,* 18–34. (a)

Wozniak, R. H. Dialectics and structuralism: The philosophical foundations of Soviet psychology and Piagetian cognitive developmental theory. In K. F. Riegel & G. Rosenwald (Eds.), *Structure and transformation: Developmental aspects.* New York: Wiley, 1975. (b)

Wozniak, R. H. Metaphysics and science, reason and reality: The intellectual origins of genetic epistemology. In J. M. Broughton & D. J. Freeman-Noir (Eds.), *The cognitive-developmental psychology of James Mark Baldwin: Current theory and research in genetic epistemology.* Norwood, N.J.: Ablex, 1982.

2 Methodology

Victoria Seitz
Yale University

INTRODUCTION

There is no one best method for studying human development. Occasionally, theoreticians will promote one particular method as the ideal against which all others should be viewed as inadequate. Laboratory experimentation has sometimes been championed in this manner; naturalistic observation has also had its surprisingly vociferous adherents. When one considers, however, the astonishing breadth of subject matter studied by developmental psychologists, it is easier to defend the proposition that developmental researchers need a corresponding breadth of methodology. Studying the elderly will almost inevitably require different procedures from those suitable for studying infants. Hypotheses about the determinants of physical growth may necessitate the use of biochemical laboratory tests, whereas hypotheses about the development of moral reasoning probably would not. Even within a single topical domain—sex role differentiation for example—one researcher might focus on hormonal influences while another scientist might study cultural differences in how adults socialize boys and girls. In short, developmental psychology provides so diverse and rich a topical terrain that a very broad spectrum of methodology is necessary to do justice to it. The present chapter provides an overview of these methods. In the following three sections, we consider procedures by which data are gathered, including naturalistic observations, experiments, and correlational studies. Then, we consider the ways in which people are selected for study and the problem of obtaining representative individuals from whose behavior valid generalizations can be made. In the next two sections, we consider statistical issues; first general principles, then specifically developmental concerns. Finally, we consider ethical issues involved in performing research.

OBSERVATIONAL METHODS OF OBTAINING
DATA

By naturalistic observations, we mean simply observations of events occurring in nature. Sometimes these observations are made with a clear hypothesis in mind; sometimes they are made to gain a better understanding of the kinds of events that would be interesting to study further. There are many observational methods (Boehm & Weinberg, 1977; Flanders, 1970; Wright, 1960). Wright (1960) has classified them as *open* methods in cases where the observer does not have any preconceived idea of what to look for, and as *closed* methods in cases where the observer decides in advance exactly what and when to observe.

Open Methods

The *case history*, or *diary*, is one example of an open observational method. In a case history, information is recorded with no fixed plan about events that seem interesting to the observer. If a preschool child offers a visitor objects at "a dime for each one. Or you can have two for a nickel," the child's mother may be so amused by this evidence of quantitative confusion that she may record it in a diary. The case history provides rich and detailed information, but it is also an unsystematic and subjective source of data. Consider, for example, the following record written by the parent of an 18-month-old:

> She broke a plastic highball spoon the other day. The loud snap scared her and perhaps a small piece stung when it hit her. Anyway, she cried and cried "back!" and pushed the broken pieces on me. I tried to demonstrate that they would not go "back" and at last she seemed to get the idea. Maybe she was just tired and gave up for that reason (Peterson, 1974, p. 74).

As this description shows, case histories often suggest interesting hypotheses, but it is difficult—if not impossible—to test hypotheses by referring to case history data.

A second open method is *specimen description*. Here the observer tries to record everything that is happening, in effect, trying to be a camera. With the advent of ever more sophisticated technological devices, observers can increasingly approximate the ideal of simply recording what is there. Although this is a more systematic approach than the case history, the chief problem is that specimen description yields too much information if it is continued for very long. One investigator, for example, followed an 8-year-old child for a single day, recording everything the child said and did. The resulting output, called *One Boy's Day,* required a 435 page book (Barker & Wright, 1951).

Closed Methods

Closed observational methods are based on the strategy of choosing only some aspects of behavior to record. Closed methods lose much of the richness of detail that can be obtained in case histories and specimen descriptions, but what they lose in richness they gain in precision of measurement. It is usually much easier to test a scientific hypothesis using data from systematic sampling methods than from narrative descriptions.

Event sampling is a procedure for recording certain behaviors each time they occur. For example, an observer could record instances of crying in a group of preschool children, or instances of quarrels among children at a day care center. Usually the observer records additional descriptive information as well. In studying quarrels, for example, the investigator might note the number of children involved, their sexes, who began the incident, how long it lasted, and whether it terminated spontaneously or required adult intervention. Usually, event sampling takes place over a relatively long time period. *Trait rating* is similar to event sampling, except that instead of recording events, the observer records a judgment. The observer may thus rate a child's friendliness, aggressiveness, cheerfulness, and so forth.

In a procedure called *time sampling,* the occurrence of specific kinds of behavior is observed during preselected time periods. The rationale behind time sampling is that people continue to behave in more or less the same way for relatively long periods of time, and that examining behavior only occasionally will yield a valid overall estimate of normal behavior. The length of each time interval may be only a few seconds, for some kinds of behavior, or several minutes or hours for others. The key feature is that the same time span is used according to a predetermined plan. During these times, the observer records either a single check mark (if the behavior of interest occurred) or a tally of the number of times the behavior occurred. To use the quarreling example again, the researcher might decide to observe for the first 10 minutes of four successive hours, tallying the number of quarrels that occurred during these periods. Rich information, such as why these quarrels occurred, would not be obtained by this method. But time sampling would probably permit a better comparison of the harmoniousness of two different preschoolers than would the event sampling procedure.

In a method called *field unit analysis,* the observer uses "behavior units" rather than time or events as the basis for segmenting behavior. A new behavior unit is said to begin whenever either the child's behavior or the child's environment changes. If a child who is playing in a sandbox suddenly puts sand in another child's hair, for example, or if a child is hit by another child, a new behavior unit is scored. For each behavior unit, the observer records both whether the child's behavior has changed and whether the child's environment has changed. When the observation period is completed, the observer examines the behavior units in order to analyze them.

An example of the field unit analysis method is provided in a study of 2- and 3-year-old children's responses to each other in an interracial nursery school (Stevenson & Stevenson, 1960). The investigators recorded behavior units, then found that these units could be classified into eight categories. Examples were "friendliness," where the child actively sought out the company of others, and "lack of social participation," where the child played in a solitary manner. Analyzing the behavior units, these investigators discovered that even though these young children were sensitive to the sex of other children in their social interactions, they were surprisingly insensitive to race. As the observers put it, "They might as well all be blue" (Stevenson & Stevenson, 1960, p. 370).

Special Considerations in Observing

Reliability. In all observational methods, an important goal is to achieve inter-observer reliability. If two or more observers watch the same behavior, it is important that they be able to produce accounts that coincide. As trial lawyers know, untrained observers are often unreliable. One eyewitness to a crime may assure the jury that the criminal was "tall—about 6'4"—with sandy hair" while another contends that the culprit was "about medium height, with brown hair, and shifty eyes." Unless observers could be trained to see and report the same events in the same manner, observational data would be purely subjective and therefore worthless for scientific purposes. In general, it is easier to achieve inter-observer reliability with closed than with open observational methods. In psychological research, observers are usually given practice before the study begins until they can score behavior with nearly perfect (at least 90%) agreement. It is also a common practice to have two or more observers in observational studies. When films, videotapes, or tape recordings have been made, the investigator can refer to the original behavior if there are disagreements about what happened. Before beginning a study, a researcher can also use such recorded data for pilot subjects to establish good coding systems and thereby increase inter-observer reliability.

Functions of Observations. Observational studies may serve two different purposes. The first is a *hypothesis-generating function,* which is most useful when one knows relatively little about the subject being observed. When first studying a particular population, such as preschool children, or a particular topic, such as aggression or play, a good strategy is to observe by using an open method. After a period of open observation, one is more likely to have a better idea of what could be worth studying systematically. One might then use observations in their second capacity; that is, in their *hypothesis-testing function,* employing a time sampling procedure or selecting certain individuals or behaviors for more concentrated observation.

If one were to observe infants in their homes, for example, one might notice that fathers seemed to be more playful with babies than mothers. One might then formulate a hypothesis that the nature of an infant's social interactions differs depending on the sex of the parent. To test this, one could systematically observe interactions, using event sampling, for example, to study all those episodes in which adults hold their infants. One would then confirm the hypothesis, finding that mothers most often hold infants to perform caretaking acts, such as feeding or changing diapers, while fathers most often hold babies to play with them (Lamb, 1977).

EXPERIMENTAL STUDIES

Definition and Examples

While it is impossible to draw a clear line between experimental and nonexperimental methods, generally speaking, experimental procedures imply the ability to *create* the event to be studied and to *control* factors that would interfere with the interpretability of the study's results. Before performing an experiment, a researcher formulates a hypothesis, which is a statement of how constructs in a theory are related. For example, a researcher might hypothesize that the exposure to violence increases children's aggression. The researcher then translates the hypothesis into a specific, measurable prediction, such as "if children see an hour of TV violence every day for a month, they will behave more aggressively than if they do not see the violence." To test the prediction, the experimenter could randomly assign some children to see an aggressive television program for an hour every day and other children to see a nonaggressive program (such as a nature program).[1] The assumption in using random assignment is that other factors that might cause aggressive behavior, such as the hours of violent TV programs children watch at home, will be similar in randomly assigned groups and, being similar, will not be the cause of any differences between the groups at the end of the experiment. The prediction would be confirmed if the two groups were initially equivalent in aggression, but after a month of seeing the daily hour of televised violence the first group had become more aggressive than the second.

The causal part of the hypothesized relationship, televised violence, is called an *independent variable*. The consequence, children's aggressive behavior, is called a *dependent variable*. In general, to perform an experiment, a researcher creates conditions that represent different levels of the independent variable and assigns groups of subjects to receive each different condition. An experiment therefore requires a minimum of two groups: an *experimental group*, which

_____

[1] We will discuss ethical issues in how such research might be conducted later in this chapter.

receives some kind of special treatment, and a *control group*, which is initially equivalent to the experimental group but which does not receive the treatment. In the example just given, the experimental group received one hour's worth of the independent variable—televised violence—while the control group received none. Sometimes there are several experimental groups, as when some children see films with many aggressive episodes and others see films with only a few. There can also be several control groups, as when a nature film is shown for one group and no film at all is shown for another group. The critical part of the experimental method, however, is that all of the groups must be exactly the same with the exception of the kind of treatment they receive during the experiment. If this ideal can be achieved (and random assignment to groups is the usual method of trying to accomplish it), then changes in the dependent variable (aggression) can reasonably be believed to have been caused by changes in the independent variable (TV violence).

Threats to Experimental Validity

Although the experimental method is the most powerful means of testing whether a cause–effect relationship exists, there are some special problems raised by the method. One problem is that just being part of an experiment evidently changes the behavior of some individuals. When this occurs, the results of an experiment may not be valid for real-life events (Roethlisberger & Dickson, 1939). In medical research, this problem is called the *placebo effect*. As amazing as it may seem, almost any kind of symptom can be alleviated in some individuals by giving them a placebo—a treatment that theoretically should not have curative properties, such as a sugar pill or an injection of saline solution. Once regarded as a nuisance, the placebo is now viewed by many medical researchers as an alternative treatment, reflecting the action of some not yet well-understood mechanism by which people's feelings affect their physical well-being. Often, special control groups of people who believe they are receiving a treatment, but who actually are not, are therefore included in an experiment to assess this effect.

A second problem is that random assignment to conditions may cause negative reactions to being a part of an experiment. *Resentment* at being denied a desired service can lead to a subject's refusal to participate in or to an early withdrawal from a study. Changes in control groups, such as demoralization or compensatory rivalry (the John Henry effect), may arise from having been denied a treatment rather than as a reflection of its simple absence. Thus, rather than improving the validity of a study, random assignment can sometimes create attitudes that threaten it. This may be especially true in the realm of social intervention projects, such as the provision of day care services to poor, working families (Seitz, 1982).

A third problem of the experimental method is that the apparatus and conditions in the experiment may cause people to believe that they are supposed to behave in a particular manner (Orne, 1962). In effect, certain experimental arrangements almost demand a certain kind of response that is not actually what the person would do when not participating in the experiment. An example of this *experimental demand* problem is making available a large number of aggressive toys, such as knives and guns, and very few nonaggressive toys. Such a procedure could cause children to behave more aggressively than they normally do. Even the most docile child is unlikely to play "house" or "tea party" with guns and knives.

A fourth problem is that the *experimenter's expectations* may influence the results of the experiment (Rosenthal, 1963). A researcher who believes strongly in his or her hypothesis may unwittingly create conditions confirming that hypothesis. The experimenter may, for example, give subtle cues to the subjects, causing them to behave in the expected manner. For this reason, experiments are often conducted in a "double-blind" manner. In such a procedure, neither the subjects nor the person who observes the subjects know who is receiving a particular treatment until the study is completed.

Quasi-Experimental Studies

In cases where true experiments cannot be performed, it is often possible for a researcher to introduce some degree of control over potentially interfering extraneous factors and to approximate the conditions of an experiment. A number of such approximate or "quasi-experimental" designs exist, and there is now considerable literature on their advantages and disadvantages (Bryk & Weisberg, 1977; Cook & Campbell, 1979; Cronbach, 1982; Glass, Willson, & Gottman, 1975; Schaie, 1977). Suppose, for example, that an investigator wishes to study the effects of day care on children's social development. Conducting a true experiment would require that the independent variable (day care versus no day care) come under the researcher's control: children would be randomly assigned either to receive day care or to remain at home under parental care for the duration of the experiment. Most parents would be unwilling or unable to permit their children to participate in an experiment of this kind, and most studies of such potentially important socializing events as day care, preschool intervention programs, or public versus private schooling cannot be conducted with true experiments. Quasi-experimental studies sometimes permit a more controlled approach to such problems than do simple correlational studies.

Quality.   Quasi-experimental designs vary greatly in quality. One of the best of these designs involves using people who are on waiting lists for the treatment or program in question as control subjects. Cochran (1977), for example, has studied the effects of day care with a waiting list design, and Zigler and Butterfield (1968) used this kind of quasi-experimental design to study the effects of Project Head Start. While waiting list subjects may differ in some ways from the people who actually receive the program (perhaps they are procrastinators, or somewhat less well informed about scarce community resources), they are comparable in that they are a self-selected group of people who explicitly desire to receive the program. Therefore, they provide a far superior alternative to using a group of "no day care" or "no Head Start" subjects whose families have not attempted to enroll them in the programs. Parents who choose to enroll their children in day care may be presumed to differ in many ways from parents who do not (Hock, 1980; Sibbison, 1973). Some of these differences—perhaps family size, family income, or parental educational level—could easily be more important than the day care itself in producing differences later observed between children who receive day care and those who do not.

At the opposite end of the spectrum are very poor quasi-experimental procedures that often produce misleading results. One example is the matched group design, in which the researcher compares two groups that are matched on a variable on which they normally differ and that might have a causal influence on the dependent variable. For example, if children who are receiving day care come from families who are poorer than those of children who are not receiving day care, an investigator might attempt to "match" the groups by selecting nonday-care families who have the same income level as does the day-care sample. Comparing two such groups is, unfortunately, likely to yield results that cannot be interpreted as a reflection of the true effects of day care on the children. Because it is so commonly encountered, we discuss the matching problem more extensively later in this chapter.

On the "Relevance" of Experiments

Artificiality.   One criticism of experimentation is that it is often conducted in such artificial settings with such a restricted range of conditions that we cannot apply it to the complex, real world. A great deal of research in developmental psychology has been conducted in university laboratories where children are taken into a quiet room by an adult and given tests or other psychological tasks to perform. This kind of laboratory research has been criticized as being too far removed from the children's real-life experiences to give a good picture of how they actually behave (Bronfenbrenner, 1977; Brooks & Baumeister, 1977). As Bronfenbrenner has phrased it, such research can produce a "science of the strange behavior of children in strange situations with strange adults for the briefest possible periods of time" (1977, p. 513).

This criticism has its merits. Nevertheless, controlled studies conducted in artificial settings can be very useful. The critical point is that where and how one chooses to study development depends on the questions one is asking. Some types of experiments can only be performed in a laboratory, yet the information obtained is almost certainly valid in real-life situations. If one wishes to know how well infants see color, one needs to use precision equipment that can deliver light of exactly the right brightness and wavelength (e.g., Bornstein, Kessen, & Weiskopf, 1976). The way in which infants respond to color in the laboratory is almost certainly the same way they would respond elsewhere, but the laboratory setting is necessary to measure their responses with scientific accuracy. If one is studying social behavior, however, it is possible that children do behave differently in familiar and unfamiliar places. The place where behavior is studied probably matters more for some kinds of behaviors than for others.

It is useful to think of studies as falling along a *continuum of naturalness* (Parke, 1976). Naturalistic observations usually represent studies at one end of the continuum, while controlled experiments are usually at the other end, representing relatively contrived situations. However, there is nothing about the experimental method that *requires* that experiments be conducted in artificial settings or in laboratories. To return to the example of studying the effects of televised aggression, Friedrich and Stein (1973) have established a very naturalistic setting for an experiment. Children were shown television programs as part of the ordinary activities of a nursery school session. Familiar programs (e.g., "Batman" and "Misterogers' Neighborhood") were used. The routine of the nursery school allowed a greater degree of control over the children's activities than would have been possible if the study was conducted in the children's homes. Yet the conditions were neither artificial nor laboratory-like. As we will see in later chapters, many psychologists are turning to procedures that combine the control and precision possible in experiments with the advantages of observing children in their everyday surroundings (see the chapter by Rogoff, Gauvain, and Ellis).

Theory Testing.   It is also important to recognize that experiments that seem trivial and irrelevant to real life can provide an important test of a theory. A scientist may have a very complex theory, yet the predictions based on the theory may be quite simple: either a given event will occur under specified circumstances or it will not. Physicists employ this approach when they create in a cyclotron particles that cannot exist under ordinary conditions but that their theory predicts should exist if those conditions are made proper. Finding these particles is extremely important, because it suggests that the theory is correct—it is a "go-ahead" signal for applying the explanatory theory to events in the real world. In psychology, an example of this kind of experiment is one in which language researchers have created nonsense words to study young children's acquisition of grammatical rules. When a child is shown a drawing of a strange animal and told that it is a "wug," psycholinguists have been interested to discover how the child refers to two of them (Berko, 1958). When children reply "wugs," the researcher can be confident that they have learned a linguistic rule they can apply correctly, and that they are not simply remembering a word they have heard others use. Such nonsense words do not exist in the natural language, but the way the child responds to them provides information that can be important in theory testing.

CORRELATIONAL STUDIES

Definition and Examples

In a correlational study, the researcher measures at least two variables and calculates the degree of relationship between (or among) them. Correlational studies are often performed with only one group of subjects. For example, an investigator could ascertain the number of hours of homework that children complete nightly and the children's scores on an academic achievement test in order to determine the relationship between these two variables. Correlational studies are also frequently used to compare groups, as discussed below.

There are two important features to notice about a correlation coefficient: its size and its sign. The *size* of the correlation indicates the strength of the relationship, while the *sign* indicates whether the relationship is positive or negative. Several illustrations might be helpful. The size of a correlation is always a value between -1 and $+1$. Ignoring the sign, the closer the value is to 1, the stronger the relationship, and the closer to zero, the weaker the relationship. The sign shows the direction of the relationship. A positive sign means that the high values of one variable are associated with the high values of the other, and that low values similarly occur together. An example of a moderate-sized positive relationship is the correlation of $+.57$ between height and weight in mature teenage girls (Faust, 1977). This correlation reflects the fact that taller girls tend to weigh more and shorter girls less, but that there are some exceptions to the rule. A negative correlation signifies that the high values of one variable are associated with the low values of the other. An example would be temperature and the amount of clothing worn; the lower the temperature, the more clothing people wear, and the higher the temperature, the less clothing they wear.

Interpretational Problems

Correlation coefficients can be deceptively simple. A number of factors affect whether a particular correlation coefficient is a good or a poor estimate of the true degree of relationship that exists between two variables. One of the most common problems is that an investigator has sampled too narrow a range of one or both variables. *Restriction of range* reduces the size of the correlation coefficient from the value that would be found with a more representative sample. For example, there would be little relationship between age and size of vocabulary in a group limited to children who were between 10 and 11 years old. If a relationship is *curvilinear* (for example, the average daily temperature over the months of March through November), an ordinary correlation coefficient would underestimate the true degree of predictability of temperature from the calendar date. *Reliability of measurement* affects the interpretation of correlations. Correlations between unreliably measured variables underestimate the true degree of relationship. As correlations are the basis of many analyses performed in developmental research (such as multiple regression and factor analysis), it is a good idea to become familiar with these and other technical factors affecting their interpretation. Guilford (1965) and Cohen and Cohen (1975) are two good sources of such discussions; this information can also be found in many basic statistical textbooks.

Causality—A Special Problem

Correlational evidence tells us *whether* certain events are related to each other, but not *why* they are. For example, watching aggressive television programs is correlated with the amount of aggression children display: the more hours of aggressive television the child watches, the more aggressive the child is when playing with other children (Stein & Friedrich, 1975). The problem with correlational information such as this is that the cause of the relationship is not evident. Does television incite children to violence, or do aggressive children like to watch violent programs when they aren't occupied with hitting their playmates? Or does some unknown event cause children both to become aggressive and to enjoy watching violent TV programs?

Although correlations do not prove causation, they can often suggest its probable nature. It is usually more plausible to believe that the cause runs in one direction rather than the other. For example, a number of years ago, social psychologists discovered that the price of cotton and the number of lynchings in the South were negatively correlated. It is certainly more plausible that the price of cotton is the cause and the lynchings the effect, rather than vice versa. It is hard to see how having more lynchings could cause prices to drop, whereas a drop in the price of the main commodity of a region might cause hard times, anger and frustration, and so more violence.

Naturally Formed Groups and Correlational Studies

There are many occasions when investigators compare naturally existing groups in order to discover factors affecting development. For example, children from industrialized, Western societies can typically memorize isolated pieces of information more easily than can non-Westernized children (see the chapter by Rogoff, Gauvain, and Ellis). Non-Westernized children, however, excel when they are asked to recall complex three-dimensional scenes. Cross-cultural researchers have pointed out that children in nonindustrialized societies are expected to learn by observing others in everyday activities. In contrast, children in industrialized countries spend long hours in school learning verbally presented information. The memory differences that have been found may therefore be due to the extensive cultural differences in the ways children are taught.

The study of this kind of developmental factor (cultural influences) is not experimental. One cannot randomly assign one group of children to be born to parents in a village in the Mexican highlands and another to parents living in New England. Neither can one assign people to be boys rather than girls, or infants rather than adolescents. Such factors as ethnic heritage, gender, and age are, as Kenny (1975a) aptly puts it, variables that are "attached to rather than assigned to" the organism (p. 888).

Because people are not assigned to naturally formed groups, it is never possible for such groups to be truly comparable in the way that experimentally formed groups are. Thus, studies of naturally formed groups are always *methodologically* correlational (even though one can choose statistical procedures other than correlations to analyze results from them). The challenge for the researcher in studying these important kinds of factors is to attempt to eliminate rival explanations for group differences in order to make causal inferences based on the variable of interest (e.g., age, or culture).

Obtaining Comparable Groups.   As Cole and Means (1981) point out, the more scientists know about the subject populations they are studying, the better control they can exercise over important sources of unwanted differences between the groups. Consider the comparison of normal and retarded children on intellectual development, for example. Ideally, one wishes to study two groups that differ only in the variable of interest—retardation. As Zigler (1969) remarks, however, comparisons have often been made between retarded children who live in an institution and children of normal intellect who live with their own families. It is therefore unclear whether any differences that are found are due to retardation or to institutionalization. The latter experience is known to affect children's motivation in testing situations: institutionalized children are often especially wary of strangers and tend to perform more poorly than their actual cognitive abilities would permit. Knowing the importance of institutionalization, researchers can attempt to obtain groups that are comparable on this factor; for example, by studying only noninstitutionalized subjects. (Care must be exercised, however, not to fall into the matching problem, described in the following section of this chapter, when trying to equalize groups on nuisance variables.)

Obtaining Equivalent Treatments for Different Groups.   Before differences between groups can be interpreted, it is necessary that the materials, procedures, and instructions they receive be equally motivating and equally well understood by all of the groups. In the example of retarded children given above, an attempt could be made to reduce the motivational differences likely to exist between such children and the normal children with whom they are to be compared. An extra period of warm-up interactions with the examiner, for example, could be employed with retarded children, or with any children suspected of having motivational problems related to being tested by unfamiliar adults. In one study using this strategy (Zigler, Abelson, & Seitz, 1973), lower-class preschool children who received a ten minute play period with the examiner performed better than similar children who were tested without a play period. Middle-class children's performance, however, was unaffected by this experimental manipulation, suggesting that comparisons of children from different social classes should always be made with an allowance for possible motivational differences between them.

The Group X Task Strategy for Group Comparisons.   In the comparison of naturally formed groups, Cole and Means (1981) suggest searching for Group X Task interactions using at least two tasks. These tasks should be chosen in such a way that, if the hypothesis about the underlying causes of the group differences is correct, the groups will perform equivalently on one of the tasks and differently on the other. This equivalent task condition provides a kind of control condition, in that a number of potential rival explanations (group differences in motivation, understanding instructions, etc.) are less plausible when equivalence is found on at least one task. The Cole and Means (1981) book provides numerous examples of how this strategy can be employed.

Combining Methods

The most productive strategy for studying development will often be an eclectic one. In their examination of culture and thought, Cole and Scribner (1974, 1975) call attention to the many advantages of merging the "complementary and mutually enriching research approaches" of experimentation (the psychologist's traditional method) and observation (the anthropologist's). The three steps they recommend are particularly applicable to situations where naturally occurring groups are to be compared:

1. First, analyze a proposed or actual experiment to determine the possible task-specific sources of difficulty for the subjects. Become familiar with how the subject understands the experimental tasks and his role as a subject. Does the experiment seem reasonable to the subject (foreigner/child)? Are the tasks sufficiently familiar and performable?

2. Second, see if there are naturally occurring situations in which the subjects perform well, even though they may have performed poorly in an experiment. Determine how these situations differ from the laboratory.

3. Third, integrate observation and experimentation: "experiment with the experiment." Try variations of the research procedures designed to test specific hypotheses about what causes good performance in naturally occurring situations.

For example, consider this study of young children's memory. Istomina (1975) found that 3- and 4-year-olds performed poorly when they were asked to recall objects that were placed in view on a table. Yet, in naturalistic observations, children this young showed much better recall, sometimes even remembering aspects of events that adults had forgotten. Istomina hypothesized that the poor performance in the laboratory recall task had occurred because 3- and 4-year-olds were unlikely to consider recall an abstract skill. Rather, for young children, remembering things is a means to an end. Thus, tailoring the experiment to fit into the normal expectations of the children might improve their performance. Istomina therefore "experimented with the experiment," embedding the children's task within a meaningful, realistic situation. She set up a "store" in the children's preschool and equipped it with merchandise, play money, a cash register, and a "salesperson." The children were sent on a "shopping trip" by their teacher, who slowly named five items for the child to buy before sending him or her to the "store" in the next room. Recall was much better—almost twice as high for the youngest children—in the store situation than it had been in the laboratory-like task.

Summary

In developmental studies, data can be obtained through naturalistic observations, experiments or quasi-experiments, or correlational studies. Naturalistic observations may be made either with a predetermined plan (closed methods) or with no such plan in mind (open methods). Open methods are particularly suitable for suggesting hypotheses, while closed methods are superior for testing them. In both cases, inter-observer reliability is a necessity if the observations are to be valid.

Experimental methods are those in which investigators attempt to create the event they wish to study. Experiments require a minimum of two groups; an experimental group that receives a specific treatment and a control group that does not. Random assignment is used to attempt to make the groups comparable at the time the study begins. If the groups differ at the end of the experiment, there is strong reason to believe that the experimental treatment caused the difference.

Although it is easier to draw causal inferences from experiments than from other kinds of studies, problems can occur that reduce experimental validity. Attitudinal changes in subjects, the expectations of the experimenter, and the constraints placed on the subjects during the experiment can cause outcomes that are not true reflections of the experimental treatment.

Quasi-experiments are designs that do not provide the full control possible in experiments. These designs vary greatly in quality, with the best of them approximating true experiments when used appropriately.

Even though experiments have been criticized for their lack of naturalness, they vary in the degree to which they resemble real-life situations. Psychologists are becoming increasingly creative in designing experiments that have a natural, rather than a laboratory, quality. While this is often an advantage, even artificial experiments have an important place in psychological research, because they do play a role in testing theories.

In correlational studies, the investigator's interest lies in the relationship between variables. These relationships can be studied within a single group, as in the examination of how intelligence and creativity are related. They can be studied in the context of comparing groups, as in determining whether children's gender is related to their aggressiveness. Correlations can establish the magnitude and direction of relationships, but they do not provide information on causality.

Many studies in developmental psychology involve comparing naturally formed groups to which subjects could not possibly be assigned (such as boys versus girls). Because these are correlational studies, the causative role of the difference between the groups is difficult to establish. Some guidelines for dealing with this fact of developmental research were discussed, with the recommendation that searching for Group X Task interactions is a particularly good strategy.

If we contrast the methods of research, we find that the experimental method is powerful but narrow. It is a spotlight that brightly illuminates a small portion of the stage: We can see everything in that portion very clearly, but we can see nothing else. Natural observation and correlational methods are more like dim lights that permit us to see only shadows, but they illuminate a large portion of the stage. The usual sequence in scientific method is to begin with naturalistic observations, progress to correlational methods, and then use experiments. Nonexperimental methods are the best source of hypotheses for a young science. Without knowing where to look, one could easily perform an elaborate experiment only to find that one has an excellent view of a very empty corner of the stage.

THE SELECTION OF PEOPLE TO STUDY

Representativeness

The most important question a researcher asks about the people being studied is: How *representative* are they? Ideally, one would like to be able to conclude that what is true of the subjects studied is true of others as well. In practice, however, research is usually conducted with groups of people who may easily be unrepresentative in some way. They may, for example, all be from a university community or from middle-class families.

In order to reconcile the limitations of information from particular samples with the ideal of studying people in general, a common strategy is to repeat a study (to *replicate* it) with new groups of subjects. Suppose we find in one study that middle-class, American 13-year-olds from San Francisco can reason abstractly while their 8-year-old brothers and sisters cannot. We can be more confident that we have described a genuine developmental change in logical thinking if someone replicates the study with other children, such as American children from other locales and social class backgrounds, and especially with children from other countries.

Some research involves subjects who are unusual in some way, such as juvenile delinquents or infants who were born blind. The study of unusual development is valuable in illuminating the nature of normality. The study of blind infants, for example, has taught us much about the role of smiling in normal social development (Fraiberg, 1977). Because blind children smile at the same age as do sighted children, it is clear that some kind of maturational mechanisms must be involved and that the children are not simply imitating their caregivers. In the study of unusual people, representativeness remains important in the sense that we try to study individuals who are typical of others like themselves. Studying blind children, for example, we would try to be sure that they were not unusual in some other way as well, such as being physically disabled or mentally retarded.

Comparing Individuals of Different Ages

Cross-Sectional Studies.   One way to compare the behavior of individuals of different ages is by conducting a *cross-sectional* study in which the subjects are of different ages. The major advantage of such a study is that it produces information about typical age differences relatively quickly. By studying emotional behavior in people of different ages, we could discover that temper tantrums are common among 2-year-olds but unusual in 12-year-olds without having to wait ten years for the 2-year-olds to mature. Because of this key advantage, cross-sectional studies are very common in developmental research.

The results from cross-sectional studies, however, must always be interpreted cautiously. In a cross-sectional study, there is no assurance that the younger subjects would actually come to resemble the older subjects as they develop. There are two main reasons for this. First, there may be sampling problems, especially if it is harder to obtain representative groups of individuals at one age than at another. Finding typical 12-year-olds, who are likely to be attending a local school, may be easier than finding typical 2-year-olds, some of whom are at home, some with babysitters, and some in day care centers. Cross-sectional sampling error often occurs when researchers choose their subjects by grade level rather than by age. Because children are not necessarily promoted to a new grade each year, children in a classroom can differ in age and life history (in having experienced school failure). It is, therefore, a poor idea to compare "first graders" with "fourth graders" without checking the children's ages and school records. The percentage of children who have failed a grade is likely to be higher among the fourth graders, since they have had more opportunity to fail than have the first graders. Any cause of unrepresentativeness in the sample for any age group will bias the results of a cross-sectional study.

A second problem with cross-sectional study designs is that societal changes may be responsible for some of the differences observed in persons of different ages. If IQ tests are given to adults, groups of older adults almost always score lower than do younger ones (Kimmel, 1974). Results from cross-sectional studies suggest that IQ begins to drop at about age 45 and declines slowly but continuously thereafter. However, in many of these studies, the older adults tested grew up during a time when few people attended college, and many did not even complete high school. Lack of education may have made them perform less well than the more educated younger adults, who may continue to score well on IQ tests as they grow older. Other studies of IQ test performance, in fact, show that when the *same* individuals are tested as they grow older, there does not appear to be a drop in IQ until very late in life (Botwinick, 1967). Due to the difficulties in interpreting results from cross-sectional studies, the results are often tested by other means as well, in order to permit us to be confident of the findings.

Longitudinal Studies.   In a *longitudinal* study, the same people are studied as they grow older. Although the advantage of this approach is that it yields a convincing picture of how particular individuals change over time, an obvious disadvantage is the long time required to complete it. One investigator, Lewis Terman, began a study of intellectually gifted children in 1921. Now, over half a century later, information about what became of these children is still being analyzed and reported (P. Sears & Barbee, 1978; R. Sears, 1977). A longitudinal study need not continue for an entire lifetime, but even if it continues for only a year or two, it is relatively costly in time and effort.

The most serious methodological limitation of longitudinal research is that it produces results specific to a particular *cohort* measured at particular times. (The term ''cohort'' was the Roman name for legions of soldiers who fought together; to present day demographers, it refers to persons born in the same year and thus, figuratively, marching through the life-span together.) The group one chooses to study longitudinally may differ, for both genetic and environmental–cultural reasons, from other groups one might instead have studied. Considering societal changes, for example, gifted children in the 1980s—particularly girls and minority group children—may have different opportunities from those that were available to them when Terman began his study sixty years ago. A new longitudinal study to determine what becomes of such individuals might yield quite a different set of findings from Terman's.

Another problem in longitudinal work is that subjects may cease to be available for study. People move, or become tired of participating. As a result of the loss of subjects from a study, which is called *attrition*, the subjects still participating at the end of the project may be unusual. They may be more cooperative, healthier, or better educated than people in general, and therefore not a good group upon which to base conclusions about human development. Problems also arise from measuring the same people many times. Taking IQ tests every year might cause people to become better at them. One might therefore erroneously conclude that people's IQs increase as they grow older.

Despite its limitations, longitudinal research is a very useful method in developmental psychology. As we will see later, a number of longitudinal studies have now been completed, and from them we now know a great deal about change and constancy in people's lives (Bloom, 1964; Jones, Bayley, MacFarlane, & Honzig, 1971; Thomas & Chess, 1977). As is the case with cross-sectional studies, researchers usually try to test the conclusions from longitudinal research by other means.

Cohort Sequential Designs.   One good test of the validity of the findings from a longitudinal study is simply to repeat the study at a different time and with a different group of individuals. If the same results continue to be obtained, then we can have a great deal of confidence in them. The *cohort sequential* method refers to performing a replication of a longitudinal study with subjects from a new cohort. For example, suppose social development were studied over a 10-year period beginning in 1980 with people who were 15 years old when the study began. At some later time, say five years later, the researcher would repeat the identical procedures using a new group of subjects who were 15 years old. The two different cohorts of subjects would each be studied from ages 15–25, but one of the groups would have been born in 1965 and the other in 1970. If the two groups showed similar age changes in social behavior from ages 15–25, this would strengthen the case for interpreting the changes as age-specific.

Cross-Sequential Designs.   Cross-sectional designs can also be extended into *cross-sequential* designs by re-measuring each subject in at least one followup test. The value of this kind of design is illustrated in a study of adult cognitive abilities conducted by Schaie and Labouvie-Vief (1974). These investigators measured subjects at three separate times over a 14 year time span. Using the cross-sequential method, several different kinds of information were obtained, providing an overall picture that is very informative. Figure 2.1, for example, presents the cross-sectional findings from Schaie and Labouvie-Vief's study using a test of Spatial Reasoning Ability from the Primary Mental Abilities Test (Thurstone, 1958).

As the data in Fig. 2.1 show, in each of the three years that the study was conducted, cross-sectional comparisons suggested a steady decline in spatial ability with age. In contrast, however, consider Fig. 2.2, where the data represent a 14 year picture of performance on this test by the same subjects retested longitudinally. These data suggest that, across almost the whole adult life-span, a person's ability in this area will remain constant, or may even improve. What these data—and most of the data on other tests used by these investigators—also show is cohort differences. On a wide range of intellectual tests, subjects who were born earlier were less competent as adults than were subjects born later. A

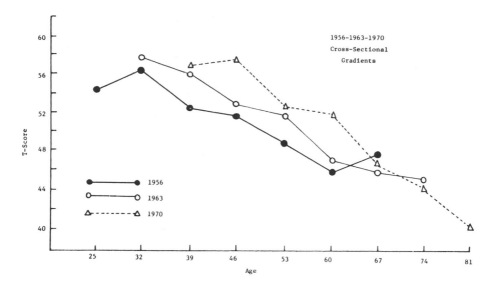

FIG. 2.1.   Spatial Ability for Subjects of Different Ages (Cross-Sectional Methodology). (From K. W. Schaie and G. Labouvie-Vief, *Developmental Psychology*, 1974, Volume 10, p. 309. Reprinted by permission of the publisher and authors.)

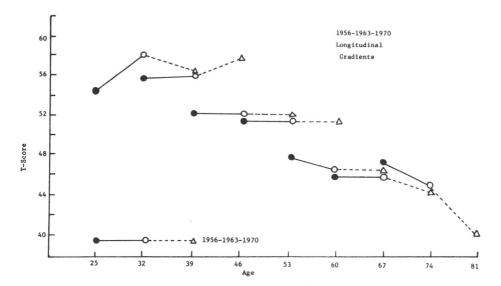

FIG. 2.2.   Spatial Ability for Subjects of Different Ages (7 Longitudinally Studied Groups). (From K. W. Schaie and G. Labouvie-Vief, *Developmental Psychology*, 1974, Volume 10, p. 309. Reprinted by permission of the publisher and authors.)

summary of this kind of information is shown in Fig. 2.3, for the Space test as well as for a composite IQ measure and for a test of educational aptitude (Thurstone, 1958).

From these data, the authors conclude, "that most of the adult life span is characterized by an absence of decisive intellectual decrements. In times of rapid cultural and technological change it is primarily in relation to younger populations that the aged can be described as deficient . . ." (Schaie & Labouvie-Vief, p. 317). As computer usage becomes more generalized in our society, this trend for young adults to outperform the levels reached by their parents on many kinds of cognitive tests when they were the same age may well be even greater than was true for the cohorts studied by Schaie and Labouvie-Vief.

Numerous other refinements of the longitudinal and cross-sectional methods exist. Discussions of these variations and statistical methods of analyses appropriate for disentangling cohort, age, and time of measurement effects may be found in Schaie (1977) and in Nesselroade and Baltes (1978).

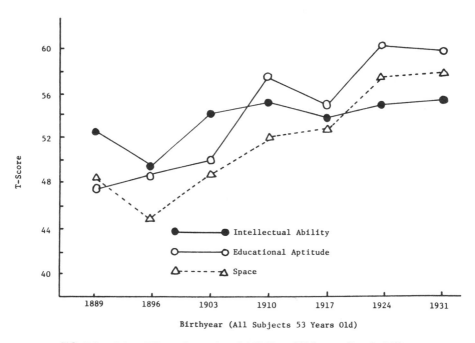

FIG. 2.3.   Cohort Effects: Comparison for 53-Year-Old Persons Born in Different Years. (From K. W. Schaie and G. Labouvie-Vief, *Developmental Psychology,* 1974, Volume 10, p. 316. Adapted and reprinted by permission of the publisher and authors.)

Representativeness in Naturally Formed Groups

Thus far, we have discussed representativeness primarily in terms of age group comparisons. As noted earlier, a common problem in the comparison of any naturally formed groups is the existence of correlated "nuisance" variables. It is important to consider how this fact affects the representativeness of samples. Suppose one wishes to compare children from two social classes on a measure of creativity. It is likely that children from different socioeconomic backgrounds will differ significantly on IQ test scores. If creativity test performance is influenced by general cognitive level, as indexed by the IQ, some method is needed to deal with this correlated nuisance variable. One strategy is to match the groups on IQ and compare the performance of the resulting *matched samples*. Another strategy is to sample randomly from the two populations, and then employ some form of *statistical "correction"* for the known difference. In one case one controls procedurally, in the other statistically. This choice can make a considerable difference in the results.

Matching.   If a variable is distributed in a different way in two populations, the chief problem with matching on it is that the resulting samples are unrepresentative of the populations (Campbell & Erlbacher, 1970; Cook & Campbell, 1979; Meehl, 1970, 1971). For example, IQ is typically distributed differently in lower- and middle-class populations, with the mean for the latter group being higher than that for the former. If lower- and middle-class children are selected for a study only if their IQs are between 90 and 110, the result will be a group of lower-class children who have relatively high IQs compared with their classmates, and a group of middle-class children for whom the reverse is true. To whom, one may wonder, could the results of such a study be generalized? Although one might wish the answer to be "children of average intellect who happen to have been raised in different socioeconomic circumstances," it is clear that this may not be true. The effects of years of social comparisons with their peers, for example, might have given both groups of children somewhat odd life experiences for children of their social class group.

A related problem is that the atypical samples created by matching are likely to be subject to unequal *regression* effects that make it difficult to study change over time. In this context, "regression" refers to the tendency for any group that is selected on the basis of extreme performance to perform in a more average manner when retested. (Furby [1973] provides a relatively nontechnical explanation of the regression problem and the reasons it occurs.) The more extreme the sample is, relative to its parent population, the greater is the expected regression. For example, taking a cutoff point of 145 on an IQ test and defining such children as "gifted" is a procedure virtually guaranteed to result in a group that will perform more poorly when retested.

Typical Samples.   Rather than risking unrepresentative sampling, it is almost always better to obtain representative samples and to attempt to deal with a nuisance variable statistically. Covariance analyses, multiple regression analyses, and techniques based on partial correlations can be helpful. This is a very complex, problematical area in statistical analysis, however, and no general principle that will cover all cases can be given. Reichardt (1979) devotes a chapter to the problem and possible solutions involved in attempting to perform such statistical adjustments, and there are a number of useful articles on the problem (Bryk & Weisberg, 1977; Kenny, 1975a; Linn & Werts, 1977; Lord, 1960, 1967; Overall & Woodward, 1977; Werts & Linn, 1970).

Dual Sampling Strategies.   A final approach to the nuisance variable problem is to employ both matched and representative samples and to compare the results, a strategy suggested by Meehl (1970, 1971). The consequences of Meehl's strategy can be seen in results from a study of personality and motivational characteristics in lower- and middle-class children (Yando, Seitz, & Zigler, 1979). With samples of children matched on age and IQ, there were few differences among social class and ethnic groups on a large battery of measures. With typical samples and a covariance analysis there were many differences. Some variables showed significant group differences regardless of the sampling procedure employed. The effort needed for such a double approach can sometimes be rewarded by the strength of the generalizations that emerge from it. As Meehl comments, ''we know more if we have both to think about'' (1971, p. 147).

Summary

Representative samples are important in order to be able to generalize validly from their performance. As truly representative samples usually cannot be obtained, replicating a study's results with new samples is the usual procedure to test whether a finding can be generalized or not.

The nature of age changes in behavior can be studied either cross-sectionally (using different subjects at each age level) or longitudinally (measuring the same subjects at different ages). Both methods are vulnerable to sampling error and societal change, although in different ways. Both methods can be strengthened by combining their best features in either a cohort sequential or a cross-sequential design.

Obtaining equally representative samples for two or more naturally formed groups is usually complicated by the existence of correlated nuisance variables. Matching on such variables is usually a poor idea, resulting in unrepresentative samples.

METHODS OF ANALYZING DATA

The spectrum of statistical techniques appropriate for developmental research is as broad as the range of methods that are used to obtain the data. It is not possible in a brief chapter to provide technical details for even a few of these statistical procedures. Instead, I concentrate on guidelines for how to seek out such information. I also discuss basic concepts such as statistical power and the importance of satisfying common assumptions. Finally, I consider some specifically developmental issues in analysis, including the assessment of change.

Sources of Information

There is usually more than one acceptable solution to the problem of how to analyze a particular set of data, and some methods have greater power, efficiency, or elegance than others. Most procedures also have specific limitations and can yield misleading conclusions when applied inappropriately. Before analyzing data, therefore, researchers find it worthwhile to become familiar with current literature on the statistical methods that others have used for similar problems.

One good method is to examine recently published articles dealing with similar research problems. This provides a sense of the current state of the art for analyzing the kind of data in question. Recent issues of the *Psychological Bulletin* are likely to contain specialized articles that may be useful. It is also worth consulting two or three textbooks. Reading a few pages on the same method from several different books often makes the method clearer. Finally, don't be afraid to ask others. Colleagues may be helpful. Departments of statistics often have a consulting service and are both approachable and well informed.

Descriptive and Inferential Statistics

In general, there are two different aims of statistical procedures. The first is to describe efficiently the characteristics of data. *Descriptive* statistics, such as means, medians, proportions, standard deviations, and correlation coefficients, convey well-understood information about the samples one has studied. In almost all research, some descriptive statistics are necessary; in some cases, they are sufficient to meet the researcher's statistical needs.

Inferential statistics were developed to meet the second aim, that of inferring characteristics of an unstudied population from information gathered on only a part of it. These procedures are based on *sampling theory,* a mathematical exploration of how well samples represent the populations from which they are taken. Some inferential procedures, such as *t-tests,* or *F ratios* in the analysis of variance, are used to infer whether or not differences between groups could reasonably have arisen through chance sampling error. In other cases, a researcher's interest lies in estimating from a descriptive statistic (e.g., a proportion) what the comparable value would be for the whole population.

Statistical Power

Effect Sizes.   The usefulness of inferential statistical methods depends on the size of the effect one is trying to detect. In comparing two groups—boys versus girls, for example—one is usually interested in the size of the difference between the means of those two groups. More technically, the interest lies in how two means differ relative to the amount of variation in the groups. I follow Cohen's (1977) terminology here and define this particular kind of *effect size* as the difference between the two population means divided by their standard deviation. (The latter is presumed to be equal in the two populations for the purposes of most statistical tests.)

Examples of Effects of Different Sizes.   Consider the Wechsler Intelligence Scale for Children (WISC), in which the standard deviation for most age groups is about 15 points. If the means of two groups differed by 12 points, the effect size would equal .8—the groups would differ on the average by eight-tenths of their common standard deviation. This can be considered a "large" effect size because it can be shown that it implies the existence of considerable separation, or nonoverlapping, in the two groups, as shown in Fig. 2.4. Cronbach (1960) estimates that the mean IQ difference between typical college freshmen and people with Ph.D. degrees is of this magnitude (p. 174). Again, using Cohen's definition, an effect size of .2 could be considered a "small" effect. Using IQ scores, a 3-point true difference between the means of two groups would represent such a small effect. A "medium" effect can be defined as .5, or half a standard deviation's separation between two group means. Fig. 2.4 illustrates the nature of the true population differences for such small, medium, and large effects.

If an effect is a *very* large one (greater than 2 or 3), there is actually no need to use statistical procedures to document its existence. It is perfectly obvious that 15-year-olds are taller than 5-year-olds. In such a case, in which there is a minimal overlap between two populations, one may simply be seeking "statistical sanctification," as Tukey has phrased it, in calculating a *t*-value or a correlation coefficient (*r*) and reporting the infinitesimal probability of its chance occurrence if the populations are equivalent. It is perhaps for this reason that ethologists and cultural anthropologists have traditionally made less use of formal statistical procedures than have psychologists. Effects such as imprinting, or effects involving such distinctive cultural practices as breastfeeding children until the age of 4 to 5 years versus weaning them at 6 months, are sufficiently obvious that they meet Leonard Savage's "interocular-traumatic" test, in which one knows what the data mean because they leap up and hit one between the eyes.

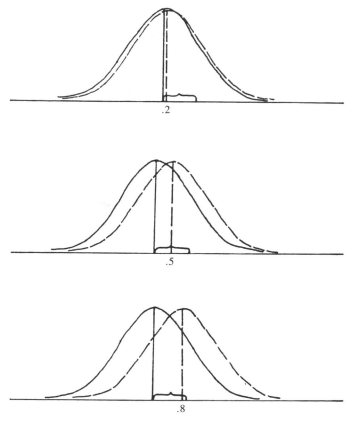

FIG. 2.4. Population Differences Corresponding to ''Small,'' ''Moderate,'' and ''Large'' Effect Sizes.

Oddly enough, if an effect size is very small, statistical procedures may also be relatively impractical. It may be important for purposes of building or testing *theories* to search for small true effects. It is interesting, for example, that the average IQ for twins has been reported to be approximately 3 points lower than the average IQ for nontwins (Husen, 1959). Detecting small true effects requires taking large samples, however, and this can be expensive or difficult to do. Also, as very large samples have enough statistical power to detect small effects, findings that are *statistically significant* (e.g., improbable based on chance alone) can be found for effects that have little practical importance.

The most useful area for employing statistical procedures lies in detecting moderate effects. In correlational terms, a moderate effect does not seem impressive: the correlation corresponding to an effect size of .5 is .24, indicating that only about 6% of the variance is accounted for by group membership. But in terms of the overlap of the populations, as Fig. 2.4 shows, the practicality of such a difference is clearer. If both populations have normally distributed scores with equal variances, almost 70% of the individuals in the lower population (for example, a control group) would fall below the median for the upper population (an experimental group). If an experimental procedure could produce such an effect, it would be a reasonably useful difference, but not such an obvious one that it could readily be seen without the aid of statistics.

As the true effect size is usually not known, it might seem that this discussion of power is pointless. However, it is usually possible to produce an educated guess about the nature of population differences, based on earlier findings and theoretical expectations. Conceptualizing theoretical questions in terms of the size of the population effects that the researcher would consider worth detecting can lead to a better decision as to which statistical procedures are necessary and so to the design of studies that will have sufficient power to determine these effects. Cohen's (1977) book provides advice concerning the desired size of samples when the investigator wishes to be relatively certain that an effect of a given size is statistically significant.

Assumptions

All statistical procedures are based upon at least a few underlying assumptions. Real data often fail to conform perfectly to textbook assumptions, even when they have been carefully collected. A large part of the challenge involved in using statistical procedures well consists of determining the most appropriate procedure, given the degree to which one's data are imperfect.

Random and Independent Observations. Two key assumptions for most statistical procedures are that the samples to be studied were drawn randomly from the population(s) of interest and that each member of the sample is independent from all others. Randomness is a cruel taskmaster of an assumption. In the early days of election forecasting, political poll takers often came to grief for their neglect of this fundamental basis for valid statistical inference. Probably the most famous example was the misprediction of the 1948 American presidential election. On the basis of data from biased samples, the editors of one major newspaper published headlines announcing the election of Thomas E. Dewey as the new president. Photographs of President Harry S. Truman smilingly holding the paper aloft the following morning are sometimes printed in books on sampling theory to provide a cautionary note. Recently, respect for the principle of careful sampling has led to some rather breathtaking demonstrations of the rewards that mathematical statistics has to offer for those who are able to meet its demanding theoretical requirements. It is now routine for many election outcomes to be predicted accurately from samples of less than 1% of the total vote.

For many problems of developmental psychology, random or well-stratified sampling procedures may not be necessary, as the processes that are being studied are relatively universal (e.g., many aspects of language development, physical development, or preschool children's learning). But for other research purposes, investigators need to specify their sampling procedures very carefully and limit their generalizations to the population that the sample actually represents until their findings have been replicated.

Independence of observations is not usually so difficult to achieve. As developmentalists have become more concerned with ecological validity, however, they have begun more often to study what Bronfenbrenner (1979) terms "second order effects"—the influences of other people on the subjects. Studies of these effects can raise problems for the independence of observations, even when subjects are assigned randomly to certain conditions. Consider, for example, the design of a study conducted by Jacklin and Maccoby (1978) that examines preschool children's social behavior in same-sex versus mixed-sex pairs. Viewed one way, there are six groups of children in the study. Given girl-girl, boy-boy, and girl–boy pairs, there are three groups to which a girl could be randomly assigned, and the same is true for boys. In this kind of study, however, there are not actually six independent groups, because of the children's influences on each other. Consider what might occur with measures of aggression. If Billy the Bully is paired with Arthur Average, Arthur may well be provoked to become more aggressive than he normally is. Such socially induced changes in behavior multiplied over several pairs of children would produce a positive correlation for the scores in the group. Negative correlations might also be found: If Billy's partner is Mikey Meek, Mikey might become even less aggressive than normal, crying and cowering in the corner. As these examples illustrate, the exact kind of interdependence may not be predictable, but the fact that the scores are related, rather than independent, must be dealt with by statistical procedures that take this fact into account. As researchers have ventured into the exciting territory of studying second-order effects, there has been an increasing need to deal with the statistical problems created due to the nonindependence of paired scores.

Normality and Homogeneity of Variance.   Two common assumptions for many statistical procedures' validity are normality and homogeneity of variance. Comparing the means of two samples, for example, the populations from which the samples are selected ideally would have normally distributed values of the variable in question and the variances of the two populations would be similar. In comparison with the need for random, independent sampling, these assumptions are usually much less important sources of concern. Bock (1975) and Harris (1975) provide good discussions of the consequences for the validity of many statistical tests of violating these and other common assumptions. Harris, for example, concludes that as long as sample sizes are 10 or more, and the populations are unimodal, normal-curve-based tests on a single correlation coefficient can almost always be considered valid. For F- and t-tests, again there is considerable latitude in the conditions under which the tests are probably valid, e.g., "so long as two-tailed tests are used; the ratio between the largest and smallest sample variance is no greater than about 20 to 1; the ratio between the largest and smallest sample size is no greater than about 4; and the total degrees of freedom for the error term is 10 or more (Harris, 1975, p. 23).'' These are fairly generous conditions and are likely to be met in most cases.

Scale of Measurement.   Most statistical procedures are intended for data that represent at least an interval scale of measurement of the underlying conceptual variable. That is, the numbers are presumed to be assigned to the data in such a way that equal differences between numbers reflect equal real differences in the conceptual, underlying variable. The Fahrenheit and Celsius scales used to measure temperature are interval scales because the difference between 10 and 20 degrees Fahrenheit represents the same magnitude of true temperature change as the difference between 20 and 30 degrees. If an interval scale can be constructed so that an assigned value of zero corresponds to a conceptual absence of the underlying variable, then the scale is called a ratio scale. (This is not true for the Fahrenheit scale, as 0 degrees does not mean an absence of temperature.) The use of inches to measure length qualifies as an example. Data based on ratio scale measurement satisfy the most stringent level-of-measurement requirements needed for any statistical procedure. Unfortunately, this quality of measurement, or even the slightly less elegant interval scale, is relatively uncommon for behavioral science data.

More commonly, the numbers that are generated by measurement procedures in the behavioral sciences bear only an ordinal relationship to the conceptual variable the researcher wishes to assess. A measure of achievement motivation can be based on children's interview responses in a manner that appears to be meaningfully related to the conceptual variable. But the best that can be said of the resulting numbers may well be that the larger they are, the greater the child's achievement motivation.

In many cases, it is probably not misleading to use statistical procedures designed for data produced by interval scale measurement, even if the measurement does not achieve this level. As Harris (1975) points out, alternative procedures that are supposed to be more appropriate for less than interval scale data often yield very similar results to those that are produced by using the procedures designed for interval scale data. In his opinion, ''searching out statistical procedures and measures of relationship especially designed for nominal or ordinal data is usually a waste of time'' (p. 228).

Care is needed, however, in the way in which generalizations are made from the results of analyses performed on numbers that bear only an ordinal relationship to the underlying variable. There is a particular need for caution in interpreting *interactions* that are found to be significant when the level of measurement is no better than ordinal (Stanovich, 1976). As Cole and Means (1981) discuss, if one can assume a monotonic relationship (e.g., for any increase in the conceptual variable, there is an increase of *some size* in the response measure), then *cross-*

over interactions can be interpreted. A crossover occurs if one group is better than the other in one condition but worse than the other in a different condition. For example, if Westernized children score better than non-Westernized children on one test (recalling isolated bits of information), but they score more poorly than non-Westernized children on a second test (recalling information from complex scenes), it would be considered a crossover interaction. Krantz and Tversky (1971) also discuss interactions and provide a method for determining whether or not an interaction would disappear if the data were to be transformed nonlinearly. As the search for Group X Task interactions is a basic strategy for comparing naturally formed groups (discussed earlier), these references are worth examining before conducting such research.

Nonparametric Procedures

When data fail to meet assumptions such as normality or interval scale measurement, an investigator can often choose a nonparametric statistical procedure. Nonparametric tests, such as the Chi-square Test, typically require that very few assumptions be met in order for the test to be valid. Unfortunately, they also tend to be low in statistical power; that is, they are less likely to detect moderate true effect sizes than are parametric procedures such as F- or t-tests.

As an example, consider the results of a study of the long-range effects of an intervention program given to children during their infancy (Seitz, Rosenbaum, & Apfel, 1983). When these children were in elementary school, the boys who had received the intervention showed much better school adjustment than did control boys who had not received the program. The cost of remedial and other special school services needed by the boys averaged about $400 for the intervention boys and $1500 for the control boys, a difference that was significant when analyzed by a t-test. A nonparametric chi-square analysis, comparing the fact that 4 of the 11 intervention boys, versus 8 of the 11 control boys, were receiving some kind of special services, would not have been significant. Often, a nonparametric procedure involves sacrificing important information; in this case, the fact that the kind and cost of the services were very different for the two groups. To choose a low power procedure if a stronger analysis would be reasonable because of only minor violations of statistical assumptions, is to fail to do justice to one's data. In those cases in which nonparametric procedures do seem to be the best choice, good sources of information on how to choose and when to use them are Hollander and Wolfe (1973) and Siegel (1956).

Multivariate procedures

Multivariate procedures are those that permit the simultaneous analysis of multiple dependent variables (Bock, 1975). One example is the multivariate analysis of variance (MANOVA), in which groups are compared on several outcomes. Thus, rather than comparing an experimental and a control group on a single outcome such as an overall IQ score, the investigator might use a MANOVA to compare them on two measures, such as a verbal IQ and a performance IQ. As the two scores are correlated, the MANOVA would probably be a good choice. It would be better, for example, than performing an ordinary analysis of variance (ANOVA) on each of the two scores, as separate tests on correlated scores provide redundant information. The MANOVA is designed to provide correction for correlated outcomes. Another multivariate procedure is canonical correlation, which is a means of determining relationships between two sets of variables (instead of between two single variables as in ordinary correlation). For most univariate statistical procedures (with one dependent variable), there is an analogous multivariate procedure.

There are a number of texts that describe multivariate statistical procedures with special reference to their use in the behavioral sciences (Bock, 1975; Harris, 1975; Tatsuoka, 1971; Timm, 1975). These techniques are increasingly popular, probably due to the increased availability of suitable computer programs to perform them. Multivariate assumptions are often straightforward generalizations of the assumptions on which univariate procedures are based (e.g., multivariate normality). Not as much is known as yet about the consequences of violating assumptions for multivariate procedures. It is therefore advisable to be more careful in using them to follow good basic statistical practice, such as obtaining samples that are of equal size and that are reasonably large (preferably 30 or more).

An important principle in using multivariate methods is that the variables to be analyzed must not be linearly dependent. That is, none may provide information that is fully redundant with the information already given by the other variables. This happens in practice when the unwary analyst tries to use all the subscales of a test and also the overall test score in a single analysis. It can also happen when any two variables are very highly correlated. As the probability of adding redundant information increases as the number of variables increases (Belsley, Kuh, & Welsch, 1980), this leads to a second principle: the number of variables to be included in the analysis should not be large relative to the total number of subjects. A wise practice is to limit the number of variables on which groups are to be compared to no more than half the size of the smallest cell in the design. If the study has 16 boys and 16 girls, 8 variables would be a reasonable upper limit to the number of variables included.

Summary

In order to select the best procedure for analyzing data, it is often advisable to seek out specialized information from recent articles, basic texts, colleagues, and—for unusually complex problems—from professional statisticians. Simple descriptive statistics are sufficient to meet the needs of some research projects; inferential statistics, usually involving significance tests to determine whether results could have occurred through sampling error alone, are often required as well.

The usefulness of inferential statistical procedures is related to the size of the effect the researcher is studying. Statistical methods vary in power, just as a telescope does. As a general rule, too, power increases as the size of the sample does. High power methods (or large sample studies) can detect tiny effects that are metaphorically equivalent to distant stars. Low power (or small sample) methods may be able to detect only large true effects—the equivalent of looking for a planet. Researchers should speculate on the size of the effect that is likely to exist and plan the size of their experiments and the choice of their statistical procedures accordingly.

Deciding whether data meet assumptions for statistical procedures is an area in which considerable judgment is required. Reviews of some of these basic assumptions were provided. Nonparametric procedures are often appropriate if basic assumptions cannot be met. The validity of multivariate procedures may be more affected by violation of basic assumptions than is the case for the validity of univariate procedures; multivariate methods should therefore be used more cautiously.

DEVELOPMENTAL ISSUES AND STATISTICS

Aims of Developmental Research

Developmental Functions.   One common aim of developmental psychologists is to establish the "developmental function" for a behavior (McCall, 1981; Wohlwill, 1973). This is the process of describing what is typical, average, behavior at different ages. The data shown in Figs. 2.1 and 2.2 are examples of developmental functions for cognitive abilities during adulthood. The documentation of basic developmental functions was a key interest early in the history of developmental psychology. Normative patterns for physical growth, language development, and so forth are now a standard feature of developmental textbooks.

Individual Differences.   Another common developmental research aim is the study of individual differences and the stability or instability of a trait across time. For example, is IQ stable: is a bright child always a bright child? Will an unusually tall 12-year-old girl become an equally unusually tall woman?

Statistical Implications of the Two Aims.   The first of these two aims is usually addressed statistically by methods that allow the comparison of means. If there are two times of measurement, the means can be compared with a *t*-test. If there are three or more measurement occasions, some possible choices are an analysis of variance (ANOVA), multivariate analysis of variance (MANOVA), planned trend analysis, or a repeated measures ANOVA. If the data are obtained longitudinally, there will usually be significant positive correlations between the scores for any two times. The procedure chosen should therefore be one that takes this fact into consideration (e.g., a t-test for correlated observations). For three or more times of measurement, either a MANOVA or a repeated measures ANOVA can be used for longitudinal data (see McCall & Appelbaum, 1973, for comparisons of the procedures). With a repeated measures ANOVA, it is usually necessary to introduce a correction for the fact that correlations between tests given close together in time are found to be higher than correlations between the same tests given a long time apart; Winer (1971) provides the necessary information for doing so.

With three or more age levels, a planned trend analysis is a more powerful procedure for detecting age effects and interactions with age than is a standard ANOVA. If developmental change can reasonably be expected to be in the same direction—the scores are either steadily increasing or decreasing, but not both—across the age span in question, trend analysis is more appropriate (Hale, 1977). Hays (1963), Kirk (1968), and Winer (1971) all counsel the use of planned comparisons when justified by reasonable theoretical expectations, rather than the use of an overall ANOVA F-test. Winer (1971, pp. 482–485) specifies how to explore interactions in trend analysis.

The second aim requires information about correlations at each time. As McCall (1977) points out, correlational methods are of little value in determining developmental functions, because correlations are insensitive to differences in mean values across time. Correlational methods are fundamental to the individual differences approach because they preserve information about rank order for all testings. Ordinary correlations, partial correlations, and multiple regression procedures can provide efficient descriptions of the relationships of interest (see Cohen & Cohen, 1975; Draper & Smith, 1981; Kerlinger & Pedhazur, 1973).

Comparison of Groups

Sometimes both aims interest the researcher simultaneously. For example, the investigator may wish to determine whether there are meaningful individual differences in developmental functions. It is also possible to use the data to identify groups of individuals who have recognizably different patterns of development. For example, an investigator might wish to determine if children born to teenage mothers show a different pattern of cognitive development from that of children born to older mothers.

Although comparisons for naturally formed groups are correlational, the statistical analyses applied to the data from such studies need not be. The choice of method depends on whether the researcher's primary interest lies in the group means or in the percentage of variance that is accounted for by group membership status. One can compare the mean from a group of boys with the mean from a group of girls by a t-test. It is equally feasible to calculate a correlation coefficient to describe the relationship between sex and performance. All that is necessary is to assign numerical values to the sex "variable" (e.g., 0 = male, 1 = female, or vice versa), and to compute the correlation between sex coded in this manner and performance scores. Similarly, analysis of variance (ANOVA) problems can be analyzed as multiple regression problems (an extension of simple correlational analysis) by assigning numerical values to different levels of the classifying variables. A Sex X Race ANOVA design might thus be recast as a multiple regression predicting performance from sex and racial group membership.

As Cohen and Cohen (1975) point out, a comparison of means is most informative when measures impart a direct sense of the magnitude of the effect. Dollars of welfare costs, age at first childbearing, height, and number of ounces of alcohol consumed daily are directly meaningful numbers. To be told that teenage mothers had an average age of 16 years at the birth of their first child, while a control sample had an average age of 22 would be immediately understandable. Many social science data are based on arbitrary units of measurement, however. To be told that teenage mothers had an average "family conflict" score of 10 while the control sample had an average value of 2 would not be readily interpreted. If one were told, however, that the younger–older mother distinction in the sample accounted for 50% of the variance in family conflict scores, it would be much more easily understood. Cohen and Cohen (1975) argue that multiple regression analysis tends to be more useful, therefore, with data of this kind.

Measuring Change

The single issue that is perhaps the most basic interest in developmental research—the assessment of change over time—is also one of the most difficult problems to address statistically. The principal reason for this fact is that detecting change requires highly reliable measures. (Unreliability, by its very definition, means that scores are likely to be different the next time a measurement is taken.) Using completely reliable measures, it is legitimate to calculate a simple difference score between time 2 and time 1 and to analyze these difference scores. Physicists can calculate changes in temperature, or pressure, or volume, with exactitude. Data in psychological research are usually only moderately reliable, and psychologists cannot measure change so easily.

Psychological change is also difficult to study because a trait can be differently manifested at different ages, and its causes may not remain constant. Aggression, for example, is not likely to be displayed in the same way by a 10-year-old as by a 2-year-old, nor are the causes of aggressive behavior (considered relatively normal in 2-year-olds) the same for the two ages. Change scores comparing the number of times someone bites a peer would thus not only be statistically ill-advised, but also psychologically ridiculous. Studying developmental change requires the researcher to deal both with problems of reliability of measurement and with changing manifestations of, and causes of, the traits the researcher is tracking.

There are technical reasons, deriving from measurement theory, why the difference between unreliable scores is even more unreliable. Discussions of these reasons may be found in many textbooks and in some specialized articles (Cronbach & Furby, 1970; Reichardt, 1979; Werts & Linn, 1970). As a concrete illustration, consider what scores should be like if children receive an IQ test at two different times, about a week apart. If one were asked to place a bet on a child's second score, based on one's knowledge of the first score, one might be willing do so within a range of 5 points or so. But if one were asked to bet on the specific number of points the score would change and whether the direction would be up or down, it would be much riskier. One has a much better (more reliable) idea of what the child's basic cognitive level is than one does of how much it will change from one testing occasion to another. Even with quite reliable variables ($r = .80$), it is easy for the difference score between them to have a reliability as low as .50. Cohen and Cohen (1975) describe the situation well: "the danger in using difference scores is a real one, since they frequently cannot be expected to correlate very substantially with anything else, being mostly measurement error" (p. 64).

A number of alternative procedures to difference scores have been suggested for studying change. Cohen and Cohen's recommendation (1975, chapter 9) is to use regressed change scores. Sociologists and economists likewise tend to favor methods based on multiple regression or partial correlation (Goldberger, 1971; Heise, 1970). Kenny (1975a) points out that cross-lagged panel correlation can be a good choice for ascertaining possible causes of change in a longitudinally studied sample. As Kenny points out, multiple regression presumes causative relationships between predictors and the criterion for study and is vulnerable to measurement error and to unmeasured third variables. Cross-lagged panel correlation presumes both measurement error and unmeasured third variables and attempts to deal with them. This method, along with suggestions for when it should and should not be used, is described in several sources (Cook & Campbell, 1979; Kenny, 1973, 1975a; Rickard, 1972; Rozelle & Campbell, 1969). In practice, it is usually necessary to have relatively large samples to use cross-lagged panel correlation effectively.

There are also a number of procedures that can be applied to the more complex problem of comparing the amount of change in two or more groups. Discussion of these procedures is beyond the scope of this chapter; interested readers may consult Kenny (1975b) and Reichardt (1979) for details.

The choice of a method for analyzing change depends on how the data are gathered (e.g., as judgments in a scaling procedure or scores on tests), on the reliability of the measures, on the underlying pattern of change (increasing or decreasing, linear or not), and on whether the causes of the behavior are assumed to be the same at each time of measurement. Choosing a method is not necessarily as difficult as it sounds. Some simple scatterplots of performance at time one versus time two, and graphs showing the mean performance of each group at each time, can be useful aids in determining what kind of situation the data fit into. By comparing these diagrams with the theoretical ones shown in Reichardt (1979) or Kenny (1975b), it may be possible to decide on an appropriate treatment of the data.

As suggested above, the better the investigator's understanding of the causes and measurement problems involved, the better the statistical analysis of the results is likely to be. What is really needed to study change intelligently is a good working model of causality (Blalock, 1964; Kenny, 1979). As more substantive information becomes available on an issue and a better theory is developed, it is possible to develop increasingly plausible causal models and to use statistical procedures to test them. As Kenny notes, "Ideally the researcher starts with a model or formulates one. Then the researcher determines if the data to be analyzed can estimate the parameters of the model and if the data can falsify the model. Such estimation and testing reveal whether the model is too general, too simple, or just plain wrong" (1979, p. 6).

Kenny's book on nonexperimental causal inference (1979) shows that estimates of causal parameters can be made in a number of ways, including regression coefficients, partial correlations, factor loadings, and canonical coefficients. Nonexperimental causal inference has long been of interest to economists and sociologists, who are generally unable to manipulate the variables—such as interest rates, money supply, crime rates, or urban density—that are important in their theory development. In many cases, developmental psychologists may find these methods useful as well.

Summary

The two chief aims in developmental research are determining what is typical behavior at different ages (establishing the "developmental function") and studying the stability of behavior across time. Statistical procedures for the former involve comparisons of means; addressing the second aim requires methods based on correlations.

The measurement of change is of particular interest to developmental psychologists; yet it is complicated due to the unreliability of measurement, and because of normal developmental changes in the causes and expression of traits. There is no simple solution to these problems. A number of approaches that are sometimes appropriate were discussed. It is likely that causal modeling will prove to be the best strategy for conceptualizing change and that, as substantive knowledge and theory improve in an area, so also will the measurement of change.

ETHICAL ISSUES IN DEVELOPMENTAL RESEARCH

Historical Reasons for Concern

Human beings are not guinea pigs to be experimented with at will. The history of science, however, contains some chilling episodes of science run amok. In the 1920s, medical investigators allowed a group of prisoners suffering from syphilis to remain untreated to prove the effectiveness of the penicillin cure they provided to others (U. S. Public Health Service, 1973). In the 1930s, two psychologists raised a pair of infant twin girls in a single room, rarely speaking to or playing with them, to see if they would develop normally despite these deprivations (Dennis & Dennis, 1941). It is now recognized that the potential emotional and intellectual damage to the children was much too great to permit such a study to be attempted. Due to a growing awareness of ethical issues in research, studies such as these would never be permitted today.

A more recent study that raised the ethics issue in public awareness was performed by Stanley Milgram (Milgram, 1965). Milgram designed the study because of his concern about the obedience Nazi officials had shown in carrying out inhumane acts during World War II. In an effort to learn more about this frightening phenomenon, Milgram studied it in a laboratory, having American college students perform the role of "simply following orders." The results were disturbing: Many students continued to press buttons that had been described as delivering painful electrical shocks, even when they could see the "victim" in the next room, evidently suffering and finally becoming unconscious. Although the subjects were later told the truth—that no shock had been employed and that the "victim" was an actor—the possibility of psychological damage to these subjects was clearly present. This study raised a storm of controversy (see Baumrind, 1964).

Due to the potential for harm, there are some who feel that research with human subjects should never be performed. This extreme position, however, also carries risks for society. Advances in the treatment of diseases such as rabies and yellow fever are clear examples of how scientific knowledge has reduced human misery, and research with human subjects was essential to produce this knowledge. Similarly, practices such as placing children in institutions were once more common than they are today because research has demonstrated that alternative methods of care are usually less harmful. Society needs the knowledge that science can produce, although it must always be careful of the cost.

It is also now recognized that special ethical problems arise when young children are subjects for research. There are many important questions about child development that research might answer to the benefit of all children. But children are vulnerable and may suffer more extensively than an older person from any negative effects of experimental procedures. Children are also unlikely to be able to weigh the potential risks and benefits of participating in a study.

There is no simple solution to the problem of how to balance the benefits of research against the risks involved. A common approach is to have special ethics committees examine proposed research before it is conducted to determine whether it might pose risks and, if so, whether it should be conducted. Federal regulations now require that institutions receiving governmental support for research have an ethics committee screen all proposals for research involving human subjects. There are a number of guidelines that these ethics committees must employ (National Commission for the Protection of Human Subjects of Biomedical and Behavioral Research, 1977).

Guidelines for Ethics in Research

One guideline for ethics in research is that the research should be *scientifically sound and significant*. People have a right not to be asked to participate in studies that are so trivial or poorly designed that they cannot yield useful information. The first decision of an ethics committee, therefore, is whether or not the research is worth doing from a scientific point of view.

A second guideline is *justifiable risk*. The ethics committee must decide whether there are any potential risks and, if so, how serious these risks are. In developmental psychology, most research involves what is called "minimal risk"; that is, no more likelihood of harm than the child normally encounters in daily life. When the risk is more than minimal, however, ethics committees must wrestle with the question of whether the risks are justifiable. If the subjects are likely to receive important benefits, such as a cure for an illness or psychological disturbance, and if the researcher is using the safest possible method, the committee may decide that the risks are justified in that case.

A third ethical principle is the necessity for *informed consent*. People have a right to know exactly what will happen to them if they agree to participate in a study, the nature of any possible risks, and the manner in which the results of the study will be reported. They also have the right not to be coerced in any way and to withdraw from the research at any time. The principle of informed consent does not mean that deception can never be practiced in an experiment. If the deception is mild and is necessary for the purpose of the study, the committee may decide it is permissible. In order to study gambling behavior, for example, it might be necessary to "rig" apparatus so that what the subject thinks is a game of skill is actually a game of chance. If any deception is employed, the researcher is required to provide the truth before the subject leaves the experimental setting.

Obtaining informed consent from children poses special problems, as they are less able to understand the purpose and nature of the research than are adults. Law and long-time practice therefore dictate that the consent for children's participation in a study be obtained from the child's parents or legal guardians. When children are old enough, their own assent is also required, and, as with adults, they must always be allowed to discontinue participating if they wish to do so. As children become adolescents, their best interests sometimes require that they, rather than their parent, should be the only people asked for consent. Ethics committees have special guidelines as to how researchers should obtain consent for participation in programs dealing with drug addiction, teenage pregnancy, and other areas in which the requirement of parental permission might cause the adolescent to avoid participating in a program that he or she would otherwise like to be a part of.

Another guideline is the *right to privacy*. The results of a subject's performance should not be publicized in any way unless the person does not object. In most developmental research, this is not a problem, as results are reported as averages or correlations from groups of subjects. Reporting an individual's performance would require the individual's permission if that person could be identified in any way.

A final guideline is that *principles of justice* must be followed in choosing subjects. If there are any risks in research, they should be borne equally by all members of a society. People who are especially weak or vulnerable, such as children, the sick, and the poor, should not be participants in research more often than other groups of people unless the research is especially designed to benefit them.

In summary, balancing competing ideals in performing research is often not easy. On the one hand, freedom of inquiry is a basic scientific ideal that deserves to be vigorously defended. On the other hand, the protection of individual rights is equally basic. Although there is probably no one "best" solution to the problem of weighing the alternatives, the trend toward ethics committees is a welcome one that should help to maximize the information science can produce, while minimizing its risks and costs.

SUMMARY AND CONCLUSIONS

In this chapter, a number of methods used by developmental psychologists to gather their data and to analyze their results have been discussed. A key emphasis throughout has been the need for flexibility and breadth in locating and adapting methodology. There is no single, best method to study all of the issues that are important in development. The contributions of ethologically trained researchers to our understanding of children's attachment and emotional development has been enormous. These researchers have extensively favored observational methods, rather than experiments, for good and practical reasons. The contributions of cognitive psychologists to our understanding of children's learning has also been enormous. Many of these researchers have used carefully controlled experiments in laboratory settings, again because the method was reasonable and appropriate. It is simply not possible to single out one method of choice for all cases.

To a considerable extent, developmental researchers are becoming increasingly creative in their studies, blending and merging features from different research traditions into their methods. The procedures suggested by Cole and Scribner are a good example of this. So is the trend toward conducting experiments in real-life settings, such as day care centers (Friedrich & Stein, 1973).

Technological advance is aiding research in many ways. Reliable observations are much more easily obtained from videotaped sessions, as investigators can re-examine the behavior as often as is necessary to establish a good coding system. Innovations such as split-screen videotaping have made possible excellent studies of dyadic interaction, as the behavior of both partners to an interaction can easily be directly compared (Brazelton, Koslowski, & Main, 1974; Stern, 1977). Technological advances in medicine, too, are playing a role in the greater sophistication now possible in psychological research. The recent development of PET (Positron Emission Tomography) scan technology has made it possible to view the cerebral blood flow in prematurely born infants—information that may soon help to explain why some of these infants have much better long-term psychological outcomes than do others.

Statistical advances are also occurring, primarily in the greater availability of computer packages for statistical procedures, This is, at present, a mixed blessing. Complex analyses are often not good choices for relatively unreliable data obtained on relatively few subjects. The easy availability of multivariate analyses is a temptation that is not always avoided when it should be. In the long run, however, the increased availability of good computer packages cannot help but benefit developmental researchers.

This is an exciting time to be performing developmental research. The field is rich and stimulating. There is a niche for people of all manner of talents, from the technologically oriented person interested in studying basic perception to the more socially oriented student of children's friendships. The following chapters bear witness to this diversity.

REFERENCES

Barker, R. G., & Wright, H. F. *One boy's day: A specimen record of behavior.* New York: Harper & Row, 1951.

Baumrind, D. Some thoughts on ethics of research: After reading Milgram's "Behavioral study of obedience." *American Psychologist,* 1964, *19,* 421–423.

Belsley, D. A., Kuh, E., & Welsch, R. E. *Regression diagnostics: Identifying influential data and sources of collinearity.* New York: Wiley, 1980.

Berko, J. The child's learning of English morphology. *Word,* 1958, *14,* 150–177.

Blalock, H. M. *Causal inferences in non-experimental research.* Chapel Hill, N. C.: University of North Carolina Press, 1964.

Bloom, B. S. *Stability and change in human characteristics.* New York: Wiley, 1964.

Bock, R. D. *Multivariate statistical methods in behavioral research.* New York: McGraw-Hill, 1975.

Boehm, A. E., & Weinberg, R. A. *The classroom observer: A guide for developing observation skills.* New York: Columbia Teacher's College, 1977.

Bornstein, M. H., Kessen, W., & Weiskopf, S. Color vision and hue categorization in young human infants. *Journal of Experimental Psychology: Human Perception and Performance,* 1976, *2,* 115–129.

Botwinick, J. *Cognitive processes in maturity and old age.* New York: Springer, 1967.

Brazelton, T. B., Koslowski, B., & Main, M. The origins of reciprocity: The early mother-infant interaction. In M. Lewis & L. G. Rosenblum (Eds.), *The effect of the infant on its caregiver.* New York: Wiley, 1974.

Bronfenbrenner, U. Toward an experimental ecology of human development. *American Psychologist,* 1977, *32,* 513–531.

Bronfenbrenner, U. *The ecology of human development.* Cambridge, Mass.: Harvard University Press, 1979.

Brooks, P. H., & Baumeister, A. A. A plea for consideration of ecological validity in the experimental psychology of mental retardation. *American Journal of Mental Deficiency,* 1977, *81,* 407–416.

Bryk, A. S., & Weisberg, H. I. Use of the nonequivalent control group design when subjects are growing. *Psychological Bulletin,* 1977, *84,* 950–962.

Campbell, D. T., & Erlbacher, A. How regression artifacts in quasi-experimental evaluations can mistakenly make compensatory education look harmful. In J. Hellmuth (Ed.), *Compensatory education: A national debate.* Vol. 3 of *The disadvantaged child.* New York: Brunner/Mazel, 1970.

Cochran, M. A comparison of group day and family child-rearing patterns in Sweden. *Child Development,* 1977, *48,* 702–707.

Cohen, J. *Statistical power analysis for the behavioral sciences* (Rev. ed.). Hillsdale, N. J.: Lawrence Erlbaum Associates, 1977.

Cohen, J., & Cohen, P. *Applied multiple regression/correlation analyses for the behavioral sciences.* Hillsdale, N. J.: Lawrence Erlbaum Associates, 1975.

Cole, M., & Means, B. *Comparative studies of how people think: An introduction.* Cambridge, Mass.: Harvard University Press, 1981.

Cole, M., & Scribner, S. *Culture and thought: A psychological introduction.* New York: Wiley, 1974.

Cole, M., & Scribner, S. Theorizing about socialization of cognition. *Ethos,* 1975, *3,* 249–268.

Cook, T. D., & Campbell, D. T. *Quasi-experimentation: Design and analysis issues for field settings.* Chicago: Rand-McNally, 1979.

Cronbach, L. J. *Essentials of psychological testing.* (2nd ed.). New York: McGraw-Hill, 1960.

Cronbach, L. J. *Designing evaluations of educational and social programs.* San Francisco: Jossey-Bass, 1982.

Cronbach, L. J., & Furby, L. How we should measure "change"—or should we? *Psychological Bulletin,* 1970, *74,* 68–80.

Dennis, W., & Dennis, M. G. Infant development under conditions of restricted practice and minimum social stimulation. *Genetic Psychology Monographs,* 1941, *23,* 147–155.

Draper, N., & Smith, H., Jr. *Applied regression analysis* (2nd ed.). New York: Wiley, 1981.

Faust, M. S. Somatic development of adolescent girls. *Monographs of the Society for Research in Child Development,* 1977, *42,* No. 1. (Serial No. 169).

Flanders, N. A. *Analyzing teacher behavior.* Reading, Mass.: Addison-Wesley, 1970.

Fraiberg, S. *Insights from the blind: Comparative studies of blind and sighted infants.* New York: Basic Books, 1977.

Friedrich, L. K., & Stein, A. H. Aggressive and prosocial television programs and the natural behavior of preschool children. *Monographs of the Society for Research in Child Development,* 1973, *38* (Serial No. 151).

Furby, L. Interpreting regression toward the mean in developmental research. *Developmental Psychology*, 1973, *8*, 172–179.

Glass, G. V., Willson, V. L., & Gottman, J. M. *Design and analysis of time-series experiments.* Boulder, Co.: Associated University Press, 1975.

Goldberger, A. S. Econometrics and psychometrics: A survey of communalities. *Psychometrika*, 1971, *36*, 83–107.

Guilford, J. P. *Fundamental statistics in psychology and education.* (4th ed.). New York: McGraw-Hill, 1965.

Hale, G. A. On the use of ANOVA in developmental research. *Child Development*, 1977, *48*, 1101–1106.

Harris, R. J. *A primer of multivariate statistics.* New York: Academic Press, 1975.

Hays, W. L. *Statistics for the social sciences* (2nd ed.). New York: Holt, Rinehart, & Winston, 1973.

Heise, D. R. Causal inference from panel data. In E. F. Borgatta & G. W. Bohrnstedt (Eds.), *Sociological methodology 1970.* San Francisco: Jossey-Bass, 1970.

Hock, E. Working and nonworking mothers and their infants: A comparative study of maternal caregiving characteristics and infant social behavior. *Merrill-Palmer Quarterly*, 1980, *26*, 79–101.

Hollander, M., & Wolfe, D. A. *Nonparametric statistical methods.* New York: Wiley, 1973.

Husen, T. *Psychological twin research.* Uppsala, Sweden: Almquist & Wiksell, 1959.

Istomina, Z. M. The development of voluntary memory in preschool-age children. *Soviet Psychology*, 1975, *13*, 5–64.

Jacklin, M., & Maccoby, E. Social behavior at 33 months in same-sex and mixed-sex dyads. *Child Development*, 1978, *44*, 557–569.

Jones, M. C., Bayley, N., MacFarlane, J. W., & Honzig, M. P. *The course of human development.* Waltham, Mass.: Xerox Publishing, 1971.

Kenny, D. A. Cross-lagged and synchronous common factors in panel data. In A. S. Goldberger & O. D. Duncan (Eds.), *Structural equation models in the social sciences.* New York: Seminar Press, 1973.

Kenny, D. A. Cross-lagged panel correlation: A test for spuriousness. *Psychological Bulletin*, 1975, *82*, 887–903. (a)

Kenny, D. A. A quasi-experimental approach to assessing treatment effects in the nonequivalent control group design. *Psychological Bulletin*, 1975, *82*, 345–362. (b)

Kenny, D. A. *Correlation and causality.* New York: Wiley, 1979.

Kerlinger, F. N., & Pedhazur, E. J. *Multiple regression in behavioral research.* New York: Holt, Rinehart, & Winston, 1973.

Kimmel, D. C. *Adulthood and aging.* New York: Wiley, 1974.

Kirk, R. E. *Experimental design: Procedures for the behavioral sciences.* Belmont, Calif.: Brooks/Cole, 1968.

Krantz, D. H., & Tversky, A. Conjoint-measurement analysis of composition rules in psychology. *Psychological Review*, 1971, *78*, 151–169.

Lamb, M. E. Father-infant and mother-infant interaction in the first year of life. *Child Development*, 1977, *48*, 167–181.

Linn, R. L., & Werts, C. E. Analysis implications of the choice of a structural model in the nonequivalent control group design. *Psychological Bulletin*, 1977, *84*, 229–234.

Loftus, G. R. On interpretations of interactions. *Memory and Cognition*, 1978, *6*, 312–319.

Lord, F. M. Large-sample covariance analysis when the control variable is fallible. *Journal of the American Statistical Association*, 1960, *55*, 307–321.

Lord, F. M. A paradox in the interpretation of group comparisons. *Psychological Bulletin*, 1967, *68*, 304–305.

McCall, R. B. Challenges to a science of developmental psychology. *Child Development*, 1977, *48*, 333–344.

McCall, R. B. Nature–nurture and the two realms of development. *Child Development*, 1981, *52*, 1–12.

McCall, R. B., & Appelbaum, M. I. Bias in the analysis of repeated-measures designs: Some alternative approaches. *Child Development*, 1973, *44*, 401–415.

Meehl, P. E. Nuisance variables and the ex post facto design. In M. Radner & S. Winokur (Eds.), *Minnesota studies in the philosophy of science* (Vol. 4). Minneapolis, Minn.: University of Minnesota Press, 1970.

Meehl, P. E. High school yearbooks: A reply to Schwartz. *Journal of Abnormal Psychology*, 1971, *77*, 143–148.

Milgram, S. Behavioral study of obedience. *Journal of Abnormal and Social Psychology*, 1963, *67*, 371–378.

National Commission for the Protection of Human Subjects of Biomedical and Behavioral Research. *Report and recommendations: Research involving children.* Washington, D. C.: Superintendent of Documents, U. S. Government Printing Office, 1977.

Nesselroade, J. R., & Baltes, P. B. (Eds.). *Longitudinal research in human development: Design and analysis.* New York: Academic Press, 1978.

Orne, M. T. On the social psychology of the psychological experiment: With particular reference to demand characteristics and their implications. *American Psychologist*, 1962, *17*, 776–783.

Overall, J. E., & Woodward, J. A. Nonrandom assignment and the analysis of covariance. *Psychological Bulletin*, 1977, *84*, 588–594.

Parke, R. D. Issues in child development: On the myth of the field-lab distinction. *Newsletter of the Society for Research in Child Development*, 1976, 2–3.

Peterson, C. C. *A child grows up: Watching a child develop through a baby-diary and an annotated text.* New York: Alfred Publishing Co., 1974.

Reichardt, C. S. The statistical analysis of data from nonequivalent group designs. In T. D. Cook & D. J. Campbell (Eds.), *Quasi-experimentation.* Chicago: Rand-McNally, 1979.

Rickard, S. The assumptions of causal analysis for incomplete causal sets of two multilevel variables. *Multivariate Behavioral Research*, 1972, *7*, 317–359.

Roethlisberger, F. L., & Dickson, W. J. *Management and the worker.* Cambridge, Mass.: Harvard University Press, 1939.

Rosenthal, R. On the social psychology of the psychological experiment: The experimenter's hypothesis as an unintended determinant of experimental results. *American Scientist*, 1963, *51*, 268–283.

Rozelle, R. M., & Campbell, D. T. More plausible rival hypotheses in the cross-lagged panel correlation technique. *Psychological Bulletin*, 1969, *71*, 74–80.

Schaie, K. W. Quasi-experimental research designs in the psychology of aging. In J. E. Birren & K. W. Schaie (Eds.), *Handbook of the psychology of aging.* New York: Van Nostrand Reinhold Company, 1977.

Schaie, K. W., & Labouvie-Vief, G. Generational versus ontogenetic components of change in adult cognitive behavior: A fourteen-year cross-sequential study. *Developmental Psychology*, 1974, *10*, 305–320.

Sears, P. S., & Barbee, A. H. Career and life satisfaction among Terman's gifted women. In J. Stanley, W. George, & C. Solano (Eds.), *The gifted and the creative: Fifty-year perspective.* Baltimore, Md.: Johns Hopkins University Press, 1978.

Sears, R. R. Sources of life satisfaction of the Terman gifted men. *American Psychologist*, 1977, *32*, 119–128.

Seitz, V. A methodological comment on the problem of infant day care. In E. Zigler & E. Gordon (Eds.), *Day care: Scientific and social policy issues.* Boston, Mass.: Auburn House Publishing Co., 1982.

Seitz, V., Rosenbaum, L. K., & Apfel, N. H. *Day care as intervention.* Paper presented at the Biennial Meeting of the Society for Research in Child Development, Detroit, Michigan, April 24, 1983.

Sibbison, V. H. The influence of maternal role perceptions on attitudes toward and utilization of early child care services. In D. Peters (Ed.), *A summary of the Pennsylvania day care study*. University Park, Pa.: Pennsylvania State University Press, 1973.

Siegel, S. *Nonparametric statistics*. New York: McGraw-Hill, 1956.

Stanovich, K. E. Note on the interpretation of interactions in comparative research. *American Journal of Mental Deficiency*, 1976, *81*, 394–396.

Stein, A. H., & Friedrich, L. K. Impact of television on children and youth. In E. M. Hetherington (Ed.), *Review of Child Development Research* (Vol. 5). Chicago: University of Chicago Press, 1975.

Stern, D. *The first relationship*. Cambridge, Mass.: Harvard University Press, 1977.

Stevenson, H. W., & Stevenson, N. G. Social interaction in an interracial nursery school. *Genetic Psychology Monographs*, 1960, *61*, 37–75.

Tatsuoka, M. M. *Multivariate analysis: Techniques for educational and psychological research*. New York: Wiley, 1971.

Thomas, A., & Chess, S. *Temperament and development*. New York: Brunner/Mazel, 1977.

Thurstone, T. G. *Manual for the SRA Primary Mental Abilities 11-17*. Chicago: Science Research Associates, 1958.

Timm, N. H. *Multivariate analysis with applications in education and psychology*. Monterey, Calif.: Brooks/Cole, 1975.

U. S. Public Health Service. *Final report of the Tuskeegee Syphilis Study Ad Hoc Advisory Panel*. Washington, D. C.: U. S. Public Health Services, 1973.

Werts, C. E., & Linn, R. L. A general linear model for studying growth. *Psychological Bulletin*, 1970, *73*, 17–22.

Winer, B. J. *Statistical principles in experimental design* (2nd ed.). New York: McGraw-Hill, 1971.

Wohlwill, J. F. *The study of behavioral development*. New York: Academic Press, 1973.

Wright, H. F. Observational child study. In P. H. Mussen (Ed.), *Handbook of research methods in child development*. New York: Wiley, 1960.

Yando, R. M., Seitz, V. R., & Zigler, E. F. *Intellectual and personality characteristics of children: Social class and ethnic group differences*. Hillsdale, N. J.: Lawrence Erlbaum Associates, 1979.

Zigler, E. Developmental versus difference theories of mental retardation. *American Journal of Mental Deficiency*, 1969, *73*, 536–556.

Zigler, E., Abelson, W. D., & Seitz, V. Motivational factors in the performance of economically-disadvantaged children on the Peabody Picture Vocabulary Test. *Child Development*, 1973, *44*, 294–303.

Zigler, E., & Butterfield, E. C. Motivational aspects of changes in IQ test performance of culturally deprived nursery school children. *Child Development*, 1968, *39*, 1–14.

3 Perceptual Development

Marc H. Bornstein
New York University

> . . . *all that a mammal does is fundamentally dependent on his perception, past or present.*
>
> D. O. Hebb (1953, p. 44).

INTRODUCTION

We begin with two questions: Why study perception? Why study early perceptual development?

Why Study Perception? Perception underlies our basic awareness, experience, and interpretation of the world. Philosophers, psychologists, physiologists, and physicists study perception for two broad categories of reasons related to this privileged position of perception. Both reasons also have roots in philosophy.

Even on casual introspection, our everyday experiences raise a series of intriguing questions about perception. Some are quite general. How do properties or objects or events in the real world differ from our perceptions of them? How do those properties or objects or events come to be perceived as stable amidst continuous environmental flux, and how do they come to be invested with meaning? Other questions provoked by perceptual experiences are more specific. How does the quality of "bitter" differ from the quality of "red"? How do we see a three-dimensional world when visual processing begins with only a two-dimensional image in the eye? How are the individual features of things we perceive synthesized into organized wholes?

The second reason for studying perception is epistemological, impelled by the question of the origins of human knowledge. For centuries, philosophers have appealed to perception to address epistemological questions of knowledge and the origins of knowledge. Extreme views have been put forward by *empiricists*, who assert that all knowledge comes through the senses and grows by way of experience, and by *nativists*, who reason that some kinds of knowledge could not possibly rely on experience or be learned, and thus humans enter the world (at

81

minimum) with a sensory apparatus equipped to order and organize rudimentary knowledge.[1] These positions define the classic "nature–nurture" debate.

Perceptual study by philosophers had two prominent characteristics. First, the philosophical approach consisted mainly of theoretical speculation, and it was not until the marriage of physics and psychology in psychophysics that experimentation and fact were introduced into perceptual study. Second, philosophy focused its attention on the development of perception, and especially on the study of perception near the beginning of life, as this was the period in which epistemologically meaningful issues related to the *origins* of knowledge could be addressed. This consideration leads us to the second question.

Why Study Early Perceptual Development? The study of perceptual development originally captured the imaginations of those who were interested in the nature and growth of knowledge because it promised to reveal how much and what kind of knowledge was inborn in humans, and how much and what kind of knowledge had to be learned. Perception is the necessary first step in information gathering about the environment; understanding perception is therefore important—early in life, and especially in infancy—to our understanding of the development of knowledge. In this sense, studies of early perception essentially constitute *experimental tests of nativist and empiricist theories* of knowledge. Further, the developmental study of perception provides *information on normative processes* in early perception; namely the quality, limits, and capacities of the sensory systems as they normally develop and function early in life. Not long ago, textbooks in pediatrics portrayed the infant as "perceptually incompetent"; studies of infant perception assess the accuracy of this characterization. Additionally, determining how the senses function in infancy helps toward *specification of the perceptual world* of babies. If a substance tastes sweet to adults they may suppose that it does for infants also, and even that infants like it, when in fact taste receptors for sweet may not even be present in infants or, if present, may not function so early in life. Defining normative capacity early in life also permits *developmental comparisons* among individuals over time. That is, the comparison of mature versus immature perceptual function is predicated on

---

[1]Both early empiricists and nativists were interested in epistemology for philosophy and also to reach other goals, including theology and morality. Empiricist reason, which was championed by Locke, Berkeley, and Hume, arrived in the eighteenth century and was greeted into a milieu of religious belief, deeply rooted in social institutions and in the hearts of men. This dogma was not easily uprooted. If ideas—faith and morals—were inborn in men, then God would transcend. But the empiricists rejected this supposition on epistemological grounds, and thereby inadvertently questioned articles of faith. If the mind of the babe is a "tabula rasa," knowledge (even of God) must be acquired materially, through sense experience. But no one has experience with God or can know God this way. (Moreover, through Berkeley and Hume's analyses, even mind degenerated into frail perceptions, memories, and feelings.) Kant's *Critique of Pure Reason* parried for science as well as for religion: Perhaps skepticism is not an ultimate, but a limited, authority, Kant wrote, and there is room for instinct and emotion *and* for knowledge and morality inherent in the nature and structure of the mind.

knowing what is developmentally appropriate at a given age in infancy. Finally, studies of perception in infancy provide *baseline data* against which the course of maturation and the effects of experience over time can be assessed.

For these reasons, much of the impetus to study perceptual development has derived from philosophy, and much perceptual study has focused on infancy. Further, in the study of perceptual development, both theory and methodology have played central roles. Our consideration of perceptual development in this chapter begins with a discussion of the philosophical foundations and motivations for studying perceptual development and then turns, almost immediately, to the contribution of theory—in particular, to the "nature–nurture" controversy—for our understanding of perceptual development. The views of some traditional and modern theorists are then outlined, and a logical structure for considering the interactive roles of nature and nurture is described. The next section of the chapter presents a taxonomy of the methodologies used in studying perceptual development. This taxonomy is organized both to reflect different contemporary strategies of attacking questions in perceptual development and to underscore the fact that different methodologies require different degrees of inference in assessing perception. Following this discussion, a summary of the substance of what these methods have revealed about early perceptual development is provided. Although the chapter focuses on perceptual development in infancy, reflecting the evolution of theory and research in this area, principles of perceptual development in childhood and in old age are also reviewed. The chapter concludes with a brief evaluation of the developmental sequelae of altering the world perceptually, as by modification, deprivation, or enrichment.

A few additional words should be offered about what this chapter does and does not do. Sensation and perception are broad topics in psychology with long research traditions. Wilhelm Wundt (1832–1920) established the first laboratory of experimental psychology more than a century ago to investigate sensation and perception. Study in this area embraces the physics of the stimulus, the physiology of the sensory systems, the psychology of perception, and diverse philosophies of epistemology. Not even a portion of these background topics can be covered here; rather, this chapter concentrates on theory and data in perceptual development. Finally, the chapter emphasizes (though not exclusively) visual development, reflecting the persistent interest of psychologists concerned with perceptual development.

In the past, many investigators have been reluctant to add a developmental perspective to the formal study of sensation and perception—alleging that developmental psychology is a *different* field—and the experimental study of sensation and perception was confined largely to adults and to animal models. Today, after major research efforts with infant, child, and aged populations, the contribution of the developmental point of view is acknowledged as more than informative, and it is esteemed by students of sensation and perception generally. Let us see why.

PHILOSOPHICAL UNDERPINNINGS

Among all of the different subject disciplines of developmental psychology, perception has historically been the most intimately tied with nature–nurture questions. What do we know before we have any experience in the world? How do we acquire knowledge about the world? The two main positions are empiricism and nativism.

Empiricism

The empiricist argument has several parts. First, empiricists assert that there is no endowed knowledge at birth; second, that all knowledge comes through the senses; and third, that perceptual development proceeds through associative experience. Specifically, empiricists argue that stimuli in the world naturally provoke bodily sensations that, occurring close together in space or in time, give rise to more global "ideas" and thereby begin to invest the perceptual world with meaning. It is through association, empiricism explains, that separate raw sensations aggregate into meaningful perceptions. Today we see, with some hindsight, that the empiricist's view of the nature of the mind in early life has been fostered by two separate, if similar, schools of thought. One derives from John Locke (1632–1704) who is reputed to have expressed the opinion that the infant mind is a "tabula rasa." In the Lockean sense, mental life begins with nothing, and an understanding of the world depends wholly on the accretion of experiences. A slightly different empiricist view can be attributed to William James (1842–1910). James conceived of the world of the infant as a "blooming, buzzing confusion" out of which, presumably, the infant's experience helps to organize and create order and knowledge.

　　According to the empiricist account, the naive infant does not share the perceptual world of an experienced adult. Empiricism is an inherently developmental viewpoint since, by whatever mechanism of growth is postulated, children develop from a perceptually naive state to a perceptually experienced one.

Nativism

The belief that humans begin life empty-headed, so to speak, has been conceived by many to be both philosophically intolerable and logically indefensible. Nativists originally argued that God did not create human beings as mindless, and that the knowledge that humans possess could not be achieved by learning alone in so short a span of time as early childhood. As a consequence, nativist philosophers including René Descartes (1596–1650) and Immanuel Kant (1724–1804) viewed humans as being endowed from birth with ideas or categories of knowledge that assist perceptual functions. They postulated innate perceptual categories, such as size, form, position, or motion, as well as more abstract conceptions, such as space and time. Contrary to the empiricist argument, the nativist argument holds that the mind naturally, and from the beginning of life, imposes order on sensory input, thereby transforming sensations into meaningful perceptions.

According to the nativist account, the infant possesses many of the same perceptual capacities as does the experienced adult, and the two perceive the world in much the same way. For abilities that are congenital, nativism is not a developmental theory; for abilities that mature, nativism is developmental in outlook.

Reflecting on the extreme nativist and empiricist opinions that have been championed and the vigor with which they have been advanced, many psychologists have argued that perceptual development stands as a kind of "battle ground" between nativists and empiricists on how the mind works. Let us examine in detail one exemplary skirmish, the question of how we perceive depth in space. This example is selected for several reasons. First, depth perception is crucial to determining the spatial layout of the environment, to mediating object recognition, and to guiding motor activity. Second, the study of depth perception harbors a central question in perception, namely how do we recover the three-dimensional model of the environment from two-dimensional information laid out on the retina. Third, debate on this question follows the typical historical programme in the study of perceptual development: It originates with hotly contested nativist–empiricist philosophical controversies that spanned the seventeenth to nineteenth centuries and culminates with experimentation in infancy and with the contributions of animal physiology in the twentieth century.

A Nativist–Empiricist Debate

How Do We Come to Perceive Depth in Visual Space?   Writing in *La Dioptrique* in 1638, René Descartes offered a simple answer to this question based on classical ideals of the mind's intuitive grasp of pure mathematics. For Descartes, humans and human thought operated as systems driven by natural law; knowledge was inborn. Thus Descartes theorized: Our two eyes form the base of a triangle whose apex is the object under our gaze. When we look at a faraway object, our eyes are nearly parallel and the base angles of the triangle approach 90°, whereas when we converge our eyes on a nearby object, the base angles are acute. The closer the object, the more acute the angles. Distance, Descartes (1638/1824, pp. 59–66) concluded, is given by "an act of thinking which, being simple imagination [pure thought], does not entail [explicit] reasoning."

Descartes had a point. All of us are born with two eyes, and our eyes converge more for near than for far points of interest. Indeed, the degree of convergence is directly related to the object's distance from us. But are we born with trigonometric tables in our heads?

A counter explanation for depth perception (one actually built on Descartes' theory) was later set forth by the empiricist George Berkeley (1685–1753) in his *Essay towards a New Theory of Vision* of 1709. Berkeley (1709/1901) argued that humans do not deduce distance by "natural geometry":

> Since I am not conscious, that I make any such use of the Perception I have by the Turn of my Eyes. And for me to make those Judgments, and draw those Conclusions from it, without knowing that I do so, seems altogether incomprehensible (Sect. xix).

Rather, Berkeley argued, we come to know depth and distance through our experiences; we learn that the things whose size we know appear smaller when they are at a distance, and we associate visual cues in the environment with feedback from our tactile and motor experience with them. Berkeley reflected:

> When an *Object* appears Faint and Small, which at a near Distance I have experienced to make a vigorous and large Appearance; I instantly conclude it to be far off. And this, 'tis evident, is the result of *Experience;* without which, from the Faintness and Littleness, I should not have infer'd any thing concerning the Distance of *Objects* (sect. iii).

In essence, Berkeley claimed that we associate the large apparent size of objects (their "vigorousness") with bringing our two eyes close together and the small cost of small arm movements when we reach for nearby objects, and we associate the small apparent size of objects (their "faintness") with the parallel position of our two eyes and the large cost of large arm movements when we reach for faraway objects. Berkeley hypothesized that infants' constant reaching in association with convergence of the eyes and the appearance of objects eventuates in visual understanding of depth and distance.

Nativist replies to this experiential argument first countered with logic. In the *Critique of Pure Reason* of 1781, Immanuel Kant asserted that the human mind does not originally rely on experience for meaning, but innately organizes sensations in such a way that they are meaningful. Kant (1781/1924) argued that "Space is a necessary *a priori* idea":

> Space is not an empirical conception, which has been derived from external experiences. For I could not be conscious that certain of my sensations are relative to something outside of me, that is, to something in a different part of space from that in which I myself am. . . . No experience of the external relations of sensible things could yield the idea of space, because without the consciousness of space there would be no external experience whatever (pp. 22–29).

Kant's theoretical argument was buttressed by two compelling observations: The emergence of depth perception early in life could not wait on extensive experience and learning, and, relatedly, individuals with limited experience and even young babies give evidence that they perceive depth. The philosopher Arthur Schopenhauer (1788–1860), for example, invoked the case of Eva Lauk in this connection. Born without limbs and consequently restricted in her experience, Eva reportedly possessed normal intelligence and perceptions of space. (Eva could, of course, move about, so that the case of space perception in infants is more compelling.) Fueled thus, nativists argued that (at least) some capacity to perceive depth must be inborn or directly given. This deduction impelled some investigators to seek specific biological substrates that might underlie the ability to perceive depth. At first, such mechanisms were only postulated, as for example by the notable nineteenth century physiologist Ewald Hering (1834–1918). In more modern times, sensory physiologists have found evidence for them.

Immediately after Kant, however, the debate continued with a defense of empiricism. In his classic 1866 *Handbook of Physiological Optics*, Hermann von Helmholtz (1821–1894) rebutted nativism with the logical and rational argument that "intuition theory is an unnecessary hypothesis." Helmholtz (1866/1925) asserted that it is uneconomical to assume mechanisms of innate perception, especially when:

> It is not clear how the assumption of these original "*space sensations*" can help the explanation of our visual perceptions, when the adherents of this theory ultimately have to assume in by far the great majority of cases that these sensations must be overruled by the better understanding which we get by experience. In that case it would seem to me much easier and simpler to grasp, that all apperceptions of space were obtained simply by experience, instead of supposing that the latter have to contend against intuitive perceptual images that are generally false[2] (Vol. III, sect. 26).

After this blow by Helmholtz, turn-of-the-century Gestalt psychologists restored credibility to the nativist views of Kant; moreover, they appealed primarily to experimentation in doing so. At this time in the history of science, empiricism began to supplant speculation, and with the movement of questions such as these away from pure philosophy to psychology, more and more experimentation was introduced. In fact, experimental psychology, which began with this century, was specifically organized to address issues such as these. Given the enormous significance attributed to these questions and the power of an argument submitted to the test of trial, it is hardly surprising that an experimental

---

[2]Helmholtz (1866/1925) also appealed to his own childhood recollections:

the . . . relation between size and distance . . . can only be acquired by long experience, and so it is not surprising that children are . . . apt to make mistakes. I can recall when I was a boy going past the . . . chapel . . . where some people were standing in the belfry. I mistook them for dolls and asked my mother to reach up and get them for me, which I thought she could do (pp. 282–283).

psychology of infancy captured the imagination, effort, and energy of subsequent generations of researchers.

Let us now look briefly at several exemplary lines of research which developmental investigators have taken up to address the question of depth perception in infants. The starting point for the first is familiar:

> Human infants at the creeping and toddling stage are notoriously prone to falls from more or less high places. They must be kept from going over the brink by side panels on their cribs, gates on their stairways, and the vigilance of adults. As their muscular coordination matures, they begin to avoid such accidents on their own. Common sense might suggest that the child learns to recognize falling-off places by experience—that is, by falling and hurting himself. But is experience really the teacher? Or is the ability to perceive and avoid a brink part of the child's original endowment? (Gibson & Walk, 1960, p. 64)

Faced with this lingering conundrum, in the early 1960s Eleanor Gibson and Richard Walk (1960) began to investigate the development of depth perception experimentally in human infants using a "visual cliff." Babies were placed on a centerboard to one side of which was an illusory precipitous drop, whereas the other side clearly continued the platform of the centerboard. In fact, however, a glass sheet provided firm support for the babies on *both* sides of the centerboard. Gibson and Walk found that 27 out of 30 infants between 6 and 14 months would crawl across the "shallow" side of the apparatus from the centerboard when their mothers called them, and only 3 infants would crawl across the "deep" side. From this, Gibson and Walk concluded that perception of depth must be present in infants as early as 6 months.

As should be clear, however, the method used in these studies to assess depth perception is limited by the capacity of infants to locomote, which they only begin to do in the second half of the first year of life. By this time, the child may have plenty of experience with depth. To meet the challenge of this consideration, Campos, Langer, and Krowitz (1970) monitored a different behavior, heart rate, in precrawling babies who were exposed to the visual cliff. They lay the babies face down on the visual cliff and suddenly exposed them either to the deep or to the shallow drop. By 2 months of age, those babies who were exposed to depth showed heart-rate changes, whereas the babies exposed to the shallow side showed no comparable heart-rate change. These differences suggest that babies may perceive depth long before the ability to locomote begins. Further work along these lines has revealed that although young infants may discriminate depth, fear of depth may not begin until infants actually begin to crawl (Campos, 1976).

The "visual cliff" experiments are one way developmental investigators sought to tease out an infant's capacity to perceive depth. Another related situation that taps the perception of depth in space is "looming." Looming describes the action of an object moving directly toward us on a "hit path," and our reaction normally is to avoid the impending collision as the object moves closer in space. Bower, Broughton, and Moore (1970) and Ball and Tronick (1971) reported that babies only a half month of age show an "integrated avoidance response" to impending collision: They observed that babies threw back their heads with regularity and also shielded their faces with their hands and even cried when an object moved at them along a hit path, but failed to show these defensive reactions when the same object moved along a miss path, or when it receded into space. In the experimental situation these investigators created, infants were not actually threatened with a solid object but viewed instead a translucent screen onto which a silhouette of the three-dimensional object was cast; this technique cleverly avoids cueing infants with air changes on the face that an actual object approaching an imminent collision would cause. However, Yonas (1981) reasoned insightfully that, insofar as the magnification of an object's outline is the optical cue to an impending collision, an object's upper contour itself naturally moves upward in the field of view as the object advances. In "throwing their heads back," infants may simply be tracking the rapidly changing upward contour of the advancing image, giving only an *impression* of "avoiding." Yonas conducted a series of control experiments that employed babies of different ages and a variety of different response measures in conditions in which an object's image remained on a hit path, but its upper contour either remained at a constant level or rose. He determined that babies probably do track upper contours and that the "looming response" could not be demonstrated reliably until babies are approximately 4 months of age. However, Yonas has also observed that, as early as 1 month, babies show a reasonably consistent eye-blink response to approaching objects. Thus, if very young babies do show components of a looming response at all, they show only weak ones.

These two lines of research attacked the question of depth perception in highly functional ways, examining infants' reactions to and appreciation of depth. A different strategy has been to study infants' responses to isolated cues that may signal depth. The visual system can use binocular or monocular information in perceiving depth. Each eye registers a separate image of the visual world, and discrepancy or disparity between them provides information about depth (stereopsis). In turn, stereopsis depends on the organism's capacity, first, to fixate an object binocularly and, second, to fuse the two disparate retinal images. Thus, one requisite of stereopsis harks back to the original observations of Descartes and Berkeley on binocular convergence. If convergence of the eyes cues depth, convergence needs to be present early in life for infants to see depth. We have all noted, however, that in some babies one eye wanders, and that many babies seem unable to fix both eyes on an object at all times (strabismus). Empirical studies of infants' eye movements while tracking dynamic targets have shown only minimal vergence at 1 month but regular vergence at 2–3 months (e.g., Aslin, 1977; Maurer, 1975). Binocular disparity is also an adequate stimulus for stereopsis. Empirical studies of infants' detection of disparity in random-dot stereograms have shown that only infants older than about 3 months possess stereopsis (e.g., Fox, Aslin, Shea, & Dumais, 1980). Monocular cues, such as familiar size, linear perspective, and interposition, also specify depth (Hochberg, 1978), but only older 5–7-month-olds seem to be able to take advantage of these cues alone to discriminate depth.

Studies of the visual cliff, looming, and binocular and monocular cues with human babies cumulatively suggest that depth perception is relatively poor up until about 2 months after birth, after which this perceptual ability develops rapidly. We still do not know, however, precisely when depth perception arises or what course it follows in early development. Though empirical studies such as these clearly advance our understanding of psychological function beyond philo-sophical debate, psychological investigation does not necessarily bring us to a resolution. Psychologists on both sides of the issue are quick to point out that there can be no final triumph for nativism or for empiricism. *No matter how early in life depth perception can be demonstrated, the ability must still rest on some experience; no matter how late the demonstration, it can never be proved that only experience has mattered.*

Other arguments and data bear on the nature versus nurture question. When perceptual psychologists working in infancy reach an impasse in their efforts to resolve issues such as these, they frequently resort to behavioral or physiological sources of information provided by infrahuman animals. Animals offer special circumstances for research, as they lend themselves to experimentation and manipulation that is sometimes not possible with humans.

Animals have provided valuable behavioral information about the ontogeny of depth perception. Some species can be more readily studied earlier in postnatal life than can humans, and they can be "asked" about their perceptions of depth. A variety of species has been tested in the visual cliff, for example, some of which, like chicks, move about on their own within a day after hatching. All avoid the cliff, suggesting that depth perception may develop very early and unfold independent of motor experience. Of course, it is still possible that depth perception is innate and congenital in some species but not in others, including human beings.

The general premise of the developmentalist's appeal to physiological data is that perceptual behaviors ought to have identifiable neural substrates, and, if those substrates are found, they can contribute evidence to the nativist–empiricist argument. To continue the example from depth perception, Hubel and Weisel (1970) and Barlow, Blakemore, and Pettigrew (1967) have identified single cells in the visual systems of cats and of monkeys that are exquisitely sensitive to binocular disparity. Although these sorts of results suggest some physiological basis for perception, developmentalists need to be cautious about reductionism of this sort. Because these cells exist in other mature species does not mean that they exist in the infant forms of those species; because these cells exist in lower species does not mean they exist in human beings; and, because these cells exist at all, of course, does not mean they signal "depth" in a psychologically or functionally meaningful way.

Looking back over this example, we can see that theoretical, philosophical, and theological differences of opinion about epistemology burned like embers over centuries in the minds of men, now and again igniting into controversy over whether human ideas, abilities, or capacities were innately given or a product of experience. The sparks of speculation that flew during those times generated more heat than light. In modern times, psychology has added experimental evidence, in addition to observations from animal behavior and physiology, to fuel these ancient fires. Psychology's contribution has continued to generate heat, but it has also shed more light on the original issues. To show that the embers still burn, however, we have only to consider the opinions of major contemporary developmental theorists about these and other classical questions in perceptual development.

Capsule Views of Some Major Contemporary Theorists

Hebb. One of the more prominent contemporary developmental theorists is Donald O. Hebb (1949), whose motor-neurological theory of perceptual development combines some nativist with strongly empiricist views. Hebb reasoned that a few rudimentary perceptual abilities must be inborn; among these he counted the ability to distinguish between figure and ground. Beyond this limited innate ability, Hebb theorized that perception develops based on motor behavior and neural activity in the brain. When we see a form, we scan it and thereby develop an internal representation of the form related to the motor activity of our eyes, as well as to the activity of cortical neurons repeatedly excited by the form. The pathways in the brain activated by the form eventually aggregate into "cell assemblies" that go on to construct perceptions. In essence, the spatial and temporal contiguities of excited cells promote the organization of cell assemblies, and metabolic changes (presumably via neurotransmitters) facilitate connections among cells to organize "perceptual" pathways. Over time and with experience, Hebb argued, the likelihood that particular stimuli will excite particular pathways through reduced synaptic resistance increases. In this way, Hebb[3] combined the basics of nativism with empiricist doctrine that places extreme importance on experience for higher pattern perception and thought. In this view,

---

[3]Hebb's theorizing has provoked three lines of research that have contributed additional fundamental insights to our understanding of perception and how it develops. Most directly, Hebb's work suggests that the motion of the eyes is necessary to perception. Intriguingly, it has been shown that when an image is stabilized on the retina, it "disappears." More generally, Hebb's work addresses issues related to perceptual deprivation and enrichment. Some investigators have found that enriched early experience augments eventual perceptual performance, and others have indicated that some amount and range of stimulation is necessary to maintain normal functioning.

perceptual development, then, is "integration through repetition and association in neural processes." For Hebb, some rudiments of space and depth perception are given innately ascribable to the innate differentiation of figure and ground, but by and large depth is learned through experience.

Soviet motor-copy theories (e.g., Zaporozhets, 1965) view perceptual development in a similar way. An infant's sensorimotor investigations of the world—through tactile and/or visual exploration—result in motor images that aid memory and cognition and contribute to filling in perception.

Wertheimer.   Max Wertheimer (1923/1958, 1945) was one of the founders of the Gestalt school of perceptual psychology, which included Koffka (1927) and Köhler (1947). For Gestalt psychologists, perceptual organization constitutes a primitive, direct, and basic element of mental activity, and they maintain that perceptual organizations of various kinds are innate, the byproducts of brain activity. The Gestaltists point to several general laws of perception that, they assert, exist and function universally; these laws include grouping forms by similarity and contiguity, seeing closure, and perceiving wholes and relations among parts, as opposed to just concentrating on parts. The significance of infancy studies for Gestalt perceptual theory is obvious, though surprisingly few infant studies have been designed to test Gestalt principles directly. For Gestalt psychologists, experience is clearly less essential, and the rudiments of depth perception, for example, are present at or near birth based on how the visual system naturally functions.

The Gibsons.   Eleanor Gibson (1969, 1982) and James Gibson (1979) have asserted that in some ways perceptions are direct and in others perceptual learning proceeds through a developmental process of differentiation. According to the Gibsons, the environment is information, and the sensory systems have evolved so as to perceive that information directly. Texture gradients, for example, cue visual depth directly and ought to be perceived early in life. Through time, exposure, and practice, organisms perceive—discover and extract—environmental information. The information potential is available all the time; perception consists in the ultimate detection of invariants in environmental stimulation. As the perceptual processes mature, children adopt increasingly economical modes of discovering invariant properties of the rich ambient array. The Gibsons also maintain that perceptual development consists of an increasing response specificity—children move from primitive global distinctions to progressively finer discriminations. The process of development in perception is essentially tripartite, therefore, consisting, first, in abstracting central differences among sources of information; second, in rejecting irrelevant cues; and third, in selectively orienting the senses to optimize reception of critical environmental information.

Piaget.   Although best known for his studies of cognitive development, Jean Piaget (1946/1971, 1961/1969; Piaget & Inhelder, 1948/1967) also brought his constructivist viewpoint to the study of perceptual development. Piaget proposed that, through manipulation and motor activity, the child actively structures sensory information into mental representations of the world rather than passively receiving representations of the environment. Prior to about the age of 18 months, the child's mental schemes are actually percepts evoked by sensory stimulation; after 18 months, schemes are signifiers that stand for stimuli and are independent of sensory and perceptual input. Piaget's theorizing about perception has not been as influential as his theorizing about cognition (see Kuhn, in this volume), although perception does play a broadly significant role within his scheme of cognitive development. For example, intelligence in infancy is identified with sensorimotor competence, and, later, centering (the child's perceptual focus on concrete properties of the world) captures the young child's cognitions and holds him or her in the stage of concrete operations. In general, for Piaget, analytical thought in early life is subordinate to perceptual thought, but perceptions develop: The perception of visual depth, for instance, is built up over time through motor feedback and increasing visual experience as the child acts on stimuli more and more and becomes increasingly mobile.

Summary

No simple or abbreviated summary of the theories of perceptual development could do justice to any one or to the overall richness of theoretical viewpoints in this area. Rather, the foregoing is an attempt only to invoke major themes in the theories of perceptual development.

By far the two most prominent themes have been nativism and empiricism— opinions on how much or how little infants are capable before they have had experience, and what sorts of roles experience plays in development. One connected line of thought and research, extending from Locke and Berkeley through modern empiricists, holds that perception and perceptual development arise because of our experiences in the world. A parallel line, extending from Descartes and Kant through contemporary nativists, holds that perception and perceptual meaning are competences that are already a part of the armamentarium of even the very young child. Different theorists' arguments for depth perception exemplify these divergent points of view: Nativists see the child as immediately capable of perceiving depth on account of the way in which the nervous system functions; empiricists feel the child is able to perceive depth only after continued, repeated experiences associating movements of the eyes, arms, and other body parts with small and large images of objects in the visual world. Thus, constructivist theories, such as Piaget's, assume that the two-dimensional retinal image must be supplemented with movement to give a scale of depth; but direct perception theories, such as the Gibsons', maintain that space is automatically perceived in relations among higher-order variables (such as texture), to which the sensory systems have evolved. Not every theory or theorist fits neatly into a nativist or an empiricist perspective; of course, there are elements of both in all developmental theories. Although sometimes conceived as either-or contributors, nature and nurture interact to influence developmental outcomes. Nevertheless, as Hochberg (1962) observed, perhaps in no other area in psychology has the nativism–empiricism controversy been perceived as so meaningful or legitimate as it is in the study of perceptual development.

NATURE AND NURTURE

Nature and nurture define two extremist philosophical positions, but each, as has been suggested, contributes to perceptual development. Indeed, normative perceptual development involves the interaction of both these forces. The potential ways in which nature and nurture can interact in the course of development can be conceptualized in a simple and comprehensive manner. The accompanying figure (Fig. 3.1) shows different possible courses of development before the onset of experience and the several possible ways in which early experience can influence eventual perceptual outcomes. If we take as a convenient developmental marker the onset of experience (usually, but not necessarily, birth), we can compare the period before experience against the period after experience. Several logically possible interactions of nature and nurture unfold. First, there is the possibility that perceptual abilities or functions develop to a high level before the onset of experience, after which they require experience only to be maintained. Without relevant experience, these abilities or functions may be lost. Second, perceptual abilities or functions may develop only partially before the onset of experience, after which experience functions in one of three ways: (a) relevant experience can facilitate further development of an ability or function or fine-tune that ability or function; (b) experience can serve to maintain the ability or function at the incomplete level of development it attained before the onset of experience; or (c) without relevant experience, the ability or function can be lost. Of course, experience per se may not be altogether necessary where the perceptual ability or function would continue to mature automatically as a reflection of the genetic blueprint. Finally, a perceptual ability or function that is undeveloped at the onset of experience can be induced by relevant experience; without such experience, the function or ability will not emerge.

To flesh out this skeletal introduction to some of the major ways nature and nurture can interact in perceptual development, let us examine, however briefly, a perceptual domain in which these several possibilities have actually been investigated. The domain is a narrow but important one: speech perception. It requires just a little background before going into the scheme itself. Sounds are essentially different sine wave frequencies that are produced simultaneously, and

POSSIBLE DEVELOPMENTAL OUTCOMES

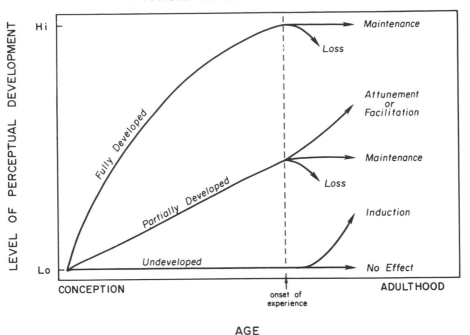

FIG. 3.1. Possible developmental outcomes given different levels of perceptual development before the onset of experience and different experiences afterwards. (Figure 2.1 from R. N. Aslin, Experiential influences and sensitive periods in perceptual development: A unified model. In R. N. Aslin, J. R. Alberts, & M. R. Peterson (Eds.), *Development of perception. Psychobiological perspectives (Vol. 2): The visual system.* New York: Academic Press, 1981.)

speech is the complex collection of different frequencies produced over time. Languages extract from the universe of all possible speech sounds (phonetics) particular subsets that they invest with meaning (phonemics). One dimension along which certain phonemes in many languages are distinguished is their "voicing." Differences in voicing are articulated by a speaker's producing different frequencies at slightly different times. Clearly the relative onsets of the low- and high-frequency components of a sound may vary *continuously;* that is, a high-frequency component may lead a low-frequency component by different amounts of time, the two may begin simultaneously, or the low-frequency component may lead the high-frequency component. However, adult perceptions of differences in voicing are more or less *categorical;* that is, although we can distinguish differences in the relative onset times of low- and high-frequency bands, we classify many different such sounds as similar. Interestingly, cross-language research has discovered that adults in nearly all cultures hear only one, two, or three categories of voicing: The three are known as prevoiced, voiced, and voiceless. Categorical perception means that across a nearly infinite spectrum of possibilities, only three tokens are functionally distinguished and that the same three are distinguished by nearly all peoples, despite their wide language differences. In English, we distinguish voiced and voiceless versions of initial stop–consonant phonemes, as for example /b/ − /p/, /d/ − /t/, or /g/ − /k/.

Many people assume that phenomena so ubiquitous, consistent, circumscribed, and significant in human behavior as perceptual categories of speech might have a biological foundation. To test this assumption, Eimas, Siqueland, Jusczyk, and Vigorito (1971) sought to discover whether preverbal human infants perceived acoustic changes in voicing categorically; that is, in a manner parallel to adult phonemic perception. Using a technique that relies initially on babies getting bored when the same sight or sound is presented over and over again and then their expressing renewed interest in something new (the technique is called "habituation"), these investigators arranged to ask infants some simple same–different questions about their auditory perceptions. They found that 1- and 4-month-olds behaved as though they perceived speech sounds in the adultlike categorical manner: Babies distinguished /b/ from /p/, but did not distinguish between two different /b/s. That is, babies categorize different sounds as either voiced or voiceless long before they use language, or even have extensive experience hearing language. This might suggest that categorical perception is essentially innate. Returning to Figure 3.1, it would seem that the categorical perception of phonemes most closely fits the topmost developmental function.

However, this experiment does not conclusively rule out the role of experience in development. The babies tested were born into monolingual English-speaking families in which the voiced–voiceless distinction they discriminated is common. It could be true, then, that categorical perception is partially developed at the onset of experience, and that its further development is facilitated or attuned over the 1–4 months of experience these babies had had prior to the experiment (or more, as fetuses may "hear" in the uterus; see below). It could also be true that categorical perception is undeveloped at the onset of experience, and that experience with the language, however little, readily induces sophisticated auditory perception. Cross-cultural developmental research is of help here.

Surveys of the world's languages show that only three categories of voicing are common—prevoiced, voiced, and voiceless—yet not all languages make use of all of these categories. Eimas et al. (1971) had only tested an English category. Are all or are only some voicing categories universal among infants? That is, do infants from communities where different patterns of voicing prevail in the adult language make the same categorical distinctions? If infants everywhere have some or all of the same three categories, even though the adults in their cultures do not, the data would go a long way toward specifying the possible developmental courses of categorical perceptions of speech. To address this question, Lasky, Syrdal-Lasky, and Klein (1975) tested infants from Spanish (Guatemalan) monolingual families. Spanish was chosen because the voiced–voiceless distinction is not the same as in English. Spanish 4- and 6-month-olds were found to discriminate using the English voiced–voiceless sound contrast rather than the Spanish one. Likewise, Streeter (1976) found that Kikuyu (Kenyan) 2-month-olds categorized both the English voicing contrast that is not present in Kikuyu as well as a Kikuyu prevoiced–voiced contrast that is not present in English. These two studies confirm that at least some perceptual capacities develop before the onset of experience, and the Kikuyu study also shows that perceptions can be induced with just 2 months of experience (unless Kikuyu babies and American babies are biologically different in some way). Interestingly, Spanish and Kikuyu adults perceive (though they do not use) the universal English voicing contrast, but they perceive it only weakly. Between infancy and maturity, therefore, a perceptual discrimination that is present at birth atrophies (but is not lost), probably on account of lack of experience.

The literature on the categorical perception of phonemes is replete with many additional examples and has developed so as to illustrate the scheme shown in Figure 3.1. Certain perceptions seem to be universal and developed at birth; these are maintained by the linguistic experiences of the child, but attenuate if absent from the language. Other perceptions, present at birth, can be altered by experience. Still other perceptual capacities can be induced in children by their experiences in the linguistic environment.

A TAXONOMY OF METHODOLOGY

Perception is private. There is no way for one person to know what another person's perceptions of *red, C-sharp, sweet, pungent,* or *soft* are like. We must infer the perceptions of others from their reports or from their behaviors. From a developmental point of view, the study of perception between young adulthood and old age poses little difficulty in this respect, as adults can readily be instructed to report on, or to behave in, certain ways relative to their perceptions. In childhood, and especially in infancy, however, the communication barrier poses a fundamental problem for perceptual study. Moreover, infants are motorically intractable. As a consequence, our knowledge of infant and child perception must be inferred from reports and behaviors of varying fidelity and credibility.

This section presents an overview and illustrates several methodologies that have been adopted by psychologists to study perception in infancy and in early childhood. As described earlier, this period in the life cycle has historically captured much of the concern of perceptual developmentalists. Moreover, this is the period during which most significant developments in perception are taking place. The diversity of techniques we review here have led directly to major discoveries of perceptual capacity and its development.

Despite important differences among methodologies, virtually all techniques developed for the study of perception have been engineered to address a surprisingly small number of questions. Two important ones have to do with whether the observer detects the presence of a stimulus—in the psychophysicist's terms, whether the stimulus passes *absolute threshold*—and whether the stimulus is meaningful for perception. Another related question has to do with whether the observer detects the difference between two stimuli—whether the stimuli surpass a *difference threshold.*

Further, different methodologies vary in the power of *inference* they allow about an observer's actual perceptions. If perception is private and we cannot communicate directly with an observer, our conclusions about an observer's perceptions must be inferred from our methods. Some methods, as we shall see, yield only weak inference; other methods yield stronger inference. The term inference can best be defined with reference to an illustration. If we ascertain that an auditory stimulus applied at the ear yields a regular pattern of electrical response in the brain, then we can feel certain that some internal connections between the peripheral sensory system (the ear) and the central nervous system (the brain) are present or, in the case of the fetus or infant, that these connections have (at least) structurally matured. However, a regularity of brain response tells us nothing, unfortunately, about how, or even whether, the auditory stimulus is actually *perceived;* hence, the inference about perception based on elec-trophysiological data is weak. (Even if two different stimuli gave rise to two distinctly different patterns of electrical activity, we would still not know whether the two stimuli were perceived or whether they were perceived as different.) If, however, we were able to instruct (or in the case of fetuses, infants, and young children, train) the observer to respond behaviorally in one way to one sound and in another way to another sound, our inference would be so strong that, barring artifact, we would possess incontrovertible evidence of per-ception. The two main response systems for the study of perception in nonverbal observers that have been explored are psychophysiological and behavioral; as we shall see, several different techniques have been developed in each. For purposes of comparison, the methods reviewed here are roughly ordered along a hypo-thetical continuum of inference; and for purposes of illustration, examples are drawn mainly from the now extensive infant literature.

Psychophysiological Techniques

Psychological investigations of perceptual development that have adopted phys-iological techniques have approached development via both the central and auto-nomic nervous systems. We first review examples of central and then autonomic nervous system function.

Central Nervous System (CNS) Function.   Research efforts related to percep-tual development focused in the central nervous system have been pitched, roughly speaking, at three distinct levels—neurological anatomy, single-cell physiology, and gross cortical electrical activity. The first level of investigation encompasses anatomical development. Here the questions asked concern the ontogeny of the structure of the perceptual apparatus, with an eye to its relation to function. A presumption of this research strategy in perceptual development is that structure (anatomy) is necessary for function (perception) and so our understanding of perception is, in a sense, bounded by our knowledge about underlying structure. (In the past, perceptual theorists have turned this argument on its head and postulated the existence of structures based on known function. This is true in infancy as well, as discussed by Teller & Bornstein, 1984.) Note, however, that structure is a necessary, but not a sufficient, condition for function: Babies have legs but do not walk. Thus, insofar as inference about perception is concerned, evidence that is based solely on anatomical structure is very weak.

The course of the anatomical development of the sensory systems has received more than modest attention, leading to the conclusion that human beings are reasonably well prepared to perceive once extrauterine life begins. By the second trimester of prenatal life, the eye and visual system (Bronson, 1974; Maurer, 1975), the ear and auditory system (Hecox, 1975), the nose and olfactory system (Tuchmann-Duplessis, Auroux, & Haegel, 1975), and the tongue and gustatory system (Bradley & Stearn, 1967; Humphrey, 1978) have developed so that they are essentially structurally complete and nearly functionally mature. In general, two principles of development operate within and among sensory systems. Within sensory systems, maturation tends to proceed from peripheral to central locations so that, for example, the eye differentiates structurally and reaches functional maturity before the visual cortex (e.g., Abramov, Gordon, Hendrickson, Hainline, Dobson, & LaBossiere, 1982; Conel, 1939–1959). Among sensory systems, different senses tend to come into functional maturity at different times (Gottlieb, 1971), and Turkewitz and Kenny (1982) have persuasively argued for the biopsychological advantages of this staggered programme of development.

The second level of psychophysiological investigation has focused even more narrowly on the development and specificity of individual neurons in different sensory systems. Since the advent of microelectrode recording techniques in physiology, it has been possible to study the sensitivities of single neurons in the brain. Such neurophysiological recording has revealed that individual cells code specific physical characteristics of the environment. So-called "trigger features" of environmental stimulation to which individual neurons in the visual system, for example, have been found to be sensitive include wavelength of light, orientation of form, direction of movement, and so on. Although this area of research is exciting and very provocative for the study of perceptual development, several questions render it of limited current value and indicate that such findings should be applied with caution. For example, although single neurons are sensitive to properties of environmental stimulation, their actual role (if any) in perception is largely undefined. Further, because virtually all studies of single units have been conducted in infrahuman species, usually in cats or monkeys, the direct relevance or applicability of single-unit studies to human perception is still open to question. Finally, a very intriguing, but still largely unresolved, question for perceptual development in this field is whether single units are innately sensitive to their "trigger features"; it could be that sensitivity grows with, or reflects, experience.

The third level of research into the contributions of the central nervous system to perception speaks most directly to the perceptual development of the intact human being. It derives from measures of overall electrical activity of the developing brain. In this line of research, the principal electrophysiological technique involves the cortical evoked potential. This evoked potential derives from the complex sequence of electrical currents that are normally produced in the brain and can be seen in the electroencephalograph (EEG). When a stimulus is presented to the eye or to the ear it gives rise to a characteristic wave form of activity in particular parts of the brain. Through the use of computer averaging techniques, this wave form can be isolated from the EEG as a whole.

Studies of the development of the evoked potential show that the wave form begins simply, is slower to start in response to a stimulus in infancy than in adulthood, but has a relatively stable amplitude across the life cycle. As shown in the top panel of Figure 3.2, the evoked potential for a visual stimulus can be detected in preterm babies when it assumes a simple form, and it is already relatively complex at birth. The wave form remains quite variable up to 3 years, however. As shown in the bottom panel of the same figure, the time between stimulus onset and the appearance of the major positive crest (P_2) of the evoked potential shows a reasonably orderly decrease with age until it reaches adult values. The amplitude of the cortical evoked potential (not shown) follows a more complex course of development: It diminishes with age up to term, then increases to 3 years, then decreases again so that, in essence, adult and newborn show similar amplitudes.[4] It is important to note that these principles, though broad (Berg & Berg, 1979; Hecox & Galambos, 1974; Schulman-Galambos & Galambos, 1975), describe normal infants who are shown particular stimuli; variations among infants or stimuli can perturb these generalizations.

Sound sensitivity in infants has also been measured by means of the evoked potential. Indeed, through the unique placement of a miniature loudspeaker next

---

[4]Insight into the developmental history of sensory and perceptual systems from early life, such as that documented here, has been obtained through the adventitous study of babies born prematurely; these infants are available for observation at conceptional ages that are otherwise closed to research (see Humphrey, 1978; Friedman & Sigman, 1981). Importantly, preterm infants can contribute to the understanding of biological development, as here, as well as to behavioral development. For example, Sarnat (1978) has found that preterm infants as young as 7 months gestational age would presumptively suck or increase motor activity when a peppermint extract was placed under their nose, evidence that suggests that the olfactory system is functional considerably earlier in development than term.

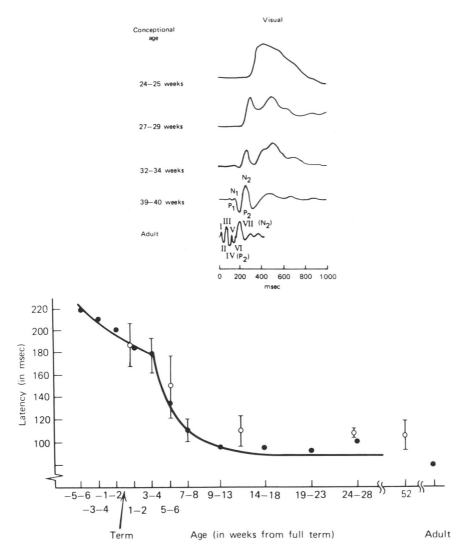

FIG. 3.2. *Top:* Cortical responses evoked by visual stimuli in preterm infants, term newborns, and adults. Derivations are bipolar: Oz-Pz for the visual response. Surface negativity is plotted upwards. *Bottom:* Latency of the major positive component of the visual-evoked response as a function of age in weeks from term. The solid and open dots represent data from two different experiments. The vertical lines passing through the open dots signify ± 1 SD for a group of 21 subjects. (From W. Berg & K. Berg, 1979. Copyright John Wiley. Reprinted with permission.)

to the ear and an electrode clipped to the scalp of the fetus *in utero,* Scibetta, Rosen, Hochberg, and Chik (1971) have recorded auditory evoked potentials in the last trimester of pregnancy. As the middle ear reaches maturity in structure by the sixth month after conception (Hecox, 1975), and at this point fetuses respond to auditory stimuli behaviorally (Bench, 1978), it may be that babies still in the womb can "overhear" parental conversations.[5] Of course, it is also important to consider that human voice qualities may be altered for the fetus, given the acoustic transduction characteristics of the uterus, the amniotic fluid, and the abdominal wall of the mother.

Studies of anatomy, single-cell physiology, and gross electrical activity of the brain all contribute to our understanding of perception, its bases, and its development. Perhaps evoked potential studies have provided the most useful data to date.

Autonomic Nervous System (ANS) Function.   A second, widely applied psychophysiological approach to gaining information about perception in early life has been the monitoring of infants' autonomic nervous system responses in perceptual settings. Orienting reflexes, respiration, and heart rate are common sites of measurement, used even with the youngest observers (Berg & Berg, 1979; Kessen, Haith, & Salapatek, 1970). For example, when Charles Darwin (1877) described the growth of his young son Doddy in the first English language account of an infant, he reported an informal psychophysiological experiment: "with respect to vision,—his eyes were fixed on a candle as early as the 9th day, and up to the 45th day nothing else seemed thus to fix them. . . ." (pp. 286–287). Since Darwin's time, the use of infant autonomic system response to index perceptual function has become increasingly complex: Figure 3.3 shows a newborn baby "wired" for perceptual study.

Heart rate has proven particularly useful in research on early perception (Berg & Berg, 1979; Porges, 1974). We have already witnessed, for example, how heart rate substituted for crawling in testing babies' perceptions of depth on the visual cliff; heart rate has also been used in other paradigms to assess visual, auditory, gustatory, and olfactory perceptions in infants. Still other studies have connected heart rate to more complex social–cognitive perceptions. Campos (1976), for example, has collected heart-rate data in the context of 5- and 9-month-old infants' global responses in unstressed and distressed situations. Infants in this age-range typically fear strangers. As a stranger enters, approaches, intrudes, and then departs from them, infants' facial expressions alter from simple interest and become increasingly negative (changing from frown to whimper to cry); concomitantly, their heart rates first decelerate from resting

---

[5]Recently, we have learned through behavioral techniques that neonates less than 3 days old prefer their mother's voice to that of a stranger, presumably based on their *past* experience with that voice (DeCasper & Fifer, 1980).

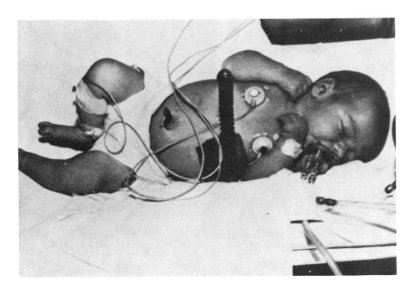

FIG. 3.3. Two-day-old infant with heart rate electrodes attached (two on chest, and the indifferent electrode on right leg), pneumobelt between the abdomen and chest (to measure respiration), and an automatic nipple in place (to deliver fluid and measure amplitude and frequency of sucking). (From L. P. Lipsitt, 1977.)

level (a common index of interest) and then accelerate during distress (as much as 30 beats per minute in 9-month-olds). Thus, heart rate accompanies affect changes and can serve, as here, as a converging measure of perception.

Our understanding of the foundations of perception has been enhanced considerably by studies of nervous system structure and function. They inform us as to the existence of perceptual structures and when connections are functionally "hooked up." In immature organisms, psychophysiological indices often substitute valuably for behavioral ones as objective and sensitive measures of perception, although many factors besides those under experimental scrutiny can influence psychophysiological responses. The psychophysiological approach has also proven valuable for the light it sheds on atypical development. For example, the evoked potential has been successfully used as an aid in the diagnosis of the etiology of deafness in infancy. If the infant does not respond to sound, the evoked potential can tell us whether or not the baby's brain pathways are intact (Hecox & Galambos, 1974; Schulman-Galambos & Galambos, 1979).

Despite these virtues, the contribution of psychophysiology to our understanding of perception is limited, and it requires the highest degree of inference. That a cortex exists, and that a stimulus presented to the eye creates an identifiable pattern of cortical activity, is no guarantee that the stimulus registers in *perceptually meaningful and functional ways* for the observer—infant or adult. Some autonomic system measures fare somewhat better in this regard, but they still are not convincing of *conscious perception,* as the body can also respond in the absence of awareness. The only way we have access to conscious perceptual function is through behavioral report. Behavioral techniques constitute the second main class of approaches to perceptual development, and, for the purposes of understanding perception generally, they provide a more solid foundation than do psychophysiological techniques.

Behavioral Techniques

Developmental psychologists have appealed to a wide variety of behavioral techniques to assess perceptual development in early life. Prominent measures use children's natural responses and reactions, preferences, and learning. Again, this list is, at least implicitly, ordered according to the strength of inference each paradigm yields about perception underlying the behavior. In this section, we look briefly at each of these techniques. Each is illustrated with data from studies of infancy or very early childhood.

Corneal Reflection. In the 1960s, William Kessen, Marshall Haith, and Philip Salapatek argued in a series of experimental reports that it is possible to assess infant vision, even at birth, simply by "looking at looking." These investigators photographed the reflection of a stimulus in the cornea of the baby's eye. They assumed that "perceiving" was to some degree implied by the infant's "fixating" the stimulus—voluntary visual orienting that brings a stimulus into the line of visual regard—thus, the direction toward which a baby looks indicates visual selectivity and, hence, visual perception. Until these studies were performed, answers to basic questions—e.g., *Do newborn babies see?*— were still elusive. In the 20 years since this technique was introduced, experimental situations in which infants' visual regard is measured have become increasingly sophisticated (see Figure 3.4), although the main data obtained from these studies, which take the form of scan plots of infants' eye movements, have remained the same. The original findings in this area are still among the most provocative, and they demonstrate some basic principles: Even in the first hours after birth infants look selectively at parts of stimuli where there is information (usually high-contrast features—in the example shown in Figure 3.5, at the angles and along the contours of the triangles) rather than scanning randomly about the background or over the central part of a figure.

Subsequent efforts of various investigators have advanced both the quality and the sophistication of the corneal reflection technique so that it addresses issues that are not only related to what the baby looks at, but also to how scan patterns develop and how babies distribute scanning over different visual patterns, as for example, faces versus geometric forms. In particular, the detailed work of Salapatek (1975), Hainline (e.g., 1978; Hainline & Lemerise, 1982), and Haith (1979, 1980) has revealed much about the extent of infants' visual

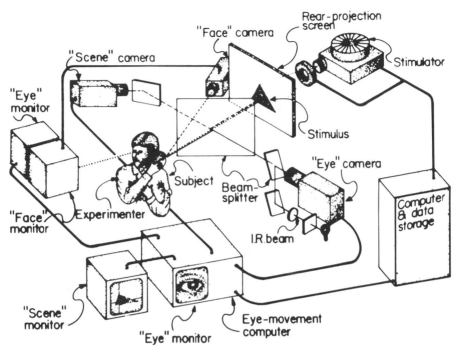

FIG. 3.4. A schematic representation of an eye-movement recording system designed for use with infants. (After L. Hainline & E. Lemerise, Infants' scanning of geometric forms varying in size. *Journal of Experimental Child Psychology,* 1982, *33,* 235–256. Copyright Academic Press. Reprinted by permission.)

inspection of the world in the first 2 months of life. For example, 1-month-old babies tend to scan in a limited fashion, whereas 2-month-olds visually scan more widely. Importantly, all of the work on scanning indicates that, from the first days of life, infants consistently and actively orient to information in the environment.

Studies of organized scanning in early infancy suggest *that* newborns see, but these studies are still not particularly informative as to *what* newborns see. After all, the fact that an infant scans the angle of a triangle does not mean that the infant perceives the triangle (or even an angle) *qua* form, as adults presumably see it. Scanning studies in slightly older infants have addressed this point and, at the same time, brought increasing social relevance to the study of perceptual development in infancy. Notably, Haith, Bergman, and Moore (1977) have traced the development of infants' scanning of the human face. These investigators showed babies in three age groups—3 to 5 weeks, 7 weeks, and 9 to 11 weeks—the live faces of their mothers and of a stranger. The face is a recurrent and highly interesting stimulus for infants, as we know, and research in facial perception has implications for both perceptual and cognitive development as

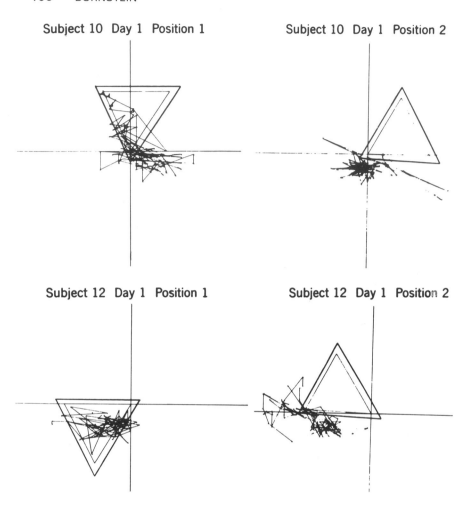

FIG. 3.5.   Records of ocular orientations of Ss in [an] experimental group. The outer triangle of each record represents the outline of the solid, black, equilateral triangle, 8 in. to a side, presented to the experimental Ss. (After W. Kessen, 1967. Copyright John Wiley. Reprinted by permission.)

well as for social and emotional development in infancy (E. J. Gibson, 1969). Most studies of face perception in early life have used two-dimensional slides or photos, or three-dimensional masks and, only very infrequently, live faces. In the majority of these studies, investigators were able to say *whether* but unable to say *where* on the face the infants were looking. Haith and his colleagues assessed where infants scanned on real faces. They found that infants spend increasing amounts of time looking at faces as they age from 3 to 11 weeks and that infants also scan different features of the face as they get older. While 3- to 5-week-olds might scan a face 22% of the available viewing time, 7- to 11-week-olds scan a face 88% of the time. Moreover, 3- to 5-week-olds scan the edges and contrasts of the head and background more than the eyes and central features of the face, while 7- to 11-week-olds scan the eyes and central features more than the outer contours (Table 3.1). Their other results showed that babies at all ages looked at their mothers as much as at a stranger; they looked at still and moving faces equally; they looked at faces that talked more than at faces that were silent; and they confined their looking more narrowly to the central features of the faces that talked. The investigators concluded that perception of the face develops over the first 2 months of life from mere concentration on contours to an appreciation of the perceptual configuration of the face as a whole.

Natural Responses and Reactions. Perception psychologists have frequently relied on babies' naive responses and reactions to stimuli to indicate their sensory or perceptual sensitivities. Thus, pupillary constriction indicates sensitivity to light, head movement indicates orientation to an external stimulus, and vocalization (or its inhibition) signals interest. One of the clearest demonstrations of this technique belongs to Steiner (1977, 1979), who has investigated babies' differential reactions to tastes and smells by studying their facial expressions. Steiner gave newborn infants sweet, sour, or bitter things to taste, and vanilla or raw fish to smell, and he photographed their "gustofacial" and "nasofacial" reactions—all prior to the very first time any of the babies ate. Figure 3.6 shows the results. Truly a picture is worth a thousand words in a Results section!

Preference. One day, while playing with his daughter, James Mark Baldwin, one of the founders of modern developmental psychology, observed that the young girl would consistently reach for a yellow cube over a blue one. The girl's preference of one over the other was independent of where the toy cubes were located. Baldwin deduced that young Helen saw colors because her preferential reaching gave evidence that she discriminated yellow from blue. Although Baldwin's logic met with some resistance in the 1890s, in the late 1950s and early

TABLE 3.1
Distribution of Face Fixations by Babies in Different Age Groups

Age Groups (weeks)	Percentage of Face Fixations			
	Eyes	*Nose*	*Mouth*	*Edges*
3 to 5	29.8	7.9	4.9	57.4
7	54.8	7.2	4.2	33.8
9 to 11	48.9	12.7	5.7	32.7

[a]Adapted from M. M. Haith, T. Bergman, and M. J. Moore, Eye contact and face scanning in early infancy. *Science,* 1977, *198,* 853–855.

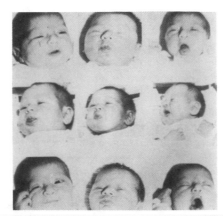

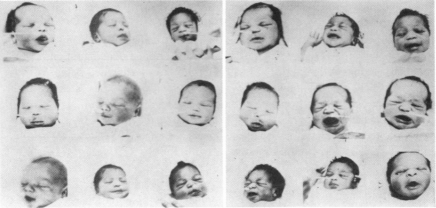

FIG. 3.6.   *Top:* Infants' gustofacial response to the taste of sweet (left column), sour (middle column), and bitter (right column). *Bottom:* Infants' nasofacial response to the smell of vanilla (left panel) and raw fish (right panel). (After J. Steiner, 1977.)

1960s, Robert Fantz revived Baldwin's argument, grounding it this time in infant looking, rather than reaching. Fantz argued that if a baby looked preferentially at one stimulus over another in a paired-choice design, and the baby's looking preference was consistent irrespective of the spatial location of the two stimuli, that preference could be taken to indicate detection or discrimination. Today, Fantz's argument is the bedrock of many infant research techniques. Infants visually prefer faces over nonfacial configurations of the same elements, they prefer some pattern organizations over others, and some colors over others. In the auditory realm, infants orient and attend preferentially to certain sounds. Studies that use this simple technique not only give evidence that some stimuli are preferred to others, but show that expressed preference itself implies discrimination.

Early on, Fantz used this preference technique to examine visual form perception and visual acuity in the first year of life. To study acuity Fantz, Ordy, and Udelf (1962) capitalized on the observation that infants consistently prefer heterogeneous to homogeneous patterns. They posted pairs of patterns for babies to look at, in which one member of the pair was always gray and the other a set of stripes that varied systematically in width. (The two stimuli were always matched in brightness.) If pattern is consistently preferred, the stripe width that fails to evoke a preference from the baby is the one that marks the limit of the baby's ability to tell stripes from the solid gray. (At some point, stripe width can become so fine as to fade into homogeneous gray for all of us.) By this measure, newborns showed 20/400 vision (in Snellen notation); babies 6 months old showed 20/100 vision. (Happily, measures of visual acuity by behavioral and electrophysiological techniques agree; see Dobson & Teller, 1978.)

Preferential looking and reaching have been used to investigate a wide variety of perceptual abilities in infancy, especially in pattern vision (Karmel & Maisel, 1975) and in color vision (Bornstein, 1981a; Teller & Bornstein, 1984). Other sorts of manifest preferences have been used to study perceptual development in other sensory systems as well. For example, Macfarlane (1977) was interested in the rapid development of newborns' olfactory identification of their mothers. He asked mothers to place a gauze swab in their brassieres before they brought their babies to the laboratory. There he presented babies with pairs of swabs—from the mother, a stranger, and out of "the box"—to assess preference. Babies in the first week of life preferentially oriented to a scented breast pad next to an unscented one and demonstrably preferred their mothers' odor to a stranger's by the second week of life. Preference has also served as one of the major techniques used to measure taste perception in infants. Newborns in the first week of life consume more sweetened fluid than plain water and consume more fluid the higher its concentration of sugar. Moreover, newborns and older infants even distinguish among sugars by preference, ingesting more fructose or sucrose than lactose or glucose (Desor, Maller, & Greene, 1977; Desor, Maller, & Turner, 1973).

Although these and other studies show that infants prefer some stimuli to others, they do not suggest why such natural preference hierarchies might exist. When organisms display consistent behaviors, such as preferences, so early in life, it is natural for investigators to look for some explanation in the biology of the organism and to look to brain–behavior relationships. In this case, Bornstein (1975, 1978), Karmel and Maisel (1975), and Haith (1979, 1980) have offered similar hypotheses—namely that, at least in vision, stimuli that excite greater cortical neuronal activity attract and hold the infant's attention. This activity is believed to have positive consequences for neurological development and sensory integration.

Demonstrable preferences offer good evidence for the existence of absolute and discriminative thresholds; unfortunately, the preference paradigm suffers from a major shortcoming. That is, the observer's *failure* to demonstrate a preference is fundamentally ambiguous and tells us nothing about the observer's ability to detect or to discriminate stimuli. A child in the laboratory, for example, may look to mother and stranger equally, but still be able to tell them apart . . . and know which to prefer under particular circumstances. This is a nontrivial methodological drawback; for example, in preferential assessments of visual acuity, the limit of visual resolution (described above) is given by equal looking between striped patterns, but equal looking does not necessarily indicate that infants could not discriminate even finer stripe widths. The infant may prefer pattern homogeneity and very narrow stripes equally, but may also be able to see a difference between the two. For this reason, many investigators have turned to paradigms that draw even more actively on definitive infant behaviors to study absolute and difference thresholds. Among the most prominent today are conditioned head rotation and habituation.

Conditioned Head Rotation.   Wise investigators always capitalize on the most developed response capacities of their organisms, and infant investigators do not differ in this respect. As is well known, physical development proceeds cephalocaudally (from the head downward) and proximodistally (from the center of the body outward); as a consequence, the eye, mouth, head, and neck regions of the body are the most highly developed at the earliest point in ontogenesis. Many of the response procedures discussed thus far call upon infants' looking or orienting or sucking for the analysis of perceptual function.

One paradigm that taps infants' voluntary motor control to assess perceptual development is conditioned head turning. The baby sits on mother's lap, otherwise unencumbered. There is a loudspeaker to one side of the baby. When a sound (a single tone or speech syllable) is played through the speaker and the baby responds by orienting to it, the baby is rewarded by the activation of a colorful mechanical toy located just above the speaker. Infants quickly learn to orient to the sound. Experimenters subsequently manipulate the sound. How loud does the tone have to be before the infant orients? By varying the intensity and the frequency of tones, developmental psychoacousticians can plot infants' absolute thresholds (e.g., Schneider, Trehub, & Bull, 1980). Do preverbal infants categorize speech sounds as adults do? By reinforcing infant head turns for some sounds but not for others, and then probing with new sounds, developmental psycholinguists can discern infants' discrimination among speech sounds (e.g., Kuhl, 1984).

Habituation.   The conditioned head rotation technique provides reasonably secure data about infant perception because babies are actively, voluntarily, and definitely responding to stimuli, thereby "communicating" their perceptions. An equally demonstrative and reliable technique, and one that has been the most widely adopted in experimental studies of perception in infancy, is habituation. This procedure has the advantage that it can be, and has been, used to investigate perception in every modality and very early in infancy; for the purposes of this exposition, we take vision as our example (Bornstein, 1984, provides a comprehensive review).

In habituation, an infant is shown a stimulus, and the infant's visual attention to the stimulus is monitored. Typically, when an infant is placed in an otherwise homogeneous environment, the infant will orient and attend to the initial presentation of a novel stimulus. If the stimulus is available to the infant's view continuously, or if it is presented repeatedly, the infant's attention to the stimulus will wane. This decrease in attention, or habituation, presumably reflects two component processes: the infant's developing a mental representation of the stimulus, and the infant's continuing comparison of whatever stimulus is present with that representation. If the external stimulus and the mental representation match and baby "knows" the stimulus, there is little reason to continue to look; mismatches, however, maintain the infant's attention. A novel discriminable stimulus, introduced after habituation to a familiar one, will typically re-excite infant attention. Habituation to familiarity and recovery to novelty have proven the most versatile and fruitful infant methods, giving a large number of investigators the wherewithal to assess myriad aspects of perception and cognition in infancy.

Specifically, this basic paradigm permits an investigator to address questions (a) about detection and discrimination; (b) about perceptual categorization; (c) about recognition memory; and (d) about conceptual abilities in infants and young children. Here are some examples: (a) Can babies tell the difference between two expressions on the same face? If an infant is habituated to a face wearing a neutral expression and is afterward shown the same face wearing a smiling expression, the infant will recover looking to the smiling expression. This pattern of looking indicates that the infant discriminates between (at least) two expressions of the same face (Caron, Caron, & Myers, 1982). (Of course, the finding says nothing about how the baby may interpret expressions.) (b) Do babies see the world partitioned into general categories of color? If a baby is habituated to a blue, and then tested with the same blue, with a second but different blue, and with a green, the baby will recover looking selectively to the new green, but not to the new blue. This finding indicates that babies discriminate green from blue and co-classify different blues (Bornstein, 1981a, 1981b; Bornstein, Kessen, & Weiskopf, 1976). (Of course, babies can still discriminate among various shades of blue.) Figure 3.7 shows the parallel divisions of the spectrum in infancy and in adulthood. (c) Do babies remember particular stimuli? If a baby is habituated to a face, for example, and after a delay is shown both the original face and a novel face, the baby will look more at the novel face. This pattern indicates that babies can recognize a familiar face even after a delay (Fagan, 1979). The habituation paradigm is a very powerful one for the study of recognition memory: Experimenters can vary the time delay so as to test short- or long-term recognition memory, and they can fill the delay between habituation and test with interference (material from the same dimension as the to-be-remem-

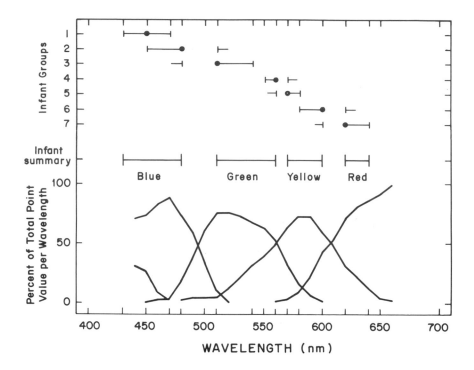

FIG. 3.7.   *Top:* Results of infant experiments on hue categorization. Closed dots stand for habituation stimuli, and vertical bars for other test stimuli. A horizontal connection indicates perceived similarity between wavelengths, and a gap indicates a perceived difference. Thus, in the example described in the text (Group 2), infants habituated to one blue (480 nm) perceived another blue (450 nm) as similar, but treated a green (510 nm) as different. *Middle:* The infant summary indicates ranges of wavelengths infants treat as similar—their "hue categories"— and probable locations of interhue transitions. *Bottom:* Adult color-naming functions. (The curve rising below 470 nm is for red.) Note the correspondences in the ranges of wavelengths infants and adults treat as similar and in the locations of crossovers between hues. (After M. H. Bornstein, W. Kessen, & S. Weiskopf, 1976.)

bered stimulus or from a different dimension). In these ways, it is possible to assess the fidelity and durability of infant recognition memory for different stimuli. (*d*) When do babies begin to form concepts of conventional objects in the world? If an older, but still preverbal, child is habituated over a series of trials with a variety of items of food and is then tested with a novel item of food and a piece of furniture, the infant will reach for and look more at the furniture. This finding indicates that during habituation the child developed the concept of a "class" of stimuli (food) and used this rudimentary concept accurately (Ross, 1980).

Habituation has also been combined with learning to yield a variant procedure. Siqueland and DeLucia (1969) observed that babies who sucked at a baseline rate would suck more frequently and with greater force if their forceful sucks (via an electronic arrangement) brightened a visual image the babies were looking at, or produced a sound they could hear. However, repeated presentation of the same image or sound would not maintain the babies' new high rate of sucking, but would eventually result in a decrease in the frequency of high-amplitude sucking and in a return to the baseline rate of sucking. The introduction of a new discriminable stimulus, however, would re-excite infant sucking. This procedure is conceptually akin to the habituation of attention procedure described earlier, but it has additional advantages and disadvantages. The drawbacks are that the sucking procedure requires considerably more experimental paraphernalia and that it places babies who participate in a much more onerous task than just looking; as a consequence, the infant drop-out rate is high. The advantages of the sucking procedure are that it has proved to be applicable with considerably younger infants than has the looking procedure (1 month vs. 3 months are the approximate lower age limits), and that sucking can be used in auditory experiments as well as in visual ones. In one study that used the sucking habituation procedure to study visual discrimination, Milewski (1976) habituated babies of two ages to a two-component stimulus (▢) and then tested the babies with the same stimulus; with a stimulus that changed the external form but not the internal one (△); and with a stimulus that changed the internal form but not the external one (△). One-month-olds discriminated change in the external form, but not the internal; 4-month-olds, by contrast, detected alterations in both. These developmental results are also noteworthy because they are consonant with the data on infant scanning patterns discussed earlier, viz. younger babies first scan external elements of patterns and only later scan internal elements.

The high-amplitude sucking paradigm has proven remarkably felicitous in studies of infant audition. In a well-known study discussed earlier, Eimas et al. (1971) adapted the procedure to study speech perception by 1- and 4-month-old infants. These investigators made the presentation of one stop–consonant phoneme (/b/) contingent on infants' sucking, and they habituated infants to it. Later, the investigators divided the infants into three groups: One group heard a physically different stop consonant from a different adult phoneme category (/p/); a second group heard a physically different stop consonant from the same category (/b'/); and a third group continued to hear the habituation stimulus (/b/). The two new test stimuli (/p/ and /b'/) differed from the habituation stimulus (/b/) equally in physical terms (milliseconds of voice-onset time), but the two presumably differed unequally in psychological terms (as adults categorize the two /b/ sounds together and distinguish them from /p/). Babies at both ages responded according to expectations that they perceived these ''speech'' sounds in an adultlike categorical fashion: Those in the between-consonant group recovered sucking—indicating their perception of novelty in the change stimulus—while those babies in the within-consonant and control groups continued to habituate sucking. The technique has now been used to investigate a host of perceptions of speech and nonspeech sounds (see Jusczyk, 1984, for a review).

Summary: Methodology and Substance of Early Perceptual Development

Investigators of early perceptual capacity have overcome the major impediment infants present to experimental research—their silence—by establishing communication with infants in a variety of ingenious ways. Some investigators have relied on psychophysiological measurements of the central and autonomic nervous systems; others have relied on behavioral measures of attention, response and reaction, and learning. In so doing, modern investigations have systematically and forever eradicated the view of the perceptually incompetent infant.

Approaching perceptual development via a taxonomy of methodology, as we have done here, stresses technique and tends to underemphasize the substance of what is developing. But perception itself, for the reasons already detailed, merits attention. Through the development of diverse methodologies, perceptual developmentalists have glimpsed the perceptual world of the infant. In précis, what is that world like?

At birth, infants can see, hear, taste, feel, and touch; in this sense, they are well prepared for the new world that surrounds them. An important general aspect of sensation is that even from the very beginning of life babies actively seek out information in their environment; moreover, babies show distinct preferences for some kinds of information over others. For example, soon after birth, newborns seek out contours and edges, where visual information is rich, and they prefer saturated colors, sweet tastes, and pleasant odors. Babies in the first month of life can also recognize their mothers by voice and by scent, though whether they can by face is open to question.

By the age of one month, the infant's perceptual world has become clearer and more organized in many ways. Babies' visual acuity and convergence are rapidly developing toward mature levels, and they are beginning to perceive complex, as well as simple, visual patterns. At this age, babies see color and hear speech (perhaps not as speech per se but at least in a speechlike way). By the end of their third month, babies' vision has further developed: They can focus on near or far objects, and they possess the rudiments of shape and size constancies. By 4 to 5 months, babies perceive Gestalts and recognize objects two- *or* three-dimensionally; they are perceiving speech *qua* speech and discriminating sound differences at the beginning, in the middle, or at the end of syllables. By 6 months, visual–auditory and visual–tactual information is already integrated so as to fuse perceptual wholes.

These exciting, sometimes startling results of the perceptual observations of young infants do not mean that newborns possess fully developed perceptual capacities at birth. Even if rudimentary function is present, qualitative information is still lacking; in some sensory systems, it is not known what functions exist at birth. In some cases, technical problems still limit access to knowledge; in other cases, it is clear that development simply has not yet occurred. Much perceptual development remains to the period after infancy, and much of this development is, as is well known, bound up with more comprehensive developments in cognition.

PERCEPTION IN CHILDHOOD, ADULTHOOD, AND OLD AGE

It has been implicit in this chapter so far that the study of perceptual development can be thought of as synonymous with the study of perceptual development *in infancy*. Three principal reasons may be given for this state of affairs. The first is that perceptual study as a whole was given strong impetus by the nature–nurture debate. To study perception, therefore, was to address this controversy, and to address this controversy effectively was to study perception near the beginning of life. The second reason why expositions of perceptual development have tended to focus on the period of infancy is that the study of perception at most other periods in the life cycle, for example adulthood, is normally outside the province of developmental psychology and belongs to a different area in psychology— sensation and perception. If an investigator's ambitions focus on understanding how the sensory systems function normally, it is in that researcher's best interest to work with observers who possess mature sensory systems and who will give the most stable data with the highest reliability and the greatest ease of communication. (Infants fail all these criteria.) Adult sensation and perception is a venerable and stalwart area in psychology—indeed, it is the oldest in experimental psychology—but adult research is only included in the study of perceptual development when developmental comparisons are called for. There is a third substantial reason why the study of perceptual development has been circumscribed to early life. By the time human beings are toddlers, their perceptions are reasonably mature. Much of the "action" in perceptual development seems to take place very early in life; that is, in infancy.

Nevertheless, two periods in the life span other than infancy, childhood and old age, hold some interest for developmentalists. These life phases provide important basic information, as well as tests of theories. For example, understanding perceptual capacities in childhood and in old age is important for practical reasons; in childhood because of the role of perception in learning to read (e.g., Bornstein & Stiles-Davis, 1984; Gibson & Levin, 1975; Kavale, 1982), and in old age because of the significance of perceptual capacity for autonomy and self-reliance (Bromley, 1966/1974). Understanding the course of perceptual development from childhood through old age is also interesting theoretically to uncover whether deterioration of perceptual capacity follows a course that parallels its evolution (Comalli, 1970).

Childhood

Many applied investigators have been interested in perceptual development in childhood, particularly form perception, because of its importance in schooling. Preschoolers attend to form, but the significance of form and of changing form is only truly brought home when children have to pay attention to letters; that is, when they begin to learn how to read (Gibson & Levin, 1975).

Perhaps the best-known experiments on the early development of form perception are those conducted by the Gibsons to test a "differentiation" theory of perceptual learning. The Gibsons adopted the position (described earlier) that perceptual development involves an increasingly efficient abstraction of invariants or constant stimulus features from the environmental array. Perceptual life begins undifferentiated and diffuse, and, through experience, it differentiates and becomes more selective and acute. The Gibsons (1955) demonstrated perceptual differentiation of form in one cross-sectional experiment comparing children 6–8 and 8.5–11 years of age with adults. Each subject was shown a coil-like figure (Ɛ) and then asked to point it out again when shown a series of similar coils one at a time in a test. The foils or distractors in the test looked very much like the original standard coil, except that they differed in number of turns, degree of compression, or orientation. Thus, successful identification depended on perceiving distinctive features of coils on these dimensions. There were 18 standards in all. Among the three age groups, the adults had the most correct initially and reached 100% recognition after only three exposures to each standard stimulus; the older children had fewer correct at first and took longer than adults to reach perfect recognition; and the younger children had the fewest correct initially and never met a learning criterion. Both measures present a good indication of children's increasing ability to differentiate perceptual features with age. In perception, we learn what to look for and what is distinctive versus what is irrelevant.

The Gibsons and their colleagues later applied this finding directly to the educational question of children's letter learning (Gibson, Gibson, Pick, & Osser, 1962). In this experiment, the investigators wanted to assess how 4–8-year-olds learn to distinguish letter-like forms, a basic problem for shape constancy and a prerequisite for reading. This experiment also used a matching task. This time, however, letter-like forms were used (Ц), and foils varied systematically from the standard to assess what specific confusions children might make and whether their confusions might vary with age. Twelve types of foils were used; these included breaks (Ц), rotations (⊏), reversals (Ц), and perspective transformations (Ц). Across ages, the children detected figural breaks best, rotations and reversals next, and perspective transformations the least proficiently. Regardless of transformation, the children's performance improved with age. The fact that youngsters have particular difficulty with reversals reminds us of common left–right reading and writing confusions in young children (e.g., *s* for *z*, *b* for *d*, etc.) Bornstein, Gross, and Wolf (1978) offered a perceptual interpretation for this phenomenon: These investigators reasoned that because left–right reversals only occur in nature when they are twin aspects of the same thing (e.g., an object and its silhouette) they ought to be treated as the same thing (as with a constancy) and need not be differentiated. In support of this hypothesis, Bornstein et al. (1978) showed that, under many conditions, very young infants treat left–right reversals of patterns as similar, though they distinguish other rotations. In the case of reversals in letters, children must apparently *un*learn a natural perceptual constancy.

Further investigation of the growth of form perception has focused on young children's perceptions of parts versus wholes of complex stimuli (Elkind, 1975). When shown a man made out of fruit, to which do children respond: the man (the whole) or the fruit (the parts)? It turns out that whether the young child tends more strongly to focus on the whole or on the parts depends on the perceptual salience of wholes versus parts; older children and adults, who are more analytic and decentered (in Piaget's terms) or differentiated (in the Gibsons' terms), tend to see both wholes and parts.

Do children literally search forms in ways different from the ways adults do? Gibson and Yonas (1966) asked children aged 7, 9, and 11 years to pick target letters out of arrays of target and foil letters. Across a variety of conditions, in which the ratio of foils to targets changed, and so on, the children consistently improved with age. Later, Vurpillot (1968) coordinated an assessment of children's actual looking movements with the accuracy of their psychological judgments. She recorded eye movements of children between 3 and 10 years of age as they compared pairs of patterns for similarity or difference. The patterns were pairs of houses, each with six windows, and corresponding windows in the two houses could have similar or different object silhouettes showing in them. When the houses differed by only a single window, young children were inaccurate in their similarity–difference judgments, and Vurpillot's eye-track records showed that these children only searched about half the windows before responding; older children compared all corresponding windows systematically and were more often correct in their judgments. It would appear that systematic search also increases with age.

Although there is a large and growing body of literature that is concerned with children's perception of form, little of it has been directly applicable to practical questions regarding reading (Gibson & Levin, 1975). It is not really known how children gain perceptual access to this important symbol system, and, although some success rests on cognitive and social factors (Vellutino, 1977), clearly some success in reading depends as well on childrens' visual perceptual skills (e.g., Kavale, 1982). This is one important area in which the need for more research is clear.

Old Age

One of the main principles of aging is that, from a peak in early adulthood and through a complex sequence of changes, the body dies a little every day. Select intellectual functions and almost all bodily or vegetative functions decline in this way (Bromley, 1966/1974). The consequences include changes and deterioration in perceptually related structures and functions: Brain weight declines, cells in the CNS die and do not regenerate, nerve conduction velocity slows. Across the senses, perceptual deterioration is common and often regular.

A major and open question surrounding the decline of sensory-perceptual function in old age turns on the relative contributions of organ impairment, nervous system degeneration, and deterioration of psychological judgment. Some phenomena that tell of poor performance in old age seem clearly to be based on adverse physiological change. For example, the lens of the eye grows like an onion over the entire course of the life span, adding layer upon layer. Each layer is pigmented, and, as the lens grows, light must traverse more and more absorptive material before it reaches the retina and is effective in vision. As lens pigment selectively absorbs short-wavelength (blue) visible light, the perception of blue systematically attenuates in old age.

Other detriments to performance in old age may depend on the combination of central nervous system deterioration and changes in judgment. A major example is the precipitous increase in traffic accidents among drivers older than about 50. It is well known that the conduction velocity of nerve fibers drops approximately 15% between the ages of 20 and 90, and that simple reaction time to lights and sounds drops 50% over the same period (Bromley, 1966/1974). These and other related psychological factors, including changes in patterns of attention and judgment, are certainly implicated in vehicular accidents.

The study of perception in aging is of further interest for the theoretical information it brings to bear on the question of perceptual change across the lifecycle. There is considerable evidence to support progressive–regressive patterns in the life-span development of some psychological abilities (Strauss, 1982). For example, many perceptual functions seem to improve during childhood, reach a peak or high plateau during adulthood, and subsequently decline in old age: Illusion susceptibility, the apparent horizon, performance on the Rod-and-Frame Test, part–whole differentiation, visual span, and tachistoscopic form discrimination are just some capacities reported to wax and then wane during the lifecycle (see Comalli, 1970).

Reprise: Nature and Nurture

The discussion of old age permits us the opportunity, if only briefly, to consider again the roles of nature and nurture in perception, this time in a somewhat different light. The implications here are practical as well as theoretical and heuristic. Consider the following set of facts.

Auditory sensitivity is measured by assessing the absolute threshold for perceiving sounds of different frequencies. One of the consequences of aging is deterioration in auditory sensitivity. In essence, the elderly require more energy to hear certain frequencies than do younger people. As the top panel of Figure 3.8 shows, among Americans hearing loss in aging is more pronounced at higher frequencies. One prominent and simple explanation for this finding has been that aging entails the natural and regular deterioration of the anatomical and physiological mechanisms that subserve hearing. An alternative hypothesis is that

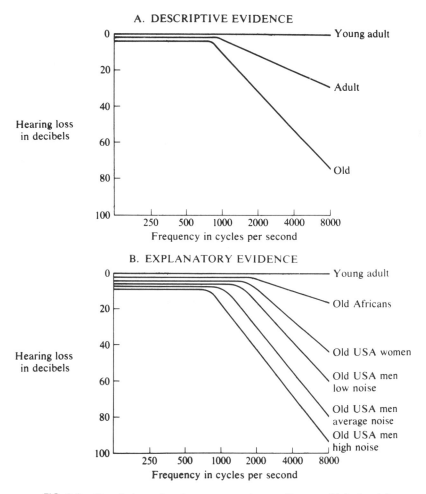

FIG. 3.8.   Descriptive and explanatory research on auditory sensitivity in adulthood. (From *Life-Span Developmental Psychology: Introduction to Research Methods*, by P. B. Baltes, H. W. Reese, & J. R. Nesselroade. Copyright 1977 by Wadsworth Publishing Company. Reprinted with permission of the publisher, Brooks/Cole Publishing Company, Monterey, California.)

cumulative exposure to noise over the course of the life span deleteriously affects the perception of high frequencies and is the prime cause of physiological change (rather than any natural aging process). How can we decide between the nature and nurture explanations?

Additional data, first, from individuals in other societies and, second, from individuals in our own society who have different life histories of exposure to noise help to distinguish between these two hypotheses. As the bottom panel in Figure 3.8 shows, older American women evidence less hearing loss than older American men, and Sudanese Africans, who show no sex differences in hearing with aging, evidence even less deterioration than Americans of either sex. Contrary to the original biological hypothesis, data from these two additional research programs—on gender and culture—suggest that aging alone is probably not the key factor in hearing loss. (It could still be, however unlikely it may seem, that sexes or races differ biologically in the integrity of their auditory mechanisms.) The data on elderly American men exposed to different amounts of noise over the course of their lifetimes lend further support to the experiential interpretation. Data from this third research program—on noise history—strongly support the view that hearing loss in old age is related less to natural physiological processes than to the deleterious effects of the amount of exposure to noise. The three research programs together supplement the "descriptive evidence" with "explanatory evidence" and lend credence to a nurture view. Of course, the fact that noise history selectively affects high frequencies indicates that nature and nurture interact in development.

In developmental theory, the influences of nature and nurture interact and are often difficult to disentangle. Yet an assessment of their relative contributions is critical to the growth of knowledge about the ontogeny of sensory and perceptual as well as other psychological processes. One special virtue of developmental investigations derives from the information they afford to prevention. Although the descriptive evidence alone strongly implicates physiological deterioration, the alleviation of which might be achieved through specialized hearing aids for the elderly, the explanatory evidence that derives from diverse biological and experiential developmental comparisons suggests more important and more productive intervention strategies that would prevent sensory deterioration and hearing loss in the first place.

PERCEPTUAL MODIFICATION, ENRICHMENT, AND DEPRIVATION IN DEVELOPMENT

Research with Diverse Human Populations

How do special perceptual rearing circumstances—modification, enrichment, or deprivation—affect development? As developmental research has evolved, this single question has reformulated itself into two. The first is quite literal: How does perceptual modification, etc., affect perceptual development per se. Two opposite views have competed—without clear resolution—for the answer to this question. Consider, as a concrete example, how deprivation in one perceptual system—e.g., blindness—might affect the development of other systems. One view is that the unaffected senses, such as hearing, might literally develop to a higher level of function, or at least to a heightened level of awareness to compensate for the blindness. Thus, true auditory function in the blind might be enhanced as some sort of physiological compensation for blindness; alternatively, because they are visually deprived, blind people might attend more closely to information arriving via other sensory channels, or perhaps analyze that information more efficiently. The second, opposite view is that the absence of information processing in one modality adversely affects the eventual level of development or awareness in other modalities. On the first view, psychophysics has developed techniques (e.g., signal detection theory) that help to distinguish differences in sensory function from differences in psychological judgment. There is no good evidence, based on these procedures, that surviving systems reach a higher perceptual level, although there is good evidence that attention and awareness, may be enhanced or strategy may differ in surviving perceptual systems (Hoemann, 1978; Warren, 1978). The degree to which shifts in attention or strategy in one modality compensate for the loss of another is, of course, uncertain. On the second view, perceptual deprivation, like blindness, is specifically debilitating to the sensory system and information processing directly involved, but is not necessarily generally debilitating.

The second formulation of our original question on how special perceptual rearing might affect development has been much more general. The question has been asked this way: What effects does perceptual modification, enrichment, or deprivation early in life have on the later development of perceptual, cognitive, or social development? Two major approaches to this question have also evolved. The first approach involves the study of congenitally handicapped populations, and the second involves normal populations who, by chance, have experienced special rearing circumstances, either in institutions or in cultures or ecologies that vary widely in the perceptual experiences they provide. In evaluating effects of perceptual modification on development in these diverse populations, it is necessary to keep in mind that the extraordinary constellation of conditions that impact upon development in these populations may surpass in significance their different perceptual experiences. Blindness, deafness, or other perceptual handicaps, as well as institutionalization or cultural variation, can have such profound concomitant social and emotional effects on development as to render studies of perception alone problematic. For example, practical research problems revolve around defining the severity of a handicap; determining at what age the handicap began; disentangling the physical, emotional, and intellectual disabilities produced by the handicap; and separating the handicapped child's limited general experience from his limited perceptual function.

Unfortunately, these criticisms have no ready replies. As a consequence, what we have learned about perceptual development from investigations of the handicapped is much more limited and confounded than is commonly supposed.[6]

Turning to the other populations, viz. the perceptually deprived or culturally diverse, has presented some new solutions, and many new problems as well. Most studies involving institutionalized or deprived populations have understandably been principally concerned with elucidating the effects of deprivation on the development of cognitive and social skills. As a consequence, studies designed to assess the effects of perceptual modification of this sort on human perceptual development are understandably scarce. What role has perception for cognitive and social function? Though some have argued that such effects are important only inasmuch as they may be mediated by the concomitant absence of important human beings in the child's life (Clarke-Stewart, 1973), several major investigations have yielded direct associations between perceptual experiences (or lack thereof) and cognitive development (e.g., Casler, 1968; Elardo, Bradley, & Caldwell, 1977; Fantz, Fagan, & Miranda, 1975; Parke, 1978; Rheingold, 1960; Yarrow, Rubenstein, & Pedersen, 1975). For example, Wachs and his associates (1979, Wachs, Uzgiris, & Hunt, 1971) conducted investigations that attempted to overcome socioeconomic status (SES), institutional, and other confounds to delimit how early exposure to inanimate physical stimulation—via perception—influences cognitive development in the first 3 years of life. Their findings support an "optimal match hypothesis," which posits that understimulation and overstimulation, as well as disorganized stimulation, are deleterious for development in specific different populations. This hypothesis is also held to explain such diverse findings as why noise confusion in the home is negatively related to cognitive advance (Wachs et al., 1971) and to reading ability (Cohen, Glass, & Singer, 1973), as well as why general enrichment might fail to accelerate development in babies (White & Held, 1966).

The third human group to whom researchers have turned to answer the question of how perceptual experience may influence development includes children reared in vastly different perceptual environments. Indeed, one of the major ways in which extremes of perceptual experience have been investigated safely in humans has been to take advantage of "natural experiments" in which children are reared in widely varying perceptual ecologies (Bornstein, 1980; Serpell, 1976; Witkin & Berry, 1975). All humans are believed to be endowed with roughly the same anatomy and physiology. It is reasonable to expect, therefore, that most perceptual systems or abilities are essentially universal, and that humans begin life on the same footing. Do varying perceptual rearing circumstances influence perception or cognition differently after the onset of experi-

---

[6]Of related interest are modern studies of profoundly handicapped infants (thalidomide babies), which demonstrate that the inability to act motorically does not inhibit the development of normal perception and cognition—echoing Eva Lauk (Décarie, 1969).

ence? Some perceptions seem to be affected, others not. Although Western children are reared in environments that are largely constructed of geometric verticals and horizontals, Zulu children in South Africa are reared in curved visual environments. Allport and Pettigrew (1957) reported that these different ecologies influence the inferences children and adults make about what they see. On the other hand, children from rural areas of New Guinea, Ethiopia, and Ghana, who are reared with little or no exposure to representational arts, seem immediately able to recognize two-dimensional representations of familiar three-dimensional objects (Bornstein, 1980, provides a more comprehensive discussion).

In summary, our perceptual systems are in some degree plastic to experience and in others unperturbed by large, but normal, variation in environmental stimulation. Moreover, our physical and perceptual experiences seem to be sufficiently common to render most perceptions nearly the same for everyone, everywhere.

Some Notes on Perceptual Research with Animals

Although this chapter concentrates on the theories, methods, and substantive findings concerning perceptual development in human beings, it would be remiss to omit some consideration of comparative research. Perceptual development has been studied in nonhuman animals for three reasons. First, animals are often used to answer general biological questions (e.g., Brown & Deffenbacher, 1979). Second, animal research is undertaken as a valuable and informative tool in its own right, as in ethological study (e.g., Marler, Dooling, & Zoloth, 1980; von Uexküll, 1934). Third, studies with animals have provided unique experiments that inform our understanding of principles of perceptual development in general, just as animal analogs help to clarify perceptual development in human beings, specifically. Some animals, like monkeys, are very close to humans physiologically, but permit experimental manipulations that are not possible with human infants. Investigators who use monkey babies can attain greater control, can test repeated times, can manipulate experience, and can investigate brain-behavior relationships. These conditions often afford clearer, or even unique, findings. Even though they are closely related, however, monkeys and humans traverse different developmental pathways; for example, monkey visual development is accelerated relative to that of the human (by a ratio of about 4:1). Consequently, inferences about anatomical and perceptual development in humans from monkeys (or any infrahuman species) must be made cautiously.

Animal research has played an important role in investigating and in explicating human perceptual development. Let us examine briefly three exemplary lines of investigation. Suppose, first, that you wanted to develop an animal model to specify the effects of early limited vision or blindness on later visual ability. Minimally, this would require establishing the facilities of a monkey colony and the procedures by which monkeys could be born and reared as naturally as possible, but in the dark. As you might intuit, research that requires the rearranging and controlling of an organism's environment from birth necessitates enormous experimental motivation and investment. After Riesen (1947) reared two chimpanzees in the dark for 16 months, he found that his subjects still could not be used properly to answer this first experimental question because dark rearing had caused physical damage to their eyes. Later studies showed that if chimps were exposed for brief periods to diffuse light, they would not sustain visual system damage; these chimps scored greater successes on visual tasks, but they had not been totally deprived.

Many perceptual theorists, including Piaget and Hebb, have argued that variation of visual stimulation is essential to perceptual development. However, the question of whether such perceptual stimulation may be experienced passively or must be experienced actively to be effective—our second example line of research—remained unresolved until Held and Hein (1963). These investigators examined whether and how perceptual feedback from movement produced by the animal itself would affect the animal's visually guided behavior. To do this, they reared cats in the dark and kept them there except for brief periods of visual experience. During these periods, the experimenters literally "yoked" litter mates in a carousel apparatus so that as one animal wandered and actively experienced its visual world (the inner striped surface of a barrel) contingent upon its self-produced movements, its partner experienced the same visual world only passively by mechanical transfer from the first. This was the only visual experience for either animal. Afterward, Held and Hein tested the pairs of cats for their performance on a variety of visually coordinated behaviors. The "active" cats were more accurate at locating things spatially, they blinked at approaching objects, and they avoided the visual cliff significantly more often than their yoked "passive" controls. In other words, Held and Hein found that motor outflow is important in conjunction with visual feedback to effect positive perceptual development; visual–motor development depends not only on stimulation, but on active exploration as well. (If deprived animals were later given appropriate experience, their deficits abated.) This second line of research shows that activity plays a critical role in normal perceptual development.

Among the most intensive and successful of all animal research in perception has been that concerned with delineating the ways in which diverse perceptual rearing experiences alter neural sensitivities in the visual system. Usually a cat or monkey visual cortex is selected as the preparation of study. This third line of animal research has yielded at least three important sets of general findings about perceptual development (e.g., Movshon & Van Sluyters, 1981): (a) Single cells in the sensory system are specialized for orientation, binocular disparity, and a large number of other properties of the visual world; (b) early visual experience influences anatomy, neural sensitivity, and behavior toward a mutual consonance; and (c) the application of perceptual alterations at different times has isolated "sensitive periods," or temporal windows during which early selective environmental experience is especially effective in influencing the nature of anatomy, neural sensitivity, and behavior.

Summary

Perceptual stimulation is necessary for normal development, and the lack of it, too much of it, or its disorganization are detrimental. Further, studies of perceptual modification, enrichment, and deprivation in humans and in animals have led to the discovery of important general principles of perception, including the influences of experience on anatomical and behavioral development; the delineation of critical periods when such influences are especially effective; and the significance of activity for normal perceptual development. In contrast, our understanding of compensatory perceptual function and capacity among the profoundly handicapped is, for diverse methodological reasons, severely limited.

SUMMARY AND CONCLUSIONS

Perception is one of the oldest fields in psychology and one of the most closely tied to psychology's philosophical origins. It is also one of the most popular areas in developmental study. Studies of infancy constitute the bulk of perceptual developmental research, and studies of perceptual development have, until recently perhaps, constituted the bulk of research in infancy. The several reasons for this state of affairs are outlined at the beginning of this chapter.

In recent years, many secrets of infancy and early childhood—formidable and intractable as they once seemed—have been revealed through a variety of ingenious techniques. From the research that has been discussed in this chapter we now know that even the very young of our own species perceive beyond mere "sensing." We have also learned about a few signal aspects of perceptual processing as, for example, the role of activity. But several old and important questions about perceptual development are still open, left unanswered even by the wealth of research amassed in the last two decades. Moreover, many of the startling revelations we derive from our simplest introspections as adults continue to spark our curiosity about perceptual development. How do we get from patterns of sensation received and transduced at the sensory surface to what we effortlessly perceive to be integrated wholes of objects in the real world? How does a world that is constantly in flux come to be perceived as stable? As context is so influential in perception, how do we come to attend selectively to signal and figure and to eliminate the influence of noise and ground? How do objects we perceive come to be invested with conventional (or idiosyncratic) meaning?

The study of perception in children is also very practical. For example, the relevance of perceptual research to social and emotional development, or to medicine and education, is readily apparent. Physical and social stimulation are perceptual stimulation, and generally, many aspects of social development depend initially on perceptual capacity: Specific examples abound—from the neonates' perception and consequent imitation of facial expressions (Meltzoff & Moore, 1983), to the toddlers' acceptance of photographs to mediate separation from their mothers (Passman & Longeway, 1982). Perception has been equally invoked in the assessment of hyperactivity (Douglas, 1972), and in the study of prerequisites for reading (Bornstein et al., 1978; Bornstein & Stiles-Davis, 1984; Gibson & Levin, 1975; Kavale, 1982).

Perceptual development could serve as a model of developmental studies just as well as any field that is described in this text. It encompasses philosophy and methodology, and it confronts the overarching substantive issues in developmental study. Some perceptual capacities are given congenitally—even in the functioning of the sensory systems—whereas between infancy and maturity other perceptual capacities develop. This ontogenetic change, in turn, has several possible sources: It can be genetic and occur largely as a reflection of maturation, or change can be experiential and largely reflect the influences of the environment and particular events. Perceptual development after birth (or the onset of experience) is doubtless some complex transaction of these two principal sources of variation. At one time or another each of these possibilities has been proposed as determinative. Modern studies have informed a modern view, however. Through their systematic efforts in infancy and early childhood, perceptual developmentalists have determined that basic mechanisms in many cases impose perceptual structure near the beginning of life, and that perceptual development is as much determined and guided by these structural endowments as it is by experience. Thus, neither nativism nor empiricism hold sway in perceptual development; rather, innate mechanisms and experience both have their place in the way in which a child comes to perceive the world.

ACKNOWLEDGMENTS

This chapter was prepared while the author was a Guggenheim Fellow and was partly supported by a research grant (R01 HD17423) and a Research Career Development Award (K04 HD00521) from the National Institute of Child Health and Human Development. April Benasich, Helen Bornstein, Jane Gaughran, Sharon Krinsky, Michael Lamb, Janet Mindes, Madeleine Tress, and Martha Vibbert provided invaluable comments and assistance.

REFERENCES

Abramov, I., Gordon, J., Hendrickson, A., Hainline, L., Dobson, V., & LaBossiere, E. The retina of the newborn human infant. *Science*, 1982, *217*, 265–267.

Allport, G. W., & Pettigrew, T. F. Cultural influence on the perception of movement: The trapezoid illusion among Zulus. *Journal of Abnormal and Social Psychology*, 1957, *55*, 104–113.

Aslin, R. N. Development of binocular fixation in human infants. *Journal of Experimental Child Psychology*, 1977, *23*, 133–150.

Aslin, R. N. Experiential influences and sensitive periods in perceptual development: A unified model. In R. N. Aslin, J. R. Alberts, & M. R. Peterson (Eds.), *Development of perception: Psychobiological perspectives (Vol. 2): The visual system.* New York: Academic Press, 1981.

Ball, W., & Tronick, E. Infant responses to impending collision: Optical and real. *Science,* 1971, *171,* 818–820.

Baltes, P. B., Reese, H. W., & Nesselroade, J. R. *Life-span developmental psychology: Introduction to research methods.* Monterey, Calif.: Brooks/Cole, 1977.

Barlow, H. B., Blakemore, C., & Pettigrew, J. D. The neural mechanism of binocular depth discrimination. *Journal of Physiology,* 1967, *193,* 327–342.

Bench, J. The auditory response. In U. Stave (Ed.), *Perinatal physiology.* New York: Plenum, 1978.

Berg, W. K., & Berg, K. M. Psychophysiological development in infancy: State, sensory function, and attention. In J. D. Osofsky (Ed.), *Handbook of infant development.* New York: Wiley, 1979.

Berkeley, G. *An essay toward a new theory of vision.* Oxford: Clarendon Press, 1901. (Originally published, 1709.)

Bornstein, M. H. Qualities of color vision in infancy. *Journal of Experimental Child Psychology,* 1975, *19,* 401–419.

Bornstein, M. H. Visual behavior of the young human infant: Relationships between chromatic and spatial perception and the activity of underlying brain mechanisms. *Journal of Experimental Child Psychology,* 1978, *26,* 174–192.

Bornstein, M. H. Cross-cultural developmental psychology. In M. H. Bornstein (Ed.), *Comparative methods in psychology.* Hillsdale, NJ: Lawrence Erlbaum Associates, 1980.

Bornstein, M. H. Two kinds of perceptual organization near the beginning of life. In W. A. Collins (Ed.), *Minnesota symposia on child psychology* (Vol. 14). Hillsdale, NJ: Lawrence Erlbaum Associates, 1981. (a)

Bornstein, M. H. Psychological studies of color perception in human infants: Habituation, discrimination and categorization, recognition, and conceptualization. In L. P. Lipsitt (Ed.), *Advances in infancy research* (Vol. 1). Norwood, NJ: Ablex, 1981. (b)

Bornstein, M. H. Habituation of attention as a measure of visual information processing in human infants: Summary, systematization, and synthesis. In G. Gottlieb & N. A. Krasnegor (Eds.), *Measurement of audition and vision in the first year of postnatal life: A methodological overview.* Norwood, NJ: Ablex, 1984.

Bornstein, M. H., Gross, C., & Wolf, J. Perceptual similarity of mirror images in infancy. *Cognition,* 1978, *6,* 89–116.

Bornstein, M. H., Kessen, W., & Weiskopf, S. Color vision and hue categorization in young human infants. *Journal of Experimental Psychology: Human Perception and Performance,* 1976, *2,* 115–129.

Bornstein, M. H., & Stiles-Davis, J. Discrimination and memory for symmetry in young children. *Developmental Psychology,* 1984, *20,* in press.

Bower, T. G. R., Broughton, J. M., & Moore, M. Infant response to approaching objects: An indication of response to distal variables. *Perception and Psychophysics,* 1970, *9,* 193–196.

Bradley, R. M., & Stearn, I. B. The development of the human taste bud during the foetal period. *Journal of Anatomy,* 1967, *101,* 743–752.

Bromley, D. B. *The psychology of human ageing.* Harmondsworth, England: Penguin Books, 1974. (Originally published, 1966.)

Bronson, G. W. The postnatal growth of visual capacity. *Child Development,* 1974, *45,* 873–890.

Brown, E. L., & Deffenbacher, K. *Perception and the senses.* New York: Oxford University Press, 1979.

Campos, J. Heart rate: A sensitive tool for the study of emotional development in the infant. In L. P. Lipsitt (Ed.), *Developmental psychobiology: The significance of infancy.* Hillsdale, NJ: Lawrence Erlbaum Associates, 1976.

Campos, J. J., Langer, A., & Krowitz, A. Cardiac responses on the visual cliff in prelocomotor human infants. *Science,* 1970, *170,* 196–197.

Caron, R. F., Caron, A. J., & Myers, R. S. Abstraction of invariant face expressions in infancy. *Child Development,* 1982, *53,* 1008–1015.

Casler, L. Perceptual deprivation in institutional settings. In G. Newton & S. Levine (Eds.), *Early experience and behavior.* Springfield, Il: C. C. Thomas, 1968.

Clarke-Stewart, K. A. Interactions between mothers and their young children: Characteristics and consequences. *Monographs of the Society for Research in Child Development,* 1973, *38* (6–7, Serial No. 153).

Cohen, S., Glass, D., & Singer, J. Apartment noise, auditory discrimination, and reading ability in children. *Journal of Experimental Social Psychology,* 1973, *9,* 407–422.

Comalli, P. E. Life-span changes in visual perception. In L. R. Goulet & P. B. Baltes (Eds.), *Life-span developmental psychology.* New York: Academic Press, 1970.

Conel, J. L. *The postnatal development of the human cerebral cortex* (Vols. 1–6). Cambridge, Mass.: Harvard University Press, 1939–1959.

Darwin, C. A biographical sketch of an infant. *Mind,* 1877, *2,* 286–294.

DeCasper, A. S., & Fifer, W. P. Of human bonding: Newborns prefer their mothers' voices. *Science,* 1980, *208,* 1174–1176.

Décarie, T. G. A study of the mental and emotional development of the thalidomide child. In B. M. Foss (Ed.), *Determinants of infant behavior* (Vol. 4). London: Methuen, 1969.

Descartes, R. *La dioptrique.* In V. Coursin (Ed.), *Oeuvres de Descartes* (M. D. Boring, trans.). Paris: np, 1824. (Originally published, 1638.)

Desor, J. A., Maller, O., & Greene, L. S. Preference for sweet in humans: Infants, children and adults. In J. Weiffenbach (Ed.), *Taste and development.* Washington, DC: DHEW, 1977.

Desor, J. A., Maller, O., & Turner, R. Taste in acceptance of sugars by human infants. *Journal of Comparative and Physiological Psychology,* 1973, *84,* 496–501.

Dobson, V., & Teller, D. Visual acuity in human infants. A review and comparison of behavioral and electrophysiological studies. *Vision Research,* 1978, *18,* 1469–1483.

Douglas, V. I. Stop, look and listen: The problem of sustained attention and impulse control in hyperactive and normal children. *Canadian Journal of Behavioral Science,* 1972, *4,* 259–282.

Eimas, P. D., Siqueland, E. R., Jusczyk, P., & Vigorito, J. Speech perception in infants. *Science,* 1971, *171,* 303–306.

Elardo, R., Bradley, R., & Caldwell, B. M. A longitudinal study of the relation of infants' home environments to language development at age three. *Child Development,* 1977, *48,* 595–603.

Elkind, D. Perceptual development in children. *American Scientist,* 1975, *63,* 533–541.

Fagan, J. F. The origins of facial pattern recognition. In M. H. Bornstein & W. Kessen (Eds.), *Psychological development from infancy: Image to intention.* Hillsdale, NJ: Lawrence Erlbaum Associates, 1979.

Fantz, R. L., Fagan, J. F., & Miranda, S. B. Early visual selection. In L. B. Cohen & P. Salapatek (Eds.), *Infant perception: From sensation to cognition* (Vol. 1). New York: Academic Press, 1975.

Fantz, R. L., Ordy, J. M., & Udelf, M. S. Maturation of pattern vision in infants during the first six months. *Journal of Comparative and Physiological Psychology,* 1962, *55,* 907–917.

Fox, R., Aslin, R., Shea, S. L., & Dumais, S. Stereopsis in human infants. *Science,* 1980, *207,* 323–324.

Friedman, S. L., & Sigman, M. (Eds.). *Preterm birth and psychological development.* New York: Academic Press, 1981.

Gibson, E. The concept of affordances in development: The renascence of functionalism. In W. A. Collins (Ed.), *The Minnesota symposia on child psychology* (Vol. 15). Hillsdale, NJ: Lawrence Erlbaum Associates, 1982.

Gibson, E. J. *Principles of perceptual learning and development.* New York: Appleton-Century-Crofts, 1969.

Gibson, E. J., Gibson, J. J., Pick, A. D., & Osser, H. A developmental study of the discrimination of letter-like forms. *Journal of Comparative and Physiological Psychology*, 1962, *55*, 897–906.

Gibson, E. J., & Levin, H. *The psychology of reading*. Cambridge, Mass.: MIT Press, 1975.

Gibson, E. J., & Walk, R. D. The "visual cliff." *Scientific American*, 1960, *202*, 64–71.

Gibson, E. J., & Yonas, A. A developmental study of visual search behavior. *Perception and Psychophysics*, 1966, *1*, 169–171.

Gibson, J. J. *The ecological approach to visual perception*. Boston, Mass.: Houghton Mifflin, 1979.

Gibson, J. J., & Gibson, E. J. Perceptual learning: Differentiation or enrichment? *Psychological Review*, 1955, *62*, 32–41.

Gottlieb, G. Ontogenesis of sensory function in birds and mammals. In E. Tobach, L. R. Aronson, & E. F. Shaw (Eds.), *The biopsychology of development*. New York: Academic Press, 1971.

Hainline, L. Developmental changes in visual scanning of face and non-face patterns by infants. *Journal of Experimental Child Psychology*, 1978, *25*, 90–115.

Hainline, L., & Lemerise, E. Infants' scanning of geometric forms varying in size. *Journal of Experimental Child Psychology*, 1982, *33*, 235–256.

Haith, M. M. Visual competence in early infancy. In R. Held, H. Leibowitz, & H.-L. Teuber (Eds.), *Handbook of sensory physiology* (Vol. 8). Berlin: Springer-Verlag, 1979.

Haith, M. M. *Rules that babies look by*. Hillsdale, NJ: Lawrence Erlbaum Associates, 1980.

Haith, M. M., Bergman, T., & Moore, M. J. Eye contact and face scanning in early infancy. *Science*, 1977, *198*, 853–855.

Hebb, D. O. *The organization of behavior*. New York: Wiley, 1949.

Hebb, D. O. Heredity and environment in mammalian behavior. *British Journal of Animal Behavior*, 1953, *1*, 43–47.

Hecox, K. Electrophysiological correlates of human auditory development. In L. B. Cohen & P. Salapatek (Eds.), *Infant perception: From sensation to cognition* (Vol. 2). New York: Academic Press, 1975.

Hecox, K., & Galambos, R. Brain stem auditory evoked responses in human infants and adults. *Archives of Otolaryngology*, 1974, *99*, 30–33.

Held, R., & Hein, A. Movement-produced stimulation in the development of visually-guided behavior. *Journal of Comparative and Physiological Psychology*, 1963, *56*, 872–876.

Helmholtz, H. von. [*Handbook of physiological optics*] (J. P. C. Southall, trans.). New York: Optical Society of America, 1925. (Originally published, 1866.)

Hochberg, J. E. Nativism and empiricism in perception. In L. Postman (Ed.), *Psychology in the making*. New York: Knopf, 1962.

Hochberg, J. E. *Perception*. Englewood Cliffs, NJ: Prentice-Hall, 1978.

Hoemann, H. W. Perception by the deaf. In E. C. Carterette & M. P. Friedman (Eds.), *Handbook of perception* (Vol. 10). New York: Academic Press, 1978.

Hubel, D. H., & Weisel, T. N. Binocular interaction in striate cortex of kittens reared with artificial squint. *Journal of Physiology*, 1970, *206*, 419–436.

Humphrey, T. Function of the nervous system during prenatal life. In U. Stave (Ed.), *Perinatal physiology*. New York: Plenum, 1978.

Jusczyk, P. W. The high amplitude sucking technique as a methodological tool in speech perception research. In G. Gottlieb & N. A. Krasnegor (Eds.), *Measurement of audition and vision in the first year of postnatal life: A methodological overview*. Norwood, NJ: Ablex, 1984.

Kant, I. [*Critique of pure reason*] (F. M. Müller, trans.). New York: Macmillan, 1924. (Originally published, 1781.)

Karmel, B. Z., & Maisel, E. B. A neuronal activity model for infant visual attention. In L. B. Cohen & P. Salapatek (Eds.), *Infant perception: From sensation to cognition* (Vol. 1). New York: Academic Press, 1975.

Kavale, K. Meta-analysis of the relationship between visual perceptual skills and reading achievement. *Journal of Learning Disabilities*, 1982, *15*, 42–51.

Kessen, W. Sucking and looking: Two organized congenital patterns of behavior in the human newborn. In H. W. Stevenson, E. H. Hess, & H. L. Rheingold (Eds.), *Early behavior: Comparative and developmental approaches*. New York: Wiley, 1967.

Kessen, W., Haith, M. M., & Salapatek, P. H. Human infancy: A bibliography and guide. In P. H. Mussen (Ed.), *Carmichael's manual of child psychology*. New York: Wiley, 1970.

Koffka, K. *The growth of the mind*. New York: Harcourt, Brace and World, 1927.

Köhler, W. *Gestalt psychology*. New York: Liveright, 1947.

Kuhl, P. Conditioned head turning as a measure of auditory discrimination and categorization. In G. Gottlieb & N. A. Krasnegor (Eds.), *Measurement of audition and vision in the first year of postnatal life: A methodological overview*. Norwood, NJ: Ablex, 1984.

Lasky, R. E., Syrdal-Lasky, A., & Klein, R. E. VOT discrimination by four to six and a half month old infants from Spanish environments. *Journal of Experimental Child Psychology*, 1975, *20*, 215–225.

Lipsitt, L. P. Taste in human neonates: Its effects on sucking and heart rate. In J. M. Weiffenbach (Ed.), *Taste and development*. Bethesda, MD: DHEW, 1977.

Macfarlane, A. *The psychology of childbirth*. Cambridge, MA: Harvard University Press, 1977.

Marler, P. R., Dooling, R. J., & Zoloth, S. Comparative perspectives on ethology and behavioral development. In M. H. Bornstein (Ed.), *Comparative methods in psychology*. Hillsdale, NJ: Lawrence Erlbaum Associates, 1980.

Maurer, D. Infant visual perception: Methods of study. In L. B. Cohen & P. Salapatek (Eds.), *Infant perception: From sensation to cognition* (Vol. 1). New York: Academic Press, 1975.

Meltzoff, A. N., & Moore, M. K. The origins of imitation in infancy: Paradigm, phenomena, and theories. In L. P. Lipsitt (Ed.), *Advances in infancy research* (Vol. 2). Norwood, NJ: Ablex, 1983.

Milewski, A. E. Infants' discrimination of internal and external pattern elements. *Journal of Experimental Child Psychology*, 1976, *22*, 229–246.

Movshon, J. A., & Van Sluyters, R. C. Visual neural development. *Annual Review of Psychology*, 1981, *32*, 477–522.

Parke, R. D. Children's home environments: Social and cognitive effects. In I. Altman & J. F. Wohlwill (Eds.), *Human behavior and environment* (Vol. 3). New York: Plenum, 1978.

Passman, R. H., & Longeway, K. P. The role of vision in maternal attachment: Giving 2-year-olds a photograph of their mother during separation. *Developmental Psychology*, 1982, *18*, 530–533.

Piaget, J. *The construction of reality in the child*. New York: Basic Books, 1954.

Piaget, J. [*The mechanisms of perception*] (G. N. Seagrim, trans.). London: Routledge & Kegan Paul, 1969. (Originally published, 1961.)

Piaget, J. [*The child's conception of movement and speed*] (G. E. T. Holloway & M. J. Mackenzie, trans.). New York: Ballatine, 1971. (Originally published, 1946.)

Piaget, J., & Inhelder, B. [*The child's conception of space*] (F. J. Langdon & J. L. Lunzer, trans.). New York: Norton, 1967. (Originally published, 1948.)

Porges, S. W. Heart rate indices of newborn attentional responsivity. *Merrill-Palmer Quarterly*, 1974, *20*, 231–254.

Rheingold, H. L. The measurement of maternal care. *Child Development*, 1960, *31*, 565–575.

Riesen, A. H. The development of visual perception in man and chimpanzee. *Science*, 1947, *106*, 107–108.

Ross, G. S. Categorization in 1- to 2-year-olds. *Developmental Psychology*, 1980, *16*, 391–396.

Salapatek, P. Pattern perception in early infancy. In L. B. Cohen & P. Salapatek (Eds.), *Infant perception: From sensation to cognition* (Vol. 1). New York: Academic Press, 1975.

Sarnat, H. B. Olfactory reflexes in the newborn infant. *Journal of Pediatrics*, 1978, *92*, 624–626.

Schneider, B. A., Trehub, S. E., & Bull, D. High-frequency sensitivity in infants. *Science*, 1980, *207*, 1003–1004.

Scibetta, J. J., Rosen, M. G., Hochberg, C. J., & Chik, L. Human fetal brain response to sound during labor. *American Journal of Obstetrics and Gynecology*, 1971, *109*, 82–85.

Schulman-Galambos, C., & Galambos, R. Brain stem auditory-evoked responses in premature infants. *Journal of Speech and Hearing Research*, 1975, *18*, 456–465.

Schulman-Galambos, C., & Galambos, R. Brain stem evoked response audiometry in newborn hearing screening. *Archives of Otolaryngology*, 1979, *105*, 86–90.

Serpell, R. *Culture's influence on behaviour*. London: Metheun, 1976.

Siqueland, E. R., & DeLucia, C. A. Visual reinforcement of nonnutritive sucking in human infants. *Science*, 1969, *165*, 1144–1146.

Steiner, J. E. Facial expressions of the neonate infant indicating the hedonics of food-related chemical stimuli. In J. M. Weiffenbach (Ed.), *Taste and development*. Bethesda, Md.: DHEW, 1977.

Steiner, J. E. Human facial expressions in response to taste and smell stimulation. In H. Reese & L. Lipsitt (Eds.), *Advances in child development and behavior* (Vol. 13). New York: Academic Press, 1979.

Strauss, S. *U-shaped behavioral growth*. New York: Academic Press, 1982.

Streeter, L. A. Language perception of 2-month-old infants shows effects of both innate mechanisms and experience. *Nature*, 1976, *259*, 39–41.

Teller, D. Y., & Bornstein, M. H. Human infant color vision and color perception. In P. Salapatek & L. B. Cohen (Eds.), *Handbook of infant perception*. New York: Academic Press, 1984.

Tuchmann-Duplessis, H., Auroux, M., & Haegel, P. *Illustrated human embryology* (Vol. 3). New York: Springer-Verlag, 1975.

Turkewitz, G., & Kenny, P. A. Limitations on input as a basis for neural organization and perceptual development: A preliminary theoretical statement. *Developmental Psychobiology*, 1982, *15*, 357–368.

Uexküll, J. von. A stroll through the worlds of animals and men. In C. H. Schiller & K. S. Lashley (Eds.), *Instinctive behavior*. New York: International Universities Press, 1934.

Vellutino, F. R. Alternative conceptualizations of dyslexia: Evidence in support of a verbal-deficit hypothesis. *Harvard Educational Review*, 1977, *47*, 334–354.

Vurpillot, E. The development of scanning strategies and their relation to visual differentiation. *Journal of Experimental Child Psychology*, 1968, *6*, 632–650.

Wachs, T. D. Proximal experience and early cognitive-intellectual development: The physical environment. *Merrill-Palmer Quarterly*, 1979, *25*, 3–41.

Wachs, T. D., Uzgiris, I. C., & Hunt, J. McV. Cognitive development in infants of different age levels and from different environmental backgrounds: An exploratory investigation. *Merrill-Palmer Quarterly*, 1971, *17*, 283–317.

Warren, D. H. Perception by the blind. In E. C. Carterette & M. P. Friedman (Eds.), *Handbook of perception* (Vol. 10). New York: Academic Press, 1978.

Wertheimer, M. Principles of perceptual organization. In D. C. Beardslee & M. Wertheimer (Eds.), *Readings in perception*. Princeton, NJ: Van Nostrand, 1958. (Originally published, 1923.)

Wertheimer, M. *Productive thinking*. New York: Harper & Row, 1945.

White, B. L., & Held, R. Plasticity of sensorimotor development. In J. F. Rosenblith & W. Allinsmith (Eds.), *The causes of behavior*. Boston, Mass.: Allyn & Bacon, 1966.

Witkin, H. A., & Berry, J. W. Psychological differentiation in cross-cultural perspective. *Journal of Cross-Cultural Psychology*, 1975, *6*, 4–87.

Yarrow, L. J., Rubenstein, J. L., & Pedersen, F. A. *Infant and environment: Early cognitive and motivational development*. New York: Wiley, 1975.

Yonas, A. Infants' responses to optical information for collision. In R. N. Aslin, J. R. Alberts, & M. R. Peterson (Eds.), *Development of perception: Psychobiological perspectives* (Vol. 2). New York: Academic Press, 1981.

Zaporozhets, A. V. The development of perception in the preschool child. *Monographs of the Society for Research in Child Development*, 1965, *30* (2, Serial No. 100).

4 Cognitive Development

Deanna Kuhn
Teachers College
Columbia University

INTRODUCTION

My primary aim in this chapter is not to provide a survey of the products of cognitive development research. Rather, the focus of the chapter is an examination of the succession of ways in which the study of cognitive development has been approached during the relatively brief period of its existence. Such an approach is based on the premise that an examination of this sort affords the greatest insight into the topic itself. The study of cognitive development, it can be claimed, has consisted of an overlapping historical succession of conceptualizations of (1) what it is that develops, (2) the process by means of which this development occurs, and (3) how the study of this development is best conducted. These conceptualizations have dictated both the questions that are selected for investigation and how the products of those investigations are understood. They have thus provided a series of "windows" through which the topic might be viewed, and it is only by examining these windows, or conceptual and methodological frameworks, themselves that one can gain a sense of how knowledge of cognitive development has progressed.

One thing a reader new to the field is likely to gain from this chapter is an appreciation of why the study of cognitive development has not yielded simple, straightforward answers to seemingly simple, straightforward, empirically researchable questions. For example, does basic memory capacity increase or remain constant as the individual develops? The reader should come to appreciate why such questions themselves, as well as their answers, turn out to be considerably more complex than they appear on the surface. Although the reader new to the field may be disillusioned to learn that the field lacks simple, easily

133

answered research questions or an accumulated body of perspective-free facts, I argue in this chapter that there is actually considerable reason to be optimistic regarding the field's past and prospective progress. As suggested later on, the field is in many ways at a turning point in its own development, with considerable promise for future progress. A number of long-standing polarities, controversies, and preoccupations that have detracted attention from the central questions crucial to an understanding of cognitive development have in recent years either been resolved, set aside, or recast, with the result that attention is now focused more directly on these key questions. Some might take the negative view that through the succession of windows in terms of which it has proceeded, the field has done no more that repeat itself and, in effect, stand still. I take exception to this view and suggest instead ways in which these windows are becoming clearer as the perspectives they entail increase in explanatory power.

THE COORDINATION OF MIND AND REALITY: BASIC PERSPECTIVES

An adequate account of cognitive development must, at a minimum, contain answers to two basic questions: What is it that develops? How does this development occur? The answer to the first question, at least, might appear obvious: The profound differences in the intellectual functions exhibited by the newborn infant and the mature adult are evident to the most casual observer. It is this development that is the obvious object of concern. In fact, the different theoretical and methodological approaches to the study of cognitive development that I examine represent a wide variety of views as to what is developing, ranging from individual stimulus–response connections to discrete, context-linked skills, to a smaller set of more general cognitive functions, to a single broad system of cognitive operations that underlies all more specific intellectual abilities and behaviors.

The second question also harbors greater complexity than is suggested on the surface. There is more to be explained than how intellectual functioning, or mind, is transformed during the course of development, though formulating such an explanation is in itself a formidable challenge. The full question that must be addressed, rather, is how the mind develops *in the particular direction,* or toward the particular end, that it does, rather than in a host of other possible directions, so as to become well-adapted to the external world of which the developing individual is a part. The two questions are, of course, not independent. The answer to the second question to a large degree determines the answer to the first, though the reverse is less true. In the following discussion, therefore, I focus on answers to the second question, noting their implications with respect to the first question.

Three broad answers to the second question have appeared and reappeared throughout the history of developmental psychology. All three, in fact, have their roots in classical philosophical traditions that predate psychology as a field of scientific study. Each of the perspectives can be classified in terms of which of these three answers it reflects.

The first answer, rooted in the philosophical tradition known as rationalism, is that mind and reality exist in pre-established coordination with one another. In other words, the particular direction in which the mind will develop is predetermined, presumably through some form of genetic coding unique to the species. The second answer, whose roots lie in the philosophical tradition known as empiricism, is that the nature of reality is imposed on the mind from without during the course of development, and it is for this reason that mind and reality come to coordinate with one another. The third answer, rooted in the philosophical tradition known as interactionism, is that mind is neither in pre-established coordination with reality nor molded by it from without; rather, through a lengthy series of interchanges between individual and environment, the coordination is gradually achieved.

Maturationism

The first of the three answers is reflected in the first theoretical perspective to have a major guiding influence on the study of child development by North American psychologists, the doctrine of maturationism.[1] Until the appearance of the work by Arnold Gesell, the major advocate of maturationism, studies of children's development had been conducted largely within the atheoretical "child study movement" that flourished in America during the early part of the twentieth century. It can be argued that the myriad of descriptive studies of children's knowledge and interests produced by the child study movement did not make a lasting contribution to our understanding precisely because these investigations were not guided by an overarching conceptual framework. Gesell's studies, in strong contrast, adhere clearly to a mold dictated by his theoretical view.

Gesell was struck by the regularity he observed in the emergence of various motor abilities during the first years of life, despite huge variability in environmental circumstances. These observations led him to posit that new skills emerge according to a regular sequence and timetable that are the product of a predetermined genetic code, similar, for example, to the code that governs the appearance of secondary sexual characteristics at puberty. Maturation, Gesell proposed, is the internal regulatory mechanism that governs the emergence of all new skills and abilities—cognitive as well as behavioral—that appear with advancing age. Thus, according to this view, it is a sequence of discrete skills that develops, and the mechanism by means of which this development occurs is one of predetermined unfolding.

---

[1]The theories of James Baldwin, as noted later, had an influence largely confined to Europe, despite the fact that Baldwin was an American.

Gesell and his coworkers engaged in meticulous cross-sectional and longitudinal observations of infants, which enabled them to describe in precise detail the sequence and timetable in terms of which early motor abilities appeared. (See Gesell, 1929, for a classic statement of his view and summary of this work.) Subsequent bodies of such research in developmental psychology have been criticized as "merely descriptive," but one cannot lodge this criticism against Gesell's work, for there is a logical link between his research strategy and his theory: If the appearance of new behaviors is the product of an innate genetic code, the researcher's task is merely to provide a precise description of this unfolding; no further explanation is necessary.

An experimental methodology would seem to have no place in Gesell's work. One experiment Gesell performed, however, has become a classic. Gesell conducted the experiment for the purpose of demonstrating the secondary role of the environment, relative to the central role he believed is played by the process of maturation. Quite unlike most modern experiments, Gesell's experiment had only two subjects, 11-month-old twin girls. At the onset of the experiment, neither twin exhibited any proficiency in the skill that was to be the focus of the experiment: stair climbing. Gesell proceeded to subject one of the twins to daily training sessions on a specially constructed staircase for a period of six weeks. At the end of this period, the trained twin was a proficient stair climber, while the control (untrained) twin still showed no ability.

At this point, the experiment would appear to show exactly the opposite of what Gesell held; i.e., it appears to show that the acquisition of motor skills is highly susceptible to environmental influence. The experiment did not end at this point, however. Several weeks later, the control twin spontaneously began to exhibit some stair climbing proficiency. At this point, Gesell instituted a two week period of training of the same type that had been administered to the experimental twin. At the end of this period, the control twin equaled her experimental twin in stair climbing proficiency, and the two remained equivalent in proficiency from then on.

What Gesell wished to demonstrate by this experiment, of course, is that the environment, or "experience," plays at most a superficial, secondary role in temporarily accelerating the emergence of a skill that is destined by the maturational code to appear at a later time. While these results were initially accepted by some as evidence of the correctness of Gesell's maturational doctrine, a major criticism of the experiment was raised. Did the experimental design adequately control for the effects of experience? The untrained twin continued to have experience of a variety of sorts, even if it was not stair climbing, during the period the experimental twin was being trained. Could this experience legitimately be ruled out as having contributed to the eventual appearance of the untrained twin's skill?

At first, the issue was regarded as a problem in research design. Were it feasible on both ethical and technical grounds to totally restrict the experience of the control twin during the training period, then experience could be ruled out as a contributing factor. Ultimately, however, the problem was recognized as a logical, not a methodological, one. As long as an organism has life, it is always undergoing some experience, by the very definition of what it is to be alive. Thus, a process of maturation can be observed only in the case of a living organism that is undergoing experience of some sort during the period of observation. It is, in turn, impossible to rule out this experience as having played a role in the emergence of new behaviors exhibited by the organism.

Following this recognition of the impossibility of eliminating experience as a contributing factor to development, interest in the maturational doctrine declined, and attention turned instead toward investigating *how* this experience influences development. Few, if any, current developmental psychologists would categorize themselves as maturationists. The modern-day theorist to whom the maturationist (or, to use the more common modern term, nativist) view is most often attributed is the linguist Chomsky. It is important to note, however, that Chomsky does not subscribe to a nativist doctrine in anything like the strong sense of Gesell. Chomsky regards the *capacity* to acquire language as an innate capacity that is unique to the human organism (in contrast to Piaget, who regards the capacity for language as evolving out of sensorimotor activity during infancy). Chomsky (as well as Piaget), however, regards experience as an essential aspect of the *process* of language acquisition.

The pure doctrine of maturationism, then, is significant because of its historical influence, rather than as a guiding perspective in the current study of cognitive development. Rejection of the doctrine of maturationism, it should be emphasized, however, does not imply the rejection of underlying physical or neurological changes as critical to the emergence of new cognitive or behavioral skills. On the contrary, developments in the brain and nervous system that appear to be critical for behavioral development have become a topic of intense interest and research effort in recent years. These physical developments, however, do not by themselves initiate related behavioral developments. At most, they are enabling conditions that make it possible for the behavioral developments to take place; the process of behavioral development itself remains to be explained.

Empiricism

Although Gesell's studies were theoretically motivated, his descriptions of developmental patterns were attended to more for their practical than their theoretical significance, as the field at this point, under the influence of the child study movement, was still very practically oriented. In fact, the series of books by Gesell and his co-workers that describe developmental norms for parents and teachers are still referred to today. It is probably accurate to say, then, that when the empiricist movement that had come to occupy the mainstream of academic psychology by the middle of this century embraced the field of child development, it was the first time that the field's research efforts became dominated by an overarching theoretical framework.

The empiricist view represented a striking counterinfluence following Gesell's maturationism. If developmental change does not arise from within the organism, then perhaps it is imposed from without by the environment. This solution represents the second of the three answers referred to earlier: Mind and reality come to be coordinated with one another because reality imposes itself on, and hence shapes, the mind over the course of development. Mind, then, is in the beginning Locke's classic *tabula rasa,* or blank slate.

The name of B. F. Skinner is the one most closely identified with the empiricist doctrine known as behaviorism that dominated the study of psychology in North America for several decades. Skinner explored the full implications of the Law of Effect originally proposed by Thorndike at the turn of the century: Organisms tend to repeat those behaviors that have satisfying consequences and to eliminate those that do not. Thus, the behaviors an organism comes to exhibit are a direct function of their environmental consequences. The organism is thereby shaped by its environment.

Bijou and Baer are the two theorists most widely known for applying Skinner's doctrine to the realm of child development. The child, they have proposed, is most appropriately conceptualized as "a cluster of interrelated responses" (Bijou & Baer, 1961). Development, in turn, consists of the progressive shaping of these individual responses by the environment. Like Skinner, Bijou and Baer held as one of their most important tenets that the temptation of relying on unobservable internal constructs to explain behavior must be avoided. Only external, observable behaviors are the proper object of scientific study. The observable behaviors, in turn, are a function of observable external events. To speculate about processes internal to the individual only obscures the direct connection between external behavior and the external stimuli that control it.

One might wonder what relevance such a doctrine could have for the study of cognition and its development, as cognition almost by definition is a process that occurs within the individual. Bijou and Baer, however, took the position that cognition is nothing more than a particular class of behavior and, as such, it is under the same environmental control as any other behavior. For example, consider what (mistakenly) might be regarded as an internal concept that a young child has of, say, animal. What this so-called "concept" actually consists of, according to Bijou and Baer, is a common behavioral response the child has learned to exhibit (as a function of external reinforcement) in the presence of objects or events that have a certain set of properties (e.g., movement, four legs, eyes, nose, mouth, perhaps fur or tail). It is thus not fruitful to regard the concept as either inside the child's head or existing in nature. Rather, such "conceptual" behavior is under the control of the environmental agents that administer the appropriate reinforcement contingencies (i.e., signify approval if the child emits the response when the defining properties are present). It could well be a different set of properties (and hence a different "conceptual" behavior) that the agents chose to reinforce. (See Bijou, 1976, Chapters 3 & 4, for an elaboration of this view of concept development.)

A few fundamental principles have governed research in cognitive development that is carried out within the empiricist framework. The most important are the principle of reductionism, the related principle of parsimony, and the principle of experimental control. Reductionism has been influential both as a theoretical principle and as a research strategy. As a theoretical principle, reductionism is the assertion that any complex behavior is in fact a constellation of very simple behaviors. As a research strategy, reductionism dictates that the smallest possible behavioral units that make up a complex behavior be isolated and investigated individually. Once the process governing each of these individual units is understood, explanations of more complex forms of behavior should follow.

The related principles of parsimony holds that an explanatory mechanism that accounts for the broadest range of phenomena is to be preferred over one that accounts for a narrower range of phenomena. In the case of behaviorist theory, this has meant that more complex explanations must be rejected if a behavior can be accounted for in terms of the simple mechanism of operant conditioning; that is, control by means of external reinforcement. Applied to the field of developmental psychology, the major implication of the principle of parsimony is that developmental phenomena can (and should) be regarded as the accumulated effects of the operation of the simple conditioning (or learning) mechanism. In other words, development can be reduced to the simpler process of learning. Hence, there is no need to retain the more complex term.

The parsimony principle is also reflected in the assumption that the basic learning mechanism functions in an identical way throughout an individual's development. One implication of this assumption with respect to research strategy is that there is no need to compare individuals at different points in their development. If a particular learning process is observed to operate at one age level, it is assumed that it will operate in the same way at any other age level. Thus, researchers studying cognitive development within an empiricist framework have tended to utilize a single age group in their studies. Rarely have they engaged in the cross-sectional and longitudinal age comparisons that characterize much developmental research.

The principle of experimental control has led to the almost exclusive choice of an experimental laboratory method. As the laboratory provides a controlled environment, the researcher can introduce the environmental variable believed to control a particular behavior in order to establish that it does in fact produce that behavior, with reasonable assurance that it is not some other (uncontrolled) variable that has actually produced the behavior, which might be the case in a natural setting.

A research program conducted within the empiricist framework that illustrates all of these principles is the laboratory study of paired-associate learning that was prevalent in the 1950s and 1960s. In a paired-associate learning experiment, a subject is exposed to pairs of nonsense syllables (e.g., PIF and LER) until a connection is established between the two members of the pair, such that the presentation of one syllable enables the subject to recite the other. The choice of arbitrary (nonsensical) material to be learned is not itself arbitrary but rather is an important part of the research strategy, dictated by the objective of experimental control. Arbitrary associations between meaningless syllables will be completely, and therefore equally, new to all learners. Individual differences in past learning and reinforcement are controlled for in this manner.

Paired-associate learning experiments were conducted both with children of different ages and with adults as subjects. The purpose of these experiments, however, was not to compare the performance of different age groups. Rather, the large number of studies conducted were all devoted to identifying the variables (for example, exposure time or distinctiveness of syllables) that affect the learning process; it was assumed that these variables would function in an identical way for all subjects.

The tremendous effort devoted to the study of paired-associate learning was justified on the assumption that it represents one of the simplest, most basic forms of learning, and that understanding how it operates would provide a key to understanding the more complex and significant forms of learning that occur in schools and other natural settings. To critics who argue that it would be preferable to devote research efforts to studying these more complex forms of learning directly, proponents of the reductionist strategy counter that the learning that occurs in natural contexts is simply too complex to be amenable to investigation. Employing the reductionist strategy, they would claim, provides the only avenue to eventual understanding. As I document later on, the controversy between pro- and anti-reductionist positions continues through the present day.

The maturationist and empiricist perspectives that have been described in this section reflect two of the three answers to the basic question posed at the outset: How does the mind develop so as to become coordinated with the external world it inhabits? The answers that underlie these two perspectives are diametrically opposed. The maturationist answer is that this coordination is pre-established within the individual, and the empiricist answer is that this coordination is imposed on the individual by the external world. Let us turn now to the perspective that reflects the third of these answers.

PIAGET AND CONSTRUCTIVISM

Rediscovering the Child's Mind

American developmental psychology was in many ways ripe for its "discovery" of Piaget in the 1950s. The Piagetian influence brought something new that many would argue had been conspicuously absent in the study of the child's cognitive (as well as social) development: the "rediscovery of the child's mind," as one observer (Martin, 1959/60) put it at the time. Some would go so far as to claim that the study of cognitive development began with Piaget; before Piaget, there existed a psychology of learning, not a psychology of development. Many of Piaget's ideas are evident in the work of the philosopher and psychologist, James Mark Baldwin (Wozniak, 1982), as well as Piaget's contemporary, Heinz Werner (1948). Yet it was Piaget who was to have the major influence on the study of cognitive development in American psychology, even though his scholarly career had been under way in Europe for several decades before American psychologists became interested in his work.

Piaget's descriptions of "childish" thought intrigued a wide audience of psychologists and educators. Young children's beliefs that the amount of liquid changes when poured into a differently-shaped container; that names are a part of the objects they represent; that the sun follows one around and thinks and feels as humans do; that one's own thoughts and dreams are material objects visible to observers; to cite a few of the most well-known examples, were startling revelations to many who regarded themselves as knowledgeable about children. These features of children's thought evidently had been "there to be seen" for centuries, but in most cases had never been noted before.

Piaget, however, found these observations of childish thought significant not so much for their own sake as for their implications regarding the mechanisms by which the mind develops. Consider, for example, the container of liquid portrayed in Figure 4.1. If asked to draw the liquid as it would appear while the container is tilted at a 45-degree angle, young children tend not to represent the liquid by a line parallel to the true horizontal (left side of Figure 4.1). Instead, they draw the line showing the liquid parallel to the top and bottom of the container (right side of Figure 4.1). No child has ever seen liquid in a container in that way. The child's drawing, therefore, cannot be a direct reflection of his or her experience with objects and events in the physical world. Instead, Piaget

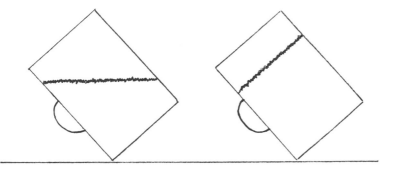

FIG. 4.1. When asked to draw a line indicating the level of liquid in a tilted container, young children typically draw the line parallel to the top and bottom of the container (right) rather than on the true horizontal.

argued, it must be an intellectual construction—the child's understanding of what he or she sees.

Each observation of this sort was significant in Piaget's view as testimony to the fact that the child is engaged in an extended intellectual "meaning–making" endeavor. In other words, the child is attempting to construct an understanding of self, other, and the world of objects. "Childish" beliefs, such as nonconservation (e.g., of the true horizontal, following a perceptual alteration such as the tilting of the container, or of quantity, following transfer to a differently-shaped container), are significant because they cannot have been directly internalized from the external world. Nor is it plausible that these beliefs are innate and simply appear, uninfluenced by the child's experience in the world.

In discounting these opposing alternatives, Piaget proposed at least the general form of a third solution to the question of how mind and reality come to be coordinated with one another. Through a process of organism-environment, or subject-object, interchanges, the subject gradually constructs an understanding of both its own actions and the external world. The most important feature of this interchange is that it is bidirectional: The organism and the external world gradually come to "fit" one another—neither makes any radical or unilateral accommodations to the other. Each new "childish belief" that is discovered, i.e., each new belief that directly reflects neither the external world nor the child's innate disposition, provides further evidence of the occurrence of this bidirectional interchange and, hence, constructive process.

The Doctrine of Stages

It has been suggested that the single, most central idea in Piaget's wide ranging theory is that the intellectual effort to understand one's own actions and their relation to the world of objects—i.e., the individual's extended "meaning–making" enterprise—motivates, or energizes, a constructive process directed toward progressively greater equilibrium between the individual and the environment. Thus, when Piaget's influence became prominent in American psychology, one might have expected that it would be this constructive, meaning–making enterprise, or at the very least the "rediscovery of the child's mind," that Piaget would represent.

Instead, it was the derivative doctrine of stages that came to identify Piaget's theory in American developmental psychology. The individual's meaning–making effort, Piaget believed, was marked by a striving for coherence, with the result that the individual's ideas had a unity to them, even if the ideas were largely incorrect by external, or mature, standards. In other words, these ideas were reflections of a broad, unified cognitive system that had its own unique form and that mediated all of the more specific manifestations of the individual's cognitive functioning.

Furthermore, it was this cognitive system as a whole that allegedly underwent developmental change. As a result of the interactive process directed toward adaptation, or greater equilibrium between organism and environment, the cognitive system underwent a series of major reorganizations, each reflecting an improved equilibrium—mind and reality were better coordinated than they had been previously. These newly and better organized mental structures, or "stages," were held to appear in an invariant sequence universal to the human species. Each new structure reflected the most probable organization to emerge from the organism–environment interactions that characterized the preceding level; each new structure represented a new set of principles or rules that governed the interaction between organism and environment. One reason the doctrine of stages may have become the focus of attention for American developmental psychologists, then, is that it represented a challenge to prevailing empiricist theories, as it implied both the inevitability of the sequence of stages and their resistance to environmental influence.

Stemming from this structuralist theoretical perspective is an inductive research strategy, aimed at inferring the nature of the underlying cognitive system by observing a varied sampling of intellectual behaviors and postulating a model of their underlying mental structure. This strategy implies that any one of these individual behaviors cannot be fully understood and appreciated in isolation. It is only by understanding their relation to each other and to the underlying mental structure they reflect that their true nature can be appreciated.

From the theoretical claim that the cognitive system undergoes a series of major transformations comes a developmental research strategy. The functional rules that describe the interaction between an organism and its environment do not remain constant, as assumed within the empiricist perspective. Rather, these rules undergo transformation, as part of the transformation of the cognitive system as a whole. Each new structure is unique, and consequently the individual at each new stage of development must be studied as a unique organism, different from what it was earlier or what it will be at a later stage of development.

In Piaget's work these postulated structures are represented in the symbolic medium of formal logic, and each of the major structures (sensorimotor, preoperational, concrete operational, and formal operational) is regarded as a broad system of logical operations that mediates, and so unites, a whole range of more specific intellectual behaviors and characteristics (Piaget, 1970). The most appropriate structure to examine as an example of Piagetian stage structures is the structure labeled concrete operations, which allegedly emerges in the age range 6–8, because it has received the most attention both in Piaget's own work and in subsequent research by others.

The central feature that defines the concrete operational thought structure and differentiates it from the earlier preoperational thought structure, Piaget claimed, is the reversibility of mental operations. Mental acts emanating from the preoperational thought structure are irreversible; they cannot be performed in the opposite direction. Thus, judging that A is smaller than B does not entail the identical judgment made from the reference point of B, i.e., that B is larger than

A. For this reason, the child conceptualizes phenomena in absolute rather than relative terms. For example, a young child who classifies a ball as *large* is likely to have great difficulty in subsequently regarding this same ball as *small* relative to another, larger ball.

The underlying irreversibility of preoperational thought, Piaget claimed, is what is responsible for many of the unique features of young children's thinking that are described in his investigations. Most central are the absence of operations reflecting the logic of relations, as just illustrated, and the logic of classes, i.e., the ability to conceptualize elements as having multiple membership in a set of hierarchical classes (e.g., living things, human beings, man, father). It is this absence of class logic to which Piaget attributed one of his most widely cited examples of preoperational reasoning: A young child asked if there are more roses or more flowers in a set of 4 roses and 3 tulips is likely to reply more roses. Such a reply, Piaget claimed, reflects the child's inability to simultaneously (and hence reversibly) regard the roses as both a subclass and a part of the larger class (flowers). Hence, the child compares the subclass *roses* to its complement *tulips*, rather than to the class *flowers*.

The complete system of operations proposed by Piaget as the concrete operational thought structure is an integrated system of reversible operations of classification—the combining of elements into groups based on their equivalence; and relation—the linking of one element to another in an equivalence relation of symmetry (A is to B as B is to A, as in the case of two brothers), or in a difference relation of asymmetry (A is less than B and B is greater than A). The evolution of this structure was postulated by Piaget to underlie the attainment of conservation also: With concrete operations the child can mentally reverse the transformation (e.g., the pouring of the liquid from the original to a differently shaped container) and hence deduce that the quantity must remain invariant, despite its altered perceptual appearance. In addition, the irreversibility of thought prior to the evolution of the concrete operational structure was alleged to underlie all of the characteristics of young children's thinking that Piaget labeled as "egocentric": the inability to assume the perspective of another, the attribution of one's own psychological characteristics to material objects (animism), and the elevation of the products of one's own psyche (thoughts, dreams) to the status of real, material events visible to others (realism).

Summary: Constructivism and Empiricism

In summary, the constructivist perspective that has just been described and the empiricist perspective described earlier have been the two major theoretical influences leading to the current study of cognitive development. The two perspectives differ from one another on a number of major dimensions. The constructivist views what develops as the internal cognitive system as a whole, the central feature of which is the individual's "meaning–making" effort to understand his or her own actions and those of the external world. The empiricist views what develops as independent units of external, observable behavior, each under the individual control of environmental variables.

With respect to how development occurs, the empiricist posits a cumulative process in which each new behavior unit is independently acquired through the operation of the same basic mechanism of environmental shaping. The constructivist posits a bidirectional, rather than a unidirectional, interaction between the individual and the environment, leading to a series of major qualitative reorganizations in the cognitive system as a whole, and reflecting progress in the individual's "meaning–making" enterprise.

The research strategy employed by the empiricist is a nondevelopmental experimental laboratory strategy devoted to examining the process through which individual behavior is shaped by environmental contingencies. Empirical investigations are therefore devoted to detailed analyses of a single simple behavior. The research strategy employed by the constructivist is inductive, as well as developmental. The researcher samples a wide range of behaviors as a basis for hypothesizing the nature of the underlying cognitive system that is presumed to generate these behaviors. Cross-age comparisons are then conducted as a basis for inferring changes that occur in the cognitive system.

It is probably because the two perspectives are so diametrically opposed that the study of cognitive development during the 1960s to a large extent polarized into two camps, with a good deal of the research and theoretical writing during this period directed toward demonstrating the merits of one of the approaches and deficiencies of the other. Since that time, serious weaknesses have become apparent in each of the approaches. As a result, few theorists or researchers studying cognitive development today would classify themselves as adherents of either the empiricist or the constructivist perspectives in the pure forms in which they have been described here. In turn, several new perspectives have evolved and gained adherents; although each of these new perspectives retains certain aspects of empiricism or constructivism, none is in such polar opposition to another as the original constructivist and empiricist views that preceded them. We turn now to the weaknesses that became apparent in the empiricist and constructivist perspectives.

THE LIMITS OF EMPIRICISM

It has been suggested that researchers who conducted studies of children's learning and memory in the 1950s within the empiricist tradition dominant at the time had no interest in childhood per se, but used children as subjects of convenience to investigate those processes of learning that were the real focus of their interest. Whether this claim is justified or not, a sizeable accumulation of such research supported a conclusion that gained wide acceptance: The basic mechanisms of learning function in an identical way across species and across humans of different ages. A psychology of learning is therefore applicable to children and adequate to explain development.

The Study of Learning

Subsequent research has forced a modification of this basic conclusion. The most influential series of studies by Kendler and Kendler stemmed directly from the discrimination learning paradigm that was prevalent at the time. (See Kendler & Kendler, 1975, for an interesting historical review of their work.)

An example of the stimuli and reinforcement contingencies used in the basic experimental paradigm is shown in the left column of Figure 4.2. Reinforcement is always administered if the response is made in the presence of either of the two top stimuli (designated +) and is never administered if it is made in the presence of either of the bottom stimuli (designated −). This initial "training" phase of the experiment continues until the subject reaches a pre-established criterion of some number of errorless trials, i.e., repeated presentations of the four stimuli during which the subject always makes the response in the presence of a reinforced (+) stimulus and never in the presence of a non-reinforced (−) stimulus. This basic experimental paradigm was employed with diverse subjects, and so the response and the reinforcer themselves might be anything from a lever press and a food pellet in the case of an animal, to verbal responses and reinforcers in the case of a college student.

At this point the training phase of the procedure ends and the test phase begins. The stimuli remain unchanged during the test phase; only the reinforcement contingencies associated with them are different. The contingencies are changed in one of two ways. One of the two ways (labeled reversal shift) is portrayed in the center column of Figure 4.2. The other (labeled an extradimensional shift) is portrayed in the right column of Figure 4.2. The question of interest is how long it takes the subject to learn the new response so as to reattain

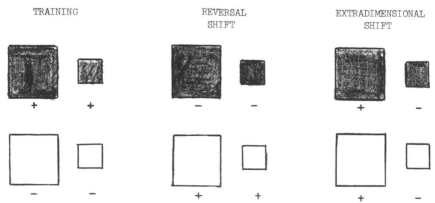

FIG. 4.2.   An example of the stimuli and reinforcement contingencies used in the basic experimental paradigm.

the criterion of errorless responding, i.e., to respond consistently in the presence of the + stimuli and never in the presence of the − stimuli. In particular, which of the two altered contingency patterns portrayed in Figure 4.2 should result in more rapid learning, i.e., more rapid reattainment of the criterion? Readers unacquainted with this research may wish to study Figure 4.2 and make their own prediction before reading on.

Classical empiricist theories of learning yield a clear prediction. The response (or nonresponse) to each stimulus is regarded as an associative bond that is built up as a function of the reinforcement contingencies. When the shift to the test phase occurs, at least some of these bonds must be relearned. The number of bonds that need to be relearned, however, depends on the type of shift. The reader can verify from Fig. 4.2 that in one case (extradimensional shift) only two bonds must be relearned; the other two remain unchanged. In the other case (reversal shift), however, all four bonds must be relearned. It can be predicted, therefore, that the former will be easier to master.

Kendler and Kendler (1975) compiled substantial evidence confirming this prediction in the case of animals and young human subjects (under 6 years of age). Uncharacteristically, however, they also studied subjects at a range of older age levels, including adulthood. These older subjects performed contrary to the learning theory prediction: For them, the reversal shift was easier to relearn than the extradimensional shift.

The inability of traditional learning theory to account for the performance of older subjects in these experiments led the Kendlers to develop a new, modified theory that they termed "mediation theory." What the older subject is learning in the training phase of the experiment, the Kendlers proposed, is not a set of discrete associations between stimuli and responses, but a covert (internal) "mediational" response. In the instance portrayed in Figure 4.2, for example, a subject may in effect say to herself, "Oh, it's the color that matters; the size has nothing to do with it." This covert response mediates, or controls, the overt responses (i.e., responding in the presence of the black stimuli and inhibiting response in the presence of the white stimuli). The Kendlers initially emphasized the verbal nature of these mediating responses, that is, older subjects had learned and applied verbal labels to the stimuli (size, color; black, white), which they then verbalized to themselves during the experiment. Subsequently, however, the Kendlers broadened their theory somewhat, regarding mediating responses as any covert symbolic responses the subject makes to common features of the stimuli.

If older subjects do indeed make mediational responses during the training phase, then the predicted relative difficulty of the two shifts changes. In the extradimensional shift, not only the overt response, but also the covert mediating response must be relearned (e.g., size rather than color). In the reversal shift, only the overt responses must be relearned (e.g., respond to white, not black). Therefore, the reversal shift should be easier, which was exactly what the Kendlers found for subjects over the age of 5 or 6.

The Kendlers therefore proposed what was in effect a developmental theory of learning. The traditional model of the formation of discrete stimulus–response bonds characterizes the learning of children under the age of 5 or 6. At about this age, children develop mediational learning capacity, and at this point the mediational model becomes a more accurate description of the learning process. The historical significance of the Kendlers' formulation of mediation theory is twofold. First, their theory represents a refutation of the behaviorist maxim that claims that the basic learning process functions in an identical way across the life-cycle. The way an individual learns, the Kendlers' work indicates, depends on the individual's developmental level—as a result, learning cannot be studied independently from development.

Second, mediation theory represents a departure from the behaviorist maxim that observable behavior is the only proper object of scientific study, and that it is not fruitful to postulate unobservable internal constructs that mediate this observed behavior. The Kendlers' work indicates that speculating about internal processes was, in this case, the only route to an adequate conceptualization of the external behavior that was observed. By not doing so, one ran the risk of serious misinterpretation. In the shift experiments, the achievement of laboratory rats, 5-year-olds, and college students appears equivalent at the end of the training phase (though one group may require more trials to reach the criterion than another). The performances of the respective subject groups during the test phase, however, indicate that the learning that takes place during the training phase—although it appears equivalent in its external manifestations—is actually quite different across subject groups. A theory that would make reference to the processes underlying these seemingly equivalent observable performances seemed the only way to explain the differences in performance that the subsequent test phase revealed to be present. In other words, the Kendlers' work pointed to the importance of a distinction that would become critical in future work in cognitive psychology: the distinction between product (performance) and the process that generated it.

The Study of Memory

Some notable parallels exist between historical developments in the study of learning and historical developments in the study of memory. In this section, some of the latter are summarized and common characteristics are noted.

Memory as Storage.   According to the empiricist perspective that dominated psychology in the 1940s and 1950s, learning and memory were but two sides of a single coin. Consider, for example, the paired-associate paradigm discussed earlier. Learning refers to the process by which the associative bond (between the two nonsense syllables) is formed, memory to the retention or storage of that bond, once it has been formed. Because the stimuli are meaningless to the subject, i.e., because the subject has no prior history of associations to them, they were considered as the ideal medium in which to study the basic processes of learning and retention in their pure form. By employing these elementary, "neutral" stimuli, basic properties of the human learning and memory apparatus might be identified. For example, how many exposures are required for an association to be formed and what is the organism's storage capacity for these associations, once they are formed?

Memory as Construction. Memory became a popular research topic in the 1960s, and many laboratory studies were conducted using both children and adults as subjects. The findings from much of this research, however, were difficult to reconcile with the concept of memory as a storage of associations. Consider, for example, memory for an arrangement of chess pieces on a chessboard after a subject studies the board and it is then removed. One might anticipate that studies of this nature would provide indices of the capacity of the human visual memory system. Such estimates, however, have been found to be dependent on the subject's familiarity with the stimulus material and the constraints imposed on the stimulus material to be remembered, that is, whether the pieces are arranged on the board randomly, or in a pattern that conforms to the rules of chess. If the arrangement is random, chess experts and non-chess players show equal memory capacity; if the arrangement is legitimate, however, chess experts display greater memory capacity than non-chess players, even when the chess experts are children and the non-players adults (Chi, 1978). Thus, one cannot speak of any absolute memory capacity, even one that increases in an age-linked manner. It all depends on what is being remembered, relative to the individual's existing knowledge and cognitive system.

A great many other studies have suggested that, when processing a piece of information to be remembered, an individual does not store it in its intact form as an isolated unit. Instead, the individual assimilates the new information to a framework provided by the individual's existing knowledge, often altering or elaborating this new information in a way that is consistent with this existing knowledge base. In a series of studies, Paris and his coworkers asked children simple questions to assess their memory of short narratives. Even young children were willing to reply "yes" to a question such as "Did she use a broom?", when the story stated only, "She swept the kitchen floor" (Paris & Carter, 1973). Moreover, by the age of 9 children were able to recall a sentence such as the preceding one from the cue "broom" as effectively as from the cue "swept" (Paris & Lindauer, 1976), even though one had been explicitly and the other only implicitly present.

It would appear, then, that subjects integrate new material into a framework provided by their existing knowledge and draw on this existing knowledge to make inferences that go beyond what is explicitly presented. As a result, newly acquired material cannot be clearly separated from what is already known. Memory, then, is more aptly conceptualized as a process of construction, or reconstruction, than as a process of storage. As such, it cannot be strictly separated from broader processes of reasoning and comprehension, i.e., from the individual's more general "meaning–making" activity.

Memory and Development.   If memory is part of the broader cognitive system, then developmental changes in this system ought to have implications for memory functions. This has been demonstrated in both a narrow and a broad sense. In the narrow sense, the level of comprehension of material to be remembered should affect how and how well it is remembered. A simple demonstration of this influence has been provided by studies of children's ability to draw an ordered set of sticks of graduated length after they have viewed it and it has been removed (Inhelder, 1969; Liben, 1977). Children who do not comprehend the logic of asymmetrical relations (as revealed by their inability to construct a seriated array from a set of randomly ordered sticks of different lengths) are less able to draw a seriated array from memory after viewing one; rather, they report very different configurations as what they "remember" having seen (Figure 4.3).

In the broad sense, transformations of the cognitive system ought to affect the memory function itself. Indeed, a wide range of studies indicating such developmental changes have been conducted. The bulk of these studies have centered

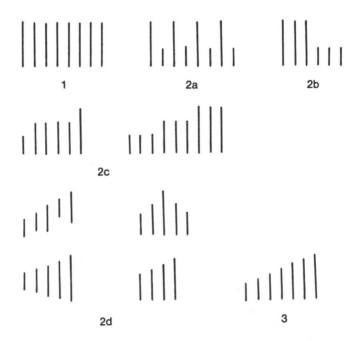

FIG. 4.3.   Various arrays produced by subjects in Inhelder's studies of memory development in children (Inhelder, 1969).

around the utilization of strategies to enhance memory. Organizing the material to be remembered into conceptual categories and rehearsal, for example, are both strategies that aid memory. Children under the age of Piaget's concrete operational stage show negligible use of these or other strategies to aid memory (Brown, Bransford, Ferrara, & Campione, 1983). For example, given a list of items to memorize containing foods, animals, toys, and items of clothing in a random order, older children and adults tend to recall the individual items within these superordinate categories; young children show no such organizational tendency in their recall. The absence of strategic devices in young children's performance on memory tasks is further substantiated by the finding that young children perform equivalently in a memory task whether they are instructed to try to remember the presented items or simply to look at them (Flavell, Beach, & Chinsky, 1966). Later, we shall consider further what governs the development and utilization of cognitive strategies such as these. The most important implication to note here is that, as the Kendlers' work demonstrated with respect to learning, memory functions cannot be studied without regard to the subject's developmental status.

Summary: The Limits of Reductionism

In summary, I have traced the ways in which both the study of learning and the study of memory came to take on a more cognitive as well as a more developmental cast. The work described suggests that neither learning nor memory can be studied profitably as a basic process that functions uniformly independent of what it is that is being learned or remembered and its relation to what the learner already knows. Given this, two implications for the study of the development of learning and memory follow, each of which has received considerable empirical support (Brown, Bransford, Ferrara, & Campione, 1983; Paris & Lindauer, 1982; Siegler, 1983; Siegler & Klahr, 1982). Developmental change in the cognitive system influences learning and memory performance in the narrow sense that the level of comprehension of new material affects how and how well it is both learned initially and remembered. Developmental change in the cognitive system affects learning and memory in the broad sense that it influences the learning or memory function itself, i.e., the strategies the individual utilizes in executing the task.

Perhaps the most telling indicator of the evolution that has been described is that in contrast to the 1950s and 1960s, few current psychologists classify their work as exclusively devoted to the study of learning or of memory. Rather, they tend to classify themselves as cognitive psychologists, interested in study of the cognitive system as a whole. In some ways, the evolution described might be interpreted as a failure of the principle of reductionism. As discussed earlier, the principle of reductionism and the related principle of parsimony led to the invocation of a single basic mechanism that accounted for the acquisition of new behavior, irrespective of the behavior, the organism, or the relation between the two. The research reviewed here indicates that this assumption is unwarranted. As a research strategy, reductionism dictated that very simple behaviors were to be isolated and studied independently. Once the acquisition mechanism governing these very simple isolated behaviors was understood, an understanding of more complex and significant forms of behavior would follow. It is fair to say that this promise has not been realized. It is now largely accepted that the search for a single content- and context-free acquisition mechanism will not be fruitful, and that mastery of new cognitive material cannot be investigated isolated from the broader context of the meaning the subject attributes to the material and to the task.

The implications for methodological practice are substantial. In the case of the paired-associate research paradigm described earlier, strong critics (e.g., Riegel, 1978) have characterized the studies themselves, not just the task material, as nonsensical and doomed to failure on the grounds that the learning that is observed is of no meaning or relevance to the learner; that is, it occurs completely out of any context, and therefore cannot possibly provide insight into natural context-bound processes of learning. At a minimum, it has been well established that context and meaning have a profound effect on performance. Preschoolers asked to memorize a list of items, for example, on the average remembered only half as many items as they remembered when asked to retrieve a series of items from a make-believe grocery in the next room (Istomina, 1977). Thus, studying the acquisition of arbitrary (meaningless) material in artificial settings offers, at best, limited insight into the acquisition of meaningful material as it occurs in complex, meaning-rich contexts. This limitation has been particularly severe in the study of memory development, in which work has largely been confined to the laboratory study of memory for arbitrary stimuli (Brown & DeLoache, 1978; Brown et al., 1983). As will be noted later, however, the last ten years have seen an increasing concern with the investigation of cognitive functions and their development in contexts (such as Istomina's) that are meaningful to the individuals being studied.

Even a rejection of reductionism, and the resulting theoretical and methodological concepts of a context-free acquisition mechanism, however, does not force a total repudiation of the empiricist view. A few theorists, such as Bijou and Baer (1961), have retained an orthodox behaviorist perspective. More common, however, are the "neo-behaviorist" formulations proposed by the Kendlers and several others (Gagné, 1968; Gholson, 1980; Rosenthal & Zimmerman, 1978). Largely abandoned by the neo-behaviorists are the refusal to speculate about internal processes, reductionism in its radical form, and the nondevelopmental research strategy. Common to all of these neo-behaviorist formulations, however, is the endorsement of the empiricist solution to the question of mechanism: Mind is shaped from without by the unidirectional effects of the environment.

THE LIMITS OF CONSTRUCTIVISM

Empirical evidence incompatible with the theory brought into focus the limitations of orthodox behaviorism as an explanatory framework for cognitive development. During the 1960s and 1970s, American developmental psychologists
conducted extensive research related to Piaget's work, much of it disconfirming
predictions derived from Piagetian theory. One might have expected, then, that
this work, in a similar way, would have brought into focus the limitations of
constructivism as an explanatory framework for cognitive development. In this
case, however, matters are more complex, for it was not to constructivism that
researchers principally addressed their studies, but to Piaget's doctrine of stages.

Stages

The most straightforward prediction derived from stage theory is that the various
behaviors that are the alleged manifestations of the underlying stage structure
ought to emerge in synchrony, as indicators of the emergence of the underlying
structure. In the case of the various behaviors alleged to be manifestations of the
concrete operational structure, a large number of studies were performed replicating Piaget's findings that these behaviors emerge between the ages of 6 and
8. Researchers then went on to investigate whether, within individual children,
these behaviors appear synchronously at some point during this age period—an
issue with respect to which Piaget himself had not reported empirical data. A
substantial amount of data has now been collected, none of which has yielded
strong evidence that concrete operational concepts, such as hierarchical classification, seriation, transitivity, conservation, and various forms of perspective-
taking, emerge synchronously, even though they all appear during the same
general age range.

In the face of these findings, some developmentalists came to Piaget's defense, objecting that Piagetian theory does not proclaim a precisely synchronous
emergence of behaviors but rather only their emergence during a period of
several years, by the end of which they are consolidated into the structured whole
specified by the theory. Others objected to this apparent lack of synchrony on
methodological grounds: The set of tasks administered to a subject to assess the
various concepts, they claimed, had not been equated with respect to their more
superficial performance demands, which had little to do with the concept itself.
One assessment task, for example, may have been presented in a manner that
made greater demands on the subject's verbal skills than did the other tasks, and
for this reason the display of the concept being assessed by this task was delayed
relative to the concepts assessed by the other tasks.

This second objection, however, points to what is an even more fundamental
problem for stage theory: Even slight, and what one would expect to be insignifi-
cant, modifications in task format can drastically alter the likelihood that subjects
will exhibit the concept being assessed. For example, whether children will

recognize the subclass as part of the class (class inclusion) in the earlier example of roses and flowers is affected by the numerical ratio between the two. Thus, even *within* a single task or concept domain, whether the concept is judged to be present or absent depends to a considerable extent on the particulars of the assessment procedure. The sizeable literature that has accumulated on children's attainment of Piagetian concepts shows this to be the case for every one of the concepts investigated. Using one assessment procedure, for example, 30% of 6-year-olds might be assessed as having attained a particular concrete operational concept. Using a slightly different procedure, perhaps 70% of the same group of 6-year-olds would be assessed as having attained the concept. On what basis does one decide which procedure yields the "true" incidence of attainment?

These demonstrations of so-called task variance were particularly significant because they suggested that Piagetian assessment tasks are not "pure" measures of an underlying reasoning competency, in the way that Piaget's descriptions of them tended to imply. Rather, a number of distinguishable skills appeared to be involved in the successful performance of a task, many of which were not an integral part of the reasoning competency that was the focus of the assessment. Consider, for example, the concept of transitivity, allegedly part of the concrete operational structure. Once the child's mental actions involving relational comparisons of the form $A > B$ are organized into a reversible mental structure, such that $A > B$ is recognized as entailing $B < A$, Piaget theorized, this reversibility should enable the child to mentally construct a seriated array, i.e., $A > B > C > D$, as well as to derive additional order relations from those that are given. For example, given $A > B$ and $B > C$, the child should be able to make the inference $A > C$. Because it is understood that B participates in dual relationships, one as less than A and another as greater than C, it can serve as the mediator that links A and C. Piaget referred to this inference as the inference of transitivity.

A number of subsequent studies of the transitivity inference, by Trabasso, Bryant and others (Trabasso, 1975; Bryant & Trabasso, 1971), aimed to demonstrate that there is more involved in making an inference of transitivity than the inference itself. Each of the individual relations, i.e., $A > B$ and $B > C$, must first be attended to and encoded by the subject. Each relation must then in some manner be represented and retained in the subject's cognitive system. Failure to achieve any of these steps would be sufficient to prevent the inference from being made, for example if the subject forgot one of the initial relations. The studies by Trabasso and Bryant endeavored to show that if the successful execution of these initial components were ensured (for example, by exposing subjects to extended training with respect to the initial relations), children several years younger than the ages reported by Piaget showed successful performance on a transitivity task. Similar analyses of other concrete operational concepts have been proposed, for example, Trabasso et al.'s (1978) analysis of the class inclusion concept.

In addition to suggesting that multiple skills enter into performance on a Piagetian reasoning task, the Trabasso and Bryant studies are examples of the numerous so-called "training" studies conducted in the 1960s and 1970s, which will be examined in more detail later, in a discussion of methods for studying developmental change. In these studies, attempts were made to induce a particular concept alleged to be part of the Piagetian stage structure, by exposing children who had not yet attained the concept to some form of training in an experimental laboratory session. Whether the changes from pretest to posttest assessment that occurred in many of these studies were superficial or genuine became the topic of extended debate. At the very least, however, the studies demonstrated that with relatively minimal instruction children could be taught to display some of the behaviors characteristic of the stage structure they had not yet attained naturally, bringing into question the claim that such behaviors are integral parts of a structured whole.

All the forms of evidence described so far—evidence of asynchrony in emergence, of heterogeneous skills contributing to performance on assessment tasks, and of the susceptibility of this performance to environmental influences—contributed to an increasing disenchantment with the Piagetian doctrine of stages during the 1970s. Positing a single, unified structure, the evolution of which is totally responsible for all of the more specific changes in intellectual functioning that occur over the course of development, appeared an oversimplification that did not accord with a growing body of research data. In a certain sense, stage doctrine in its strongest form appeared to be a kind of reductionism of an opposite sort to that employed by those working within the empiricist framework: Instead of the accumulation of large numbers of individually governed small behavioral units, development could be reduced to the evolution of a single, unitary, all-encompassing structure. (For further discussion of the debate surrounding stage theory, the reader is referred to articles by Brainerd [1978] and by Flavell [1982].)

The disenchantment with stage theory was furthered by the fact that Piaget's descriptions of the major stage structures, such as concrete operations, were not closely linked to the actual mental processes in which a subject might engage when responding to one of the typical assessment tasks. Rather, these structures were described in terms of formal logical models that were so abstract and removed from surface behavior that readers of Piaget's descriptions were left uncertain as to how such models might ever be validated as true portrayals of the individual's mental functions or structure.

In the absence of satisfying answers to these questions, large numbers of developmental psychologists turned away from stage theory, in search of what they hoped would be more promising models of cognitive development. The problem came, however, in articulating a replacement for stage theory. To conclude that the positing of a single, unified structure as what develops is an oversimplification does not dictate the opposite extreme: that discrete competencies develop entirely independent of, and unrelated to, one another. The truth almost certainly lies between these two extremes (Flavell, 1982). The central theoretical and research challenge, then, becomes one of characterizing the inter-dependencies that exist between developments that occur within distinct domains. Note, however, that the question posed is one about the developmental process: To what extent and in what manner do developmental changes that occur within domains interact with one another as they take place?

In many ways, theorists and researchers in cognitive development were not in a strong position at this point to formulate theoretical models or research hypotheses regarding the developmental process. As we have observed, Piaget's views on developmental process had received relatively little attention from American developmental psychologists in favor of the derivative theory of stages. The tendency in many circles, then, was to discount Piaget's theory in its entirety in rejecting the stage doctrine. On the other hand, there was little enthusiasm, following American developmental psychology's absorption with Piaget, for a return to an empiricist conception of mechanism, which had become widely perceived as inadequate.

I shall describe the directions in which the study of cognitive development did turn, following this disillusionment with Piaget's stage doctrine. First, however, it is important to mention the evolution that has occurred with respect to the understanding of developmental process, for during the field's preoccupation with stage theory, a few developmentalists continued to focus their attention on questions of process, or mechanism, and, therefore, on an examination of the merits of Piaget's constructivist hypothesis.

Constructivism

Questions about structures, it was suggested, are really questions about the process of construction of these structures, and it is understanding of the former that provides a key to conceptualizing the latter. It can be argued that the study of stages within American developmental psychology reached a dead end because one cannot study structures independently of the constructive processes that give rise to them. Piaget, however, viewed the constructive process in somewhat the same manner as he did structures, that is, in a very general, abstract form, and to some extent this mode of characterization has given rise to a similar set of problems. The process Piaget described is one in which the individual's own actions on the external world generate feedback that leads to the modification of those actions and their reorganization into new interrelationships with one another. In other words, individuals themselves produce their own development (Lerner, 1982; also this volume). To many, this conception of developmental change seemed a welcome and desirable alternative to the empiricist view of the individual as the passive recipient of effects produced by the environment.

The efforts of those who undertook to explore Piaget's constructivist model, either theoretically or empirically, however, led to the articulation of two related weaknesses in the model. First, the actions generated by the individual's cognitive system that give rise to change are described by the model in such general, abstract terms that it is not easy to draw on the model in conceptualizing the varieties of more specific, cognitively salient acts the individual engages in and their likely influence on cognitive development. For example, cross-cultural findings indicating that conservation of quantity developed more rapidly in cultures that emphasized certain kinds of experiences (Newman, Riel, & Martin, 1983) were not incongruent with Piaget's model, but the model offered no way of predicting the effects of such specific variations in experience.

The second limitation, closely related to the first, is that in emphasizing the role of the individual's own self-generated actions, the constructivist model neglects the social context in which these actions, and therefore cognitive development, necessarily occur. The constructive process, whatever its precise nature, does not take place in a vacuum. In the course of their everyday experiences, children encounter all sorts of implicit or explicit examples of the higher-level concepts that they themselves will acquire. This does not imply that they internalize these examples in any direct or automatic way. But it is equally unlikely that they systematically ignore them. Indeed, specific evidence is now accumulating to show that children attend to external models of higher-level concepts in a sustained and deliberate manner (Morrison & Kuhn, 1983). The objective, then, must be to understand the specific ways in which the individual's constructive activity utilizes these external data.

Summary: Neo-Constructivist Directions

In the preceding discussion, I briefly traced the impact that Piaget's work has had on American developmental psychology from its introduction in the 1950s to the present day. During this period, American researchers collected data suggesting asynchrony in the emergence of stage-related competencies, the contribution of heterogeneous skills to performance on assessment tasks, and the susceptibility of this performance to environmental influence. All of these kinds of evidence contributed to a disillusionment with stage doctrine in its strong form—the doctrine that all of cognitive development can be accounted for by the evolution of a single, unitary structure. The lesser attention devoted to Piaget's constructivist hypothesis also revealed a set of serious problems and limitations, however, centering around the effects of specific forms of experience on the individual's cognitive development.

Faced with the limitations they perceived in Piaget's constructivist formulation, a number of developmentalists concerned with questions of process sought ways to modify or to expand on the Piagetian model to take into greater account the specific influence of the environmental context in which development takes place. Fischer (1980), for example, while maintaining many of the central features of Piaget's structuralism, proposed a model in which new cognitive skills are at least initially wedded to the concrete contexts in which they are acquired; they are not the totally general, content-free acquisitions implied by Piaget's theory.

Also to a large extent in reaction to the neglect of social context in Piaget's constructivism, a renewed interest has occurred in developmental theories originating within Soviet psychology, notably those of Luria (1976) and Vygotsky (1978). As I indicate later, the Soviet perspective has had a substantial impact in recent years on methodology, as well as theory. In contrast to Piaget, both Luria and Vygotsky emphasized the major role played by the social environment in the development of more advanced forms of mental functioning within the individual. It is the child's first social relations, and in particular the resulting exposure to a language system, that give rise to mental development, according to the Soviet view. In Luria's (1976, p. 9) words: "Children assimilate language—a ready-made product of sociohistorical development—and use it to analyze, generalize, and encode experience. They name things, denoting them with expressions established earlier in human history, and thus assign things to certain categories and acquire knowledge." The mode of such transmission is social interaction: What start out as interpersonal regulations, e.g., a mother guiding her child in performing a task the child is unable to do alone, gradually become intrapersonal regulations—the child becomes capable of regulating his or her own actions to produce the performance, without external guidance. Wertsch (1979) has conducted interesting observational studies of this process as it occurs during the course of a mother helping her child do a puzzle.

This view of development is appropriately classified as neo-behaviorist according to the criteria specified earlier—development is conceptualized as the product of a unidirectional influence of the environment on the individual. Accordingly, although this view balances Piaget's exclusive focus on the role of individuals in producing their own development by emphasizing the external influences stemming from social interaction, it ignores the complementary part of the individual–environment interaction, i.e., the role of the individual: Little attention is given to how children attribute meaning to the social interactions they are involved in, and how this attributed meaning mediates the process by which society affects mind. Descriptions of the shift from interpersonal to intrapersonal regulation in parent–child interaction provide an insightful conceptualization of how parents structure their behavior in efforts to aid the child, but offer little insight into the cognitive processes that enable the child to make use of the adult's input.

Despite the essential factors it highlights, it is thus unlikely that the Soviet view on development would prove a wholly satisfactory substitute for Piaget's constructivism. But it is also unlikely that, for the time being, it will have such an opportunity, for the attention of a large number of researchers in cognitive development has turned in another direction.

THE INFORMATION-PROCESSING APPROACH

The information-processing approach to the study of cognitive development is not as readily classified as the theoretical perspectives examined up to this point. The major reason is that it is, by the admission of its own adherents, not a comprehensive theory of development, or even of cognition; rather, it is an approach to the study of cognition and, to a lesser extent, its development. Thus, it does not take an explicit position on some of the questions that must be addressed by a theory of cognitive development.

The Computer Metaphor

The origins of the information-processing approach are in cognitive, rather than developmental, psychology. A major impetus for its development was the technological innovation of the modern electronic computer. At the heart of the approach is the concept that the human intellect may function as an information-processing system, for which a mechanical information-processing system (i.e., the computer) is a fruitful model. How did this approach attract the attention and enthusiasm of a large number of developmental psychologists so rapidly? It is not difficult to trace the major reasons.

Consider the example of the transitivity inference cited earlier. Piaget attributed the child's ability at the level of concrete operations to infer $A < C$, given the information $A < B$ and $B < C$, to the underlying thought structure acquiring the characteristic of reversibility: The operation $A < B$ entailed the reverse operation $B > A$, and B could thus be regarded as simultaneously greater than A and less than C, thereby serving as the mediator linking A and C. This explanation in terms of underlying logical structure, however, does not identify the specific mental processes by which the child produces a judgment of transitivity in a particular instance. Thus, critics of Piaget's structural approach complained that there was no way ever to prove or disprove the correctness of such models as explanations of the child's behavior.

Furthermore, researchers studying the transitivity inference identified a number of specific processes that must go into its correct performance, e.g., encoding and retention of the initial relations. From this work it is only a short step to the suggestion that the performance of a cognitive task is made up entirely of the serial execution of a number of individual processes such as these. The computer-inspired information-processing model from cognitive psychology offered a formal model of just such a possibility, for it is by means of such serial execution of operations that a computer functions. The guiding assumption underlying the model is that human cognitive functioning is composed of a set of individual processes that operate sequentially and that are not necessarily governed by the same principles of operation. The information-processing approach can be characterized, then, as one that focuses on these individual processes and the manner in which they operate individually and combine serially to produce the final performance.

What are these individual processes? The major source of influence in defining them has been the information-processing operations executed by a computer. It is thus assumed that information from the environment must be encoded and stored in symbolic representational form. Various processes then operate on the contents of this representation, manipulating and transforming it in ways that create new representations. These processes may be constrained by the fixed processing capacity of the system, and representations may be constrained by a fixed storage capacity. When processing is completed, output is generated in the form of a final performance, or solution to the problem.

A few information-processing psychologists have taken the computer metaphor literally and have attempted to describe the cognitive operations generating a performance by means of a very exact and detailed model that could actually serve as a computer program for the performance. This approach has the attractive feature of containing a ready test of the model's sufficiency: Does the program successfully simulate performance on a computer? Klahr and Wallace (1976), for example, developed models of the performance of a number of Piagetian concrete operational tasks using a collection of "condition-action" links termed "productions" as the basic elements of their models. In contrast to the study of "condition–action" (or stimulus–response) links by behaviorists in the 1950s, the work of information-processing psychologists like Klahr and Wallace is focused squarely on modeling those processes inside the black box that behaviorists sought to bypass. An example of the production system proposed by Klahr and Wallace to produce a transitivity judgment is shown in Figure 4.4, which illustrates the extremely precise, detailed nature of such a model. Every minute aspect of the process must be represented explicitly or the model will fail to meet the sufficiency criterion. The computer cannot make any decisions that the program has left unspecified.

Klahr and Wallace's models were criticized as replacing one formalism (i.e., Piaget's models employing symbolic logic) with another; and indeed, following their pioneering effort only a few attempts to construct similar models appeared. A good deal of work followed, however, by researchers who endorsed the general spirit of Klahr and Wallace's approach without casting their models in the form of explicit computer simulations. Interestingly, these researchers continued to employ Piagetian tasks in their work, although they began to include tasks from Piaget's formal operational stage as well as the concrete operational stage.

In an approach advocated by Siegler (1983), for example, the child's performance on a task is described by the "rule" to which that performance conforms. The rule specifies a sequence of acts that are performed in order to execute the task. One test of the adequacy of the rule in characterizing the child's behavior is the extent to which it predicts performance over a variety of specific task items.

```
03000   QUANTIFIER:(CLASS SUBIT COUNT ESTIMATE)
03100
03600   APPQUANT:(OPR CALL) simulate quant opr selection
03700              results in (GOAL * QQQQ(X)) where QQQQ
03800              is SUBIT, COUNT or EST
03900
04200   REL.WORD:(CLASS MORE LESS LONGER SHORTER BIGGER SMALLER EQUAL SAME)
07900
08000                    transitivity rules
08100   PTRAN:((* GOAL TRAN)(X QREL Y QREL Z) --> SAT (X ===> OLD X) SEREAD)
08200   PTR789:((* GOAL TRAN)(X QREL Z)(X QREL Y)(Y QREL Z) --> MARKREL (X QREL Y QREL Z))
08300   PTR1:((* GOAL TRAN) (X QGT Y)(Y QGT Z) --> (X QGT Z))
08400   PTR2:((* GOAL TRAN) (X QLT Y)(Y QLT Z) --> (X QLT Z))
08500   PTR3:((* GOAL TRAN) (X QEQ Y)(Y QEQ Z) --> (X QEQ Z))
08600   PTR.RE:((* GOAL TRAN)(X QREL Y)(Z QREL X) --> (NTC (Z QREL X)))
08700   PTR4:((* GOAL TRAN)(X QGT Y) --> (X ===> OLD X)(Y Q< X))
08800   PTR5:((* GOAL TRAN)(X QLT Y) --> (X ===> OLD X)(Y Q> X))
08900   PTR6:((* GOAL TRAN)(X QEQ Y) --> (X ===> OLD X)(Y Q= X))
09000   PTRAN.FAIL:((* GOAL TRAN) --> (* ==> -))
09100
09200   MARKREL:(ACTION (NTC (X Y)(OLD **)(NTC (Y Z)(OLD **)
09300              (NTC (X Z)(OLD **))
09400   SEREAD:(OPR CALL) read series for desired relation
11400
11600                    main productions
11700   P1A:((* GOAL GET.REL X Y)(X QREL Y) --> SAT (NTC (X QREL)(OLD **) SAY.IT)
11900   P1B:((* GOAL GET.REL Y X)(X QREL Y) --> SAT (NTC (X QREL)(OLD **) SAY.IT)
12100   P2:((* GOAL GET.REL)(TS)(- GOAL CON) ABS --> (* GOAL CON))
12200   P3:((* GOAL GET.REL)(- GOAL TRAN) ABS --> (* GOAL TRAN))
12300   P4:((* GOAL GET.REL X Y) --> (* GOAL COMPARE X Y))
12600   P6A:((* GOAL COMPARE X Y) (X QREL Y) --> SAT)
12700   P6B:((* GOAL COMPARE Y X) (X QREL Y) --> SAT)
12800   P7:((* GOAL COMPARE X Y) (QS (X)) (QS (Y))   --> RELATE)
13100   P9A:((* GOAL COMPARE X Y)(VALUE X) -->(VALUE ===> OLD VALUE) (* GOAL QUANTIFY (X)))
13300   P9B:((* GOAL COMPARE X Y)(VALUE Y) --> (VALUE ===> OLD VALUE)(* GOAL QUANTIFY (Y)))
13500   P10:((* GOAL QUANTIFY (X)) (GOAL + QUANTIFIER (X)) --> SAT)
13600   P11:((* GOAL QUANTIFY (X)) --> APPQUANT )
14500
14700   PS.TRAN:(PTRAN PTR789 PTR1 PTR2 PTR3 PTR.RE PTR4 PTR5 PTRAN.FAIL)
14800   PSM2:(P1A P1B P2 P3 P4 P6A P6B P7 P9A P9B P10 P11)
14900   PSEXEC:(PA PZ PSVERB PSVS PS.TRAN PS.CON PSM2 PQ)
```

FIG. 4.4.   PS.QC6, a model for quantitative comparison, including conservation and transitivity rules (from Klahr & Wallace, 1976).

The most widely cited example is Siegler's (1976) rule-based model of performance on Piaget's balance scale task. The subject is shown a balance scale on which weights are placed at various distances from the center, and the subject must predict whether one or the other (or neither) side of the scale will go down following the removal of a supporting block. Siegler showed that the performance of 5- and 6-year-old children on such problems conformed to what he termed Rule I, in which only the number of weights is considered: Predict that the side with more weights will go down; if the weights are equal, predict balance. Older children's performance conformed better to Rule II: in the case of equal weights, predict that the side with weights at a greater distance from the fulcrum will go down; or to Rule III, which involved processing both weight and distance information without a consistent rule for integrating them. Not until mid- to late adolescence did a fully correct rule (Rule IV) begin to characterize some subjects' performances (consistent with Piaget's findings on this task). The major virtue of this kind of rule-based model of performance on a cognitive task is its explicit characterization of the sequence of mental operations that the individual allegedly utilizes to execute the task.

A somewhat different approach originated with Pascual-Leone (1970) and later Case (in press). At the heart of their work lies what they term the "task analysis" of the operations a subject would have to perform in order to execute a cognitive task. An example is their task analysis of Piaget's isolation of variable task. In one form of the task Piaget asked children and adolescents to experiment with a set of rods that differed on several dimensions (e.g., length, thickness, material) to discover what determined their flexibility. Not until early adolescence, Piaget found, do subjects employ an isolation of variables strategy, i.e., hold the level on all other variables constant while systematically varying the level of one variable to assess its effect. Piaget linked this development to the emergence of the cognitive structure of formal operations.

Based on his task analysis, Case argued that what the subject needs to perform this task is very simple:

> All the subject must do is to identify an object with an extreme position value on the dimension to be tested (e.g., a long stick), then identify an object with an extreme negative value (e.g., a short stick), and then check to see if there is any *other* difference between these two objects that might affect the result of interest (e.g., bending). (1978, p. 199)

More formally, the subject must execute the set of procedures shown in Figure 4.5 (from Case, 1978).

The virtues of the information-processing approach for analyzing performance on cognitive tasks are readily apparent, and it is easy to see why the approach was particularly attractive to those developmentalists who had become disillusioned with Piagetian stage theory. In contrast to the Piagetian models of cognitive competence—which seemed vague, abstract, removed from specific behavior, and unverifiable—information-processing analyses offered explicit, precisely articulated models of the series of cognitive operations a subject actually executed when performing a cognitive task. Less readily apparent, however, were several of the strengths of the constructivist approach that were sacrificed in the adoption of the information-processing approach. The reason this loss was less apparent has to do with what we have already noted with respect to the way American psychologists interpreted Piaget, that is, their focus on the theory of stages at the expense of the theory of constructivism.

A Return to Reductionism

The constructivist and information-processing perspectives differ radically in two respects. One is the information-processing perspective's explicit commitment to reductionism, in contrast to the constructivist perspective's explicit commitment to anti-reductionism, or holism. The other is the focus, within the constructivist perspective, on what has been termed "metacognition," in con-

Detailed Model for Control of Variables[a]

	Step or Operation		Specific Schemes	Symbol[b]
1.	Identify the object with extreme positive value on the dimension to be tested (e.g., long).	(1)	Operative scheme corresponding to the working definition of the positive pole of the dimension to be tested (e.g., for length, if the object sticks out the most, call it the longest).	ψ Dimension to tested (+)
		(2)[c]	Figurative scheme representing the array of the objects in the visual field.	φ Array
2.	Identify the object with value at the other extreme of dimension to be tested.	(1)	Operative scheme corresponding to the working definition of the other pole of dimension to be tested (e.g., for length, if the object is recessed the most, call it the shortest).	ψ Dimension to be tested (−)
		(2)[c]	Figurative scheme representing the array of the objects in the visual field.	φ Array
3.	Check to see if there is any difference between the two objects, other than the one to be tested.	(1)	Figurative scheme representing the dimension to be tested.	φ Dimension to be tested.
		(2)	Operative scheme representing the routine for scanning back and forth between the two objects and isolating any salient difference between them.	ψ Find difference
		(3)	Figurative scheme representing object A.	φ Object A
		(4)[c]	Figurative scheme representing object B.	φ Object B
4.	If a difference is found recycle to Step 2.			
5.	If no difference is found, conduct the test for property (i.e., see if object A > B on property of interest, e.g., bending).			

Note: Adapted from "Structures and Strictures: Some Functional Limitations on the Course of Cognitive Growth" by R. Case, Cognitive Psychology, 1974, 6, 544-573. Copyright 1974 by Academic Press. Reprinted by permission.

[a]Problem Question: Given a set of multidimensional objects with property X (e.g., bending), does dimension Y effect magnitude of X?
[b]ψ = operative scheme; φ= figurative scheme.
[c]Scheme activated by perceptual field. No M-power necessary.

FIG. 4.5.   Detailed model of control of variables (from Case, 1978).

trast to its de-emphasis within the information-processing perspective. Let us consider the issue of reductionism first.

The dual respects in which the information-processing approach is committed to reductionism closely parallel the respects in which the behaviorist approach of the 1950s and 1960s was committed to reductionism. First, in a theoretical vein, molar behavior is regarded as being composed of a number of smaller, individually controlled elements. Second, in a methodological vein, the most fruitful research strategy is considered to be the focus on a particular, well-specified task domain (see our earlier example of paired-associate learning), which, once well understood, will permit generalization to broader (and more significant) domains of behavior. Piagetian theory and research strategy, of course, are notable, in contrast, for their non-reductionistic perspective—individual elements can be properly interpreted only in relation to the whole.

Methodologically, the result has been a series of exceptionally meticulous, detailed analyses of the procedures subjects employ in performing a particular task, ones that serve as pioneering models of the precision to which psychological analyses might aspire. One of the criticisms, however, that has been levelled

against these task analyses of specific cognitive tasks pertains to their ver-
ifiability. Although closer to observable performance than Piaget's logical models, task analyses by no means constitute a magical key that unlocks the secret of
how a correct (or incorrect) performance is produced. How do we know that a
particular task analysis is correct? Researchers might collect converging behavioral evidence, such as eye movement patterns or reaction times, that are in
accordance with what would be predicted by a given task analysis, but alternative
hypotheses always remain possible (Brown et al., 1983; Sternberg & Powell,
1983). Indeed, researchers engaged in task analyses of cognitive tasks have
tended to produce as many analyses of the same task, e.g., conservation, as there
are analyzers of it. Empirical data have not, as yet, served in the role of *discon-*
firming a proposed task analysis.

Another criticism of task analysis and the information-processing approach
more generally has been that it limits itself to proposing models of performance
on specific tasks and has not integrated those models into a broader theory of
human cognitive performance. Adherents of the information-processing approach, on the other hand, defend this omission as a matter of appropriate
sequence: Precise models of performance in very specific, restricted domains are
alleged to be prerequisites for the formulation of broader, more comprehensive
theories. Stated differently, the information-processing psychologist justifies, in
the short term at least, sacrificing explanatory breadth for explanatory precision.
Here again the parallel to the earlier reductionist research strategy adhered to by
behaviorists is clear. And so the debate over reductionism continues, with the
information-processing approach assuming the pro-reductionist role.

Theoretically, the concept promoted by the information-processing approach
that multiple, largely independent processes are likely to be involved in the
performance of a cognitive task has contributed valuably to thinking about cognitive development, particularly as an antidote to Piagetian stage doctrine, which
treated performance as the manifestation of a single underlying stage structure.
But the problem, and the reductionism debate, arises in deciding whether it is
justified to go on to maintain that the performance is nothing but the serial
execution of a specified set of individual processes, or whether some higher-
order organizing entity must be invoked. This brings us to the second major way
in which the constructivist and information-processing perspectives differ.

The most serious criticism that has been lodged against the information-
processing approach is that it has concerned itself predominantly with "strategy
execution," and scarcely at all with "strategy selection." In other words, it has
largely ignored the processes of "executive" control through which individual
strategies are selected, assembled, and monitored. Stated in still different terminology, it has ignored "metacognition."

Consider for example Case's analysis of the isolation of variables strategy
portrayed in Figure 4.5. One can agree with Case that the sequence of strategies
he specifies is not difficult to execute, and it is not surprising to learn that he was

successful in teaching 8-year-olds to do so (Case, 1974). But, if not specifically directed to do so, how would an individual know that this set of strategies ought to be applied to such a problem? Without this knowledge, knowledge of how to execute the strategies is of limited value.

In comparison to knowledge of the first type, i.e., knowledge of how to execute the strategies, which is to a considerable extent ascertainable from the surface features of the performance, knowledge of this second type is subtle and complex (Kuhn, 1983). In order to select a strategy as appropriate for solving a particular problem, the individual must understand the strategy, understand the problem, and understand how the strategy and the problem intersect or map onto one another, which entails understanding the range and limits of the strategy's appropriate application. In the case of the isolation of variables strategy represented in Figure 4.5, this kind of knowledge includes an understanding of: (1) why the isolation or "all other things equal" method is the only means of achieving the task objective; (2) how and why each component of the strategy (such as ". . . check to see if there is any *other* difference between these two objects that might affect the result") constitutes an essential step in correct application; and (3) why any other strategy would not yield a correct solution.

To be convinced of the importance of this second kind of knowledge, one need only note that it is this knowledge that will determine whether or not an individual utilizes the new strategy when an appropriate situation arises in the natural environment, in the absence of direct instruction. It is the absence of such knowledge that is responsible for the common failures of generalization following training interventions: The subject learns the strategy in the particular context in which it is taught, but fails to apply it subsequently in other contexts in which it is equally appropriate (Brown et al., 1983).

Knowledge of one's own cognitive strategy as it applies to a task implies a *reflection on* the strategy that clearly differentiates it from the *execution of* the strategy. The reader may recognize such a developing reflection on one's actions as the heart of the constructivist account of cognitive development that originated with Baldwin and Piaget. It is just this kind of reflection that is involved in strategy selection, to use the language of information processing, but is difficult to incorporate into the information-processing model.

A slightly different aspect of this reflection is implicated in another concept central to Piagetian theory, that of logical necessity. Consider once again the example of the transitivity inference. In the research of Trabasso and his colleagues (1975) described earlier, young children who did not show the transitivity concept were trained with respect to each of a set of individual relations, i.e., $A < B$, $B < C$, $C < D$, $D < E$, using a set of sticks of graduated lengths. It was hypothesized that the subjects encoded and represented the set of relations as a visual image, i.e., $A < B < C < D < E$. If so, this would explain how a child was able to answer questions about the relation between nonadjacent elements, e.g., A and C, correctly: The child could simply refer to the internal pictorial array that had been formed and produce the information A < C. These findings have prompted an extended debate as to whether these children had indeed mastered the concept of transitivity (Breslow, 1981), and Piagetians were quick to make the distinction between an "empirical" judgment of transitivity and a judgment of transitivity that had the characteristic of logical necessity. In other words, the child just indicated might "read off" of her mental representation the fact that A < C, but it does not follow that she sees the relation A < C as an inevitable logical necessity following from the relations A < B and B < C, rather than as an empirical fact that happened to be true but could have been otherwise. This distinction is a difficult one to assess empirically, yet it is this logical necessity of the transitivity judgment that was the heart of the matter for Piaget. And such concepts of logical necessity can only come about as a product of reflection on one's own mental actions, or metacognition—in this case, the mental actions of relating A to B and B to C.

Why is it that those utilizing an information-processing approach tend not to focus on the processes of reflection on one's own cognition that are the core of the constructivist perspective and that are implicated in the concept of logical necessity or the exercise of strategy selection? Rather than an accident, this neglect is most likely ascribable to the fact that the information-processing perspective does not lend itself readily to the incorporation of this aspect of cognition, precisely because its underlying metaphor, the information-processing computer, does not—indeed, it cannot—reflect on what it is doing at a level differentiated from the "doing" itself. Unlike humans, computers do not "know" what they are doing. The computer can contemplate or evaluate its own actions only in the limited sense represented by the programmer specifying the operations that will constitute such an "evaluation," e.g., a condition–action link directing that processing be terminated once a certain set of conditions is met, but again, these "evaluating" operations are not at a level that is distinct from the processing operations themselves.

Summary: Toward a Developmental Information-Processing Model

It has been attempted here to highlight both the strengths and the limitations of the currently popular information-processing approach to the study of cognitive development. The major strength noted is the explicitness and precision with which it attempts to model specific kinds of cognitive performances. In addition, the information-processing approach is responsible for the concept that performance is composed of a set of sequentially operating individual processes. This specificity and precision, however, is tied closely to a significant limitation—the scant attention that has been paid to the integration of specific models into a broader theory of cognition and, particularly, cognitive development.

The major limitation that has been focused on is the lack of attention to what have been termed metacognitive processes. If the information-processing approach is not to restrict its explanation of cognitive development unduly, it will eventually have to go beyond the literal model of the computer to incorporate the reflective, or evaluative, components of cognition and cognitive development. One indication that it is attempting to do just that is the increasing attention that researchers working within the information-processing approach are paying to so-called "executive" strategies. One impetus for this interest has been the frequent finding that subjects are able to execute all of the component strategies that a task analysis deems are required for performance of a certain task, and yet do not assemble those components to produce the performance. Something else appears necessary for success. The term metacognition, as both Brown et al. (1983) and Sternberg and Powell (1983) note, has been employed very broadly to refer to both the regulation of one's own cognitive processes and knowledge about those cognitive processes. Research pertaining to metacognition thus far has been largely confined to attempts to assess metacognitive knowledge. Is a child aware, for example, that the organization of items into categories is a strategy that is useful to employ to enhance recall? Younger children, we noted, show little awareness of the utility of these types of strategies.

The increasing attention given the topic of metacognition suggests a growing belief in the significant role it is likely to play in understanding cognitive development. What is necessary, however, is a fruitful conceptual and methodological framework in terms of which metacognitive processes can be studied. Despite its centrality in his theory, Piaget's treatment of the topic has proven too abstract and divorced from specific contexts to generate much empirical research. On the other hand, the computer model that underlies the information-processing approach is not well-suited to capture metacognitive processes.

One further limitation of the information-processing approach, only alluded to until now, is one that has been widely noted and acknowledged by both followers and critics of the approach: Information-processing models offer no explanation of change. This limitation is obviously crucial if the approach is to provide an account of development. Why and how is the information-processing system modified over the course of development? However, information processing is in good company here, for it is the mechanism of change that has proven the most difficult and formidable problem for all theories of cognitive development. Let us turn again, then, to the more general question of mechanisms of developmental change.

MECHANISMS OF DEVELOPMENTAL CHANGE

Only a decade or two ago, it appeared as if the question of mechanism in cognitive development was a clear-cut one. There were only two possibilities, and it seemed, moreover, that the data from a set of critical experiments would make it easy to choose between the two. Either the learning theorists were right, and the same basic processes of learning could account for development as well, or Piaget was right and a small number of reorganizations of the cognitive system as a whole that occurred only a few times during the course of the individual's development were sufficient to account for all developmental change.

To decide between these two alternatives, it was thought, one needed only to conduct some so-called "training" studies. In a training study, the investigator attempts to induce via simple learning mechanisms competencies held by Piaget to be manifestations of a global stage structure. If these studies were successful, the developmental process could be explained by simple learning mechanisms. If they were unsuccessful, Piaget's concept of global stage transformation would be implicated.

Remarkably, several hundred training studies were carried out in the decade from the early 1960s to the early 1970s. Even more striking, the vast majority of these studies were devoted to inducing a single Piagetian competency, conservation of quantity. The one thing that can be concluded about these studies is that they did not clearly decide the issue, and "the issue" indeed is now recognized to be much more complex than what we have just portrayed. Many of the studies showed significant changes in children's performance on conservation tasks following training of a variety of different kinds, ranging from telling the children the correct answer ("The amount doesn't change") and rewarding them for making it, to more cognitively oriented attempts to get them to appreciate the logic that dictates the invariance. Exactly what these results implied about how and why children shift during the natural course of development from believing that quantity varies with perceptual rearrangement to believing that it is invariant, however, is far from clear.

In what is perhaps the most widely cited conservation training study, one often praised as a model of elegant experimental design, Gelman (1969) claimed that young children fail to conserve because they do not attend to the relevant attribute, e.g., the number of elements rather than the length of the row in the case of number conservation. She demonstrated that by reinforcing children over many trials for choosing as "same" (as a standard) the row with the same number of items but different length (rather than the row of the same length but a different number of items), she could induce many of them to subsequently respond correctly in the standard conservation task, i.e., to respond that the number of items in two rows remained the same after one of them was spread out to be of greater length than the other. In Gelman's terms, she taught such children to discriminate which of two possibilities (spatial magnitude or number) the term "same" refers to. Gelman, however, quite pointedly did not go on to draw from her findings the conclusion that natural attainment of the conservation concept involves "nothing but" (i.e., is reducible to) simple processes of discrimination learning and reinforcement. Nor have the many others who have cited her study been prepared to draw such a conclusion.

Exactly what conclusions ought to be drawn from such studies, then, is far from clear. Much of the uncertainty can be traced to two major sources of ambiguity surrounding experiments that have utilized the training study methodology. First, many observers questioned the validity of the experimentally induced attainments: Had the child merely acquired the surface behaviors indicative of an understanding of conservation or had some genuine change in understanding, i.e., cognitive reorganization, taken place? Although much debate ensued, the matter was largely unresolvable inasmuch as opinion differed widely as to what conservation attainment in fact consists of: Is some underlying cognitive reorganization involved or is it merely the acquisition of a simple empirical fact or rule (quantity doesn't change through perceptual rearrangement)? In others words, what is it that is developing?

Even if these fundamental issues were agreed on, however, and the experimentally induced change were accepted as genuine, a second and even more fundamental and troubling issue remains with respect to the method itself: the issue of *can* versus *does*. If a particular treatment is sufficient to produce a behavior in an experimental laboratory situation, it does not follow that the salient features of this treatment are always, or ever, involved in the emergence of that behavior during the natural course of development. It is this second issue that is probably most responsible for the disillusionment that developed with the training study as a tool for investigating mechanisms of developmental change. Perhaps the most striking testimony to its limitations is the fact that despite the 200 or more training studies of conservation conducted in the last two decades, there continues to exist a wide variety of diverse theories regarding the process through which conservation is attained (Acredolo, 1981; Anderson & Cuneo, 1978; Brainerd, 1979; Pinard, 1981; Shultz, Dover, & Amsel, 1979; Siegler, 1981). Thus, the vast conservation training study literature has not significantly constrained theories of the developmental process that underlies the attainment of conservation.

Multiple Dimensions and Mechanisms of Change

Along with the abandonment of the idea of training studies as providing a critical test of empiricist versus constructivist explanations of change came a gradual abandonment of the idea that either view could provide a comprehensive theoretical account of developmental change in cognitive functioning. One reason is that, following in part from work done within the information-processing approach, a considerably more complex picture of what it is that is developing has emerged—a ''what'' that encompasses a diverse set of competencies, rather than only a single entity. As a result, it is likely to require a more complex process, or set of processes, to explain that development. A range of possibilities exists with respect to what it is that may develop, including basic processing capacity, processing efficiency, processes of encoding and representation, strategy possession and execution, and metacognitive processes of strategy selection and regulation. Developmental changes in each of these could conceivably be governed by different mechanisms; moreover, changes in some (e.g., processing capacity) might be invoked to account for changes in others (e.g., strategy usage).

Processing Capacity. A possibility that is very attractive because of its simplicity is that the change responsible for most, if not all, advances in cognitive functioning with age is an increase in basic processing capacity, presumably as the result of neurological development. Thus, this alternative attributes cognitive development most directly to an underlying biological process of maturation. Pascual-Leone (1970) has advanced an elaborate "neo-Piagetian" theory of cognitive development founded on the assumption of age-linked increases in absolute processing capacity. The fact that performance increases with age on tests of basic processing such as digit span appears to support such a view. A 3-year-old can repeat an average of only 3 digits, while a 10-year-old can repeat an average of 6 digits.

That such improvements in performance are attributable to increases in processing capacity, however, is extremely difficult, if not impossible, to prove, since a number of hard-to-discount alternative explanations exist. In the instance of digit span, for example, the older child may be employing some strategic device, such as rehearsal or chunking, that the younger child is not. In other words, it is difficult to prove that children of the two ages are executing the task in exactly the same way, the only difference being that the older children have a quantitatively greater capacity. Furthermore, as discussed earlier, capacity is highly influenced by familiarity with the material: If the domain is one in which a young child is highly experienced (e.g., chess boards), that child's recall performance may exceed that of much older children less familiar with the domain. Similarly, Case and his colleagues demonstrated that the capacity of adults drops to that of 6-year-olds if adults are required to execute a digit memory task using a newly learned set of digit symbols (Case, Kurland, & Goldberg, 1982).

Processing Efficiency. Case (in press), in opposition to Pascual-Leone, has argued that improvements with age in performance on tests such as digit span only appear to be the result of an absolute capacity increase. Actually, he claims, improved performance is ascribable to an increase in the efficiency with which basic operations, such as encoding, are executed; accordingly, less capacity is required for their execution. This leaves the individual with a greater remaining "functional" capacity for holding the products of those operations in memory, even though the total capacity remains unchanged. In support of his perspective, Case cites recent evidence that performance on measures of basic operations (e.g., counting an array of objects) becomes faster and more efficient with age, making plausible his view that increases in efficiency are at least in part responsible for increases in functional capacity, and hence in performance on processing tests such as digit span. Whether the fundamental change is one of processing efficiency, as Case claims, or of total processing capacity, as Pascual-Leone claims, both believe that this change is itself a function of underlying neurological development (though Case raises the possibility that experience of a very broad, general sort may also contribute to increased efficiency).

The issue even more critical to debate, however, is the extent to which age-related increases in processing capacity (whether absolute or only "functional") underlie all forms of developmental change in cognitive functioning, as both Case and Pascual-Leone claim. The fact that performance on measures of basic processing improves with age has already been established, as indicated above. But we also know that cognitive functioning changes developmentally in many other ways. Children acquire new, qualitatively different strategies they did not have previously; they integrate existing strategies in new ways; they encode new and different kinds of information and represent it in new and different ways; and they develop new forms of executive, or metacognitive, control over their cognitive functioning. Most developmentalists today would agree with the view that increases in basic processing efficiency and/or capacity are implicated at most as necessary conditions for many of these other kinds of changes. They fall far short of being by themselves sufficient to explain how these changes come about. Let us turn, then, to these other kinds of changes and the mechanisms that may underlie them.

Encoding and Representation.   Another factor that undergoes developmental change, and might account for improvements in performance on many kinds of cognitive tasks, is improved encoding and representation of information essential to successful execution of the task. No matter how efficiently they are developed, operations cannot be performed on material that has not been attended to, encoded, and in some manner represented within the cognitive system. Siegler and Klahr (1982) emphasize this point nicely in the case of the balance scale task described earlier: At a certain level children encode information about weight but do not encode information about the distance of the weight from the fulcrum, as evidenced by their ability to reproduce weight but not distance information in tests of recall. The encoding of distance information is an obvious prerequisite to the execution of the more advanced strategies in which distance is taken into account, though Siegler's work does not prove that it is a change in encoding behavior that causes the change in strategy. Conceivably, the causal relationship is in some sense the reverse: The child's intent to use a new strategy leads the child to encode new kinds of information.

Strategy Execution.   Through what process does an individual come to use new or modified strategies in performing a cognitive task? Constructivist accounts have traditionally emphasized the role of self-regulatory mechanisms within the individual: The individual gradually constructs a more adequate, comprehensive, and better equilibrated set of cognitive operations to be applied to the external world. But, as noted, these accounts have tended to minimize the role of the external environment. Within some versions of the constructivist account, exposure to material reflecting the higher-level structure toward which the individual is developing is a necessary condition for change, while others theorizing within the constructivist framework hold to the more radical position (reflected in Piaget's writings) that the individual literally constructs anew each more advanced mode of cognitive functioning based on the discrepant feedback produced by actions executed at the existing level. According to this formulation, then, the functioning of the cognitive system leads to its modification, a view endorsed by theorists operating from such disparate frameworks as Piaget (1971) and Klahr and Wallace (1976).

This stronger version of constructivism ignores the fact that models of the more advanced concepts or strategies the individual will acquire are often prevalent in the individual's environment, as emphasized by the Soviet theories of Luria (1976) and Vygotsky (1978) mentioned earlier. Case's (1978) work on the isolation of variables strategy suggests that an individual can be taught to execute this strategy through social facilitation, at least in a laboratory context. The role of social influence in its acquisition in natural contexts is another question. But the role of both of these processes (individual construction and social facilitation) must be considered in positing an explanation of how an individual acquires a new strategy. Even though external models are not directly or automatically internalized, it is most unlikely that they are systematically ignored.

Strategy Selection and Regulation.   With respect to one final factor, namely the individual's metacognitive decision to utilize particular strategies, the power of social facilitation is less clear. An individual might be instructed successfully in exactly how to execute a particular strategy and even be instructed regarding the conditions under which it is appropriate to apply the strategy, provided these conditions can be well specified. But whether the individual will choose to use the strategy in contexts that are not identical to the one instructed is more problematic. For example, children might be taught to use rehearsal to facilitate memory and yet not employ the strategy in their own activities, a finding that has, in fact, been reported by Paris and Lindauer (1982). As suggested earlier, whether a strategy is selected in noninstructed, natural contexts is likely to depend on individuals' metacognitive understanding of the strategy itself, i.e., their understanding of their own actions. In other words, the individual must understand the value and significance of the strategy as well as how to execute it; and the acquisition of this appreciation, or metacognitive understanding, is likely to be the more difficult, complex attainment of the two.

Piaget proposed that the mechanism underlying the development of both strategies and metacognitive strategies was *equilibration,* the functioning of which he described only in rather general and formal terms. Strategies become consolidated and coordinated with one another through exercise. The feedback from this exercise, however, causes the individual to perceive the limitations of these strategies and provides the impetus, or disequilibrium, necessary for the construction of new strategies that will be more adequate for dealing with the tasks encountered and so leave the organism in a state of improved equilibrium with its environment. Several information-processing theorists have undertaken to introduce a developmental mechanism into their models by describing this kind of process in the language of information processing. Klahr and Wallace (1976), for example, talk about a self-modifying production system with features such as consistency detectors, which lead strategies to become more efficient. Case (1978) likewise describes a process whereby a set of strategies becomes modified during the course of their own functioning. Thus far, however, these efforts have not gone beyond the description of the general features of the process, in language that is very different from Piaget's. What would be most useful now are models that would generate new, testable hypotheses about how the process operates.

Summary: New Approaches to Studying Change

Two major factors that have limited progress in understanding the mechanisms of developmental change have been discussed. One is the lack of satisfactory methods of empirical investigation. The other is the scarcity of specific hypotheses that are amenable to empirical test. On the positive side, we now have a considerably more sophisticated conception of what it is that is developing and of the mechanism—or more likely mechanisms—that will be necessary to account for this development.

Also on the positive side is the fact that in recent years, after being diverted by a number of subsidiary issues, such as the existence of stages, modern developmentalists of virtually every theoretical orientation have identified a better understanding of the process of change as their primary objective, and a great many of them have begun to focus their research efforts on investigating the mechanisms of developmental change. In particular, researchers interested in both learning and development have begun to explore the use of new "microgenetic" methods as a means of obtaining detailed observations of the change process as it occurs. These methods differ markedly from the classical training study methodology discussed earlier, in that the focus is on the change process itself rather than on a comparison of pretest and posttest performance.

Microgenetic methods show promise in affording insight into the change process, though the approaches used do not fit into traditional categories of research methods. Lawler (1981), for example, observed a single subject over several months, during the course of which the child mastered some elementary mathematical concepts. His observations led him to emphasize as a central feature of the developmental process the integration of strategic knowledge that initially functions within isolated, unintegrated domains. Similarly, Kuhn and Phelps (1982) observed preadolescent subjects in repeated encounters with a problem-solving task over a period of months. Most subjects' progress, they found, occurred only very gradually and involved the prolonged use of both less and more advanced strategies in conjunction with one another. It was during this period of observation, Kuhn and Phelps proposed, that the subject was gaining metacognitive understanding of which strategies were effective and why, as well as gaining practice in the execution of the more advanced strategies. Their observations also pointed to an aspect of the change process that has been largely ignored. The most formidable problem for subjects appeared to be not the acquisition and consolidation of new strategies but the ability to abandon old, less adequate strategies, which is a reversal of the way development has typically been conceived. Other current approaches to the microgenetic study of developmental change are reflected in work by Feldman (1980) within a constructivist framework, and in work by Paris and his colleagues (Paris, Newman, & McVey, 1982) within an information-processing framework; the work by Paris also points to the importance of the metacognitive regulation of strategy usage.

PAST PROGRESS AND FUTURE DIRECTIONS

In this chapter, I have undertaken to describe how the study of cognitive development has been conceived and conducted in American psychology over a period of almost half a century, culminating in the current focus on gaining better understanding of the mechanisms of developmental change. How might we summarize the progress that is reflected by this evolution?

Evolution in Theory

One way to summarize this evolution is as the successive rejection of a series of explanatory mechanisms on the grounds that they are too simple to explain what a theory of cognitive development must account for—in other words, they are too simple to answer the question posed at the outset of this chapter as underlying the study of cognitive development: How do mind and reality come to be coordinated with one another?

A biologically governed unfolding of developmental forms without regard to environmental influence is no longer taken seriously as a model of psychological development. The more recent hypothesis of a biologically governed, quantitatively increasing processing capacity has similarly been criticized as inadequate to explain how and why cognitive development occurs.

Also rejected as too simple to account for the complexity of cognitive functioning and its development are explanatory mechanisms that bypass the internal functioning that takes place within the organism. Influences of external variables on the developmental process are now widely accepted as mediated by characteristics internal to the individual.

Likewise rejected are simple acquisition mechanisms that are purported to function in an identical manner irrespective of the material being acquired and its relation to what is already known by the acquirer and to the capabilities of his or her cognitive system. Put another way, it is now widely accepted that mechanisms of learning and retention do not function independently of the individual's intellect as a whole. Existing conceptual structure provides the basis for the interpretation of new information.

Although the individual's intelligence, or active structuring of experience, is thus recognized, there has also been criticism and widespread rejection of explanatory mechanisms that attribute cognitive development to the progressive restructuring of this intelligence as an activity of the individual that takes place isolated from social contexts that might influence it. Individuals develop within a social context of other individuals, and the interdependence of cognitive and social processes must therefore be acknowledged and investigated.

Parallel with this evolution in the concepts of an adequate explanation of developmental process has been an evolution in concepts of what it is that is developing. The concept of isolated competencies that accumulate independently has been rejected for ignoring the crucial organizational features of behavior and knowledge. But the concept of a single, structured whole that develops as an integrated entity and mediates all more specific components of cognitive functioning has also been rejected. A major contribution of the information-processing approach has been to highlight the fact that there exist a number of distinct cognitive functions, each of which may undergo developmental change. A unique contribution of the constructivist perspective, on the other hand, and one difficult for the information-processing approach to encompass, is its focus on what is now termed metacognition and its development—in other words, the individual's reflection on his or her actions and the ''meaning–making'' endeavor that this reflection is a part of.

The preceding summary conversely serves to prescribe the features a fully satisfactory explanatory account of cognitive development would need to possess:

1. It would need to refer to the mental processes that take place within the organism, including those processes termed metacognitive.
2. It would need to characterize development as a gradual coordination of individual mind and external physical and social reality, in which neither internal nor external forces predominate over the other.
3. It would need to address the social contexts in which development occurs and the ways in which those contexts relate to individual development.
4. It would need to account for context specificity of cognitive attainments as well as transsituational commonalities in cognitive functioning.

5. It would need to specify the mechanisms by which developmental change occurs.

During the next several decades, theories that are proposed to account for cognitive development are likely to possess at least the preceding characteristics, as well as others not yet clear. That this is so serves as an indication that the field has progressed, despite the absence of an accumulation of the "hard facts" a reader of this chapter might have anticipated.

Evolution in Method

Not surprisingly, as the field of cognitive development has evolved in its theoretical sophistication, so it has also evolved with respect to its methods, and this latter evolution also gives reason for optimism regarding the field's future. A decade or so ago, researchers in the field of cognitive development could be portrayed, with some justification, as preoccupied with a narrow range of cognitive phenomena investigated in experimental laboratory contexts, where both phenomenon and context were of uncertain relevance to children's cognitive functioning and development in natural settings. Meanwhile, crucial practical decisions as to how children might be reared and educated so as to maximize their cognitive potential and their productivity and fulfillment as adults were left to others outside the academic enterprise of cognitive development.

Today, these characterizations of the field of cognitive development are much less accurate than they were. As we have indicated, recognition of the profound effect that context and meaning have on performance has grown, and more and more researchers are undertaking to examine cognitive functioning within the natural contexts of meaningful activities that children engage in—in school as well as in non-school environments. Cognitive abilities such as reading are currently of great interest to cognitive and developmental psychologists to a large extent because of, rather than despite, their practical importance.

One impetus for this research trend has been the work on cognition and culture by Cole, Scribner and others (see Rogoff chapter, this volume), work that has been inspired to a large extent by the "contextualist" theoretical perspective of Vygotsky and Luria. A number of cross-cultural investigations have shown that non-schooled populations do poorly on Western IQ test items, which are of course closely related to the kinds of activities engaged in in school (Sharp, Cole, & Lave, 1979). This finding is, by itself, trivial and uninterpretable and highlights the necessity of examining cognition and cognitive development in the context of those cognitive activities that are meaningful and salient in the lives of the individuals being investigated, if meaningful conclusions are to be drawn. The appropriate unit of investigation, it has been suggested, should become cultural practices, not psychological tests and experiments (Laboratory of Comparative Human Cognition, 1983).

This point is equally applicable to research within our own culture. The study of cognitive development in contexts that are not clearly linked to contexts in which cognitive development occurs naturally seriously constrains the insight this study can yield. There are signs that developmental researchers are beginning to take this admonition seriously, and that future academic study of cognitive development will not be as divorced from practical or "applied" concerns as it has been.

This issue of "ecological validity" has been highlighted even further by another trend of the last decade: The study of cognitive development is no longer limited to an exclusive focus on the childhood years. There are indications that it may be fruitful to conceptualize cognitive functioning in adulthood—particularly the substantial individual variation in cognitive functioning among adults—from a developmental perspective. Parallel to what has been recognized to be the case in cross-cultural work, however, it is apparent that it will be essential to study cognitive functioning beyond the childhood years in contexts that are meaningful and salient to the individuals studied, if our interpretations are to be meaningful (Baltes, this volume; Kuhn, Pennington, & Leadbeater, 1983).

This expansion of the traditional child-focused study of development to encompass the latter 80% of the life-span promises benefits not only for our understanding of adult cognition, but for our understanding of cognition and cognitive development during childhood as well. The process of cognitive development during childhood can be fully appreciated only to the extent that we understand the end points toward which it is evolving. The study of cognitive development as a process that takes place throughout life, then, will most likely enrich the conceptual perspectives that, over the next several decades, will be the historical successors of those that have been described in this chapter.

ACKNOWLEDGMENT

Preparation of this chapter was supported by the Redward Foundation.

REFERENCES

Acredolo, C. Acquisition of conservation: A clarification of Piagetian terminology, some recent findings, and an alternative formulation. *Human Development,* 1981, *24,* 120–137.

Anderson, N., & Cuneo, D. The height and width rule in children's judgments of quantity. *Journal of Experimental Psychology: General,* 1978, *107,* 335–378.

Bijou, S. *Child development: The basic stage of early childhood.* Englewood Cliffs, NJ: Prentice-Hall, 1976.

Bijou, S., & Baer, D. *Child development: A systematic and empirical theory.* New York: Appleton-Century-Crofts, 1961.

Brainerd, C. The stage question in cognitive–developmental theory. *Behavioral and Brain Sciences,* 1978, *1,* 173–213.

Brainerd, C. Markovian interpretations of conservation learning. *Psychological Review,* 1979, *86,* 181–213.

Breslow, L. Reevaluation of the literature on the development of transitive inferences. *Psychological Bulletin,* 1981, *89,* 325–351.

Brown, A., Bransford, J., Ferrara, R., & Campione, J. Learning, remembering, and understanding. In P. Mussen (Ed.), *Carmichael's manual of child psychology* (4th ed.). New York: Wiley, 1983.

Brown, A., & DeLoache, J. Skills plans, and self-regulation. In R. Siegler (Ed.), *Children's thinking: What develops?* Hillsdale, NJ: Lawrence Erlbaum Associates, 1978.

Bryant, P., & Trabasso, T. Transitive inferences and memory in young children. *Nature,* 1971, *232,* 456–458.

Case, R. Piaget and beyond: Toward a developmentally based theory and technology of instruction. In R. Glaser (Ed.), *Advances in instructional psychology,* Vol. 1, Hillsdale, NJ: Lawrence Erlbaum Associates, 1978.

Case, R. Structures and strictures: Some functional limitations on the course of cognitive growth. *Cognitive Psychology,* 1974, *6,* 544–573.

Case, R. *Intellectual development: A systematic reinterpretation.* New York: Academic Press, in press.

Case, R., Kurland, D. M., & Goldberg, J. Operational efficiency and the growth of short-term memory span. *Journal of Experimental Child Psychology,* 1982, *33,* 386–404.

Chi, M. Knowledge structures and memory development. In R. Siegler (Ed.), *Children's thinking: What develops?* Hillsdale, NJ: Lawrence Erlbaum Associates, 1978.

Feldman, D. *Beyond universals in cognitive development.* Norwood, NJ: Ablex, 1980.

Fischer, K. A theory of cognitive development: The control and construction of hierarchies of skills. *Psychological Review,* 1980, *87,* 477–531.

Flavell, J. On cognitive development. *Child Development,* 1982, *53,* 1–10.

Flavell, J., Beach, D., & Chinsky, J. Spontaneous verbal rehearsal in a memory task as a function of age. *Child Development,* 1966, *37,* 283–299.

Gagné, R. Contributions of learning to human development. *Psychological Review,* 1968, *75,* 177–191.

Gelman, R. Conservation acquisition: A problem of learning to attend to relevant attributes. *Journal of Experimental Child Psychology,* 1969, *7,* 167–187.

Gesell, A. Maturation and infant behavior pattern. *Psychological Review,* 1929, *36,* 307–319.

Gholson, B. *The cognitive-developmental basis of human learning: Studies in hypothesis testing.* New York: Academic Press, 1980.

Inhelder, B. Memory and intelligence in the child. In D. Elkind & J. Flavell (Eds.), *Studies in cognitive development.* London: Oxford University Press, 1969.

Istomina, Z. The development of voluntary memory in preschool-age children. In M. Cole (Ed.), *Soviet developmental psychology.* White Plains, N.Y.: Sharpe, 1977.

Kendler, H., & Kendler, T. From discrimination learning to cognitive development: A neo-behavioristic odyssey. In W. K. Estes (Ed.), *Handbook of learning and cognitive processes,* Vol. 1. Hillsdale, NJ: Lawrence Erlbaum Associates, 1975.

Klahr, D., & Wallace, J. *Cognitive development: An information-processing view.* Hillsdale, NJ: Lawrence Erlbaum Associates, 1976.

Kuhn, D. On the dual executive and its significance in the development of developmental psychology. In D. Kuhn & J. Meacham (Eds.), *On the development of developmental psychology.* Basel, Switzerland: Karger, 1983.

Kuhn, D., Pennington, N., & Leadbeater, B. Adult thinking in developmental perspective. In P. Baltes & O. Brim (Eds.), *Life-span development and behavior* (Vol. 5). New York: Academic Press, 1983.

Kuhn, D., & Phelps, E. The development of problem-solving strategies. In H. Reese (Ed.), *Advances in child development and behavior* (Vol. 17). New York: Academic Press, 1982.

Laboratory of Comparative Human Cognition. Culture and cognitive development. In P. Mussen (Ed.), *Carmichael's manual of child psychology* (4th ed.). New York: Wiley, 1983.

Lawler, R. The progressive construction of mind. *Cognitive Science*, 1981, *5*, 1–30.

Lerner, R. Children and adolescents as producers of their own development. *Developmental Review*, 1982, *2*, 342–370.

Liben, L. Memory in the context of cognitive development: The Piagetian approach. In R. Kail & J. Hagen (Eds.), *Perspectives on the development of memory and cognition*. Hillsdale, NJ: Lawrence Erlbaum Associates, 1977.

Luria, A. *Cognitive development: Its cultural and social foundations*. Cambridge, Mass.: Harvard University Press, 1976.

Martin, W. Rediscovering the mind of the child. *Merrill-Palmer Quarterly*, 1959/60, *6*, 67–76.

Morrison, H., & Kuhn, D. Cognitive aspects of preschoolers' peer imitation in a play situation. *Child Development*, 1983, *54*, 1041–1053.

Newman, D., Riel, M., & Martin, L. Cultural practices and Piagetian theory: The impact of a cross-cultural research program. In D. Kuhn & J. Meacham (Eds.), *On the development of developmental psychology*. Basel, Switzerland: Karger, 1983.

Paris, S., & Carter, A. Semantic and constructive aspects of sentence memory in children. *Developmental Psychology*, 1973, *9*, 109–113.

Paris, S., & Lindauer, B. The role of inference in children's comprehension and memory for sentences. *Cognitive Psychology*, 1976, *8*, 217–227.

Paris, S., & Lindauer, B. The development of cognitive skills during childhood. In B. Wolman (Ed.), *Handbook of developmental psychology*. Englewood Cliffs, NJ: Prentice-Hall, 1982.

Paris, S., Newman, R., & McVey, K. Learning the functional significance of mnemonic actions: A microgenetic study of strategy acquisition. *Journal of Experimental Child Psychology*, 1982, *34*, 490–509.

Pascual-Leone, J. A mathematical model for transition in Piaget's developmental stages. *Acta Psychologica*, 1970, *32*, 301–345.

Piaget, J. Piaget's theory. In P. Mussen (Ed.), *Carmichael's manual of child psychology* (3rd ed.). New York: Wiley, 1970.

Piaget, J. *Biology and knowledge*. Chicago: University of Chicago Press, 1971.

Pinard, A. *The conservation of conservation: The child's acquisition of a fundamental concept*. Chicago: University of Chicago Press, 1981.

Riegel, K. *Psychology mon amour: A countertext*. Boston: Houghton Mifflin, 1978.

Rosenthal, T., & Zimmerman, B. *Social learning and cognition*. New York: Academic Press, 1978.

Sharp, D., Cole, M., & Lave, J. Education and cognitive development: The evidence from experimental research. *Monographs of the Society for Research in Child Development*, 1979, *44* (Serial No. 178).

Shultz, T., Dover, A., & Amsel, E. The logical and empirical bases of conservation judgments. *Cognition*, 1979, *7*, 99–123.

Siegler, R. Three aspects of cognitive development. *Cognitive Psychology*, 1976, *4*, 481–520.

Siegler, R. Developmental sequences within and between concepts. *Monographs of the Society for Research in Child Development*, 1981, *46* (Serial No. 189).

Siegler, R. Five generalizations about cognitive development. *American Psychologist*, 1983, *38*, 263–277. (b)

Siegler, R. Information processing approaches to development. In P. Mussen (Ed.), *Carmichael's manual of child psychology* (4th ed.). New York: Wiley, 1983. (a)

Siegler, R., & Klahr, D. When do children learn? The relationship between existing knowledge and the acquisition of new knowledge. In R. Glaser (Ed.), *Advances in instructional psychology* (Vol. 2). Hillsdale, NJ: Lawrence Erlbaum Associates, 1982.

Sternberg, R., & Powell, J. The development of intelligence. In P. Mussen (Ed.), *Carmichael's manual of child psychology* (4th ed.). New York: Wiley, 1983.

Trabasso, T. Representation, memory, and reasoning: How do we make transitive inferences? In A. D. Pick (Ed.), *Minnesota symposia on child psychology* (Vol. 9). Minneapolis: University of Minnesota Press, 1975.

Trabasso, T., Isen, A., Dolecki, P., McLanahan, A., Riley, C., & Tucker, T. How do children solve class-inclusion problems? In R. Siegler (Ed.), *Children's thinking: What develops?* Hillsdale, NJ: Lawrence Erlbaum Associates, 1978.

Vygotsky, L. *Mind in society: the development of higher psychological processes.* Cambridge, Mass.: Harvard University Press, 1978.

Werner, H. *Comparative psychology of mental development.* New York: International Universities Press, 1948.

Wertsch, J. From social interaction to higher psychological processes. *Human Development,* 1979, *22,* 1–22.

Wozniak, R. Metaphysics and science, reason and reality: The intellectual origins of genetic epistemology. In J. Broughton & D. J. Freeman-Moir (Eds.), *The cognitive-developmental psychology of James Mark Baldwin: Current theory and research in genetic epistemology.* Norwood, NJ: Ablex, 1982.

5 Current Issues in Language Learning

Lila R. Gleitman
University of Pennsylvania

Eric Wanner
Alfred P. Sloan Foundation

INTRODUCTION

Language is learned, in the normal course of events, by children bright or dull, pampered or neglected, exposed to Tlingit or to English. In Leonard Bloomfield's words, "This is doubtless the greatest intellectual feat any one of us is ever required to perform" (1933, p. 29). Appreciation of the enormity of this human capacity, given the intricacy and variety of the languages of the world, has motivated an intense exploration of language learning by linguists and psychologists alike. Both in topic and in theoretical orientation, these approaches vary marvelously. If there is an anchoring point for the disparate efforts, it is Chomsky's break with the Bloomfieldian tradition of language study and, as a particular consequence, his analysis of the logic of language learning. In this chapter, we first review this paradigmatic change in the theory of language learning. Thereafter, we organize current findings in the field as they bear on these two opposing theoretical positions.

BLOOMFIELD AND CHOMSKY ON LANGUAGE LEARNING

Leonard Bloomfield and Noam Chomsky, in succession, utterly dominated the field of linguistics for periods extending over three decades. Within these time periods it is small overstatement that investigating language was a matter of agreeing or disagreeing in detail with the programs developed by these thinkers. Such a history is commonplace in science; for example, the study of learning in

American psychology, for five decades, was a series of responses pro and con to a general problem as framed by Thorndike. For language, it is of some interest that Bloomfield and Chomsky appear to have been in close agreement on the essential nature of the problem. Both their most influential works (Bloomfield, 1933; Chomsky, 1965) open with an analysis of language acquisition, supposing that the problem of learning a first language and the problem of language description are at bottom one and the same.

According to both these accounts, language is a pairing of forms to meanings. These pairings differ from language to language, e.g., in English the sound /si/ is paired to the meaning ''gaze at with the eyes'' while in Spanish the sound /si/ is paired to the meaning ''yes.'' This variability implies that learning must take place by direct exposure to some particular language. But if there were nothing more to language than such associative pairings between sounds and meanings, learning would probably not be hard to describe. For both Bloomfield and Chomsky, the mystery of the learning feat derives from two further crucial facts about the human use of language: It is rule governed, and it is creative. Bloomfield (1933) wrote:

> It is obvious that most speech forms are regular, in the sense that the speaker who knows the constituents and the grammatical patterns can utter them without having heard them; moreover, the observer cannot hope to list them since the possibilities of combination are practically infinite. For instance, the classes of nominative expressions in English are so large that many possible actor–action forms—say, *a red-headed plumber bought six oranges*—may never have been uttered. (p. 275)

Bloomfield's learner came into the world scantily endowed. He could hear. And he had a single principle of data manipulation that allowed him to classify together materials that occurred in the same positions within utterances. For example, the fact that *the* and *a* both occur sentence-initially, before adjectives and nouns, etc., would be the basis for assigning them to the same class. Bloomfield's learning device could also draw inductive generalizations from the distributional properties of the grammatical classes so formed, and so be able to utter new sentences that exhibited the same regularities: ''A grammatical pattern (sentence type, construction, or substitution) is often called *an analogy*. A regular analogy permits the speaker to utter speech-forms which he has not heard; we say that he utters them *on the analogy* of similar forms which he has heard'' (1933, p. 275).

For Bloomfield, then, a grammar is a description of the analogies that hold for a language, and learning is the set of discovery procedures (the data manipulations) by which the child forms these analogies. The learner first discovers that the continuously varying sound wave can be analyzed into discrete segments (the *phones*), which appear in discoverable recurrent patterns (the *words*), which appear in yet larger recurrent patterns (the *phrases* and *sentences*), all discovered by extracting generalizations about their relative distribution in the corpus presented to the ear (see Harris, 1951, for detailed proposals about discovery procedures at each of these linguistic levels). The child learns to use each sentence appropriately by connecting the learned situation of its use (the stimulus) with its form (the response).[1]

In all fairness to history, Bloomfield was not as explicit as Chomsky in identifying linguistic theory with the problem of language learning, but his position ("The only useful generalizations about language are inductive generalizations," 1933, p. 29) derives coherently from the assumption that child and linguist are in the same position, each required to identify from scratch a linguistic system that potentially might be anything at all: "Features which we think ought to be universal may be absent from the very next language that becomes accessible" (1933, p. 20). If there are no constraints on the form of a natural language, then each child must be endowed with a set of discovery procedures of an entirely unbiased sort to guarantee equally facile learning of any language.

Chomsky's analysis of the learner's problem began in much the same way, with the joint assumptions that the input data are heard sentences (in context) and that the learning procedure must be some sort of inductive generalization from such a corpus. But Chomsky asserted that these assumptions answer the questions about learning only by begging them. After all, how does the child manage to generalize (learn by analogy) always and only from old grammatical sentences to new grammatical sentences? How is the learner to avoid wrong analogies and seize on the right ones? For example, consider a child who has been exposed to the following sentences:

---

[1]Bloomfield (1933) emphasized that the pairing between speech and event must be complex: "Even if we know a great deal about a speaker and about the immediate stimuli which are acting upon him, we usually cannot predict whether he will speak or what he will say." He put this problem down to

"the fact that the human body is a very complex system . . . so that a very slight difference in the state of the body may result in a great difference in its response . . . [we could predict] whether a certain stimulus will lead someone to speak, and, if so, the exact words he will utter . . . if we knew the exact structure of his body at the moment or, what comes to the same thing, if we knew the exact makeup of his organism at some early stage—say, at birth or before—and then had a record of every change in that organism including every stimulus that had ever affected the organism" (p. 33).

Thus, Bloomfield had the courage of his materialist convictions. (See Skinner, 1957, for a modern variant of the same position, but keep in mind that Bloomfield was a professional linguist and made a series of exquisite technical contributions to the study of language structure and history.) Probably no avowed mentalist would disagree with this global claim that speech events are ultimately "caused" by a combination of internal structures and states and the external events they confront. But a large disagreement is whether the description of such speech-to-event relations would constitute an appropriate theory of language knowledge or performance. The problem is that only certain states, events, etc., are relevant to language organization. That is, the relations between sentences and events are mediated by the relations between sentences and their meanings. Presumably, the latter relations constitute a theory of language. (For further discussion, see the final section of this chapter).

1. John painted the barn red.
2. John painted the barn blue.
3. John painted the red barn.
4. John saw the red barn.

By an analogy based on shared relative position, *blue* and *red* can be substituted for one another in Sentences 1 and 2. The child can therefore try the same substitution in Sentences 3 and 4, correctly inducing new sentences such as:

5. John painted the blue barn.
6. John saw the blue barn.

By similar analogy, the child can substitute *saw* for *painted* in Sentences 3 and 4. However, if the child tries this same substitution for Sentences 1 and 2, he or she will make the *false* induction that

7. John saw the barn red.
8. John saw the barn blue.

are acceptable sentences of English. The problem is that some analogies are the right ones and others the wrong ones, but Bloomfield's learner has no means for making these decisions and hence—according to Chomsky—no sure means for acquiring his native tongue.

Chomsky therefore reasoned that the natural languages could not vary arbitrarily from each other, else Bloomfield's claims must hold and language learning would be impossible. Rather, Chomsky argued that the natural languages must share universal properties, and human infants must be biologically disposed to consider only languages embodying these properties. In sum, the problem now becomes one of clothing Bloomfield's learner with a variety of presuppositions about the system to which it is being exposed, narrowing the hypothesis space on which inductions are performed. At the same time, these predispositions must be cast in some very abstract form so as to accommodate the detailed differences among the real languages:

> The real problem is that of developing a hypothesis about initial structure that is sufficiently rich to account for the acquisition of language, yet not so rich as to be inconsistent with the known diversity of language. (Chomsky, 1965, p. 58)

The focal supposition here is that an unbiased problem-solving device, guessing inductively at a grammar from a finite corpus of instances, cannot be guaranteed to arrive at the correct solution. As one more demonstration of this impasse, consider the question of how the learner is to know whether the sample of sentences heard so far come from the language consisting of exactly those sentences, or from some larger corpus. How could the learner know from a sample of English sentences that the correct grammar is not the union of English grammar and Bantu grammar—although, so far, no Bantu sentences are in the corpus (for a discussion, see Fodor, Bever, & Garrett, 1974)? To the retort "Such hypotheses are mad!" comes the counter-retort "But that is the point!" The problem of explaining language learning is essentially the problem of stating which hypotheses are mad and therefore never to be entertained, and which are sane, for a human learner.

One might, of course, propose that children do launch mad hypotheses in the course of learning their native tongues, only to be reined in by parents who correct them. This proposal faces severe problems. The first comes from examining the real interactions of caretakers with young children: Adults rarely correct their fledglings' syntax (Brown & Hanlon, 1970) and even when they do, children rarely pay attention (McNeill, 1966). Still, one could object that negative information might be available to the child in subtle form. A blatantly ungrammatical utterance by the child may fail to elicit the desired response from an adult who might misunderstand it, and this mismatch between childish expectation and adult reaction may be enough to signal the child that something is amiss.

But true as it may be that negative information of this subtle sort could be available to the child, the objection misses two points. One has to do with the complexities in the child's social environment, an environment in which many things other than language learning and teaching are going on. Owing to this complexity, many of the child's utterances are objected to by caretakers on grounds that have nothing to do with syntax, but instead pertain to the truth or social acceptability of what the child says (Brown & Hanlon, 1970). For example, the perfectly grammatical sentence "I'll color the wall red" may be rejected by the mother. How is the child to know that this is a correction of action, not grammar, while the (much rarer) rejection of sentences such as "Me wuvs yer, Mom" is in aid of grammaticality, not social correctness? Woe to the child— both as social being and as speaker of English—who guesses wrong about the basis for these two rejections of what she has said.

Beyond this practical difficulty, the theory that children learn by correction misses a logically prior point: Children hardly ever *require* correction of either direct or subtle varieties. For the overwhelming number of linguistic generalizations the child never errs at all, and therefore no opportunity to correct him ever arises. To be sure, as we shall detail later on, children do make some errors, such as saying "foots" for "feet" or "Mail come" instead of "The mail comes." In such cases, it is possible to believe that children acquire the right forms because they are corrected when they say the wrong forms. But such cases of overt error, while very noticeable to parents and to investigators of child language, are really the exception when compared to the huge number of semantic and syntactic generalizations each child learns without committing any overt errors along the way. To continue with an example mentioned earlier, children learning English do sometimes hear noun-phrases in which an adjective follows a noun, as in "I painted the town red" or "That ice is paper thin" or "Her cheeks were rose red" or "I'm dog tired." But they never overgeneralize, e.g., to "I saw the house red." This failure to make a mistake means that the parent never gets the chance to correct such attempts, either overtly or tacitly.

Thus by and large, it is necessary to assume that the child learns from the "good" sentences he or she hears, i.e., learning from *positive examples,* rather than from being corrected for the "bad" sentences he or she utters, i.e., learning from *negative examples.* Thus the job for investigators of language learning is to explain how, among the myriad grammatical generalizations that children might draw from their limited experience with language, somehow they seem to draw the right ones or very nearly the right ones from the start. That they do so is evident even from examples that are sometimes marshaled to argue just the reverse.

For instance, Ervin (1964) has shown that children are good—all too good— at forming inductive generalizations. Children who at two and three years of age spontaneously and appropriately produce both weak (*talked, pushed*) and strong (*brought, sang*) past-tense endings for English verbs, frequently around age four produce weak endings almost exclusively; that is, they now say "*bringed*" and "*singed*" in systematic violation of the input corpus. For the stock of most frequent English verbs (the ones children are likely to hear), the weak tense ending occurs far less than half the time on types and still less on tokens. This is no formal proof, but it is a clear suggestion that young children are inclined to draw grand inductive generalizations even over noisy data. The corpus violates the generalization the majority of the time; still, the learner evidently prefers a bad generalization to none at all. But now the question must be just how many false generalizations are true of English sentences 30 or 40 percent of the time. For example, it has been noted that substantives preceding *-hood* are very predominantly kinship terms (*childhood, motherhood, neighborhood*) and yet no child supposes that *robin* is a kinship term.

To approach these issues, Chomsky (1965) designed a hypothetical language learner who would be spared these never-ending inductive pitfalls. In some ways, Chomsky's model is an odd candidate for the attention it has received in developmental psycholinguistics, since it was never offered as a serious empirical account of how a child acquires a language. In fact, Chomsky's model is really no more (or less!) than a description of the problem of language acquisition, and it is a description framed from a particular point of view—namely, that in acquiring language the child must master the rules of a generative grammar. However, Chomsky was able to develop a number of very strong claims about acquisition simply by stating the problem in this way, and much of the empirical work in the field can be seen as an effort to develop these claims, to test them, or to reject them outright.

Chomsky's analysis begins with the unarguable claim that children receive little or no formal instruction about the rules that presumably underlie adult performance. Rather, or so it would seem, the child is exposed only to some finite sample of utterances, different for each child, in the presence of certain events and circumstances in the world. Sometimes, though surely not always, these utterances will be appropriate to the circumstances in some way. For instance, a lucky learner may hear "A rabbit is running by" as a rabbit runs by. From such exposure to utterance/situation pairs, the learner must induce a finite representation of the language that projects to an infinite set of sound/meaning pairs.[2]

According to Chomsky's idealization, the child has the internal wherewithal to assign a "partial and tentative" structural description to the input utterance, aided by its context (Chomsky, 1965, p. 32). The child is also armed with an innate linguistic theory that includes all the logical apparatus necessary to construct candidate transformational grammars. An innate learning theory tests these grammars against the input, by matching the structural descriptions generated by the candidate grammar with those given in the primary linguistic data. In case more than one grammar survives this test, Chomsky endowed his hypothetical child with an evaluation measure that provides a way of ranking all the empirically successful grammars. If correct, such a ranking would favor just the grammar that the real child actually emerges with from his encounter with the primary linguistic data.

According to Chomsky's idealization, this process of grammar acquisition takes place instantaneously; that is, grammar construction occurs in the presence of a large body of primary linguistic data, and the evaluation procedure will immediately choose the most highly valued grammar appropriate to these data. Although this is clearly counterfactual, it has never been the source of much controversy because Chomsky was more interested in demonstrating the logical prerequisites to language learning than in making claims about the details of the process. In general, those who have accepted Chomsky's instantaneous model have assumed that it could be "slowed down" without changing any of its essential properties (see, e.g., Roeper, 1982). Those who have rejected this model have objected on other grounds.

We organize our discussion of language learning against the backdrop of Bloomfield's and Chomsky's formulations of the task. Such an organization leaks, in part, for some work in this field verges on issues outside these idealizations. Granting this, we adopt a historical method that is unblushingly Thucydidean, interpreting the varying research efforts in a way that maximizes their joint

---

[2]Note that, although the environment could pair only utterances to situations, the character of learning must be more general than this: To a remarkable degree, adults can assign a compositional meaning to sentences on request, in the absence of external context. And they can comprehend books about ancient history. The theoretical task then becomes: asking how the child recruits information of a certain sort (primary linguistic data, or utterance/situation pairs) and constructs a system of a different sort (sound/meaning, or deep-structure/surface-structure pairs).

coherence. This coherence resides, we believe, in their relation to the logic expressed by these two great linguists, even though some investigators will deny, quite correctly, that they were explicitly influenced by them.

THE CONTENT AND FORM OF THE PRIMARY LINGUISTIC DATA

As Bloomfield and Chomsky would agree, the nature of learning crucially depends on how the learner naturally organizes what he hears; how he represents the input to himself. On Bloomfield's story, the organizing principles must be very general and subject to revision all along the line, for what is to be learned varies arbitrarily. On Chomsky's story, the languages "out there" are of an antecedently well-defined type, so innate knowledge about them is useful; in fact, to the extent that the forms and categories of language are distinct from the forms and categories of cognition in general, innate knowledge of the language principles is the requirement for learning. In detail, the specification of a learning procedure requires the answer to two prior questions having to do with the state of the organism as learning begins: (a) How does the child make a relevant semantic analysis of the situation while listening to adults talk about it; and (b) How does the child analyze the sound wave that results from the adult talk? We address these two issues here. Afterward, in the presence of a tentative specification of the initial state, we address the learning problem: How does the child develop a system that maps between the sounds and the meanings?

Extracting Meaning from the Situation

On Chomsky's formulation, the child is assumed to hear utterances in situations from which she can recover partial and tentative structural descriptions including, of course, some characterization of meaning. No matter the theoretical stance, the same assumption seems to be made by all investigators. For Bloomfield, each "situation" was that extralinguistic event (stimulus) connected by temporal contiguity to a particular linguistic event (response). That all parties agree to the requirement for extralinguistic sources of information is not surprising, for this follows from prior agreement about the analysis of the task: Since a language is a pairing of sounds (linguistic forms) to meanings, and since languages *vary* in these pairings, learning logically requires that samples of the forms be presented, paired with samples of the meanings; the main source for discovering these meanings seems to be in the situations accompanying the speech events. It follows that the prerequisite ability to interpret the real world in a linguistically relevant fashion must exist *ab initio*, if the child is to acquire her native tongue (for an informative discussion, see Wexler, 1982).

It is sometimes assumed that these claims for a learner are quite innocent, that language learning is easy to explain because the child can "rely on meaning from the context." However, it is hard to conceive how such claims could be brought to ground at all. The difficulty is that neither words nor sentences, nor even propositions, are in any direct way encodings of scenes or situations in the world.

As a simplest instance of problems here, consider the fact that a child observing a cat is observing, *a fortiori*, an animal, an object, the nose of a cat, Felix the cat, and the nose-plus-ear of a cat at the same time. Should someone now say "cat," this is presumably the situational context from which the child is to learn that "cat" means 'cat.' But what is to prevent the child from assuming that the meaning is *nose-ear-complex of a cat*, instead? If a (currently unknown) representational principle of mind automatically excludes this as a possible human concept, it is still the case that the child must learn *nose* and *Felix*, as well as *cat*, under these frightful circumstances (Quine, 1960).

These problems re-arise at every level of the linguistic hierarchy, reaching their ultimate exacerbation for the case of the sentence unit. A child who observes a cat sitting on a mat also observes, *a fortiori*, a mat supporting a cat, a mat under a cat, a floor supporting a cat and a mat, and so on. If the adult now says, "The cat is on the mat," even while pointing to the cat on the mat, how is the child to choose among these interpretations of the situation? Especially as the less probable (whatever this means) choices are sometimes made: The adult sometimes does say "What a good bed that mat makes for the cat." Such problems are materially worsened by the fact that the adult may speak of one thing while the child attends to another. The adult may say "Time for your nap" as the child regards the cat on the mat. Worst of all, certain structures in a language, among them those most frequently used with children, are specifically reserved for mismatches with the world: The felicitous occasion for positive imperatives such as "Eat your peas!" or "Go next door to Granny and borrow an egg!" is the absence of pea eating, Grannys, and eggs.

In sum, there is no innocence to the claim that the child learns language by relying on "meaning" or "the world." Nevertheless, it seems impossible to avoid the posit that the child will, in some crucially exploited cases, feel justified in assuming that a sound wave that enters his ear refers in some particular way, from some particular point of view, to a situation he is currently observing, as, for example, cat-on-mat rather than mat-under-cat. Three kinds of evidence bear on (though they do not explain) ways children solve this puzzle: As learning begins, children naturally represent concepts (1) lexically and (2) propositionally; and (3) caretaker and child conspire to converse in ways that map as transparently as possible from these initial lexical and propositional representations to the contexts in which they occur.

The Word Is the Natural Domain of Simple Concepts

Theories of the Lexicon. The classical view of word meaning (Locke, 1690/1965) holds that most words are not simple, but rather are cover labels for a bundle of simpler meaning-atoms, usually called elements, features, or attributes. These basic elements are taken to be those that sensory (or low-level perceptual) experience yields *directly*. Consider a hue experience such as 'red,' assumed (at least for present expository purposes) to be an automatic neural response to specifiable light stimulation. According to the classical theory of word meaning, when a child hears the speech sound "red" while having this experience, he associates the sound with that experience; that association is the meaning of the word *red*.

But on the classical view, the number of basic elements (such as *red*) is rather small, certainly much smaller than the number of words eventually acquired by children. The complex words are built up by combining the simple elements. The basis for combination is generally taken to be the co-occurrence of more than one of the simple elements in experience, and the mechanism for combination is again taken to be association. For example, suppose that *round* and *object*, like *red*, are among the basic elements of experience. If some object that is red and round is usually seen while hearing some speech sound, say, "blitso," then the child will *compose* a new category: the category *blitso* with the meaning 'red round object.' To repeat, the category is constructed because of the co-occurrence of simple elements in experience with each other and with that word.

Compositional theories usually invoke the simple elements for more than learning: The basic elements are taken to be involved in comprehension performances, even those of adults. Pursuing the example above, the learner stores with the sound *blitso*, as its meaning, the list of its elements; i.e., the meaning entry for *blitso* is 'red and round and object.' To speak, the user pulls out *blitso* whenever he wishes to mean 'red and round and object.' To understand the heard word "blitso," the listener looks up this word in his mental dictionary, but does not understand this word directly. Rather, he pulls out its components (red, round, object) and understands these instead. In short, to comprehend words, the listener *decomposes* them into their primitive atoms.

A potential problem for such theories is that not all associates of a word, say, *ball*, could be permanently stored in the head as parts of the meaning of that word. This would be an embarrassment of representational riches, and would sometimes do more harm than good for speaking and understanding. For example, sometimes *ball* is heard in the presence of a red thing, and sometimes in the presence of a green thing. Presumably the learner could not and would not want to store all these color associates as part of the meaning of *ball*. On the contrary: English speakers come to know that *ball* can be used appropriately in total disregard of the color of the object observed. To model this fact, compositional theories of meaning limit the number of elements stored as a word's meaning. In the best-known variant, words are semantically represented by their *definitions*, a smallish subset of the basic elements: just those that are individually necessary and jointly sufficient to determine category membership (Locke, 1690/1965; for recent discussions see, e.g., Katz, 1972). The color of a ball is irrelevant to its category membership and so is not chosen as one of the elements stored as its meaning.[3]

In some more recent variants of compositional semantic theory, the necessary and sufficient conditions of the classical view are dropped, and instead the words are semantically represented as a cluster of elements (Wittgenstein, 1953; for recent discussions, see Rosch, 1975; Rosch & Mervis, 1975). In this variant, there is no criterial (necessary and sufficient) list of the features. Rather, there is a set of features associated with each lexical concept, but an individual falls into the class by partaking of some of them. For example, perhaps a bird is characterizable in terms of such attributes as flying, having feathers, being two-legged, and laying eggs. If these features were jointly necessary for 'birdness,' then neither an ostrich nor a bird amputee could be considered a bird. But according to the cluster theories, it will often be sufficient, for an entity to be identified properly as a bird, simply to have feathers and to lay eggs.

Details aside, the two positions just sketched agree in supposing that most words do not represent elementary concepts, but represent certain combinations of those elementary concepts. Whenever the listener hears a word spoken, she identifies it by the sound of its cover label (e.g., "blitso," in our example) but then extracts its meaning elements (*red, round, object*) as a step in the comprehension process.

A radically different position denies the compositional character of word meaning (for discussion, see Fodor, 1975; Fodor, Garrett, Walker, & Parkes, 1980; Armstrong, Gleitman, & Gleitman, 1983). According to this third kind of theory, both the learning and use of words is *holistic*. The bulk of vocabulary items in a language directly encode the elementary categories of experience rather than being constructs out of some very limited, covert, mental vocabulary of "features." To understand the implications of this view, it is easiest to consider a concrete example of how compositional and holistic theories would describe early word learning.

Consider how the word *cat* is to be acquired. Both approaches agree in assuming that the required condition for learning is that someone says "cat" in

---

[3]The machinery by which these choices are to be made is not easy to describe. Presumably, successive exposures will reveal to the learner that balls are not limited to any particular color. Yet it is logically possible to envisage a machine that would represent such facts by adding to a disjunctive definition, i.e., "a ball is a round thing that is red, or green, or violet, or blue and red striped, or . . ." Further machinery would be necessary to conclude that "any color" is closer to the facts about items standardly called balls. But a further problem is that "any color" is sensibly excluded from the definition too, despite the fact that each observed ball is some color. Redundancy rules are often invoked to handle this problem. All physical objects must be some color—whether they be balls, giraffes, pebbles, or sofas. An efficient dictionary would filter the specification *colored* up to the highest level at which it obtains. That is, balls would be described as colored only insofar as balls are described as being physical objects. Since physical objects are described as colored, balls would inherit this property, but *colored* would not be among the necessary and sufficient features specified for *ball*.

the presence of a cat. But the compositional learner has no way of *directly* perceiving 'catness.' Rather, she is able to experience (out there in the world), say, a shape, whiskers, fur, movement, a sinuous tail (or whatever the elementary experiences really are). Her entry for *cat* is a list of such features—and that list may be modified by subsequent events in which someone says ''cat'' in the presence of some new cat, e.g., a tailless cat. In contrast, the holistic learner is postulated to be able to observe a cat out in the world, under the same conditions, so he directly learns that ''cat'' means 'cat.' This means that, in advance of any learning, the holistic learner is assumed to have the internal (innate) wherewithal sufficient to represent 'catness' and to recognize an instance of that category in the world. Of course this learner, just like the compositional learner, may make errors during learning. Since by hypothesis he can experience animals, giraffes, statues, etc., as well as cats, he may on occasion misidentify and form a wrong meaning for *cat*. Subsequent exposures may cause him to change his entry for the sound ''cat,'' therefore, but that change is not an addition or subtraction of more elementary features.

Lexical Concept Attainment by the Young Child.   Empirical study of the child word learner has some relevance to the issues just addressed. According to the compositional views, it would be reasonable to suppose that the child's innate equipment, that allows him to interpret the world, consists of the elementary features. Moreover, learning word meanings would consist of learning feature by feature. It has been demonstrated that this position can make sense of some of the child's early word use. Specifically, the young child often overgeneralizes the use of a word; for example, he or she may use the word *ball* to refer to all round things, including faces and the moon as well as balls (things perceptually close to balls, see Clark; 1973), or all things she plays with, including dolls and blocks (things functionally close to balls; see Nelson, 1973).

A number of further investigations appeared to offer more detailed support for the compositional approach to lexical learning. For example, one set of experiments seemed to show that children first learned only one or two features of the meaning of *more* and *less,* those sufficient to establish that these words are *comparative* and have to do with *numerosity* (Donaldson & Balfour, 1968; Palermo, 1973): Two- and three-year-old children will change the number of apples on a magnetic tree if told either to ''Make it so there are *more* apples'' or ''Make it so there are *less* apples.'' But to perform this task correctly, i.e., to *add* apples in response to *more* and to *subtract* apples in response to *less,* the children would also have to know that *more* represents the positive pole (greater than some standard numerosity) and that *less* represents the negative pole (smaller than the standard numerosity). The investigators showed that the children did not seem to have this additional information. When asked to ''Make it so there are *less* apples,'' they *added* apples, just as they did for ''Make it so there are *more* apples.'' The compositional theory of meaning handles this outcome by claiming that the young learners had acquired the features *comparative* and *numerosity,* that these words share, but not the features that distinguish them from each other, *positive pole* and *negative pole.*

Unfortunately, this apparent success of compositional theories in describing word learning has turned out to be largely illusory. Carey (1977) asked young children who made the errors on *less* one more question, involving a nonsense syllable: "Make it so there are *tiv* apples on the tree." The children who had added apples for *less* added them for *tiv* as well. This begins to suggest that a partial meaning for *less* is not what led the children astray in the original demonstrations. They stray in just the same way when they have no lexical entry at all. The simplest answer seems to be that children err on *less* (and *tiv*!) just when they have no idea of what the word means. Given the situation of movable apples, their response bias is to add apples rather than to remove them, but this does not imply that they have "partial knowledge" of words like *less.* Thus the original findings cannot be interpreted as supporting a compositional theory any more than they support a holistic theory.

Carey and Bartlett (1978) subsequently studied word learning in a more direct way, by introducing new words to young children in settings that seem natural. For example, they introduced the unknown word *chromium* (to be assigned the meaning 'olive green') to two- and three-year-olds during play in the following way: Interrupting the ongoing activity, the experimenter pointed toward two trays (one red, one olive green) and said to the child "Get me the chromium tray; not the red one, the chromium one." The contrast color (here, *red*) was always one that pretests had established were known to the child. The children were tested about a week later for what they had learned from this single introducing circumstance. That half the children failed to remember anything about *chromium* is no surprise. But fully half of them had made an initial mapping between *chromium* and color concepts. To be sure, they differed in what they had learned; some children knew that *chromium* meant 'olive green,' others knew only that it was a color word, others that it was a synonym for *green,* and so on. Two properties of this learning are of special interest for evaluating the feature-by-feature learning hypothesis. The first is the rapidity of mapping—learning a meaning from a single introducing event. This is inconsistent with the idea that word meaning always is built up through repeated exposures, that dissociate necessary features from adventitious properties of a single event. The second is that the children's entries for *chromium,* while sometimes "wrong," could rarely be characterized as wrong in the sense of being incomplete. The results seem best characterized by saying the children learned a whole word concept, sometimes the one intended by the experimenter ('olive green') and sometimes some other one (e.g., 'green').

The Carey and Bartlett experiments thus provide a first evidentiary basis for a holistic theory of early word learning. Examination of the lexicons of very young children gives further support to this position, though only in a negative way: by displaying more of the difficulties of the feature-by-feature view. If children were initially sensitive to a very small set of properties that were constitutive of word meanings, it is plausible to suppose that the (relatively few) words that encoded only these elementary properties would be among the first vocabulary items acquired. For example, if a bird is, notionally, a two-legged, feathered, flying, animal, we would expect items such as *feather(ed)*, *fly(ing)* and *animal* to appear earlier than *bird* in the child's lexicon. But the facts seem to be otherwise, with these terms usually appearing in just the opposite order to that predicted: Property terms and superordinate terms are late, compared to basic object terms, in the vocabularies of child learners (cf., Nelson, 1973; Rosch, 1973; Rosch, Mervis, Gray, Johnson, & Boyes-Braem, 1976). Similarly, children learn verbs with many features (if they have features) as easily as verbs with few (if they have features). *Walk* and *run* must have *move* as one of their features; and yet the former words are usually learned before *move*, and there is no obvious stage of learning at which *run* means only *move* (Gentner, 1978, 1982; see Carey, 1982, for an important general discussion of lexical concept attainment).

Despite the descriptive difficulties of compositional theories that we just reviewed, there is good reason to be cautious about accepting the holistic theory of lexical concept attainment as the correct position. For one thing, componential theories of word meaning and word learning are hardly dead in the water. Various rescue operations are very much alive, often proceeding by increasing the power of the logical combinatorial machinery that organizes featural descriptions (Katz, 1972). Moreover, the underlying implications of the holistic view are so awesome as to dictate a wary stance. To embrace it, one must be prepared to suppose that there are as many *simple* categories of experience as there are, say, easy vocabulary items in a language, i.e., that the learner's innate conceptual furnishings are much more extensive and various than are supposed by compositional theories (Fodor, 1975, 1983). In the light of this implication and the fragmentary nature of currently available evidence, a certain agnosticism on these matters may be the best stance to adopt. We do accept as a tentative state-of-the-art generalization that the child selects the linguistic formative *word* as the repository for his elementary experiences with the world. This is the framework principle according to the holistic approach, but at present it is best interpreted more as a program for research than as a theoretical conclusion. Appropriately, Carey's and related early work just cited have been the basis for a burgeoning exploration designed to discover the conditions of learning, the kinds of words learned under varying exposure conditions, the organization of words in the lexicon as a whole, and so on (for further discussion, see Keil, 1979; Markman, Horton, & McLanahan, 1980; Waxman & Gelman, unpublished manuscript).

Before leaving this topic, it is important to note that in present guises neither of the approaches just discussed really touches the problem with which we began: How, when, and why does the learner who can putatively observe Felix, a cat, an animal, a thing (or elements constitutive of these), decide which such representation of the world is apposite to a particular external event? This problem area is certainly being addressed, e.g., in the work of Eleanor Rosch and her collaborators on the child's bias towards so-called "basic-level" concepts (Rosch et al., 1976). But general solutions are not likely to be just around the corner.

The Three Bears Description: Formatives Higher and Lower Than the Word Are Learned Late

Details aside, we have organized the literature as suggesting that single words encode single concepts for very young children. But many words are morphologically complex and encode more than one concept at a time. One case is the word *walked*, which encodes tense as well as the lexical content 'walk.' How is the child to treat such items, if he or she associates the linguistic notion *word* with a single conceptual notion? We believe that early speech is consistent with the idea that the child rejects such complexity within the word. Moreover, the child seems to take a very strict view of the way words function as components of propositions; namely, that *each word must code exactly one of the arguments of a predicate, the predicate itself, or a logical word* (such as *and* or *or*). Let us term this The Three Bears description of the roles words play in earliest sentences: To the extent a received word codes more than one of the countenanced functions, it is too big; less than one, it is too small; exactly one, and it is just right. It is because this equation of propositional functions with single words is untrue of the adult language that the child's interpretation of the scope of a word will often differ from the adult's.

One line of evidence comes from the acquisition of American Sign Language (ASL). This manual communication system has by now been studied sufficiently to determine that it is formally and substantively equivalent to other natural languages, differing from these mainly in the modality (eye and hand, rather than ear and mouth) that carries the information (Klima and Bellugi, 1979). Therefore, the case of ASL is not too far afield to consider here, and for the present issue it is particularly informative. Newport and Ashbrook (1977) have shown an early tendency to map each relational element of this system as a separate lexical (sign) item. Certain ASL predicates morphologically incorporate some of their arguments. For example, the actor of *give* is uniformly expressed in the mature language as a modulation of the *give* sign, not as an independent sign. But child learners, systematically violating these input data, express the agent of *give* as a separate sign. The generalization is to the effect that each argument and the predicate ought to be carried by a separate wordlike item. No single word can be both predicate and argument (that would be "too big"), so *give* is first interpreted as carrying only one of these functions.

Even more common is the young learner's indifference to further meanings and functions (other than predicate, argument, logical vocabulary) coded inside the word unit; for example, tense or number. (They are "too small".) Evidence suggests that complex words such as *knew* (know + ed) and *don't* (do + not) are treated as unanalyzed wholes by the youngest learners, and only much later unpacked. Errors such as *knowed* developmentally succeed instances of *knew,* as we mentioned earlier (also see Klima & Bellugi, 1966, for this treatment of first negative words). Newport (1981, 1982) has demonstrated for a range of items that young ASL users acquire holistic "frozen signs," only later analyzing these into a root form with associated derivational and inflectional modulations; Gleitman and Gleitman (1970) offer a similar discussion of children's holistic treatment of English compound nouns. The appropriate generalization seems to be that semantic information within the word (e.g., tense) that is neither argument, predicate, nor logical word simply goes unanalyzed at earliest stages, as our Three Bears description predicts.

Morphological analysis of the word item is not only late: it is variable in the linguistic population. Gleitman and Gleitman (1970) have shown that the bulk of mature speakers have difficulty analyzing the internal morphology of English compound nouns. Freyd and Baron (1982) have shown that vocabulary size for academically average eighth-graders and for precocious fifth-graders is about the same for morphologically simple items, but the talented fifth-grade youngsters have a massive advantage for morphologically complex items. Indeed, certain kinds of creative activities involving productive morphological analysis do eventually appear in the repertory of the developing child. For one such process, see Clark (1982) on the creation of denominative verbs by young speakers of English, French, and German. For another, see Bowerman (1982) on the emerging understanding of English lexical causatives. Although such analyses do take place, the authors just cited agree that these are not among the first developments. In fact, Bowerman tenders the same interpretation of her findings as do we: Each early word is an unopened package; only much later does productive lexical analysis begin to appear.

This formulation of early lexical concept attainment allows us to reapproach a famous incident recorded by McNeill (1966) and to interpret it further. McNeill's 2-year-old subject remarks "Nobody don't like me." His mother corrects him: "No, say 'Nobody likes me'." The child mulishly repeats himself. The mother stubbornly recorrects. This interchange repeats itself seven times. On the eighth correction, the child says "Oh: Nobody don't likes me." McNeill takes this as a very strong indication that overt corrections do not very much affect language learning, and we concur. But perhaps we can say more about what the child is willing to revise (adding the *s*) and what he is not (omitting the negative). He is indifferent to the *s* on the grounds just stated—it is not a predicate, an argument, or a logical word—so he can take it as well as leave it. But he cannot apparently conceive that the logical notion *negative* does not have its own separable lexical reflex. He cannot accept that, in a cranky rule of English, the negative can be incorporated into the subject nominal (and, what is more, still have the verb phrase in its semantic scope).

Summarizing, children seem to approach language learning equipped with conceptual interpretive abilities for categorizing the world. As Slobin (1973) has proposed, learners are biased to map each elementary semantic idea (concept) onto the linguistic unit *word*. We have interpreted Carey's findings of holistic word learning as one explication of this proposal: Internal analysis of the word unit is a late and variable step in cognitive–linguistic development. We have also just examined the word as a functional unit in the sentence, concluding that the lexical items are at first stages the linguistic expressions of predicates, their arguments, and logical items.

The Sentence is the Natural Domain of Propositions

A fascinating line of research, beginning with Bloom's (1970) groundbreaking work on children's spontaneous speech, provides evidence at another level about how children meaningfully interpret the world. From the earliest two-word utterances, the ordering of the component words interpreted against their context of use suggests that they are conceived as playing certain thematic roles, such as *agent, instrument,* and the like, within a predicate–argument (propositional) structure (Bloom, Lightbown, & Hood, 1975; Bowerman, 1973; Braine, 1976; Brown, 1973). Greenfield and Smith (1976) have maintained that even isolated first words betray, by their relation to events, rudiments of this propositional conception. Feldman, Goldin-Meadow and Gleitman (1978) have shown that a similar componential analysis describes a manual system of communication developing in isolated deaf children who received no specifically linguistic input, who neither heard speech nor saw formal signing (for further discussion, see Goldin-Meadow, 1982).

To be sure, as Braine (1976) has pointed out, it is by no means clear precisely what these first relational categories are, whether terms such as *agent* are appropriate in scope and content to describe them (see, for example, Braine & Hardy, 1982, for experimental manipulations designed to extract the detailed content of these categories in young children). But whatever the initial categories, there seems to be little doubt that the child approaches language learning equipped with a propositional interpretation of the scenes and events in the world around him. This is not particularly surprising. After a modest number of observations, Premack's chimpanzee, Sarah, can learn to put a sticky star on the agent and a sticky circle on the patient, as shown in brief video movies (Premack, forthcoming). If Sarah, why not human children?

The question remains how much this tells about learning a language. This depends on whether the categories and forms of natural language sentences are simple with respect to the preexisting meaning structures. From varying perspectives, a number of authors have assumed that linguistic categories and forms map transparently from the meaning structures, and hence that the bulk of explanatory apparatus—for child learner and for developmental psycholinguist—exists when these categories are isolated and described (e.g., Bates & MacWhinney, 1982; Braine & Hardy, 1982; Bloom, 1973, 1983). This view is not unreasonable on the face of it. After all, we previously subscribed to the view that the mapping between words and concepts may be quite direct. The question now on the table is whether the relation between sentences and propositional thought is as straightforward as the relation between words and concepts may be (see also Section 3.1 for further discussion of this issue).

A singularly interesting source for understanding this issue is Slobin (1982). Using evidence from a variety of natural languages, he argues that an explanation of language learning from the cognitive–interpretive basis is strictly limited by the real variation among languages. Partly different aspects of meaning are coded in the syntax of different languages. As one of many examples, the child will have to discover whether his language codes tense or aspect, or both, in the syntax. Moreover, even within a single language, it is obvious that there are many ways to say the same thing. So in this sense, too, it is massively overexuberant to hope that knowing meaning is tantamount to knowing language. As Bowerman (1982) has argued, the learner must eventually transcend his initial semantic-categorial organization of language to acquire certain grammatical categories and functions that crosscut these.

Motherese: Saying the Obvious

It is possible to suppose that caretakers' speech to young children has properties that respond to the problems we have been discussing, properties that enhance the probability that learner and teacher will be referring to the same matters from the same perspectives (for the clearest statement of this hypothesis, see Bruner, 1974/75). When speaking to the youngest learners, mothers use language that is propositionally simple, limited in vocabulary, slowly and carefully enunciated, repetitive, deictic, and usually referring to the here and now (Broen, 1972; Cross, 1977; Newport, 1977; Phillips, 1970; Snow, 1977). These same properties of speech to young children have been reported in various language communities (Blount, 1970; Schieffelin, 1979) and social classes (Snow et al., 1976) and among various caretaker types, even including the 4-year-old playmates of 2-year-old learners (Sachs & Devin, 1976; Shatz & Gelman, 1973). Although the syntactic forms vary considerably both within and across caretakers, topics to the youngest listeners are interestingly narrow in range. They are mostly a matter of focusing the listener's attention on a present scene or thing and getting him or her to act upon, or at least gaze upon, that thing: *action directives* (Newport, Gleitman & Gleitman, 1977; Shatz, 1978).

These descriptive facts about maternal speech cohere on the view that it is a matter of getting together with the young listener on what is meant. The motivation for the caretakers is not hard to find, nor need it be explicitly linguistic-tutorial. We need only suppose that the mother wishes to be understood and obeyed, and these properties will fall out.[4]

---

[4]These properties fall out because, apparently, no matter what you say to a young child, it responds by acting, if it responds at all. Shatz (1978) has shown that there is a good match between what mothers say (mothers' speech consists largely of *action directives;* whatever the syntactic form,

But one's enthusiasm for the explanatory potential of these findings requires a good deal of tempering. They suggest only *that* mother and child endeavor to represent the ongoing scene "in the same way" but do not suggest *how* they manage to do so. The explanation rests on the (unknown) cognitive system that learner and teacher share, such that in some critically exploited cases they will interpret the same scene in the same way. To be sure, contributions to the solution of such problems are currently appearing; an exemplary discussion, based on syntactic analyses, of bridges between linguistic and conceptual categories has been provided by Jackendoff (1983; see also Landau & Gleitman, in press), and we have also mentioned such experimental work as Keil's (1979), which attempts to describe the child's ontological categories. But the question here is how the *caretaker,* by special manipulations, may be helping the child understand the words and sentences she hears. Contributors to the literature on maternal speech assert—both innocuously and probably truly—that mothers say "what is obvious" or "what is salient" to children, but this terminological fiat does not seem to resolve anything. The question is why is what's obvious or salient as obvious or salient as it is. If the caretaker's special manipulations help the child understand what is obvious to the caretaker, what is it that allows the child to understand the special significance of these manipulations?

As an instance of the underlying problems here, it is instructive that children blind from birth learn the same lexical items and thematic relations in about the same order as do sighted children (Landau, 1982; Landau & Gleitman, in press), though clearly what is "here" or "now" must differ for the blind and the sighted listener. A blind 3-year-old knows, for example, that she is to perform different acts if told to *show* an object or to *give* it to a sighted listener. It is not at all obvious how the mothers of blind children differentially model the here and now so as to secure these surprising competencies.[5] Such findings of course

---

the intent is to get the child to act) and what children are inclined to do. Children "behave" in response to speech acts they even partly understand. They are likely to pick up the blocks if you say "Pick up your blocks" or "Could you pick up your blocks?" but they are just as likely to act even if your intent is merely to get information. For example, if you ask, "Can you jump to the moon?" you are liable to get a little jump from the child listener. If the mother is implicitly aware that this is the child's bias, and her motive is to be obeyed—or, what comes to the same thing, to display for herself and others the child's competence—she will select action directives when she speaks to the child. All descriptive evidence supports the view that action directives occur far more often (proportionally) in speech to younger children than in speech to older children and adults. These joint motivations in tutor and learner probabilistically increase the likelihood that the child's interpretation of the meaning of the maternal speech act will be correct.

[5]The finding here is that the blind child holds up an object for the sighted listener to perceive at a distance when told to "show" but delivers it to that listener when told to "give." Moreover, the child evidently adapts perceptual-cognitive terms to her own requirements, again in ways that are hard to explain as effects of maternal modeling. She distinguishes *touch* (contact manually) from *look* as used of herself (apprehend manually). For example, she touches her back to "Touch behind you"

cannot vitiate the claim that children learn language by "relying on meaning in the world." Rather they suggest that—since language clearly *is* learned by relying on meaning in the world—explaining language learning is more mysterious than ever.

Extracting Form from the Sound Wave

Though children may have their own devices for extracting meaning from situations, they will need other kinds of devices for extracting linguistically functioning units from the sound wave. Recall that Bloomfield's learner (and hence structural linguistics [cf. Bloch, 1941; Harris, 1951]) approached the gloriously confusing, continuously varying sound wave in a spirit of complete open-mindedness. This learner, like any objective physicist, would have no excuse to chop the complex and continuous wave form into discrete, linguistically functioning units, and even less excuse to classify these units as real speakers–listeners do. The problem of discovering the language forms from the sound waves, then, is directly comparable to the problem of discovering the meanings from the situations: What makes the learner digitalize the wave, break it into whole phones rather than halves of phones, whole words and phrases rather than nonintegral sequences of these, and so on? The analyses chosen are not inevitable inductions from the wave forms. We ask here what kinds of evidence are available to a listener with the right capacities and inclinations, to determine the forms of particular languages.

The Unit "Phone"

Chao (1934) demonstrated in a brilliant analysis of Chinese that no unified discovery procedure for a classificational scheme for sound-segments was likely to be discovered, because the criteria sufficient to isolate the phones of a particular language could not simultaneously be met (i.e., they were mutually contradictory). Classical phonemics nevertheless continued for some twenty years more to try, apparently on the plausible assumption that, if babies can do it, why not linguists? But babies could not. Therefore, language learners all over the world must be grateful to the Haskins Laboratory group of researchers who have

---

but feels in the space behind her for "Look behind you," without turning her head. She taps a cup when told to touch it, but explores it all over, manually, when told to look at it. She happily stabs at the air above in response to "Touch up" but is angry (when there's nothing to be found there) when responding to "Look up." She responds by touching when told "Touch it but don't look at it" but with confusion when told "Look at it but don't touch it." What claims about the natural categorial representations of humans account for the fact that blind and sighted children represent perceptual exploration so similarly, despite different sources of exposure to the world? It seems that the developmental literature substitutes semantic categories for syntactic ones successfully only by failing to define the former. For the present instance, we will require a semantic description of a term like *look* that subsumes the blind experience.

saved them the bother: The children need never learn to segment the acoustic wave phonetically just because they perceive such a segmentation "automatically" (see particularly Liberman, 1970; Liberman, Cooper, Shankweiler, & Studdert-Kennedy, 1967; for studies of infant phonetic perception, see Eimas, Siqueland, Jusczyk, & Vigorito, 1971; Jusczyk, 1980).

There is much controversy about the size and specific nature of the phonetic segments (for a summary discussion, see Foss & Hakes, 1978)—about whether they are the unique property of human organisms or belong to chinchillas and macaques as well (Kuhl & Miller, 1975), and about whether they derive from properties of speech perception in particular or auditory perception in general (Cutting & Rosner, 1974; Liberman & Pisoni, 1977; Newport, 1982). But these problems do not mitigate the case for rejoicing among the aspiring language learners. For them, it is enough to note that no learning apparatus is required for an initial segmentation of the acoustic wave into discrete phones. This segmentation has already been provided in the nervous system.

At this level, then, an objective, highly instrumented sequence of empirical investigations shows that the language learner has relevant information in advance about the inventory of possible phonetic elements (see Jakobson, 1941, for a seminal discussion in this context). It is interesting that in light of these findings from the acoustics laboratory, American psychology has felt entirely comfortable in adjusting to the fact of innate prespecification at this level. The curiosity is that findings of this sort seem not at all to suggest to many psychologists that higher-level language units may be prespecified in the same or a related sense. However, further findings from language learning suggest that the child has more in his bag of tricks than the phones, as learning begins.

The Unit "Word"

The learner must recover words, word classes, and phrases from their encoding in the wave form. Distributional properties of the phonetic sequences are inadequate bases for these further discoveries, for the phonetic sequences woefully underdetermine the identification of words (is it *an adult* or *a nuhdult*?), word classes (is *yellow* a noun, verb, or adjective?), and phrase boundaries (e.g., *I saw a man eating fish*). Our question, then, is whether there are units—above and beyond the phonetic distinctive features—that physically are manifest in the wave form and operative in the child's induction of language structure.

In an earlier discussion we claimed that the child selects the word unit and identifies it as the linguistic repository of simple concepts. But how does the child extract this linguistic unit from the utterance-context in which it is embedded? The child is rarely offered single words, so this problem is real. Slobin (1973) rightly conjectured that there must be some "acoustically salient" and "isolable" property of words that children can discover prelinguistically, else these claims about word and concept learning beg the question that is at issue. Here, we organize the known facts about the emergence of speech in a way we believe bears on this problem. We will try to demonstrate that there *is* an acoustically salient property well correlated with the linguistic unit *word*. This property, we argue, is an abstract characterization of the sound wave whose surface manifestation in English and other stress–accent languages is the *stressed syllable*. And we will try to show that early speech is consistent with our claim that the child is especially sensitive to this feature of the incoming property of the wave forms.[6]

The most striking fact about the English speaker's first utterances is that the little "functor" words are approximately absent; hence, the speech sounds "telegraphic" (Brown & Bellugi, 1964). To this extent, the child's early linguistic behavior again deviates systematically from the environmental model. Children have their own ideas about the forms, just as they have their own ideas about the meanings. It is particularly interesting that youngsters learning Russian omit the inflectional affixes that are the main device for marking the thematic roles in that language, adopting instead a word order strategy that has poor support in the input data (i.e., the speech of their Russian mothers; see Slobin, 1966). In light of this finding, it is impossible to suppose that the functors are omitted on the grounds that they are not semantically important. Surely it is important to distinguish between the do-er and the done-to and, as just stated, the youngest Russian learners do make this distinction, but by means of word ordering, not inflections. Given these findings, it is not surprising that some investigators have supposed that word order is easy and inflection is hard for the youngest learners. That is to say, they have described these findings as facts about earliest *syntax* (see, e.g., Feldman et al., 1978). Note, however, that it is not easy to bring this syntactic claim to bear on all the little words that are missing from earliest speech. The personal pronouns, the prepositions, the specifiers, are approximately as absent as the inflectionally functioning auxiliaries (e.g., *will*) and affixes (e.g., *-ed*). A bias toward word ordering rather than inflection does not describe these facts very satisfactorily. But if we claim instead that *the unstressed items* are what are missing, we approximate the real facts about early speech very well (see Kean, 1977, for a related hypothesis and the argument that it is relevant to describing aphasic speech).

One immediate objection to this proposed generalization is that, if the child learner is differentially sensitive to stress in the speech signal, he should not be able to tell—for a language such as English—the difference between an un-

---

[6]The specific acoustic correlates of primary stress in English include longer duration, higher fundamental frequency, and intensity (see Lehiste, 1970, for general discussion and the evidence from analysis of the speech wave and its perception). For the following argument to hold, it would be necessary to show that the same, or definably analogous, acoustic properties are available and exploited to mark phrase boundaries in the nonstress-accent languages, and that these are the properties reproduced in early child utterances. This prediction seems plausible enough, e.g., features such as rhythmicity and prepausal lengthening seem to be universal properties of speech, differing only in the details of how they map onto the phrasal units.

stressed morpheme and the unstressed syllables of monomorphemic words. However, there is good evidence, widely known but rarely mentioned, that young speakers cannot make this distinction very well. For example, it is striking that words are often first pronounced as their stressed syllables, e.g., "raff" for *giraffe* and "e-fant" for *elephant*. Moreover, when the unstressed syllables begin to be uttered, it is often in undifferentiated form (as the syllable schwa, /ə/, for all instances), for example "əportcard" for *report card,* "tape-ə-cor-də" for *tape recorder*.[7] Particularly interesting at this stage is the frequent misanalysis of clitic pronouns as the unstressed syllables of preceding words, e.g., "read-it" and "have-it," yielding such utterances as "Readit ə book, Mommie?" and "Have-it ə cookie." These properties of earliest speech suggest that the child analyzes stressed syllables reasonably well, but is less successful in rendering the unstressed syllables and in segmenting the wave form into words on this basis (see also Blasdell & Jensen, 1970, who have shown that young children are better at repeating stressed syllables than unstressed syllables in words presented for imitation; Spring & Dale, 1977, who demonstrated that young infants can discriminate the acoustic correlates of stress location in di-syllables; and Fernald, 1982, 1983, who has shown that infants prefer to listen to speech with the exaggerated prosodic properties of "motherese" even when this speech is filtered to remove all of its segmental content).

Later stages of speech development lend weight to the same generalization. Bellugi (1967) has demonstrated that when the elements of the English verbal auxiliary make their first appearance in children's speech, the items are in their full, rather than their contracted, form—e.g., "I will go" rather than "I'll go"—for some developmental time. This is in contrast to the input corpus (mothers' speech) in which, as Bellugi has shown, these items are contracted in the overwhelming majority (over 90%) of instances. Evidently, the contracted version of a word fails to be the acoustically salient element the child requires, if we take *stressed syllable* to be the appropriate specification of "salience."

Further evidence comes from investigations of input effects on learning. Newport, Gleitman, and Gleitman (1977) provided correlational evidence that the rate of learning of English verbal auxiliary elements is accelerated for children whose mothers used them proportionally most often in the noncontractable, stressed, sentence-initial position (by asking many yes/no questions, such as "Will you pick up the blocks?"). In contrast, the sheer frequency of auxiliary use (ignoring stress and position) is uncorrelated with learning rate. These results are very reliable. The correlations between yes/no questions and the child's rate

---

[7]These phenomena have not been closely studied, to our knowledge, doubtless because their theoretical interest has not been very clear. Hence, we can give no quantitative evidence about how often errors of this kind occur, though surely they are not rare. Anecdotal evidence favoring the view that the unstressed items are at first undifferentiated is quite persuasive. For example, the child of our acquaintance who said "əportcard" at an early stage of development said "Can we go to grandma's repartment house?" just as she switched to "report card."

of auxiliary growth are in the range of .80 even after partialing to correct for baseline differences among the children studied (see Furrow, Nelson, & Benedict, 1979, for a replication of this effect; and Gleitman, Newport, & Gleitman, 1984, for further discussion). It is reasonable to hypothesize either that initial position favors learning (a prediction that would follow from any theory of learning in which memory is a factor) or that the noncontracted, stressed form favors learning. We consider it likely that both these properties are relevant to the observed learning effects.

Intriguing new evidence for the same generalization comes from Slobin (1982), who has studied comprehension among 2- to 4-year-old learners of English, Italian, Serbo-Croatian, and Turkish. The Turkish children comprehended Turkish inflectional cues to thematic roles earlier in life than the learners of Serbo-Croatian comprehended Serbo-Croatian inflectional cues to thematic roles. This is exactly the prediction we would have to make on the supposition that stressed items are available earlier in development than are unstressed items: According to Slobin, the relevant inflectional items in Turkish are a full syllable long, are stressed, do not deform the surrounding words phonetically, and do not contract or cliticize. In Kean's (1979) terms, these items are phonologically *open class*. The late-comprehended Serbo-Croatian inflectional items are subsyllabic, stressless, and phonetically deformed by adjacent material (phonologically *closed class*). In sum, these two languages differ according to whether the inflectional cues to the thematic roles are encoded onto isolable stressed syllables, or not. This distinction predicts the differences in learning rate.

In the other two languages investigated by Slobin, English and Italian, the thematic roles are cued primarily by word order, not inflection. Thus, as with Turkish, they do not require the young learner to notice stressless grammatical items in order to recover the relational roles. Accordingly, there are no main-effect differences in the rate of the relevant comprehension development between Turkish and these two other languages. Only Serbo-Croatian stands apart, showing a clear delay at each point in development.

Our position is that a single principle, the advantage of stressed materials over unstressed materials, accounts for Slobin's main finding: The one language among the four investigated that requires attention to stressless materials for recovering thematic roles is the one for which comprehension is delayed. Inflection itself poses no severe problem for the learner when it is encoded on stressed materials, as in Turkish, nor does sequence pose a severe problem under the same circumstances. Recent evidence from the acquisition of Quiche Mayan (Pye, 1983) is particularly informative. For many verbs in certain syntactic environments, this language stresses inflectional suffixes, while the verb root is unstressed. Young learners often pronounce only one of these two syllables; that is, they are forced to make the choice between the semantically salient root and the perceptually salient suffix. They very consistently choose perceptual salien-

cy, pronouncing the inflection and omitting the root. In fact, morpheme boundary and syllable boundary often do not coincide in this language, providing a
good testing ground for what it is the child is actually picking up and reproducing
of the verb that he or she hears. According to Pye, these children reproduce the
syllable unit rather than the morpheme unit: Often, they pronounce the whole
syllable consisting of the final consonant of the unstressed verb root and the
whole terminus, the inflectional suffix.

Summarizing, the cross-linguistic evidence strongly supports the view that the
unit *stressed syllable* is highly salient perceptually and organizes early speech.
Stressed verb roots are pronounced early (English, Turkish, Italian, and Serbo-
Croatian) and unstressed verb roots are often omitted (Mayan); symmetrically,
stressed inflections are pronounced early (Turkish, Mayan) and unstressed inflections are often omitted (English, Serbo-Croatian). Insofar as attention to
unstressed inflections is crucial to recovering the argument structure, the child
will show some delay in comprehension (Serbo-Croatian). Insofar as the pronun-
ciation of the verb roots is obviously necessary to the adult's comprehension of
the child's message, child messages in those languages that contain unstressed
roots will be hard to understand (Mayan, as noted by Pye, 1983).[8]

The generalizations we have been considering are perforce limited to the
stress–accent languages. As Chomsky has pointed out (see Section 1), the trick
is not to make the learning of some languages easy to describe, if the cost is
rendering the learning of others forever mysterious. That is, something more
abstract than the notion *stress* in the sound wave may be required to account for

---

[8]Notice that Mayan is the only one of the languages just discussed that does not usually confound
inflection with stress. This confound is what makes the extraction of the currect learning variables so
difficult. The same confound between inflectional items and unstressed items complicates interpretation of the many studies of related distinctions in adult performance. Thus there is controversy as to
whether the phonological or syntactic properties of the closed class account for their different
patterning in various tasks with various populations. For example, Kean (1979) has explained certain
speech and comprehension impairments in Broca's aphasics on the phonological hypothesis, while
Marin, Saffran, and Schwartz (1976) emphasize the syntactic distinctiveness of the items these
aphasics cannot manage. Current evidence, for the various task domains, is insufficient to give
overwhelming support to one or the other hypothesis, though only the phonological hypothesis can
serve as part of the explanation—rather than mere description—of language learning. But for the
learning hypothesis to do work, it must be that the acoustic facts correlate with the syntactic facts to
be learned, and so either or both properties could account for distinctive adult performance with open
and closed class. Whatever the correct analysis, it has recently become clear that the open-
class/closed-class distinction has highly reliable effects in a broad range of adult linguistic performances. For example, speech errors differ for the two classes (Fromkin, 1973; Garrett, 1975); lexical
access differs for the two in normals but not in Broca's aphasics (Bradley, Garrett, & Zurif, 1979);
intrasentential code-switching constrains the two classes distinctively (Joshi, 1983); and forgetting
differs in language death (Dorian, 1978). Reading acquisition also differs for the two classes (Labov,
1970; Rozin & Gleitman, 1977), as does the historical development of writing systems (Gleitman &
Rozin, 1977) and the reliability and patterning of judgments of anomaly and paraphrase (Gleitman &
Gleitman, 1979).

this aspect of learning, given the real diversity among the natural languages (see fn. 6 to this chapter). The only well studied case we know of, apart from stress–accent languages, are studies of ASL by Newport and her colleagues (Newport & Ashbrook, 1977; Newport, 1981, 1982). We have noted that learners of ASL first treat each sequentially produced sign as an unanalyzed whole, a "frozen form." The extraction of derivational and inflectional substructures within these signs appears only in later developmental steps (see also Klima and Bellugi, 1979). The question is how to describe the physical, visually observable, manifestation called a separable *sign*.

The linguistic analyses by this group seem to us to suggest physically based distinctions between the frozen-form morphological means of ASL (e.g., handshapes) and the inflectionally and derivationally functioning morphology (e.g., certain movement types that modulate form and meaning). The latter, specially formed and specially functioning properties of manual language, are acquired later. That is to say, there seems to be evidence here for "visually salient," "isolable" properties of visible signs that are analogous to the "acoustically salient" isolable properties of speech signals. Whether there is a substantive principle of similarity underlying this analogy remains, of course, a matter for further investigation.

Whatever the ultimate description of the child's predispositions toward linguistic forms, when framed broadly enough to encompass the real languages and narrowly enough to tame induction so that language can be learned, it will almost certainly show that the child does not approach the speech wave or the visible stream of sign like an objective physicist or structural linguist. To the extent that the child must learn language by discovering the distributional properties of the input corpus (as Bloomfield stipulated), the inductive machinery appears to be constrained by the way the organism represents the materials on which induction operates (as Chomsky stipulated). In addition to discrete, featural descriptions at the phonetic level, we have argued that the child has at his or her disposal another analysis of the input. For certain well-studied languages, a physical distinction between stress and nonstress is an interim characterization. For ASL, there seems to be a related physical distinction. Appropriate characterization of the unit awaits investigation of the acquisition of nonstress–accent languages.

Sequence

We have so far determined that the child is sensitive, from earliest developmental moments, to (1) phonetic segments and (2) stressed syllables. There is clear evidence, again from early points in language learning, that the child is sensitive to the ordering both of the phonetic segments and of the stressed syllables. For the phonetic segments, it is enough to say that children seem to know *tap* from *pat* from *apt*. Errors that can be characterized as phone-order confusions are rare (though not altogether absent, e.g., transpositions such as "pə-sketti" for *spaghetti*). There is also very good evidence that sensitivity to the order of words in sentences emerges early.

During the period when the unstressed syllables are mostly missing and ill-analyzed, the child starts uttering more than one word at a time. There is massive evidence that at this point the words are sequenced in the rudimentary sentence. To be sure, the child's observance of ordering constraints are less exact than the adult's; moreover, there is controversy about the nature of the units so sequenced. That is, these might be grammatical units such as *subject,* thematic units such as *agent,* discourse units such as *topic,* or *old information:* All of these postulated units make much the same predictions about which noun-phrase (NP) the child will utter first, and which second, in declarative sentences. This overlap, taken together with the fact of the child's inexactness in honoring these ordering constraints, makes it difficult to identify the psychologically functioning units among these choices (see Section 3). But whatever their correct description, these units are sequenced fairly reliably from the first two-word utterances (for analyses of English, see, e.g., Bloom, 1970; Bowerman, 1973; Brown, 1973). As we have seen, sequencing is common even where the data base provides little support for it, as in the Russian cases reported by Slobin. Most remarkably, the sequencing of signs according to their thematic roles arises without any input support among the deaf isolates studied by Goldin-Meadow and her colleagues.

Given these strong and stable findings, it is surprising that some authors, particularly Slobin (1982), seek to discount sequential ordering in children's speech as theoretically uninteresting. Slobin adopts this stance because of his cross-linguistic finding that competence with inflection precedes competence with word order in certain comprehension tasks (encoding of the thematic roles in Turkish seems to be understood earlier than it is for English). However, as Slobin also acknowledges, attention to word order is clear from the earliest moments in speech—an inconvenient fact for the developmental generalization "inflection first, word order second." We have argued that the facts about what comes first, inflection or word order, are artifacts of phonological properties of the particular languages studied (see also Gleitman & Wanner, 1982): Unstressed material is the hardest to learn; hence, if the inflectional resources of a language are unstressed, they will appear relatively late in the child's speech; if they are stressed, they appear earlier. If we are correct, there seems little reason to take comprehension performances more seriously than speech performances—or the reverse—as indicants of the child's language organization. Findings in both domains are adequately handled by acknowledging that the child is first sensitive to stressed syllables, interpreted as words, and to orderings of these.

Nonetheless, it is important to note that a characterization of the child's word order is not really simple with respect to the adult's word order (the real utterances the learner hears from his caretakers). Only a small proportion of the sentences a child hears, in English, are subject first, because well over half the input sentences are questions and imperatives (Newport, 1977). Moreover, there is suggestive evidence that children do not reproduce the subject-first property of the heard language; rather, they may produce something of their own, perhaps agent first (see Section 3). We have already noted that the noncanonical position of the verbal auxiliary (stressed initial position, as in "Could you jump to the moon?") favors the *learning* of these auxiliaries. Still, the child first *utters* auxiliaries in declarative sentences, where they appear medially ("I could jump to the moon"). The learner, then, seems biased toward a notion of canonical word order, a notion that can arise only very abstractly from properties of the input. This is most striking for instances in which the input language *demands* noncanonical order for certain functions: Young English speakers sometimes express questions by intonation ("I could jump to the moon?") but do not invert the order of subject and auxiliary; this phenomenon is very frequent for wh-questions ("Where I could jump?"), although the inversion appears in just about every yes/no and wh-question that children hear (see Slobin & Bever, 1982, for a detailed discussion of the canonical form bias in young learners).

In summary, we must believe that the child learner is sensitive to sequence, for she orders the words in her utterances from the time there are two words to order, and the orderings she chooses conform in general to canonical or preferred orderings in the language to which she is being exposed. But learners preserve this canonical ordering even if it is not present in the input speech (as in English interrogatives); or if the ordering of the input speech is only a nonsyntactic statistical preference (as in Russian); or if there is no input at all (as in the home sign of the deaf isolates studied by Feldman et al., 1978). Hence, though sequence is a property of the wave form that the learner clearly notes and exploits, this property does not explain the character of what is learned.

The Unstressed Subcomponent of the Lexicon

As we will see in the discussion of inductive processes in language learning, the distinction between open and closed class may play a role in the child's discovery of linguistic structure. This is because, though this distinction may be discovered through a physical property (i.e., stress, in the languages we have discussed), it is well correlated with syntactic analyses that the child will have to recognize in order to recover the structure of sentences. We have seen that the closed class is acquired late. The pattern of development within this class is also distinctive. For example, Brown (1973) has shown that the closed class is learned in an item-by-item fashion over a lengthy developmental period, and in a very regular sequence (for instance, *-ing* is almost always learned before *-ed*). Moreover, learning rate is dependent on properties of the input corpus much more clearly for closed class than for open class (Landau & Gleitman, in press; Newport et al., 1977). In certain cases of linguistic isolation, the closed class may not emerge (Bickerton, 1975; Feldman et al., 1978; Goldin-Meadow, 1982; Newport & Supalla, 1980).

Slobin (1973, 1977, 1982), citing evidence from language learning, language change, and creolization processes, has conjectured that the closed class arises through the fluent user's need to be quick and efficient in language use. In homely terms, the phonological squeezing of closed class items (e.g., in English, the fact that *will* becomes *'ll* and *him* becomes *'əm*) may be an inevitable concomitant of rapid, fluent communication among linguistic experts. There is good evidence in favor of this hypothesis: The phonologically short, stressless forms of closed class items make their appearance at late stages of acquisition, in the presence of increasing fluency. An independently interesting fact is that these distinctive properties of the closed class are fully achieved only as they are filtered through the learning process by children who are native speakers. Learning a language later in life, even in the presence of adequate fluency and habitual use, does not yield these same properties (Bickerton, 1975; Newport, 1982).

One sample case has been discussed by Sankoff & Laberge (1973). They have made extensive studies of Tok Pisin, an English-based pidgin developed and acquired by linguistically heterogeneous adults in Papua New Guinea. They have shown that, in its historically earliest forms, this language had only impoverished inflectional resources. Notions such as *future* were expressed by optional, sentence-initial adverbs (such as *baimbai,* from the English *by and by*). In a second stage of evolution—a stage at which the learners were still adults acquiring Tok Pisin as a second language—this item moved into the verb-phrase (VP) and became syntactically obligatory as the marker of the future tense. In fluent usage, the item is often shortened to *bai,* thus erasing the residue of its original semantic content. This seems to show that adults are quite capable of expanding the syntactic resources of their language, as it comes into broad use as the ordinary means of communication. But at this point the new inflectionally functioning item (either *baimbai* or *bai*) is still a word with regular stress, not a clitic; that is, it is phonologically open class, even though it performs a syntactic role—tense marking—that is often reserved for the closed class in fully elaborated languages.

Recently, the use of Tok Pisin has become so general that children are acquiring it as their native language. However, the language they are hearing has little closed class morphology, so there is little for them to omit in the so-called telegraphic stage; in short, as Bickerton has argued, pidgins share interesting properties with early child speech. These learners, approximately in the period from 5 to 8 years of age, make a further move: *Baimbai* or *bai* is shortened and destressed to /bə/, becoming an obligatory verb prefix. This is an intriguing suggestion that, at a late stage of the learning process, the (phonological) closed class makes its appearance even though it is absent from the input language (see also concordant findings from Bickerton for Hawaiian creoles).

Newport (1982) has provided related evidence from the acquisition of ASL. Very often ASL is learned relatively late in life, either because it is not used by the deaf child's hearing parents (in which case ASL may still be the learner's first language, though exposure begins only when she comes into contact with other deaf individuals) or because deafness is acquired (in which case ASL is acquired as a second language). Newport has demonstrated that learners first exposed to

ASL after the age of about 7 years fail to acquire fully the inflectionally and derivationally functioning substructure of the signs (the gestural equivalents of the closed class). Again, the product of late learning is much like the utterances of native speakers at first stages.

In sum, young learners are biased to notice phonetic features, stressed syllables, and the sequences in which these are ordered. Learning a language later in life seems to show sensitivity to these same properties of the wave form. Unlike adults, children in the later stages of language acquisition become sensitive to the unstressed subcomponent of the language. At the limit (i.e., in the absence of such features in the speech heard), children can add to the stock of language resources by inventing the closed class.

The Unit "Phrase"

If we are right, the stressed syllable stands out from the rest of the wave form approximately as figure stands out from ground in the child's innate visual analysis of space (cf., Spelke, 1982). Although the stressed syllable is by no means equivalent to the mature word form, the evidence strongly suggests that its acoustic correlates (i.e., fundamental frequency, intensity, and duration) are available to the child as a bootstrap into the morphological scheme of the language. Evidence from recent studies of adult speech production and perception shows that potential bootstraps exist in the wave form for other linguistic units. For example, speech timing is affected by major syntactic boundaries, by deletion sites, and by lexical category assignment (cf., Klatt, 1975, 1976; Nakatani & Dukes, 1977; Nakatani & Schaffer, 1978; Sorensen, Cooper, & Paccia, 1978; Streeter, 1978; and many other sources). Whether learners exploit these additional acoustic cues is an open question, but recent work in infant speech perception makes this appear likely (for an informative study, see Fernald & Simon, in press). We discuss here some ingenious evidence, from older children, that suggests a continuing reliance on prosodic cues for phrasal classification.

Read and Schreiber (1982) taught 7-year-olds to play a game in which the children must listen to a sentence and then repeat some portion of it that corresponds to one of its major constituents. Children are remarkably successful at this task, learning to pick out such constituents as surface subject NP with impressive accuracy. However, they show one curious weakness: If the subject NP is only a single word (e.g., a pronoun or a generic nominal), children are regularly unable to disentangle it from the rest of the sentence. Read and Schreiber track this clue to its source, showing that, of all the many properties of single word NP's, it seems to be their intonational contour (or lack of one) that accounts for the difficulty that children experience. Unlike longer NP's, single word phrases are not rendered with falling fundamental frequency and lengthened final vowel at the close of the phrase. It is this phonological merging of the single word NP with the following VP that throws the children for a loop. Apparently phrase boundaries are largely a matter of intonation for these children. They do not appear to be able to locate these boundaries by syntax alone.

It would be perilous to reason in a straight line from 7-year-olds to 1-year olds. Simply because a second-grader shows heavy reliance upon the intonational correlates of phrases, it does not necessarily follow that he or she began learning phrases as an infant through their intonational correlates. Neither do the studies of infant sensitivity to these properties settle the case for whether these perceptions play a causal role in the discovery of syntax. Bever (1970) has argued that the mastery of an abstract syntactic rule can precede the development of heuristic perceptual strategies that come to replace the rule in practice, because they are easier to apply in the rapid-fire business of understanding or producing speech. It is not impossible that phrase-structure learning conforms to Bever's developmental sequence. Read and Schreiber's seven-year-olds may have learned the syntactic structure of phrases first and only then have come to appreciate the intonational correlates of phrases—and even if, as is likely, the discrimination of intonation patterns came well before. It is also possible that Read and Schreiber's judgmental task captures metalinguistic knowledge, or "accessible" knowledge that is partly at variance with linguistic knowledge (Gleitman & Gleitman, 1979). But it is also possible that the seven-year-old's heavy reliance on intonation is a remnant of a dependency formed at the earliest stages of acquisition. If this is the case, it would have important consequences for the way we think about the acquisition of syntax. For, as we argue later, an infant who is innately biased to treat intonationally circumscribed utterance segments as potential syntactic constituents would be at considerable advantage in learning the syntactic rules of his or her language.

Before closing, it is worth mentioning one more (indirect) source of evidence that strengthens the case for the prosodic guidance of syntax acquisition. Morgan and Newport (1981) have shown in an artificial language learning task that different physical cues to phrase grouping, such as intonation contour (when "sentences" from the language are presented orally) or physical closeness of within-phrase items (when sentences are presented visually) are sufficient for an adult subject to induce rather complex phrase-structure grammars, whose elements are nonsense phrases comprised of nonsense syllables. When sentences are presented without these phrasal cues (and without alternative semantic cues to the phrases), adults generally fail to learn the language. Again, this is no guarantee that infants are equally disposed to exploit intonational clues. But the Morgan and Newport result adds one more reasonable basis for entertaining this possibility.

Motherese: Saying it Obviously

We have expressed considerable caution about how caretakers could make special adjustments to render "meanings" easier for children to acquire. This is largely because meanings are not the sort of things that are out there in the world, available to be emphasized to one who (presumably) is not in control of the linguistic—semantic facts of the matter in advance. Barring language knowledge itself, there is no obvious way to remove the multiple possibilities of 'animalness' or 'Felixness' from cat-situations. However, we have just implicitly accepted an opposing position about the role caretakers may well play in revealing the language *forms* to their infants, for the sounds of speech *are* out there in the world, and are, in principle, available for exaggeration (of the "important" properties) and suppression (of the less important properties) so as to help the novice learn. Briefly, we now make this hypothesis more explicit.

As Newport and her colleagues (1977) have shown (see pp. 228–231 of the current chapter for further discussion), it is difficult in the extreme to show specific syntactic and semantic adjustments that mothers make, or to show effects on acquisition predicted by those adjustments that seem relatively stable (e.g., the relative shortness of maternal utterances, or their very heavy use of the imperative structure). The few adjustments that seem to work to aid the learner are largely restricted to rate-effects on closed class acquisition, e.g., of the English verbal auxiliary. In contrast, it is easy to point to universal properties that are specific to "motherese," if attention is restricted to prosody. These have been noted by many investigators, but have been systematically investigated by Fernald and her collaborators (Fernald, 1983), who have shown that motherese is special in having higher pitch, wider pitch excursions, shorter utterances, and longer pauses than speech between adults. These prosodic adjustments occur in all language communities that have been studied and, according to Fernald, they may represent a complementary adaptation by mother and child. Adapting remarks from Darwin, Fernald holds that maternal vocalizations are "sweet to the ears of the species," and so facilitate the mother–infant interaction. Specifically, Fernald and other investigators we have cited have demonstrated that infants are sensitive to the prosodic features characteristic of motherese, and prefer hearing motherese to hearing adult-to-adult speech. As stated earlier, such demonstrations do not constitute a knockdown causal argument, but they do lend persuasiveness to the view that prosodic cues help in the discovery of syntactic form. As we will now argue, the wise child should accept such available bootstraps with some alacrity, for the acquisition of syntax is no mean trick. In short, because help is clearly available in the sound wave, the best guess is that the learner is prepared to recruit it.

THE PROJECTION PROBLEM: PAIRING THE MEANINGS AND THE FORMS

In the preceding discussion, we have summarized the information available about the state of the child requisite to language learning; namely, some means for representing input speech signals and some means for representing the real-world context that co-occurs with the signals. We have asserted that input signals are interpreted as ordered phonetic strings bracketed by stress into words and bracketed by intonation into phrases. Acknowledging that some input may be physically too imperfect or indistinct to allow these analyses, we took the findings from the maternal speech literature to suggest that this problem is not greatly damaging to the position; that is, the mother's speech is generally slow, intonationally exaggerated, and almost always grammatical. As for the meaning representations, we have stated that information about these is currently orders of magnitude more fragmentary. The literature does suggest that the child assumes that words represent concepts and function as the markers of predicates and thematic roles in a propositional structure, carried by the sentence. What the concepts are and just how the sentence heard relates to a particular proposition (the cat-on-mat/mat-under-cat problem) is unknown, but we interpreted the maternal speech literature to suggest a caretaker–child conspiracy designed to respond to these problems. Just as for the speech signals, we assume that the child will have to filter out, as unusable data, those utterances whose interpretation is particularly ambiguous or murky. Granting that almost everything is unresolved here, all parties seem to agree that the preconditions for learning are that the child be able to interpret and represent the sound wave to himself in linguistically relevant ways, and also interpret and represent real-world events to himself in linguistically relevant ways. Having granted these prerequisites, we now raise the question: How does a child learn a language? That is, how does the child project from these data a general system that pairs each possible meaning with each possible form?

Directions for an answer proposed by contributors to the field differ radically. Not only do investigators disagree, they do not even seem to be addressing the same topics. Some investigators (e.g., Braine & Hardy, 1982; Schlesinger, 1971) seek to explain how the child connects semantic-relational (thematic) roles to positions in surface strings. Other investigators (e.g., Maratsos & Chalkley, 1980) ask how the child discovers such syntactic categories as noun and verb. Still others (e.g., Roeper, 1982; Wexler & Culicover, 1980) ask how an abstract learning device might acquire transformational rules. Partly, it is possible to understand all these undertakings as attempts to resolve different subparts of the syntax acquisition question. But we believe that in large part the disparity of topics investigated arises from a much deeper disagreement among these investigators about the complexity of the mapping between form and meaning. Believing this mapping to be essentially simple, some authors propose that it can be learned as a direct projection from thematic roles to the surface string. Others view the relation between form and meaning as more complex, but still believe that it can be learned by a direct projection, albeit in quite the opposite direction: from form to meaning. Still other theorists have held that no such direct projection is possible. For them, the relation between form and meaning is so complex that it must be learned through the mediation of another level of representation.

As a result of their differing beliefs about the complexity of the mapping between sound and meaning, child language investigators have offered an embarrassing variety of hypotheses about what is to be learned: case grammar, constituent structure grammar, and transformational (or lexical-functional) grammar, among others. We take up these hypotheses in turn, concentrating discussion on some current major proponents of each view. In each case, the authors are asking about the discovery of sentence structure—the main battleground of linguistic and psycholinguistic theorizing over the last two decades.

Learning a Case Grammar

In 1966, McNeill put forward the claim that children essentially "talk deep structure" at earliest developmental moments. That is, the ordering of words looks much like the left-to-right sequence of terminal nodes in deep-structure descriptions of the Chomsky (1965) variety. The retort from developmental psycholinguists (e.g., Bowerman, 1973; Braine & Hardy, 1982; Schlesinger, 1971) has been that the child's categories are semantic-relational ones, e.g., *theme, source, goal,* or *agent, instrument, patient* (depending on the particular account). It is these categories that explain the patterning of young children's speech, rather than categories such as *subject noun-phrase.*

Although this view seems plausible, the evidence in its favor is not overwhelming. One problem has to do with the analysis itself. It is not easy to define "semantic roles" nor to assign such roles to the nominals in child sentences, so as to determine whether these categories actually organize the facts about early grammars (see Braine, 1976, for a discussion of these issues). As Wexler & Culicover (1980) have pointed out, the lists of children's productions, so analyzed, themselves seem to contain counterexamples, if the definitions of the semantic roles are accepted literally. For instance, among the examples Schlesinger (1971) gives of agent + action constructions is the child utterance "Mail come"; *mail* cannot be an agent according to accepted definitions for it is not the *animate instigator* of an action. Another difficulty is that the semantic-relational analyses of children's speech may be artifacts of another variable. For a large class of English action verbs of special interest to toddlers, the subject is the agent. If the tots are really biased to use action verbs, for cognitive and motivational reasons, then a coding of the child utterances will pretty well identify subjects with agents. But, especially in light of the occasional counterexamples, it does not follow that the children believe *in principle* that subjects must be agents. A final problem with these analyses is their failure to cover the full range of phenomena observed early in the acquisition period. Young children do acquire certain linguistic subsystems that are known not to be semantically organized. For example, in the earliest learning period, German children acquire gender systems in which *masculine, feminine,* and *neuter* as conceptual categories map only very inexactly onto inflectional categories; similar effects have been reported for young Hebrew speakers (Levy, 1980, 1983; Maratsos & Chalkley, 1980).

Despite all these provisos, there is some intuitive appeal and correlational evidence supporting the semantics-based categorial view. Our question is how this supposition helps to explain language learning. It is our impression that many investigators believe they are making this problem easier by pointing to these functional semantic categories as the ones that operate in early child speech, and by supposing that these categories map onto the child's word orderings or inflectional markings in a *simple* and *direct* way. But to the extent that the child really makes these suppositions of simplicity in the mapping of form to meaning, they can only complicate the problem of learning a language. The reason is that the supposition is false for any adult language. And the reason for *that* (among many others) is that so many subtle semantic dimensions are encoded syntactically that it is literally impossible to find a single linearization for them all.

One outcome of this complexity is that the position of semantically definable propositional components (thematic roles) varies with the predicate. John's role, but not his sentential position, differs in *John is easy to please* and *John is eager to please,* as well as in *John sold a book to Mary* (where he is *source*) and *John bought a book from Mary* (where he is *goal*). John's sentential position, but not his role, differs in *John received a tie from Mary* and *Mary gave a tie to John;* in *John collided with Bill* and *Bill collided with John;* and in *Bill resembles John, John resembles Bill,* and *Bill and John resemble each other.* These old saws are no less problematical for being old saws. Moreover, the phenomenon of constructional ambiguity is understandable only if we acknowledge the complexity of relations between surface and logical forms, e.g., *These missionaries are ready to eat* allows two interpretations of the relational role of the missionaries, at least if the listeners are cannibals. Note that none of these examples, nor all of them taken together, argue that the relation between phrase order and sentential meaning is arbitrary—maybe it is arbitrary and then again maybe it is not. The examples show only that these relations cannot be simple or direct; rather, they must be mediated through, and derived from, the interaction of a number of distinct linguistic organizing principles (for discussion, see Chomsky, 1981).

A related problem is that, beyond the puerile sayings of the first 3 years of life, it is difficult indeed to describe sentences as syntactically organized by known or even stateable semantic functions. To understand the descriptive problems here, consider the following first sentence from a recent Letter to the Editor appearing in *TV Guide:*

> How Ann Salisbury can suggest that Pam Dauber's anger at not receiving her fair share of acclaim for *Mork and Mindy's* success derives from a fragile ego escapes me.

This writer, whatever his odd preoccupations, displays some formidible syntactic skills. It is hard to state that the first 27 words of his sentence represent some semantic role. What role would that be? Still, the 27 words function together as a linguistic unit; namely, the unit that determines that word 28 is to end with an *s*. Mature language knowledge involves, in addition to many semantically coherent classes, knowledge of such incoherent surface categories as noun-phrase, subject of the clause, and so forth, as the domains of these categorial contingencies. Moreover, if there is anything like an agent or do-er in the sentence above, it would have to be *me*. For its predicate (*escape*), this do-er is the second noun-phrase. But for predicates of quite similar meaning, the do-er is the first noun-phrase. That is, the sentence could be recast:

I fail to understand how Ann Salisbury can suggest that Pam Dauber's anger at not receiving her fair share of acclaim for *Mork and Mindy's* success derives from a fragile ego.

The point, an old point, is that the grammatical notion *subject* (the NP immediately dominated by S, the NP that agrees in number with the verb) is only complexly related to semantic notions such as the agent or experiencer. Thus, if we claim the child is preprogrammed to construct a semantic representation to match each sentence that he hears, we have arrived only at the beginning of the language learning problem. The rest of the problem involves acquiring the system of rules that relates surface forms to their underlying meanings. Recapitulating, we do not deny the relations between form and meaning, for learner or for user. We only deny that these relations are simple and direct.

Many developmental psycholinguists reject the standard arguments we have just given. Certain investigators suppose, to the contrary, that a grammar based simply on semantic-relational categories can describe the facts about natural language, as used both by children and adults. Such *case grammars* are described below. Another group of investigators accept a more abstract grammar for adults, but postulate that case grammar is the appropriate description for young learners. This latter description implies that the language organization of the child undergoes reorganization sometime during the learning process. We discuss this position in the following section.

Case Grammar as the Outcome of Learning

Some investigators have proposed that case grammar (of roughly the type envisaged by Fillmore, 1968) is the appropriate "psychologically real" descriptive mechanism for human language. In Fillmore's proposal, the combining categories are semantic-relational. The surface configurations of sentences arise by rule from these semantic-categorial (deep case) representations; hence, no separate interpretive device would be required for the semantic interpretation of the syntactic configurations. It has sometimes gone unnoticed that Fillmore postulated a mediating system of rules operating on the initial case representations to account for the complex relations between surface orderings and semantic roles. To our knowledge, Fillmore never argued that these relations would be simple—that is, immediate. In addition, a number of questions have been raised about the descriptive adequacy of this approach. For instance, Chomsky (1972) has pointed out that the same case descriptions would apply to *pinch* and *pull,* accounting for the surface manifestations *John pulled Mary's nose* and *John pinched Mary's nose.* But then it is hard to explain why *John pinched Mary on the nose* is acceptable but *John pulled Mary on the nose* is anomalous, on the relevant reading. Chomsky's approach has been to state the syntactic-categorial facts and, separately, an interpretive system that carries the grammatical structures to the logical structures. Another approach is to list the case relations for each predicate, and surface specifications for that predicate, as lexical information (Bresnan, 1978, 1982). Yet another approach seeks to discover certain limited semantic domains or fields and study the syntactic encodings that apply to predicates within the domain but not to predicates that fall outside it (e.g., Gruber, 1968; Jackendoff, 1983; Landau & Gleitman, in press). It remains for extensive further research to discover the extent to which semantic fields may constrain syntactic formats. However, in our opinion it is hopeless to suppose that there are a very few semantic-functional categories that transparently determine phrase orders and other syntactic properties. In general, although linguists disagree on *how* to state the relations between semantic roles and grammatical dependencies, none (to our knowledge) assert that these relations will turn out to be simple.

Nevertheless, many developmental psycholinguists have argued for such a view. For example, Braine & Hardy (1982) have conjectured that a sane creator who had the language learning problem in mind would write a case grammar that mapped semantic-relational roles onto surface structures in simple ways. We do not disagree with these directions to a good God, but we have just argued that the real deity has not been so benevolent (probably this is only one of many grounds for questioning the goodness of God). That is, the evidence of natural language design fails to suggest a transparent mapping between meanings and sentence forms. Rather, successful descriptions have had to postulate transformational rules, or lexical rules of a complexity just as great, or rules of like complexity that generate phrase-structure rules recursively, and so on. Though the complexity can be moved, then, from component to component of a grammar, it evidently cannot be *re*moved.

Case Grammar as a Stage in Learning: The Problem of Reorganization

We have argued that the relationships between form and meaning are not simple in adult grammars, i.e., that a very simple case grammar is inadequate to describe the final outcome of learning. Many investigators hold, however, that the youngest learners' grammars are organized by semantic categories, but later change (e.g., Bowerman, 1973). They reject the supposition that the child's early language is just like the adult's—but somewhat less complete—arguing instead that it is different in kind. These differences may be of units (e.g., agents but not subjects) and of combinatorial rules (e.g., serial orderings but not hierarchical arrangements or transformational rules).

The question, then, is whether language acquisition is a relatively seamless progression, characterizable in terms of the steady accretion of knowledge, or whether it involves qualitative changes in organization during the course of growth. Recent investigations seem to support the latter view: Although acquiring more information is surely a part of the learning process, the reorganization of previously acquired information is also a part of the story of language acquisition.

Some of the most interesting empirical investigations of such postulated reorganizations have been carried out by Bowerman (1982). Her primary method is to look at the "errors" a child makes during language learning. With a variety of contents and structures, she has shown that the child uses certain accepted language forms at early stages without error. For example, children will use such known lexical causatives as "I broke the window" (causative of "The window broke") or "I melted the wax." Presumably what is going on here is an item-by-item adoption of heard forms. At a later stage, errors suddenly make their appearance. The child says "Don't eat the baby—she's dirty" (presumably, this is an invented lexical causative corresponding to "The baby eats," i.e., the child means "Don't feed the baby"). As Bowerman argues, through the internal analysis of these late-appearing errors, the novel usages imply that the learner has seen through to a new organization that relates the items that were previously learned separately. This new organization allows the child to project beyond the heard instances in various ways, some of them wrong. (For a related and very interesting example, see Clark, 1982, and Clark & Clark, 1978, on the emergence of denominative verbs in speakers of English, French, and German. And see also Bever, 1970, for an interesting account of reorganization, based on the learning curves for comprehension of English passive voice constructions).

Apparently, there is a significant reorganization of knowledge during the learning period. At the extreme, this makes it reasonable to describe "stages" of language learning that are quite distinct from each other. In particular, an early stage of learning may be well characterized as a simple case grammar. However, if the concept of reorganization is adopted in the language acquisition theory, a new question immediately arises: What causes the child to reorganize his or her grammar—especially to reorganize it in a way that increases the abstractness of the relations between forms and meanings?

One kind of answer is strictly maturational: There may be relevant biological changes in the learner that cause her to revist old linguistic evidence and interpret it differently. Put another way, it could be that there is a succession of learners, each of whom organizes the linguistic data as befits her current mental state. If these learners are really quite separate—if they literally dismantle the old system and substitute a new one—then it becomes quite reasonable to do as many developmental psycholinguists have done: write a (case) grammar for the 2-year-old, and assume no responsibility for that description as a basis for describing the 3-year-old (for discussion, see Gleitman, 1981). But notice that this is a kind of metamorphosis, or tadpole-to-frog, hypothesis. It is not easy to defend, for there is no evidence that we know of to suggest that old principles and categories are literally discarded during the learning period.

The opposing view is that language learning is continuous. One version of this position is that reorganization is motivated by a data-driven process. The learner is presumed first to acquire information about the language essentially one piece at a time, e.g., generalizations that are applicable only to one or a few verbs or nouns (Bowerman, 1982; Braine, 1976). This relatively unorganized method eventually leads to an unmanageable clutter of facts. Organization into general rule systems will both simplify the storage of information and, sometimes, vastly increase the generative capacity of the system.

Another explanation of apparent reorganization has to do with the modular nature of the language system itself. It is possible that language consists of a number of distinct processes and principles that are at least partly autonomous (Chomsky, 1981). The acquisition of some of these modules may be logically contingent on the acquisition of others. If this is the correct view, then the child's usage may look radically different from an adult's, while in reality the underlying knowledge is of a proper subpart of the adult language. For example, suppose that the learner has control of the thematic-role system and some version of a phrase-structure hierarchy (or even a linearization of phrases), but lacks knowledge of a syntactic module that in the adult language stands between these and mediates their relations. By default, the learner may map one-to-one between the modules that he currently controls.

Summary

We have argued against the view that semantic roles in a language map one-to-one onto syntactic configurations. Nonetheless, case grammar may be a useful device for describing the linguistic organization of very young learners. Even if so, as usually stated this hypothesis is at best a data summary for the speech of the youngest learners, giving no hint as to how learning could progress toward the real complexities of the adult language. We have suggested two main ways out of this pickle. The first is biological: The 2-year-old molts linguistically and becomes a 3-year-old, discarding virtually all principles of the prior system. The second also acknowledges that the character of early and late stages of acquisition look very different from each other, but holds that the learning process is at bottom continuous. In one variant, the learner is motivated by the accumulation of information: Groaning under the burden of storing myriad separate facts, he or she tries some higher-order generalizations that subsume more instances. In another variant, the child maintains the original system essentially without change, but adds semiautonomous new modules at the interface between old ones, radically changing the linguistic outcomes at the surface.

Learning a Bloomfieldian Grammar

The case grammar approach to language learning takes as certain the child's mastery of a small set of semantic distinctions (agent–patient, possessor–possessed, etc.) and attempts to build the rest of syntax acquisition on this base. In contrast, the neo-Bloomfieldian position, to the extent that one exists, builds in an altogether different direction and begins with an entirely contrary certainty; namely, the unarguable fact that adults control some syntactic categories that have little if any direct correlation with matters semantic. More than anyone else, Maratsos and his colleagues (Maratsos, 1979, 1982; Maratsos & Chalkley, 1980; Maratsos, Kuczaj, Fox, & Chalkley, 1979) have been identified with the renovation of Bloomfieldian ideas. Chief among their labors has been the simple but essential reminder that adult grammatical categories, such as *noun, verb,* and *adjective,* cannot summarily be reduced to the semantic definitions of grade school. It follows that such categories must be acquired on some basis that is at least partly independent of semantics, a fact that is something of a conundrum for any theory of acquisition run exclusively on semantic machinery.

In his most recent paper, Maratsos (1982) makes a new and interesting pass at this argument. He begins with the fact that there are some syntactic distinctions, such as the German gender distinction, that are notorious for their failure to show any semantic correlation. For these categories, there is no alternative but to learn category members word-by-word on the basis of the syntactic contexts in which they appear. For example, upon hearing "das machen," one can unequivocally assign *machen* to the neuter gender (semantics be damned) and predict that *machen* will pronominalize via *es,* take *das* in the accusative, and so forth. It is this correlated set of syntactic effects that, according to Maratsos, makes up the German neuter gender. To learn the neuter gender is to learn that these syntactic phenomena predict each other, and nothing more.

From here, the argument moves to interesting ground. In effect, Maratsos argues, if *some* syntactic categories must be learned as clusters of distributional facts, then why not *all* syntactic categories, including the major grammatical categories such as noun and verb, as well as the major constituent categories, such as noun-phrase and verb-phrase? Why postulate more than one sort of language acquisition unless forced to it? A very good question, one worth some pursuit.

Maratsos' learning device is basically an inductive scheme that is capable, in principle, of classifying words together on the basis of shared contexts. We have argued from the beginning the failure of unbiased induction to account for the fact of language learning. Nonetheless, learning must ultimately be by inductive generalization. This follows from the fact that languages differ from one another and hence must be learned, in the classical sense of the term (just Bloomfield's point, as we stated in our introductory remarks). The problem is to isolate units on which induction takes place, given the capacities and inclinations of a human language learner. Maratsos explicit proposal seems to be for a general distributional analyzer that recognizes associations among *any* morphemes. We believe, however, that to the extent this proposal seems plausible, it is because it really (albeit implicitly) builds upon a quite narrow and interesting hypothesis about the nature of these units; specifically, the distributional analyzer Maratsos sketches seems to be particularly sensitive to the open-class/closed-class distinction that we described earlier. The bulk of Maratsos' *co-predictors* (correlations exploited to determine word-class membership) turn out to be associations between a closed-class item and an open-class position. For instance, "takes plural *-s*" predicts noun status for a stress-bearing word; "takes *-ed* and *will*" predicts verb status for other words. Note that a blind inductive device might focus on quite different, and ultimately useless, potential correlations, such as the correlation of *black* with *coal, night,* and *ink* vs. the correlation of *white* with *swan, milk,* and *snow;* no syntactically functioning units are picked out by these latter correlations. To the extent that Maratsos' distributional analyzer is plausible, then, it is because it has eyes for something like an open-class/closed-class distinction. These eyes rescue Maratsos analyzer from contemplating the limitless false analogies it might otherwise be forced to consider as potential bases for grammatical categories. But this rescue raises problems of its own.

First, there is serious empirical doubt as to whether the closed-class items are generally available to children to support the initial construction of grammatical categories. The evidence we have presented thus far suggests that the closed-class and relevant distinctions among the closed-class items are beyond the grasp of the youngest learners. If this is so, these items would not be available to the inductive device at the stage—a very early stage, as the literature tells us—when the initial distinction between noun and verb is acquired (as evidenced by ordering). Moreover, nouns and verbs apparently emerge without difficulty in early stages of Turkish, which has few closed-class resources, according to Slobin's analysis, and in the historically early version of Tok Pisin which, according to Sankoff, has virtually no inflectional resources. Hence, whatever the facts for normally circumstanced English speaking learners, it cannot be maintained that the distinction between noun and verb, in general, arises from a distributional analysis of open-class/closed-class relations.

Maratsos tries to resolve these problems, but succeeds only by means of weakening the pure Bloomfieldian strain of his proposal. Following Braine (1976), he acknowledges that in the initial stages of language acquisition, grammatical categories (perhaps they should be called pregrammatical categories) are probably formed on semantic grounds. Subsequently, when the closed-class distinctions have been mastered (at about age three), the child is in a position to renovate these categories on the basis of distributional properties. Postulating such a renovation is necessary to account for the fact that children make so few category errors based on semantic uniformities. Thus the verb *like* and the adjective *fond (of)* mean much the same thing. Yet children are not heard to invent *John was fonded of by Mary* on the analogy of *John was liked by Mary* (note that this is just the kind of issue that case grammars have difficulty explaining). Presumably, it is the child's growing appreciation of the ways in which verbs and adjectives co-vary with closed-class items that prevents over-generalizations of this sort.

All this seems plausible enough, but it leaves rather mysterious the acquisition of the closed class itself. Notice that this is not simply a problem of picking out phonetic segments that seem to have low initial salience in the wave form. The child must also learn the grammatical significance of these phonetic elements. It is not, for instance, the location of a word just prior to the appropriate sounds for an *-ed* ending that predicts verb status. Consider, as evidence, that there are no verbs *to lightheart, to lighthead,* or *to lightfinger,* corresponding to the adjectives *lighthearted, lightheaded,* and *lightfingered.* There *is* a distributional regularity here characteristic of verbs, but it holds only when the *-ed* form has been assigned the morphemic value, *past tense.* It follows that if the child learns the verb category partly by learning about its deployment with respect to *-ed* as a marker of past tense, then she first must have learned that *-ed* marks past tense. This much Maratsos specifically acknowledges. But the unanswered question is just how the child manages to accomplish this crucial prior feat. Put generally, the child's move from categories based on semantic properties to categories based on the syntactic distribution of grammatical morphemes is not just a matter of changing the basis of induction. The child's new syntactic base *presupposes* the analysis of grammatical morphemes, and this analysis requires an explanation of its own.

We have left the child with a problem that neither Maratsos nor Bloomfield has solved: to induce the morphemic values of the closed-class items. We will now try to show that, armed with tentative semantic heuristics and exploiting phonological properties of the input strings, the child can in principle bootstrap from partial information to converge on the correct solution. This involves a bottom-up attempt to parse the string from its physical form, combined with a top-down attempt to establish its semantically functioning lexical and phrasal categories.

So far we have granted the learner the open-class/closed-class distinction, at least roughly (that is, as picked out by associated phonological properties). We have also adduced some of the evidence demonstrating that the child is sensitive to the sequencing of open-class elements from the earliest stages. From this it is reasonable to conclude that the learner has established rough precursors to these basic open-class categories, perhaps partly on primitive semantic grounds, as Maratsos and Braine both suppose (see also Pinker, 1982). Perhaps the child is willing to guess, based on preliminary correlational evidence, that concrete objects are encoded by nouns and actions and states are encoded by verbs, a few counterexamples notwithstanding.

However, even more detailed information about strings is required to solve the problem we have just raised: particularly, to find out that *-ed* in *lighthearted* is participial, but might be a finite verb ending in, say, *hotfooted*. The problem still exists because neither the meaning nor the morphology of *hotfooted* renders it more or less verb-like than *lightfingered* or *lighthearted;* that is, there is no semantic heuristic basis in the contrast between action and thing for establishing the open-class categories of these particular words. And then there is no basis for establishing the closed-class morphemic value either, as we have already shown. To repeat, this is because the value of *-ed* can be assigned as *past* only if the learner has secure knowledge that it is bound to a verb.

It is now clear that knowing something approximate about semantic correlates of open-class lexical categories is not enough information for resolving the *-ed* discovery problem. Most generally, this is because not every verb is an action and not every noun is a person, place, or thing. Thus the discovery procedure cannot be reduced to the class definitions of grade-school grammar courses (ask yourself on what semantic basis, for example, *thunder* is both a noun and a verb, while *lightning* is a noun only). As we will show, further analysis of the global phrase structure of the sentence is required.

As we have already described, there are a variety of cooperating cues in the sound wave—stress, rhythm, prepausal lengthening, etc.—to help the learner group formatives into phrases, and we have presented evidence (Read & Schreiber, 1982; Morgan & Newport, 1981) that learners are probably disposed to exploit these cues. Moreover, recent formal demonstrations suggest that phrase labeling can be derived from the bracketings (Levy and Joshi, 1978). If a child has such a phrase structural analysis in hand, based on such cues, we can at least in principle describe how she or he learns the facts about *ed*.

One traditional way in which the syntactic values of grammatical morphemes have been determined in linguistics is by means of their relative position in the phrase structure of the sentences in which they appear. The advantage of the phrase-structure representation is that it permits global description of the sentence, as divided into an integral sequence of phrases, hierarchically organized together. At the point at which we are now engaging the learner, he or she is in possession of a partial open-class parse, but (a) one that specifically identifies only open-class elements, and among these (b) only items that conform to the semantic heuristic for identifying nouns with objects and verbs with actions. For example, we now are assuming that the child possesses the mental equivalent of grammatical rules that allow her to construct a parse tree like this:

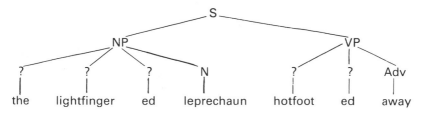

The categorial assignment of *leprechaun* is presumed to be established based on the semantic heuristic, because it is a concrete noun ("a thing"); and differential labeling of the phrasal categories is established by the procedure described by Levy and Joshi (1978). What remain to be specified are the values for *lightfinger* and *hotfoot,* as well as those for the closed-class elements: *the* (determiner), *ed* (participle), and *ed* (finite verb ending). For present purposes, we ignore the solution for *the.* Given the parse tree above, there can be little, if any, uncertainty about the appropriate syntactic categorization of *lightfinger* and *hotfoot,* or the correct assignment of the morphemic value *past* in the second case but not the first. The reasons are straightforward: *Lightfinger* occurs cophrasally before the noun and within the noun-phrase, and hence in a position appropriate to an adjective; that is, before a noun. *Hotfoot* occurs in a verb-phrase, in the position appropriate to the verb. As the first *ed* is bound to an adjective, it cannot be assigned a finite verb interpretation. In contrast, the second *ed* occurs within the verb-phrase and postposed to the verb. Thus, *past* is a possible analysis of *ed.*[9] Assuming that a similar analysis deals with the *the* case, the learner can now construct the final labelings for the parse tree:

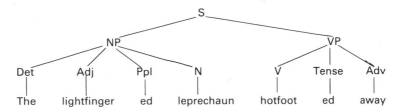

If we accept the moral of this story, the child must learn to parse (though tacitly and unconsciously) and must acquire the syntactic rules on which parsing

---

[9]The fact remains that, given our own prior discussion, the charge can be laid that we have been highhanded (if not lightfingered) in assuming that the learner is disposed to believe properties (adjectives) are of nouns, and times (tenses) are of actions (verbs). We acknowledge that we are assigning such meaningful interpretations of the world, as coded by language, to the child *ab initio,* even though the extent and usefulness of this knowledge is sharply limited by issues mentioned earlier: The interpretation of sentences by reference to scenes is a tricky business; languages vary in the properties of the world that they encode syntactically; and in any case the correlation between form-class and meaning is quite loose. Following Pinker, we here grant only a rough and tentative bias to associate whole concrete objects with the nouns and whole activities with the verbs. Even this, presumably, can be accomplished only in particularly dramatic or compelling circumstances. However the issues here may work out in detail, we submit, without such a rough ability to interpret the world in terms of forms and structures not too distant from the ones used by natural languages, there is simply no account for the acquisition of language (for discussion, see Wexler & Culicover, 1980). As for evidence, it is at least relevant that the creolizing languages we have mentioned (Bickerton, 1975; Sankoff & Laberge, 1973), developed by preliterate societies, move time markers into verb-phrases. And we have mentioned the evidence that even 18-month-olds distinguish actions from objects in their utterances by the order of the words.

depends, to determine the placement and syntactic class values of the closed class. Neither unabetted semantic learning (that *ed* means *past*) nor induction over surface regularities (that *ed* often follows verbs) escapes this conclusion. As we have mentioned in connection with the *thunder/lightning* example, this problem is not specific to such rare items as *hotfooted,* but is a general consequence of the fact that semantic properties are only loosely correlated with the formal lexical classes. To converge on the real richness of the lexical and phrasal properties of any real language, then, the child is forced to consider a deeper and more formal analysis. Detectable clues to the correct analysis can be found in the wave form, by an organism so constructed as to seek them out.

Learning a Transformational Grammar

The question of how syntactic rules are acquired returns us to the first principles of the debate between Chomsky and Bloomfield. Now, however, we can restate the issues in terms of the territory since covered:

1. Given that the child is innately able to "hear" the wave form of parental speech as an ordered string of words, intonationally bracketed into major phrases (possibly, labeled phrases); and

2. Given that the child can, by dint of his own conceptual abilities and through parental efforts to direct his attention (for which, see Bruner 1974/75), achieve an accurate interpretation of some of the sentences he encounters—even before achieving a full grasp of the language he is learning; and

3. Given that the mapping between the semantic interpretation and the surface string is not sufficiently simple to be learned either as a direct projection from semantic representation to the surface string (Braine & Hardy) or vice versa (Maratsos); it follows that

4. We must provide some independent account of how the rules that map between the semantic interpretation and the surface string are acquired.

This task is severely complicated by the fact that there is no single grammatical system now known to be the one psychologically valid statement of these mapping rules. Among the best studied of the alternative grammatical systems are transformational grammar in its several incarnations (Chomsky, 1965, 1975, 1981; Fiengo, 1980); lexical functional grammar (Bresnan, 1982); arc pair grammar (Johnson & Postal, 1980); and relational grammar (Perlmutter, 1980). Given the uncertain choice among these and other alternative descriptions of the adult system, it is difficult to achieve definite results about the process of acquisition. However, it is possible to study some of the boundary conditions under which this acquisition could conceivably take place. It is noteworthy that the study of such conditions can place constraints on the choice among possible grammatical systems because, whatever else is true of adult grammar, it must be learnable by the child. Kenneth Wexler and several colleagues have carried out an extended study of such constraints (see Wexler, 1982, for an overview). Put very simply, Wexler's work is an examination of the compatibility of holding two assumptions: (1) that children learn a mapping between form and meaning (equivalent to our assumption *1* in the preceding list); and (2) that the mapping they learn is, at least in part, a transformational grammar of the so-called "Standard Theory" vintage.

Wexler examined the consistency of these two claims by designing a hypothetical learning device for transformational grammars and determining under what conditions it will converge on the correct transformational grammar for a given language. His earliest result (Wexler & Hamburger, 1973) showed that no such convergence is possible so long as the learner has access only to positive examples of sentences in the target language. This negative result motivated Wexler and his colleagues to examine an altered scenario in which the child is considered able to derive the meaning of adult utterances from extralinguistic circumstances (our assumption 2 in the preceding list) and is also able to derive the deep structures of a transformational grammar from these meanings. On these assumptions, the child is confronted with data consisting of a word string paired with a deep structure for every sentence he or she can interpret in this fashion. Wexler's learning device is extremely simple. Whenever a string/deep-structure pair arrives, it attempts to find a set of transformations in its current grammar that will map from the deep structure to the string. If it is successful, it makes no change in its grammar. If it is unsuccessful, it either deletes one of its current rules at random or attempts to formulate a new transformation (given only its knowledge of elementary transformational operations) that will permit a successful mapping of the current input pair. If such a new rule can be found, it is added to the current grammar.

Hamburger and Wexler (1975) were able to prove that, with this kind of a learning device of this simple type can successfully converge in the limit on the target transformational grammar, but only if the grammar includes certain *new* constraints on the operation of transformational rules. These constraints (for which, see Wexler & Culicover, 1980) are necessary to insure that if the learner makes an error (i.e., infers an incorrect transformation), it will not require a sample sentence of unbounded complexity to reveal that error. A learner requiring examples of unbounded complexity might have to wait an unbounded amount of time to stumble onto even one such example. Hence, convergence could not be guaranteed.

One of the chief thrusts of Wexler's work is linguistic. In collaboration with Culicover, he has attempted to show that the constraints required to guarantee learnability have independent linguistic motivation. Very roughly, the theory imposes constraints on the application of transformational rules under general conditions that would lead to undetectable (from information available in the surface string) errors when deriving a phrase-structure analysis of the sentence derived by the transformation. Wexler and Culicover (1980) have shown that these constraints, put forward to guarantee learning, offer an explanation for certain otherwise mysterious constraints on the applicability of rules that have had to be proposed simply on descriptive grounds: to explain away some nonoccurring structures in adult languages. To the extent that the learnable grammar is also the most successful description of the adult language, it becomes possible to offer learnability as an explanation of descriptive success: The language is as it is just because it must be learned.

No one, incuding Wexler, would propose that his learning device is a full model of how children acquire syntax. It may be that Wexler's current scenario assumes both too much and too little about the input to the child: Too much because it is not known how the child gets from meaning to deep structure without additional learning to supply this mapping, as Wexler acknowledges; too little because, as we have suggested, the child may have intonational access to major phrase boundaries, while Wexler has worked from the assumption that the learner begins by recognizing only the linear string of words. If even partial phrase structure is available to the learning device, certain "undetectable" errors in Wexler's system would become "detectable." Whether the prelinguistic availability of approximate phrase bracketing might have a sufficiently general effect on detectability to render unnecessary any of Wexler and Culicover's transformational constraints is a question that may be worth attention.

Whatever the final dctails, Wexler's study of learnability is an important move in developmental psycholinguistics. Where much work in the field seems aimed at description for its own sake, Wexler's program serves to refocus attention on explanatory goals. Moreover, it sets exacting standards for the acceptability of explanatory proposals that are a model for future work. How many current notions about how language is learned can offer hard proof that language is, even in principle, learnable in the proposed way? Many arguments in developmental psycholinguistics rest upon unexamined assumptions about learnability that prove to be false once their consequences are examined by more formal techniques. An example of just this sort, and further discussion of Wexler's formal results, will concern us in the following section, describing the "Motherese Hypothesis."

Although the Wexler group's work is surely the most extensive effort to examine the conditions under which a transformational grammar might be acquired, several investigators have taken up the formal approach to studying language learning, sometimes from quite different perspectives about the nature of the learning device and the grammar that is being learned (for further discussion, see Pinker, 1979, 1982, and the collection of learnability studies in Baker & McCarthy, 1981). In fact, as transformational grammar has evolved away from the so-called standard theory, and as the complexity and variety of the transformational rules has steadily diminished, it has become increasingly clear that the learning of transformations is only a small part of the task of learning a generative grammar. Moreover, the very difficulty of establishing rapid convergence for a learning system that proceeds by enumerating grammars has led Chomsky (1981) and others to consider a more restrictive framework in which the child's innate knowledge of universal grammar hypothetically goes well beyond the elementary transformational operations countenanced by Wexler, including instead a rich knowledge of universal rule schemata. In theory, these schemata contain empty slots (where languages vary) that the child needs only to fill in to learn his or her own language. Under this idealization, which is often called "parameter setting" to distinguish it from the hypothesis-testing framework, the child might come pre-armed with schema for core grammar rules informing him that (say) an NP is composed of a head noun plus specifier, but leaving open the problems of determining what order these elements appear in, how specification is marked in this language, and so on. Although some empirical work has recently appeared within this framework (see Roeper, 1982), it is still too early to estimate reliably the value of this alternative way of looking at grammar acquisition.

Saying It Won't Make It So: Caretakers' Role in the Learning Process

As we mentioned earlier, a number of investigators have suggested that the properties of caretaker speech can, in addition to easing the utterance-meaning inductions, contribute causally to solution of the projection problem: relating the forms to the meanings; that is, acquisition of grammar. The idea behind this approach is that the caretaker could order the presentation of syntactic types, so as to narrow the candidate generalizations the child would be in a position to entertain, consistent with his or her data. Certain properties of caretakers' speech to young children give some support to this claim. The caretakers' earliest utterances to children are short and propositionally simple; hence, they are uniclausal. Possibly, mothers say easiest sentences first to littlest ears, successively adding the complications as learning proceeds, and so being responsive at all times to the requirements of an environmentally dependent learning device. This has been called the "fine tuning" hypothesis. (See Cross (1977) and Gleitman et al. (1984) for arguments pro and con.)

There are a number of problems in making good this claim. First, if it is intended to remove requirements for endowments supporting language learning, it could succeed only by transferring this claim from learner to tutor; that is, by placing apparatus in the mother so that she could effectively determine (a) the syntactic simplicity of her potential utterances and (b) the current grammar of the child, plus (c) machinery for rapid implementation of these ideas during her speech planning, so that she could monitor her performance to the child on line, in order to carry out her tutorial aims. It is not obvious why "endowment with linguistic tutorial skills" of this sort should be any more palatable than "endowment with linguistic-learning skills.'' At the very least, this is an empirical question.

Apart from this problem, the evidence of maternal speech does not add plausibility to the view that it would materially aid the acquisition of syntax. For example, the earliest utterances to children are by and large not canonical sentences of the language, and a sizable percentage are not full sentences at all, but are isolated (but well-formed) NP's and interjections. The majority of the full sentences are imperatives and questions. If a transformational grammar is the envisioned end point of learning, it is clear that the child is not selectively receiving simple syntactic structures (i.e., the straightforward, least transformationally deformed outputs of base rules and the obligatory transformations). More generally, it would seem that *any* syntactic theory would have to regard the active, declarative sentences as simplest, but these are not the forms favored by caretakers in their speech to the youngest learners. Moreover, as the child grows older, the percentage of canonical declaratives said to him increases rather than decreases, while the noncanonical forms decrease in proportion. Reliable predictions of the child's growth rate from properties of the maternal speech style that vary among mothers are also limited. In fact, they are limited to the acquisition of the closed-class morphology. Many correlations of other kinds between child's linguistic stage and mother's current usage disappear once these are corrected for baseline differences among child learners. These empirical outcomes limit the extent to which the child's learning of syntax can be assigned to the effects of ''intelligent text presentation'' by the mother (for discussion, see Gleitman et al., 1984; Wexler & Culicover, 1980, ch. 2).

Other problems with this hypothesis are logical. Chomsky (1975) and Wexler (1982) have pointed out that narrowing the learner's data base, although it might do no harm, certainly cannot do good if the outcome of learning is to be a grammar covering the full range of the language. The narrower the range of data, the more hypotheses can describe them. In fact, the difficulty of proving the learnability of language formally would be considerably reduced if it were plausible to suppose that the learner received and could analyze complex input data. This is because the trans-clausal relations within sentences (the transformations, on one formulation) are revealed only in complex sentences, quite obviously.

The major result achieved by the Wexler group thus far has been to devise a set of constraints on transformational operations such that learning is demonstrable from ''degree 2'' input (sentences that are constituted, at maximum, of a clause within a clause within a clause). If the child were assumed able to deal with yet more complex input than this—thus deriving further information about the character of derived phrase structures—fewer constraints (i.e., *less* innate apparatus) would be required, as Wexler and Culicover have shown in detail. To summarize their position, the formal description of learning is *complicated* by the plausible assumption that mothers speak *simply* to their young offspring. Constraints on transformations are required just so that learning can take place, even though the real data are simple (of no more than degree 2 complexity). Why this point has been so hard for developmental psycholinguists to grasp is itself hard to grasp. It seems reasonably obvious that learning should be more difficult from limited and biased (''degenerate,'' in Chomsky's wording) data than from rich and unbiased data. The degree 2 result, along with the constraints on transformations required to make it work, provides a formal demonstration that would seem to render unassailable the logical point that partial (''simplified'') input does not ease the problem of acquiring complex systems.

Despite the logical and empirical difficulties just described, the Motherese Hypothesis continues to be pursued in the developmental psycholinguistic literature (see, for example, the collection of essays in Snow & Ferguson, 1977). This is usually done by claiming that maternal speech aids the young learner in some other and more subtle ways: Perhaps it is the gestures accompanying maternal speech that secure learning; perhaps the mother limits herself, in using a certain form, to a single semantic function for that form. Shatz (1982) has delivered the *coup de grace* to many of these fallback positions by submitting them to a series of observational and experimental tests. She has found that the form–function relations are not materially simplified in maternal speech to young learners, and that these children are quite insensitive to whatever gestural supports to comprehension their parents might be giving (see also Landau, 1982, on language learning in blind children for another kind of support for Shatz's position). It should go almost without saying that the Goldin-Meadow group's demonstrations of the survival of syntax in the absence of formal linguistic input similarly diminish hope that the environment of the learner straightforwardly determines the character of what he or she learns.

There are counterattacks, however, that were not considered by Shatz. One is the conjecture that pragmatics-based theories of language can capture the real richness of human language organization, swallowing what have usually been conceived as syntactic theories (for interesting general discussions, see Clark & Clark, 1978; Searle, 1975; and for a description that specifically attempts to account for the child's acquisition of denominal verbs, see Clark, 1982). How far these approaches, that attempt to incorporate general inferential capacities and richer analyses of situations into the description of language structure, can go is an open question, for understandably there are as yet no well-specified theories of appropriate scope within this framework (at least to our knowledge).

It is worth mentioning that at least one group of investigators has claimed that general social-interactive properties of the mother–child discourse will causally determine the actual form–meaning pairings the child learns. This position has been explicated by Bates and MacWhinney (1982). Their discussion is important, for it recognizes the essentially social nature of language and tries to bring this to bear on the problem of acquisition (see also Fernald, in press, for related arguments). This *functionalist* approach to language and its learning is in its infancy, and to this extent the discussion by Bates and MacWhinney is programmatic. At present, it is difficult to say whether social properties of conversations that differ in England and in Germany will account for the fact that English babies put the verb in the middle while German babies put it at the end; that English babies learn to say ''I won't put up with that'' but not ''I won't tolerate with that,'' and ''I painted the wall blue'' but not ''I painted the wall beautiful''; that they can interpret the *he* in ''When he sang, John entranced the audience'' anaphorically, but not the one in ''He sang, when John entranced the audience''; and all the myriad other facts about how to interpret English sentences meaningfully. On functional grounds, so far as we can see, these issues threaten to require independent explanations, yielding an infinite variety of things that must, and therefore cannot, be learned. Perhaps a functionalist grammar can be written for adults and for children that will bring this approach under control, but for the reasons just stated we must remain pessimistic. However, the descriptive apparatus does not now exist on which to support or falsify the various detailed suggestions about learning that Bates and MacWhinney have proposed.

FINAL THOUGHTS

At the bottom of any scientific paradigm lies a set of beliefs that are usually called metaphysical. It is sometimes claimed that these deep beliefs about the nature of theories and the things they describe cannot be confirmed or disconfirmed by empirical means. It is, however, quite possible to compare different metaphysical beliefs according to the degree of success of the scientific programs they support. Moreover, substantive arguments for one set of metaphysical assumptions over others can be constructed on this basis.

At its deepest level, Chomsky's break with Bloomfield is just this sort of argument. If a grammar can be construed, not as a physical description of linguistic behavior a la Bloomfield, but instead as a description of the linguistic knowledge represented in the human mind, then—so Chomsky argued—it will be possible to construct a more successful and interesting theory of language. Chomsky's familiar commitment to linguistic competence as an object of study is at once a metaphysical decision as to what sort of thing a theory of language is about, and a very practical decision as to what sorts of data the theory will be responsible for and what sorts of constraints on the theory will prove most fruitful. If a grammar describes the speaker's linguistic knowledge, then it is only indirectly revealed in linguistic behavior, and it is not to be held accountable for the physical facts about linguistic behavior for which Bloomfield's grammar must take responsibility. There is a basis (in linguistic judgments) for making an empirical distinction between acceptable and unacceptable sentences, and grammars that aim at describing linguistic knowledge can reasonably restrict themselves to sentences that speakers know to be acceptable. In contrast, attempts, such as Bloomfield's, to construct a grammar that describes behavior directly can at best account for unacceptable sentences (such as slips of the tongue) as improbable utterances, no different qualitatively from the mass of other linguistic-behavioral data.

Although Chomsky's move allows the grammar to escape responsibility for accounting in detail for linguistic behavior, it also imposes a heavy explanatory burden on linguistic theory, and on the theory of language learning in particular. For if a grammar is to be interpreted as a psychological description of human knowledge, then it necessarily raises questions about how this knowledge is acquired. Much of our discussion has attempted to summarize just how well these questions have been answered.

Recently, however, Katz (1981) has mounted an argument against Chomsky's psychologistic interpretation of grammar, one that formally parallels Chomsky's argument against Bloomfield's physicalistic interpretation of grammar. In effect, Katz argues that it is possible to achieve a better theory of language if we drop both the idea that grammar describes human knowledge and the attendant responsibility for showing how such grammatical knowledge is learnable. This can be achieved in Katz's view only if we adopt a Platonic (or realistic) interpretation of the grammar, in which grammatical principles are supposed to describe an abstract reality entirely independent of human knowledge of it, much as the reality of a mathematical relationship (e.g., the Pythagorean Theorem) is sometimes held to be true independent of human appreciation of that truth. According to Katz, this metaphysical interpretation is to be preferred because it permits a full-blooded account of necessary linguistic truths (such as lexical entailments of the "vixen is a fox" variety), which would otherwise have to be held contingent on the nature of the human mind. Moreover, Katz holds that Platonist metaphysics permits simpler solutions to certain thorny problems of grammatical description once the grammar is freed of the requirement that it be rendered in a form learnable by human beings. It may be worth noting that this is exactly the opposite of the views advanced by certain other authors we have discussed (e.g., Wexler, 1982; Newport, 1982), who take the position that the requirement of learnability and its incorporation into linguistic theory explain otherwise mysterious grammatical facts.

Bever (1982) has explored the possible consequences of the Platonist challenge to the Chomskian paradigm for theories of language acquisition. First among these consequences would be the unhooking of linguistic theory and acquisition theory. Linguistic theory describes the set of possible natural languages, and acquisition theory describes the set of languages learnable by humans. According to Platonist assumptions, there is no theoretical reason to expect these two sets to be identical. Thus, Bever argues, the Platonist paradigm remains unembarassed when it turns out that certain cognitive operations never show up in language, just as certain linguistic operations never appear elsewhere in cognition. The Chomskian paradigm can handle such facts by postulating the mental segregation of the linguistic faculty: Language is as it is because of the structure of the human mind, but language is unlike the rest of mind in some respects because the mental organ devoted to language is unlike the rest of mind (in just those respects necessary to explain the difference). Bever claims there is circularity in this formulation: "It is not a literal contradiction to maintain . . . that the essence of language is caused by an organ of the mind. But it does present a picture of language as resulting from a capacity that is mentally isolated in sporadic ways. That is, many aspects of cognition as a whole are reflected in language use and structure; why are the specific exclusions the way they are?" (1982, p. 436). By this route, Bever rejects what he takes to be Chomsky's claim that the essence of language is necessarily caused by the structure of the mind: If there is no independent evidence (independent, that is, of the evidence provided by language itself) for the shape of the mental organ devoted to language, then the claim that the essential structure of language is caused by that mental organ is only a hypothesis, no more certain—although certainly more testable—than the Platonist claim that language is independent of mind.

But once Chomsky's claim has been shown to be hypothetical, one must ask whether the Katz–Bever revelation really changes the empirical problem of explaining language acquisition. Bever argues that one consequence of Platonist assumptions is that it becomes *unnecessary* to hold that language is acquired by a mental organ specifically designed for the task. Fair enough. But it does not follow from this that language acquisition can have a *sufficient* explanation in terms of general learning mechanisms. Even if *language* is caused by the exigencies of some abstract, Platonic reality as Bever suggests, human beings' *knowledge of language* must be psychologically caused. Children must come to know their native tongue. And, as we have been at pains to argue, this knowledge cannot be acquired through unconstrained induction. Exactly what these constraints are and just how they relate to linguistic theory and to general cognition are, we take it, open empirical questions. Indeed, they are the central questions that motivate investigation, and shape our current theories of language and its learning.

ACKNOWLEDGMENTS

This chapter is a revised version of an earlier work (Gleitman & Wanner, 1982), and we thank the Cambridge University Press for allowing us to reprint highly overlapping materials here. The original chapter was constructed as the introduction to a volume of essays from a small group of investigators of child language, and hence organizes the field around these individuals' particular contributions. Although a variety of other sources were cited and discussed, certainly a chapter so constructed will distort credit that is due to many important investigators, by emphasizing particular works and passing too lightly over cognate information contributed by others. Exigencies of time constraints for the present volume prohibited large-scale revision for the current version, which exhibits various technomorphic traces of the prior work. We therefore apologize to contributors to the literature whose work has been inadvertently omitted from this discussion. However, individuals aside, the present chapter does succeed in reviewing our own current vision of the field of language learning and does state our own—to some extent idiosyncratic—beliefs and views about the generalizations to be drawn from currently available data and discussion. We thank The National Foundation for the March of Dimes and the Alfred P. Sloan Foundation, whose continuing support of our work made possible the writing of this paper. And we thank our colleagues, Henry Gleitman, Barbara Landau, and Elissa Newport, whose criticisms of prior drafts materially improved what we have been able to say.

REFERENCES

Armstrong, S. L., Gleitman, L. R., & Gleitman, H. What some concepts might not be. *Cognition*, 1983, *13*, 263–308.

Baker, C. L., & McCarthy, J. J. (Eds.). *The logical problem of language acquisition*. Cambrige, MA: MIT Press, 1981.

Bates, E., & MacWhinney, B. Functionalist approaches to grammar. In E. Wanner & L. R. Gleitman (Eds.), *Language acquisition: State of the art*. New York: Cambridge University Press, 1982.

Bellugi, U. *The acquisition of negation*. Unpublished doctoral dissertation, Harvard University, 1967.

Bever, T. G. The cognitive basis for linguistic structures. In J. Hayes (Ed.), *Cognition and the development of language*. New York: Wiley, 1970.

Bever, T. G. Some implications of the nonspecific bases of language. In E. Wanner & L. R. Gleitman (Eds.), *Language acquisition: State of the art*. New York: Cambridge University Press, 1982.

Bickerton, D. *Dynamics of a creole system*. New York: Cambridge University Press, 1975.

Blasdell, R., & Jensen, P. Stress and word position as determinants of imitation in first language learners. *Journal of Speech and Hearing Research*, 1970, *13*, 193–202.

Bloch, B. Phonemic overlapping. *American Speech*, 1941, *16*, 278–284.

Bloom, L. *Language development: Form and function in emerging grammars*. Cambridge, MA: MIT Press, 1970.

Bloom, L. *One word at a time*. The Hague: Mouton, 1973.

Bloom, L., Lightbown, P., & Hood, L. Structure and variation in child language. *Monographs of the Society for Research in Child Development*, 1975, *40* (Serial No. 160).

Bloomfield, L. *Language*. New York: Henry Holt, 1933.

Blount, B. G. Parental speech and language acquisition: Some Luo and Samoan examples. *Anthropological Linguistics*, 1972, *14*, 119–30.

Bowerman, M. Structural relationships in children's utterances: Syntactic or semantic? In T. Moore (Ed.), *Cognitive development and the acquisition of language*. New York: Academic Press, 1973.

Bowerman, M. Reorganizational processes in lexical and syntactic development. In E. Wanner & L. R. Gleitman (Eds.), *Language acquisition: The state of the art*. New York: Cambridge University Press, 1982.

Bradley, D. C., Garrett, M. F., & Zurif, E. G. Syntactic deficits in Broca's aphasia. In D. Caplan, (Ed.), *Biological studies of mental processes*. Cambridge, MA: MIT Press, 1979.

Braine, M. D. S. Children's first word combinations. *Monographs of the Society for Research in Child Development*, 1976, *41*, Serial No. 164.

Braine, M. D. S., & Hardy, J. A. On what case categories there are, why they are, and how they develop: An amalgam of *a priori* considerations, speculation, and evidence from children. In E. Wanner & L. R. Gleitman (Eds.), *Language acquisition: State of the art*, New York: Cambridge University Press, 1982.

Bresnan, J. A realistic transformational grammar. In M. Halle, J. Bresnan, & G. A. Miller (Eds.), *Linguistic theory and psychological reality*. Cambridge, MA: MIT Press, 1978.

Bresnan, J. (Ed.). *The mental representation of grammatical relations*. Cambridge, MA: MIT Press, 1982.

Broen, P.A. The verbal environment of the language learning child. *Monograph of American Speech and Hearing Association*, 1972, *17*.

Brown, R. *A first language: The early stages*. Cambridge, MA: Harvard University Press, 1973.

Brown, R., & Hanlon, C. Derivational complexity and order of acquisition in child speech. In J. Hayes (Ed.), *Cognition and the development of language*. New York: Wiley, 1970.

Brown, R., & Bellugi, U. Three processes in the child's acquisition of syntax. *Harvard Educational Review*, 1964, *34*, 133–151.

Bruner, J. S. From communication to language: A psychological perspective, *Cognition*, 1974/75, *3*, 255–87.

Carey, S. Less may never mean more. In R. Campbell & P. Smith (Eds.), *Recent advances in the psychology of language*. New York: Plenum, 1977.

Carey, S. Semantic development: The state of the art. In E. Wanner & L. R. Gleitman (Eds.), *Language acquisition: The state of the art*. New York: Cambridge University Press, 1982.

Carey, S., & Bartlett, E. Acquiring a single new word. *Papers and reports on child language development*. Department of Linguistics, Stanford University, 1978, *15*, 17–29.

Chao, Y-R. The non-uniqueness of phonemic solutions of phonetic systems. *Bulletin of the Institute of History and Philology, Academia Sinica*, 1934, *4*, 363–397.

Chomsky, N. *Aspects of the theory of syntax*. Cambridge, MA: MIT Press, 1965.

Chomsky, N. Some empirical issues in the theory of transformational grammar. In S. Peters (Ed.), *Goals of linguistic theory*. Englewood Cliffs, N.J.: Prentice-Hall, 1972.

Chomsky, N. *Reflections on language*. New York: Random House, 1975.

Chomsky, N. *Lectures on government and binding*. Dordrecht: Foris Publications, 1981.

Clark, E. V. What's in a word? On the child's acquisition of semantics in his first language. In T. Moore (Ed.), *Cognitive development and the acquisition of language*. New York: Academic Press, 1973.

Clark, E. V. The young word maker: A case study of innovation in the child's lexicon. In E. Wanner & L. R. Gleitman (Eds.), *Language acquisition: State of the art*, New York: Cambridge University Press, 1982.

Clark, E. V., & Clark, H. H. When nouns surface as verbs. *Language*, 1978, *55*, 767–811.

Cross, T. G. Mothers' speech adjustments: The contribution of selected listener variables. In C. E. Snow & C. A. Ferguson (Eds.), *Talking to children*. Cambridge, MA: Cambridge University Press, 1977.

Cutting, J., & Rosner, B. Categories and boundaries in speech and music. *Perception and Psychophysics*, 1974, *16*, 564–70.

Donaldson, M., & Balfour, G. Less is more: A study of language comprehension in children. *British Journal of Psychology*, 1968, *59*, 461–71.

Dorian, N. The fate of morphological complexity in language death. *Language*, 1978, *54*(3), 590–609.

Eimas, P. Siqueland, E. R., Jusczyk, P., & Vigorito, J. Speech perception in infants. *Science*, 1971, *171*, 303–6.

Ervin, S. Imitation and structural change in children's language. In E. Lenneberg (Ed.), *New directions in the study of language*. Cambridge, MA: MIT Press, 1964.

Feldman, H., Goldin-Meadow, S., & Gleitman, L. Beyond Herodotus: The creation of language by linguistically deprived deaf children. In A. Lock (Ed.), *Action, symbol, and gesture: The emergence of language*. New York: Academic Press, 1978.

Fernald, A. *Acoustic determinants of infant preference for "motherese."* Unpublished Ph.D. dissertation, University of Oregon, 1982.

Fernald, A. The perceptual and affective salience of mothers' speech to infants. In C. Feagans, C. Garvey, & R. Golinkoff (Eds.), *The origins and growth of communication.* New Brunswick, N.J.: Ablex, 1983.

Fernald, A., & Simon, T. Expanded intonation contours in mothers' speech to newborns. *Developmental Psychology,* in press.

Fiengo, R. *Surface structure: The interface of autonomous components.* Cambridge, MA: Harvard University Press, 1980.

Fillmore, C. J. The case for case. In E. Bach & R. J. Harms (Eds.), *Universals in linguistic theory.* New York: Holt, Rinehart, and Winston, 1968.

Fodor, J. A. *The language of thought.* New York: Crowell, 1975.

Fodor, J. A. *The modularity of mind.* Cambridge, Mass.: MIT Press, Bradford Books, 1983.

Fodor, J. A., Bever, T. G., & Garrett, M. F. *The psychology of language: An introduction to psycholinguistics and generative grammar.* New York: McGraw-Hill, 1974.

Fodor, J. A., Garrett, M. F., Walker, E. C., & Parkes, C. H. Against definitions. *Cognition,* 1980, *8,* 263–367.

Foss, D. J., & Hakes, D. T. *Psycholinguistics: An introduction to the psychology of language.* Englewood Cliffs, N.J.: Prentice-Hall, 1978.

Freyd, P., & Baron, J. Individual differences in the acquisition of derivational morphology. *Journal of verbal learning and verbal behavior,* 1982.

Fromkin, V. A. *Speech errors as linguistic evidence.* The Hague: Mouton, 1973.

Furrow, D., Nelson, K., & Benedict, H. Mothers' speech to children and syntactic development: Some simple relationships. *Journal of Child Language,* 1979, *6,* 423–442.

Garrett, M. F. The analysis of sentence production. In G. H. Bower (Ed.), *The psychology of learning and motivation,* Vol. 9. New York: Academic Press, 1975.

Gentner, D. On relational meaning: The acquisition of verb meaning. *Child Development,* 1978, *49,* 988–98.

Gentner, D. Why nouns are learned before verbs: Linguistic relativity vs. natural partitioning. In S. Kuczaj (Ed.), *Language development: Language, culture, and cognition.* Hillsdale, N.J.: Lawrence Erlbaum Associates, 1982.

Gleitman, H., & Gleitman, L. R. Language use and language judgment. In C. J. Fillmore, D. Kempler, & W. S-Y. Wang (Eds.), *Individual differences in language ability and language behavior.* New York: Academic Press, 1979.

Gleitman, L. R. Maturational determinants of language growth. *Cognition,* 1981, *10,* 103–114.

Gleitman, L. R., & Gleitman, H. *Phrase and paraphrase.* New York: Norton, 1970.

Gleitman, L. R., Newport, E. L., & Gleitman, H. The current status of the Motherese hypothesis. *Journal of Child Language,* 1984, *11.*

Gleitman, L. R., & Rozin, P. The structure and acquisition of reading I: Relations between orthographies and the structure of language. In A. Reber & D. Scarborough (Eds.), *Toward a psychology of reading.* Hillsdale, N.J.: Lawrence Erlbaum Associates, 1977.

Gleitman, L. R., & Wanner, E. Language acquisition: The state of the state of the art. In E. Wanner & L. R. Gleitman (Eds.), *Language acquisition: The state of the art.* New York: Cambridge University Press, 1982.

Goldin-Meadow, S. The resilience of recursion: A study of a communication system developed without a conventional language model. In E. Wanner & L. R. Gleitman (Eds.), *Language acquisition: The state of the art.* New York: Cambridge University Press, 1982.

Greenfield, P., & Smith, J. *The structure of communication in early language development.* New York: Academic Press, 1976.

Gruber, J. Look and See. *Language,* 1968, *43,* 937–47.

Hamburger, H., & Wexler, K. A mathematical theory of learning transformational grammar. *Journal of Mathematical Psychology,* 1975, *12,* 137–77.

Harris, Z. S. *Methods in structural linguistics.* Chicago: University of Chicago Press, 1951.

Jackendoff, R. *Semantics and cognition.* Cambridge, MA: MIT Press, 1983.

Jakobson, R. *Kindersprache, Aphasie, und alllgemeine Lautgesetze.* Stockholm: Almqvist and Wiksell, 1941.

Johnson, D. E., & Postal, P. *Arc-pair grammar.* Princeton, N.J.: Princeton University Press, 1980.

Joshi, A. K. Processing of sentences with intra-sentential code-switching. In D. Dowty, L. Kartunnen, & A. Zwicky (Eds.), *Syntactic theory and how people parse sentences.* New York: Cambridge University Press, 1983.

Jusczyk, P. W. Auditory versus phonetic coding of speech signals during infancy. *Proceedings of the CNRS Conference,* 1980.

Katz, J. J. *Semantic theory,* New York: Harper & Row, 1972.

Katz, J. J. *Language and other abstract objects.* Totowa, N.J.: Rowman and Littlefield, 1981.

Kean, M. L. Agrammatism: A phonological deficit?, *Cognition,* 1979, *7*(1), 69–84.

Keil, F. C. *Semantic and conceptual development.* Cambridge, MA: Harvard University Press, 1979.

Klatt, D. H. Vowel lengthening is syntactically determined in a connected discourse. *Journal of Phonetics,* 1975, *3,* 129–140.

Klatt, D. H. Linguistic uses of segmental duration in English: acoustic and perceptual evidence. *Journal of the Acoustic Society of America,* 1976, *59,* 1208–1221.

Klima, E., & Bellugi, U. Syntactic regularities in the speech of children. In J. Lyons & R. Wales (Eds.), *Psycholinguistics papers.* Edinburgh: Edinburgh University Press, 1966.

Klima, E., & Bellugi, U. *The signs of language.* Cambridge, MA: Harvard University Press, 1979.

Kuhl, P. K., & Miller, J. D. Speech perception by the chinchilla, Voiced-voiceless distinction in alveolar plosive consonants. *Science,* 1975, *190,* 69–72.

Labov, W. The reading of the -ed suffix. In H. Levin & J. P. Williams (Eds.), *Basic studies on reading.* New York: Basic Books, 1970.

Landau, B. *Language learning in blind children.* Unpublished Ph.D. dissertation, University of Pennsylvania, 1982.

Landau, B., & Gleitman, L. R. *The language of perception in blind children.* Harvard University Press, in press.

Lehiste, I. Suprasegmentals. Cambridge, MA: MIT Press, 1970.

Levy, L. S., & Joshi, A. K. Skeletal structural descriptions, *Information and Control,* 1978, *5*(39), No. 2.

Levy, Y. *Gender in children's language: A study of first language acquisition.* Unpublished doctoral dissertation, Hebrew University, 1980.

Levy, Y. The acquisition of Hebrew plurals: The case of the missing gender category. *Journal of Child Language,* 1983, *10*(1), 107–122.

Liberman, A. M. The grammars of speech and language. *Cognitive Psychology,* 1970, *1,* 301–323.

Liberman, A. M., Cooper, F. S., Shankweiler, D. P., & Studdert-Kennedy, M. Perception of the speech code. *Psychological Review,* 1967, *74,* 431–461.

Liberman, A. M., & Pisoni, D. B. Evidence for a special speech-perceiving subsystem in the human. In T. H. Bullock (Ed.), *Recognition of complex acoustic signals.* Berlin: Dahlem Konferenzen, 1977.

Locke, J. An essay concerning human understanding. New York: Macmillan, 1965 (originally published 1690).

Maratsos, M. How to get from words to sentences. In D. Aaronson & R. Reiber (Eds.), *Perspectives in psycholinguistics.* Hillsdale, N.J.: Lawrence Erlbaum Associates, 1979.

Maratsos, M. The child's construction of grammatical categories. In E. Wanner & L. R. Gleitman (Eds.), *Language acquisition: State of the art.* New York: Cambridge University Press, 1982.

Maratsos, M., & Chalkley, M. A. The internal language of children's syntax: The ontogenesis and representation of syntactic categories. In K. Nelson (Ed.), *Children's language,* Vol. 2. New York: Gardner Press, 1980.

Maratsos, M., Kuczaj, S. A., Fox, D. E., & Chalkley, M. A. Some empirical findings in the acquisition of transformational relations. In W. A. Collins (Ed.), *Minnesota symposia on child psychology*, Vol. 12. Hillsdale, N.J.: Lawrence Erlbaum Associates, 1979.

Marin, O., Saffran, E., & Schwartz, M. Dissociations of language in aphasia: Implications for normal function. *Annals of the New York Academy of Sciences*, 1976, *280*, 868–884.

Markman, E. M., Horton, M. S., & McLanahan, A. G. Classes and collections: Principle of organization in the learning of hierarchical relations. *Cognition*, 1980, *8*, 227–241.

McNeill, D. The creation of language by children. In J. Lyons & R. Wales (Eds.), *Psycholinguistics papers*. Edinburgh: Edinburgh University Press, 1966.

Morgan, J., & Newport, E. L. The role of constituent structure in the induction of an artificial language. *Journal of Verbal Learning and verbal behavior*, 1981, *20*, 67–85.

Nakatani, L. H., & Dukes, K. D. Locus of segmental cues for word juncture. *Journal of the Acoustic Society of America*, 1977, *62*(3), 714–724.

Nakatani, L. H., & Schaffer, J. A. Hearing "words" without words: Prosodic cues for word perception. *Journal of the Acoustic Society of America*, 1978, *63*(1), 234–245.

Nelson, K. Structure and strategy in learning to talk. *Monographs of the Society for Research in Child Development*, 1973, *38*, 1–2.

Nelson, K. Concept, word, and sentence: Interrelations in acquisition and development. *Psychological Review*, 1974, *81*, 267–285.

Newport, E. L. Motherese: The speech of mothers to young children. In N. J. Castellan, D. B. Pisoni, & G. Potts (Eds.), *Cognitive theory*, Vol. 2. Hillsdale, N.J.: Lawrence Erlbaum Associates, 1977.

Newport, E. L. Constraints on structure: Evidence from American sign language and language learning. In W. A. Collins (Ed.), *Aspects of the development of competence: Minnesota symposia on child psychology*, Vol. 14. Hillsdale, N.J.: Lawrence Erlbaum Associates, 1981.

Newport, E. L. Task specificity in language learning? Evidence from speech perception and American Sign Language. In E. Wanner & L. R. Gleitman (Eds.), *Language acquisition: The state of the art*. New York: Cambridge University Press, 1982.

Newport, E. L., & Ashbrook, E. F. The emergence of semantic relations in American sign language. *Papers and Reports on Child Language Development* (Dept. of Linguistics, Stanford University), 1977, *13*, 16–21.

Newport, E. L., Gleitman, H., & Gleitman, L. R. Mother, I'd rather do it myself: Some effects and noneffects of maternal speech style. In C. E. Snow & C. A. Ferguson (Eds.), *Talking to children: Language input and acquisition*. Cambridge: Cambridge University Press, 1977.

Newport, E. L., & Supalla, T. The structuring of language: Clues from the acquisition of signed and spoken language. In U. Bellugi & M. Studdert-Kennedy (Eds.), *Signed and spoken language: Biological constraints on linguistic form*. Dahlem Konferenzen. Weinheim/Deerfield Beach, Fl./Basel: Verlag Chemie, 1980.

Palermo, D. S. More about less: A study of language comprehension. *Journal of verbal learning and verbal behavior*, 1973, *12*, 211–21.

Perlmutter, D. M. Relational grammar. In E. Moravcsik & J. Wirth (Eds.), *Syntax and semantics*, Vol. 13. New York: Academic Press, 1980.

Phillips, J. *Formal characteristics of speech which mothers address to their young children*. Doctoral dissertation, Johns Hopkins University, 1970.

Pinker, S. Formal models of language learning. *Cognition*, 1979, *7*, 217–283.

Pinker, S. A theory of the acquisition of lexical interpretive grammars. In J. Bresnan (Ed.), *The mental representation of grammatical relations*. Cambridge, MA: MIT Press, 1982.

Pye, C. Mayan telegraphese. *Language*, 1983, *59*(3), 583–604.

Quine, W. V. *Word and object*. Cambridge, MA: MIT Press, 1960.

Read, C., & Schreiber, P. Why short subjects are harder to find than long ones. In E. Wanner & L.

R. Gleitman (Eds.), *Language acquisition: State of the art*. New York: Cambridge University Press, 1982.

Roeper, T. The role of universals in the acquisition of gerunds. In E. Wanner & L. R. Gleitman (Eds.), *Language acquisition: State of the art*. New York: Cambridge University Press, 1982.

Rosch, E. On the internal structure of perceptual and semantic categories. In T. Moore (Ed.), *Cognitive development and the acquisition of language*. New York: Academic Press, 1973.

Rosch, E. Cognitive representation of semantic categories, *Journal of Experimental Psychology: General*, 1975, *104*, 192–233.

Rosch, E., & Mervis, C. B. Family resemblances: Studies in the internal structure of categories. *Cognitive Psychology*, 1975, *7*, 573–605.

Rosch, E., Mervis, C. B., Gray, W. D., Johnson, D. M., & Boyes-Braem, P. Basic objects in natural categories. *Cognitive Psychology*, 1976, *8*, 382–439.

Rozin, P., & Gleitman, L. R. The structure and acquisition of reading II: The reading process and the acquisition of the alphabetic principle. In A. Reber & D. Scarborough (Eds.), *Toward a psychology of reading*. Hillsdale, N.J.: Lawrence Erlbaum Associates, 1977.

Sachs, J., & Devin, J. Young children's use of appropriate speech styles in social interaction and role-playing. *Journal of child Language*, 1976, *3*, 81–98.

Sankoff, G., & Laberge, S. On the acquisition of native speakers by a language. *Kivung*, 1973, *6*, 32–47.

Schieffelin, B. B. Getting it together: An ethnographic approach to the study of the development of communicative competence. In E. Ochs & B. B. Schieffelin (Eds.), *Developmental pragmatics*. New York: Academic Press, 1979.

Schlesinger, I. M. The production of utterances and language acquisition. In D. I. Slobin (Ed.), *The ontogenesis of grammar: A theoretical symposium*. New York: Academic Press, 1971.

Searle, J. R. Indirect speech acts. In P. Cole and J. Morgan (Eds.), *Syntax and semantics: Vol. 3: Speech acts*. New York: Academic Press, 1975.

Shatz, M. Children's comprehension of question-directives, *Journal of Child Language*, 1978, *5*, 39–46.

Shatz, M. On mechanisms of language acquisition: Can features of the communicative environment account for development? In E. Wanner and L. R. Gleitman (Eds.), *Language acquisition: State of the art*. New York: Cambridge University Press, 1982.

Shatz, M., & Gelman, R. The development of communication skills: Modifications in the speech of young children as a function of listener. *Monographs of the Society for Research in Child Development* 1973, No. 152, *38*(5).

Skinner, B. F. *Verbal behavior*. New York: Appleton-Century-Crofts, 1957.

Slobin, D. I. The acquisition of Russian as a native language. In F. Smith & C. A. Miller (Eds.), *The genesis of language: A psycholinguistic approach*, Cambridge, MA: MIT Press, 1966.

Slobin, D. I. Cognitive prerequisites for the development of grammar. In C. A. Ferguson & D. I. Slobin (Eds.) *Studies of child language development*. New York: Holt, Rinehart, & Winston, 1973.

Slobin, D. I. Language change in childhood and in history. In J. Macnamara (Ed.), *Language learning and thought*. New York: Academic Press, 1977.

Slobin, D. I. Universal and particular in the acquisition of language. In E. Wanner & L. R. Gleitman (Eds.), *Language acquisition: State of the art*. New York: Cambridge University Press, 1982.

Slobin, D. I., & Bever, T. G. Children use canonical sentence schemas: A crosslinguistic study of word order and inflections. *Cognition*, 1982, *12*(3), 229–266.

Snow, C. E. Mothers' speech research: From input to interaction. In C. E. Snow & C. A. Ferguson (Eds.), *Talking to children: Language input and acquisition*. New York: Cambridge University Press, 1977.

Snow, C., Arlman-Rupp, A., Hassing, Y., Jobse, J., Joosten, J., & Vorster, J. Mothers' speech in three social classes, *Journal of Psycholinguistic Research*, 1976, *5*, 1–20.

Snow, C. E., & Ferguson, C. A. (Eds.). *Talking to children*. Cambridge: Cambridge University Press, 1977.

Sorenson, J. M., Cooper, W. E., & Paccia, J. M. Speech timing of grammatical categories. *Cognition*, 1978, *6*(2), 135–54.

Spelke, E. S. Perceptual knowledge of objects in infancy. In J. Mehler, M. F. Garrett, & E. C. Walker (Eds.), *Perspectives in mental representation*. Hillsdale, N.J.: Lawrence Erlbaum Associates, 1982.

Spring, D. R., & Dale, P. S. Discrimination of linguistic stress in early infancy. *Journal of Speech and Hearing Research*, 1977, *20*, 224–231.

Streeter, L. A. Acoustic determinants of phrase boundary perception. *Journal of the Acoustic Society of America*, 1978, *64*, 1582–92.

Waxman, S., & Gelman, R. *Preschoolers' use of superordinate relations in classification*. Unpublished manuscript, University of Pennsylvania.

Wexler, K. A principle theory for language acquisition. In E. Wanner & L. R. Gleitman (Eds.), *Language acquisition: State of the art*. New York: Cambridge University Press, 1982.

Wexler, K., & Culicover, P. *Formal principles of language acquisition*. Cambridge, MA: MIT Press, 1980.

Wexler, K., & Hamburger, H. On the insufficiency of surface data for the learning of transformational languages. In K. Hintikka, J. Moravcsik, & P. Suppes (Eds.), *Approaches to natural languages*. Dordrecht: Reidel, 1973.

Wittgenstein, L. *Philosophical investigations*. New York: Macmillan, 1953.

6

Social and Emotional Development in Infancy

Michael E. Lamb
University of Utah

INTRODUCTION

Over the last century, the attention paid to emotional phenomena and to social and emotional development has waxed and waned. These increases and decreases in the popularity of social and emotional issues among researchers and theorists have coincided respectively with optimism, occasioned by the emergence of new theoretical perspectives, and with pessimism, attributable to the apparent empirical intractability of emotions and emotional phenomena. Empirical advances have also been hampered by the absence of a clear, consensually acceptable definition of "the emotions." Because each investigator or theorist appears to have had an idiosyncratic definition and focus (see for example Plutchik, 1980) each pursued her or his unique questions in near isolation. Where conflicts or disagreements have arisen, they might often have been avoided if researchers had shown greater awareness of differences in emphasis, definition, and approach. As I show in this chapter, many of the competing theories address different questions and are thus not necessarily inconsistent with one another. Thus a synthesis of the most useful contributions of each approach is not only possible, but necessary.

Although I describe other perspectives, let me briefly provide my definition of "the emotions." Following the approach taken by researchers such as Campos (e.g., Campos & Stenberg, 1981; Klinnert, Campos, Sorce, Emde, & Svejda, 1983), I view emotions and emotional expressions as phenomena having two important purposes. First, emotional states or affects facilitate and potentiate behavioral reactions to external events. Second, emotional expressions serve a communicative function, alerting others to the emotional state, and thus to the

241

behavioral predisposition of the individual. As discussed later most theorists have focused on one or the other of these functions. The psychoanalysts and cognitive developmentalists, for example, have emphasized the covert relationships between emotional states and behavior, whereas the ethological-adaptational and social cognitive theorists have focused on the communicative functions of emotional expressions. These differences are explored further when the principal explanations of socioemotional development are discussed in sections two (Major Theories and Approaches) and four (Explanations and Interpretations of Socioemotional Milestones).

Curiously, there has been considerably less disagreement about the central question to be addressed in research and theorizing concerning social development than regarding emotional development. In this area, the principal concern has always been with the mechanisms underlying the formation of enduring emotional bonds or relationships to specific people, notably parents, and the effects of varying social experiences on later personality. However, the major theorists have attempted to provide somewhat different types of explanations, ranging from descriptions to explanations that focus on proximal causes and mechanisms to explanations that dwell on ultimate causes. Nevertheless, a consensus has emerged in the last decade, thanks to the pioneering work of John Bowlby (1969), who brought the perspective of evolutionary biology to bear on social and emotional aspects of early human development.

In this chapter, I deal only with aspects of socioemotional development in infancy. The decision to restrict the focus to this phase of life was made because although researchers have given attention to social and emotional development in older children, theoretical issues have always been clearest and the empirical data base is greatest where infancy is concerned. However, many of the issues discussed here are pertinent to the study and understanding of socioemotional development in older children.

In the second section, concerned with theories and approaches, I briefly review the major perspectives on social and emotional development, focusing on five approaches—psychoanalysis, learning theory, ethology-adaptation theory, cognitive-developmental theory, and social cognition—roughly in the order in which they attained prominence so as to provide some appreciation of the history of the area.

In the third section, I describe five milestones of social and emotional development: the emergence of social smiling, stranger anxiety or wariness, separation anxiety, social attachment, and the fear of heights. The explanations provided by the major theories for each of these milestones are discussed and evaluated in the fourth section. Here we find, as mentioned earlier, that each approach is able to explain some, but not all, of the developments on which we focus, and that in several cases, different theorists have identified different issues to explain. The origins and nature of individual differences in socioemotional development are described and discussed in the fifth section. A summary and conclusion comprise the final section.

MAJOR THEORIES AND APPROACHES[1]

Although many theorists and developmentalists have pondered the nature of socioemotional development, most have provided explanations that can be categorized into one of five major theoretical approaches. In this section, I describe only major theorists characteristic of each approach in an attempt to illustrate the nature of these diverse perspectives.

Psychoanalysis and Its Derivatives

Systematic attention to social and emotional development in infancy began with Sigmund Freud's construction of psychoanalytic theory in the first decade of the twentieth century. Freud's work (e.g., 1940) was of seminal importance for two reasons. First, he was the first theorist to speculate about the formative significance of those early experiences such as feeding, infantile sexuality, and toilet training, which had formerly been considered relatively unimportant. Second, Freud was perhaps the first theorist to pose questions about the development of emotions, rather than about their nature and significance in adults.

Freud (1923/1962) proposed that the human mind was organized into three mental systems—the id, ego, and superego.

The superego, which governs the moral and ethical conduct of the individual, develops in early to middle childhood and is thus not a factor in infant development.

By contrast, the interplay between the id and the ego is critically important to psychoanalytic theorizing about infancy. Freud viewed the id, which strives for immediate gratification by any available means, as the source of all human motivation.

Unlike the id, which is present at birth, the ego develops slowly and attempts to establish control over the id by ensuring that gratification is obtained only at appropriate times and places. Among the crucial psychological functions of the ego are: the delay of gratification; perception, thought, and language; and the experience and expression of emotions (external expressions) and affects (internal feeling states). The development of the ego can thus be assessed by observing the emergence of these three general functions.

Throughout most of his life, Freud focused on the development of the superego; his concern with infancy and thus with ego development, was one that crystalized only in the last few years of his life (e.g., Freud, 1940). As a result, most psychoanalytic theory concerning early social and emotional development is attributable to Freud's followers, notably Anna Freud (his daughter) and René Spitz.

---

[1]Most theorists speculate about social influences on socioemotional development, and in this regard almost all deal exclusively with maternal influences. In most cases, the crucial factor is the social role (caretaker) played by the mother, not her biological gender or biological relationship to the child.

It was Spitz (e.g., 1965) who proposed that ego development is not simply a function of biological maturation; instead, he argued, the emergence of ego processes is primarily determined by the quality of mother-infant interaction. In Spitz's view the major milestones of socioemotional development were "organizers" that reflected the attainment of a new stage of ego development. When maternal care was adequate, biological maturation ensured that these milestones occurred at a predictable time; but when the infant's care was deficient, ego development was retarded and thus the milestones were attained more slowly, if at all.

Psychoanalysts link the major milestones in socioemotional development to ego development, which, in their view, is affected by mother-child interaction, separation, and the child's perception of the mother's physical and emotional accessibility or inaccessibility. According to the psychoanalysts, mother-infant interaction is related to affect development in two ways. First, the mother as primary caretaker assures gratification of the infant's physical needs and this in itself guarantees formative importance. Second, she must often frustrate the child in order to facilitate its integration into society. These frustrations begin early with attempts to train the child to sleep through the night and to feed on schedule. By being the source of both gratification and frustration, the mother is thus responsible for both increases and decreases in drive. Because drive increases produce displeasure, while drive reductions produce quiescence (absence of unpleasure) or pleasure, the mother is inextricably tied into the infant's affective life.

The affects that result from need gratification help to organize the ego processes of perception, cognition, and memory. They facilitate perception by giving salience to stimuli in the environment that coincide with need and need reduction. When mother-infant interaction is generally gratifying, the stimuli that become salient are likely to be those that relate to the mother, particularly her face.

Learning Theory

Shortly after the psychoanalytic movement was launched by Freud in Vienna, behaviorism was born in the United States. It was founded by John Watson, who was frustrated by the tendency, especially on the part of European theorists, to speculate about the effects of unobservable events or unobservable mental structures and processes. If psychology was to be a science, argued Watson (1913), it must limit itself to phenomena that are empirically verifiable. Impressed by Pavlov's then recent research on classical conditioning in dogs, Watson proposed that emotional development proceeded as a result of learned associations with, or modifications of, one of the three basic (i.e., unlearned or innate) emotions he posited: fear (elicited by loud noises or the loss of support), rage (elicited by the restriction of bodily movements), and love (elicited by stroking, patting, or stimulating an erogenous zone).

Watson's major empirical contribution was the demonstration that fears could be developed through classical conditioning (Watson & Rayner, 1920) and could be eliminated in the same way (Jones, 1924). Watson and Rayner, for example, by associating the appearance of a rat with the loud fear-eliciting sound of a gong produced a conditioned fear of rats (and, indeed of all white, furry things). Watson assumed that the same process must underlie all conditioned emotions, not only fears. For Watson, and the learning theorists who followed him, only emotional expressions were of interest; internal affective states were not independently explorable or verifiable and were thus to be ignored.

While classical conditioning aims to account for the transfer of an already existing response to new stimuli that did not initially elicit the reaction, operant conditioning is useful for explaining increases or decreases in the frequency of emotional reactions that occur spontaneously. The operant conditioning of emotional reactions in infants only became the focus of attention in the 1950s, several decades after the learning theory approach was promoted by Watson. Researchers such as Rheingold, Gewirtz, and Ross (1959), Brackbill (1958), and Gewirtz (Etzel & Gewirtz, 1967) showed that rates of smiling, vocalizing, and crying could be experimentally manipulated by the discriminating application of rewards or punishments. A further development of this general approach took place a decade later, when Bandura and Walters (1959, 1963) reintroduced the notion of learning through mere observation, which they called observational learning. They argued that many behavior patterns, including emotional expression, could be learned simply by seeing them displayed by other people. However, they did not explicitly consider infant emotional behavior.

Ethological-Adaptational Theory

Unlike psychoanalysts and learning theorists, ethological-adaptational theorists such as Bowlby (1969) consider the communicative functions of emotions to be of paramount importance. As a result, they tend to focus on why people perceive emotions and experience affects, and what purpose emotions and social relationships serve. During infancy, they argue, emotional expressions such as smiles and cries affect the behavior of parents and caretakers and thus play a special role in regulating social relationships. More specifically, Bowlby proposed that these signals promote proximity to protective adults, and thus would have had great survival value in the environment in which humans originally evolved.

Bowlby went further, suggesting that the repeated association of proximity-promoting signals with appropriate (i.e., proximity-promoting) responses on the part of adults underlies the formation of attachment bonds between infants and adults. In so doing, Bowlby not only provided an answer to questions about why emotions and social relationships exist in infancy (they exist because they have survival value), but also proposed a mechanism whereby social bonding might proceed. Bowlby, who was trained as a psychoanalyst, believed that his theory, based on the principles of modern evolutionary biology, provided a more defensible model of emotional dynamics than did Freud's notion that emotional energy was regulated by the hypothetical mental structures, id, ego, and superego.

Cognitive-Developmental Approaches

While recognizing the potential function of emotional states and expressions, another group of theorists has, since the 1940s, been concerned with the cognitive processes that are the proximate causes of emotions or affects. In a seminal contribution, Hebb (1946, 1949) sought to explain how fear came to be elicited by the appearance of a novel stimulus—one that by definition could not have been associated with unpleasant consequences because it had never been encountered before. Hebb provided a physiological explanation in terms of the discrepancy between the pattern of stimulation occasioned by previous encounters with familiar stimuli and the stimulation produced by the novel stimulus. This discrepancy produces the distress which we call fear, Hebb argued. Modifying Hebb's formulation, developmental psychologists such as Kagan (e.g., 1971, 1974) and McCall (e.g., McCall & McGhee, 1977) provided an explanation of the same sort, in which they attributed fear or distress to the discrepancy between memories (or schemata) and the features of novel objects.

In terms of the discrepancy model, the magnitude of an emotional response varies depending on the degree of similarity between the novel stimulus and the schemata to which it is compared. When there is great similarity, there is little discrepancy, and thus little distress is occasioned. As the magnitude of the discrepancy increases, the amount of distress increases, up to the point at which discrepancy becomes so great that the stimulus cannot be assimilated. The amount of distress thereupon starts to decrease—producing an inverted U-shaped curve relating distress to degree of discrepancy. Kagan (1971, 1974; Kagan, Kearsley, & Zelazo, 1978) has argued that the discrepancy model can account for emotional phenomena such as smiling, separation anxiety, and stranger anxiety or wariness.

Social Cognition

The most recent perspective to gain prominence is the social-cognitive approach. There is really no unified theory here, but an approach which—like the cognitive-developmental theory—emphasizes the infant's attempts to make sense of or interpret its experiences. Many of those who take this perspective have attempted to make their perspective an adjunct to Bowlby's ethological-adaptational theory.

Despite similarities with the cognitive developmentalists, those who have proposed a social-cognitive approach differ in important ways from them. Where the cognitive developmentalists focus on discrepancy, one group of social-cognitive theorists has emphasized ambiguity, and has emphasized the communicative function of emotional expressions. For example, Campos and his colleagues (Klinnert et al., 1983) have shown that when in ambiguous situations, infants of 10 months of age and older will examine their mothers' faces for emotional cues—presumably because this information may help them to disambiguate the situation. The child then modifies its emotion and behavior in accordance with the mother's emotional expression.

The propensity to both seek and utilize the information thus obtained may vary depending on the degree of trust the infants have in their mothers. The development of trustful relationships has itself been an issue of concern to social-cognitive theorists. Following Ainsworth (1973, 1979), Lamb (1981a, 1981b) has suggested that variations in the responsiveness and sensitivity of parents to their children's signals may produce differences in the extent to which children come to count on their parents' reliability, consistency, and appropriateness of response.

Summary

Although each group of theorists has attempted to explain central aspects of socioemotional development, the approaches, emphasis, and assumptions are remarkably different. Notice, however, that each group has asked a slightly different question. Psychoanalysts have focused on the way in which social experiences retard or accelerate the endogenous processes underlying development. Learning theorists have focused on the way in which social experiences affect the emergence or later development of certain emotional reactions in the absence of any underlying endogenous developmental process. The ethological-adaptational theorists have asked what purpose these emotional reactions might currently serve or might have served during the evolutionary history of the species. The cognitive-developmental theorists have asked what basic cognitive processes underlie changes in social and emotional behavior, while those who adopt a social-cognitive perspective propose that we may obtain a broader view of socioemotional development if we assume that children actively try to make sense of, or to understand, their social and nonsocial experiences.

Thus we find both differences in basic assumptions and differences in focus. This means that while perspectives which make incompatible assumptions are obviously inconsistent with one another (e.g., psychoanalysis and learning theory), the others may all contribute something to our understanding of socioemotional development, with the joint insights being more useful than those provided by any one approach on its own.

MILESTONES IN SOCIOEMOTIONAL DEVELOPMENT

Despite great differences in approach and emphasis, all of the approaches described above have attempted to explain a narrow set of social and emotional phenomena. As far as emotional development is concerned, focus has fallen on the emergence of social smiling, fearful reactions to strangers, and distressed reactions to separation from the parents. The major milestone in social development is the formation of discriminating social attachments, which is, in most accounts, temporally linked to the emergence of separation anxiety. In this section, I describe the onset and nature of these five milestones, and then in the next section, discuss the way in which each group of theorists has attempted to explain these aspects of emotional development.

Social Smiling

Although newborns and even preterm infants produce facial expressions that resemble smiling, these expressions usually occur when the infant is either drowsy or sleeping, and seem to represent involuntary physiological reactions. Voluntary smiling (e.g., smiles elicited by social bids from adults) in a waking state usually does not occur until the infant is 4 to 6 weeks of age. Initially, smiles are elicited by a variety of stimuli, including faces, bells, and bull's-eyes (Emde & Harmon, 1972) but gradually they are limited to social stimuli and contexts, with the human face, viewed full-on, becoming the most effective stimulus for eliciting smiles. At first, the eyes appear to be most important, as a stimulus containing little more than two dots is effective in eliciting smiles. Over time, however, the infant comes to require a richer, more facelike stimulus if smiles are to be elicited (Ahrens, 1954). From the second and third months, the infant appears capable of recognizing specific faces, and thereafter, the faces of familiar people—such as family members and perhaps regular babysitters—elicit smiles most readily. Less familiar individuals elicit weaker smiles and must work harder to elicit any.

Stranger Anxiety or Wariness

Although positive reactions to strange adults are somewhat muted from late in the first quarter year (Bronson, 1972), frankly negative reactions typically do not occur until the third quarter year of life. The intensity of these reactions varies from infant to infant: Some infants may only sober when they encounter a stranger, whereas others may cry intensely and retreat rapidly. Initially called "eight month anxiety" because Spitz believed that these reactions predictably emerged at eight months, it has now become clear that the onset of negative stranger reactions is highly variable from one infant to the next, although all infants seem to pass through a phase of adverse responses to strangers, usually beginning between 6 and 15 months of age (Emde, Harmon, & Gaensbauer, 1976). One group of researchers (Scarr & Salapatek, 1970) reported a second peak around 18 months, but this is not well established. Situational characteristics also affect the intensity of stranger reactions, as Rheingold and Eckerman (1973) and Sroufe, Waters, and Matas (1974) have shown. Specifically, the intrusiveness and strangeness of the adult's behavior, as well as the proximity and accessibility of the parent, and the familiarity of the location, all affect the intensity of distress or wariness. In many cases, signs of wariness, distress, or avoidance alternate with indices of positive affiliation, indicating that infants are often attracted to strangers as well as alarmed by them (Bretherton, 1978; Bretherton & Ainsworth, 1974).

Separation Anxiety

When distress occurs following separation from parents in infants under 6–8 months of age, it appears related to the termination of enjoyable activities; infants are readily mollified by substitutes who take up where the departing person leaves off. Hereafter, however, distress appears related to separation from specific persons, and children are often dissatisfied with substitutes. If the separation is prolonged, the reaction changes from distress, agitation, and anger (termed protest) to despondency and apparent depression (called despair), to apparent recovery (otherwise known as detachment) as the child regains responsiveness to social overtures (Bowlby, 1973, 1980; Robertson & Bowlby, 1952). Long-term separations that take place prior to the onset of separation anxiety around 6–8 months (as, for example, when a child is moved from a foster home to an adoptive home) may produce temporary disequilibrium as the child adjusts to new routines and styles, but there is no comparison with the intensity of protest and despair observed when older infants experience the same separations (e.g., Yarrow & Goodwin, 1973).

Social Attachments

The emergence of discriminating separation protests is usually viewed as evidence that children have formed specific attachment bonds to the person concerned (Ainsworth, 1973; Bowlby, 1969). Other indices of these bonds include: Use of the adult as a 'secure base,' whose presence facilitates exploration; selective use of the adult for comfort or protection in the event of distress or fear; and a preferential desire for proximity to, or contact with, the adult.

As mentioned earlier, infants begin to show preferences for familiar over unfamiliar adults from the first quarter-year of life. Although they are clearly part of the process leading up to attachment, theorists have been unwilling to describe these early preferences as indices of attachment. Most theorists believe that the emergence of separation protest signals a major qualitative change in the nature of social relationships. For the first time, the child reacts differentially to the absence of a person, rather than simply to his or her presence. This suggests a change in the child's cognitive capacity—perhaps the onset of recall memory or object permanence (Piaget, 1952)—which allow the child to remember, and therefore miss, the parent when s/he is not present. This qualitative change, manifest behaviorally by the emergence of separation anxiety, is often viewed as a sign that true social attachments to specific individuals have been formed.

Fear of Heights

The second half–year of life is noted not only for the emergence of fear of strangers and separation anxiety; it is also a time when several nonsocial emotional changes take place.

The best studied of these is the emergence of a fear of heights, even though psychologists have only in the last decade come to recognize that the fear of heights is as much an aspect of emotional, as of perceptual, development. Because some animals appear fearful on the deep side of the visual cliff from birth or from the time they are able to see, many had speculated that the fear of heights was innate (e.g., Walk, 1978). This does not appear to be the case in humans. The first crucial study was one by Campos, Langer, and Krowitz (1970) in which it was shown that by 2–3 months of age infants could distinguish between deep and shallow drop-offs when suspended over them: their heart rate predictably decreased when they viewed depth, indicating attention and interest. Later Fox, Aslin, Shea, and Dumais (1980) used a more complex procedure to show that the stereoptic perception of depth emerged around 3–4 months. Interestingly, however, infants of this age do not show any signs of fear when suspended over a deep "cliff." Fearful reactions—including heart rate acceleration, distress, and refusal to cross the deep side of the visual cliff, despite the support provided by clear perspex—typically does not emerge until around 8 months of age, although there is individual variability (Campos, Hiatt, Ramsay, Henderson, & Svejda, 1978). These findings show that the *fear* of depth emerges several months after the capacity to *perceive* depth. Campos and his colleagues propose that the decalage is attributable to the fact that the sensation of depth does not initially have any fearful meaning. Once the infant is able to locomote and fall, however, depth becomes a very meaningful clue to danger, and thus begins to elicit fear.

Summary

Social smiling usually begins in the second month, and becomes common and reliable within a few weeks. After an initial period of promiscuous sociability, infants come to reserve their broadest and readiest smiles for familiar people. Five or six months later, several new emotional reactions—including stranger anxiety, separation anxiety, the fear of heights, and social attachment—all emerge at roughly the same time. Stranger reactions, separation anxiety and social attachment have often been linked in attempted explanations of their emergence, although the contemporaneous emergence of the fear of heights at least raises doubts about these links, as does evidence that stranger and separation anxiety have different origins and times of onset. These issues are explored further in the next section, where the focus is on explanations and interpretations of these milestones of socioemotional development.

EXPLANATIONS AND INTERPRETATIONS OF SOCIOEMOTIONAL MILESTONES

Social Smiling

Psychoanalytic Theory.   As mentioned earlier, the pleasurable sensation of need gratification helps to organize perception by making certain stimuli salient. When mother-infant interaction develops favorably, the stimuli that become salient are likely to be features of the mother, especially of her face. At first, this perceptual learning is rather crude: It involves discriminating certain specific aspects of the face—a configuration consisting of forehead, eyes, and nose. Once this percept is discriminated from the background stimulation, it becomes a social releaser that elicits the smiling response automatically. Thereafter, any oval stimulus containing the features of eyes can elicit smiles, even if the stimulus does not otherwise look much like a face.

Need and need reduction also help organize memory: The child learns that the appearance of the facial stimuli means that drive reduction is about to take place. Hence, Spitz (1965) uses the term ''sign gestalt'' to refer to the facial features that elicit social smiles.

In terms of this theory, infants do not learn to smile; they learn to notice the features of the face which *automatically* elicit smiling. Of course if there was no consistent caretaker, or no regular coincidence of certain stimuli and certain drive states, the face gestalt would not be noticed until later, if at all. Early, albeit methodologically weak, studies seemed to support the psychoanalysts' contentions: Ambrose (1961) found that social smiles occurred earlier in family-reared than institutionally reared infants, while Spitz and Wolf (1946) found that social smiling was delayed by cold or hostile mother–infant interaction.

The onset of social smiling heralds what Spitz called the stage of the preobject, during which the child does not yet understand the identity of the mother. During this stage, many face-like stimuli elicit smiling, while familiar faces in profile do not. Continued interaction promotes further perceptual refinements until, with time, the recognition of mother becomes so affectively laden that an important new set of cognitive and emotional processes emerge, including evocative (recall) memory, separation anxiety, and stranger anxiety.

The psychoanalytic explanation of the onset of social smiling has a fatal flaw, in that 6–12 week old infants smile not only at faces, but also at a wide range of nonsocial stimuli, such as bells and bull's-eye patterns (Emde & Harmon, 1972). The theory cannot explain this, and we must thus doubt the veracity of its explanation regarding the onset of social smiles.

Learning Theory.   Learning theorists explain the emergence of social smiling by proposing that the features of the face are associated, through a process of classical conditioning, with the pleasurable state that was brought about by drive reduction or need gratification (resulting from feeding, drinking, keeping warm). Later increases in the frequency of social smiling can be affected by operant contingencies: Parents respond enthusiastically when the infant smiles and thus reward or reinforce smiling. Two crucial studies have demonstrated the classical conditioning and deconditioning of emotions (albeit fear rather than smiling: Watson & Rayner, 1920; Jones, 1924), while others have demonstrated that the frequency of smiling can indeed be increased by reinforcement (e.g., Schwartz & Rosenberg, 1968; Etzel & Gewirtz, 1967). Thus, there appears to be some empirical support for this theory's predictions.

Unfortunately, learning theory appears better able to explain the transfer of emotional reactions from one stimulus to another and variations in the frequency of smiling and other emotional expressions than to explain the initial emergence of emotional reactions. In the case of social smiling, for example, we know that—contrary to Watson's predictions—feeding, holding, or stroking babies does not elicit smiling. Nor does any other form of drive reduction (Spitz, 1965). Thus there is no known unconditional stimulus that initially and innately elicits smiles, which is crucially important if conditional stimuli (like faces or voices) are later to become effective elicitors of smiles through conditioning. Imitation and observational learning likewise cannot explain the onset of social smiling, because blind babies begin smiling to their parents' voices at the same age as sighted infants (Fraiberg, 1974, 1977). And although the frequency of smiling can be shaped through operant conditioning, it is not plausible to suggest that infants' mouth movements are shaped in successive approximations until recognizable smiles are evident.

Cognitive-Developmental Theory.   Drawing on several of Piaget's notions, cognitive developmentalists like Kagan have expanded Hebb's theory to account for the occurrence of smiling as a result of both social and nonsocial stimuli. Kagan (1971) proposed that smiling occurs when an environmental event is assimilated to (i.e., fitted into) a central schema. Smiling at faces thus reflects the emergence of recognition memory, and mastery of the task of recognizing, first, faces in general, and later, the mother's face. Smiling at nonsocial stimuli, such as bells and bull's-eyes, is explained by hypothesizing that a new perceptual skill—the ability to perceive curvilinear stimuli—emerges in the third month.

Before then, infants do not perceive curvilinearity, hence pay little attention to such stimuli, and thus do not smile at them. When the skill first emerges, however, it permits the successful but effortful processing of information, and smiling is thus elicited. After three months, sounds are also processed differently: Earlier, they were only listened to, whereas now they can also be looked at. Practicing this new schema results in smiling.

Cognitive theories such as Kagan's predict inverted U-shaped functions relating the probability of emotional response to the amount of experience infants have had: Smiling should not occur when a schema is first being established nor should it occur when the schema is so well developed that the stimulation is no longer novel. Smiling should be greatest when the stimulus is somewhat novel, and thus somewhat difficult to assimilate to an existing schema. There is, in fact, some empirical support for this hypothesis (Zelazo, 1972), albeit in a study concerned with the elicitation of smiles by success in nonsocial tasks, varying in the degree of difficulty. Unlike either the psychoanalytic or learning theory explanations, the quality of the infant-mother interaction is of no consequence to Kagan's theory although the amount of interaction may be important. Emotional developments should occur on schedule, regardless of the child's relationship with its mother, provided that some alternative sources of stimulation are available.

Not all cognitive theorists emphasize discrepancy between stimuli and memory schemas as much as Kagan and Hebb do. Sroufe, for example, has shown that degree of discrepancy can account for the *intensity,* but not for the *hedonic quality,* of an emotional reaction. As a result, the same stimulus can elicit very different emotional responses, depending on the context in which testing takes place (Sroufe & Wunsch, 1977; Sroufe, Waters, & Matas, 1974). For instance, when mothers wear a mask, 9–12 month old infants will tend to smile or laugh, whereas if it is worn by unfamiliar adults, infants may cringe, turn away, or cry. These findings suggest that infants are capable of much more complex cognitive activities than memory and the perception of discrepancy. Following Bowlby, Sroufe (1977, 1979) interprets these findings to mean that infants (like adults) are capable of rudimentary cognitive inferences or appraisals, designed to determine whether stimuli are potentially pleasurable or harmful. Kagan (1974), on the other hand, denies the existence of these abilities in the first year of life.

Although the cognitive theory appears to explain the emergence of social smiling more successfully than either the psychoanalytic or learning theory, it can be criticized for underemphasizing biological and biogenetic determinants of behavior. There is a clear developmental progression from biological, internal elicitation to external environmental elicitation of smiles. Newborns smile quite readily, but only in rapid eye movement states (Emde & Harmon, 1972). For a few weeks after birth, they also smile when they are drowsy but not when they are awake. Only after 4–6 weeks of age do infants smile in response to environmental stimulation. This developmental sequence appears to be under maturational control, because premature infants begin to smile at environmental stimuli at the same conceptional age as full-term infants, which is, of course, longer after birth and thus after much more postnatal experience (Dittrichova, as cited by Bower, 1977). Twin studies show that monozygotic twins are more alike than dizygotic twins in their tendencies to smile during the first four months of life, suggesting that genetic factors influence individual differences in emotional reactions (Freedman, 1974). Experimental studies confirm the importance of innate determinants of emotional development—at least in monkeys. When rhesus monkeys who had been raised in isolation were shown pictures of other monkeys making threats, they responded with aversion or fear, whereas they showed positive reactions when shown pictures of infant monkeys (Sackett, 1966). These reactions did not occur before 8 weeks of age, and could not have been learned or affected by internal schemata given the monkeys' prior isolation. In any event, discrepancy from existing schemata cannot explain why some stimuli elicited positive reactions, while others elicited negative reactions. Thus, at least some complex emotional reactions appear to be elicited innately, despite minimal social experience.[2]

In addition, Kagan's model depends on the development (presumably by maturation) of the capacity to perceive and attend to curvilinear stimuli. There is little independent evidence that such a development takes place. Without this new perceptual skill, Kagan is unable to explain the onset of smiling, not only to faces, but also to bells and bull's-eyes. Sroufe similarly proposes the existence of cognitive mechanisms (appraisal processes) for which there has yet to be independent verification.

Ethological-Adaptational Theory.   Evidence concerning maturational and biogenetic influences of emotional development led psychologists to turn toward evolutionary biology, in the form of the ethological-adaptational theory, for insight into the nature of socioemotional development. As mentioned earlier, this theory challenges the notion that emotions are mere expressions of internal states by proposing that emotions are essentially communicative in nature. From this viewpoint, social smiles are viewed as signals indicating that stimulation should be maintained or increased (Emde, Kligman, Reich, & Wade, 1978; Frodi, Lamb, Leavitt, & Donovan, 1978). This view of emotions as communicative signals is supported by findings that interaction is adversely affected when emotional signals deviate from the species-specific norm. Thus, for example, mothers are disappointed by the bland facial expressions of blind babies (Fraiberg, 1974) or babies whose expressions are muted because they have Down's syn-

---

[2]Of course, these data are also inconsistent with the psychoanalytic and learning theory accounts of emotional development.

drome (Emde & Brown, 1978), and infants are upset when adults sit impassively and unresponsively in front of them (Tronick, Als, Adamson, Wise, & Brazelton, 1978; Fogel, Diamond, Langhorst, & Demos, 1979).

Ethological theorists believe that the emergence of social smiling is maturationally determined, and that the emergence of social smiling marks the beginning of a sensitive period for the development of social attachments—a period that is said to end with the emergence of stranger anxiety or wariness. This "explanation" only tells us *why* infants smile—focusing on the hypothetical adaptive value of the behavior—but tells us nothing about *how*—by what psychological, cognitive, or neurophysiological mechanism—the behavior is elicited. Thus the ethological-adaptational theory provides a different sort of explanation than do the psychoanalytic, learning, and cognitive theories. The ethological explanation is not open to conclusive verification or refutation but, viewed in the context of mechanisms proposed by the cognitive developmental theorists, may provide the most useful perspective on the development of social smiling.

Stranger Anxiety or Wariness

Psychoanalytic Theory. In terms of Spitz's (1965) psychoanalytic theory, the onset of stranger anxiety is predicated on ego development sufficient to permit evocative (i.e., recall) memory. Spitz believed that stranger anxiety results from a rudimentary inference process in which the child compares the stranger to an internal representation of mother. If mother is absent, the child anticipates that she will not be available to meet its needs. As a result, distress occurs. Spitz felt that, as with smiling, the quality of mother–infant interaction affects the expression of stranger anxiety, and as predicted, studies show that negative reactions to strangers are either absent or mild among infants raised in institutions (e.g., Rheingold, 1961).

One problem with this explanation is that the emergence of stranger anxiety around 6–9 months of age coincides with the emergence of fear to a variety of events or stimuli, such as heights, looming stimuli, masks, and jack-in-the-boxes (Campos, 1976; Scarr & Salapatek, 1970; Sroufe, 1979). It seems unlikely that these emotional changes result from ego development mediated by mother-infant interaction, and thus one wonders whether the explanation of stranger anxiety is correct. Another problem is that the intensity of reactions to strangers appear more related to the amount of experience with strangers than to the quality of infant–mother attachment (Konner, 1977; Kagan, 1974).

Learning Theory. Learning theory is similarly unable to explain the emergence of stranger anxiety. Strangers generally do not hurt or discomfort infants, making a conditioning explanation unlikely. Furthermore, parents are not usually afraid of strangers (especially when the stranger is a relative), so observational learning is clearly not involved. And we are aware of no operant contingencies that can plausibly explain the phenomenon.

Cognitive-Developmental Theory. Cognitive theorists, as in the case of smiling, initially proposed that discrepancies between the features of the stranger and some internal memory or schema explain the occurrence of stranger anxiety, because the child is unable to assimilate the stranger's features to any existing schema. One major problem with this explanation, however, was that infants can visually discriminate between mothers and strangers by 3 months of age but they do not show fear or distress until 4 or 5 months later (Bronson, 1972; Haith & Campos, 1977). Consequently, Kagan, Kearsley, and Zelazo (1978) have amended Hebb's basic notions quite substantially, adding the proposition that in the third quarter-year, infants develop the capacity to generate hypotheses, and thereafter actively attempt to understand how the environment operates, instead of merely registering sensory inputs passively. Before this capacity develops, a discrepancy between environmental stimulation and a schema yields interest rather than fear; after 8 months, however, fear or distress results when children attempt to understand environmental events and their hypotheses fail. Kagan thus portrays wariness to unfamiliar stimuli, as well as separation distress, as the predictable results of failures to understand the environment. If the child knew where mother went, when she would return, or what the stranger would do, no negative reactions would result.

Because the quality of mother-infant interaction is not viewed as a determinant of stranger anxiety, Kagan would expect distress or wariness to emerge according to a normative timetable, regardless of differences in prior social experiences. Substantiating this prediction, he has argued that stranger anxiety emerges at about the same time in infants from Israeli kibbutzim, the Kalahari desert, Greek orphanages, Guatemalan Indian groups, and middle-class Massachusetts families (Kagan, 1974; Kagan et al., 1978).

As mentioned earlier, however, Sroufe (1977, 1979) believes that discrepancy can account for the intensity, but not the hedonic quality, of emotional reactions to strange people or objects. In his view, hedonic quality is determined by the physical and social context as well as by the child's past experiences. For example, the stranger's approach is more likely to elicit cardiac acceleration and fussing in an unfamiliar setting than in the home. The parents' proximity, as well as their perceived accessibility, also affect reactions to strangers. According to Sroufe, these effects occur because infants have the capacity to *appraise* both stimuli and their contexts in order to determine whether there is reason for fear. Sroufe (1977) showed that differences among studies in the amount of wariness observed could be attributed to differences in the contexts in which the observations took place. Thus, when the mother was close by, the infant was familiarized with the stranger, and the stranger did not behave intrusively, stranger distress was often weak, subtle, and intermixed with positive, affiliative behaviors. On the other hand, when a stranger intrusively approached in a bizarre manner, or when the infant had little control over the stranger's behavior, stranger distress occurred in the majority of infants tested cross-sectionally and was nearly universal when infants were tested longitudinally.

The notion of an appraisal process thus helps to integrate diverse and apparently inexplicable findings, but unfortunately, it is a hypothetical construct that cannot be observed or studied directly. An additional problem with cognitive theories is, as mentioned earlier, that they deny the impact of biogenetic and innate determinants of emotional development. Twin studies showed genetic influences on individual differences in reactions to strangers (Freedman, 1974; Lamb, 1982; Plomin & Rowe, 1979), while Sackett's (1966) study showed that fear emerged on a predictable schedule in rhesus monkeys, despite minimal social experience.

Ethological-Adaptational Theory.   These findings are consistent with the assumptions of the ethological-adaptational theory, which holds that stranger anxiety occurs because it is adaptive for infants to avoid potential dangers, just as it is adaptive for them to seek the proximity of protective adults, especially when distressed or frightened. The purpose of stranger distress, from this point of view, is to summon the protective parent (Bowlby, 1969). While the other signs of fear mediate flight, ethologists argue that the fear of strangers does not emerge earlier in life than it does because emotions and emotional expressions only emerge when they are biologically adaptive (Izard, 1977). One explanation for the onset of stranger anxiety at around 8 months, therefore, might be that it coincides with the emergence of independent locomotion (by crawling), which allows infants to wander unsupervised into contact with strange adults. Another is that since fear mediates flight, it should not emerge until flight is possible— that is, after locomotion is achieved. Ethological theorists also propose that infants may be biologically prepared to respond to certain cues to danger. Among these are individuals who loom large over infants: strangers who tower over infants are feared more than persons at the infants' level (Weinraub & Putney, 1978). Likewise, unfamiliar full-size adults are feared more than midgets, and both are feared more than strange children (Brooks & Lewis, 1976). As mentioned earlier, however, the ethological theory attempts to explain only the whys of stranger anxiety; it does not attempt to explain how, i.e., by what psychological and physiological mechanisms negative stranger reactions are mediated.

Social Cognition.   The social-cognitive approach in a sense builds on the notions advanced by Sroufe. Instead of proposing that unfamiliar stimuli are inherently fearful because their behavioral dispositions are unknown, theorists such as Campos (Campos & Stenberg, 1981) propose that such stimuli may be *ambiguous.* In an attempt to resolve the ambiguity, infants look at their mothers' faces for cues about how to respond. If mother looks relaxed and happy, the infant concludes that there is nothing to fear and that the stranger may be fun; if mother looks fearful or unhappy, however, the infant concludes that there is reason to fear or avoid the individual. Consistent with this notion, studies have shown that the mother's expressions have a remarkable effect on the child's willingness to play with novel, attractive toys or to cross the deep side of the visual cliff (Klinnert, 1981; Svejda, 1981). This explanation does not of course preclude situations in which the adult's behavior is sufficiently bizarre, and the context so threatening, that fear is elicited immediately; it deals only with the situation in which ambiguity exists. Campos and Stenberg (1981) propose that infants begin to seek information from their parents' emotional expressions by 5 months of age, by which time they clearly seem capable of discriminating among various expressions (Oster, 1981). Although the social-cognitive approach does not provide a comprehensive account of stranger reactions, the best explanation of stranger wariness is probably provided by an amalgam of the cognitive-developmental, ethological-adaptational, and social-cognitive approaches, each of which seeks to explain different aspects of the phenomenon.

Separation Anxiety

Psychoanalytic Theory.   Each of the major theories proposes an explanation of separation anxiety very similar to its explanation of stranger anxiety. In the case of psychoanalytic theory, Spitz (1965) proposed that stranger anxiety actually occurred because the infant feared separation from its mother. In his view, separation anxiety first becomes possible when evocative memory develops between 6 and 8 months of age; this allows the infant to retrieve an image of mother in her absence. Prior to this time, the infant could recognize mother, but could not recall her image in her absence. Out of sight was out of mind. The ability to remember mother, even in her absence, permits the baby to feel threatened by her absence, and this threat is signaled by anxiety. The belief that recall memory is available by 6–8 months contradicted Piaget's belief that this is not possible until the second year, but Spitz argued that there was a decalage attributable to the organizing effect of affect on cognitive growth. Specifically, he proposed that the ability to understand mother's permanence precedes the ability to understand the permanence of objects, because mother is more affectively salient. This crucial assumption has not been empirically supported, however. Jackson, Campos, and Fischer (1978) found that when hide-and-search tasks are made comparable, infants show an equivalent appreciation of object and person permanence and search in very similar ways for both their mothers and toys. This constitutes a fatal flaw in the psychoanalytic explanations of separation anxiety and stranger anxiety.

Learning Theory. Learning theorists explain separation anxiety by suggesting that it represents the withdrawal of a source of both positive gratification and contingent responding (Gewirtz, 1972). This explanation can satisfactorily explain the onset of distress when the separation occurs, but it cannot explain the later emergence of a qualitatively different reaction, despair, and the subsequent emergence of detachment (Rajecki, Lamb, & Obmascher, 1978). Qualitative changes in the reaction to prolonged separation suggest that something more complex occurs than is proposed by learning theorists.

Cognitive-Developmental Theorists. To theorists like Kagan, separation produces a discrepancy from the familiar schema in which mother is present. The child thus generates hypotheses in an attempt to explain what happened to mother. Not knowing what happened to her, or when she will return, the child's hypotheses fail and distress results. Separation protest does not occur before 6–8 months because younger infants are not capable of generating hypotheses. The viability of this explanation thus depends on the assumption that the capacity to demonstrate hypotheses emerges around 6–8 months of age. No evidence of this sort has yet been presented.

Ethological-Adaptational Theory. Theorists such as Bowlby (1969) perceive separation distress as a signal by the infant designed to summon the absent parent back into proximity. Separation protest is thus viewed as one of several attachment behaviors that promote proximity between infants and attachment figures. Some attachment behaviors, like separation protest, bring about proximity only when the infant's signal successfully elicits an approach by the adult. Others, like locomotor approach, depend on the infant's behavior alone. Attachment behaviors, like separation protest, are said to emerge around 7–8 months of age because this is the age at which infants first appreciate person permanence, and thus can be said to have established social relationships. This assumption is the same as that made by Spitz, and is similarly unsupported by the empirical evidence. Thus, while the ethological-adaptational theory may have been correct in identifying the adaptive purpose of separation protest, Bowlby was unsuccessful in his attempt to explain the emergence of separation protest at 6–8 months of age. A better explanation, consistent with the ethological perspective, might be that separation protest does not emerge until the onset of locomotor capacities makes it possible for the child to wander off, and thus find itself separated from an attachment figure.

Social Cognition. Proponents of a social-cognitive approach have not attempted to explain the onset of separation protest. However, researchers (such as Lamb, 1981a) have used this perspective to help understand individual differences in infants' behavior upon reunion after brief separations. These explanations are discussed in the next section.

Social Attachment

There is considerable overlap between the predictions and assumptions regarding social attachment and those concerning separation anxiety, stranger anxiety, and (to a lesser extent) social smiling. This is because some theorists view social attachment simply as a summary term referring to all discriminating social behaviors, while others believe that such behaviors mediate and manifest an underlying social bond, which continues to exist even at times when no attachment behaviors are occurring. To psychoanalysts, for example, the onset of separation and stranger anxiety is determined by ego development bringing about the capacity for evocative memory. Separation and stranger anxiety are viewed simply as behavioral manifestations of a change in the infant's inner socioemotional world.

Psychoanalytic Theory. Psychoanalytic theorists have, since the time of Freud, emphasized the crucial importance of the infant-mother relationship, which Freud described as "unique, without parallel, established unalterably for the whole lifetime as the prototype of all later love relations" (1940, p. 45). This emphasis derived from the assumption that the most important interactions between parents and young infants were those around feeding. Bonds were deemed most likely to form to those who satisfied the infant's hunger, on the grounds that drive reduction was gratifying and that bonds were thus formed to those consistently responsible for this gratification.

Learning Theory. The psychoanalysts' secondary drive interpretation was adopted nearly intact by learning theorists like Hull, who attempted a reinterpretation in learning terms of central psychoanalytic mechanisms and processes (Dollard & Miller, 1950). Later learning theorists also emphasized the association between features of the caretaker and the gratification implicit in feeding. In the most popular recent interpretations of early attachment in the context of learning theory, Gewirtz (1972) and Bijou and Baer (1961, 1965) have provided operant conditioning models in which the mother becomes a discriminant reinforcer. One major difference between learning theorists and the psychoanalysts is that learning theorists eschew discussion of hypothetical structures like the ego, and deny the existence of emotional bonds independent of observable behaviors.

Both the psychoanalytic and learning theory explanations were fatally compromised by research showing that feeding does not play a crucial role in attachment. In one famous study, Harlow and Zimmerman (1959) showed that infant monkeys sought comfort from, and preferred to cling to, a terrycloth mother surrogate rather than a wire surrogate, which fed them. These studies, coupled with the general fall from favor of drive reduction theories, led developmental psychologists to abandon both psychoanalytic and learning theory accounts of social attachment, and paved the way for Bowlby's new ethological-adaptational theory. Gewirtz's theory also cannot explain why abused infants cling to, rather than flee, abusive parents; why infants first protest and then grieve over the loss of parents; and why infants use attachment figures as "secure bases" from which to explore (Rajecki et al., 1978). All of these behavior patterns are consistent with the ethological-adaptational model, which links the formation of attachments to the infants' need for protection from more powerful and competent adults.

Ethological-Adaptational Theory.   Like the psychoanalysts, Bowlby (1969) believed that separation anxiety reflected the establishment of a bond between infant and mother. However, he attempted to replace the secondary drive explanation, implicit in psychoanalytic theory, with an explanation that was more consistent with the postulates of contemporary biology. As mentioned earlier, he believed that infants were equipped with a repertoire of behaviors that served to promote proximity and contact with adults and were thus of survival value. In young infants, the proximity-promoting behaviors initially consisted of signals (such as smiles and cries) that were effective in achieving proximity or contact only when they elicited the responses with which adults were preprogrammed to respond. The fact that proximity depended on the association of infant behaviors and complementary adult responses is important because attachments apparently form to those individuals who are consistently available and respond in appropriate fashion to the infant's signals.

Bowlby proposed that there were several discrete stages in the development of attachment. Initially, the child is promiscuously sociable, not caring who responds to its proximity-promoting signals (0–6 weeks). Once it achieves the capcity to distinguish among individuals, it begins to demonstrate preferences, which become increasingly marked over the ensuing months. However, attachments are not said to form until the appreciation of person permanence, around 7–8 months of age, makes it possible for the child to remain aware of the adult's existence even when s/he is not audible or visible. At this point, an attachment bond is said to exist. The bond can be identified by seeing to whom the infant directs its proximity-promoting signals, but (and this is a crucial assumption) these behaviors only mediate the bond—they are not equivalent to the bond. Among the attachment behaviors are separation protest, locomotor approach, clinging, asking to be held, staying close, directed crying, and use of the adult as a "secure base" from which to explore.

Cognitive-Developmental Theory.   Cognitive theorists like Kagan do not attempt to explain the development of attachment bonds. They believe that the bond is really a composite of behavioral changes that can be attributed to emergent cognitive capacities. Others, such as Sroufe, accept Bowlby's explanation of the development of attachment. However, Sroufe has drawn upon cognitive development to explain the appraisal process by which infants determine how much proximity/contact they need (the set goal) given the existing circumstances and their locomotor capacities, and compare that with the degree of proximity/contact currently being enjoyed. Any discrepancy between present status and the set goal sets in motion behaviors designed to restore the balance.

Social Cognition.   Finally, social cognitive theorists focus not on the forma-
tion of social bonds, but on the way in which differences in parental behavioral styles presage the development of distinctive social expectations of those adults' future behavior (e.g., Lamb, 1981a, 1981b). The latter issues is discussed further in the section on individual differences.

Fear of Heights

The psychoanalysts and learning theorists have not attempted to explain the emergence of the fear of heights. The cognitive-developmental and ethological-
adaptational theorists offer explanations—one focused on proximal mechanisms and one on the adaptive value of the fear. The proponents of a social-cognitive approach have also considered ways in which the intensity of fear can be modulated.

Cognitive-Developmental Theory.   Theorists such as Kagan (1974) propose that the fear of heights can be explained in the same way as the fear of strangers. In each case, there is a discrepancy between the current percept and the child's mental schemata, which are based on past experiences. Discrepancy is perceived by 2–3 months, but it elicits interest rather than distress prior to the emergence, around 8 months of age, of the capacity to generate hypotheses. The failure of these hypotheses is said to underlie the emergence of frank distress. As before, a crucial problem with this explanation is the lack of independent evidence that the capacity to generate hypotheses indeed emerges at this time.

Ethological-Adaptational Theory.   From this point of view, the fear of heights is an adaptive emotion that mediates avoidance of heights and, in so doing, protects the infant from the danger of falling. As mentioned earlier, theorists such as Izard (1977) believe that emotions emerge when they are adaptive, and thus it is not surprising that the fear of heights emerges when the child acquires the ability to locomote independently (by crawling) and is thus exposed for the first time to the danger of falling. Consistent with this, Campos and his colleagues (1978) have shown that the fear of heights predictably emerges shortly after the acquisition of the ability to locomote independently. Age is not the critical variable, because the emergence of fear can be accelerated by giving infants the opportunity for independent locomotion using walkers before they are able to crawl. It is not yet clear, however, whether the experience of falling is also crucial.

Social Cognition.   Campos and his colleagues (Sorce, Emde, & Klinnert, 1981; Svejda, 1981) have also shown that the magnitude of fear can be manipulated by varying the emotional cues provided by the child's mother in ambiguous situations. For example, when the drop-off is small (e.g., one foot on the visual cliff), the child is uncertain whether the depth is sufficient to elicit fear, and looks to its mother's face for disambiguating information. If mother smiles and talks in a positive tone, infants are likely to cross the deep cliff to mother, whereas if mother produces a fear face and talks in a negative or fearful tone, infants are very unlikely to cross the same cliff. Of course if there was no depth or the cliff was clearly very deep, the mother's cues would be less influential because there would be little ambiguity in the child's mind, and thus little reason to seek disambiguating information.

Summary

With the exception of the ethological-adaptational theory, all the theories reviewed here attempt to explain the proximal mechanism whereby emotional reactions are mediated. Learning theory does a poor job of explaining the discrete and abrupt emergence of emotional milestones, while the psychoanalytic theory is flawed by the unwarranted linking of stranger and separation anxiety, and by the recourse to unobservable and unverifiable aspects of ego development. Kagan's cognitive-developmental theory has uncertain status until it is possible to demonstrate that the ability to generate hypotheses indeed emerges around 8 months of age; it also has to acknowledge the importance of biogenetic factors as determinants of emotional development. Sroufe's cognitive-developmental theory is more successful in explaining both the intensity and hedonic quality of emotional reactions, and is most readily integrated with Bowlby's ethological-adaptational theory. The ethological-adaptational theory has been extremely influential because it has provided a way of explaining why we should expect to see certain emotions developing, and why they should emerge when they do. However, only in the case of social attachments have theorists like Bowlby attempted to explain the proximal mechanisms involved.

    In part because of the lack of alternatives, most researchers and theorists today accept Bowlby's theory as the most useful, and agree that a major change in the nature of the infant's social world takes place around 6–8 months of age although (ironically) the empirical evidence shows that this change cannot be attributed to the emergence of person permanence. Bowlby's emphasis on the survival functions of infant behavior has been tremendously valuable, because it has allowed researchers to perceive organization and purpose in infant behavior that formerly appeared merely disorganized and incompetent. Further, his suggestion that bonds form as a result of consistent and appropriate adult responses to proximity-promoting behaviors provides a plausible and testable explanation of the way in which adult-child interaction affects the formation of infant-adult attachments. On the other hand, Bowlby's belief that infants are limited to forming one attachment initially has been disproved by evidence that infants generally form attachments to both parents at the same time (Lamb, 1976b, 1977) even though (consistent with Bowlby's emphasis) most seem to establish preferential relationships with their primary caretakers (Lamb, 1976a, 1976c). These preferences are evident in times of stress, when the infants' need for proximity to trusted protective adults is at its greatest. Most researchers agree that the *amount* of interaction is not critical to the formation of attachments or even to the establishment of preferences; the *quality* of interaction (as manifest by the adult's characteristic degree of responsiveness to the infant's signals) is more important. In the case of traditional fathers who spend relatively little time interacting with their infants, a propensity for exciting playful stimulation seems to increase the salience of their interactions and permit infants to establish attachment relationships to them (Clarke-Stewart, 1978; Lamb, 1977; Lamb, Frodi, Hwang, & Frodi, 1983).

INDIVIDUAL DIFFERENCES IN SOCIOEMOTIONAL DEVELOPMENT

In this section, we turn from normative developmental events and their explanation to a discussion of the origins, nature, and implications of individual differences in socioemotional development. In the social development area, the study of individual differences has been the major concern of theorists and researchers in the last decade, with focus being placed on the quality or security of infant-adult attachment. Coherence in this area has been facilitated greatly by the availability of a procedure—the Strange Situation—by which security of attachment can be assessed; almost all recent research on this topic has involved this procedure. As far as emotional development is concerned, dimensions of expressiveness or emotionality, as well as sociability or friendliness, have been of paramount concern, but there has been less agreement about how these are to be defined, much less studied. Consequently, the literature appears non-programmatic and disjointed.

Social Development

Both the psychoanalytic and (implicitly) learning theory approaches to the study of social development deal with individual differences in socioemotional development, to the extent that variations in the quality of mother-infant interaction may retard development. However, most of the relevant, empirical work undertaken by psychoanalytic theorists involved comparing children raised in home settings with those raised in institutions such as orphanages, where care by a succession of shift nurses replaced normal mother-infant interaction (e.g., Spitz, 1950; Spitz & Wolf, 1946). Variations within the normal range have been explored by psychoanalysts only in the context of case reports. Learning theorists, by contrast, seemed able to explain the effects of a wide variety of mother–child interaction patterns, until it was demonstrated that individual differences, as assessed by discrete behavioral measures, were highly unstable even over short periods of time (Coates, Anderson, & Hartup, 1972; Masters & Wellman, 1974; Waters, 1978). Since the learning theorists refused to acknowledge constructs other than those at the discrete behavioral level, these findings undercut the theory's ability to describe or explain stable individual differences. Cognitive theorists like Kagan, meanwhile, had placed such great stress on normative maturational events that there was no room to accommodate individual differences: Indeed, several reports focused on the absence of developmental variation despite vast differences in rearing environments (e.g., Fox, 1977; Kagan et al., 1978; Kotelchuck, 1976; Lester, Kotelchuck, Spelke, Sellers, & Klein, 1974).

By contrast, the ethological-adaptational theorists seem to have been most successful in their efforts to explore the origins, characteristics, and consequences of individual differences in infant-parent attachment (e.g., Ainsworth, Blehar, Waters & Wall, 1978; Lamb, 1981a, 1981b; Lamb, Thompson, Gardner, Charnov, & Estes, 1984). Perhaps the major reason for the apparent success of these theorists is their focus, not on discrete behaviors, but on the patterned organization of behavior.

As mentioned earlier, the ethological-adaptational theorists believe that infants are born with a repertoire of proximity-promoting signals to which adults are predisposed to respond (Ainsworth, 1973; Bowlby, 1969). The formation of attachments depends on the continued presence and responsiveness of specific adults during the first 6 months or so of life. Adults differ in their responsiveness to infants, however, and these differences in responsiveness are viewed as the antecedents of individual differences in the later quality of infant-adult attachments.

According to theorists such as Ainsworth, these individual differences can best be assessed by observing the effect of stress on the infant's behavior, because stress should increase the infant's desire for proximity to and/or contact with the protective parent or attachment figure, thus leading to the intensification of the "attachment behavior system" that controls a variety of behaviors (as diverse as crying, approaching, and clinging) that have the common function of helping infants attain or maintain proximity/contact. Thus, as the stress increases, infants should reduce their exploration and affiliation (for example, with strangers) and increasingly organize their behavior around their parents. Specifically, they should evince distress when separated from their parents, attempt to search for them, and greet them with bids for renewed interaction, either in the form of proximity/contact or in the form of distance interaction.

Operationally, individual differences in response to stress are usually assessed using a procedure—the Strange Situation—developed by Ainsworth and Wittig

(1969). The procedure (see Table 6.1) is designed to subject 10–24-month-old infants to gradually increasing amounts of stress, induced by the strange setting, the entrance of a strange female, and two brief separations from the parent.

Ainsworth's research, and that of other researchers in this tradition, has repeatedly shown that when American infants and parents are observed in the Strange Situation, about 65–75% behave in the pattern described above, which is termed the secure (or B) pattern because the infant seems to gain security and comfort from the parent to whom it turns in times of stress or alarm (Ainsworth, Blehar, Waters, & Wall, 1978; Lamb, 1978; Main & Weston, 1981; Thompson, Lamb, & Estes, 1982; Vaughn, Egeland, Stroufe, & Waters, 1979). The remainder display one of two types of reactions. Typically, 20–25% behave in an avoidant (A) fashion, turning away from, rather than toward the adult, especially upon reunion, when one would expect proximity-seeking behaviors to be at their most intense. Another group, the resistant, or C, group comprising 10–15% of most samples, consists of infants who are unable to use the adult as a base for exploration even in the preseparation episodes. These infants behave in an ambivalent fashion upon reunion—both seeking contact and angrily rejecting it when offered. These patterns of behavior seem to be characteristic of specific relationships, because infants may behave differently with their mothers and fathers (e.g., Grossmann, Grossmann, Huber, & Wartner, 1981; Lamb, 1978; Lamb, Hwang, Frodi, & Frodi, 1982; Lamb, Sagi, Lewkowicz, Shoham, & Estes, 1982; Main & Weston, 1981). The patterns are not ephemeral, however; infants who are seen in the Strange Situation more than once with the same adult tend to behave similarly in each observation, provided that no major changes in family circumstances or caretaking arrangements take place between the two assessments (Thompson & Lamb, 1984; Thompson, Lamb, & Estes, 1982; Vaughn et al., 1979; Waters, 1978). The fact that changes in family circumstances affect behavior in the Strange Situation supports the assumption that this

TABLE 6.1
The Strange Situation

Episode	Persons Present	Change
1	Parent, Infant	Enter room
2	Parent, Infant, Stranger	Strange adult joins the dyad
3	Infant, Stranger	Parent leaves
4	Parent, Infant	Parent returns Stranger leaves
5	Infant	Parent leaves
6	Infant, Stranger	Stranger returns
7	Parent, Infant	Parent returns Stranger leaves

All episodes are usually three minutes long, but episodes 3, 5, and 6 can be curtailed if the infant is too distressed, and episodes 4 and 7 are sometimes extended. (After Ainsworth and Wittig [1969].)

behavior is determined by prior patterns of infant-parent interaction, as does evidence that abused infants are more likely to develop insecure attachments to their abusive mothers (Egeland & Sroufe, 1981; Lamb, Gaensbauer, Malkin, & Schultz, in preparation).

Further evidence in support of this assumption was gathered by Ainsworth and her colleagues in a small longitudinal study (Ainsworth, Bell, & Stayton, 1974). Infants who behaved in the normative or secure pattern in the Strange Situation had mothers who responded promptly and appropriately to the infants' signals and needs when observed at home. Those who behaved avoidantly or resistantly had less sensitively responsive mothers. One difference between these two groups was that the mothers of avoidant infants were conspicuously rejecting and, since they found physical contact distasteful, their attempts to soothe were often abrupt. The behavior of the mothers of resistant infants was inconsistent and unpredictable.

Although these findings are frequently considered definitive, it is important to note that they were obtained in a small exploratory study using a methodology that would be inappropriate for hypothesis testing. The findings have not been independently replicated despite several attempts to verify or replicate them (see Lamb et al., 1984, for a review). At this point, findings only show clearly that low-quality maternal care is associated with the development of insecure attachments (Lamb et al., 1984). Considerably more research is needed on the antecedents of security of attachment.

Drawing upon Ainsworth et al.'s (1974) findings, nevertheless, Lamb (1981a, 1981b) has attempted to explain the relationship between security of attachment and prior patterns of infant-adult interaction by proposing that behavior in the Strange Situation reflects the infants' expectations about the adult's likely behavior based on the infants' past experiences with that adult. Thus securely attached infants have come to count on or trust the adult, who has in the past responded promptly and appropriately to the infant's signals or needs. By contrast, some infants behave avoidantly because, on the basis of their past experiences, they expect rebuffs rather than comfort in the Strange Situation. To avoid rebuffs, they turn away from the person whose responses have tended to be aversive in the past. Resistant infants do not know what to expect of adults whose behavior has been so unreliable and unpredictable in the past. This inability to predict the adults' behavior may underlie the ambivalent and confused behavior of resistant infants in the Strange Situation. In the absence of reliable information about the antecedents of attachment security, these interpretations are, of course, highly speculative.

Individual differences in Strange Situation behavior appear to predict the infants' future behavior, and this has enhanced the popularity of the Strange Situation. Researchers have shown that securely attached infants are more friendly and sociable with unfamiliar peers and adults, both contemporaneously and as much as several years after assessment in the Strange Situation, than are infants who were insecurely attached (Lamb, Hwang, Frodi, & Frodi, 1982; Lieberman,

1977; Main, 1973; Pastor, 1981; Sroufe, 1983; Thompson & Lamb, 1983; Waters, Wippman, & Sroufe, 1979).

Other studies suggest that securely attached infants are more persistent and resourceful in challenging tasks, at least through 5 years of age (Arend, Gove, & Sroufe, 1979; Matas, Arend, & Sroufe, 1978; Sroufe, 1983). However, predictions over long periods of time are only significant when there is stability in security of attachment, family circumstances, and/or caretaking arrangements (Lamb et al., 1984). Perhaps, therefore, the apparent "predictive validity" simply involves relationships between the outcome measures and characteristics of the contemporaneous (rather than former) attachment relationship. Consequently, it is not clear just how important an effect security of attachment has on later development.

Emotional Development

Individual differences in emotional development have received little attention other than in the late 1940s and early 1950s, and in the last several years. Interest in the 1940s and 1950s was prompted by evidence concerning the effects of institutionalization on social and emotional development. Children who had grown up in institutions frequently seemed to display a listless, affectless demeanor, showed no interest in social interaction, and failed to display appropriate emotions in situations that should have elicited either pleasure or distress (Bowlby, 1951).

Bowlby (1944, 1951) attributed this "affectionless personality" to a history of "maternal deprivation," and his interpretation played a major role in prompting development of the ethological-adaptational theory. The studies from this era have been soundly criticized, however, mainly for their reliance on retrospective research strategies. In the most thorough critique, Rutter (1972, 1979) has shown that long-term effects on personality are not inevitable; they depend on the child's constitutional vulnerability or invulnerability, as well as on the occurrence of other traumatic experiences before or after parent-child separation. This casts doubt on the ballistic view of social and emotional development typically held by psychoanalysts.

In the last few years, researchers have focused on variations in the quality of infant–mother relationships, rather than on the effects of separation. Interest in the origins of individual differences in emotional development was rekindled by evidence that (1) there were patterns of emotional expression that had similar communicative meanings around the world (Izard, 1971; Ekman, 1973); (2) emotional expressions were "appropriately" displayed by young infants in affect-eliciting contexts (e.g., Hiatt, Campos, & Emde, 1979; Stenberg, Campos, & Emde, 1983). Once researchers knew that they could code and interpret infant expressions, reliable and valid research became possible and a variety of experiential influences on emotionality have since been studied. Researchers such as

Gaensbauer (Gaensbauer & Harmon, 1982; Gaensbauer & Sands, 1979), for example, have compared the emotional expressions of abused and neglected infants with those who have no history of abuse or neglect. Gaensbauer and his colleagues showed that abused infants evinced a flattening of emotional expressiveness reminiscent of the emotional blunting observed in institutionalized infants. In a detailed case study, Stern (1974) showed that intrusive overstimulation led an infant to become avoidant of eye-contact with its mother, whereas mothers who were sensitive to their infants' readiness for stimulation had infants who were more sociable and expressive.

Another strategy has involved comparing infants who behaved differently in the Strange Situation, on the assumption that differences in Strange Situation behavior are consequences of differences in the quality of infant-mother interaction. Thus Thompson and Lamb (in press) found that securely attached infants were more emotionally expressive in the Strange Situation than either avoidant or resistant infants were. They speculated that these differences could be attributed to differences in the patterns of early interaction, suggesting that compared with less sensitive mothers, sensitively responsive mothers were more likely to (1) provide emotionally arousing stimuli at times when their infants were best able to appreciate them; (2) reinforce and encourage emotional displays; (3) be more sensitive to subtle variations in infant expressions. Those infants who were highly expressive facially were also most expressive vocally, suggesting that a general cross-modal dimension of expressiveness exists. This dimension is probably not of direct temperamental origin, because there are few relationships between parental reports of infant temperament and measures of facial or vocal expressiveness (Thompson & Lamb, 1982, 1984).

Another aspect of emotional expressiveness is "sociability", the infant's social attractiveness, friendliness, and willingness to respond positively to social bids by others. Individual differences in sociability appear to be consistent across contexts (Stevenson & Lamb, 1979) and moderately stable over a period of several months, provided there is stability in the security of attachment (Thompson & Lamb, 1984). This suggests that individual differences in sociability are affected by prior social experiences. However, although there is a modest relationship between security of attachment and sociability with unfamiliar adults and peers (Easterbrooks & Lamb, 1979; Lamb, Hwang, Frodi, & Frodi, 1982; Main & Weston, 1981; Pastor, 1981; Thompson & Lamb, 1984), there is no significant relationship between sociability and amount of experience with adults (Clarke-Stewart, Umeh, Snow, and Pederson, 1980; Stevenson, in preparation), maternal employment (Thompson & Lamb, 1982, 1984) or the amount of non-maternal care (Thompson & Lamb, 1983). Infants appear to be modestly more sociable when their fathers are highly involved in child care (Lamb, Hwang, Frodi, & Frodi, 1982).

Whereas the experiential determinants of individual differences in sociability remain unknown, there is mounting evidence of biogenetic influences (Lamb,

1982; Goldsmith & Campos, 1984). The fact that the similarities between monozygotic twins pairs are greater than those between dizygotic twins (Freedman & Keller, 1964; Goldsmith & Gottesman, 1981; Plomin & Rowe, 1979; Matheny, 1980) suggests that sociability is at least somewhat heritable.

Research on the heritability of sociability is related to research on temperament, typically defined as a constitutionally determined behavioral style which is somewhat stable over time (Goldsmith & Campos, 1982; Rothbart & Derryberry, 1981). Most studies have focused on some or all of the nine dimensions described by Thomas, Chess, Birch, Hertzig, and Korn (1963) in their New York Longitudinal Study: rhythm, persistence, threshold, approach, adaptability, activity, intensity, mood, and distractability. Studies using both objective measures as well as more subjective parental reports suggest that there is substantial heritability in at least some dimensions of temperament. Currently, the most exciting research regarding temperament has to do with the relationship between objective indices and parental reports (Bates, Olson, Pettit, & Bayles, 1982; Goldsmith & Campos, 1984; Rothbart & Derryberry, 1981), the heritability of temperament (Goldsmith & Campos, 1984; Plomin & Rowe, 1979), and the way in which child and parent characteristics combine to affect the child's development (Lee & Bates, in preparation).

Summary

Theorists concerned with the origins of individual differences in social and emotional behavior have generally assumed that these differences are determined by differences in the child's early social experiences. Major focus has fallen on the concept, parental sensitivity, which is rather loosely defined and operationalized. This has made it difficult to identify which aspects of parental behavior are especially important, and whether the effects on security of attachment are influenced by the same aspects of parental behavior as emotional expressiveness or sociability. More recently, researchers have recognized that at least some aspects of socioemotional development are affected by heredity. Future work is likely to focus on the ways in which inherent differences interact with aspects of the child's environment to determine individual differences.

GENERAL CONCLUSION

This chapter attests to the diversity of approaches characterizing the study of social and emotional development and to the amount of attention currently being paid to this area. On the basis of evidence now available, it seems that the understanding of socioemotional development, and of infancy in general, is considerably advanced by the perspective of evolutionary biology, which has provided a way of making sense of infant behavior simply by proposing that we consider the adaptive significance and function of infant behavior. This has provided answers to questions about why social smiling, stranger anxiety, separation anxiety, social attachment, and the fear of heights occur at all, and why they emerge when they do. This perspective, however, tells us little about the mechanisms whereby these phenomena are mediated, and nothing about the way in which individual differences in social and emotional development are to be explained. With respect to the hows of development, the most useful answers have come from the cognitive-developmental theorists, especially those like Sroufe who have attempted to make their propositions consistent with the ethological-adaptational theory. Biogenetic approaches emphasizing heritability, the analysis of social interaction, and social-cognitive perspectives seem most likely to contribute to our understanding of individual differences.

There remains, of course, much that we do not know. While much progress has been made, it is clear that we should expect considerable ferment and advance in the years that lie ahead.

REFERENCES

Ahrens, R. Beitrag zur Entwicklung des Physiognomie—und Mimskerkennens. *Zeitschrift fur experimentelle und angewandte Psychologie*, 1954, *2*, 412–454.

Ainsworth, M. D. S. The development of infant–mother attachment. In B. M. Caldwell & H. N. Ricciuti (Eds.), *Review of child development research* (Vol. 3). Chicago: University of Chicago Press, 1973.

Ainsworth, M. D. S. Attachment as related to mother–infant interaction. In J. S. Rosenblatt, R. A. Hinde, C. Beer, & M. Busnel (Eds.), *Advances in the study of behavior* (Vol. 9). New York: Academic Press, 1979.

Ainsworth, M. D. S., Bell, S. M., & Stayton, D. J. Infant–mother attachment and social development: 'Socialisation' as a product of reciprocal responsiveness to signals. In M. P. M. Richards (Ed.), *The integration of a child into a social world*. Cambridge, England: Cambridge University Press, 1974.

Ainsworth, M. D. S., Blehar, M. C., Waters, E., & Wall, S. *Patterns of attachment*. Hillsdale, N.J.: Lawrence Erlbaum Associates, 1978.

Ainsworth, M. D. S., & Wittig, B. A. Attachment and exploratory behavior of one-year-olds in a strange situation. In B. M. Foss (Ed.), *Determinants of infant behaviour* (Vol. 4). London: Methuen, 1969.

Ambrose, J. The development of the smiling response in early infancy. In B. Foss (Ed.), *Determinants of infant behaviour* (Vol. 1). London: Methuen, 1961.

Arend, R., Gove, F. L., & Sroufe, L. A. Continuity of individual adaptation from infancy to kindergarten: A predictive study of ego-resiliency and curiosity in preschoolers. *Child Development*, 1979, *50*, 950–959.

Bandura, A., & Walters, R. H. *Adolescent aggression: A study of the influence of child-rearing practices and family interrelationships*. New York: Ronald, 1959.

Bandura, A., & Walters, R. H. *Social learning and personality development*. New York: Holt, Rinehart, & Winston, 1963.

Bates, J. E., Olson, S. L., Pettit, G. S., & Bayles, K. Dimensions of individuality in the mother-infant relationship at six months of age. *Child Development*, 1982, *53*, 446–461.

Bijou, S. W., & Baer, D. M. *Child development I. A Systematic and empirical theory*. New York: Appleton-Century-Crofts, 1961.

Bijou, S. W., & Baer, D. M. *Child development II: Universal stage of infancy.* New York: Appleton-Century-Crofts, 1965.

Bower, T. G. R. *A primer of infant development.* San Francisco: Freeman, 1977.

Bowlby, J. Forty-four juvenile thieves: Their characters and home life. *International Journal of Psychoanalysis,* 1944, *25,* 107–128.

Bowlby, J. *Maternal care and mental health.* Geneva: WHO, 1951.

Bowlby, J. *Attachment and Loss* (Vol. 1). *Attachment.* New York: Basic Books, 1969.

Bowlby, J. *Attachment and Loss* (Vol. 2). *Separation: Anxiety and anger.* New York: Basic Books, 1973.

Bowlby, J. *Attachment and loss.* (Vol. 3). *Loss.* New York: Basic Books, 1980.

Brackbill, Y. Extinction of the smiling response in infants as a function of reinforcement schedule. *Child Development,* 1958, *29,* 115–124.

Bretherton, I. Making friends with one-year-olds: An experimental study of infant-stranger interaction. *Merrill-Palmer Quarterly,* 1978, *24,* 29–52.

Bretherton, I., & Ainsworth, M. Responses of one-year-olds to a stranger in a strange situation. In M. Lewis & L. Rosenblum (Eds.), *The origins of fear.* New York: Wiley, 1974.

Bronson, G. Infants' reactions to unfamiliar persons and novel objects. *Monographs of the Society for Research in Child Development,* 1972, *32,* (4, Serial No. 112).

Brooks, J., & Lewis, M. Infants' responses to strangers: Midget, adult, and child. *Child Development,* 1976, *47,* 323–332.

Campos, J. Heart rate: A sensitive tool for the study of emotional development in the infant. In L. P. Lipsitt (Ed.), *Developmental psychobiology: The significance of infancy.* Hillsdale, N.J.: Lawrence Erlbaum Associates, 1976.

Campos, J., Hiatt, S., Ramsay, D., Henderson, C., & Svejda, M. The emergence of fear on the visual cliff. In M. Lewis & L. Rosenblum (Eds.), *The origins of affect.* New York: Plenum, 1978.

Campos, J., Langer, A., & Krowitz, A. Cardiac responses on the visual cliff in pre-motor human infants. *Science,* 1970, *170,* 195–196.

Campos, J., & Stenberg, C. Perception, appraisal, and emotion: The onset of social referencing. In M. E. Lamb & L. R. Sherrod (Eds.), *Infant social cognition.* Hillsdale, N.J.: Lawrence Erlbaum Associates, 1981.

Clarke-Stewart, K. A. And daddy makes three: The father's impact on mother and young child. *Child Development,* 1978, *49,* 466–478.

Clarke-Stewart, K. A., Umeh, B. J., Snow, M. E., & Pederson, J. A. Development and prediction of children's sociability from 1 to 2 1/2 years. *Developmental Psychology,* 1980, *16,* 290–302.

Coates, B., Anderson, E. P., & Hartup, W. W. Interrelations in the attachment behavior of human infants. *Developmental Psychology,* 1972, *6,* 218–230.

Dollard, J., & Miller, M. E. *Personality and psychotherapy.* New York: McGraw-Hill, 1950.

Easterbrooks, M. A., & Lamb, M. E. The relationship between quality of infant–mother attachment and infant competence in initial encounters with peers. *Child Development,* 1979, *50,* 380–387.

Egeland, B., & Sroufe, L. A. Attachment and early maltreatment. *Child Development,* 1981, *52,* 44–52.

Ekman, P. Cross-cultural studies of facial expression. In P. Ekman (Ed.), *Darwin and facial expression: A century of research in review.* New York: Academic Press, 1973.

Emde, R. N., & Brown, C. Adaptation to the birth of a Down's syndrome infant. *Journal of the American Academy of Child Psychiatry,* 1978, *17,* 299–323.

Emde, R. N., & Harmon, R. J. Endogenous and exogenous smiling systems in early infancy. *Journal of the American Academy of Child Psychiatry,* 1972, *11,* 177–200.

Emde, R. N., Harmon, R. J., & Gaensbauer, T. J. Emotional expression in infancy: A biobehavioral study. *Psychological Issues,* 1976, *10* (whole No. 1).

Emde, R., Kligman, D., Reich, J., & Wade, T. Emotional expression in infancy. I. Initial studies of social signaling and an emergent model. In M. Lewis & L. Rosenblum (Eds.), *The development of affect*. New York: Plenum, 1978.

Etzel, B., & Gewirtz, J. Experimental modification of caretaker-maintained high rate operant crying in a 6- and a 20-week-old infant (Infans tyrannotearus): Extinction of crying with reinforcement of eye contact and smiling. *Journal of Experimental Child Psychology*, 1967, *5*, 303–317.

Fogel, A., Diamond, G. R., Langhorst, B. H., & Demos, V. *Alteration of infant behavior as a result of "still-face" perturbation of maternal behavior*. Paper presented to a meeting of the Society for Research in Child Development, San Francisco, April 1979.

Fox, N. Attachment of kibbutz infants to mother and metapelet. *Child Development*, 1977, *48*, 1228–1239.

Fox, R., Aslin, R., Shea, S., & Dumais, S. Stereopsis in human infants. *Science*, 1980, *207*, 323–324.

Fraiberg, S. Blind infants and their mothers: An examination of the sign system. In M. Lewis & L. Rosenblum (Eds.), *The effect of the infant on the caregiver*. New York: Wiley, 1974.

Fraiberg, S. *Insights from the blind*. New York: Basic Books, 1977.

Freedman, D. *Human infancy: An evolutionary perspective*. Hillsdale, N.J.: Lawrence Erlbaum Associates, 1974.

Freedman, D. G., & Keller, B. Inheritance of behavior in infants. *Science*, 1964, *140*, 196–198.

Freud, S. *An outline of psychoanalysis* (1940). New York: Norton, 1940.

Freud, S. *The ego and the id* (1923). New York: Norton, 1962.

Frodi, A. M., Lamb, M. E., Leavitt, L. A., & Donovan, W. L. Fathers' and mothers' responses to infant smiles and cries. *Infant Behavior and Development*, 1978, *1*, 187–198.

Gaensbauer, T. J., & Harmon, R. J. Attachment and affiliative systems under conditions of extreme environmental stress. In R. W. Emde & R. J. Harmon (Eds.), *Development of attachment and affiliative systems*. New York: Plenum, 1982.

Gaensbauer, T. J., & Sands, K. Distorted affective communications in abused/neglected infants and their potential impact on caretakers. *Journal of the American Academy of Child Psychiatry*, 1979, *18*, 238–250.

Gewirtz, J. L. Attachment, dependency, and a distinction in terms of stimulus control. In J. L. Gewirtz (Ed.), *Attachment and dependency*. Washington, D.C.: Winston, 1972.

Goldsmith, H. H., & Campos, J. J. The concept of temperament in human development. In R. N. Emde & R. J. Harmon (Eds.), *Development of attachment and affiliative systems*. New York: Plenum Press, 1982.

Goldsmith, H. H., & Campos, J. J. The development of temperament: A biobehavioral study. In M. E. Lamb, A. L. Brown, & B. Rogoff (Eds.), *Advances in developmental psychology* (Vol. 4). Hillsdale, N.J.: Lawrence Erlbaum Associates, 1984.

Goldsmith, H. H., & Gottesman, I. I. Origins of variation in behavioral style: A longitudinal study of temperament in young twins. *Child Development*, 1981, *52*, 91–103.

Grossmann, K. E., Grossmann, K., Huber, F., & Wartner, U. German children's behavior towards their mothers at 12 months and their fathers at 18 months in Ainsworth's Strange Situation. *International Journal of Behavioral Development*, 1981, *4*, 157–181.

Haith, M., & Campos, J. Human infancy. *Annual Review of Psychology*, 1977, *28*, 251–294.

Harlow, H. F., & Zimmerman, R. R. Affectional responses in the infant monkey. *Science*, 1959, *130*, 421.

Hebb, D. O. On the nature of fear. *Psychological Review*, 1946, *53*, 259–276.

Hebb, D. O. *The organization of behavior*. New York: Wiley, 1949.

Hiatt, S., Campos, J., & Emde, R. Facial patterning and infant emotional expression: Happiness, surprise, and fear. *Child Development*, 1979, *50*, 1020–1035.

Izard, C. E. *The face of emotion*. New York: Appleton-Century-Crofts, 1971.

Izard, C. E. *Human emotions*. New York: Plenum Press, 1977.

Jackson, E., Campos, J., & Fischer, K. The question of decalage between object permanence and person permanence. *Developmental Psychology*, 1978, *14*, 1–10.

Jones, M. C. The elimination of children's fears. *Journal of Experimental Psychology*, 1924, *7*, 382–390.

Kagan, J. *Change and continuity in infancy*. New York: Wiley, 1971.

Kagan, J. Discrepancy, temperament and infant distress. In M. Lewis & L. Rosenblum (Eds.), *The origins of fear*. New York: Wiley, 1974.

Kagan, J., Kearsley, P., & Zelazo, P. *Infancy: Its place in human development*. Cambridge, Mass.: Harvard University Press, 1978.

Klinnert, M. D. *The regulation of infant behavior by maternal facial expression*. Unpublished doctoral dissertation, University of Denver, 1981.

Klinnert, M., Campos, J., Sorce, J., Emde, R., & Svejda, M. Emotions as behavior regulators: Social referencing in infancy. In R. Plutchik & H. Kellerman (Eds.), *The emotions* (Vol. 2). *Emotions in early development*. New York: Academic Press, 1983.

Konner, M. Evolution of human behavior development. In P. H. Leiderman, S. Tulkin, & A. Rosenfeld (Eds.), *Culture and infancy: Variations in human experience*. New York: Academic Press, 1977.

Kotelchuck, M. The infant's relationship to the father: Experimental evidence. In. M. E. Lamb (Ed.), *The role of the father in child development*. New York: Wiley, 1976.

Lamb, M. E. Effects of stress and cohort on mother– and father–infant interaction. *Developmental Psychology*, 1976, *12*, 435–443. (a)

Lamb, M. E. Interactions between eight-month-old children and their fathers and mothers. In M. E. Lamb (Ed.), *The role of the father in child development*. New York: Wiley, 1976. (b)

Lamb, M. E. Twelve-month-olds and their parents: Interaction in a laboratory playroom. *Developmental Psychology*, 1976, *12*, 237–244. (c)

Lamb, M. E. Father–infant and mother–infant interaction in the first year of life. *Child Development*, 1977, *48*, 167–181.

Lamb, M. E. Qualitative aspects of mother– and father–infant attachments. *Infant Behavior and Development*, 1978, *1*, 265–275.

Lamb, M. E. Developing trust and perceived effectance in infancy. In L. P. Lipsitt (Ed.), *Advances in infancy research* (Vol. 1). Norwood, N.J.: Ablex, 1981. (a)

Lamb, M. E. The development of social expectations in the first year of life. In M. E. Lamb & L. R. Sherrod (Eds.), *Infant social cognition: Empirical and theoretical considerations*. Hillsdale, N.J.: Lawrence Erlbaum Associates, 1981. (b)

Lamb, M. E. Individual differences in infant sociability: Their origins and implications for cognitive development. In H. W. Reese & L. P. Lipsitt (Eds.), *Advances in child development and behavior* (Vol. 16). New York: Academic Press, 1982.

Lamb, M. E., Frodi, M., Hwang, C.-P., & Frodi, A. M. Effects of paternal involvement on infant preferences for mothers and fathers. *Child Development*, 1983, *54*, 450–458.

Lamb, M. E., Gaensbauer, T. J., Malkin, C. M., & Schultz, L. *The effects of abuse and neglect on security of infant–adult attachment*. Manuscript in preparation.

Lamb, M. E., Hwang, C.-P., Frodi, A., & Frodi, M. Security of mother– and father–infant attachment and its relation to sociability with strangers in traditional and non-traditional Swedish families. *Infant Behavior and Development*, 1982, *5*, 355–367.

Lamb, M. E., Sagi, A., Lewkowicz, K., Shoham, R., & Estes, D. *Security of infant–mother, –father, and –metapelet attachments in kibbutz-reared infants*. Paper presented to the Denver Psychobiology Research Group Retreat, Estes Park, Co., June 1982.

Lamb, M. E., Thompson, R. A., Gardner, W., Charnov, E. L., & Estes, D. Security of infantile attachment as assessed in the Strange Situation: Its study and biological interpretation. *Behavioral and Brain Sciences*, 1984, *7*, 127–147.

Lee, C. L., & Bates, J. F. Mother–child interaction at age two years and perceived difficult temperament. Manuscript in preparation.

Lester, B. M., Kotelchuck, M., Spelke, E., Sellers, M. J., & Klein, R. E. Separation protest in

Guatemalan infants: Cross-cultural and cognitive findings. *Developmental Psychology*, 1974, *10*, 79–85.

Lieberman, A. F. Preschoolers' competence with a peer: Relations with attachment and peer experience. *Child Development*, 1977, *48*, 1277–1287.

Main, M. *Exploration, play and cognitive functioning as related to child–mother attachment*. Unpublished doctoral dissertation, Johns Hopkins University, 1973.

Main, M. B., & Weston, D. R. Security of attachment to mother and father: Related to conflict behavior and the readiness to establish new relationships. *Child Development*, 1981, *52*, 932–940.

Masters, J. C., & Wellman, H. M. The study of human infant attachment: A procedural critique. *Psychological Bulletin*, 1974, *81*, 213–237.

Matas, L., Arend, R. A., & Sroufe, L. A. Continuity of adaptation in the second year: The relationship between quality of attachment and later competence. *Child Development*, 1978, *49*, 547–556.

Matheny, A. P. Bayley's Infant Behavior Record: Behavioral components and twin analyses. *Child Development*, 1980, *51*, 1157–1167.

McCall, R., & McGhee, P. The discrepancy hypothesis of attention and affect. In F. Weizmann & I. Uzgiris (Eds.), *The structuring of experience*. New York: Plenum Press, 1977.

Oster, H. ''Recognition'' of emotional expression in infancy? In M. E. Lamb & L. R. Sherrod (Eds.), *Infant social cognition: Empirical and theoretical considerations*. Hillsdale, N.J.: Lawrence Erlbaum Associates, 1981.

Pastor, D. L. The quality of mother–infant attachment and its relationship to toddlers' initial sociability with peers. *Developmental Psychology*, 1981, *17*, 326–335.

Piaget, J. *The origins of intelligence in children* (1936). New York: International Universities Press, 1952.

Plomin, R., & Rowe, D. Genetic and environmental etiology of social behavior in infancy. *Developmental Psychology*, 1979, *15*, 62–72.

Plutchik, R. *Emotion: A psychoevolutionary synthesis*. New York: Harper & Row, 1980.

Rajecki, D. W., Lamb, M. E., & Obmascher, P. Toward a general theory of infantile attachment: A comparative review of aspects of the social bond. *Behavioral and Brain Sciences*, 1978, *1*, 417–463.

Rheingold, H. The effect of environmental stimulation upon social and exploratory behavior in the human infant. In B. Foss (Ed.), *Determinants of infant behavior* (Vol. 1). London: Methuen, 1961.

Rheingold, H., & Eckerman, C. Fear of the stranger: A critical examination. In H. Reese (Ed.), *Advances in child development and behavior* (Vol. 8). New York: Academic Press, 1973.

Rheingold, H., Gewirtz, J., & Ross, H. Social conditioning of vocalizations in the infant. *Journal of Comparative and Physiological Psychology*, 1959, *52*, 68–73.

Robertson, J., & Bowlby, J. Responses of young children to separation from their mothers. *Courrier*, 1952, *2*, 131–142.

Rothbart, M. K., & Derryberry, D. Development of individual differences in temperament. In M. E. Lamb & A. L. Brown (Eds.), *Advances in developmental psychology* (Vol. 1). Hillsdale, N.J.: Lawrence Erlbaum Associates, 1981.

Rutter, M. *Maternal deprivation reassessed*. Harmondsworth, England: Penguin, 1972.

Rutter, M. Maternal deprivation, 1972–1978: New findings, new concepts, new approaches. *Child Development*, 1979, *50*, 283–305.

Sackett, G. P. Monkeys reared in isolation with pictures as visual input: Evidence for an innate releasing mechanism. *Science*, 1966, *154*, 1468–1473.

Scarr, S., & Salapatek, P. Patterns of fear development during infancy. *Merrill-Palmer Quarterly*, 1970, *16*, 53–90.

Schwartz, A. N., & Rosenberg, D. *An analysis of the components of social reinforcement of infant vocalization.* Masters Thesis, University of Denver, 1968.

Sorce, J., Emde, R., & Klinnert, M. *Maternal emotional signaling: Its effect on the visual cliff behavior of one-year-olds.* Paper read at the meetings of the Society for Research in Child Development, Boston, 1981.

Spitz, R. A. Possible infantile precursors of psychopathology. *American Journal of Orthopsychiatry,* 1950, *20,* 240–248.

Spitz, R. A. *The first year of life.* New York: International Universities Press, 1965.

Spitz, R. A., & Wolf, K. M. Anaclitic depression. *Psychoanalytic Study of Child,* 1946, *2,* 313–342.

Sroufe, L. A. Wariness of strangers and the study of infant development. *Child Development,* 1977, *48,* 731–746.

Sroufe, L. A. The coherence of individual development. *American Psychologist,* 1979, *34,* 834–841.

Sroufe, L. A. Individual patterns of adaptation from infancy to preschool. In M. Perlmutter (Ed.), *Minnesota symposium in child psychology* (Vol. 16). Hillsdale, N.J.: Lawrence Erlbaum Associates, 1983.

Sroufe, L. A., Waters, E., & Matas, L. Contextual determinants of infant affective response. In M. Lewis & L. Rosenblum (Eds.), *The origins of fear.* New York: Wiley, 1974.

Sroufe, L. A., & Wunsch, J. The development of laughter in the first year of life. *Child Development,* 1972, *43,* 1326–1344.

Stenberg, C., Campos, J., & Emde, R. The facial expression of anger in seven-month-old infants. *Child Development,* 1983, *54,* 178–184.

Stern, D. Mother and infant at play: The dyadic interaction involving facial, vocal, and gaze behaviors. In M. Lewis & L. A. Rosenblum (Eds.), *The effect of the infant on its caregiver.* New York: Wiley, 1974.

Stevenson, M. B. Changes in sociability, cognitive performance, and the caretaking environment from 12 to 24 months and causal interrelations among these. Manuscript in preparation.

Stevenson, M. B., & Lamb, M. E. The effects of sociability and the caretaking environment on infant cognitive performance. *Child Development,* 1979, *50,* 340–349.

Svejda, M. *The development of infant sensitivity to affective measures in the mothers' voice.* Unpublished doctoral dissertation, University of Denver, 1981.

Thomas, A., Chess, S., Birch, H. G., Hertzig, M. E., & Korn, S. *Behavioral individuality in early childhood.* New York: New York University Press, 1963.

Thompson, R. A., & Lamb, M. E. Stranger sociability and its relationship to temperament and social experiences during the second year. *Infant Behavior and Development,* 1982, *5,* 277–288.

Thompson, R. A., & Lamb, M. E. Security of attachment and stranger sociability in infancy. *Developmental Psychology,* 1983, *19,* 184–191.

Thompson, R. A., & Lamb, M. E. Continuity and change in socioemotional development during the second year. In R. Emde & R. Harmon (Eds.), *Continuity and discontinuity in development.* New York: Plenum, 1984.

Thompson, R. A., & Lamb, M. E. Security of attachment and emotional responsiveness in the Strange Situation. *Infant Behavior and Development,* in press.

Thompson, R. A., Lamb, M. E., & Estes, D. Stability of infant–mother attachment and its relationship to changing life circumstances in an unselected middle-class sample. *Child Development,* 1982, *53,* 144–148.

Tronick, E., Als, H., Adamson, L., Wise, S., & Brazelton, T. B. The infant's response to entrapment between contradictory messages in face-to-face interaction. *Journal of the American Academy of Child Psychiatry,* 1978, *17,* 1–13.

Vaughn, B., Egeland, B., Sroufe, L. A., & Waters, E. Individual differences in infant–mother attachment at twelve and eighteen months: Stability and change in families under stress. *Child Development,* 1979, *50,* 971–975.

Walk, R. Depth perception and experience. In R. Walk & H. Pick (Eds.), *Perception and experience*. New York: Plenum Press, 1978.

Waters, E. The reliability and stability of individual differences in infant–mother attachment. *Child Development*, 1978, *49*, 483–494.

Waters, E., Wippman, J., & Sroufe, L. A. Attachment, positive affect, and competence in the peer group: Two studies in construct validation. *Child Development*, 1979, *50*, 821–829.

Watson, J. B. Psychology as the behaviorist views it. *Psychological Review*, 1913, *20*, 158–177.

Watson, J., & Raynor, R. Conditioned emotional reactions. *Journal of Experimental Psychology*, 1920, *3*, 1–14.

Weinraub, M., & Putney, E. The effects of height on infants' social responses to unfamiliar persons. *Child Development*, 1978, *49*, 598–605.

Yarrow, L., & Goodwin, M. The immediate impact of separation: Reactions of infants to change in mother figures. In L. J. Stone, H. T. Smith, & L. B. Murphy (Eds.), *The competent infant*. New York: Basic Books, 1973.

Zelazo, P. Smiling and vocalizing: A cognitive emphasis. *Merrill-Palmer Quarterly*, 1972, *18*, 349–365.

7 Moral Development

Martin L. Hoffman
University of Michigan

INTRODUCTION

Moral development has been a topic of research interest in psychology for over six decades; before then, moral issues preoccupied philosophy from the time of Aristotle. The sustaining interest in the topic may lie in its importance for the organization of society as well as the fact that it epitomizes the existential human dilemma of how people come to grips with the inevitable conflicts between their personal egoistic needs and their moral obligations. Philosophers have postulated several answers to this dilemma that have parallels in current psychological theory. One is the doctrine of original sin, associated with early Christian theology, that states that people are born egoistic and only through punitive socialization experiences that subordinate their egoistic drives can they acquire a sense of moral obligation. This doctrine is reflected in Fruedian theory and certain social learning theories that stress the importance of punishment in moral development. The doctrine of innate purity, associated with writers like Rousseau, that sees children as inherently good though vulnerable to corruption by society, has its parallel in Piaget's view that adults are constraining and moral development requires the give and take of unsupervised interactions with peers. Philosophers like Kant, who attempted to derive universal moral principles, provided part of the inspiration for Kohlberg's efforts to construct an invariant sequence of moral developmental stages. And the British utilitarian tradition, represented by David Hume and Adam Smith, who focused on empathy as a necessary social bond, finds expression in current theory and research on empathic morality (Hume, 1751/1957; Smith, 1759/1965).

The flavor of the moral development literature, which is by now quite vast, can perhaps best be communicated by organizing it into three broad categories: stage theories of moral development; processes in the internalization of moral standards; and social influences on moral development.

279

STAGE THEORIES

A major preoccupation of cognitive developmental research has been the building of a series of stages that depict growth in an individual's moral conceptions. We review the moral-cognitive stage theories of Piaget, whose views are over 50 years old but remain a rich source of research ideas; of Kohlberg, whose work has dominated research in this area for two decades; and of Damon, who has described moral stages in young children. Hoffman's stage scheme for moral motivation and affect is also reviewed.

MORAL-COGNITIVE DEVELOPMENT

Piaget's Theory

Piaget's two stages derived from the attitudes expressed by different aged children toward the origin, legitimacy, and alterability of rules in the game of marbles, and childrens' responses to stories such as the well-known one in which children are asked to judge who is naughtier, a boy who accidentally breaks several cups or a boy who breaks one cup while trying to get jam out of the cupboard (Piaget, 1932). In Piaget's first stage—referred to as moral realism, morality of constraint, or heteronomous morality—the child feels an obligation to comply with rules because they are sacred and unalterable. He or she tends to view behaviors as totally right or wrong and thinks everyone views them in the same way. He or she judges the rightness or wrongness of an act on the basis of the magnitude of its consequences, the extent to which it conforms to established rules, and whether it is punished. He or she believes in "imminent justice"— that violations of social norms are followed by physical accidents or misfortunes willed by God or by some inanimate object.

The child in the more advanced stage—called autonomous morality, morality of cooperation, or reciprocity—views rules as established and maintained through reciprocal social agreement and thus subject to modification in response to human needs. He or she recognizes a possible diversity in views. The child's judgments of right and wrong place stress on intentions as well as consequences. Punishment should be reciprocally related to the misdeed (e.g., through restitution) rather than painful, arbitrary, and administered by authority. Duty and obligation are no longer defined in terms of obedience to authority but in terms of conforming to peer expectations, considering their welfare, expressing gratitude for past favors, and, above all, putting oneself in the place of others.

Piaget believes that both cognitive development (hence, maturation) and social experience play a role in the transformation from one stage to the next. Although he is not clear about how the two interact, one can interpret the threads of his argument as follows. The young child's moral immaturity is based on (a) two cognitive limitations, namely, "egocentrism" (assuming that others view events the same as he or she does) and "realism" (confusing subjective with objective experience, e.g., perceiving dreams as external events); and (b) the child's heteronomous respect for adults—a syndrome of feelings including inferiority, dependency, affection, admiration, and fear, which produces feelings of obligation to comply with adults' commands and to view their rules as sacred and unchangeable. Moral growth requires that the child give up egocentrism and realism and develop a concept of self that is distinct from others, who have their own independent perspective about events. This shift occurs in children's interactions with peers in two ways:

1. In growing older, the child attains relative equality with adults and older children, which lessens his or her unilateral respect for them and gives the child confidence to participate with peers in decisions about applying and changing rules on the basis of reciprocity. This new mode of interaction renders the child's initial conception of the rules no longer tenable. These rules are no longer seen as having an infinite past and a divine or adult origin, but as products of cooperation and agreement based on the human goals they serve, and they are amenable to change by mutual consent.

2. Interacting with peers often requires taking alternate and reciprocal roles with them, which facilitates the awareness that one is coordinate with others—that one reacts to similar situations in similar ways, that the consequences of one's acts for one's peers and theirs for oneself are similar, and yet these events seem different when viewed from different vantage points. The child thus becomes sensitized to the internal states that underlie the acts of others, which contributes, among other things, to the tendency to take their intentions into account.

Social experience, then, serves to stimulate and challenge children because it contradicts their expectations. The resulting cognitive disequilibrium motivates children to utilize their newly-attained cognitive capabilities to resolve the contradiction; it is through this effort that pre-existing patterns of moral thought are reorganized.

Although Piaget's theory appeared in the late 1920s, most of the published research based on it was done in the 1950s and 1960s. The earlier findings, critically reviewed by Hoffman (1970a), provide considerable support for Piaget's postulated age-developmental sequence in Western countries (England, Switzerland, the United States), although adults may sometimes use earlier forms of moral reasoning in certain situations. The data do not indicate that the same sequence occurs in other types of societies. The assumption of consistency across stage attributes (subjects with high scores on one attribute such as "consequences" are also high on other attributes such as "imminent justice") is generally not upheld, but the research appears to lack some of the controls needed for a critical test. Nor has a critical test been made of Piaget's central hypothesis that peer interaction is necessary for moral growth. (The influence of peers will be discussed in some detail later.) More recently, the level of moral judgment has been found to relate positively to the cognitive level displayed in solving mathematics and physics problems and to the role-taking ability of children at various ages (e.g., Ambron & Irwin, 1975; Damon, 1975).

A series of experiments done in the 1960s and 1970s attempted to test Piaget's assumption that progress from one stage to the next requires cognitive disequilibrium, by seeing if one's level of moral reasoning could be changed by simple exposure to models who verbalize moral judgments at higher or lower levels than one's own. The social learning theorists who did most of this work expected that such exposure would produce changes, whereas cognitive-developmentalists would not ordinarily expect social influences to operate in such a direct manner. In general, these experiments showed that the subjects' moral judgments were affected by the model's verbalizations. The earlier experiments (e.g., Bandura & McDonald, 1963) were criticized for demonstrating nothing more than momentary, specific response shifts rather than actual changes in level of moral reasoning (Turiel, 1966). Later research, however, indicates that children not only shift their verbal responses toward the model but also increase their understanding of the principle that intentions should be taken into account when making moral evaluations of behavior. Furthermore, in some cases the effects appear to last up to a year (e.g., Sternlieb & Youniss, 1975).

That mere exposure to models can produce such shifts has been interpreted as evidence against cognitive developmental theory (e.g., Kurtines & Greif, 1974). Another interpretation (Hoffman, 1979) is that the children did not merely imitate the model. Rather, they knew that acts may or may not be intentional but gave intentions less weight than consequences, perhaps because the stories used, like Piaget's, portrayed more harmful consequences for accidental than for intended acts. This fits the evidence (e.g., Imamoglu, 1975) that children as young as 5 years use intentions when the consequences of accidental and intended acts are equal (the modeling studies in question used older children). Repeated exposure to an adult model who consistently assigns greater weight to intentions despite the disparity in consequences might then have produced cognitive disequilibrium, which the subjects could have reduced by reexamining and changing their views. This interpretation is consonant with cognitive developmental theory but it does not make the cognitive developmental assumption that movement is always progressive, since a model that exposes "consequences," the less mature response, might also produce cognitive disequilibrium. This interpretation could be tested by having subjects report their thoughts and feelings on hearing the models' expressed views.

Kohlberg's Universal Stage Model

In developing his model, Kohlberg attempted to retain the best of Piaget's analysis and fit it into a more refined, comprehensive, and logically consistent framework. Thus, Kohlberg sees moral development as occurring in a series of six qualitatively distinct stages. The end product of these stages is a sense of justice (rather than other moral principles, such as love for humanity). This sense of justice enables one to determine the legitimate moral claims of people in a situation and to balance these claims in a way that best handles the perspectives of all contending parties. Each stage is a homogeneous type of moral reasoning strategy or a conceptual framework designed to answer moral questions and evaluate issues; moral reasoning within a stage is thus consistent across different moral problems and situations. Each stage builds upon, reorganizes, and encompasses the preceding one and is therefore more comprehensive, providing new perspectives and criteria for making moral evaluations. The content of moral values does not play a role in defining a stage.

An important feature of Kohlberg's approach is that all individuals, regardless of culture, are viewed as going through the stages in the same order, varying only in how quickly and how far they move through the stage sequence. The stages are held to be constructed by the individual as he or she tries to make sense out of his or her own experience, rather than implanted by culture through socialization. And, progress always moves forward through the stage sequence, never backward.

Kohlberg's six stages are based on extensive case analyses of boys ranging from 10 to 16 years of age (Kohlberg, 1969). The data were obtained from two-hour interviews that focused on nine hypothetical moral dilemmas in which acts of obedience to laws, rules, or commands of authority conflict with the needs or welfare of other persons. The child was asked to choose whether one should perform the obedience-serving act or the need-serving act and to answer a series of questions probing the thinking underlying his choice. Kohlberg's interest was not in the action alternatives selected by the children, which presumably reflected the content of their moral values, but in the quality of their judgments as indicated by the reasons given for their choices and their ways of defining the conflict situations.

Each stage was initially defined in terms of its position on 30 different moral issues that the children brought into their thinking. The six stages were ordered into three levels of moral orientation, the basic themes and major attributes of which were as follows:[1]

1. In the first, premoral level, control of conduct is external in two senses: one's standards consist of external commands or pressures, and one's motive is to avoid external punishment or obtain rewards. In Stage 1, one's definition of good and bad is based on obedience to rules and authority, but this is not a heteronomous stage in Piaget's sense, because punishment is feared like any other aversive stimulus. In Stage 2, acts that are instrumental in providing satisfaction to the self, and occasionally to others, are defined as ''right.''

---

[1]I say ''were'' because certain nuances in the stage descriptions have been altered owing to changes in the scoring system that will be mentioned later.

2. The second level defines morality as conforming to the expectations of others and maintaining the social order. Control of conduct is external in that standards consist of rules and expectations held by those who are significant others by virtue of personal attachment or delegated authority. Motivation, however, is largely internal: Although based on anticipation of praise or censure by significant others, the child now takes their role and respects their judgment. Thus, the personal reactions of authority now serve as cues to the rightness or wrongness of an act and the moral virtue of the actor. In Stage 3, the orientation is to gain approval and to please and help others; the morally good person is one who possesses moral virtues, and, when judging others, considers their intentions. Stage 4 is an authority and social order maintaining morality in which the orientation is to "doing one's duty," showing respect for authority, and maintaining the social order for its own sake. People at this stage believe that virtue should be rewarded, and they take the perspective of others who have legitimate rights and expectations in situations.

3. The third level is that of moral principles. Morality is defined as acting in accord with shared or sharable standards, rights, and duties. The possibility of conflict between two socially accepted standards is acknowledged, and attempts at rational adjudication are made. Control of conduct is internal in two senses: The standards have an internal source, and the decision to act is based on an internal process of thought and judgment concerning right and wrong. In Stage 5, the norms of right and wrong are defined in terms of laws or institutionalized rules that are seen to have a rational base; for example, they express the will of the majority, maximize social utility or welfare, or are necessary for institutional functioning. Although recognized as arbitrary, sometimes unjust, and one of many alternatives, the law is generally the ultimate criterion of what is right. Duty and obligation are defined in terms of contract, not the needs of individuals. When conflict exists between the individual and the law or contract, though there may be sympathy for the former, the latter ordinarily prevails because of its greater functional rationality for society. Stage 6 is the morality of individual principles of conscience. The orientation is not only to existing rules and standards but also to conscience as a directing agent, to mutual respect and trust, and to those principles of moral choice that involve an appeal to logical universality and consistency. Conduct is controlled by an internalized ideal that exerts pressure toward action that seems right regardless of the reactions of others present. If the individual acts otherwise, self-condemnation and guilt result. Although Stage 6 people are aware of the importance of law and contract, moral conflict is generally resolved in terms of broader moral principles such as the Golden Rule or the greatest good for the greatest number.

Individuals progress through these six stages, according to Kohlberg, primarily because of experiences of cognitive disequilibrium. This is an extension of the concepts of disequilibrium and equilibration in Piaget's theory of intellectual (rather than moral) development. The hypothesis, developed mostly by Turiel (1966), is that one's moral growth results from exposure to levels of moral reasoning that are moderately higher than one's own current level. The resulting cognitive conflict or disequilibrium produces tension, which results in the person's attempting to make sense out of the contradiction.

These moral stages, according to Kohlberg, also reflect a sequence of successive changes in role-taking ability. The ability to take another person's perspective is seen as having special significance in the transition from premoral to conventional morality (i.e., from Stage 2 to Stage 3). Indeed, Kohlberg at times seems to imply that role-taking is the defining characteristic of conventional morality. At other times, however, role-taking is seen as functioning primarily in the service of cognitive conflict; that is, role-taking experiences provide the individual with different perspectives and so instigate cognitive conflict and its resolution by modifying the existing moral structure. In any case, role-taking ability is fostered by opportunities to discuss people's points of view with them and to participate in decision-making with others, notions that resemble Piaget's.

Kohlberg devised an elaborate Moral Judgment Scale to determine an individual's stage of moral development (Kohlberg, 1969). Subjects make judgments about nine hypothetical moral dilemmas and justify each judgment. The scoring is based primarily on the reasons given to support these judgments. Kohlberg's initial scoring system, on which most of the reported research is based, underwent several drastic revisions in the 1970s. The most recent procedure (Colby, Gibbs, Kohlberg, Speicher-Dubin, Power, & Candee, 1980) is extremely complex. Among other things, it puts emphasis on fewer moral issues and more weight on the highest stage attained by the subject on each issue. It requires that an idea in the subject's protocol must be explicitly stated to credit the subject with that idea, and it removes Stage 6 as a scoring possibility.

An earlier, relatively minor change in the scoring was prompted by the finding in the Kohlberg and Kramer (1969) longitudinal study that a number of subjects attained higher scores (usually Stage 4) in high school than in their early college years (often Stage 2). This finding initially appeared to challenge the theory, which postulates forward rather than backward movement. For a time, it was also viewed as possibly reflecting a kind of temporary disorganization that may characterize movement from conventional to principled morality. Careful examination of the protocols, however, indicated that the Stage 2 responses of the retrogressors did not show the unconcerned, self-centered, hedonistic reasoning characteristic of the "natural" Stage 2 responses of younger subjects. Rather, these subjects appeared to view morality in conventional Stage 4 terms, to have thought about it and questioned its validity. In the revised scoring system these responses were assigned stage scores of 4.5. It should be noted that by age 25 all of these subjects are reported by Kohlberg as having developed strong, principled reasoning (Stages 5 or 6).

Relevant Research.   There have been many studies using various versions of Kohlberg's scale, and Rest's far more practical Defining Issues Test (Rest, Davidson, & Robbins, 1978) that appears to tap similar moral concepts. Much of this research is peripheral to Kohlberg's theory and will not be discussed here; they include, for example, studies relating moral judgments to IQ, to Piaget's cognitive developmental levels, to ideology, and to political activism. We discuss those findings that bear on the central tenets of the theory—the postulated stage sequence is invariant, moral growth is fostered by cognitive conflict and role-taking opportunities, the stages are homogeneous—and on the relation between Kohlberg's stages and moral behavior.

a. Regarding the assumption of stage sequence invariance, Rest (1983) has reviewed a dozen cross-sectional and longitudinal studies and reports that they show significant developmental changes in the direction postulated by Kohlberg's theory. Rest adds several important qualifications, however: Many subjects show no improvement in moral judgment over time, especially adults who are not in school; about one out of 14 subjects who are in school actually move downward; and there is no clear longitudinal evidence that Stage 6 follows Stage 5. Rest also reviews several short-term intervention studies modeled more or less after Turiel's (1966) experiment, in which subjects were exposed to moral arguments one or more stages above or below their own predominant stage. The invariant sequence assumption predicts that subjects exposed to arguments one stage above their own would show the greatest change on a post-test, because in this condition subjects could grasp the significance of the argument and would experience the disequilibrium necessary for moral-cognitive growth. Arguments more than a stage above the subjects would be too far advanced for them to understand, and arguments below the subjects' stage would be seen by them as less adequate than their own and not worthy of consideration. Rest concludes that the findings in these studies are inconclusive. He also discusses the difficulties in using experiments such as these to discover the determinants of development. All things considered, the invariant sequence assumption cannot be said to be supported by the research.

b. The studies just discussed also bear on the importance of cognitive disequilibrium, but in view of the inconclusive findings they cannot be seen as providing support for the idea that cognitive disequilibrium promotes moral growth. As for role-taking, a review by Kurdek (1978) shows that it generally relates positively to the level of moral judgment, although only about half the reported associations are significant. In any case, these correlational studies do not address the issue of whether role-taking is an antecedent or a consequence of moral judgment development or whether moral judgment is a form of role-taking, with development in moral and nonmoral role-taking occurring simultaneously or through mutual influence. In a one year follow-up of 10 subjects who had initially scored low on both role-taking and moral reasoning, Selman (1971) found that more children advanced in role taking than in moral reasoning, and the two who did advance in moral reasoning were among those who advanced in role-taking. He interprets this finding as suggesting that the development of role-taking skills may be a necessary but not sufficient condition for the development of moral thought. This interpretation, however, overlooks the fact that a year earlier a third of the children with high moral reasoning scores in Selman's initial, larger sample had *low* role-taking scores. Thus, although it seems reasonable that cognitive conflict and role-taking could help foster growth in moral thinking, clear empirical evidence is still lacking.

c. Kohlberg assumes that each stage is homogeneous and that there is a high degree of uniformity in a person's moral reasoning level in different situations. The homogeneity assumption cannot be tested in most of the published research because total moral maturity scores or dominant stage scores are given with no indication of the individual moral dilemma scores. The few studies reporting such data do not support the assumption. Thus, not one subject in a sample of 75 college students obtained the same stage score in five Kohlberg dilemmas (Fishkin, Keniston, & MacKinnon, 1973). The scores obtained by adolescent boys and also by their mothers showed considerable "scatter" (Hudgins & Prentice, 1973). And two-thirds of a large college sample used different stages in Kohlberg's dilemmas than in evaluating a social protest movement (Haan, 1975). A small amount of situational variation might be expected due to random errors of measurement and might justify invoking Piaget's concept of "décalage." The high degree of variation obtained in these studies, however, argues against décalage, and therefore perhaps against the assumption that the stages are homogeneous.

d. Kohlberg's theory does not predict a direct relationship between moral reasoning and behavior. Individuals may exhibit the same behavior for different reasons, or different behaviors for the same reason. There should be some relationship between moral reasoning and behavior, however, and Langer (1969) has suggested a possible mechanism: A discrepancy between one's level of moral reasoning and overt behavior creates a state of disequilibrium, and to reduce this the individual is compelled to lessen the discrepancy by bringing behavior and reasoning closer together. Whatever the mechanism, there is evidence of a generally positive relationship between moral reasoning and moral behavior (Blasi, 1980; Rest, 1983). Some interesting anomalies in these findings, due perhaps to variations in testing and scoring procedures, have been pointed out by Kurtines and Greif (1974). Examples are the fact that Stage 3 could characterize both the delinquents in a study by Fodor (1972) and the conformers in a study by Saltzstein, Diamond, and Belenky (1972); and that Haan, Smith, and Block (1968), in their study of participation in student protests, found many Stage 2s among college students, whereas Schwartz, Feldman, Brown, and Heingartner (1969) found none. In general, there appears to be a positive relationship between moral reasoning scores and moral behavior, but there is no clear evidence that any distinctive pattern of behavior is associated with any particular moral stage.

It seems evident that the research as yet provides no clear support for Kohlberg's claim that the stages are homogeneous, that their postulated sequence is universal and invariant, and that moral growth results from role-taking opportunities and exposure to moderately higher levels of moral reasoning. Whether the problem lies in the inadequacies of method, as Kohlberg (1975) has suggested, or in the theory itself remains to be seen.

Aside from the issue of empirical verification, Kohlberg's theory has been taken to task by Simpson (1974) for being a culturally biased approach that claims universality but is actually based on the style of thinking and social organization that is peculiar to Western culture. Stage 5, for example, makes sense only in a constitutional democracy; and Stage 6 requires a level of abstract thought that may disqualify most people in the world. The theory has also been criticized from various philosophical perspectives (e.g., Alston, 1971; Baier, 1974; Peters, 1971).

Perhaps the most fundamental problem with Kohlberg's theory is that it rests on the assumption that there is a universal principle of justice or fairness. Kohlberg relies heavily on Rawls (1971) who proposed an ingeniously simple, seemingly objective analytic device, the "veil of ignorance," for generating universally valid moral principles. That is, if one does not know what one's position in society will be, then even a purely rational, egoistic point of view will lead one to prefer a just society—a society that best represents the interests of everyone. It seems clear, however, that any number of competing justice notions that sound like universal principles may be applied in a given situation. For example, some may think it is fair to allocate society's scarce resources according to the individual's need; others may define fairness as equity and advocate the allocation of resources on the basis of one's productivity or effort; and still others may think the only fair way to allocate resources is to give everyone the same amount. Need, equity, and equality may all be advocated from the "veil of ignorance" perspective—though by different people. People who view themselves as more capable than others, for example, may equate fairness with equity, on the expectation that they will do well in an equitable society. Furthermore, even if the veil of ignorance paradigm could generate a universal principle of justice, it tells us nothing about what would motivate people to act in accord with this principle once they know their position in society and their relative competence. The principle one chooses, and especially one's actual behavior in life, may then reflect one's personal interests rather than a universal principle. Indeed, one may choose a principle that justifies one's expected actions, as has long been suggested by certain "emotive theorists" in philosophy (Brandt, 1967).

The lack of a universally accepted justice principle raises serious questions about any theory (like Kohlberg's) that postulates a moral development stage sequence that is invariant, and in which movement through the stages brings one closer to a universal principle of justice. Until a universally accepted justice principle is found, there may be no grounds for assuming that one stage is higher than another.

Domain-specific Approaches. An important contribution of Kohlberg's work is that it has stimulated others. Most notable among the new cognitive developmental approaches are those by Turiel (1983) and Damon (1977). Turiel distinguishes between moral and conventional thinking, viewing each as a distinct conceptual domain with its own developmental history. Damon makes distinctions within the moral domain and has studied the development of moral concepts in four areas: friendship, justice and fairness, obedience and authority, and social rules and conventions. Damon views moral thinking as task-specific, and he sees the child as having separate, potentially distinct moral concepts that are applied in different arenas, rather than being parts of a homogeneous, unified moral system. The child may, for example, use one kind of concept when dealing with the distribution of rewards and another kind of concept when considering issues involving authority relationships. To study concepts of justice, Damon asked 4- to 8-year-olds what they thought would be a fair way to divide candy, money, or toys in several hypothetical situations (illustrated with pictures). In one story, three children worked together to make bracelets for an adult. One child made the most and the prettiest bracelets; another was the biggest child; and the third, the youngest, could not work as well or as fast as the others. The adult rewarded the group with ten candy bars. The children being studied were asked what they thought would be the fairest way to divide the candy. In the responses to these and other stories Damon found evidence of age progression—from making little or no distinction between what a child would want for himself and what he thought was fair; to favoring an equal division; to recognizing that some children deserve more because they produced more; and finally, to understanding that several valid conflicting claims (e.g., between productivity and need) could exist and that a proper balance must be struck.

Damon's work raises questions for further research. The young child's concepts of justice and fairness appear to be more sophisticated than one would expect for this age group, given Piaget's and Kohlberg's depictions of childhood morality. Where do these early moral concepts come from? To what extent do they affect children's actual behavior, especially when the concepts conflict with the children's own self-interests? How do these early conceptions relate to moral thought and action later in life? Do they have any bearing, for example, on a person's later acceptance of the ideologies that they at least superficially resemble (e.g., ideologies involving the distribution of wealth)?

MORAL MOTIVATION AND AFFECT DEVELOPMENT

Hoffman's Empathy Scheme

Hoffman's empathy scheme highlights motivation and affect in two types of situations: (1) One is an innocent bystander who witnesses someone in pain, danger, or some other needful stage and experiences conflict between the motive to help the victim and the egoistic motive to continue what one was doing and avoid the cost of helping; (2) One experiences conflict between one's egoistic motives and feelings of obligation to another with whom one is in a relationship. When moral development is cast in motivational terms, it raises these questions: What prompts people to go to the aid of someone at a cost to themselves . . . to refrain from doing something they want to do simply because it might have a harmful effect on someone . . . to feel badly about themselves when they realize that their actions have hurt someone? Hoffman's answers are empathy—especially empathic distress—and empathy-based guilt. This is not new. As noted earlier, philosophers have long seen the value of empathy as a socially cohesive, moral force. There are also good evolutionary reasons for expecting empathy to serve as a reliable moral motive (Hoffman, 1981). And, there is considerable empirical evidence that empathy and guilt function as moral motives; that is, they dispose one toward moral action (Hoffman, 1978, 1982). We now summarize the main concepts in Hoffman's developmental scheme for empathy and point out its limitations.

Development of Empathy.   Hoffman defines empathy as a vicarious affective response that is more appropriate to someone else's situation than to one's own. Though an affect, empathy has a fundamental cognitive component: Older children and adults know that they are responding to something happening to someone else, and, based on their knowledge about others and their own past experience, they have an idea of what the other may be feeling; young children who lack the self–other distinction may be empathically aroused without these cognitions. Thus, the level of empathy depends on the level of cognition; and empathy development corresponds, at least partly, to the development of a cognitive sense of others. Hoffman suggests four broad social-cognitive levels (Hoffman, 1975a) that, when combined with empathic affect, result in the following four developmental levels of empathic distress:

1. For most of the first year, witnessing another person in distress may result in a global empathic distress response. Distress cues from the dimly perceived "other" are confounded with unpleasant feelings empathically aroused in the self. Because infants cannot differentiate themselves from the other, they may at times act as though what happened to the other happened to themselves. An 11-month-old girl, on seeing a child fall and cry, looked as if she were about to cry herself, and then put her thumb in her mouth and buried her head in her mother's lap, which is what she would do if she herself were hurt.

2. With the acquisition of "object permanence," including the gradual emergence of a sense of the other as physically distinct from the self, Hoffman hypothesizes that the affective portion of the child's global empathic distress is transferred to the separate image-of-self and image-of-other that emerge. The child can now be aware that another person, and not oneself is in distress, but the other's internal states are unknown and may be assumed to be the same as one's own. An 18-month-old boy fetched his own mother to comfort a crying friend

although the friend's mother was also present—a behavior that, although confused, is not entirely egocentric because it indicates that the child is responding with appropriate empathic affect.

3. With the beginning of role-taking, at about 2–3 years, one becomes aware that other people's feelings may differ from one's own and are based on their own needs and interpretations of events, and so one becomes more responsive to cues about what the other is feeling. Furthermore, with language, children can empathize with a wide range of increasingly complex emotions, and eventually with several conflicting emotions. Empathizing with a victim's distress, they may also empathize with the victim's desire not to feel obligated, hence not to be helped.

4. By late childhood, owing to the emerging conception of oneself and others as continuing people with separate histories and identities, one becomes aware that others feel pleasure and pain not only in the immediate situation, but also in their larger life experience. Consequently, though one may still respond empathically to another's immediate distress, one's empathic response is intensified when one realizes the other's distress is not transitory but chronic. Thus, one's empathically aroused affect is combined with a mental representation of another's general level of distress or deprivation. It also seems likely that, along with the ability to form social concepts, one's empathy arousal may be combined with a mental representation of the plight of an entire group or class of people (e.g., the poor, oppressed, outcast, or retarded). This empathic level can provide a motive base, especially in adolescence, for the development of certain moral and political ideologies that are centered around alleviation of the plight of unfortunate groups (Hoffman, 1980).

When one has advanced through these four levels and encounters someone in pain, danger, or distress, one is exposed to a network of information about the other's affective state. The network may include verbal and nonverbal expressive cues from the victim, situational cues, and one's knowledge about the other's general affective experience that goes beyond the immediate situation. These sources of information are assumed to be processed differently: Empathy aroused by nonverbal and situational cues is mediated by largely involuntary, cognitively "shallow" processing modes. These include: (a) classical conditioning of empathic affect resulting from co-occurrences of distress cues from others and one's own experiences of actual distress (Aronfreed & Paskal, 1965), or from similarities between the other's current situation and one's own past distress experiences (Humphrey, 1922); and (b) a two-step process involving the imitation of the victim's facial and postural movements (mimicry) and the resulting afferent feedback that contributes to one's understanding and feeling of the victim's affect (Lipps, 1906). Empathy that is aroused by verbal messages from the victim, or by one's knowledge about the victim, requires more complex processing, such as semantic interpretation or imagining oneself in the other's place (Stotland, 1969).

Hoffman suggests the various cues, arousal modes, and processing levels usually contribute to the same affect, but contradictions occur, as between different expressive cues (e.g., facial expression and tone of voice) or between expressive and situational cues. If one's knowledge of the other's life condition conflicts with the other's immediate expressive cues, the latter may lose much of their force for an observer who knows they only reflect a transitory state. Imagine someone who does not know that he has a terminal illness, laughing and having a good time. A young child might respond with empathic joy, whereas a mature observer might experience empathic sadness or a mingling of sadness and joy. The most advanced empathic level thus involves some distancing—responding partly to one's mental image of the other rather than only to the other's immediate stimulus value. This fits Hoffman's definition of empathy, not as an exact match of another's feelings, but as an affective response that is more appropriate to the other's situation than to one's own.

Sympathetic Distress. The transition from the first to the second empathic level can, according to Hoffman, involve an important qualitative shift in feeling: Once children are aware of others as distinct from themselves, their own empathic distress, which is a parallel response—a more or less exact replication of the victim's presumed feeling of distress—may be transformed, at least in part, into reciprocal concern for the victim. That is, they may continue to respond in a purely empathic manner—to feel uncomfortable and highly distressed themselves—but they may also experience a feeling of compassion, or "sympathetic distress," for the victim, along with a conscious desire to help because they feel sorry for the victim, not just to relieve their own empathic distress.

Hoffman's evidence for this shift comes from observational research (Murphy, 1937; Zahn-Waxler, Radke-Yarrow, & King, 1979) and anecdotes such as those cited earlier, which show that: (a) children progress developmentally from first responding to someone's distress by seeking comfort for the self, to later trying to help the victim rather than the self; and (b) there appears to be an in-between stage, in which children feel sad and comfort both the victim and the self, that occurs at about the same time that they first become aware of others as distinct from themselves.

What developmental processes account for this shift? Hoffman suggests that the unpleasant, vicarious affect that is experienced as a part of the child's initial global, undifferentiated self is transferred to the separate image-of-self and image-of-other that emerge as part of the self–other differentiation process; as is the wish, not necessarily conscious, to terminate the unpleasant affect. Consequently, the child's empathic distress response now includes a wish to terminate the other's distress—the sympathetic distress component—and a more "purely" empathic wish to terminate distress in the self. The last three empathy development levels therefore apply to sympathetic as well as empathic distress.

Causal attribution and empathy. In Hoffman's view, the partial transformation of empathic into sympathetic distress occurs when the other is clearly perceived as a victim, as in an accident or illness. Other causal attributions are possible, depending mainly on cues that are relevant to causality. If these cues indicate that the victim is responsible for his or her own plight, this may be incompatible with empathic or sympathetic distress because the other may no longer appear as a victim; the observer may feel indifferent or even derogate the victim. If the cues indicate a third person is to blame, one may feel anger at that person, which can interfere with empathy, or, one might alternate between feelings of anger and feelings of empathy. If one were to discover that the victim had previously harmed the attacker, one might blame the victim and empathize with the attacker.

When situational cues are ambiguous, personality differences can play a role. Some observers may blame the victim, to reduce the discomfort of empathic distress. There may also be a general tendency to attribute the cause of another's condition to his or her own disposition (Jones & Nisbett, 1971), or, more specifically, to blame others for their own misfortune in order to support one's assumptions about a "just world" (Lerner & Simmons, 1966). However, research showing a widespread tendency for people to respond empathically to another's distress (Hoffman, 1981) indicates that derogatory attitudes are not incompatible with empathic responses. Culture can play a role too: The misery of a person who belongs to an outcast group can either be attributed to false cues or responded to with indifference regardless of the situation.

Guilt Feeling.   A special case is one in which the cues indicate that the observer is the cause of the other's distress. It seems reasonable to assume that empathic distress occasioned by pain or distress in others that is caused by the observer will be transformed by self-blame into a feeling of guilt. Guilt feelings not only have the same cognitive requisites as empathy but others as well. Included are the awareness that one has choice over one's actions and that one's actions have an impact on others, and the ability to contemplate or imagine an action and its effects on others. These cognitive abilities are necessary for anticipatory guilt feeling and for guilt over omission or inaction. Hoffman has presented a scheme for guilt, along with modest observational evidence, that highlights the parallel development of guilt and empathy (Hoffman, 1982). The scheme, briefly, is as follows: (1) before children become aware of others as separate physical entities they respond to simple expressions of pain in others with empathic distress; they may also at times experience a rudimentary guilt feeling, even though they may lack a keen sense of being the causal agent, simply because of the contiguity of their actions and distress cues from others. (2) Once they know that others are separate physical entities, children experience empathic distress when observing someone who is physically hurt, but the empathic distress can be transformed into guilt if they perceive that their own actions are responsible for the hurt. Similarly, (3) once aware that others have internal states, the empathic distress experienced in the presence of someone having painful or unhappy feelings can be transformed into guilt if one perceives one's actions as causally related to these unpleasant feelings. Finally, (4) once aware of the identity of others beyond the immediate situation—groups as well as individuals—one's empathic response to their general plight can be transformed into guilt if one feels responsible for that plight.

The combination of empathy and a feeling of responsibility for the plight of others (perhaps guilt over inaction) can render the individual receptive to certain moral, as well as political and economic ideologies—ideologies, for example, that pertain to the ways in which society might change to benefit its disadvantaged members. Erikson (1970) notes that adolescents are often motivated to search for a moral ideology that contributes to a sense of identity; ideologies are the "guardians of identity" because they locate one's self in the world and provide coherence for one's affective and cognitive experiences. If one succeeds in finding or constructing an ideology that fits one's empathic and guilty dispositions, then one's new moral viewpoint may be considered a developmental advance because it incorporates social realities previously ignored.

The Role of Socialization.   The discussion so far has dealt with the natural processes that may occur under ordinary conditions in most cultures due to the human tendency to respond vicariously to others. People also have egoistic needs, however, and socialization, which in part reflects the larger social norms, may build upon the child's empathic or egoistic proclivities in varying degrees. Hoffman (1970b) suggests that there may be little conflict between empathic and egoistic socialization in early childhood, even in individualistic societies. At some point the two may begin to clash as one learns that one's access to society's limited resources depends partly on how well one competes. Parents know this, and it affects their childrearing practices. For this and other reasons (parents' personal needs and stresses), wide variations in these practices, and so in children's capacity for empathy and guilt, can be expected. Specific hypotheses about socialization are presented elsewhere (Hoffman, 1982, 1983).

Relevant Research.   Research bearing on aspects of Hoffman's empathy theory has been reviewed elsewhere (Hoffman, 1975a, 1978). Briefly, observations by Murphy (1937) and by Zahn-Waxler et al. (1979) suggest that when children under a year old witness someone being hurt, they may stare at the victim, appear to be agitated themselves, often cry, and seek comfort for themselves. In the second year they cry less often but their faces typically show empathic distress; they may do nothing, make tentative approaches, or actively try to comfort the victim—usually inappropriately due to their cognitive limitations. By 3 or 4 years they show empathic distress but also try to help in more appropriate ways, which is also true of older children and adults. Further, in both children and adults the intensity of empathic affect and the speed of overt helping responses appear to increase as the intensity of distress cues from victims increases (Gaertner & Dovidio, 1977; Geer & Jarmecky, 1973; Murphy, 1937); the intensity of empathic affect appears to drop following acts of helping, and high levels of intensity continue if one does not attempt to help (Darley & Latane, 1968; Murphy, 1937). These findings fit the expected pattern if empathic distress operates as a prosocial moral motive, and they fit with Hoffman's stage scheme. Direct tests of the scheme have not been made, however, although there is experimental evidence for the hypothesis that arousing empathic distress in school-age children intensifies the guilt they feel over harming others (Thompson & Hoffman, 1980).

Limitations of Empathic Morality.   There are some potentially important limitations. First, there is evidence (reviewed by Hoffman, 1978) that people empathize more with others who are perceived as similar to themselves than with those perceived as dissimilar. People *do* empathize with others perceived as dissimilar, however, which suggests that they are responsive to the moral claims of strangers, though to a lesser extent than they respond to the moral claims of kin. Another potential bias is that empathy may lead to moral evaluations that favor people who claim society's resources on the basis of their needs—society's victims—as opposed to those who claim resources on the basis of their productivity or effort (which is not to say the latter claim is free of bias).

Second, because empathic distress is aversive, we might expect it to be intense enough at times to direct one's attention to one's own distress, with the result that one does not try to help the victim. There is suggestive evidence for such an "overarousal" effect in highly empathic children (Kameya, 1976). And, highly empathic student nurses have been found to experience conflict between the desire to help their terminally ill patients and their own intense empathic distress that made it difficult for them to remain in the same room with those patients (Stotland, Mathews, Sherman, Hansson, & Richardson, 1979). As empathic distress usually does lead to helping (see review by Hoffman, 1981), the overarousal effect suggests that there may be a broad range of empathic arousal—perhaps determined by one's general level of distress tolerance—within which one is most responsive to another's distress. Beyond that range, one may be too preoccupied with one's own aversive state to help. Or, one might employ perceptual or cognitive strategies to reduce the empathic distress, such as looking away from the victim, thinking distracting thoughts, or making derogatory attributions. This overarousal effect surely limits the effectiveness of empathic morality. The limitation should not be overdrawn in the absence of further research, however, because the overarousal effect may enable humans to preserve their energies in hopeless situations and thus be more readily available to help others when that help might be more effective. Stotland's nurses may have spent more time with other patients.

Empathy is especially vulnerable to overarousal when it is mediated only by semantic interpretation. If people are asked about their thoughts and feelings on hearing about someone's misfortune by letter, two role-taking processes emerge: (1) one simply focuses attention on the other's misfortune and imagines how the other is feeling (other-focused role-taking). This is often enough to arouse empathy. The resulting empathic feeling may be heightened if one visualizes the other's behavioral responses to his or her plight—facial expressions, posture, tone of voice, sound of cries. One may then respond empathically to that image, almost as though the other was present. (2) One pictures oneself in the other's place and imagines how one would feel (self-focused role-taking). That is, one imagines that the stimuli impinging on the other are impinging on oneself; one then responds affectively to the imagined event. The empathic affect may be heightened if one is also reminded of similar events in one's own past when the same affect was experienced.

The second process appears to have a built-in limitation: When one focuses on one's own affective experience, the image of the other and the other's situation that initiated the process may slip out of focus and fade away, a phenomenon Hoffman (in press) calls "egoistic drift." This appears to contradict Stotland's (1969) finding that subjects instructed to imagine how someone undergoing a painful heat treatment felt (other-focused) showed less empathic distress than subjects instructed to imagine how they themselves would feel in that situation (self-focused). A possible explanation of both findings is that self-focused role-taking arouses more intense empathy because it directly connects the victim's affective state to the observer's need system, but it is this very connection that makes self-focused role-taking vulnerable to "egoistic drift." Self-focused role-taking thus generates more intense, but less stable, empathic affect. Whatever the explanation, these findings show the fragility of empathic responses that rely entirely on verbal statements of the victim's plight, and raise questions about the strength of empathic moral systems. In defense of empathic morality, one need not often rely on verbal cues alone. Victims may be present and direct expressive cues of their feeling, usually visual or auditory, or situational cues may supplement verbal messages and keep the empathic processes "alive" because these cues may be salient, vivid, and hold the observer's attention. Empathic morality may thus be effective in face-to-face interpersonal encounters.

Another limitation of empathic morality pertains to its scope. There are aspects of moral action for which it may have little relevance. Thus, empathy alone cannot explain how children learn to negotiate and achieve a proper balance between the consideration of others and egoistic motives in situations. Empathy may also have little to say about a morality of justice—unless a clear victim is involved, perhaps someone who is treated unfairly—or about behaving morally out of a sense of duty. And, although empathy may make one receptive to certain moral ideologies, as suggested earlier, it alone cannot explain how these ideologies are formulated and applied in given situations.

Perhaps the most general limitation of an empathy-based morality's scope is that although it may provide a reliable motive base for helping, caring, and considering others, it may not contribute to making appropriate moral judgments when several behaviors are to be compared, or competing moral claims are to be evaluated. It is in these complex situations that the empathic bias noted earlier is apt to be disruptive. To make appropriate moral judgments in these situations probably requires moral principles that go beyond empathizing with and considering other people, and against which anyone's behavior can be assessed with minimal bias. Such moral principles would enable one to decide which moral claims deserve priority and to do so with more objectivity than mere empathy can provide.

MORAL INTERNALIZATION THEORIES

Whereas stage theories describe moral modes and attempt to delineate qualitative differences in the modes children employ as they grow up, internalization theories deal with those experiences and processes that provide people with a moral sense and motivate them to act morally in situations involving conflict between their own needs and the needs of others, without regard to social approval and other egoistic concerns. Since Freud and Durkheim, social scientists have agreed that most people do not go through life viewing society's moral norms, many of which deal with this conflict, as external, coercively imposed pressures. The norms may be initially external and often conflict with one's desires, but they may eventually become a part of one's motive system to some extent, and help guide behavior even in the absence of external authority. There is disagreement, however, in the definition of moral internalization. Thus, a given theory of what fosters moral internalization—sometimes called moral autonomy, moral motivation, or introjection—may deal with a particular facet of morality (affective, behavioral, cognitive) and treat a certain aspect of the child's experience that is ignored by other theories.

Psychoanalytic Theory

The first complete theory of moral internalization was Freud's. Although it is not presented in any one place, the theory can be pieced together through two decades of Freud's published work (e.g., Freud, 1925/1961). The central thrust of the theory, which applies mainly to males, is as follows. The young child inevitably suffers many frustrations—some ascribable to parental interventions—that contribute to the development of hostility toward the parents. The child also desires close bodily contact with the mother for erotic pleasure. The main rival is the father, and the child's rivalrous behavior and expressed desires for the mother are often punished. Due to anxiety over the anticipated punishment, especially the loss of parental love and abandonment, children repress their hostile and erotic feelings. To master the anxiety and maintain repression, as well as to avoid punishment and elicit continuing affection from their parents, children adopt certain rules and prohibitions emanating from their parents that often reflect society's moral norms. Children also acquire a generalized motive to emulate the behavior and adopt the internal states of their parents, especially fathers. Finally, they adopt the parents' capacity to punish themselves when they violate a prohibition or are tempted to do so—turning inward the hostility they originally directed toward their parents. This self-punishment is experienced as a guilt feeling dreaded for its intensity and resemblance to earlier anxieties about punishment and abandonment. Children therefore try to avoid guilt by acting in line with incorporated parental prohibitions, and erecting defense mechanisms against conscious awareness of contrary impulses. These basic conscience formation processes are accomplished by 5 to 6 years of age, and are worked through and solidified during the remaining, relatively calm years of childhood.

Moral internalization (superego formation) is thus a product of the child's introjection of parental prohibition, which is motivated largely by the child's fear of losing parental love. The result is a disciplinary agency within the child that can detect transgression and mete out punishment as guilt feelings. This all occurs early in life, before children can process complex information. Consequently, these moral norms become part of an inflexible, primarily unconscious, and often strict impulse control system. It is interesting to note that the superego rests on an egoistic motive base (anxiety avoidance), although it presumably results in moral action.

This theory is widely accepted by psychoanalytic writers with minor variations, although its main support comes from the scattered observations of adult patients. The hypothesis that anxiety over the loss of parental love contributes to moral internalization finds little support in parent-discipline research (see review by Hoffman, 1970a): Love-withholding discipline does not correlate with moral internalization (although it does correlate with the inhibition of anger). The hypothesis that parent identification fosters moral internalization receives limited support: Identification correlates with some visible moral behaviors, such as helping or making moral judgments about others. It does not correlate with guilt, an index of using moral standards for the evaluation of one's own behavior (Hoffman, 1971, 1975d), which makes sense because parents rarely communicate the source of their guilt to young children, who cannot make the necessary inferences about the parent's internal states without this information.

More fundamentally, it is unlikely that a largely unconscious, internalized control system can be adaptive, let alone account for the complexities of moral behavior. That this system is quasi-pathological has long been noted by Freud and other psychoanalytic writers (e.g., Freud, 1930/1955; Lederer, 1964). Some have tried to modify it to account for "positive" aspects of morality, but the processes invoked remain close to Freud's (see reviews by Hoffman 1970b, 1980). Others have suggested that, although the superego persists through childhood, it is disrupted in adolescence owing to hormonal changes, social demands, and new information about the world that may contradict it (cf., Blos, 1976; Erikson, 1970; Settlage, 1972). Considerable anxiety results from this disruption and from the resulting threat to the close, dependent relation with the parents that supported the superego. The child must therefore find a new, more mature moral basis, or erect defenses to ward off uncontrollable impulses and maintain the superego intact. These writers suggest mechanisms for a mature morality in adolescence, but the mechanisms are not clearly defined and persuasive data support is not offered (see review by Hoffman, 1980).

Social Learning Theory

Social learning theorists typically avoid terms such as *moral internalization* pertaining to internal psychological states that are several steps removed from observable behavior, but they do attempt to explain a similar phenomenon: Overt moral action (defined by cultural norms) or the absence of deviant action under conditions of temptation and non-surveillance. One social learning theory states that, owing to a history of experiences in which one has been punished for deviant acts, painful anxiety states may become associated with these acts; that is, with the kinesthetic and perceptual cues produced by the acts and the cognitive cues associated with them (e.g., Aronfreed & Reber, 1965; Mowrer, 1960). This anxiety over deviation may subsequently be experienced when one deviates or contemplates deviating even when no one is present, and it can best be avoided by inhibiting the act. Individuals may thus appear to behave in an internalized manner, although they are actually responding to a subjective fear of external punishment. When deviation anxiety becomes diffuse and detached from the conscious fear of detection, the inhibition of a deviant act can be seen as a primitive form of internalization that has much in common with the concept of the superego. Indeed, the initial inspiration for this theory was Mowrer's (1960) attempt to translate psychoanalysis into learning terms.

Social learning theories also deal with the child's exposure to models who behave in a moral manner or are punished for behaving in a deviant manner. In the former case, it is assumed that children learn by observing and emulating the model in future situations when the model is absent. In the case of punishment to a deviant model, it is assumed that the child is punished vicariously or, anticipating the model's fate, avoids the deviant behavior.

Social learning theory has inspired a lot of research that, unfortunately, has serious problems (Hoffman, 1977b). In experimental studies designed to simulate the effects of punishment by parents, the entire socialization process is usually telescoped into a single adult–child interaction; that is, the child's immediate response to a particular punishment by the experimenter is used to indicate the presence or absence of moral behavior. This use of a single instance of compliance as the moral index blurs the distinction between moral action and mere compliance with an arbitrary request by authority; besides, compliance is a questionable moral index to begin with, as is evidenced by Milgram's (1963) finding that compliance can, at times, lead to immoral action. The research on models also has other problems and the findings do not provide clear support for the theory (see review by Hoffman, 1977b). Although observing models who deviate from a moral norm clearly increases the likelihood of deviant behavior in children, observing models who resist temptation and adhere to the norm does not appear to increase the likelihood of moral behavior. This may indicate that simply observing models who act morally does not arouse motives powerful enough to overcome the child's egoistic tendencies. The research also suggests that although observing models who deviate and are not punished fosters deviant behavior in the child, observing models who are punished has relatively little effect. The relevance of the latter research to internalization may be questionable, quite apart from the findings, because the children may be using punishment to the model only as an index of what might happen to them if they were to behave in the deviant manner.

There is another, more subtle social learning approach that derives from the notion that one may engage in an act in order to gain reward from oneself (Bandura, 1977). It follows that if children are socialized to act morally and to experience self-rewards afterward, they will come to guide their behavior in accord with the moral norms even in the absence of external authority. This conception of internalization seems plausible, although there is as yet no evidence for it, and it does leave certain important questions unanswered. For example, why should self-reward contribute to moral action? People may reward themselves for any behavior, as Bandura states. But the behaviors for which they reward themselves depend on the cultural norms guiding their socialization, and in our highly individualistic society these norms are as apt to include competitive aggressive behavior as they are morally considerate behavior. Self-reward may not be a reliable mediator of moral action, therefore, for most people in individualistic societies. Furthermore, the self-reward concept does not explain how the self that is rewarded develops in the first place and what the mechanisms are by which moral actions come to reward that self.

Hoffman (1981) has suggested a type of self-reward that may meet some of these objections; namely, the self-reward that is inherent in empathy. A person who helps others may experience a decrease in empathic distress, as noted earlier, but beyond that, when the victim shows visible signs of relief or joy after being helped, the helper may also feel empathic relief or empathic joy. Experiencing these pleasurable empathic feelings, one may be subsequently motivated to help others in order to experience those feelings once again. This view of empathic pleasure as a moral motive still lacks empirical evidence: As noted elsewhere (Hoffman, 1982), the available evidence indicates that although people feel good after helping others, they do not generally help others in order to feel good.

"Self-awareness" theory should also be mentioned here (Duvall, Duvall, & Nealy, 1979; Duvall & Wicklund, 1972), although it may not properly be classed as a social learning theory. Self-awareness theory assumes that one's moral norms for correct actions are an intrinsic part of one's "self." Anything in a situation that focuses attention on oneself may therefore activate and make one aware of one's moral norms. If one's behavior deviates from an activated moral norm, a state of tension may result that can be reduced by bringing one's behavior into line with the norm. Focusing people's attention on themselves can therefore lead to moral actions. In one field experiment, trick-or-treating children entering a home were told from another room to take only one piece of candy from a large bowl on a table near the front door (Beaman, Klentz, Diener, & Svanum, 1979). Children were more likely to take only one candy in the self-focus condition (the candy bowl was placed in front of a large mirror) than in the control condition. This theory, as well as the finding, is intriguing and potentially important, but as yet it contributes little toward an understanding of moral internalization because, as with the self-reward conception, it ignores the problem of how the self develops, how a person's moral norms become linked to the self, and why the egoistic aspects of the self are not activated when attention is focused on oneself.

Attribution Theory

The earliest attributional explanation of moral internalization is simply this: If the pressure put on children is just enough to get them to change their behavior and comply with a moral norm but is not enough for them to notice the pressure, they will then attribute their compliance to their own will rather than to the pressure (Festinger & Freedman, 1964). A more elaborate version of this basic theory is Lepper's (1983) "minimal sufficiency principle," which specifies that internalization is facilitated by parental discipline that puts the least amount of pressure on children needed to gain their compliance. When children are induced to behave in a manner that goes against their initial inclination, they seek to explain their resulting compliant behavior to themselves. If the external pressure is clear and unmistakable, the compliance is simply attributed to the external pressure; in future temptation situations in which there is no external pressure, there is no reason to comply. If the pressure by the parent is not salient, it allows children to generate internal explanations for their compliance; for example, they may see their conformity as stemming from their own intrinsic motivation to be good. When confronted with a later temptation to break the rule even in the absence of surveillance, they will not be able to do so without violating their own attitude, or their own self-image of being a good person. Although these formulations have an elegant simplicity, they bypass the question of why children should subordinate their desires and change their behavior against their will when they are unaware of any pressure to do so.

An attribution theory advanced by Dienstbier (1978) is unusual in that it attempts to deal with affect and motivation. According to Dienstbier, the child is emotionally aroused when disciplined by the parent. The aroused emotion is at first undefined but is then given meaning as the child attributes it either to the punishment the child expects to receive (if the parent has made punishment salient) or to the deviant act and its harmful effects (if explanation is used and punishment is mild). At a later date, when the temptation to behave in a similar deviant manner occurs again, the emotional discomfort that the child feels when contemplating the deviant act will likewise be attributed either to the anticipated punishment or to the deviant act. If no authority is present and detection is unlikely, attributing the aroused emotion to anticipated punishment—which is likely in the child for whom punishment has been made salient—is irrelevant to the situation, and the child has no reason to resist temptation and refrain from the deviant act. Attributing the emotion to the act itself, however—which is likely in the child who is frequently exposed to explanations—is relevant even when no one is present and can be expected to play a role in facilitating the child's resistance to temptation. The use of explanations and mild punishment therefore contributes to moral internalization.

This explanation, which is in keeping with Schachter and Singer's (1962) formulations about the necessity of cognitive appraisal for experiencing specific emotions, is also elegant and simple. But here, too, the elegance may have been gained at the cost of ignoring certain important details. According to Dienstbier's theory, if punishment is salient the child attributes the aroused emotion to punishment; if explanation about the act is salient the child attributes the aroused emotion to the act and the harm done. That is, the particular attribution made by the child is isomorphic with respect to the aspect of the situation that is made salient by the parent's behavior. The attribution may thus be little more than a labeling of the emotion according to the stimulus highlighted by the parent's behavior. What is lacking is an explanation of why the emotion is aroused in the first place and how it contributes to moral internalization. We may also ask, how it is possible for the emotion aroused in discipline encounters to remain in an undefined state until appropriate attributions are made. Isn't it likely that the parent's action (e.g., threatening to strike the child) elicits an *immediate* and specific emotional response in the child, such as fear, rather than an undefined feeling that is experienced as fear only after it is attributed to the parent's action? What is gained by introducing the concept of attribution? Another limitation of this and the other attribution approaches is that, like some social learning paradigms, it seems to view moral internalization as nothing more than compliance without awareness of the external pressure that led to that compliance. Compliance without awareness may be part of moral internalization, but it is surely not the whole thing.

Cognitive-Developmental Theory

Cognitive developmentalists, like social learning theorists, tend to avoid terms like *moral internalization* but for a different reason: The term seems to suggest something outside the child that becomes part of his or her internal moral structure. The child thus appears relatively passive in acquiring moral norms, rather than actively constructing them. Although these writers avoid the term, they do appear to have an implicit moral internalization concept that may have been apparent in the earlier description of Kohlberg's stage theory. Namely: (a) When people are exposed to new and morally relevant information that is more comprehensive and in keeping with a level of moral thought optimally higher than their own, they engage in active mental efforts to process this information and integrate it with their own prior view; (b) the normal human tendency is to move toward the higher level; and (c) the highest levels are autonomous and principled, and one may be said to have internalized them by virtue of having constructed them oneself.

This concept of internalization involves two assumptions. One assumption, implicit in stage theory, is that the new information must be at an optimally higher level than one's own and that one tends to move toward higher, more principled levels. This assumption may be questioned, especially in view of the serious limitations of stage theory summarized earlier. The other assumption, which is implicit in most cognitive theories, including non-stage theories, is that the process of construction is active and involving and, as a result, the products of construction, regardless of their domain (e.g., moral, physical), become part of one's system of knowledge structures and it is in that sense that they are internalized. This notion of internalization, which may be divorced from stage theory, remains plausible, and it has a certain appeal because the individual is viewed as capable of thinking matters through and accepting moral and other concepts on more or less rational grounds.

Affective–Cognitive Synthesis

In Hoffman's view of internalization, moral norms are internalized to the degree that one feels an obligation to act in accord with them, and the obligation is no longer based on the fear of punishment or disapproval. The moral norm in question is simply that people should consider the welfare of others as well as themselves. As with other moral norms, it presumably has motivational, affective, and cognitive components. Thus, one is motivated to consider and avoid harming others; one feels good after acting in accord with the norm and guilty (in the sense discussed earlier) after violating it; and one has cognitive representations of the reasons why certain actions are right or wrong—the prohibitions against acting in various ways that might harm others, and the probable consequences of one's actions for others. When a norm is internalized it is usually experienced as deriving autonomously from within oneself, with little recollection of where it actually originated. The question Hoffman tries to answer is what socialization experiences are necessary for developing such a complex network of moral cognition, affect, and motivation. His answer, the rationale for which is presented elsewhere (Hoffman, 1983), is that the relevant socialization experiences consist primarily of discipline encounters with parents that result in children's feeling empathy and empathy-based guilt over acting in a harmful manner toward others.

The central finding in a rather large body of research (see review by Hoffman, 1977b) indicates that a moral orientation that is characterized by the independence of external sanctions, as well as by high guilt, is fostered by the frequent use of inductions. These are disciplinary techniques that point up the effects of the child's behavior on others, either directly ("If you keep pushing him, he'll fall down and cry.") or indirectly ("Don't yell at him. He was only trying to help."). They become more complex as the child grows older and may often include suggestions of reparative acts, such as apologies. In contrast, a moral orientation that is based primarily on the fear of punishment is associated with the excessive use of power-assertive discipline—force, deprivation of privileges, threats, or commands. There is evidence, however, that occasional power-assertion—to let children know the parent feels strongly about something, or to control children's unreasonably defiant behavior—when administered by parents who normally employ inductions, contributes positively to moral internalization (e.g., Zahn-Waxler et al., 1979). There is no relation between moral internalization and love-withdrawal techniques, which are direct but non-physical, expressions of the parent's anger or disapproval (e.g., the mother ignores, turns her back on, refuses to speak or listen to, explicitly states dislike for, isolates, or threatens to leave the child). Love-withdrawal, however, does appear to contribute to children's inhibition of anger. Hoffman's explanation of these findings is an information-processing type of theory (Hoffman, 1977b, 1983) that can be summarized as follows:

1. Most disciplinary techniques have a power-assertive or love-withdrawal component that may be needed to get children to stop what they are doing and pay attention to the information contained in the inductive component that may also be present. This inductive component points up the harmful consequences of the child's action. Too little power-assertion or love-withdrawal may result in children ignoring the parent. Too much power-assertion or love-withdrawal may produce fear, anxiety, or resentment in children, which may interfere with the effective processing of the induction; whether they comply or not, these feelings may direct children's attention to the consequences of their actions for themselves. Techniques that include a salient inductive component ordinarily achieve the best balance, and if phrased in terms that the child can comprehend they draw the child's attention to the consequences for the victim. This will often engage the child's empathic response system at whatever empathic level the child has attained (see earlier discussion of developmental levels of empathic distress).

2. Inductions help make it clear that the child caused the other's distress. This is especially important for young children who may not spontaneously see causal connections between their acts and other's states because of motivation, cogni-

tive limitations, intense affect, or the ambiguity of the situation. The result of pointing out the connection is that children may then attribute blame to themselves. Self-blame may combine with empathic distress, as discussed earlier, to produce a feeling of guilt. These guilt feelings, aroused in countless discipline encounters over time, may produce a moral motive in children.

3. Inductions also give children information pertaining to the cognitive component of the norm of considering others. Aside from indicating the harmful consequences of children's action, inductions may also communicate a prohibition against harming others, the reasons why particular actions are right or wrong, and the parent's value in considering others. This information may be stored and cumulatively organized over time, and the resulting structure may constitute the cognitive component of the child's emerging moral norm. Because guilt feelings have accompanied the initial processing of this information in discipline encounters, the resulting moral-cognitive structure is charged with guilty affect and so acquires the characteristics of a motive. The norm of considering others may thus become a "hot cognition" resulting from the synthesis of affect and cognition in discipline encounters. In future situations, when the child acts or contemplates acting in a harmful manner, cues from the other person or the situation may activate one or another component of the norm, which may then enter into the balance of the forces determining how the child acts quite apart from any concerns about punishment or disapproval. The norm can then be considered internalized.

4. The child's mental activity in processing inductions—the semantic interpretation of the informational content and relating it to his or her action and to the victim's condition—makes the child's own internal processes salient. For this reason, and also because of the way information appears to be stored in memory (semantically processed material is cumulatively organized and integrated into one's enduring knowledge structures, whereas situational details are processed in a shallower fashion and forgotten relatively quickly), children may come to perceive themselves, rather than their parents, as the source of this information. And they may feel that the guilt feelings originally generated in discipline encounters have come from within themselves.

Although this theory stresses discipline by parents, in acquiring an early motivational base the child may be receptive to inductions from other adults as well. Interaction with peers may also contribute under certain conditions (Hoffman, 1980), expanding the domain of situations in which the norm may be activated. This domain is also expanded as children acquire the language and social-cognitive skills that enable them to comprehend the effects of their actions on others beyond the immediate situation, or to anticipate these effects ahead of time.

This theory is consistent with the discipline research that it was designed to explain. It is also in keeping with research that shows that: (a) optimal levels of anxiety foster the semantic processing of verbal messages, whereas intense anxiety fosters attention to the physical details of the message and the relative neglect of semantic processing (Kahneman, 1973; Mueller, 1979); (b) when people observe someone in distress they typically experience empathic distress, and when they are aware of being the cause of the other's distress they ordinarily feel guilty (Hoffman, 1982, in press); and (c) semantic processing by children and adults is cumulatively organized and enduring, whereas processing of situational details is relatively short-lived (Brown, 1975; Craik, 1977; Stein & Glenn, 1979; Tulving, 1972). The theory gains plausibility from its fit with these bodies of research, but research is needed that tests hypotheses that are derived directly from it, for example, that guilt is often aroused by inductive discipline, that guilt adds motive force to moral structures resulting from children's processing and integration of the content of inductions, and that the resulting moral motive is activated in later temptation situations and contributes to the balance of forces that determine how a person acts.

The Role of Moral Internalization in Society

Sociologists have long noted that there are not enough overt control forces to keep societies running smoothly, and moral values and norms have emerged to aid in this task. But although society benefits when individuals act in accordance with its moral values, this action does not generally reward the individual actor unless the value has been internalized. Internalization, then, serves the function of integrating the goals of the individual with those of society by translating the "social" into the "moral." As stated by Simmel over 80 years ago, "The tendency of society to satisfy itself as cheaply as possible results in appeals to 'good conscience' through which the individual pays to himself the wages for his righteousness, which otherwise would probably have to be assured to him in some way through law or custom" (Simmel, 1902, p. 19).

Other sociologists argue against excessive reliance on internalization and draw attention to *external* social controls and the vulnerability of moral standards to external pressure. There is evidence for their contention. Milgram's (1963) experiments have shown that people sometimes obey requests by respectable authority figures to behave in ways that contradict their professed, and presumably internalized, standards. In a survey conducted by Baumhart (1961), most business executives agreed with the statement "businessmen would violate a code of ethics whenever they thought they could avoid detection." In another survey, Harvard graduate students in political science, presented with details of cases of official duplicity, gave responses indicating "an orientation toward seeing things not in ethical but in cost-benefit terms and whether one might get caught" (reported by Otten, 1974). Ross and DiTecco (1975) cite instances in which morality actually broke down on a large scale when policing agencies were removed. These examples, together with familiar Watergate and corporate bribery revelations should help us to discard any simplistic notion that a person's internal moral standards persist unchanged through life without environmental support, and to accept the fact that internalized standards are vulnerable to external pressure and temptation.

Moral internalization may nevertheless be important for society. As an example, when many members of a society have internalized its moral standards these internalized standards may act as a brake and soften the impact of external (e.g., technical, economic) pressures for social change. The situation is complicated because subgroups—age, socioeconomic, ethnic—vary in the extent to which their members internalize moral standards and are exposed to external pressures against those standards. As a result, conflicts between subgroups, as well as between internalized standards and external pressures within subgroups, are to be expected. All of these conflicts constitute a major dynamic in social change. Moral internalization, then, although it is vulnerable to external pressures, can nevertheless serve a central, primarily stabilizing function in the social process.

THE INFLUENCE OF SOCIALIZATION ON MORAL DEVELOPMENT

The research on moral socialization, half a century old, has generally been empirical, with little concern for theory. The exception is child-rearing research, which was inspired largely by psychoanalytic notions and eventually provided the basis for many internalization theories. Only recently has the search for socialization influences expanded to include peers, television, and sex roles, although this research remains scanty. The influence of school experiences, possibly very profound, has been totally neglected.

Childrearing Practices and Moral Internalization

The moral norm studied in most childrearing research is simply that people should consider the needs and welfare of others (e.g., they should tell the truth, keep promises, help others; they should not lie, steal, betray a trust, physically attack others or hurt others' feelings). The focus has been on two aspects of the parent's role: disciplinarian and model.

Discipline and Moral Internalization.   There is an empirical generalization, noted earlier, that induction relates positively to moral internalization and power-assertion relates negatively. Most of this research was done with children ranging from 4 to 12 years of age, although there is evidence that the generalization holds up for children as young as 2 years (Zahn-Waxler et al., 1979). The generalization is also supported by laboratory research (Kuczynski, 1983; Sawin & Parke, 1980).

One argument against the generalization states that because most of the findings are correlational, causal inferences cannot be made (Bell, 1968). Although the general point is beyond dispute, it has been argued on theoretical, logical, and empirical grounds that the weight of the evidence in this case is far more favorable to one causal inference—i.e., the type of discipline affects moral internalization—than to any other (Hoffman, 1975c), and that it is therefore scientifically indefensible to assume we know nothing about causality in this domain.

The argument, in part, is this. First, parents begin to discipline their children in earnest by the time they are 2 years of age, which is several years before children show the earliest signs of moral internalization. Thus, by 2 years, parents are found to attempt to change children's behavior against their will on an average of about once every 6 to 7 minutes (cf., Minton, Kagan, & Levine, 1971), and they are usually successful. Second, parents exert far more control over children's behavior than the reverse (Lytton, 1979; Schoggen, 1963; Wright, 1967). Third, the internal states presumably elicited for the first time in children in disciplinary encounters (e.g., guilt over harming others, fear of punishment, or loss of love for a misdeed) resemble the internal states elicited later in moral encounters or temptation situations in children who have or have not internalized the moral norm in question. These findings suggest that the effects of parental discipline predate children's moral internalization, and that the primary causal influence is from parental discipline to child morality, although this influence may be mutual once the process is set in motion.

Three findings have been offered in rebuttal: Altering children's behavior can affect discipline-like actions by adult experimenters (Keller & Bell, 1979); and parental discipline is influenced by the nature of the child's deviant behavior, and also by the extent to which the child is distracted (Chapman, 1979; Grusec & Kuczynski, 1980). The first is irrelevant because the adult was a stranger with no power over the child. The last two miss the point of the argument as it has been presented: Given a particular deviant act, parents can use whatever discipline technique they choose. The same argument can be made regarding genetic influences: If parents of children who were temperamentally abrasive at birth used few inductions, it would show that temperament affects the use of induction but it would not be evidence against the contribution of induction to moral internalization. Many factors—possibly including genetics, social class, and IQ—can affect the parents' use of induction, but this does not negate the immediate, "proximal" impact of induction on the child's internal states in disciplinary encounters. The immediate effects, cumulatively integrated over time, are presumably what count in moral internalization. In any case, two of the internalization theories discussed earlier, those of Dienstbier (1978) and of Hoffman (1975c), represent attempts to explain the ways in which inductions contribute to moral internalization.

Parent as Model.   Since the time of Freud, it has generally been assumed that children identify with their parents and adopt their parents' ways of evaluating their own behavior. The motive for identification is to avoid physical attack or the loss of parental love. For nonpsychoanalytic writers, children identify with their parents in order to acquire desired parental characteristics (privileges, control of resources, power over children). As the relevant research has been summarized at different points in this chapter and some of the methods criticized, it is only necessary to review the main findings here. The research (see reviews by Hoffman, 1971, 1975d) suggests that identification may contribute to those aspects of morality that are reflected in parents' words and deeds, though not to feeling guilty over violating moral standards (Hoffman, 1971) perhaps because parents rarely communicate the source of their guilt feelings to children. Children's motivation to identify with their parents may also not be strong enough to overcome the pain of self-criticism that accompanies guilt feelings.

In the early 1960s, Bandura suggested that identification is an unnecessarily complex concept; imitation is simpler, more amenable to research, yet equally powerful as an explanatory concept. Numerous experiments followed. Those that study the effects of adult models on children's moral judgment and resistance to temptation (reviewed by Hoffman, 1977b) are especially pertinent. The results include the following: (a) Children readily imitate adult models who yield to temptation (e.g., leave an assigned task to watch a movie), as though the model serves to legitimize the deviant behavior, but they are much less likely to imitate a model who resists temptation; and (b) when children who make moral judgments of others on the basis of the consequences of their acts are exposed to adult models who judge acts on the basis of intentions, those children show an increased understanding of the importance of intentions—and this effect may last for several months. (The theoretical implications of these findings were discussed earlier.)

It seems reasonable to conclude tentatively that identification can contribute to the adoption of visible moral attributes requiring little self-denial, and to the adoption of standards of moral evaluation that are internalized in the sense that children use them as criteria of right and wrong in judging others. However, identification does not—as inductive discipline apparently does—contribute to the use of moral standards as evaluative criteria for examining one's own behavior.

Peer Influences

Despite longstanding interest in the topic, peer interaction and its effects on children have only recently been studied systematically, and much of the research is descriptive. There has been little research on how interaction with peers affects the child's moral development. The dominant theoretical orientation is Piaget's (discussed earlier) in which unsupervised interaction with peers is essential for moral development: The absence of gross differentials of power provides children with the experiences—such as role-taking or decision-making—necessary to develop moral norms and belief systems that are based on mutual consent and cooperation among equals. More recently and in a similar vein, Youniss (1980) has suggested that friendship among children is an obvious context in which they begin to understand cooperation and jointly discover principles that serve mutual ends. An opposite conception is reflected in Golding's novel *Lord of the Flies* (1962) and derivable from Freud's view that one's morality may be thrown off in large groups where "all individual moral acquisitions are obliterated and only the most primitive, the oldest, the crudest mental attributes are left (Freud, 1924, p. 288)." This conception is that unsupervised peer interaction may release the child's inhibitions and undermine the effects of previous socialization at home.

The research provides tentative answers concerning the effects of peer interaction on aggression, as well as suggestive insights about moral development. First, there is support for the widespread assumption that peer influence increases as children grow older, with the peak occurring in adolescence (e.g., Berndt, 1979). By early adolescence most children are aware of operating in two separate and sometimes conflicting social tracks—a peer track and an adult track. As for the direction of peer influences—Do peer groups support or undermine adult values? The answer is less clear. Most of the research on high school subcultures finds broad areas of agreement with adult values, along with modest differences in emphasis, such as greater stress on athletics and popularity rather than on academic achievement (e.g., Coleman, 1961). A significant exception is the use of drugs by adolescents, which was found to be associated with the use of drugs by their friends (Kandel, 1971).

Regarding the role of peer interaction in the socialization of aggression, the experimental research reviewed by Hoffman (1977b) indicates that if a child observes a peer who behaves aggressively and is not punished, the likelihood of that child also behaving aggressively is increased; if the aggressive peer is punished, there is no measurable effect. This suggests that when children express aggression and are not punished, which often occurs in unsupervised peer settings, the effect may be to stimulate other children in the vicinity to act aggressively. Even if the aggressive children are punished, however, this may *not* serve as a deterrent to others. Peer behavior may thus be more likely to weaken, rather than to strengthen, the inhibitions against aggression that the child has acquired in the home.

In a classic observational study of 11-year-old boys in an experimental summer camp Sherif, Harvey, White, Hood, and Sherif (1961) found that when two previously unacquainted groups competed in team sports, considerable animosity developed. Only working together on a superordinate goal introduced by camp counselors could reduce the negative feelings. Other,more recent studies with groups of preschool children (Patterson, Littman, & Bricker, 1967; Savin-Williams, 1979; Strayer & Strayer, 1978) suggest that aggressive behavior may emerge spontaneously and increase over time. Aggression may be reduced by an adult who alters the composition of the group or introduces new activities that stimulate cooperative interaction. Aggression may also be reduced by the spontaneous emergence of a dominance hierarchy within the group. In this case, however, a price may be paid by those children who develop a submissive pattern in which they rarely challenge others. All things considered, Piaget's contention that unsupervised peer interaction is conducive to moral development may not be entirely accurate. Certainly with respect to the expression of aggression, peers appear to offer little constructive guidance or control. And dominance hierarchies may often preclude the equal, reciprocal interactions among peers that were envisioned by Piaget as crucial for moral development.

There is a body of laboratory research that indicates that children will imitate a variety of acts by their peers, including moral acts such as helping others. This suggests that if groups can be structured to encourage these desirable behaviors in some individuals, others may act in a similar fashion. Furthermore, correlational studies have shown a negative relationship between early sociability (frequent, comfortable interaction with peers) and rates of delinquency and conduct disorders during adolescence (Conger & Miller, 1966).

More research is needed concerning the role of peers in moral socialization; for example, we need to know whether naturally forming unsupervised peer groups at various ages, in different segments of society and, operating in different settings, actually support or contradict prevailing moral norms. What types of peer interaction are most conducive to moral actions? How do children manage the different and sometimes competing messages of peers, parents, and teachers? Do dominance hierarchies control aggression, and if so, at what cost? What is the contribution of childhood friendships to moral socialization?

The Effects of Television

Children of all ages spend many hours watching television, and the trend in the amount of viewing time continues upward. Although wide variations exist depending on the segment of the audience surveyed, the average television set is on for almost seven hours a day, and children are among the most frequent viewers (Roberts & Bachen, 1981). The effect of television viewing on children has been the subject of considerable research, most of it on violence. Some argue that watching filmed violence may *reduce* one's proneness to violent behavior because of the cathartic release it provides (Feshbach & Singer, 1971). Others note that viewers, especially children, learn by observing and imitating television characters. Thus, if a child sees people (especially those presented in a positive light with whom the child might identify) handling social conflict situations in a violent manner, he or she might respond in a similar fashion when placed in a conflict situation. Repeated exposure may also blunt a sensitivity to violence, leading the child to underestimate, or to fail to anticipate, the painful consequences of aggressive acts (Thomas, Horton, Lippincott, & Drabman, 1977).

Laboratory experiments have shown fairly conclusively that children exposed to a live or filmed model behaving aggressively (or helping or sharing) are apt to behave like the model shortly afterward (see review by Hoffman, 1977b). These studies suggest that when children observe a violent television program they are likely to have an immediate tendency toward aggressive behavior. The important social issue is whether television violence has long-term effects. A review of the relevant research follows.

Researchers employing sample surveys have reported positive correlations between children's viewing of violent television programs and such measures of aggression as the amount of conflict with parents, frequency of fighting, and delinquent behavior (see review by Roberts & Bachen, 1981). These correlations do not demonstrate a causal connection, however. They may, for example, reflect a tendency for aggressive children to prefer violent television, as indicated in findings by Atkin, Greenberg, Korzenny, and McDermott (1979), and by Fenigstein (1979). Or, a third variable may predict both aggressive behavior and the preference for violent television. Efforts have been made to overcome these limitations. In several studies in which the samples were large enough to control for a variety of third variables, the relationship between viewing violence and aggressive behavior remained, although considerably weakened. A more stringent, though possibly flawed (Rogosa, 1980), technique for establishing a causal connection from correlational data is the "time-lagged" design. This method was employed by Eron, Huesmann, Lefkowitz, and Walder (1972), and by Eron (1982), who found that children who preferred violent television were rated as more aggressive in their behavior ten years later.

Perhaps the most convincing way to test for long-term effects is to control the television viewing experience of children and observe their social behavior in a natural setting over an extended period of time. This is difficult, time-consuming, and expensive research. It demands the active cooperation of parents, schools, and other institutions. Control groups that are similar to the group watching the violent program are required, but must either watch a different program or participate in other activities. Children in a control group may resent being deprived of their usual television fare and their possible anger at this change must be accounted for in analyzing the data. Children must be observed before, during, and shortly after watching the film, as well as some time later. The observers must not know whether they are observing experimental or control subjects.

Few experiments of this type have been attempted. All of them lack at least one of the above requirements, and the results are inconclusive. Feshbach and Singer (1971), in two studies in which 625 boys from 9–15 years of age in seven residential schools and institutions watched either aggressive programs (e.g., "Gunsmoke") or non-aggressive programs (e.g., "The Dick Van Dyke Show"), found no evidence that the violent programs led to an increase in aggressive behavior. Indeed, *less* aggression was found among lower-class boys, who were highly aggressive to begin with, and among low-intelligence hyperactive boys, who had watched the violent television programs. The authors concluded that because of design imperfections, the most valid interpretation of the findings is that, for the population sampled, the viewing of televised aggression did not lead to an increase in real-life violence. In a partial replication that eliminated some design flaws, no significant differences in aggressive behavior were found between boys exposed to the aggressive and nonaggressive television diets (Wells, 1973). Parke, Berkowitz, Leyens, West, and Sebastian (1977) improved the design still further and used it in three studies of adolescent boys living in reformatories. Aggressive behavior was found to increase during and immediately following violent programs, but there were apparently no prolonged effects.

In another study (Friedrich & Stein, 1973), children in a summer nursery school watched three 20-minute episodes per week for four weeks of an aggressive ("Batman" or "Superman"), neutral, or prosocial ("Mister Rogers' Neighborhood") program. Measures of interpersonal aggression, which combined physical and verbal responses, were based on observations made for two weeks before, during, and following exposure to the television programs. Overall, there were no significant differences among the three television treatments, although when the sample was divided on the basis of initial aggression scores, there was a tendency for certain subgroups to become more aggressive if they watched the violent programs. Armor (1976), as reported by Kaplan & Singer (1976), reexamined the Friedrich and Stein data and found that the children exposed to the *prosocial* programs actually exhibited the greatest post-treatment rise in aggression. Armor concluded that these data provide no evidence that violent television content raises the level of violent behavior in children. Sawin (1973) also found no evidence for an aggression-increasing effect of viewing television violence.

In short, the data suggest some relationship between television viewing and aggressive behavior, but studies employing the most stringent methods have not been performed. As one moves from the highly controlled but artificial laboratory experiments to controlled interventions in natural settings, the findings become less clear. Both types of research clearly show that televised violence can have immediate aggression-enhancing effects. Correlational research indicates long-term effects but lacks the methodological rigor to support a causal inference. Studies in which television has been introduced into a community for the first time show children behaving more aggressively, but appropriate controls are lacking (Joy, Kimball, & Zabrack, 1977). The field intervention studies show that children's aggressive tendencies in natural settings may be elevated while watching television violence and for a short time afterward, but without further research the nature of long-term effects is not certain. It could well be that the subjects' life experiences between the interventions and the observations of their violent behavior will always make the proper determination of such effects difficult.[2]

A promising, yet different line of research by Collins (1979) has revealed

---

[2]See a review by Pearl, Bouthilet, & Lazar (1982) that concludes that this research does provide relatively clear support for the long-term negative effects of television violence.

children's inability to separate the central plot from peripheral details. His data suggest that children often cannot make the proper inferences about the motives underlying acts of aggression or the consequences of an act for the victim or the actor. What they comprehend and retain is the aggressive act itself. This fragmentary experiencing of the film by young children is amplified by commercials that interrupt the flow of events from act to consequence, but it can be reduced, and the child's comprehension increased, by the addition of suitable adult commentary (Collins, Sobol, & Westley, 1981).

Other studies have examined how a child's identification with benign television characters may form a basis for influence. Can this kind of programming encourage children's prosocial behavior such as cooperation, sharing, and giving comfort? In the study by Friedrich and Stein (1973) cited earlier, the findings did not show a consistent pattern. However, when special training was added (e.g., role-taking of themes in the programs), exposure to prosocial films did lead to an increase in helping behavior. The results of this and other studies (e.g., Coates, Russer, & Goodman, 1976) suggest that the prosocial behavior of young children can be increased through television when it is supplemented by certain training procedures. This is very promising, but as most television viewing will continue to occur outside of educational contexts, further research is required on the type of programs that can increase children's prosocial behavior without requiring supplementary techniques.

Sex-Role Socialization and Moral Internalization

About 50 years ago, Freud suggested that, owing to anatomical differences, girls are not compelled to resolve the Oedipus complex quickly and dramatically and therefore do not identify with parents as fully as boys. Consequently, females have less internalized moral structures than males. In Freud's (1925/1961) words,

> For women the level of what is ethically normal is different from what it is in men. Their superego is never so inexorable, so impersonal, so independent of its emotional origins . . . they have less sense of justice, less tendency to submit themselves to the great necessities of life and frequently permit themselves to be guided in their decisions by their affections or enmities (pp. 257–258).

Freud's followers differed in the details, but drew essentially the same conclusion: Females are more dependent on the moral views of others; males more often internalize moral principles and act autonomously in accord with them. Other developmental theories have ignored sex differences in moral internalization. An exception is Aronfreed's (1961) hypothesis that our society expects males to be self-reliant and to exercise control over their actions and environments, and expects females to be more responsive to directions from without;

consequently, the moral orientations of boys rely more on inner resources than do the moral orientations of girls.

The available evidence, contrary to these views, is that females are more morally internalized than males. In a national survey, 14- to 16-year-olds were asked why parents made rules and what would happen if there were none. Boys more often said parents made rules to keep children out of trouble (Douvan & Adelson, 1966), suggesting an external orientation in boys. In an experimental study in the Milgram tradition, females more often resisted instructions to violate a norm against harming others (Kilham & Mann, 1974), which suggests that this norm is more deeply internalized in females. This finding is particularly interesting because females more often conform to instructions in experiments that do not bear on moral issues (e.g., Wallach & Kogan, 1959). In a field experiment, females more often returned valuable items found in the street when no witnesses were present; when others were present, there were no sex differences (Gross, 1972). In an extensive study of hundreds of 10- to 14-year-olds in the Detroit area, females gave strong evidence of having more internalized moral orientations than males: They were more likely to feel guilty after violating a moral norm (as indicated in story completion responses), whereas males showed more fear of external punishment (Hoffman, 1975b). Females also revealed a more humanistic moral orientation, placing a greater value on going out of one's way to help others; males placed a higher value on achievement, but this appeared to reflect an instrumental rather than a moral orientation. And finally, females appear to be more empathic than males (Hoffman, 1977a). A similar pattern of sex differences in moral orientation has been reported by Gilligan (1977).

These sex differences in moral orientation may be due partly to childrearing differences, as parents of girls more often use inductive discipline and express affection (Zussman, 1978). But the same pattern of sex differences in moral orientation has also been found in parents, indicating the need for a broader explanation. One suggestion Hoffman (1975b) has offered is that because females traditionally have been socialized into the "expressive" role—to give and receive affection and to be responsive to other people's needs—they are well equipped to acquire humanistic moral concerns. Boys are socialized this way too, but as they approach adolescence they are increasingly instructed in the "instrumental" character traits and skills needed for achievement and occupational success, which may often conflict with humanistic moral concerns. Burton (1972), for example, found that under pressure for high achievement, parents may sometimes communicate that it is more important to succeed than to be honest.

These findings, if substantiated, are potentially important. Because our society still defines masculinity largely in terms of achievement and success, the indoctrination of adolescent boys into the male role may often conflict with the moral norms they may have internalized in childhood. And, because the indoctrination pressures may be powerful, they may often override the moral norms and dull the edges of males' sensitivity to the needs of others. The instrumental world may thus often operate as a corrupting influence on the morality of males. It is important to know if this analysis is correct and whether it will apply to women who are taking on the instrumental role in increasing numbers. If it does apply to women, will this have future implications for the moral socialization of children?

CONCLUDING REMARKS

In this chapter, I have critically reviewed the major moral development literature. Rather than present a detailed summary, I shall discuss the major points in the context of suggestions for future research.

1. It seems clear that the search for an invariant developmental sequence in the direction of a universal moral principle has not borne fruit. The problem may be methodological, but it may also be more fundamental: There is no consensus as to whether a universal moral principle exists, let alone what that principle may be. Investigators like Kohlberg are thus compelled to postulate their own moral principle, construct developmental stages through which individuals advance to attain it, and devise measuring instruments and collect data showing that people do in fact progress through these stages. When research fails to demonstrate invariant sequences, instruments are scrapped, new ones are devised, and the procedure is repeated in the hopes that this time the invariant sequences will be revealed. I suggest that it may be better to start out empirically, like Damon, and search for the actual steps in children's development of moral concepts in different moral domains. The question of whether or not moral structures cut across domains and develop in an invariant order may be left for the future.

2. The evidence that empathy and guilt feeling may provide a basis for moral motivation appears to be strong. Though an empathy- and guilt-based morality thus seems plausible, it may have several built-in limitations: If the empathy aroused is too intense, it may be transformed into an egoistic concern for one's own distress; a similar transformation may occur even with less intensity if the other's distress is communicated only through language; an empathy-based morality may be biased in favor of people similar to oneself or to those perceived as victims. There may also be limitations of scope. Nevertheless, a human response system that can transform another's physical or psychological pain into one's own distress deserves continued study and recognition for its importance in moral development.

My own stage theory of empathy, which highlights the interaction of affect and cognition, gains plausibility from its fit with several domains of research, although more research is needed before the theory can be evaluated. We need research on conditions that lead to empathic overarousal, for example, as well as basic research on the empathic process itself. I single out mimicry not only for its possible role in morality but also for its potentially broader contribution to social cognition. Do humans obtain information about others' internal states by unconsciously imitating their facial expressions and posture? How early in life do they begin to do this?

3. It is surprising, given the abundant evidence for guilt feeling as a reliable moral motive, that guilt has been neglected in developmental research. Perhaps guilt is viewed negatively in psychology because of its long association with pathology. In any case, there is evidence that a seemingly adaptive type of guilt can be fostered by parental disciplinary techniques that point up the consequences of the child's actions for others. Further work is needed on the socialization practices that contribute to adaptive and maladaptive guilt. As for cognitive prerequisites, it seems reasonable to hypothesize that to feel guilty one must be aware of having choice and control over one's own actions and be able to make causal inferences relating one's actions to changes in another's state or condition. Yet Zahn-Waxler et al. (1979) have found evidence for a rudimentary guilt feeling in 15-month-old infants, who presumably lack most of these cognitive abilities, a finding I have tried to explain (Hoffman, 1982).

4. The limitations of empathy-based moral systems stem primarily from their motivational properties. Cognitive moral theories escape these criticisms because they postulate no moral motive. But without a motive these theories cannot answer certain questions: What prompts people to subordinate their own interests in the service of helping others, keeping promises, or telling the truth; and what makes them feel bad when they harm someone? Cognitive moral theories deal with principles such as justice and fairness; lacking a motive base, these theories have difficulty explaining how the principles become activated in situations in which one's egoistic motives are also involved and why people may not only advocate, but also act in accordance with, the principles even when those principles are in opposition to their own interests.

5. It follows that a comprehensive moral development theory requires both a motive and a principle component. The motive component is necessary to assure the activation of the principles and thus the enactment of moral behavior even when one's own self-interest is involved. The principle component, although perhaps inevitably lacking universality, may help clarify the objectives of moral behavior, reduce personal bias, and in general transcend many of the limitations inherent in empathy. One step toward a comprehensive theory, implicit in much of the preceding, is to recognize that moral encounters vary in complexity. Perhaps the simplest is the situation of the innocent bystander, in which the basic elements of moral conflict are immediately present—an empathy-based motive to help someone and an egoistic motive to continue what one was doing and avoid the cost of helping. The situation becomes more complex when, in addition to an empathic motive to help, one also feels an *obligation* to do so, the source of which may lie beyond the immediate situation (e.g., activation of the

general principle of reciprocity, or social responsibility). Still more complex are situations involving mutual rights and expectations. Moral principles should become more essential as situations become more complex.

6. A further step toward a comprehensive theory may be to search for developmental connections between empathic distress and the moral principles stressed in our society, such as consideration for others, justice, fairness, and reciprocity. Because empathic distress is a response to another's internal state or condition, it seems reasonable to expect that empathic distress will often evolve naturally into a motive to consider others. Although an empathic child may consider others without a sense of moral obligation, this may change in adolescence when one's self-concept begins to include one's perception of how one relates to others (Damon, in press). Considering others may then acquire an obligatory quality; that is, it may become a principle by which one more or less consciously guides one's actions and evaluates oneself.

There may also be a developmental link, albeit a less direct one, between empathy and the principles of justice, fairness, equity, and reciprocity. This may be obvious when there is a clear victim, perhaps someone treated unfairly. But even without a clear victim, an empathic observer may construct one. For example, statements of the equity principle that people deserve what they earn often have an empathic ring. Consider this response by a 13-year-old male subject to the question, Why is it wrong to steal from a store? "Because the people who own the store work hard for their money and they deserve to be able to spend it for their family. It's not fair; they sacrifice a lot and they make plans and then they lose it all because somebody who didn't work for it goes in and takes it." Responses like these suggest that empathy may provide a motive base for being receptive to principles of equity and fairness, and for guiding one's actions in accordance with them.

7. I mentioned the self only briefly, but one's moral principles sometimes are an integral part of one's self-concept, and people may be powerfully motivated to act in accordance with those moral principles that are tied to the self. If one's actions depart from these principles, they could produce feelings of shame or guilt. A morality that is closely tied to one's self-concept may not have the limitations of empathic morality. Such a morality may therefore be necessary for making extreme sacrifices for others and taking stands against agencies of established moral authority. If so, a comprehensive moral theory requires greater research attention to the relation between moral development and the development of the self.

In conclusion, I suggest three broad directions for future research: The search for developmental links between simple empathy-based moral motives and complex cognitive processes involved in choosing moral principles, building moral ideologies, and establishing moral priorities; the search for other motives that may provide a more direct and certain link than does empathy to the principles and ideologies involving justice, fairness, and reciprocity; and the search for processes in the development of a motivational self-system and its possible link to moral concepts.

REFERENCES

Alston, W. P. Comments on Kohlberg's "From Is to Ought". In T. Mischel (Ed.), *Cognitive development and epistemology.* New York: Academic Press, 1971.

Ambron, S. R., & Irwin, D. M. Role-taking and moral judgment in five- and seven-year olds. *Developmental Psychology,* 1975, *11,* 102.

Armor, D. J. *Measuring the effects of television on aggressive behavior.* Santa Monica: The Rand Corporation, 1976.

Aronfreed, J. The nature, variety, and social patterning of moral responses to transgression. *Journal of Abnormal and Social Psychology,* 1961, *63,* 223–240.

Aronfreed, J., & Paskal, V. Altruism, empathy, and the conditioning of positive affect. Unpublished manuscript, University of Pennsylvania, 1965.

Aronfreed, J., & Reber, A. Internalized behavioral suppression and the timing of social punishment. *Journal of Personality and Social Psychology,* 1965, *1,* 3–16.

Atkin, C., Greenberg, B., Korzenny, F., & McDermott, S. Selective exposure to televised violence. *Journal of Broadcasting,* 1979, *23,* 5–13.

Baier, K. Moral development. *Monist,* 1974, *58,* 601–615.

Bandura, A. *Social learning theory.* Englewood Cliffs, N.J.: Prentice-Hall, 1977.

Bandura, A., & MacDonald, F. J. Influence of social reinforcement and the behavior of models in shaping children's moral judgments. *Journal of Abnormal and Social Psychology,* 1963, *67,* 274–281.

Baumhart, R. C. How ethical are businessmen? *Harvard Business Review,* 1961, *39,* 6–19.

Beaman, A. L., Klentz, B., Diener, E., & Svanum, S. Self-awareness and transgression in children: Two field studies. *Journal of Personality and Social Psychology,* 1979, *37,* 1835–1846.

Bell, R. Q. A reinterpretation of the direction of effects in studies of socialization. *Psychological Review,* 1968, *75,* 81–95.

Berndt, T. Developmental changes in conformity to peers and parents. *Developmental Psychology,* 1979, *15,* 608–616.

Blos, P. The split parental image in adolescent social relations. *Psychoanalytic Study of the Child,* 1976, *31,* 7–33.

Brandt, R. B. Emotive theory of ethics. In P. Edwards (Ed.), *The encyclopedia of philosophy.* New York: Crowell, 1967.

Brown, A. L. The development of memory: Knowing, knowing about knowing, and knowing how to know. In H. W. Reese (Ed.), *Advances in child development and behavior,* Vol. 10. New York: Academic Press, 1975.

Burton, R. V. *Cheating related to maternal pressures for achievement.* Unpublished manuscript, Psychology Department, University of Buffalo, 1972.

Chapman, M. Listening to reason: Children's attentiveness and parental discipline. *Merrill-Palmer Quarterly of Behavior and Development,* 1979, *25,* 251–263.

Coates, B., Russer, H. E., & Goodman, I. The influence of "Sesame Street" and "Mister Rogers' Neighborhood" on children's social behavior in the preschool. *Child Development,* 1976, *47,* 139–144.

Colby, A., Gibbs, J., Kohlberg, L., Speicher-Dubin, B., & Candee, D. Standard Form Scoring Manual, Center for Moral Education, Harvard University, 1980.

Coleman, J. S. *The adolescent society.* New York: Free Press of Glencoe, 1961.

Collins, W. A. Effect of temporal separation between motivation, aggression, and consequences. *Developmental Psychology*, 1973, *8*, 215–221.

Collins, W. A. Children's comprehension of television content. In E. Wartella (Ed.), *Children communicating: Media and development of thought, speech, understanding*. Beverly Hills: Sage, 1979.

Collins, W. A., Sobol, B. L., & Westley, S. Effects of adult commentary on children's comprehension and inferences about a televised aggressive portrayal. *Child Development*, 1981, *52*, 158–163.

Conger, J. J., & Miller, W. C. *Personality, social class, and delinquency*. New York: Wiley, 1966.

Craik, F. I. M. Depth of processing in recall and recognition. In S. Dornic (Ed.), *Attention and performance*, Vol. 6. Hillsdale, N.J.: Lawrence Erlbaum Associates, 1977.

Damon, W. Early conceptions of positive justice as related to the development of logical operations. *Child Development*, 1975, *46*, 301–312.

Damon, W. *The social world of the child*. San Francisco: Jossey-Bass, 1977.

Damon, W. Self-understanding and moral development from childhood to adolescence. In J. Gewirtz & W. Kurtines (Eds.), *Morality, moral development, and moral behavior: Basic issues in theory and research*. New York: Wiley, in press.

Darley, J. M., & Latane, B. Bystander intervention in emergencies: Diffusion of responsibility. *Journal of Personality and Social Psychology*, 1968, *8*, 377–383.

Dienstbier, R. A. Attribution, socialization, and moral decision making. In J. H. Harvey, W. Ickes, & R. F. Kidd (Eds.), *New directions in attribution research* (Vol. 2). Hillsdale, N.J.: Lawrence Erlbaum Associates, 1978.

Douvan, E., & Adelson, J. *The adolescent experience*. New York: Wiley, 1966.

Duvall, S., Duvall, V. H., & Nealy, R. Self-focus, felt response, and helping behavior. *Journal of Personality and Social Psychology*, 1979, *37*, 1769–1778.

Duvall, S., & Wicklund, R. A. *A theory of objective self-awareness*. New York: Academic Press, 1972.

Erikson, E. H. Reflections on the dissent of contemporary youth. *International Journal of Psychoanalysis*, 1970, *51*, 11–22.

Eron, L. O. Parent–child interaction, television violence, and aggression of children. *American Psychologist*, 1982, *37*, 197–211.

Eron, L. O., Huesmann, L. R., Lefkowitz, M. M., & Walder, L. O. Does television violence cause aggression? *American Psychologist*, 1972, *27*, 253–263.

Fenigstein, A. Does aggression cause a preference for viewing media violence? *Journal of Personality and Social Psychology*, 1979, *37*, 2307–2317.

Feshbach, S., & Singer, R. D. *Television and aggression*. San Francisco: Jossey-Bass, 1971.

Festinger, L., & Freedman, J. L. Dissonance reduction and moral values. In P. Worchel & D. Byrne (Eds.), *Personality change*. New York: Wiley, 1964.

Fishkin, J., Keniston, K., & MacKinnon, C. Moral reasoning and political ideology. *Journal of Personality and Social Psychology*, 1973, *27*, 109–119.

Fodor, E. M. Delinquency and susceptibility to social influence among adolescents as a function of moral development. *Journal of Social Psychology*, 1972, *86*, 257–250.

Freud, S. Thoughts for the time on war and death, In *Collected Papers*. London: The Hogarth Press, 1924.

Freud, S. Some psychical consequences of the anatomical distinction between the sexes. In J. Strachey (Ed. and trans.), *Standard edition of the complete psychological works of Sigmund Freud* (Vol. 19). London: The Hogarth Press, 1961. (Originally published, 1925).

Freud, S. *Civilization and its discontents*. London: The Hogarth Press, 1955. (Originally published 1930).

Friedrich, L. K., & Stein, A. H. Aggressive and prosocial television programs and natural behavior of preschool children. *Monographs of the Society for Research in Child Development*, 1973, *38* (4, Serial, No. 151).

Gaertner, S. L., & Dovidio, J. F. The subtlety of white racism, arousal, and helping behavior. *Journal of Personality and Social Psychology,* 1977, *35,* 291–707.

Geer, J. H., & Jarmecky, L. The effect of being responsible for reducing another's pain on subject's response and arousal. *Journal of Personality and Social Psychology,* 1973, *26,* 232–237.

Gilligan, C. In a different voice: Women's conceptions of the self and of morality. *Harvard Educational Review,* 1977, *47,* 481–517.

Golding, W. G. *Lord of the flies.* New York: Coward-McCann, 1962.

Gross, A. E. *Sex and helping; Intrinsic glow and extrinsic show.* Paper presented at the meetings of the American Psychological Association, Honolulu, September, 1972.

Grusec, J. E., & Kuczynski, L. Directions of effect in socialization: A comparison of the parent's vs. the child's behavior as determinants of disciplinary techniques. *Developmental Psychology,* 1980, *16,* 1–9.

Haan, N. Hypothetical and actual moral reasoning in a situation of civil disobedience. *Journal of Personality and Social Psychology,* 1975, *32,* 255–270.

Haan, N., Smith, M. B., & Block, J. Moral reasoning of young adults: Political-social behavior, family background, and personality correlates. *Journal of Personality and Social Psychology,* 1968, *10,* 183–201.

Hoffman, M. L. Moral development. In P. H. Mussen (Ed.), *Carmichael's handbook of child psychology,* Vol. 2. New York: Wiley, 1970. (a)

Hoffman, M. L. Conscience, personality and socialization techniques. *Human Development,* 1970, *13,* 90–126. (b)

Hoffman, M. L. Identification and conscience development. *Child Development,* 1971, *42,* 1071–1082.

Hoffman, M. L. Developmental synthesis of affect and cognition and its implications for altruistic motivation. *Developmental Psychology,* 1975, *11,* 607–622. (a)

Hoffman, M. L. Sex differences in moral internalization. *Journal of Personality and Social Psychology,* 1975, *32,* 720–729. (b)

Hoffman, M. L. Moral internalization, parental power, and the nature of parent–child interaction. *Developmental Psychology,* 1975, *11* (2), 228–239. (c)

Hoffman, M. L. Altruistic behavior and the parent–child relationship. *Journal of Personality and Social Psychology,* 1975, *31* (5), 937–943. (d)

Hoffman, M. L. Sex differences in empathy and related behaviors. *Psychological Bulletin,* 1977, *84,* 712–722. (a)

Hoffman, M. L. Moral internalization: Current theory and research. In L. Berkowitz (Ed.), *Advances in experimental social psychology,* Volume 10. New York: Academic Press, 1977. (b)

Hoffman, M. L. Empathy, its development and prosocial implications. In C. B. Keasey (Ed.), *Nebraska symposium on motivation,* Volume 25. Lincoln: University of Nebraska Press, 1978.

Hoffman, M. L. Identification and imitation in children. *ERIC Reports, ED 175 537,* March 1979.

Hoffman, M. L. Adolescent morality in developmental perspective. In J. Adelson (Ed.), *Handbook of adolescent psychology.* New York: Wiley Interscience, 1980.

Hoffman, M. L. Is altruism part of human nature? *Journal of Personality and Social Psychology,* 1981, *40,* 121–137.

Hoffman, M. L. Development of prosocial motivation: Empathy and guilt. In N. Eisenberg-Berg (Ed.), *Development of prosocial behavior.* New York: Academic Press. 1982.

Hoffman, M. L. Affective and cognitive processes in moral internalization. In E. T. Higgins, D. Ruble, & W. Hartup (Eds.), *Social cognition and social development: A sociocultural perspective.* New York: Cambridge University Press, 1983.

Hoffman, M. L. Interaction of affect and cognition in empathy. In C. Izard, J. Kagan, & R. Zajonc (Eds.), *Emotion, cognition, and behavior.* Cambridge: Cambridge University Press, in press.

Hudgins, W., & Prentice, N. Moral judgment in delinquent and nondelinquent adolescents and their mothers. *Journal of Abnormal Psychology,* 1973, *82,* 145–152.

Hume, D. *An inquiry concerning the principle of morals*, Vol. 4. New York: Liberal Arts Press, 1957. (Originally published in 1751.)

Humphrey, G. The conditioned reflex and the elementary social reaction. *Journal of Abnormal and Social Psychology*, 1922, *17*, 113–119.

Imamoglu, E. O. Children's awareness and usage of intention cues. *Child Development*, 1975, *46*, 39–45.

Jones, E. E., & Nisbett, R. E. The action and the observer: Divergent perceptions of the causes of behavior. In E. E. Jones et al. (Eds.), *Attribution: perceiving the causes of behavior*. Morristown, N.J.: General Learning Press, 1971.

Joy, L. A., Kimball, M., & Zabrack, M. L. *Television exposure and children's aggressive behavior*. Presented at Canadian Psychological Association, Vancouver, 1977.

Kahneman, D. *Attention and effort*. Englewood Cliffs, N.J.: Prentice-Hall, 1973.

Kameya, L. I. The effect of empathy level and role-taking training upon prosocial behavior. Unpublished doctoral dissertation, University of Michigan, 1976.

Kandel, D. Adolescent marijuana use: Role of parents and peers. *Science*, 1971, *5*, 216–220.

Kaplan, R. N., & Singer, R. D. Television violence and viewer aggression: A re-examination of the evidence. *Journal of Social Issues*, 1976, *32*, 35–70.

Keller, B. B., & Bell, R. Q. Child effects on adult's method of eliciting altruistic behavior. *Child Development*, 1979, *50*, 1004–1009.

Kilham, W., & Mann, L. Level of destructive obedience as a function of transmitter and executant roles in the Milgram Obedience Paradigm. *Journal of Personality and Social Psychology*, 1974, *29*, 696–702.

Kohlberg, L. The cognitive-developmental approach. In D. A. Goslin (Ed.), *Handbook of socialization theory and research*. Chicago: Rand McNally, 1969.

Kohlberg, L. *Symposium on moral development*. Society for Research in Child Development, Denver, Colorado, 1975.

Kohlberg, L., & Kramer, R. Continuities and discontinuities in childhood and adult moral development. *Human Development*, 1969, *12*, 93–120.

Kuczynski, L. Reasoning, prohibitions, and motivations for compliance. *Developmental Psychology*, 1983, *19*, 126–134.

Kurdeck, L. A. Perspective-taking as the cognitive basis of children's moral development: A review of the literature. *Merrill-Palmer Quarterly*, 1978, *24*, 3–28.

Kurtines, W., & Greif, E. B. The development of moral thought: Review and evaluation of Kohlberg's approach. *Psychological Bulletin*, 1974, *81*, 453–470.

Langer, J. Disequilibrium as a source of development. In P. H. Mussen, J. Langer, & M. Covington (Eds.), *Trends and issues in developmental psychology*. New York: Holt, Rinehart & Winston, 1969.

Lederer, W. Dragons, delinquents, and destiny. *Psychological Issues*, 1964, *4*.

Lepper, M. Social-control processes and the internalization of social values: an attributional perspective. In E. T. Higgins, D. Ruble, & W. Hartup (Eds.), *Social cognition and social development: A socio-cultural perspective*. New York: Cambridge University Press, 1983.

Lerner, M. J., & Simmons, C. Observer's reaction to the innocent victim: Compassion or rejection? *Journal of Personality and Social Psychology*, 1966, *4*, 203–210.

Lipps, T. Das Wissen von fremden Ichen. *Psychologische Untersuchungen*, 1906, 694–722.

Lytton, H. Disciplinary encounters between young boys and their mothers and fathers: Is there a contingency system? *Development Psychology*, 1979, *15*, 256–268.

Milgram, S. Behavioral study of obedience. *Journal of Personality and Social Psychology*, 1963, *67*, 371–378.

Minton, C., Kagan, J., & Levine, J. Maternal control and obedience in the two-year-old. *Child Development*, 1971, *42*, 1873–1894.

Mowrer, O. H. *Learning theory and behavior*. New York: Wiley, 1960.

Mueller, J. H. Anxiety and encoding processing in memory. *Personality and Social Psychology Bulletin*, 1979, *5*, 288–294.

Murphy, L. B. *Social behavior and child personality*. New York: Columbia University Press, 1937.

Otten, A. L. Politics and people. *Wall Street Journal*, April 11, 1974.

Parke, R. D., Berkowitz, L., Leyens, J. P., West, S. G., & Sebastian, R. J. Some effects of violent and nonviolent movies on behavior and juvenile delinquents. In L. Berkowitz (Ed.), *Advances in experimental social psychology*, Vol. 10, 1977.

Patterson, G. R., Littman, R. A., & Bricker, W. Assertive behavior in young children: A step toward a theory of aggression. *Monographs of the Society for Research in Child Development*, 1967, 35, 5.

Pearl, D., Boutheilet, L., & Lazar, J. *Television and behavior: Ten years of scientific progress and implications for the 1980's*. U.S. Department of Health and Human Services. Public Health Service, 1982.

Peters, R. S. Moral development: A plea for pluralism. In T. Mischel (Ed.), *Cognitive development and epistemology*. New York: Academic Press, 1971. 237–267.

Piaget, J. *The moral judgment of the child*. New York: Harcourt, 1932.

Rawls, J. *A theory of justice*. Cambridge, Mass.: Harvard University Press, 1971.

Rest, J. R. Morality. In J. Flavell & E. Markman (Eds.), *Cognitive development*, in P. Mussen (General Editor), *Carmichael's manual of child psychology*, (4th Ed.). New York: Wiley, 1983.

Rest, J., Davidson, M. L., & Robbins, S. Age trends in judging moral issues: A review of cross-sectional and longitudinal studies of the Defining Issues Test. *Child Development*, 1978, *49*, 263–279.

Roberts, D. F., & Bachen, C. M. Mass communications effects. *Annual Review of Psychology*, 1981, *32*, 307–356.

Rogosa, D. A critique of cross-lagged correlation. *Psychological Bulletin*, 1980, *88*, 245–258.

Ross, M., & DiTecco, D. An attributional analysis of moral judgments. *Journal of Social Issues*, 1975, *31*, 91–110.

Saltzstein, H. D., Diamond, R. M., & Belenky, M. Moral judgment level and conformity behavior. *Developmental Psychology*, 1972, *7*, 327–336.

Savin-Williams, R. C. Dominance hierarchies in groups of early adolescents. *Child Development*, 1979, *50*, 923–935.

Sawin, D. B. *Aggressive behavior among children in small playgroup settings with violent television*. Doctoral dissertation, University of Minnesota, 1973.

Sawin, D. B., & Parke, R. D. Empathy and fear as mediators of resistance-to-deviation in children. *Merrill-Palmer Quarterly*, 1980, *26*, 123–134.

Schachter, S., & Singer, J. E. Cognitive, social, and physiological determinants of emotional state. *Psychological Review*, 1962, *69*, 379–399.

Schoggen, P. Environmental forces in the everyday lives of children. In R. G. Barker (Ed.), *The stream of behavior: Explorations of its structure and content*. New York: Appleton-Century-Crofts, 1963.

Schwartz, S. H., Feldman, K. A., Brown, M. E., & Heingartner, A. Some personality correlates of conduct in two situations of moral conflict. *Journal of Personality*, 1969, *37*, 41–57.

Selman, R. The relation of role taking to the development of moral judgments in children. *Child Development*, 1971, *42*, 79–91.

Settlage, C. F. Cultural values and the superego in late adolescence. *Psychonalytic Study of the Child*, 1972, *27*, 57–73.

Sherif, M., Harvey, O. J., White, B. J., Hood, W. R., & Sherif, C. *Intergroup conflict and cooperation: The robbers cave experiment*. Norman, OK: University Book Exchange, 1961.

Simmel, G. The number of members as determining the sociological form of the group. *American Journal of Sociology*, 1902, *8*, 1–46.

Simpson, E. L. Moral development research: A case study of scientific culture bias. *Human Development*, 1974, *17*, 81–106.

Smith, A. The theory of moral sentiments. In A. Selby-Bigge (Ed.), *British moralists*. New York: Dover, 1965. (originally published 1759).

Stein, N. A., & Glenn, C. An analysis of story comprehension. In R. O. Freedle (Ed.), *New directions in discourse processing*. Norwood, N.J.: Ablex, 1979.

Sternlieb, J. L., & Youniss, J. Moral judgments one year after intentional or consequence modeling. *Journal of Personality and Social Psychology*, 1975, *31*, 895–897.

Stotland, E. Exploratory investigations of empathy. In L. Berkowitz (Ed.), *Advances in experimental social psychology* (Vol. 4), New York: Academic Press, 1969.

Stotland, E. Exploratory investigations of empathy. In L. Berkowitz (Ed.), *Advances in experimental social psychology* (Vol. 4). New York: Academic Press, 1969.

Stotland, E., Mathews, K. E., Sherman, S. E., Hansson, R., & Richardson, B. Z. *Empathy, fantasy and helping*. Beverly Hills, CA: Sage, 1979.

Thomas, M. H., Horton, R. W., Lippincott, E. C., & Drabman, R. S. Desensitization to portrayals of real-life aggression as a function of exposure to televised violence. *Journal of Personality and Social Psychology*, 1977, *35*, 450–458.

Thompson, R., & Hoffman, M. L. Empathy and the arousal of guilt in children. *Developmental Psychology*, 1980, *15*, 155–156.

Tulving, E. Episodic and semantic memory. In E. Tulving & W. Donaldson (Eds.), *Organization of memory*. New York: Academic Press, 1972.

Turiel, E. An experimental test of the sequentiality of developmental stages in the child's moral judgments. *Journal of Personality and Social Psychology*, 1966, *3*, 611–618.

Turiel, E. *The development of social knowledge: Morality and convention*. New York: Cambridge University Press, 1983.

Wallach, M., & Kogan, N. Sex differences and judgment processes. *Journal of Personality*, 1959, *27*, 555–564.

Wells, W. D. Television and aggression: Replication of an experimental field study. Unpublished manuscript, Graduate School of Business, University of Chicago, 1973.

Wright, H. F. *Recording and analyzing child behavior*. New York: Harper & Row. 1967.

Youniss, J. E. Parents and peers in social development: A Sullivan–Piaget perspective. Chicago: University of Chicago Press, 1980.

Zahn-Waxler, C., Radke-Yarrow, M., & King, R. M. Childrearing and children's prosocial initiations toward victims of distress. *Child Development*, 1979, *50*, 319–330.

Zussman, J. U. Relationship of demographic factors to parental discipline techniques. *Developmental Psychology*, 1978, *14*, 685–686.

8 Sex-Role Development

Diane N. Ruble
New York University

INTRODUCTION

The study of sex-role acquisition has been of central concern to developmental psychologists for many years. Sex roles influence choices, values, and behaviors throughout the life span. As Mussen (1969) suggests, "No other social role directs more of an individual's overt behavior, emotional reactions, cognitive functioning, covert attitudes, and general psychological and social adjustment" (p. 707). Furthermore, sex-role demands have been implicated in physical health and life expectancy differences, favoring women, and mental health problems, especially depression, favoring men (Frieze, Parsons, Johnson, Ruble, & Zellman, 1978; Pleck, 1981). Sex-role development has also been a primary focus of debate among the major theories of social-personality development and is a frequent target of the nature–nurture controversy (Lamb & Urburg, 1978). In recent years, sex-role development has taken on a political flavor because of its implications for the Equal Rights Amendment, Women's Liberation Movement, and other issues of gender equality.

As with most aspects of development, the study of sex-role development has seen a number of shifts in methodological approaches and conceptual emphases. Unlike most areas, however, there has been a shift in the value placed on the final outcome of this developmental process. Until quite recently, the literature contained an implicit assumption that adopting sex-typed standards and behaviors was good—and necessary for psychological adjustment. Thus, understanding the antecedents of sex typing was viewed as providing information necessary for the optimal socialization of appropriately sex-typed individuals. In contrast, current research appears to be guided by an implicit assumption that sex-role

325

tions may be bad—placing limits on individual growth and flexibility (Bem, 1983; Lamb & Urburg, 1978; Pleck, 1981). Thus, understanding the antecedents of sex-typing can be alternatively viewed as providing information necessary for raising children with egalitarian beliefs and behaviors.

Along with shifts in approaches and emphases in the literature there came a proliferation of terms associated with the study of sex-role development. Although most of the terms appear quite similar on the surface, many of their distinctions have become important conceptually. Thus, it is necessary to provide a brief guide to terminology. (Huston, 1983, and Rosen and Rekers, 1980, provide a more detailed discussion of sex-role taxonomies and definitions.)

One very basic distinction is between the terms "sex" and "gender." These terms are commonly used as synonyms, and many dictionaries define them as such. Because the term "sex" has multiple meanings, there has been a trend toward using "gender" to refer to the various dimensions of maleness and femaleness (Rosen & Rekers, 1980). Because both terms have become associated with certain concepts and sets of literatures, however, we will use them interchangeably. Their intended meanings, then, will be linked to the terms they precede—e.g., stereotypes, identity, role, etc. The most common of these distinctions is that between gender "role" and gender "identity" or "orientation" (e.g., Kagan, 1964; Money & Ehrhardt, 1972). Although there is debate about the exact nature of the distinction (Rosen & Rekers, 1980), "role" usually refers to cultural expectation of the behaviors, characteristics, and social status of males versus females. It is the "public" face of gender. In contrast, "identity" or "orientation" usually refers to the individual's perception of his or her own consistency within these cultural expectations. Thus, it has a more "private" connotation. Other terms and distinctions will be defined as they become relevant to the discussion.

We begin our consideration of sex-role development with a discussion of the different ways males and females have been perceived, beginning with ancient history. These beliefs about the dimensions of masculinity and femininity indicate the social standards or conventions to which individuals must conform if they desire to be perceived as appropriately sex typed. Thus, in addition to discussing general cultural beliefs we will examine individual self-perceptions—how well they conform to sex-role norms, and the implications of perceiving oneself as relatively masculine and/or feminine.

In the next section, we examine whether men and women are, in reality, as different in *personality* as they are believed to be. There are a number of methodological and interpretational problems in the literature on sex differences in personality and, as a result, there is controversy about how prevalent and extensive these differences are. There is little debate, however, about the differences in male and female *roles*—differences that have implications for status and value. Thus, both of the first two sections are concerned with the "end-points" of sex-role development—what people believe about sex differences and how the two sexes behave after experiencing various developmental influences.

The remainder of the chapter examines what these influences are and how powerful they appear to be. Three types of developmental influences will be considered: (a) biological, (b) external socialization pressures, and (c) cognitive developmental structures and self-generated motivation. First, we consider how one might distinguish the biological bases of sex typing from cultural influences. We then discuss various possible biological mechanisms, using two types of sex-typed behavior as exemplars. The first concerns how hormones may influence sex differences in social behaviors, with reference to both animal and human studies. The second concerns how genetics, brain organization, and hormonal changes at puberty can influence sex differences in intellectual functioning.

Next, we consider the question of the sociocultural bases of sex typing with a discussion of the distinction between the two major theories of sex-role development. Evidence that is relevant to *social learning theory* is considered. We ask whether or not boys and girls are treated differently by socializing agents. Are children encouraged by the culture to engage in sex-appropriate activities? Is aggression or physical activity reinforced in boys, and dependence reinforced in girls? We also ask whether boys and girls may become sex typed through observational learning, and we consider what children might learn from models when, for example, they watch television.

Finally, evidence that is relevant to the *cognitive developmental bases* of sex typing is discussed. Two general questions are considered. The first concerns when one's knowledge about sex roles develops. When does basic gender labeling of oneself and others, as well as the recognition of sex stereotypes, occur? The second question concerns the ways in which this knowledge can structure children's sex-role choices and behavior. Do changes in children's concepts about gender affect what information they attend to, imitate, and remember? This evidence is pertinent to possible variations across the life span in flexibility versus rigidity, in adherence to sex roles, and in the possibility of change.

DIMENSIONS OF BEING MALE OR FEMALE

Historical Perspective

What are the "true" natures of the sexes? Interest in this question dates back to ancient time. According to Aristotle (Book IX of *The History of Animals*, Chapter 1; cited in Miles, 1935, p. 700), for example, women are "more compassionate . . . more envious, more querulous, more slanderous, and more contentious . . ."; while men are "more disposed to give assistance in danger" and "more courageous." Recent reviews of these historical beliefs and myths have identified several central themes or images (Bullough, 1973; Gould, 1976; Hunter, 1976; Hyde & Rosenberg, 1976; Tavris & Offir, 1977; Whitbeck, 1976; Williams, 1983); but, interestingly, they have tended to focus on the nature of women rather than of men. This one-sided view may have evolved because most records were kept by men (Bullough, 1973), and a male perspective is likely to focus on how women are different.

Although there are many different labels and connotations attached to images of women, depending on the writer and the period of history being examined, the themes can be categorized into two extreme views. These range from the positive pole, in which women are regarded as love goddesses and wholesome mother figures, to the extreme negative view of women as inferior and evil (Bullough, 1973; D. N. Ruble & Ruble, 1982). Tavris and Offir (1977) have labeled these extremes "the pedestal–gutter syndrome" (p. 3).

The "gutter" pole is represented by several images, with the belief in womens' inferiority as its core. Woman is viewed as a partial man, deficient in both sexual capacity and quality of mind (Whitbeck, 1976). With Eve as her representative, she is both an afterthought (an inferior being) and an evil seductress (Hunter, 1976; Tavris & Offir, 1977). The story of Samson and Delilah illustrates the common theme that being seduced by a woman drains a man of his strength (Williams, 1983). The contrasting view of woman portrays her as worthy of worship. She has been viewed as the fertility goddess, the mother of all, and as virtue incarnate (Bullough, 1973; Gould, 1976; Hyde & Rosenberg, 1976; Williams, 1977). The tradition of chivalry, which places women on a pedestal, epitomizes this image (Hunter, 1976; Yorburg, 1974). There is a negative side, however, about the side of woman's nature that is worshiped. Placing woman on a pedestal confined her to an essentially passive, powerless, and so subordinate, role (Bullough, 1973; Hunter, 1976; Williams, 1977).

Of course, beliefs about the sexes have varied considerably throughout time, just as they continue to vary across cultures (see Tavris & Offir, 1977). Nevertheless, throughout history women and men have been perceived as different in fundamental and important ways, and these differences have often been viewed as "natural," intrinsically linked to the roles of the sexes in society (Shields, 1975).

Empirical research on sex differences and sex roles has been conducted for decades (see Miles, 1935), and interest in these topics has continued to grow. In the late 1960s, after the rise of the Women's Liberation Movement, much of this research raised questions about the inferior nature of women and why women's roles and achievements are typically of lower status. More recently, questions about men, masculinity, and the restrictions associated with male roles have also appeared in the literature (Brannon, 1976; Lamb, 1976; Pleck, 1981; Pleck & Brannon, 1978). In spite of this new level of awareness, however, strong beliefs about the differences between males and females remain. Before discussing these differences and how they develop, we examine what these common beliefs are.

Dimensions of Masculinity and Femininity

Two types of questions have characterized the research on masculinity and femininity. The first concerns beliefs about people in general. What are the typical male and female like, and how do they differ? The second concerns self-perceptions. How masculine or feminine is a particular man or woman? In some respects, these two types of questions are very different. The first deals with *stereotypes*—beliefs about the personal attributes of men and women and the likelihood that an unknown male or female will possess a given trait. The second deals with sex-role *orientation*—the extent to which men and women perceive themselves to possess the characteristics associated with maleness or femaleness. These two issues are clearly related. Individuals may perceive themselves as possessing a certain set of attributes because of cultural sex stereotypes; and, reciprocally, cultural stereotypes may reflect the conglomerate reality of individual sex-role orientations. Moreover, there is a common set of problems in conceptualizing and measuring masculinity and feminity, both as stereotypes or as personal orientations.

Sex Stereotypes.   Numerous modern studies have identified characteristics that can be considered stereotypes of men and women (e.g., Bem, 1974; Broverman, Vogel, Broverman, Clarkson, & Rosenkrantz, 1972; Heilbrun, 1976; McKee & Sherriffs, 1957; Rosenkrantz, Vogel, Bee, Broverman, & Broverman, 1968; Spence, Helmreich, & Stapp, 1974, 1975). Despite the considerable conceptual and methodological inconsistencies that characterize this literature, there is some degree of consensus concerning the types of characteristics associated with one sex versus the other (D. N. Ruble & Ruble, 1982).

Rather than compiling an extensive list of the characteristics that have been identified as stereotypic, we briefly describe a few studies to illustrate both typical methods and conclusions. In one study, the investigators developed a questionnaire to assess stereotypes by starting with a list of 122 bipolar items (e.g., from Not at all Aggressive to Very Aggressive) and asked 74 college men and 80 college women to rate the extent to which each item was characteristic for an adult male and an adult female (Rosenkrantz et al., 1968). An item was considered "stereotypic" if at least 75% of the students rated one pole as more typical of one sex than it was of the other. Thus, the definition of stereotypic was based on an arbitrary criterion.

The results of several studies based on the 1968 questionnaire were summarized a few years later (Broverman et al., 1972). It was concluded that there is a strong consensus about the differing characteristics of men and women across widely divergent groups within this culture. The positively valued masculine traits formed a cluster of behaviors reflecting competence, rationality, and assertion; the positively valued feminine traits formed a cluster reflecting warmth and expressiveness, which is consistent with historical images of maternal love and virtue.

Spence, Helmreich, and Stapp (1974, 1975) refined the 1968 questionnaire to produce a new instrument, called the Personal Attributes Questionnaire (PAQ). In a procedure similar to that used by Rosenkrantz et al. (1968), 248 college men and 282 college women rated the *typical* adult male and female on 138 bipolar items (the original 122 items plus 16 new items). Another group rated the *ideal* male and female. Items this time were identified as "stereotypic" on the basis of statistically significant differences in the ratings. The ratings of the ideal male and female were used to determine whether the "masculine" pole (e.g., Aggressive) was valued more or less than the "feminine" pole (e.g., Not at all Aggressive). Based on this analysis, three types of characteristics were identified, as shown in Table 8.1. Male-valued items are those for which the ratings for *both* ideal males and ideal females were higher on the masculine side of the scale. Female-valued items are those for which the ratings for *both* ideal males and ideal females were higher on the feminine side of the scale. Finally, sex-specific items are those for which ratings for the ideal male were higher on the masculine side and ratings for the ideal female were higher on the feminine side. Inspection of Table 8.1 indicates that the positively valued male and female traits identified in this study are consistent with the conclusions of Broverman et al. (1972), despite the different criteria used to identify these traits.

Finally, the results of a recent study (T. L. Ruble, 1983) suggest that there has been little change in the stereotypes since the original study by Rosenkrantz et al. in 1968. The only item that did not show a significant difference for males versus females was "Intellectual." Thus, stereotypes of men and women, as measured by the PAQ, have apparently remained relatively stable from the 1960s to the 1980s, at least among college students, despite the increased concern with equality between the sexes.

Sex-Role Orientation.   The study of self-perceptions along sex-typed dimensions has been a central and long-standing issue in sex-role development research. In early research, masculinity and femininity were viewed as representing a bipolar continuum on a single scale, and it was assumed that a person could be either masculine or feminine, but not both. Implicit in this approach was the positive value placed on a high degree of sex typing; thus, a major question was how to promote healthy males and females by helping them acquire appropriately sex-typed attitudes, interests, and traits (e.g., Biller, 1971; Brown, 1957; Kagan, 1964).

Recently, the bipolar assumption has been criticized on the grounds that individuals can possess characteristics that are *both* masculine and feminine (Bem, 1974; Constantinople, 1973; Heilbrun, 1976; Spence & Helmreich, 1978). Bem has applied the term "Androgynous" to people who possess both masculine and feminine characteristics. Spence and Helmreich prefer the term "Dualistic" to refer to the idea that masculinity and femininity are independent dimensions of personality that can both develop in the same individual. In contrast to early work on sex-role development, these new formulations assume that an individual may possess qualities associated with masculinity (e.g., assertive) as well as qualities associated with femininity (e.g. sensitive to the needs of others) and still function effectively.

TABLE 8.1
Personal Attributes Questionnaire Items Classified as to Male-
Valued, Female-Valued, and Sex-Specific

Male-valued		
Independent	Adventurous	Self-confident
Not easily influenced	Outspoken	Feels superior
Good at sports	Interested in sex	Takes a stand
Not excitable, minor crisis	Makes decisions easily	Ambitious
Active	Not give up easily	Stands up under pressure
Competitive	Outgoing	Forward
Skilled in business	Acts as leader	Not timid
Knows ways of world	Intellectual	

Female-valued		
Emotional	Strong conscience	Creative
Not hide emotions	Gentle	Understanding
Considerate	Helpful to others	Warm to others
Grateful	Kind	Likes children
Devotes self to others	Aware, other feelings	Enjoys art and music
Tactful	Neat	Expresses tender feelings

Sex-specific	
Male	*Female*
Aggressive	Cries easily
Dominant	Excitable, major crisis
Likes Math and Science	Feelings hurt
Loud	Home-oriented
Mechanical aptitude	Needs approval
Sees self running show	Needs for security
	Religious

Source: Spence, Helmreich, and Stapp (1975), Table 1, p. 31.

Several self-report instruments have been developed to study the effects of individual differences in sex-role orientations. Individuals indicate the extent to which they personally exhibit each of a series of characteristics. (See, for example, the traits used in the Spence and Helmreich [1978] Personal Attributes Questionnaire (PAQ) presented in Table 8.1.) Individuals can then be grouped into different categories, according to their self-ratings. Bem (1977) and Spence, Helmreich, and Stapp (1975), for example, used four categories: feminine (high feminine–low masculine); masculine (low feminine–high masculine); androgynous (both high); and undifferentiated (both low).

The underlying question of the research based on these new formulations of sex-role identity is whether androgynous individuals are more behaviorally adaptive and psychologically healthy than individuals who are rigidly sex typed. Although there have been some inconsistencies across studies, the answer to this question has often been affirmative. Several studies have reported, for example, that androgynous individuals score higher on measures of self-esteem than sex-typed or undifferentiated subjects (Bem, 1975, 1977; Bem & Lenney, 1976; Orlofsky & Windle, 1978; Spence, Helmreich, & Stapp, 1975). Other research has suggested that sex-typed individuals may be more stressed in social interaction with the opposite sex than are androgynous individuals (Ickes & Barnes, 1978).

There is, however, one noteworthy limitation to the conclusion that androgyny represents a preferred orientation. Several studies have reported weak or no differences between androgynous- and masculine-typed individuals. Most studies of self-esteem, for example, have found that both androgynous and masculine groups were higher than feminine-typed and/or undifferentiated groups (e.g., Bem, 1977; Heilbrun, 1976). Furthermore, some research has suggested that flexibility and adjustment are more strongly associated with masculinity than with androgyny (Jones, Chernovetz, & Hansson, 1978). These findings have led some to question the meaning of positive correlations between an androgynous orientation and socially valued behaviors. Kelly and Worell (1977), for example, suggest that it may be primarily the masculine aspects of an androgynous orientation (e.g., instrumentality) that lead to social reinforcements in our society, a conclusion that is also supported by a more recent review (Taylor & Hall, 1982).

Additional Dimensions of Masculinity and Femininity

The view of masculinity and femininity as separate and relatively independent dimensions represents an important conceptual distinction. But this dualistic model may itself constitute a limited reflection of reality, because neither masculinity nor femininity is likely to be unidimensional. Thus, in measuring either stereotypes or self-perceptions, a single summary score of masculinity or femininity that ignores variations in the subtraits may be inappropriate (Brannon, 1978; Constantinople, 1973). Assume, for example, that the stereotype "masculinity" is composed of two relatively independent factors: achievement and assertiveness. Further, assume that we have two instruments that attempt to measure "masculinity." One instrument has 10 items related to achievement and 5 items related to assertiveness. The other instrument has 5 achievement items and 10 assertiveness items. If overall scores are obtained by simply summing items, we essentially have an achievement-dominated instrument versus an assertiveness-dominated instrument. It is obviously misleading to assume that equal scores on the two instruments represent equivalent measures of "masculinity." Recent research, therefore, has incorporated a multidimensional view of the traits associated with men and women and has attempted to identify the "core concepts" of masculinity and femininity (e.g., Ashmore & Del Boca, 1979; Brannon, 1976; Cicone & Ruble, 1978; Deaux & Lewis, 1983; Pleck, 1981).

Summary

Beliefs about the differences between men and women have existed throughout history and remain strong today. Empirical research on these beliefs takes two forms. The first concerns sex *stereotypes*—what people think the typical man and woman are like. The second concerns sex-role *orientation*—what people themselves think they are like. One major conceptual and methodological issue in measuring these beliefs is whether sex-typed traits represent a bipolar continuum on a single scale, or whether individuals can possess characteristics that are both masculine and feminine. Recent research has adopted the latter assumption, viewing people as having the capacity to be androgynous or dualistic. It is further assumed that an androgynous orientation is healthier than a sex-typed orientation, but empirical research has provided mixed support for this hypothesis. Current research is moving beyond the dualistic conceptions of masculinity and femininity to consider the multiple dimensions that comprise these constructs.

SEX DIFFERENCES: DO BELIEFS REFLECT REALITY?

Summarizing the Results

Are commonly held beliefs about the characteristics of males and females supported by data about how people actually behave? Is it true that the average man is relatively aggressive, independent, and good at mathematical tasks; while the average woman is relatively passive, dependent, and good at verbal tasks? There are no simple answers to these questions. These characteristics are difficult to define and to observe, and there are many inconsistencies in the conclusions that have been drawn by different studies.

The most comprehensive review of the sex-differences literature appears in a book published in 1974 by Eleanor Maccoby and Carol Jacklin. They compiled over 2000 studies, published mainly after 1966, that examined sex differences in personality or intellectual abilities. They then tabulated the number of studies reporting statistically significant sex differences and compared them to the number of studies in that domain that did not find statistically significant differences. On the basis of these "box score" tabulations, Maccoby and Jacklin suggested that empirical data supported the existence of sex differences in only four areas: aggressive behavior, and mathematical, spatial, and verbal skills. According to Maccoby and Jacklin (1974): (a) boys are more physically aggressive at all ages (through college age) and across cultures; (b) beginning around puberty, boys' mathematical skills increase faster than girls; (c) males tend to perform better on tasks involving spatial skills than do girls, with the difference beginning during the adolescent years; and (d) from middle elementary school through high school, girls tend to perform better than boys on tasks involving verbal skills. In other domains in which sex differences might be expected, Maccoby and Jacklin felt either that the question was still open (e.g., activity level, compliance, nurturance) or that the evidence did *not* support sex differences (sociability, analytic skills).

The Maccoby and Jacklin conclusions have generated a fair amount of controversy (e.g., Block, 1976a, 1976b). This controversy centers primarily around the "box score" approach that Maccoby and Jacklin used and the possibility that this approach may have led to erroneous conclusions. Two main problems have been noted. First, some studies are stronger methodologically than others. Giving each study equal weight, therefore, may be misleading, particularly if methodological weakness leads to a particular type of finding, such as no sex difference. Indeed, failure to find a "true" difference is more likely for studies that lack statistical power because of small sample sizes. Thus, there may be validity to the suggestion that Maccoby and Jacklin under-represented the number of true sex differences. On the other hand, studies finding sex differences are more likely to be published than those that do not. Thus, there are biases in both directions affecting the Maccoby and Jacklin conclusions.

A second problem with the box score approach is deciding how to categorize the studies. To illustrate, social sensitivity may be defined in several ways including role taking, nurturance, or empathy. If males and females differ consistently in only one of these behaviors, such as empathy, then an analysis of a category that includes all of the above indices of social sensitivity may be misleading. That is, the category may be too broad, and a large number of "no difference" results for role taking could obscure actual sex differences in empathy (M. L. Hoffman, 1977).

A few recent reviews of sex differences have been able to avoid some of the problems associated with a box score approach by using a technique called meta-analysis. Briefly, meta-analysis is a way to aggregate the results of multiple independent studies that are relevant to a single hypothesis. Statistical procedures can be applied to the combined data sets in order to assess, for example, overall effect sizes (Cohen, 1977). In general, these meta-analysis reviews conclude that differences between the sexes are very small or are restricted to studies using particular methods, even for presumably well-established differences, such as verbal and quantitative skills (Eagly & Carli, 1981; Eisenberg & Lennon, 1983; Hyde, 1981).

Interpreting the Results

An additional problem to answering the question, "Do beliefs reflect reality?" concerns the interpretation of the results of sex-differences studies. What, for example, does it mean to report finding that women conform more than men? Does it reflect a long-term characteristic of men and women, built-in and stable, or does it reflect a short-term behaviorial response to the experimental situation? What the lay public and most researchers want to know, presumably, concerns the former interpretation. Yet there are many features of a study that may elicit differential reactions of males and females, which are irrelevant to the focus of the study, but nevertheless contaminate its findings. The experimenter's sex, familiarity with the situation, or interest in the topic of the experiment are all aspects of the methods of a study that can interact with the sex of the subject and influence the results (Eagly & Carli, 1981; Karabenick, 1983; Pedersen, Shinedling, & Johnson, 1968; Sistrunk & McDavid, 1971). Thus, in some cases, apparent sex differences in personality or abilities may represent little more than demands of the situation.

Situational determinants of sex differences are particularly problematic for interpreting a research finding because they can be quite subtle. Subjects can present themselves as behaving more or less consistently with prevailing sex stereotypes on the basis of seemingly incidental aspects of the situation, such as the relative number of males and females in the room (D. N. Ruble & Higgins, 1976) or the attractiveness of the subject's partner in the study (Zanna & Pack, 1975). Insofar as studies sample situations eliciting stereotypic rather than non-stereotypic responding, the research literature may have over-represented the extent to which stable sex differences exist. If, for example, a woman is dependent in some situations and independent in others, the research literature is biased if studies are more likely to examine those situations that elicit only the woman's dependent behavior.

Although it is difficult to examine directly how prevalent this bias might be, there are several reasons to believe it is a problem. First, hypotheses tend to be formulated in terms of prior beliefs, such as stereotypes. In designing a study, the experimenter may be predisposed to select a situation or set of measures that are likely to elicit stereotyped responding, not because of overt bias but because the hypothesis makes these kinds of situations more accessible in memory. In this context, it is interesting to note that studies of conformity conducted by women are less likely to find sex differences than those conducted by men (Eagly & Carli, 1981). Second, in strange situations, such as experiments, people tend to present themselves relatively conservatively and behave more consistently with cultural beliefs than they do in familiar situations. Certainly the knowledge of a cultural belief system can influence subjects' self-reports of their own characteristics, particularly if they believe this is what the experimenter is looking for. It is not surprising, therefore, that sex differences are more likely to be found when self-report measures are used rather than studies of actual behavior (e.g., Eisenberg & Lennon, 1983). Moreover, many types of sex differences are positively related to the subjects' level of development (Frieze et al., 1978). As one's knowledge of gender-related cultural beliefs increases with age, these developmental trends also support the present assertion that sex differences reflect, in part, situational demands or expectations. Not only is there a lack of empirical support for most differences believed to exist between the sexes, but the differences that are found may represent something other than the dispositional qualities of males and females.

Implications for the Study of Sex-Role Development

If sex differences are not as prevalent or strong as commonly believed, what, then, is the study of sex-role development concerned with? Why has there been so much theoretical and empirical attention devoted to the development of sex-typing and gender-related socialization processes? One answer is that although the basic temperamental characteristics of the two sexes may be relatively similar, their roles in society are not. As adults, men and women have very different functions and responsibilities in the home and in the work place (Eccles & Hoffman, in press; Frieze et al., 1978; T. L. Ruble, Cohen, & Ruble, 1984). Although over half of all women are now in the labor force, they continue to work in the lowest paying industries. Women account for almost all nurses and secretaries while men represent almost all engineers, carpenters, and mechanics. Overall, women earn only about 60% of what men earn, and major wage differentials remain even when comparisons are made within occupational types, such as farm laborers or food service workers (Norwood, 1982; Rytina, 1982). Not only do men and women have different roles, they also appear to have different intrinsic worth, at least as measured by financial compensation.

Precursors of these role differences begin quite early; young boys and girls exhibit distinctive tastes in toys, books, sports, and other kinds of recreational activities. By adolescence, distinctive roles are evident as well in dating behavior and occupational choices. At all age levels, males and females differ in the more subtle aspects of their roles, such as dress and mannerisms. Sex-role differentiation, then, is pervasive, and the study of developmental processes can help us understand why. This kind of knowledge is important for reasons other than the satisfaction of basic scientific curiosity. On the one hand, gender differentiation may be viewed as a normal, natural outcome of development; indeed, much early research was oriented toward the value of promoting "normal" masculine and feminine identification and roles (e.g., Kagan, 1964). A related concern is the understanding of those processes that lead to atypical sex-role development, such as transsexualism, and the decisions of when (or if) to try clinical interventions that must be made in such cases (Green, 1975; Zucker, 1982). On the other hand, sex-role differentiation may be viewed as an undesirable outcome because it limits the options available to individual men and women. Social penalties are imposed on males who want to stay home and care for their children, as well as on females who do not. Discriminatory processes operate on women who seek positions of power and prestige, as well as on men who seek to pursue traditionally female occupations, such as nursing. Thus, an understanding of developmental processes is also relevant to promoting gender equality and reducing the limiting aspects of sex roles.

Summary

In spite of the large number of studies examining sex differences, the results remain inconclusive. On the basis of sheer numbers of positive results alone, reasonably strong support exists for only four differences: aggression, spatial skills, mathematical skills, and verbal abilities (Maccoby & Jacklin, 1974). These conclusions may be challenged, however, in two very different ways. First, they may *under*-represent the number of sex differences due to inadequacies in the box score approach. Second, they may *over*-represent the differences because the subjects and/or observers are affected by sex stereotypic beliefs. In spite of these problems of interpretation, it is clear that the available evidence does *not* justify existing stereotypes. The research has failed to show that the characteristics of males and females are as different as we believe them to be. Yet, men and women do play very different social roles, and these differences begin early, as reflected in boys' and girls' different interests and activities. The study of sex-role development is concerned with the antecedents of these sex-differentiated roles and values.

SEX-ROLE DEVELOPMENT: BIOLOGICAL FACTORS

For some people, the reasons for a sex-typed division of labor are no mystery. Asking why men do not stay home to raise children is like asking why humans do not flap their arms and fly. Men and women are ordained, by their biological predispositions and limitations, to fulfill certain roles. Women care for children because they have a maternal instinct and men do not; men are the providers and the protectors because they have greater strength and because women must be left free to care for children. Although this extreme form of Freud's "Anatomy is Destiny" argument is no longer accepted as legitimate, questions about the influence of biological factors on sex-role development remain. One question concerns which aspects of sex-role development are influenced by biological factors. A second question concerns the mechanisms by which biology exerts its influence.

The Search for Biological Influences

The fact that biology is involved in sexual dimorphism is indisputable. The presence of a Y chromosome leads the undifferentiated gonad in the embryo to become testes. The absence of the Y chromosome turns the gonad into an ovary. Genetic factors are also involved in the greater vulnerability of males to problems during pregnancy and birth (Maccoby, 1980). Hormones have a direct effect on prenatal anatomical and brain differentiation (McEwen, 1981; Money & Ehrhardt, 1972); and during puberty, hormones lead to further physical differentiation of the sexes, such as breast development or beard growth. But do these obvious biological differences carry over to psychological development and role differentiation? This is not an easy question to answer. How is it possible to determine whether or not biological factors are involved in these processes? Which kinds of data provide the best clues?

Sex Differences in Infants.   One possible approach is to study sex differences in infants. The basic logic of this approach is that socialization has relatively little effect on behavior during the first weeks and months after birth and so any observed differences must reflect biological influences. One problem with this approach is that it is difficult to identify those behaviors of babies that might be precursors of later sex-role differences. Which infant behaviors reflect dominance or nurturance? A second problem is that socialization can begin at birth, at the moment babies are wrapped in either pink or blue blankets. Thus, any differences that are found are difficult to attribute exclusively to biological influences.

Few consistent differences between infant girls and boys have been found, however. Males appear to be somewhat physically stronger (Maccoby, 1980). Some early studies suggested that boys may be relatively more active and irritable and girls relatively more attached to parents, but subsequent research has yielded inconsistent results (cf. Frieze et al., 1978; Maccoby & Jacklin, 1974). Thus, studies of infant sex differences provide little insight into possible biological bases of sex roles.

Cross-Cultural Universals.   A second possible approach is cross-cultural analysis. According to the logic of this approach, sex differences that are relatively consistent across cultures are thought to imply some biological basis. There are, in fact, several behaviors that show a relatively high degree of cross-cultural consistency. In virtually all cultures, women are the primary caretakers and men are the protectors during war. Furthermore, there is evidence of some consistency in related characteristics—interest in infants, dominance, and aggression (Frieze et al., 1978; Maccoby, 1980; Rohner, 1976).

Although those findings are suggestive of biological influences, their implications must be considered with caution. Cross-cultural universals can be explained by similarities in sex-role socialization across cultures (Barry, Bacon & Child, 1957). Also, there are ample indications of cultural diversity even within the relatively consistent behaviors. Perhaps the best known example is Margaret Mead's study of three primitive tribes in New Guinea (Mead, 1935). Among the Arapesh, both men and women acted as we expect women to act—gentle and nurturant. Among the Mundugamore, both men and women acted as we expect men to act—aggressive, with little indication of parental orientation. Among the Tchambuli, stereotypic roles were reversed. There is also cultural diversity in the magnitude of sex differences, even when the direction of the difference is consistent across cultures. Sex-typed division of labor, for example, is affected by variations in economic and familial structure across cultures (Rosaldo, 1974). Finally, cultural variation in some sex-related behaviors may be so extreme that the magnitude of sex differences pales by comparison. In one study, levels of aggression in several cultures were rated on a 12-point scale. Males were found to be more aggressive in 10 out of 14 cultures but the differences were slight (one or two points along the scale). The most and least aggressive cultures, however, differed by 8 points along the scale. This kind of cultural diversity leads us to question how much importance should be attached to biological influences in the development of sex-role behaviors. Cultural range appears much greater than sex differences within any given culture. Nevertheless, cultural universals in the direction of sex differences in, for example, aggression and parenting, are suggestive of biological influences operating directly or in combination with socialization.

Examining Biological Mechanisms.   A third approach to the study of the biological bases of sex roles involves a more direct examination of possible biological mechanisms. The issue is whether or not variations in certain biological factors are associated with variations in sex-role behaviors. This question has been addressed in two ways. First, the hypothesized biological mechanisms (e.g., hormone levels) can be manipulated in an experiment. This approach has the advantage of being able to infer that behavior variations (e.g., level of aggression) were *caused* by the manipulation. It has the disadvantage, though, that studies of this kind are obviously restricted to animals. Because the effects of any given manipulations may vary greatly from species to species, it is difficult to know to what extent the results of animal studies are applicable to humans. Second, naturally occurring variations in hypothesized biological mechanisms, such as the time of maturation or hormone levels, can be related to behaviors. Although this kind of analysis can be applied to humans, it has the problem of inferring causality that is intrinsic to a correlational study.

In order to illustrate these approaches to studying biological mechanisms, we describe how they apply in two frequently researched questions about the biological bases of sex differences. The first concerns the influence of hormones, particularly during perinatal periods. The second concerns the biological bases of intellectual functioning, such as mathematical or spatial abilities. This review is not intended to be exhaustive; there are many other sex-role behaviors that may have a biological basis. Rather, it is intended to illustrate possible approaches and necessary cautions.

Biological Mechanisms: (1) Social Behavior

Animal Studies.   A remarkable change occurs in the behavior of a normal adult female rodent several times a month. She displays a variety of sexual enticement behaviors, such as small hopping movements or wiggling her ears, and she is responsive to the sexual advances of a nearby male. As he mounts her, she raises her rump and her head, assuming the "lordosis" posture. If, however, the same male were to make sexual advances toward her a day later, the same female would either run away or face the male in an aggressive posture and, if necessary, kick or bite in order to repel the advance (Kimble, 1973; McEwen, 1976).

How can we account for these extraordinary changes in behavior in such a short period of time? Fulfilling the sexual sequence depends on the hormonal state of the animal. For the female, there are cyclic variations in the levels of two hormones, estrogen and progesterone, which circulate in the bloodstream. Only when she is in a state of estrus, a peak in hormone levels that occurs every fourth or fifth day, will she be sexually receptive. If these hormonal surges are stopped by removing her ovaries, sexual receptivity ceases, though it can be restored by hormone injections. The male's mounting behavior is governed by the hormone testosterone, a type of androgen that, in contrast to the female, does not show major variations. If the level of testosterone is reduced by means of castration, however, the frequency of mounting is correspondingly reduced.

These data provide clear evidence of hormonal effects on social behavior. The experimental manipulation of hormone levels has a direct effect on the sexual behavior of rodents. To further understand the mechanisms involved in hormone–behavior relationships, an additional question must be addressed. What would happen if our two normal adult male and female rodents were injected with hormones characteristic of the other sex? If the male was injected with estrogen and progesterone, would he assume the lordosis posture? Perhaps surprisingly, the answer is no. Adult rodents show little or no behavioral response to injections of the "wrong" hormones.

Hormones have two types of effects on behavior. One is an "excitatory" or "activation" influence, in which the presence of a hormone triggers a particular behavior. This is the kind of influence we have just described; estrogen and progesterone activate the adult female's lordosis response. The other effect is an "organizational" influence that occurs during development. Sexual differentiation is dependent on whether or not gonadal hormones (estrogen or testosterone) are present during a sensitive period early in development.

Numerous experiments in which hormone levels have been manipulated experimentally during this sensitive period have shown that low levels of gonadal hormones lead to the development of female characteristics, whereas high levels lead to the development of male characteristics (Hines, 1982). A genetic female rat injected with testosterone within a week after birth, for example, develops masculinized genitalia; as an adult, her sexual behavior is responsive to the excitatory influence of testosterone but not of estrogen and progesterone. That is, given testosterone, she will exhibit more mounting behavior than a normal adult female. When given estrogen and progesterone, she will exhibit fewer lordosis responses than a normal adult female. Thus, the hormones that are present around the time of birth have an organizational influence on the brain; through the development of neurons and the formation of synaptic contacts, it is irreversible (McEwen, 1976). Subsequently, the animal is sensitive only to particular hormones and is not sensitive to others, and the sexual behavior of the adult shows the clear and lasting influence of this developmental event.

The organizational influence of hormones has been linked in many nonhuman mammals to nonsexual behaviors as well (Eccles-Parsons, 1982; Hines, 1982; Lamb, 1975; Quadagno, Briscoe, & Quadagno, 1977). These include parenting behaviors, aggression, rough and tumble play, open-field exploration, and running patterns on an activity wheel. Increased aggression often results, for example, when animals exposed to testosterone during the sensitive period are injected with testosterone after puberty (e.g., McEwen, 1981). These data suggest that nonhuman mammals are predisposed to act in a masculine or a feminine manner depending on the hormonal environment present at early points during their development. The question of whether such findings are relevant to understanding sex-role differentiation in humans is considered next.

Human Studies. During normal human development, males are exposed to higher levels of testosterone prior to and shortly after birth than are females (Maccoby, 1980). Is this difference reflected in later behavior? This question cannot be answered easily. For obvious ethical reasons, it is not possible to manipulate experimentally the human hormonal environment. Thus, conclusive evidence about causal relationships between hormones and behavior cannot be gathered. There are, however, individuals who develop abnormal hormonal conditions for one reason or another. Genetic defects can change normal hormone secretions, and a fetus can be exposed to abnormal hormone levels when a pregnant woman receives hormone treatments for medical reasons. Several syndromes are possible, and these provide a kind of natural experiment for examining the effects of hormones on human behavior.

A number of different abnormal genetic/hormone combinations have been identified. One frequently studied syndrome occurs when the fetus, either male or female, is exposed to abnormally high levels of androgens. Another syndrome occurs when a genetic male is insensitive to androgen due to a genetic defect. The basic question underlying these studies is whether individuals exposed prenatally to a hormone environment that deviates from normal male or female levels exhibit concomitant masculine or feminine behavioral differences from normal controls. Do, for example, genetic females exposed prenatally to androgens exhibit more masculine behavior as young girls or women than their normally developing counterparts?

Many different aspects of femininity and masculinity have been examined. These can be grouped into three categories: (1) gender roles—e.g., personality, play behavior, interest in marriage and children; (2) sexual preference—heterosexual, homosexual, or bisexual; and (3) gender identity—degree of knowledge about, and satisfaction with, being a male or a female. Few, if any, clear-cut conclusions have emerged from this research, in part because of numerous null effects and inconsistencies across studies, and in part because of the inherent methodological and interpretational problems in this type of research.

Some very intriguing findings have emerged, however. The most consistent, and probably the best-known, result is that prenatal exposure to androgens is related to more masculine gender-role behavior in females (Baker, 1980; Eccles-Parsons, 1982; Hines, 1982). In two investigations, for example, girls exposed to androgen showed fewer wedding fantasies, less interest in infant care and dolls, increased incidences of tomboyism, and an elevated activity level, as compared either to control girls matched on demographic variables (Ehrhardt, Epstein, & Money, 1968) or to siblings (Ehrhardt & Baker, 1974). These findings suggest that prenatal hormones can predispose humans toward masculine or feminine behavior, as they do in animals. A closer look at the research, however, indicates that a firm conclusion is not yet possible. Most importantly, children exposed to abnormal prenatal hormones are typically born with physical abnormalities, such as ambiguous genitalia. It is therefore possible that a girl's "masculine" behavior reflects her own, the interviewers', or socializing agents' reactions to her masculine appearance (Eccles-Parsons, 1982; Quadagno et al., 1977). In fact, most studies of individuals exposed to abnormal prenatal hormones, but without physical abnormalities, report null effects (see Hines, 1982). Nevertheless, a few very recent studies have reported significant effects, such as higher aggression on paper and pencil measures, for affected individuals as compared to controls (Reinisch, 1981).

In short, the research on the effects of prenatal hormones in humans suggests that even when such effects are found, they tend to be small and within the range of normal behavior. Moreover, in most cases, gender identity and sexual orientation are consistent with sex of rearing, regardless of genetic sex (Baker, 1980; Money & Ehrhardt, 1972). The most striking example of this sex-of-rearing effect is a case study of monozygotic twin boys, one of whom the family decided to rear as a girl due to an accident during circumcision (Money & Ehrhardt, 1972). At 17 months of age, this child had surgery to create a vagina and was later administered steroids. Subsequent interviews with the parents suggested that this sex-reassignment and socialization effort was quite successful. In one interview, for example, the mother compared the daughter to the son as follows: "She likes for me to wipe her face. She doesn't like to be dirty, and yet my son is quite different. I can't wash his face for anything . . . She seems to be daintier. Maybe it's because I encourage it" (Money & Ehrhardt, 1972, p. 19). At age 12, the girl was reported as continuing to do well (Money & Tucker, 1975).

These data have been used to support conclusions that the effects of socialization practices are extremely powerful, in some cases even overriding genetic and biological influences (e.g., Frieze et al., 1978). This position, however, is not without controversy. With respect to the twin case study, for example, Diamond (1982) reports that a set of psychiatrists who first saw this girl at age 13 indicated that she had significant problems with sexual identity. He argues that this follow-up report supports his "strong belief in the force of an inherent male or female nervous system bias for the development of sexual identity and partner choice" (Diamond, 1982, p. 182). It should be noted, however, that the nature of the problems Diamond (1982) reported were masculine appearance, statements that being a boy is easier, a preference for a masculine occupation, and seeming unhappiness—all of which are not uncommon characteristics of early adolescent girls. Thus, exactly what conclusions should be drawn from this case study remain unresolved. It does indicate, however, some of the difficulties of identifying appropriate criteria for distinguishing between biological and socialization influences.

Recent data have stimulated another debate that is relevant to examining relative influences of socialization and biology. On the basis of various studies of individuals with abnormal prenatal hormones, Money and Ehrhardt (1972) have concluded that socialization is the primary determinant of identity and sexual orientation, as long as a clear and consistent gender assignment has been made by 3–4 years of age. They argue that after this "critical period" gender reassignment cannot be successfully accomplished. This conclusion has been called into question, however, by studies of male pseudohermaphrodites from interrelated families in the Dominican Republic (Imperato-McGinley et al., 1979). Because of a genetic disorder, these children were born with ambiguous external genitalia—even though they had normal male hormone levels—and they were reared as females. In contrast to the Money and Ehrhardt (1972) critical period hypothesis, these individuals took on male sexual orientations at puberty when physical virilization occurred. These data suggest that the effects of prenatal hormones may outweigh socialization in determining sexual orientation. Many questions about these findings have been raised, however (Baker, 1980; Rubin, Reinisch, & Haskett, 1981). Were the boys truly raised unambiguously as girls, for example, given their ambiguous appearance? Perhaps the culture provided an atmosphere of acceptance that made these transitions possible. Indeed, after a time, the culture developed three gender labels: *guevedoce* ("eggs at 12"), *guevote* ("penis at 12"), and *machihembra* ("first woman, then man"). This example, then, highlights our need to understand better the delicate and complex balance of biological and cultural influences on gender-role development.

Biological Mechanisms: (2) Intellectual Functioning

In 1980, an article was published in the prestigious *Science* magazine that re-ignited a major controversy. This article reported the results of a mathematical talent search conducted between 1972 and 1979. Seventh- to tenth-grade girls and boys were invited to take the SATs in mathematics, and the top 2–5% of those were invited to take courses at The Johns Hopkins University. The article focused on the observation that every year the test was given, more than twice as many boys as girls scored over 500. On the basis of these findings, the authors concluded: "We favor the hypothesis that sex differences in achievement in and attitude toward mathematics result from superior male mathematical ability, which may in turn be related to greater male ability in spatial tasks." In regard to causation, the authors stated that "male superiority is probably an expression of a combination of both endogenous and exogenous variables." In addition, they suggested that "environmental influences are more significant for achievement in mathematics than for mathematical aptitude" (Benbow & Stanley, 1980, p. 1264). This conclusion has been interpreted as an unusually strong statement about the biological bases of sex differences and has elicited a large number and wide range of responses from the scientific community (see Letters to *Science,* April 10, 1981) and from the popular press (e.g., *The New York Times,* Dec. 7, 1980, p. 102; *Newsweek,* Dec. 15, 1980). In this section, we consider the possible biological mechanisms that could contribute to sex differences in mathematics and other intellectual skills.

Genetic Biases.   Few contemporary researchers suggest that sex differences in intellectual skills are a direct result of genetic transmission. A few years ago, the possibility that spatial skills were influenced by a recessive gene on the X chromosome was considered (e.g., Lehrke, 1972). The basic argument was that the positive influence of this recessive gene was more likely to be expressed in males, because they do not have a second X chromosome (as do females) to offset the effects of this gene. (The principle is the same as for the transmission of color blindness.)

This hypothesis has been examined through intrafamilial correlations of performance. Because boys receive their mother's X chromosome, it was expected that higher correlations between sons and mothers would be found than between sons and fathers. Some early research has supported this prediction (see Wittig, 1976), but more recent research with larger samples has not (see Boles, 1980; Vandenberg & Kuse, 1979). Because of these inconsistent findings, as well as additional conceptual problems in interpreting the correlations reported, the X-linked hypothesis remains open (Thomas, 1983).

Brain Organization: Laterality of Function.   The two hemispheres of the brain show different specialization of function in adults; the left hemisphere is specialized for verbal skills, and the right for spatial abilities. One possible explanation for sex differences in intellectual skills is that the extent of the lateralization of function, or the time of its occurrence during development, may differ for girls and boys. Waber (1977), for example, has reported that late-maturing adolescents do better on tests of spatial skills than adolescents who mature earlier. Possible mechanisms underlying sex differences in spatial skills, therefore, may be related to the fact that boys mature later than girls (Waber, 1979). To illustrate: Boys' slower maturation may lead to greater lateralization and, in turn, to superior spatial skills. Although there is some support for Levy's (1972) hypothesis that males show greater lateralization of function than do females, definitive conclusions are not yet possible (Bryden, 1979). The issue of the differential timing of lateralization is even less clear-cut (see Eccles-Parsons, 1982, and Huston, in press). Thus, any conclusions drawn about the role of brain lateralization in sex differences in intellectual functioning would seem to be premature.

Hormonal Changes at Puberty.   The advent of puberty is marked by a number of dramatic biological changes. In terms of hormonal status, there are sharp increases in testosterone levels for boys, and in estrogen and progesterone levels for girls. If sex differences in intellectual functioning are related to hormone levels, these differences should presumably increase, or begin, during adolescence. Indeed, as noted earlier, male superiority in mathematical and spatial skills does not seem to appear until the later years of childhood or adolescence. One might predict, therefore, that higher levels of testosterone would be associated with greater skill at these kinds of tasks.

Some evidence supports this view. In one study, hormonal status, as it is inferred from measurements of body shape and genital development, was related to measures of spatial scores. As predicted, masculine body type for girls was associated with better spatial skills. For boys, however, the reverse relationship was found (Petersen, 1979). Thus, spatial abilities did not show a direct relationship to the inferred influence of testosterone, but were instead related to an androgynous body type. A more recent study, however, with a larger sample failed to find a significant relationship between an androgynous body type and intellectual performance, although the trends were in the predicted direction (Berenbaum & Resnick, 1982).

To date, no direct relationship between hormonal changes at puberty and intellectual functioning has been demonstrated. Attempts to examine the influence of hormones in terms of changes in intellectual or motor performance across phases of the menstrual cycle have also failed to demonstrate a relationship (cf., Ruble & Brooks-Gunn, 1979; Sommer, 1973). The suggestion that spatial skills may be related to an androgynous body type is quite intriguing. It is not clear, however, that these effects are necessarily related to hormone levels, as a number of social differences (e.g., self-perceptions, interpersonal relations) are also associated with variations in body type.

Summary

Men and women perform different roles in our society. One obvious question to ask about this observation is whether or not it is "natural." Are men and women biologically predisposed toward different roles, interests, and abilities? There is evidence that would support an affirmative response. Many differences are consistent across cultures, and experimental and correlational studies have identified possible biological mechanisms. On the other hand, none of the findings can be interpreted as conclusive evidence for a biological basis for sex-role behavior. There are problems with applying animal studies to humans and with demonstrating that a naturally occurring correlation between a biological factor and a sex difference is necessarily due to the biological factor rather than possible socialization alternatives. Thus, we can only describe biological processes that *might* influence sex differences in social behavior and intellectual functioning; more definitive conclusions must await future research.

SOCIAL BASES OF SEX TYPING

Cultural forces exert powerful control over our behavior. Culture dictates how long our skirts are, whether our pants are flared or straight, whether we wear makeup, or even whether we should intentionally scar our bodies. Additionally, how and where we deliver our babies, the significance of puberty, and the treatment of women during menstruation all vary dramatically from culture to culture. Regarding gender roles, biological factors can create certain predispositions and limitations, but most investigators agree that sociocultural factors act as the primary determinants of an individual's gender orientation and behavior. Controversy continues, however, over *how* the child learns these gender identity and roles and *when* in development this learning takes place.

The major current hypotheses about sex-role development are based on two theoretical orientations: social learning and cognitive development. These two approaches share a number of common features, but they also differ in two fundamental ways. First, they emphasize different sources of influence. Social learning theories emphasize those processes from the environment that act on the child. Children are viewed as being shaped by external forces toward male or female roles. It is assumed that this shaping takes place by the same learning processes involved in the acquisition of all behaviors—reinforcement and modeling. That is, boys and girls learn by being rewarded and punished for exhibiting different behaviors and by imitating the behavior of male and female models, such as their parents (Bandura, 1969; Mischel, 1970). In contrast, cognitive-developmental theory emphasizes internal rather than external forces. Children are viewed as being motivated to learn social rules because of a basic orientation toward mastering the environment. Sex-role learning, therefore, represents children's active construction of rules as they interact with their social world (Kohlberg, 1966; Kohlberg & Ullian, 1974).

A second distinction between these theories concerns the importance of the child's developmental level. Social learning theory views sex-role development as a process of cumulative experience. Age or developmental level is unimportant except as it relates to past reinforcement and modeling history. In contrast, developmental timing is a central feature of cognitive developmental theory. Children's constructions of gender rules are viewed as progressing in a series of stages, and the impact of gender-related information on children's stereotypes and behaviors depends on their level of gender understanding.

Although the two theories differ in their assumptions about the mechanisms and timing of sex-role development, they both emphasize the importance of the ready availability of gender information in our culture. Furthermore, research literature suggests that elements of both theories are necessary for a complete understanding of sex-role development. In this section, we focus on the literature most commonly associated with social learning theory, and in the next section we discuss cognitive developmental influences on sex typing.

Socializing Agents and Social Pressure

Basic to social learning theory is the concept of operant conditioning or reinforcement. Behaviors that are reinforced in some way increase, while those that are not reinforced decrease or extinguish. The effectiveness of operant conditioning has been shown across a wide range of behaviors. It is an extremely powerful shaping mechanism, and it can sometimes operate in ways that are subtle and not intuitively obvious. To illustrate: Consider the problem of a nursery school teacher desiring to reduce the amount of aggression in his classroom. He begins by punishing every aggressive act—sternly calling to the child by name, asking her to sit in a corner, etc. What the teacher discovers is that the level of aggression goes up, not down. The teacher was in effect reinforcing the child's aggression by attending to it. When the teacher attended to cooperation and ignored aggression, the amount of aggression in the classroom decreased (Brown & Elliott, 1965).

Reinforcement does affect behavior, but it is not always obvious what is reinforcing. This kind of problem has made it difficult to determine whether or not socializing agents are shaping boys' and girls' behavior through differential reinforcement. It is possible, for example, that boys and girls respond to different reinforcements. In this case, a parent who acts exactly the same way toward a son and daughter could, in fact, be providing differential reinforcement.

Conclusions about whether boys and girls receive differential treatment have been mixed. In 1974, Maccoby and Jacklin concluded that there was little evidence of direct shaping of masculine and feminine behavior. The research showed no evidence, for example, that boys are reinforced for aggression and girls are reinforced for dependency. Thus, it appeared that infant and toddler boys and girls were treated very similarly (Maccoby & Jacklin, 1974).

More recent reviews of the literature, however, suggest that these conclusions may be premature (e.g., Block, 1978; Huston, 1983). In particular, Maccoby and Jacklin (1974) may have underestimated the importance of subtle differences in treatment and neglected the role of the father. In addition, some studies not available at the time of the Maccoby and Jacklin review have employed clever techniques of observing or eliciting differential responses to boys and girls. We turn now to a consideration of the various ways that boys' and girls' sex roles are differentially shaped by the social environment. Our review emphasizes differential treatment by parents, although similar processes can operate for teachers, peers, and other socializing agents (see Eccles & Hoffman, in press, and Huston, 1983, for reviews).

Social Expectations.   From the moment a newborn is swaddled in a pink or blue blanket, different expectations about a girl versus a boy are evident. In one study, for example, within the first 24 hours of their baby's life, parents were asked to describe him or her as they would to a close friend. Even though the boys and girls were objectively very similar in terms of health, size, and weight, they were described very differently. Boys were believed to be better coordinated, more alert, stronger, and bigger than girls. Girls were believed to be smaller, softer, more finely featured, and less attentive than boys (Rubin, Provenzano, & Luria, 1974).

Whether or not these expectations are made explicit, there is now considerable evidence that people do respond differently to boys and girls on the basis of gender-related expectations. This phenomenon is shown most clearly in situations in which people's beliefs about the sex of a child is manipulated. In general, adults are more likely to offer a doll to a child they think is a girl and to offer stereotypically male toys, such as trucks, to a child they think is a boy (cf. Huston, 1983). Moreover, a few studies have shown that boys are encouraged in more physical or motor activities than are girls (Frisch, 1977; Smith & Lloyd, 1978). Those findings suggest that young boys and girls do receive differential treatment, in part because of adults' expectations of what boys and girls are like.

Parents' Treatment of Sons and Daughters.   It is possible that such expectation effects disappear when adults know a child well. Thus, it is important to ask directly whether parents treat their young sons and daughters differently. There is growing evidence of an affirmative answer to this question, and interestingly, fathers and mothers appear to be differentially affected by their child's gender. Referring back to the expectation studies, men tend to perceive infants in more stereotypic terms than do women (see Huston, 1983), and this difference extends to parents' perceptions of their own children (Rubin et al., 1974). Although parents tend to treat infants under a year old very similarly, fathers play with sons differently than mothers play with either sons or daughters (Huston, 1983; Lamb, 1977). Fathers are rougher and engage in more physical stimulation and gross motor play with their infant or toddler sons (Parke & Suomi, 1980). Fathers are also more likely to offer sex stereotypic toys to their infants, daughters as well as sons (Jacklin & Maccoby, 1983).

The differential shaping of boys and girls appears to be stronger during the toddler and preschool years. First, some research has shown that parents interact more with girls and leave boys alone more (e.g., Fagot, 1978). These differences may be important to developing a sense of personal control and independence, although the findings are not consistent (Huston, 1983). Second, several studies have suggested that boys receive more physical punishment than do girls (Jacklin & Maccoby, 1983; Maccoby & Jacklin, 1974). Third, there is evidence of differential reinforcement for sex-appropriate play. Parents provide different toys for their sons than for their daughters and encourage them to develop sex-typed interests (Cairns, 1979; Maccoby & Jacklin, 1974; Rheingold & Cook, 1975). In addition, one study reported that toddlers received more positive reactions when they engaged in sex-appropriate activities than when they engaged in activities appropriate for the other sex. A wide range of activities elicited differential response, including doll play, asking for help, manipulating objects, and climbing (Fagot, 1978). As with younger children, differential treatment is stronger for fathers than for mothers. Fathers are more likely to initiate rough-and-tumble play with boys than with girls (Jacklin & Maccoby, 1983).

Differences between fathers' and mothers' reactions to play are particularly well illustrated in a recent clever experimental study. The experimenter asked preschool children to play with a highly sex-typed set of toys—either dollhouse, kitchen play area, and women's dress-up outfits or an army game, highway tollbooth, and cowboy outfits. The children were instructed to play with the toys as boys would or as girls would, depending on which set they were given. The child's mother, father, or a same-sex playmate then entered the room and their responses to the child's sex-appropriate or inappropriate play were observed. Fathers were found to be much more negative (e.g., interference with play, signs of disgust) than were mothers or peers when their children, particularly their sons, were engaged in sex-inappropriate play. Mothers showed relatively little differential reaction, while peers exerted pressure on boys only (Langlois & Downs, 1980). Thus, there is clear evidence that young children are pressured to respond according to sex-role expectations. Boys receive more pressure than girls, and fathers exert more pressure than mothers.

A fourth area of the differential treatment of preschoolers concerns teaching behavior and achievement expectations. Parents have lower expectations for, and attach less importance to, the long-range accomplishments of daughters than of sons (L. W. Hoffman, 1977; Parsons, Ruble, Hodges, & Small, 1976). These differences are particularly pronounced in the area of mathematical achievement (Eccles-Parsons, 1983). Direct observations of interactions between parents and young children show differential behaviors that are consistent with these expectations. Parents demand more independent performance for boys and are more likely to help girls quickly. Not surprisingly, fathers tend to show more of these differences than do mothers, although mothers are more likely to help and correct the mistakes of daughters than sons (cf. Huston, 1983).

After the preschool years, boys and girls have very different experiences of freedom and restriction. Boys are allowed to investigate wider areas of the community and are expected to run errands at an earlier age (Saegert & Hart, 1976). They are also more likely to be left unsupervised after school, less likely to be picked up at school, and less likely to have restrictive rules on them about how far away from home they can go alone (cf. Huston, 1983). As Huston (1983) notes, this difference is not based on parents' lower evaluations of their daughters' competence or maturity. Rather, it appears to reflect fears of chance encounters with strange males, leading parents to chaperone and protect their daughters from possible danger. Regardless of the reason, the difference may be quite significant for the growth of personal feelings of effectance and free exploration and may lead girls toward greater conformity to cultural norms and values.

One subtle aspect of differential treatment is worth highlighting. Parents appear to respond differently to same-sex than to opposite-sex children. Parents seem to feel they play a special socialization role for same-sex children, and this sense seems to be particularly strong for fathers. Parents interact more with same-sex children, and they tend to be somewhat more restrictive and controlling with them (Lamb, 1977; Rothbart & Maccoby, 1966).

The specialness of the same-sex parent–child relationship, taken together with findings of differential play practices of mothers and fathers, suggests that children reared by a single parent may experience a very different kind of sex-role socialization from children raised by both parents. Given that fathers are particularly important in encouraging physical play and discouraging feminine play for boys, the absence of the father would be expected to result in less masculine behavior and orientation for boys. Indeed, the available literature is consistent with this prediction (see Huston, 1983). Of particular interest are the findings of a longitudinal study of preschool children of divorced parents (Hetherington, Cox, & Cox, 1979). Two years after the divorce, the boys, then 6 years of age, showed fewer masculine play preferences and behaviors than matched comparison boys from two-parent homes. Father absence shows less effect on the sex-role development of girls. These girls do, however, appear to show difficulties in social interactions with males beginning in adolescence (Hetherington, 1972). Interestingly, consistent with the apparent special role of the same-sex parent, a study of mother-absent divorced families suggested that girls' sex-role development and general adjustment is more affected in this situation than is that of boys (Santrock & Warshak, 1979).

In summary, parents provide socialization experiences that differ for boys and girls. Boys are encouraged to be physical and are allowed to be more independent, while girls are more likely to receive assistance rather than to be encouraged toward independent mastery. Both sexes receive support for engaging in sex-appropriate play. Some effects, however, vary with the sex of the parent. Fathers are more likely to encourage sex-appropriate activities in their children than are mothers, and both parents tend to be more attentive and controlling toward same-sex children. Such effects suggest that boys and girls may respond differentially to father versus mother absence, and studies of single-parent families yield results consistent with this pattern of findings.

Observational Learning

As with the acquisition of most complex behaviors, it seems unlikely that differential shaping and reinforcement are sufficient to account for the development of sex roles. Direct tuition of masculine and feminine "styles" of dress, play, communication, interests, and so on would seem to require substantially more time and effort than seem available to socializing agents. For this reason, much of the research on sex-role development has been concerned with how children learn masculine and feminine behavior by observing others. These "modeling" processes are central to both the social learning and cognitive developmental approaches.

Certainly there is a wide variety of sex-stereotypic information available that children may imitate. Consider the fairy tales that children read. In "Snow White," for example, the heroine survives because of her great beauty. The Huntsman spares her life, the seven dwarfs accept and protect her, and the King's son rescues her from death—all because she is beautiful. This emphasis on appearance and attractiveness for girls and women is pervasive throughout our culture. Beauty contests, the use of the female body in advertising, the emphasis on makeup, and many other aspects of our culture all convey the message that the path to success for women is through their faces and their bodies. This emphasis on beauty can create a double bind for women who want to achieve success through personal competence, as attractiveness and competence are viewed by many people as incompatible in women (Heilman & Saruwatari, 1979). In contrast, boys and men are portrayed as doers. On television, for example, they represent ⅔ to ¾ of the major characters in viturally every kind of program (Huston, 1983), and they show more of every kind of social behavior, except deference and passivity (McArthur & Eisen, 1976; Sternglanz & Serbin, 1974). Interestingly, even the subtle production features of television support sex stereotyping. There is a greater variety of scenes, loud music, and sound effects in commercials directed at boys than in those directed at girls (Welch, Huston-Stein, Wright, & Plehal, 1979).

In brief, it is now well demonstrated that the portrayal of the sexes throughout American society is overwhelmingly consistent with sex stereotypes (cf. Huston, 1983; D. N. Ruble & Ruble, 1982). Models of sex-stereotypic behavior are therefore readily available. The main question of interest then becomes one of how influential these models are during sex-role development.

From a social learning perspective, children acquire appropriate male and female behavior in large part by observing and imitating same-sex models. In their games, for example, children model appearance when they play dress-up and they model roles when they play doctor/nurse. There is considerable debate, however, about the strength of the evidence showing early same-sex modeling (Lewis & Weinraub, 1979; Maccoby & Jacklin, 1974). There is little evidence that children are either differentially exposed, or that they selectively attend, to same-sex models, and relatively few studies demonstrate that children are more likely to imitate a model of the same sex than of the other sex (Huston, 1983; Maccoby & Jacklin, 1974).

Recent analyses suggest that hypotheses about the role of observational learning in sex-role development may be oversimplified. That is, a large number of variables are likely to affect modeling processes. These include the attributes of the child, such as previously learned concepts, importance of gender, perception of the situation, as well as the attributes of the model, such as power, competence, and similarity (Huston, 1983). Thus, it is difficult to fully understand the impact of observational learning independent of the child's emerging constructions of gender. Accordingly, we present the evidence on observational learning along with the discussion of cognitive developmental processes in the next section.

Summary

There is considerable evidence of external pressures that are different for girls and boys, consistent with a social learning theory perspective. First, people's responses to a child depend on their expectations of his or her gender. Second, children are encouraged to engage in conventionally sex-appropriate play. Third, boys receive more physical stimulation and more physical punishment than do girls, especially from fathers. There are also differences in expectations for achievement and acceptance of independence and free exploration. Interestingly, parents respond differently to children of the same sex than they do to children of the opposite sex, and these differences may have implications for the experiences of children reared in single-parent homes. Finally, children are influenced by stereotypic models that are readily available in the society.

COGNITIVE-DEVELOPMENTAL BASES OF SEX TYPING

The influence of external pressures on children's developing sex-role orientation is undeniable. The full impact of these external forces cannot be completely understood, however, without reference to changes within the child. According to the cognitive-developmental position, changes in children's understanding of gender structure their experiences. Emerging cognitive structures may influence both the salience and the interpretation of gender information. As a result, both the quantitative and the qualitative impact of gender information may vary with the child's developmental level. In this section we consider two questions: (1) When do different kinds of gender knowledge develop? (2) In what ways do they structure sex-role choices and behavior?

The Development of Children's Sex-Role Knowledge and Identity

Knowledge and Awareness of Stereotypes. Numerous studies have examined the development of children's sex stereotypes. Both perceptions about children (their characteristics, playthings, activities) and about adults (their characteristics and activities) have been studied. The major issues are *when* children become aware of sex stereotypes, the *contents* of their perceptions, and age-related differences in the *strength* of these stereotypes. It is difficult to draw firm conclusions about these issues because the studies make use of different sets of stimuli, questions, modes of responses, and age ranges of subjects. Nevertheless, a few consistent trends can be identified.

Children's knowledge of sex roles and interests appears to develop at an early age. By preschool, children are quite accurate in assigning sex-stereotypic *labels* to activities, occupations, and playthings (Edelbrock & Sugawara, 1978; Fauls & Smith, 1956; Garrett, Ein, & Tremaine, 1977; Guttentag & Longfellow, 1977; Hartley, 1960; Masters & Wilkinson, 1976; Nadelman, 1970, 1974; Papalia & Tennent, 1975). Stereotyping of objects has even been shown in children as young as 24 months of age (Thompson, 1975). In contrast, studies examining sex-typed *traits* suggests that this kind of knowledge develops somewhat later. In one study, for example, children were asked which of two silhouette pictures (male or female) was best characterized by each of several traits (e.g., who gets into fights, who cries a lot). Only 14 of the 60 5-year-olds responded above a chance level, as compared with 60/80 8-year-olds and 47/48 11-year-olds (Best, Williams, Cloud, Davis, Robertson, Edwards, Giles, & Fowles, 1977).

In general, an increase in stereotyping with age would be expected in young children, consistent with increased experience and cognitive skills; indeed, young children do seem to demonstrate an increasing knowledge of sex stereotypes, at least through the kindergarten level (Edelbrock & Sugawara, 1978; Flerx, Fidler, & Rogers, 1976; Reis & Wright, 1982; Thompson, 1975; Vener & Snyder, 1966). After this age, however, there are mixed developmental trends. Many studies show a sharp *increase* in knowledge between 5 and 8 years of age with some leveling off after that (Best et al., 1977; Masters & Wilkinson, 1976; Nadelman, 1974; Williams, Bennett & Best, 1975). Other research, however, suggests *decreases* (e.g., Garrett et al., 1977) or *curvilinear* relationships of stereotyping with age (e.g., Guttentag & Longfellow, 1977; Ullian, 1976; Ur-berg, 1979).

One possible reason for these apparent contradictions is the differences across studies in the response measure employed. Measures that require a forced choice between males and females tend to show an increase in stereotyping during the early years of school (Best et al., 1977; Masters & Wilkinson, 1976; Nadelman, 1974; Williams et al., 1975); whereas those that allow for a "both" or "nei-ther" response typically show a decrease during these years (Garrett et al., 1977; Guttentag & Longfellow, 1977; Urberg, 1982). This pattern of results suggests that, although the older children may have more complete knowledge about what kinds of activities and characteristics are stereotypically associated with males or females, they may also apply such stereotypes more flexibly or with finer dis-criminations (Masters & Wilkinson, 1976).

The idea of increasing flexibility is supported by the results of a large survey study by Damon (1979). Reactions to sex-inappropriate acts were solicited from children aged 4 through 9 years. Children showed awareness of sex-role vio-lations, such as men wearing dresses, by age 5; from 5 to 7, they were quite insistent that these kinds of acts were wrong. After this age, however, children began to make allowance for individual flexibility in the face of sex-role conventions.

Another possible reason for inconsistent age effects is that the various dimen-sions of sex stereotypes may be differentially salient and important according to age level. Clearly, the sex-role related concerns of early elementary school children differ considerably from those of adolescents, and so one might predict peaks in the strength of stereotyping corresponding to different interests of chil-dren at differing ages. Indeed, it is frequently suggested that the nature of sex-typing changes during adolescence (Katz, 1979; Mischel, 1970; Newman & Newman, 1979), in accordance with the child's newly emerging identity as a sexual being, and with strong peer pressures (cf. Urberg & Labouvie-Vief, 1976). Lamb and Urberg (1978), for example, have suggested that the inse-curities associated with the sudden changes in, and importance of, physical appearance during adolescence may lead to a new commitment to traditional sex roles. Indeed, some research has reported a heightened degree of stereotyping in adolescence relative to middle elementary school (Guttentag & Longfellow, 1977; Stein & Smithells, 1969; Urberg, 1979). In addition, the results of a large interview study suggested a pattern of alternating acceptance and rejection of sex-role norms, based on age-related changes in perceiving sex differences as being biologically, as opposed to socially, caused (Ullian, 1976).

In summary, by the age of 5 children have a reasonably well-defined set of stereotypes about the more concrete aspects of sex roles—specific activities, playthings, and occupations. More abstract aspects of sex roles (i.e., traits) are acquired somewhat later. In general, *knowledge* of stereotypes increases to an asymptote with age, as shown by studies that require forced-choice responding. When other response options are provided, however, stereotypic versus equalitarian perceptions show fluctuations with age, depending on the nature of the stereotypes being assessed and the age range of the sample included in the study.

Gender Labeling and Identity.   A second issue in the development of sex-role knowledge occurs when children are able to apply accurate gender labels (e.g., boy or girl) to themselves and to others. Unfortunately, defining and operationalizing this construct is not as straightforward as it might initially appear, and there are wide variations in the age at which this skill is acquired, depending on which measure is used. One measure consists of categorizing people according to common noun labels (e.g., "boy" or "mommy"). Children's ability to distinguish between the sexes is first established on the basis of superficial physical characteristics (hair style, clothing, body type), with genitals acquiring increasing importance with age (Kohlberg, 1966; McConaghy, 1979; Thompson & Bentler, 1971). Early studies have indicated that children are able to identify both their own sex and the sex of others by the age of four (Brown, 1956; Rabban, 1950). More recent research suggests that this skill emerges at a surprisingly young age; 24-month-olds accurately applied gender labels to pictures of others, and by 30 months of age the children were accurately applying these labels to themselves (Thompson, 1975).

Other research, however, suggests that this simple classification represents only a rudimentary understanding of gender. Specifically, children do not appear to understand that gender is a stable and consistent aspect of identity until several years after they can accurately label males and females (De Vries, 1969; Eaton & Von Bargen, 1981; Emmerich, Goldman, Kirsh, & Sharabany, 1977; Kohlberg, 1966; Marcus & Overton, 1978; Slaby & Frey, 1975). According to Kohlberg (1966), this concept of gender identity constancy is the critical aspect of gender labeling, because it "can provide a stable organizer of the child's psychosexual attitudes only when the child is categorically certain of its unchangeability" (p. 95).

Gender constancy refers to the consistent labeling of oneself and others as male or female in spite of superficial transformations, such as hairstyle, clothing, or changes in toy interest. In one study (Slaby & Frey, 1975), this concept was measured by a series of questions and counter-questions, grouped into three aspects of gender constancy. These were: (1) identity (e.g., "Is this a woman or a man?" "Is this a [opposite sex of subject's first response]?"); (2) stability (e.g., "When you grow up, will you be a mommy or a daddy?"); and (3) consistency (e.g., "If you played [opposite sex of subject] games, would you be a boy or a girl?"). These levels showed the characteristics of developmental stages in that they were sequentially ordered (fitting the response pattern of a Guttman scale) and age-related in the sample of 2- to 5-year-olds. Identity was the easiest and was mastered by 4 years of age; stability and consistency were understood by 4½ to 5 years of age.

The developmental course of understanding gender constancy has not yet been definitively established, however. Measures of gender constancy have varied across studies, leading to differences in the age at which this kind of knowledge is exhibited. Some measures, for example, involve perceptual transformations, such as depicting male or female clothes or hair on dolls or live models that accompany the questions. These studies suggest that an understanding of gender constancy develops somewhat later and is closely associated with the development of the ability to perform accurately on Piagetian measures of the constancy of physical objects—i.e., at approximately 5 to 7 years of age in middle-class children (De Vries, 1969; Kohlberg, 1966; Marcus & Overton, 1978). Research using other criteria for gender understanding has reported that gender constancy was *not* achieved even by most 7-year-olds (Emmerich et al., 1977). Thus, there is some debate about when gender constancy develops, although it clearly develops later than simple gender labeling and some aspects of sex-role stereotyping. The developmental timing of this concept is important because it is central to theoretical statements about the acquisition of sex roles and understanding the nature of the relationships between different kinds of sex-role knowledge and sex-typed behavior.

The Influence of Sex-Role Knowledge on Behavior

To what extent does children's knowledge of sex stereotypes play a role in producing sex-typed behavior? Is the initial acquisition of sex-role behavior dependent on a prior knowledge of stereotypes or a prior knowledge of gender labelling? Direct evidence on these important questions is scarce. It is possible, however, to begin to examine these issues through an analysis of two aspects of the available evidence: (1) comparisons across studies as to the kinds of knowledge that developmentally precede different sex-role behaviors, and (2) correlations within single studies among the various components of sex roles.

Gender Constancy and Sex-Role Behavior.   According to cognitive developmental theory (Kohlberg, 1966; Kohlberg & Ullian, 1974), structural cognitive changes that allow children to perceive constancy of gender serve as organizers of sex-role behaviors. It has been hypothesized that children become interested in same-sex models and perceive sex-appropriate behaviors as reinforcing because of the newly acquired concept of the inevitability of their gender. Thus, there should be little evidence of preference for sex-appropriate models and activities until this concept emerges at approximately 5–7 years of age (Constantinople, 1979; Lewis & Weinraub, 1979; Maccoby & Jacklin, 1974).

In contrast to this hypothesis, however, the empirical evidence suggests that some aspects of sex typing are evident by ages 3–4 (Brooks-Gunn & Matthews, 1979; Constantinople, 1979; Edelbrock & Sugawara, 1978; Maccoby & Jacklin, 1974). By preschool age, children indicate preferences for sex-stereotypic toys (e.g., Fling & Manosevitz, 1972), there is sex differentiation in play (e.g., Cramer & Hogan, 1975; Fagot & Patterson, 1969), and boys tend to be somewhat more physically aggressive and active than girls (Maccoby & Jacklin, 1974). The pattern of data shows clearly that the concept of gender constancy is not a necessary precondition for observing sex-typed behavior. The attainment of gender constancy, however, may have a special impact on sex-role development in other ways. According to Kohlberg (1966), once children develop a conception of a constant, categorical gender identity, they become motivated to learn what behavior is appropriate for their gender, and to act accordingly. Thus, it is at this point in development that children should actively begin to seek information about their own gender and to attend to and imitate same-sex models.

Only a few studies are relevant to whether attention to same-sex models varies as a function of gender constancy. In one study, preschool boys at advanced stages of gender constancy spent more time selectively attending to a same-sex model in a movie than boys at lower stages, consistent with cognitive developmental theory (Slaby & Frey, 1975). In contrast, Bryan and Luria (1978) failed to find differential attention to slides of males or females in children aged 5–6 years and 9–10 years. It is not clear, however, that their results seriously question the validity of the hypothesis. Their stimuli were relatively simple and only a single model was presented at a time. Thus, there was no need to selectively attend as there was in the Slaby and Frey study, in which male and female models were presented simultaneously.

There is also little information that is directly relevant to the association between gender constancy and sex-specific behavior. Only a few of the many studies of modeling show that children differentially imitate same-sex models (Barkley, Ullman, Otto, & Brecht, 1977; Maccoby & Jacklin, 1974). Most of these studies, however, examined preschool children, who presumably had not yet attained gender constancy. Further, in most studies including older children, developmental changes have not been examined. In one study that divided children by age level, same-sex imitation was found for 7- to 8-year-olds, but not for the younger children, which is consistent with the cognitive developmental hypothesis (Ward, 1969).

A few studies have shown a direct relationship between gender constancy and differential modeling (Frey & Ruble, 1981; Perloff, 1982; D. N. Ruble, Balaban, & Cooper, 1981). In one study, for example, preschool and kindergarten children were shown a toy commercial in the middle of a cartoon in which either two boys or two girls played with a toy pretested to be perceived as equally appropriate for girls and boys. The subjects then had an opportunity to play with the target toy, as well as with other toys of interest. An analysis of the time spent playing with the target toy revealed that only children at advanced levels of gender constancy were affected by the commercial conditions. For this group, children who viewed same-sex children in the commercial subsequently played with that toy significantly longer than children who had seen opposite-sex children in the commercial. In contrast, children at low levels of gender constancy showed no effect of the sex of the models (D. N. Ruble, et al., 1981). In addition, the stereotyping of toys was influenced by the sex of the model for high but not low gender constant children in this study, and in another similar study (Frey & Ruble, 1981).

Thus, there is tentative support for the idea that the development of gender constancy is related to children's responsiveness to sex-role models. A somewhat different picture emerges, however, when the measure of sex-role behavior is preferences for sex-appropriate activities. According to Kohlberg (1966), children's increasing awareness of the unchangeability of their gender is accompanied by increasing preferences for same-sex activities. The evidence is, however, mixed on this point.

One study reported partial support for the hypothesis. When only information about gender appropriateness was available, virtually all children selected a same-sex toy, regardless of their level of gender understanding. In contrast, when the nature of the toy varied on two dimensions—activity level involved in playing with the toy, as well as sex appropriateness—children who had achieved gender stability were more likely to base their choice on sex appropriateness than those who had not (Eaton, Von Bargen, & Keats, 1981). Most studies, however, find little evidence that gender constancy development relates to toy preferences. In one study, for example, kindergartners, first- and second-grade children were asked about their preferences for games, television characters, and peers. Although there were some age-related changes in same-sex preferences, there was no relationship between gender constancy and sex-role preference (Marcus & Overton, 1978). Other research supports this finding (Emmerich, 1981).

One explanation of failures to support the cognitive developmental predictions is that neutral or opposite-sex activities may be less threatening once children understand that their gender will not change regardless of their sex-role preferences (Marcus & Overton, 1978). Alternatively, current preferences may be relatively insensitive to children's increased interest in gender-related information, because some sex differentiation of activities is readily acknowledged to be present prior to a child's *stable* identification as a boy or girl (Kohlberg, 1966). Behavioral preferences in early childhood are probably determined by such factors as reinforcement from socializing agents, what playthings are available, and characteristics of toys (Eisenberg, Murray, & Hite, 1982). Thus, the greater attention to gender-related information that is associated with the attainment of gender constancy may not have much impact on play habits, especially as the information received is not likely to deviate much from the stereotypic patterns already formed.

In summary, there is some evidence that children's changing awareness of the constancy of their gender is associated with heightened susceptibility to information from sex-role models. From this conclusion, we can draw the potentially important inference that this stage of development may represent a point at which change in sex-stereotypic behavior would be possible, if children viewed same-sex models exhibiting non-stereotypic behavior during this time of information seeking. Indeed, greater flexibility of stereotypes has been shown in children at advanced levels of gender constancy (Frey & Ruble, 1981; Urberg, 1982).

Other Gender-Related Cognitions and Sex-Typing.   Although the attainment of gender constancy has been the primary focus of the cognitive developmental perspective, other kinds of cognitions may influence sex typing and sex-role development. Consider, for example, the evidence presented in the preceding sections that some aspects of both sex-typed behavior and sex-role knowledge begin to emerge after 2 years of age. Perhaps these early types of knowledge (gender labeling and stereotyping objects) exert some organizing influence on children's preferences and activities that, in turn, helps lead to progressive cognitive awareness and differentiation. Thus, children's growing knowledge about gender and stereotyping may influence sex-typed behavior prior to achieving gender constancy.

Indeed, several recent theoretical analyses have suggested that sex-role knowledge probably influences how information is categorized and that these categorization processes play a role in guiding children's activities both before and after gender constancy is achieved (Bem, 1981, 1983; Constantinople, 1979; Martin & Halverson, 1981; Pleck, 1975). Early sex-role learning can be viewed in terms of the acquisition of a set of rules, similar to language acquisition (e.g., Constantinople, 1979; Pleck, 1975). According to Constantinople (1979), children begin to screen information from the environment in terms of sex-role categories because of the abundance of sex-related cues in the environment and because of their natural inclinations to generalize and form categories. All that is required to set this process in motion is the initial labeling of people, objects, and activities according to gender, which, as we have already discussed, occurs by ages 3–4.

Recently, the term "schema," common in the literatures on cognitive development and information processing, has been applied to the study of sex roles (Bem, 1981, 1983; Martin & Halverson, 1981). The content and importance of an individual's gender schemas—naive theories about sex roles—influence the kind of information that is encoded and recalled. Thus, once gender schemas are formed, they may help to maintain sex-typed preferences and stereotypes because they contribute to biased information processing. They should also serve as guides to behavior because they provide information about which activities are appropriate and which should be avoided.

Several studies support the prediction that gender schemas direct information processing in such a way that gender-consistent information is encoded more efficiently and better remembered (cf. Bem, 1981; Martin & Halverson, 1981). In one study, for example, highly stereotyped children remembered more pictures that were consistent with sex stereotypes than those that violated sex stereotypes (Liben & Signorella, 1980). Other research has shown that sex-typed individuals are more likely to encode information in terms of sex-linked associations and are faster to embrace sex-appropriate attributes as descriptive of themselves than are non-sex-typed individuals (Bem, 1981).

One phenomenon is a particularly interesting demonstration of the influence of gender schemas or expectations on information processing. In some circumstances, children apparently distort gender-inconsistent information, and as a result make surprising errors reporting what they saw only a short time earlier. In one study, for example, children viewed films of male and female doctors and nurses. When subsequently asked to identify in photographs what they had seen, children who had seen a male doctor and a female nurse were 100% accurate. In contrast, most of the children who saw a male nurse and female doctor said they saw a female nurse and male doctor (Cordua, McGraw, & Drabman, 1979). Other, more recent studies have reported similar effects (Frey & Ruble, 1981; Martin & Halverson, 1983). It is noteworthy that these studies involved young children (6 years and under). It is possible that extreme distortions of this kind are more likely when children are in the process of constructing gender rules. The greater flexibility in stereotyping that seems to follow gender constancy, for example, may render such distortions less necessary.

One problem with gender schema theories is that the presence of a schema does not necessarily imply that information processing biases will operate in favor of gender-consistent information. The social psychological literature suggests that under some circumstances subjects may recall schema-*inconsistent* information better than schema-*consistent* information (Crocker, Hannah, & Weber, 1983; Hastie & Kumar, 1979). Indeed, there is contradictory evidence in the sex-role development literature. One study found that children recalled gender-inconsistent information from stories better than gender-consistent information (Jennings, 1975). Thus, it is necessary to be cautious about conclusions claiming that gender schema act to maintain sex typing.

It is possible to conclude, however, that gender beliefs influence information processing. There are also indications that children's behavior is influenced by gender beliefs or labels. Children imitate a model selectively, depending on the sex appropriateness of the task (e.g., Barkley et al., 1977; Frey & Ruble, 1981; Masters, et al., 1979), and they select toys and activities that are consistent with gender labels (e.g., Schau, Kahn, Diepold, & Cherry, 1980; Thompson, 1975). Furthermore, some research suggests that children's actual performance is influenced by their perceptions of the sex appropriateness of the task (e.g., Montemayor, 1974).

One central question about gender-schematic processing remains to be addressed: Under what conditions do individuals respond according to gender schemas, and when do they not? One way to address this question is to look at the strength or salience of an individual's gender beliefs with respect to a particular situation. Bem (1981), for example, reports individual differences in gender orientation in adults that influence gender-related information processing. To understand the influence of gender-schematic processing in sex-role development, however, we need to examine relevant socialization and developmental variables. What situations make gender schemas salient in children at different age levels? Evidence presented earlier suggests that gender-schematic processing may be high when children are learning about the constancy of their gender. In addition, several of the studies reviewed earlier indicate that the nature and strength of stereotypes may undergo a fairly dramatic change during adolescence, suggesting that there may be other important developmental shifts in information processing. Thus, a developmental analysis of the relationship between different kinds of sex-role knowledge and behavior at several key points in the life span would be likely to provide some important insights concerning the relationship of these two key dimensions of sex-role development (Emmerich, 1973; Huston-Stein & Higgins-Trenk, 1978; Katz, 1979).

Summary

A vast range of studies suggest that children's growing knowledge of gender can influence their sex-role development in a number of ways. Children begin to use gender categories for themselves and others by 3 years of age, and soon after they show an understanding of a quite sophisticated range of sex stereotypes. Although cognitive developmental theory has emphasized the importance of achieving gender constancy at around 5–6 years of age, understanding this concept is clearly not requisite to exhibiting sex-typed behavior. Children's changing awareness of the constancy of their gender does, however, seem to be related to their susceptibility to information from sex-role models. In addition, there is growing evidence that earlier forms of gender knowledge help structure children's sex-typed preferences and activities. Gender beliefs can even lead young children to distort information in order to be consistent with sex stereotypes. Thus, sex-role cognitions influence both children's processing and behavioral responses to gender-related information.

CONCLUSION

It is assumed that males and females differ in a number of ways, and for many individuals, these sex stereotypes provide guidelines for self-perceptions and personal standards. Nevertheless, these standards may represent neither the reality nor the ideal. The literature on sex differences in personality traits suggests that males and females are more similar than is commonly believed. Furthermore, there is a general consensus among theorists and researchers that individuals can possess both masculine and feminine characteristics. Indeed, it may be maladaptive to be too rigidly sex typed. Yet, early in development boys and girls begin to show very different interests and activity preferences, and such sex-*role* differentiation remains strong throughout the life span. A long tradition of developmental research has been concerned with the ways in which sex-role differentiation occurs.

One approach focuses on the biological bases of sex roles. Hormone levels present at sensitive periods during development have been implicated in the emergence of sex-typed sexual and social behavior of animals and, possibly, humans. Some research also suggests that sex differences in intellectual functioning can be influenced by genetic factors, brain lateralization, and hormone changes at puberty. At present, however, there is no conclusive evidence regarding biological mechanisms in these areas as the findings are inconsistent, and often subject to alternative interpretations.

Another approach concerns the shaping of sex roles through social learning processes—e.g., reinforcement and observational learning. Boys and girls do seem to be treated differently. They receive differential encouragement to engage in physical activity, to be independent, to play with trucks or dolls, and so on. Social learning may also occur through observation, and there is no question that sex-stereotypic models are readily available to children. Again, however, there is debate about the ways in which observational learning leads to sex typing and how potent a force it is.

A third approach concerns children's internal motivations to exhibit sex-appropriate behavior because of their emerging cognitive structures or sex schemas. Consistent with cognitive developmental theory, changes in children's understanding of gender appear to structure their experiences. There is evidence, for example, that understanding the constancy of gender at about age 5 is related to the influence of same-sex models. There is debate, however, about the developmental timing of these cognitive structuring processes. Recent theoretical analyses have suggested that sex categorization processes present by age 3 may influence children's attention to and recall of gender-related information at this young age.

No doubt the development of sex roles, in all of its complexity, is multiply determined. Prenatal hormonal variation and other biological factors may create predispositions in an infant or young child toward masculine or feminine characteristics. At the same time, sex-stereotypic expectations, present from the moment of birth, exert shaping influences. These biological and social forces may even interact at various points in development. Small sex differences in, for example, activity level may be exacerbated by parents' willingness to play roughly with boys but not girls. By age 3, children begin to construct organizing principles and seek to generalize the sex-role rules they are learning. At this point, then, children's internal motivations to act appropriately are added to external pressures toward sex typing. The sex-stereotypical models, available throughout the culture, can then be integrated into children's emerging structures and serve as guidelines for behavior. Although children subsequently become more flexible in the application of the sex-role rules learned during childhood, new learning and new needs for rigid adherence to social norms probably emerge in adolescence, as well as in later periods throughout the life span.

REFERENCES

Ashmore, R. D., & Del Boca, F. K. Sex stereotypes and implicit personality theory: Toward a cognitive-social psychological conceptualization. *Sex Roles, 1979, 5,* 219–248.

Baker, S. W. Biological influences on human sex and gender. *Signs: Journal of Women in Culture and Society, 1980, 6,* 80–96.

Bandura, A. Social learning theory of identificatory processes. In D. A. Goslin (Ed.), *Handbook of socialization theory and research.* Chicago: Rand McNally, 1969.

Barkley, R. A., Ullman, D. G., Otto, L., & Brecht, J. M. The effects of sex-typing and sex appropriateness of modeled behavior on children's imitation. *Child Development, 1977, 48,* 721–725.

Barry, H., III, Bacon, M. K., & Child, I. L. A cross-cultural survey of some differences in socialization. *Journal of Abnormal and Social Psychology, 1957, 55,* 327–332.

Bem, S. L. The measurement of psychological androgyny. *Journal of Consulting and Clinical Psychology, 1974, 42,* 155–162.

Bem, S. L. Sex role adaptability: One consequence of psychological androgyny. *Journal of Personality and Social Psychology, 1975, 31,* 634–643.

Bem, S. L. On the utility of alternative procedures for assessing psychological androgyny. *Journal of Consulting and Clinical Psychology, 1977, 45,* 196–205.

Bem, S. L. Gender schema theory: A cognitive account of sex typing. *Psychological Review, 1981, 88,* 354–364.

Bem, S. L. Gender schema theory and its implications for child development: Raising gender-aschematic children in a gender-schematic society. *Signs, 1983, 8,* 598–616.

Bem, S. L., & Lenney, E. Sex typing and the avoidance of cross-sex behavior. *Journal of Personality and Social Psychology, 1976, 33,* 48–54.

Benbow, C. P., & Stanley, J. C. Sex differences in mathematical ability: Fact or artifact, *Science, 1980, 210,* 1262–1264.

Berenbaum, S. A., & Resnick, S. Somatic androgyny and cognitive abilities. *Developmental Psychology, 1982, 18,* 418–423.

Best, D. L., Williams, J. E., Cloud, M. J., Davis, S. W., Robertson, L. S., Edwards, J. R., Giles, H., & Fowles, J. Development of sex-trait stereotypes among young children in the United States, England, and Ireland. *Child Development, 1977, 48,* 1375–1384.

Biller, H. B. *Father, child, and sex role: Paternal determinants of personality development.* Lexington, Mass.: Heath Lexington Books, 1971.

Block, J. H. Debatable conclusions about sex differences. *Contemporary Psychology, 1976, 21,* 517–522. (a).

Block, J. H. Issues, problems, and pitfalls in assessing sex differences. *Merrill-Palmer Quarterly, 1976, 22,* 283–308. (b).

Block, J. H. Another look at sex differentiation in the socialization behaviors of mothers and fathers. In J. Sherman & F. L. Denmark (Eds.), *The psychology of women: Future directions of research.* New York: Psychological Dimensions, 1978.

Boles, D. B. X-linkage of spatial ability: A critical review. *Child Development,* 1980, *51,* 625–635.

Brannon, R. The male sex role: Our culture's blueprint of manhood, and what it's done for us lately. In D. David & R. Brannon (Eds.), *The forty-nine percent majority: The male sex role.* Reading, Mass.: Addison-Wesley, 1976.

Brannon, R. Measuring attitudes (toward women, and otherwise): A methodological critique. In J. Sherman & F. Denmark, (Eds.), *Psychology of women: Future directions in research.* New York: Psychological Dimensions, Inc., 1978.

Brooks-Gunn, J., & Matthews, W. S. *He and she.* Englewood Cliffs, N.J.: Prentice-Hall, 1979.

Broverman, I. K., Vogel, S. R., Broverman, D. M., Clarkson, F. E., & Rosenkrantz, P. S. Sex role stereotypes: A current appraisal. *Journal of Social Issues,* 1972, *28,* (2), 59–79.

Brown, D. G. Sex-role preference in young children. *Psychological Monographs,* 1956, *70,* no. 14, entire issue.

Brown, D. G. Masculinity–femininity development in children. *Journal of Consulting Psychology,* 1957, *21,* 197–205.

Brown, P., & Elliott, R. Control of aggression in a nursery school class. *Journal of Experimental Child Psychology,* 1965, *2,* 103–107.

Bryan, J. W., & Luria, Z. Sex-role learning: A test of the selective attention hypothesis. *Child Development,* 1978, *49,* 13–23.

Bryden, M. P. Evidence for sex-related differences in cerebral organization. In M. A. Wittig & A. C. Petersen (Eds.), *Sex-related differences in cognitive functioning.* New York: Academic Press, 1979.

Bullough, V. L. *The subordinate sex.* Urbana: University of Illinois Press, 1973.

Cairns, R. B. *Social development: The origins and plasticity of interchanges.* San Francisco: Freeman, 1979.

Cicone, M. V., & Ruble, D. N. Beliefs about males. *Journal of Social Issues,* 1978, *34,* 5–16.

Cohen, J. *Statistical power analysis for the behavioral sciences* (2nd ed.). New York: Academic Press, 1977.

Constantinople, A. Masculinity–femininity: An exception to the famous dictum? *Psychological Bulletin,* 1973, *80,* 389–407.

Constantinople, A. Sex-role acquisition: In search of the elephant, *Sex Roles,* 1979, *5,* 121–134.

Cordua, G. D., McGraw, K. O., & Drabman, R. S. Doctor or nurse: Children's perceptions of sex typed occupations. *Child Development,* 1979, *50,* 590–593.

Cramer, P., & Hogan, K. Sex differences in verbal and play fantasy. *Developmental Psychology,* 1975, *11,* 145–154.

Crocker, J., Hannah, D. B., & Weber, R. Person memory and causal attributions. *Journal of Personality and Social Psychology,* 1983, *44,* 55–66.

Damon, W. *The social world of the child.* San Francisco: Jossey-Bass, 1979.

Deaux, K., & Lewis, L. L. Assessment of gender stereotypes: Methodology and components. *Psychological Documents,* in press.

DeVries, R. Constancy of generic identity in the years three to six. *Monographs of the Society for Research in Child Development,* 1969, *34,* (3), Serial no. 127.

Diamond, M. Sexual identity, monozygotic twins reared in discordant sex roles and a BBC follow-up. *Archives of Sexual Behavior,* 1982, *11,* 181–186.

Eagly, A. H., & Carli, L. L. Sex of researchers and sex-typed communications as determinants of sex differences in influenceability. A meta-analysis of social influence studies. *Psychological Bulletin,* 1981, *90,* 1–20.

Eaton, W. O., & Von Bargen, D. Asynchronous development of gender understanding in preschool children. *Child Development,* 1981, *52,* 1020–1027.

Eaton, W. O., Von Bargen, D., & Keats, J. G. Gender understanding and dimensions of preschooler toy choice: Sex stereotype versus activity level. *Canadian Journal of Behavioral Science*, 1981, *13*, 203–209.

Eccles, J. S., & Hoffman, L. W. Sex roles, socialization, and occupational behavior. In H. W. Stevenson & A. E. Siegel (Eds.), *Research in child development and social policy: Volume 1*. Chicago: University of Chicago Press, in press.

Eccles-Parsons, J. Biology, experience and sex dimorphic behaviors. In W. Gove & G. R. Carpenter (Eds.), *The fundamental connection between nature and nurture: A review of the evidence*. Lexington, Mass.: Lexington Books, 1982.

Eccles-Parsons, J. Expectancies, values, and academic behaviors. In J. T. Spence, (Ed.), *Achievement and achievement motives*. San Francisco: Freeman, 1983.

Edelbrock, C., & Sugawara, A. I. Acquisition of sex-typed preferences in preschool aged children. *Developmental Psychology*, 1978, *14*, 614–623.

Ehrhardt, A. A., & Baker, S. W. Fetal androgens, human central nervous system differentiation, and behavior sex differences. In R. C. Friedman, R. M. Richart, & R. L. VandeWiele (Eds.), *Sex differences in behavior*. New York: Wiley, 1974.

Ehrhardt, A. A., Epstein, R., & Money, J. Fetal androgens and female gender identity in the early treated adrenogenital syndrome. *Johns Hopkins Medical Journal*, 1968, *122*, 160–167.

Eisenberg, N., & Lennon, R. Sex differences in empathy and related capacities. *Psychological Bulletin*, 1983, *94*, 100–131.

Eisenberg, N., Murray, E., & Hite, T. Children's reasoning regarding sex-typed toy choices. *Child Development*, 1982, *53*, 81–86.

Emmerich, W. Socialization and sex-role development. In P. B. Baltes & K. W. Schaie (Eds.), *Lifespan developmental psychology: Personality and socialization*. New York: Academic Press, 1973.

Emmerich, W. *Development of gender constancy and sex-typed preferences*. Paper presented at the Biennial Meeting of the Society for Research in Child Development, Boston, April 1981.

Emmerich, W., Goldman, K. S., Kirsh, B., & Sharabany, R. Evidence for a transitional phase in the development of gender constancy. *Child Development*, 1977, *48*, 930–936.

Fagot, B. I. The influence of sex of child on parental reactions to toddler children. *Child Development*, 1978, *49*, 459–465.

Fagot, B. I., & Patterson, G. R. An in vivo analysis of reinforcing contingencies for sex-role behaviors in the preschool child. *Developmental Psychology*, 1969, *1*, 563–568.

Fauls, L., & Smith, W. Sex-role learning of five-year-olds. *Journal of Genetic Psychology*, 1956, *89*, 105–117.

Flerx, V. C., Fidler, D. S., & Rogers, R. W. Sex-role stereotypes: Developmental aspects and early intervention. *Child Development*, 1976, *47*, 998–1007.

Fling, S., & Manosevitz, M. Sex typing in nursery school children's play interests. *Developmental Psychology*, 1972, *7*, 146–152.

Frey, K. S., & Ruble, D. N. *Concepts of gender constancy as mediators of behavior*. Paper presented at the Biennial Meeting of the Society for Research in Child Development, Boston, April, 1981.

Frieze, I. H., Parsons, J. E., Johnson, P. B., Ruble, D. N., & Zellman, G. L. *Women and sex roles: A social psychological perspective*. New York: W. W. Norton, 1978.

Frisch, H. L. Sex stereotypes in adult–infant play. *Child Development*, 1977, *48*, 1671–1675.

Garrett, C. S., Ein, P. L., & Tremaine, L. The development of gender stereotyping of adult occupations in elementary school children. *Child Development*, 1977, *48*, 507–512.

Gould, C. C. Philosophy of liberation and the liberation of philosophy. In C. C. Gould & M. W. Wartofsky (Eds.), *Women and philosophy: Toward a theory of liberation*. New York: G. P. Putnam, 1976.

Green, R. The significance of feminine behavior in boys. *Journal of Child Psychology and Psychiatry*, 1975, *16*, 341–344.

Guttentag, M., & Longfellow, C. Children's social attributions: Development and change. In C. B. Keasey (Ed.), *Nebraska symposium on motivation*. Lincoln, Neb.: University of Nebraska Press, 1977.

Hartley, R. Children's concepts of male and female roles. *Merrill-Palmer Quarterly*, 1960, *6*, 83–91.

Hastie, R., & Kumar, P. A. Person memory: Personality traits as organizing principles in memory for behavior. *Journal of Personality and Social Psychology*, 1979, *37*, 25–38.

Heilbrun, A. B., Jr. Measurement of masculine and feminine sex role identities as independent dimensions. *Journal of Consulting and Clinical Psychology*, 1976, *44*, 183–190.

Heilman, M. E., & Saruwatari, L. When beauty is beastly: The effect of appearance and sex on evaluations of job applicants for managerial and non-managerial jobs. *Organizational Behavior and Human Performance*, 1979, *23*, 360–372.

Hetherington, E. M. Effects of father absence on personality development in adolescent daughters. *Developmental Psychology*, 1972, *7*, 313–326.

Hetherington, E. M., Cox, M., & Cox, R. Play and social interaction in children following divorce. *Journal of Social Issues*, 1979, *35*, 26–49.

Hines, M. Prenatal gonadal hormones and sex differences in human behavior. *Psychological Bulletin*, 1982, *92*, 56–80.

Hoffman, L. W. Changes in family roles, socialization, and sex differences. *American Psychologist*, 1977, *32*, 644–657.

Hoffman, M. L. Sex differences in empathy and related behaviors. *Psychological Bulletin*, 1977, *84*, 712–722.

Hunter, J. Images of woman. *Journal of Social Issues*, 1976, *32*, (3) 7–17.

Huston, A. C. Sex-typing. In E. M. Hetherington (Ed.), *Social development*, volume in P. H. Mussen (General Ed.), *Carmichael's manual of child psychology* (4th ed.). New York: Wiley, 1983.

Huston-Stein, A., & Higgins-Trenk, A. The development of females: Career and feminine role aspirations. In P. B. Baltes (Ed.), *Life-span development and behavior*. (Vol. 1). New York: Academic Press, 1978.

Hyde, J. S. How large are cognitive gender differences? *American Psychologist*, 1981, *36*, 892–901.

Hyde, J. S., & Rosenberg, B. G. *Half the human experience: The psychology of women*. Lexington, Mass.: D. C. Health, 1976.

Ickes, W., & Barnes, R. D. Boys and girls together—and alienated: On enacting stereotyped sex roles in mixed-sex dyads. *Journal of Personality and Social Psychology*, 1978, *36*, 669–683.

Imperato-McGinley, J. et al. Androgens and the evolution of male-gender identity among male pseudo hermaphrodites with 5-reductase deficiency. *New England Journal of Medicine*, 1979, *300*, 1233–1270.

Jacklin, C. N., & Maccoby, E. E. Issues of gender differentiation in normal development. In M. D. Levine, W. B. Carey, A. C. Crocker, & R. T. Gross (Eds.), *Developmental-behavioral pediatrics*. Philadelphia: W. B. Saunders, 1983.

Jennings, S. A. Effects of sex-typing in children's stories on preference and recall. *Child Development*, 1975, *46*, 220–223.

Jones, W., Chernovetz, M. E., & Hansson, R. O. The enigma of androgyny: Differential implications for males and females? *Journal of Consulting and Clinical Psychology*, 1978, *46*, 298–313.

Kagan, J. Acquisition and significance of sex typing and sex role identity. In M. L. Hoffman & L. W. Hoffman (Eds.), *Review of child development research*, Vol. 1. New York: Russell Sage, 1964.

Karabenick, S. A. Sex-relevance of content and influenceability: Sistrunk and McDavid revisited. *Personality and Social Psychology Bulletin*, 1983, *9*, 243–252.

Katz, P. A. The development of female identity. *Sex Roles*, 1979, *5*, 155–178.

Kelly, J. A., & Worell, J. New formulations of sex roles and androgyny: A critical review. *Journal of Consulting and Clinical Psychology,* 1977, *45,* 1101–1115.

Kimble, D. P. *Psychology as a biological science.* Pacific Palisades, Calif.: Goodyear Publishing Co., 1973.

Kohlberg, L. A cognitive-developmental analysis of children's sex-role concepts and attitudes. In E. E. Maccoby (Ed.), *The development of sex differences.* Stanford, Calif.: Stanford University Press, 1966.

Kohlberg, L., & Ullian, D. Z. Stages in the development of psychosexual concepts and attitudes. In R. C. Friedman, R. M. Richart, & R. L. Vande Wiele (Eds.), *Sex differences in behavior.* New York: Wiley, 1974.

Lamb, M. E. Physiological mechanisms in the control of maternal behavior in rats: A review. *Psychological Bulletin,* 1975, *82,* 104–119.

Lamb, M. E. *The role of the father in child development.* New York: Wiley, 1976.

Lamb, M. E. The development of parental preferences in the first two years of life. *Sex Roles,* 1977, *3,* 495–497.

Lamb, M. E., & Urberg, K. A. The development of gender role and gender identity. In M. E. Lamb, (Ed.), *Social and personality development.* New York: Holt, Rinehart, & Winston, 1978.

Langlois, J., & Downs, C. Mothers, fathers, and peers as socialization agents of sex-typed play behavior in young children. *Child Development,* 1980, *1,* 1237–1247.

Lehrke, R. A theory of X-linkage of major intellectual traits. *American Journal of Mental Deficiency,* 1972, *76,* 611–619.

Levy, J. Lateral specialization of the human brain: Behavioral manifestations and possible evolutionary basis. In J. A. Kiger (Ed.), *The biology of behavior.* Corvallis, Or.: Oregon State University Press, 1972.

Lewis, M., & Weinraub, M. Origins of early sex-role development. *Sex Roles,* 1979, *5,* 135–154.

Liben, L. S., & Signorella, M. L. Gender-related schemata and constructive memory in children. *Child Development,* 1980, *51,* 11–18.

Maccoby, E. E. *Social development.* New York: Harcourt Brace Jovanovich, 1980.

Maccoby, E. E., & Jacklin, C. N. *The psychology of sex differences.* Stanford, Calif.: Stanford University Press, 1974.

Marcus, D. E., & Overton, W. F. The development of cognitive gender constancy and sex role preferences. *Child Development,* 1978, *49,* 434–444.

Martin, C. L., & Halverson, C. F. A schematic processing model of sex-typing and stereotyping in children. *Child Development,* 1981, *52,* 1119–1134.

Martin, C. L., & Halverson, C. F. The effects of sex-typing schemas on young children's memory. *Child Development,* 1983, *54,* 563–574.

Masters, J., Ford, M., Arend, R., Grotevant, H., & Clark, L. Modeling and labeling as integrated determinants of children's sex-typed imitative behavior. *Child Development,* 1979, *50,* 364–371.

Masters, J. C., & Wilkinson, A. Consensual and discriminative stereotypes of sex-typed judgments by parents and children. *Child Development,* 1976, *47,* 208–217.

McArthur, L. Z., & Eisen, S. V. Achievements of male and female storybook characters as determinants of achievement behavior by boys and girls. *Journal of Personality and Social Psychology,* 1976, *33,* 467–473.

McConaghy, M. J. Gender permanence and the genital basis of gender: Stages in the development of constancy of gender identity. *Child Development,* 1979, *50,* 1223–1226.

McEwen, B. S. Interactions between hormones and nerve tissue. *Scientific American,* 1976, *235,* 48–58.

McEwen, B. S. Neural gonadal steroid actions. *Science,* 1981, *24,* 1303–1311.

McKee, J. P., & Sherriffs, A. C. The differential evaluation of males and females. *Journal of Personality,* 1957, *25,* 356–371.

Mead, M. *Sex and temperament in three primitive societies.* New York: Morrow, 1935.

Miles, C. Sex in social psychology. In C. Murchinson (Ed.), *Handbook of social psychology.* Worcester, Mass.: Clark University Press, 1935.

Mischel, W. Sex-typing and socialization. In P. H. Mussen (Ed.), *Carmichael's manual of child psychology.* New York: Wiley, 1970.

Money, J., & Ehrhardt, A. A. *Man & woman: Boy & girl.* Baltimore: Johns Hopkins University Press, 1972.

Money, J., & Tucker, P. *Sexual signatures: On being a man or woman.* Boston: Little, Brown, 1975.

Montemayor, R. Children's performance in a game and their attraction to it as a function of sex-typed labels. *Child Development,* 1974, *45,* 152–156.

Mussen, P. H. Early sex-role development. In D. A. Goslin (Ed.), *Handbook of socialization theory and research.* Chicago: Rand McNally, 1969.

Nadelman, L. Sex identity in London children: Memory, knowledge, and preference tests. *Human Development,* 1970, *13,* 28–42.

Nadelman, L. Sex identity in American children: Memory, knowledge, and preference tests. *Developmental Psychology,* 1974, *10,* 413–417.

Newman, B. M., & Newman, P. R. *An introduction to the psychology of adolescence.* Homewood, Ill.: Dorsey, 1979.

Norwood, J. L. The male–female earnings gap: A review of employment and earnings issues. U.S. Department of Labor, Bureau of Labor Statistics, Report 673, September, 1982.

Orlofsky, J. L., & Windle, M. T. Sex-role orientation, behavioral adaptability, and personal adjustment. *Sex Roles,* 1978, *4,* 801–811.

Papalia, D. E., & Tennent, S. S. Vocational aspirations in preschoolers: A manifestation of early sex role stereotyping. *Sex Roles,* 1975, *1,* 197–199.

Parke, R. D., & Suomi, S. J. Adult male–infant relationships: Human and non-primate evidence. In K. Immelman, G. Barlow, M. Main, & L. Petrinovitch (Eds.), *Behavioral development: The Bielefeld interdisciplinary project.* New York: Cambridge University Press, 1980.

Parsons, J. E., Ruble, D. N., Hodges, K. L., & Small, A. W. Cognitive-developmental factors in emerging sex differences in achievement-related expectancies. *Journal of Social Issues,* 1976, *32,* 47–62.

Pedersen, D. M., Shinedling, M. M., & Johnson, D. L. Effects of sex of examiner and subject on children's quantitative test performance. *Journal of Personality and Social Psychology,* 1968, *10,* 251–254.

Petersen, A. C. Hormones and cognitive functioning in normal development. In M. A. Wittig & A. C. Petersen (Eds.), *Sex-related differences in cognitive functioning: Developmental issues.* New York: Academic Press, 1979.

Perloff, R. M. Gender constancy and same-sex imitation: A developmental study. *The Journal of Psychology,* 1982, *111,* 81–86.

Pleck, J. H. Masculinity–femininity: Current and alternative paradigms. *Sex Roles,* 1975, *1,* 161–178.

Pleck, J. H. *The myth of masculinity.* Cambridge, Mass.: The MIT Press, 1981.

Pleck, J. H., & Brannon, R. (Eds.), Male roles and the male experience. *Journal of Social Issues,* 1978, *34,* 1–4.

Quadagno, D. M., Briscoe, R., & Quadagno, J. S. Effect of perinatal gonadal hormones on selected nonsexual behavior patterns: A critical assessment of the nonhuman and human literature. *Psychological Bulletin,* 1977, *84,* 62–80.

Rabban, M. Sex-role identification in young children in two diverse social groups. *Genetic Psychology Monographs,* 1950, *42,* 81–158.

Reinisch, J. M. Prenatal exposure to synthetic progestins increases potential for aggression in humans. *Science,* 1981, *211,* 1171–1173.

Reis, H. T., & Wright, S. Knowledge of sex-role stereotypes in children aged 3 to 5. *Sex Roles,* 1982, *8,* 1049–1056.

Rheingold, H., & Cook, K. The content of boys' and girls' rooms as an index of parent behavior. *Child Development,* 1975, *46,* 459–463.

Rohner, R. P. Sex differences in aggression: Phylogenetic and enculturation perspectives. *Ethos,* 1976, *4,* 57–72.

Rosaldo, M. Z. Women, culture and society: A theoretical overview. In M. Z. Rosaldo & L. Lamphere (Eds.), *Women, culture and society.* Stanford, Calif.: Stanford University Press, 1974.

Rosen, A. C., & Rekers, G. A. Toward a taxonomic framework for variables of sex and gender. *Genetic Psychology Monographs,* 1980, *102,* 191–218.

Rothbart, M. K., & Maccoby, E. E. Parents' differential reactions to sons and daughters. *Journal of Personality and Social Psychology,* 1966, *4,* 237–243.

Rosenkrantz, P., Vogel, S., Bee, H., Broverman, I., & Broverman, D. M. Sex-role stereotypes and self-concepts in college students. *Journal of Consulting and Clinical Psychology,* 1968, *32,* 287–295.

Rubin, J. S., Provenzano, F. J., & Luria, Z. The eye of the beholder: Parents' views on sex of newborns. *American Journal of Orthopsychiatry,* 1974, *5,* 353–363.

Rubin, R. T., Reinisch, J. M., & Haskett, R. F. Postnatal gonadal steroid effects on human behavior. *Science,* 1981, *211,* 1318–1324.

Ruble, D. N., Balaban, T., & Cooper, J. Gender constancy and the effects of sex-typed televised toy commercials. *Child Development,* 1981, *52,* 667–673.

Ruble, D. N., & Brooks-Gunn, J. Menstrual symptoms: A social cognition analysis. *Journal of Behavioral Medicine,* 1979, *2,* 171–194.

Ruble, D. N., & Higgins, E. T. Effects of group sex composition on self-presentation and sex-typing. *Journal of Social Issues,* 1976, *32,* 125–132.

Ruble, D. N., & Ruble, T. Sex stereotypes. In A. G. Miller (Ed.), *In the eye of the beholder.* New York: Praeger, 1982.

Ruble, T. L. Sex stereotypes: Issues of change in the 1970's. *Sex Roles,* 1983, *9,* 397–402.

Ruble, T. L., Cohen, R., & Ruble, D. N. Sex stereotypes: Occupational barriers for women. *American Behavioral Scientist,* 1984, *27,* 339–356.

Rytina, N. F. Earnings of men and women: A look at specific occupations. *Monthly Labor Review,* April 1982, 25–31.

Saegert, S., & Hart, R. The development of environmental competence in girls and boys. In P. Burnet (Ed.), *Women and society.* Chicago: Maaroufa Press, 1976.

Santrock, J. W., & Warshak, R. A. Father custody and social development in boys and girls. *Journal of Social Issues,* 1979, *35,* 112–125.

Schau, C. G., Kahn, L. Diepold, J. H., & Cherry, F. The relationships of parental expectations and preschool children's verbal sex typing to their sex-typed toy play behavior. *Child Development,* 1980, *51,* 266–270.

Shields, S. A. Functionalism, Darwinism and the psychology of women: A study in social myth. *American Psychologist,* 1975, *30,* 739–754.

Sistrunk, F., & McDavid, J. W. Sex variable in conforming behavior. *Journal of Personality and Social Psychology,* 1971, *17,* 200–207.

Slaby, R. G., & Frey, K. S. Development of gender constancy and selective attention to same-sex models. *Child Development,* 1975, 849–856.

Smith, C., & Lloyd, B. Maternal behavior and perceived sex of infant: Revisited. *Child Development,* 1978, *49,* 1263–1265.

Sommer, B. The effect of menstruation on cognitive and perceptual motor behavior: A review. *Psychosomatic Medicine,* 1973, *35,* 515–534.

Spence, J. T., & Helmreich, R. L. *Masculinity and femininity*. Austin: University of Texas Press, 1978.

Spence, J. T., Helmreich, R., & Stapp, J. The personal attributes questionnaire: A measure of sex-role stereotypes and masculinity–femininity. *JSAS Catalog of Selected Documents in Psychology*, 1974, *4*, 43. (MS no. 617).

Spence, J. T., Helmreich, R., & Stapp, J. Ratings of self and peers on sex role attributes and their relation to self-esteem and conceptions of masculinity and femininity. *Journal of Personality and Social Psychology*, 1975, *32*, 29–39.

Stein, A. H., & Smithells, J. Age and sex differences in children's sex role standards about achievement. *Developmental Psychology*, 1969, *1*, 252–259.

Sternglanz, S. H., & Serbin, L. A. Sex role stereotyping in children's television programs. *Developmental Psychology*, 1974, *10*, 710–715.

Tavris, C., & Offir, C. *The longest war*. New York: Harcourt, Brace, Jovanovich, 1977.

Taylor, M. C., & Hall, J. A. Psychological androgyny: Theories, methods, and conclusions. *Psychological Bulletin*, 1982, *92*, 347–366.

Thomas, H. Familial correlational analyses, sex differences, and the X-linked gene hypothesis. *Psychological Bulletin*, 1983, *93*, 427–440.

Thompson, S. K. Gender labels and early sex role development. *Child Development*, 1975, *46*, 339–347.

Thompson, S. K., & Bentler, P. M. The priority of cues in sex discrimination by children and adults. *Developmental Psychology*, 1971, *5*, 181–185.

Ullian, D. Z. The development of conceptions of masculinity and femininity. In B. Lloyd & J. Archer (Eds.), *Exploring sex differences*. London: Academic Press, 1976.

Urberg, K. A. Sex role conceptualization in adolescents and adults. *Developmental Psychology*, 1979, *15*, 90–92.

Urberg, K. A. The development of the concepts of masculinity and femininity in young children. *Sex Roles*, 1982, *8*, 659–668.

Urberg, K. A., & Labouvie-Vief, G. Conceptualization of sex-roles: A life-span developmental study. *Developmental Psychology*, 1976, *12*, 15–23.

Vandenberg, S. G., & Kuse, A. R. Spatial ability: A critical review of the sex-linked major gene hypothesis. In M. A. Wittig & A. C. Petersen (Eds.), *Sex-related differences in cognitive functioning*. New York: Academic Press, 1979.

Vener, A., & Snyder, C. A. The preschool child's awareness and anticipation of adult sex-roles. *Sociometry*, 1966, *29*, 159–168.

Waber, D. P. Sex differences in mental abilities, hemispheric lateralization, and rate of physical growth at adolescence. *Developmental Psychology*, 1977, *13*, 29–38.

Waber, D. P. Cognitive abilities and sex-related variations in the maturation of cerebral cortical functions. In M. A. Wittig & A. C. Petersen (Eds.), *Sex-related differences in cognitive functioning*. New York: Academic Press, 1979.

Ward, W. D. Process of sex-role development. *Developmental Psychology*, 1969, *1*, 163–168.

Welch, R. L., Huston-Stein, A., Wright, J. C., & Plehal, R. Subtle sex-role cues in children's commercials. *Journal of Communication*, 1979, *29*, 202–209.

Whitbeck, C. Theories of sex differences. In C. C. Gould & M. W. Wartofsky (Eds.), *Women and philosophy: Toward a theory of liberation*. New York: G. P. Putnam, 1976.

Williams, J. E., Bennett, S., & Best, D. Awareness and expression of sex stereotypes in young children. *Developmental Psychology*, 1975, *11*, 635–642.

Williams, J. H. *Psychology of women. Behavior in a biosocial context*. New York: Norton, 1977.

Williams, J. H. *Psychology of women*. New York, Norton, 1983.

Wittig, M. A. Sex differences in intellectual functioning: How much of a difference do genes make? *Sex Roles: A Journal of Research*, 1976, *2*, 63–74.

Yorburg, B. *Sexual identity, sex roles and social change.* New York: Wiley, 1974.

Zanna, M. P., & Pack, S. J. On the self-fulfilling nature of apparent sex differences in behavior. *Journal of Experimental Social Psychology,* 1975, *11,* 583–591.

Zucker, K. J. Childhood gender disturbance: Diagnostic issues. *Journal of the American Academy of Child Psychiatry,* 1982, *21,* 274–280.

9 Aggression, Altruism, and Self-Regulation

Charlotte J. Patterson
University of Virginia

INTRODUCTION

By virtue of our lives as human beings, we are all familiar with both aggression and altruism. We have all probably puzzled over the emergence of both these tendencies in the behavior of others, and perhaps even in our own behavior as well. Why do people do the things that we call altruistic or aggressive, and how does the possibility of doing them emerge in the course of development?

Within the confines of this chapter, it would not be possible either to present an exhaustive review of research findings or to provide definitive answers to the questions we have just posed. Many more extensive and detailed reviews of recent research, from a variety of perspectives, are available elsewhere (e.g., Bandura, 1973, 1977; Baron, 1977; Berkowitz, 1962; Hartup & DeWit, 1974; Mussen & Eisenberg-Berg, 1977; Parke & Slaby, 1983; Radke-Yarrow, Zahn-Waxler & Chapman, 1983; Rushton & Sorrentino, 1981; Staub, 1978, 1979). The questions themselves have been of interest to thoughtful people, in one form or another, at least since the days of Plato, and much of the history of Western philosophy can be read as an attempt either to answer or to avoid them (see, for example, MacIntyre, 1966; and compare Cavell, 1976, 1979). The aims of this chapter, then, are more circumscribed.

This chapter presents an approach to conceptualizing both the possibility of, and the actual emergence and development of, altruistic and aggressive behavior during childhood. I shall argue that the behaviors we label as aggressive or altruistic are cases of intentional action that are best seen in the broad context of human efforts to achieve self-regulation. I then use this general approach as a framework within which to review illustrative evidence on the development of

373

aggression and altruism taken from the empirical research literature. Finally, in light of the research findings, I return to a consideration of the development of both aggressive and altruistic action in the context of self-regulation. What I hope will emerge from this discussion is not in any sense a finished theory of the development of altruistic and aggressive action, but a general perspective out of which such an understanding might grow.

AGGRESSION AND ALTRUISM AS INTENTIONAL ACTIONS

The activities that we call aggressive and altruistic are, by definition, intentional. Consider, for example, some experiences I might have when riding on a crowded bus or other public conveyance. Perhaps I am pushed or shoved by another passenger. Do I call this behavior aggressive? I may, but only if I believe that it was done *on purpose;* otherwise, I should think that it was merely inadvertent or accidental, not that it was aggressive. Perhaps I drop some packages, and a fellow passenger, a stranger, picks them up for me. Do I call this action altruistic? Possibly I do, but only if I believe that he did so in my interest; if he subsequently asks me for money, I will likely change my interpretation of his behavior.

In deciding whether a particular behavior qualifies as an example of aggression or altruism, then, it is not just the topography or physical characteristics of the behavior that count. To speak of a person as being ''aggressive by accident'' or ''altruistic for selfish purposes'' simply doesn't make sense; in these cases, we say instead that a person's behavior stems from some other motive or cause. Thus, when we say of a person's behavior that it is altruistic or aggressive, attribution of *intent* is central to what we mean.

For this reason, it is useful to view both aggressive and altruistic behavior in the broader context of people's efforts to achieve what I term ''self-regulation.'' In my definition of the term (see Patterson, 1982), self-regulation involves the successful achievement, through intentional action, of personally selected aims and goals. The aims themselves, and the actions through which they are realized, can be as varied as the people who conceive them and as different as the individuals who carry them out. Whatever is done freely and successfully to fulfill an intention or intentions can, in this sense, be regarded as self-regulated activity. In the usage adopted here, the domain of self-regulation is coterminous with the realm of effective, intentional action.

Inclusion of aggressive and altruistic practices under the rubric of self-regulation is helpful in part because it calls attention to their status not just as *behaviors,* but also as *actions.* Any movement of a person's body, whether intentional or unintentional, can be thought of as behavior. As I employ the term here, it is only that subset of behavior that we call intentional which is properly thought of as action. Thus, those movements of my fellow passenger's body that result in my being jostled as we both ride on a bus are behaviors quite apart from the stranger's intentions, or lack of them. They constitute actions, however, only insofar as they are intended. Aggression and altruism are actions, and actions are intentional behaviors.

The idea of intentional action is useful here because it highlights the importance of descriptions that we use, the importance of our interpretations. Actions are intentional, as Anscombe (1957) has shown, only under the particular descriptions or interpretations that we make of them. For example, imagine once again that I drop my packages on a crowded bus. This time, let us assume that a man I do not know stoops down to pick them up for me, and that he jostles other passengers in the process. One interpretation is that this man intended to offer me help, and that he accidentally pushed or shoved other people in his attempt to do so. In this case, we might say that his actions were altruistic.

Another interpretation might be that, for whatever reasons of his own (let us say that he was a pickpocket, or that he knew and disliked other passengers on the bus), he intended to jostle other passengers, and simply seized on my fallen parcels as an opportunity to do so. In this case, we might call his actions aggressive. In either case, however, it is our interpretation of his intentions which creates for us the meaning of his action, whether altruistic or aggressive. Seeing aggression and altruism as cases of intentional action helps to highlight the importance of interpretation in their understanding.

One implication of this view is that whether a particular behavior will be called an aggressive or an altruistic act—indeed, whether it will be called an act at all—may depend upon the viewpoint of the person who is doing the calling. The man who jostles me on the bus and I myself who am jostled may have very different interpretations of what it is that he was trying or intending to do; hence, the two of us may literally see his single set of movements as different actions. We return to this point later on, when considering research on the development of altruism and aggression in childhood, because there the possibility will emerge that what appears to us, for example, as a child's aggressive action may appear as something quite different to the child who performs it.

I have thus far suggested that aggression and altruism should be viewed as examples of intentional action, and hence that they should be seen in the context of our efforts to achieve self-regulation; and I have emphasized the centrality of interpretation in the understanding of self-regulated action. I turn now to sketch some of the possible implications of these views.

In the context of altruism and aggression, what might some of these implications be? One of them is that we ought to acknowledge a distinction between behavior that is violent or aversive on the one hand, and aggressive action on the other. An infant's cry can be extremely aversive to others without being aggressive, without arising out of any intention to hurt or to cause pain. A child's motor activities can be violent (i.e., characterized by strong physical force) and can even inadvertently injure others, without being aggressive. Violent and/or aversive behavior is a generic category, of which aggressive action is a subset.

In a similar vein, it is important to distinguish between behavior that has positive or beneficial effects on others, and altruistic action, as such. A young infant who smiles engagingly at his or her caretakers is behaving in a prosocial manner, but is unlikely to be doing so for altruistic reasons. A child who uncomplainingly performs his or her household chores is behaving in a prosocial way, but may or may not be doing this out of altruistic motives. Altruistic action is thus a subset of the much larger category of prosocial behavior.

By offering these conceptual distinctions—between antisocial behavior and aggressive action on the one hand, and between prosocial behavior and altruistic action on the other—I do not mean to suggest that the activity of distinguishing them in practice is always easy. To the contrary, as the examples considered earlier show, these distinctions can be quite difficult to apply in concrete cases. Because these distinctions are so important to our understanding, however, it is essential that even as we acknowledge the practical difficulties involved in making them, we nevertheless persist in our efforts to do so.

There are a number of reasons why these distinctions are important. One reason is that they remind us that altruistic and aggressive intentions can be realized through a wide variety of activities, including but not limited to those that appear, at a surface level, to be either aversive or rewarding. It is by no means clear, for instance, that altruistic aims cannot sometimes best be accomplished through hurtful or painful means (as, for example, when a close friend tells me something that, although painful to hear, is beneficial to my well-being). Similarly, aggressive aims are sometimes accomplished quite effectively through outwardly pleasant means (as, for example, when a cutting remark is delivered as a joke, or with a smile). Keeping in mind the distinction between topography and intention helps to remind us that the actions undertaken to realize our intentions can take many different forms.

Taking the same point from the other side, these distinctions also remind us that behavior that is antisocial or prosocial in its outward aspect does not necessarily spring from aggressive or altruistic intentions. Thus, what may at first glance appear as aggression in children may in fact have been activities undertaken to achieve quite different intentions. Hence, these distinctions help to guard against the inappropriate projection of our initial interpretations in cases where they may not fit.

I argue that, particularly when we observe the behavior of very young children, we are indeed often in danger of such inappropriate projection. In fact, I suggest that much of young children's behavior that appears, to adults, as aggression or altruism, may actually be misconceived under this label; that the emergence of true altruism or aggression is an event of real developmental significance; and that age-related changes in altruism and aggression are best understood within the framework of efforts to achieve self-regulation.

Summary

I have argued that the human activities that we term aggressive and altruistic are, by definition, *intentional* in nature. In other words, I have suggested that aggression and altruism are not simply cases of behavior, but are cases of intentional behavior, or *action* as well. From this viewpoint, it follows that not every antisocial behavior can be considered aggressive, nor can every prosocial behavior be considered altruistic. Only those antisocial (e.g., violent and/or aversive) actions that we believe to have been undertaken with intent to harm another person ought to be considered aggression; only those prosocial (e.g., pleasant and/or beneficial) actions that we believe to have been undertaken with intent to help another person ought to be considered altruistic. Hence, the interpretation of an actor's intentions is crucial to the identification of aggressive or altruistic action. Because the attribution of intentionality is so central to identification of aggression and altruism, and because various observers may interpret an actor's intentions differently, the very existence of either aggression or altruism is often subject to debate and disagreement in particular cases. This is especially likely to be true when the actor whose behavior we are seeking to interpret is a very young child.

EMERGENCE AND DEVELOPMENT OF AGGRESSIVE ACTION

Consider the following encounter between two 7-year-olds (Hartup, 1974):

> Marian is complaining to all that David . . . had squirted her on the pants she has to wear tonight. She says, "I'm gonna do it to him to see how he likes it." She fills a can with water and David runs to the teacher and tells of her threat. The teacher takes the can from Marian. Marian attacks David and pulls his hair very hard. . . . Later, Marian and Elaine go upstairs and into the room where David is seated with a teacher. He throws a book at Marian. The teacher asks Marian to leave. Marian kicks David, then leaves (p. 339).

The kicking, hair pulling, and book throwing described in this vignette are clearly intentional behavior; they are clearly actions. Moreover, they are clearly performed with the intent to injure or harm another; they are clearly aggressive actions. If we were to ask either Marian or David why they acted as they did, we would expect them to reply by expressing their dislike of and/or their desire to hurt the other.

Compare these observations made by Piaget (1952) of his infant son:

> At 6 months, I present Laurent with a matchbox, extending my hand laterally to make an obstacle to his prehension. Laurent tries to pass over my hand, or to the side, but he does not attempt to displace it. [These and similar reactions continue

essentially unchanged for several weeks. . . .] Finally, at 7 months 13 days, Laurent reacts quite differently. . . . I present a box of matches above my hand, but behind it, so that he cannot reach it without setting the obstacle aside. But Laurent, after trying to take no notice of it, suddenly tries to hit my hand as though to remove or lower it; I let him do it and he grasps the box (p. 217).

What shall we say about Laurent's behavior at 7½ months, when he strikes his father's hand out of the way so that he can reach the matchbox that is the object of his interest? Certainly, we are inclined to call it an action. Although Laurent, who has not yet uttered his first words, would not be able to offer us reasons, we are nevertheless very likely to attribute intentionality to his movements. Is it an aggressive action? Again, Laurent cannot tell us what he intended, but I think that most of us would see his action as aimed at getting the matchbox, rather than hurting his father's hand. Thus, I think that most of us would reject the idea that Laurent's action was aggressive. Even if his movements had caused his father real pain, I think we would simply say that the injury was accidental. We do not attribute the capacity for aggression to an infant of this age.

Because almost everyone would be likely to agree that Marian and David's actions were aggressive, whereas Laurent's were not, these examples raise important questions: When and how does the capacity for aggressive action first emerge? How, and to what extent, do the frequency and character of aggression change during the course of development? Why? In the following section, the research literature is examined in an effort to address these questions.

Developmental Trends

One of the earliest studies of the origins of aggression was that of Goodenough (1931), who drew her evidence from diaries kept by mothers of children ranging from 1 to 7 years of age. She found that, in terms of sheer frequencies, angry outbursts were most common among 1- to 2-year-olds. At 18 months, the children in her study averaged about one such outburst for every 6 hours they were awake. Three- and 4-year-olds, in contrast, showed only about half as many.

This finding does not, however, mean that these 1- and 2-year-olds were highly aggressive. The great majority of their outbursts of anger were not focused on any particular person or object. Most of these outbursts were, rather, what Maccoby (1980, p. 121) has called ''undirected tantrums,'' characterized by screaming, crying, and violent motor behavior, but not, apparently, by any identifiable aggressive intent. On the other hand, focused outbursts of anger, such as those occurring in retaliation for a perceived injury, more than quadrupled from the 1- and 2-year-old period to the 3- and 4-year-old group. Thus, the appropriate conclusion to be drawn from Goodenough's findings would seem to be that although the incidence of violent and/or aversive behavior reported by mothers declined after the age of 2, the incidence of reported aggression increased, at least up to 4 years of age.

Similar findings emerged from a study by Dawe (1934). Drawing on observations of naturally occurring quarrels in a nursery school environment, Dawe reported that although preschoolers (54–65 months of age) were likely to respond to conflict with physical aggression such as pushing or hitting, toddlers (18–29 months) were more likely to exhibit what she called "undirected energy," including "crying, screaming, jumping up and down or stamping, without any directed resistance" (Dawe, 1934, p. 143). It is worth noting that this latter category, although it includes much that is forceful or violent in nature, and much that would be aversive to almost any observer, nevertheless does not qualify as aggression in our terms. The results of Dawe's study are thus consistent with those of Goodenough in suggesting an increase in aggressive action, as such, over the preschool years.

There is a paradox of sorts in citing Dawe's findings to support the idea that aggression increases in frequency during the preschool years, because Dawe also reported that the frequency of conflicts between children decreases during this period. In her study, toddlers (18–29 months) were much more likely to start a quarrel, and in fact were involved in conflicts almost twice as often as older children (54–65 months). How can toddlers start more conflicts and quarrel more often, yet be less aggressive than preschool children? How can we account for this apparent discrepancy?

The answer lies in an examination of the nature of children's conflicts. The largest number of conflicts, at all of the ages Dawe studied, were those over objects. Among toddlers, object-centered quarrels accounted for almost three-quarters of all observed conflict. The proportion of disputes that were centered on objects declined steadily with age, accounting for less than 40% of conflicts by the age of 5 years. In contrast, the proportion of conflict instigated by physical violence or disagreements over social rules showed marked increases over this same age period. In short, although preschoolers' conflicts were more likely to begin over physical violence or verbal disagreements, toddlers' disputes were more likely to start over possession of objects (Dawe, 1934).

There is, in fact, good agreement among a variety of investigators that toddlers are particularly likely to experience conflict with their peers over objects (Bronson, 1975; Dawe, 1934; Hay & Ross, 1982; Maudry & Nekula, 1939). In the recent Hay and Ross study, for example, conflicts between pairs of 21-month-old children were recorded, and 84% of them proved to be struggles over toys.

If we were to imagine a prototypic object struggle between a pair of young toddlers, it might go something like this: One child (call her Marcy) is playing with a toy, a ball. Another child (call her Susan) notices the movements of the ball in Marcy's hands, becomes interested, and moves nearer. Susan reaches for the ball and takes it into her hands. In an effort to retrieve the ball again, Marcy runs into Susan, who pushes her away. Marcy loses her balance, falls, and begins to cry.

Now, the crucial question to ask about this episode is whether it is more like the encounter between David and Marian discussed earlier, or more like the one between Laurent and his father. In other words, is Susan's intention in this episode to be understood as "hurting Marcy" (and thus as aggressive like Marian) or as "getting the ball" (and hence as nonaggressive like Laurent)? It is often difficult to make this kind of judgment. When we watch episodes like this among young toddlers, however, I think we are most often inclined to see them as being more like Laurent's behavior than like Marian's.

We are inclined to say that although Susan acted in such a way that the end result was painful to Marcy, this result was unexpected or accidental from Susan's point of view. Her intention was simply to get the ball, and she had little idea that the realization of her intention might prove painful to Marcy. Had Susan been an adult, we might be inclined to think that she should have foreseen at least some of these consequences, and so to hold her responsible. Because she is so young, however, we do not expect her to know these things, and we call her innocent. In fact, Levine (1983) has suggested that possessiveness and object struggles among toddlers stem more from the participants' emerging attempts at self-definition than from selfishness or aggressive intentions.

In these terms, then, what initially seemed to be a discrepancy in Dawe's (1934) findings—that the incidence of aggression increased even as the frequency of conflict decreased during the preschool years—appears instead to be exactly what we should expect. Very young children start more quarrels because they have no idea that their desire to manipulate interesting objects may have aversive consequences for their peers. Acting in complete, or near-complete, innocence, they are simply pursuing their own aims as best they can. Unaware of the potential ramifications of their actions for others, young toddlers often precipitate conflict, but may still remain incapable of aggression.

These early conflicts between peers must, however, have important implications for the emergence of aggression among children. If we imagine Susan's encounter with Marcy to be literally the first of its kind that she has experienced, then we must also imagine that Susan is in some way surprised at its outcome. With repeated experiences of this kind, however, Susan will learn that her peers do not like to have toys taken away from them, that they are likely to attempt retrieval of toys she has snatched, that struggle and injury may ensue, and so on. She will learn what neither she nor Laurent can initially be credited with knowing: that if, for whatever reason, she hits another person, it may hurt them. In short, she will learn that she is able to hurt others and in what ways, and this knowledge in turn will make it possible for her to act aggressively if and when she chooses to do so in the future. In other words, the knowledge she acquires in this way will create for her the possibility of aggressive action.

In this view, the emergence of a capacity for aggressive action—action that is intended to hurt another person—is a momentous event, one that is dependent on cognitive achievements of a sophisticated nature. Drawing on Maccoby's (1980) discussion, we might say that the emergence of a capacity for true aggression requires, at a minimum, the understanding that there is a distinction between self and others; that others can experience distress; that one's own actions can cause distress in particular people; and that the execution of specific actions is likely to cause distress in a specific case. As Maccoby has stressed, the word "understanding" should be taken in a broad sense here; a child need not be able to recite a list of this sort in order to act in accordance with aggressive intentions. Still, it is clear that a capacity for aggressive action requires substantial cognitive development and learning; hence, this capacity might be expected to increase during the early childhood years. This view is very much in accord with the findings of what is perhaps the best known study of the development of aggression in childhood, that of Hartup (1974).

Hartup's (1974) study involved observations of preschool (4- to 6-year-old) and elementary school (6- to 7-year-old) children's activities in their normal school environments. Aggressive events were defined as "intentional physical and verbal responses that are directed toward an object or another person and that have the capacity to damage or injure" (p. 339), and observers recorded all cases of such activities witnessed during a 10-week period. These were, in turn, divided into categories that Hartup called *instrumental aggression,* violent actions that are "aimed at the retrieval of an object, territory, or privilege" (p. 338); and *hostile aggression,* violent actions that are aimed directly at harming or injuring another person. He also distinguished between verbal aggression (e.g., derogation, threats) and physical aggression (e.g., pushing, shoving).

Hartup's findings were these: Consistent with the results reported by Dawe (1934; see also Savin-Williams, 1979), older children were more likely to respond to insults verbally, whereas younger children were more likely to respond with physical aggression. In other words, the extent to which apparently aggressive intentions were carried out verbally increased with age. In addition, elementary school children were less aggressive per unit time than were preschool children, and this decline was attributable to a decrease in "instrumental aggression." A significantly higher proportion of older children's aggression was hostile in nature. These findings are often cited as evidence for the proposition that instrumental aggression declines with age during this period.

To put these findings in the context that has been used here, some efforts at translation are required. We can start by recalling the distinction made earlier between aggression as such and the more general category of violent and/or aversive behavior. Violent actions that are carried out with the intention of hurting another person are those we have termed aggressive. Those carried out for some other reason (e.g., to retrieve an object, as in the example of Laurent, or in that of Susan and Marcy) we called violent and/or aversive, but not aggressive. In our terms, then, the concept of "instrumental aggression"—aggression that is *not* aimed at hurting another person—is a misnomer, a contradiction in terms.

In our terms, what Hartup (1974) has called "instrumental aggression" is simply violent or aversive action undertaken to achieve some nonaggressive goal, such as the retrieval of an object. As adults, we may be tempted to label this an aggressive activity because if we undertook it, we would do so in anticipation of its hurtful consequences for another person. To the extent that we believe young children are without such anticipation, however, we cannot be justified in labeling their actions as aggressive; to do so would be no more than the projection of our own preoccupations onto them.

In summary, Hartup's (1974) findings seem to show both a greater frequency of true aggression and a greater reluctance to use violent means to non-hostile ends among elementary school as compared to preschool children. As such, his observations are consistent with, and also extend those of Goodenough (1931) and Dawe (1934). Thus, the most important conclusion emerging from these findings seems to be that, as they get older, children increasingly confine their use of physical violence to their pursuit of aggressive aims.

An important qualification to this conclusion, however, is that it rests on our interpretations of children's intentions. The meanings of actions are given by our interpretations of them, and our interpretations are always subject to disagreement, discussion, and debate. Thus, although we may be inclined to interpret some of children's actions as aggressive and others as nonaggressive, we should do so only in recognition that other interpretations are also possible. When we are concerned with the actions of adults, our respect for the potential range and complexity of underlying intentions makes this recognition relatively easy to achieve. Even when they seem most transparent, however, the actions of children are worthy of our respect in this regard as well. Overall, then, confidence in our conclusions should be tempered by acknowledgment of the primacy of ambiguity in the interpretation of human actions.

With this qualification in mind, we can summarize the tentative conclusions that we have reached. In the behavior of infants and very young children, it appears that violence and aggression are often distinguishable; physically violent behavior frequently occurs without aggressive intent. Increasingly with age, however, physical violence and aggression do appear to become almost interchangeable terms in practice, inasmuch as older children increasingly seem to use violent means only when their goals are aggressive. Thus, during the early childhood period, there appears to be both an increasing capacity to conceive and carry out aggressive intentions as well as a growing association of physical violence with aggressive intent in children's activities. What might account for these trends?

Underlying Factors

It has been said that even to conceive an aggressive intention is a sophisticated cognitive achievement. Certainly, then, it must represent an even more sophisticated achievement to limit the use of violence and aversive techniques to those cases in which our intentions are actually to harm. What underlies these achievements? We can begin our discussion of these questions by considering an episode related by Maccoby: "During a long ride in the car, a four-year-old boy lay down on the car seat with his head in his mother's lap. He gazed deeply into his mother's eyes. The mother felt pleased at this loving intimacy. Then the boy said, "Mom, your eyes are just like road-maps!" (1980, p. 31).

This remark, if made by an adult, might well be considered an insult; it might be interpreted as a deliberate attempt to hurt the woman's feelings or injure her pride. In other words, it might be considered aggressive. As Maccoby explains, however, "The mother was not pleased, of course, to have attention called to her bloodshot eyes. But she understood that the child did not intend to hurt her feelings." In other words, the remark could not be considered aggressive, because the little boy did not understand how his remark would make his mother feel.

As this episode suggests, efforts to comprehend the development of aggression must take into account the growth of social understanding. As I have argued, it is the growth of social understanding that makes aggression possible; certainly, the growth of social understanding can also help to explain the changes in its forms with advancing age. Let us look, then, at some of the evidence on how social understanding—in particular, the appreciation of social perspectives other than one's own—seems to affect the development of aggression.

It is an interesting but regrettable fact that research on the social understanding of aggression and violence tends (with rare exception—e.g., Rule, Nesdale & McAra, 1974) to begin with children of elementary school age. Among older children, victims' interpretations of perpetrators' intentions clearly influence their responses to violence. For example, highly aggressive children are more likely than their less aggressive peers to interpret the behavior of others as stemming from hostile intentions (Dodge, 1980; Dodge & Frame, 1982; Dodge & Newman, 1981; Nasby, Hayden & DePaulo, 1980). Both aggressive and nonaggressive children are more likely to retaliate in kind if they believe themselves to be the victims of intentional, as opposed to accidental, violence (Dodge, 1980; Dodge & Frame, 1982).

It would be useful, then, to know how very young children interpret their playmates' attempts to take toys from them. Do they regard these actions as instrumental, or as hostile? Does it matter? When one toddler inadvertently pushes or injures another in the midst of a dispute, is this regarded by the victim as accidental or intentional? And how does this affect the victim's response? There is little information available with which to answer such questions.

There is some suggestion in the literature that preschool children may interpret any of another person's movements as intentional. Smith (1978) showed 4-, 5-, and 6-year-old children videotaped sequences of adult behavior and asked them to judge its degree of intentionality (i.e., the extent to which the actor was trying, or wanted, to do the particular behavior displayed on the videotape). He found that 4-year-olds tended to regard almost all movements, even involuntary ones such as sneezing, as intentional activity. Even very undesirable effects (e.g., garbage landing on the floor instead of in the garbage can), labelled by adults as unintended, were perceived as intended by 4-year-olds. Older children, particularly 6-year-olds, recognized that even though an action might be voluntary, all of its effects might not be intended.

Smith's findings may have important implications for understanding the development of aggression because they suggest that young children may regard any outcome they encounter at the hands of their peers, no matter how negative or aversive, as intended. To the extent that young children are biased to view any effects of a person's actions as intended, they must also often overestimate the extent to which their peers' intentions are hostile. Hence, they may see their peers as more hostile than they "really are" (i.e., more hostile than adult observers would believe them to be). Such an attributional bias might increase young children's likelihood of responding to accidental violence with real aggression, and so lead to the needless escalation of many conflicts. If correct, this line of reasoning would seem partly to account for the relatively high frequencies of conflicts that begin in the context of object struggles among younger children. In the absence of relevant data, however, these suggestions remain entirely speculative.

Research on children's ability to differentiate intentional from unintentional violence in the behavior of their peers does not begin until school age. Shantz and Voydanoff (1973) told boys stories about another boy who committed some violent acts, thereby harming another child. In some stories, the violence was intentional (i.e., aggressive); in others, it was unintentional (i.e., accidental). The boys were asked to choose among different levels of physical punishment for the child who had been violent. The major finding was that while 9- and 12-year-olds chose less severe punishment for the accidental acts of violence, 7-year-olds did not differentiate between accidental and intentional (i.e., truly aggressive) violence.

In contrast, Dodge (1980) reports that 7-year-old boys did make such a distinction. In Dodge's study, boys worked on a puzzle, which was subsequently spoiled, either accidentally or on purpose, by another boy. They subsequently had an opportunity either to help or to hurt the child who had spoiled their work. Seven-year-olds showed a greater tendency to hurt, physically as well as verbally, the child who had spoiled their work on purpose. The discrepancy between Dodge's findings and those of Shantz and Voydanoff (1973) might be attributed to any of a number of procedural differences between the two studies, or it might reflect a genuine instability in children's responses at this age; further research is necessary to resolve this point.

In a related study, Ferguson and Rule (1980) have shown that by the age of eight, boys held an actor more responsible (i.e., said that the actor was more to blame) for the negative consequences of his violent behavior when they were intended than when they were not. In addition, the oldest boys (14-year-olds) not only put more blame on the actor for the intended than for the unintended negative effects of his actions, but they also differentiated between accidental-but-foreseeable versus accidental-and-not-foreseeable negative effects, attributing more blame for the former than the latter. Eight-year-olds did not make this distinction. Thus, older children apparently expect their peers to make reasonable efforts to foresee the probable consequences of their actions, and to take them into account. To the extent that the actor did not behave in these ways, and to the extent that the effects of his actions on others were negative, he was considered blameworthy by older, but not younger, children.

In a further study by Rule, Nesdale, and McAra (1974), children were asked to attribute blame for intentionally violent and/or aversive actions that were committed with hostile (angry), personal-instrumental (selfish), or social-instrumental (prosocial) intentions. In one study, 5-year-old girls labelled those actions committed with hostile intentions as more reprehensible than those performed with social-instrumental intentions. In another, 6-year-old boys called actions committted for hostile or selfish motives more reprehensible than those undertaken for prosocial purposes. It is interesting to note that personal-instrumental intentions were treated by 6-year-olds in essentially the same way as hostile ones. This finding seems consistent with the suggestion from Smith's (1978) study that young children may be likely to over-attribute intentionality to actions and their effects.

In general, the available research seems to reveal children's increasing sensitivity with age to the varying intentions that underlie the particular behaviors they observe. Although the available evidence is still fragmentary in nature, it appears that over the preschool and early elementary school years, children may become less likely to over-attribute hostile intent in the behavior of others, and more likely to recognize alternative interpretations. Thus, the decrease during this period in the frequency of peer conflicts that begin in the context of object struggles may be explained, at least in part, by developments in the social-cognitive domain.

Whereas children seem to become less likely with age to attribute hostile intentions to their peers when these attributions are not justified, they may also become more likely to notice and respond to cues of actual hostility from their peers. For instance, by the age of about 6 years, children are able to identify those facial expressions that signify their peers' unwillingness to give up possession of contested objects, and to name the emotional states portrayed by those expressions (Camras, 1980). Even 5-year-olds adjusted their behavior in disputes appropriately when their peers exhibited facial expressions of antagonism; children at this age were less likely to persist in their attempts to take possession of a desired object when a peer produced antagonistic expressions than when a peer produced more neutral facial cues while defending his or her possession of a disputed object (Camras, 1977).

It would be interesting to compare the responses of younger children in situations similar to those Camras (1977, 1980) studied. Judging from the frequency of toddlers' object-related disputes with their peers, we might expect them to be somewhat less adept at reading a peer's nonverbal signs of imminent retaliation. Very young children might also be less likely than preschoolers and elementary school children to adjust their own actions before the conflict has escalated. Until relevant data on younger children become available, however, this possibility cannot be evaluated.

By the age of 5 or 6 years children seem to understand at least some aspects of their peers' expressive behavior signaling the likelihood of resistance or compliance with their own assertive maneuvers. Children at this age also seem to be highly responsive to the degree of success or failure they experience in specific peer encounters. For example, Patterson, Littman, and Bricker (1967) observed peer conflicts in nursery schools and reported that children were less likely to initiate conflicts with peers who had retaliated successfully against them in previous encounters. To the extent that physically violent methods were unsuccessful in achieving their aims, these children increasingly turned either to other victims or to alternative forms of behavior.

Taken together, the results of the Camras (1977, 1980) and Patterson et al. (1967) studies suggest that during the late preschool and early elementary school periods, children may become increasingly sensitive to their peers' often unfavorable responses to physically violent behavior. To the extent that children of this age have learned that victims of their violent actions may retaliate, and to the extent that they have also learned to read the nonverbal signs of imminent retaliation, they might well be expected to begin to search in earnest for nonviolent methods of achieving their non-hostile (e.g., instrumental) aims. Thus, the trend during this age period for children increasingly to confine their use of violent methods to their achievement of hostile aims (e.g., Dawe, 1934; Hartup, 1974) may be partially explained by data such as these.

Summary

Although we cannot pinpoint one specific age at which the capacity for true aggression definitely appears, the available evidence nevertheless suggests both an absence of the capacity for true aggression during infancy, and an enormous expansion of that capacity over the years between infancy and the entrance into school. The frequency of verbal aggression increases markedly during this age period, while the frequency of physical aggression appears to drop. Thus, the major developmental achievement of early childhood in this regard appears to be an increasing ability to confine the use of physical violence to the pursuit of hostile aims and to develop alternative means of achieving other, non-hostile aims. Both children's increasing levels of social understanding in general and their actual experience with peers in particular seem to underlie these developmental trends.

EMERGENCE AND DEVELOPMENT OF ALTRUISTIC ACTION

Just as we earlier recognized a distinction between antisocial behavior and aggressive action, so we need also to distinguish between prosocial behavior and altruistic action. Prosocial behavior—behavior that has the effect of benefitting or sustaining others—is a large and ramified category. Altruistic action—prosocial behavior that is undertaken *with the intention of* providing such benefits to others—is a subset of this category.

Prosocial behavior includes not only such paradigm cases as contributing to charities and rescuing victims of disasters, but also a host of other everyday, conventional activities that result in benefits to others. When we operate automobiles in accordance with local traffic ordinances we contribute to the safety and welfare of others who use the same highways. When we conform to prevailing customs of dress, manners, and conduct, we benefit those around us by providing them with a relatively stable, predictable environment in which to pursue their own daily activities. When we comply with the conventions of conversation and discourse—indeed, of languages themselves—we benefit others by facilitating communication, and so rendering the pursuit of joint activities easier. It is difficult to overestimate the depth and range of the influence of convention in our lives, and it is more difficult still to overestimate the benefits that accrue to us as a result. Thus, a very large proportion of our normal, everyday activities can be considered prosocial behavior.

Although many of our everyday activities have beneficial effects on others, a much smaller proportion of them are undertaken with the intention of having these effects. When we fit our activities to the requirements of local traffic laws, customs of dress, or conventions of conversation, we most often do so almost without thinking. When we do think about such matters, most of us probably think first about our own self-interest. For instance, when we are deciding whether or not to drive in excess of posted speed limits, most of us probably evaluate first the probability of getting a speeding ticket, not the probability of injuring other drivers. Thus, while many of our activities have prosocial effects, only a small proportion of them can be classified as altruistic actions.

The ability to act in an altruistic manner involves not only the ability to distinguish between self and other, but also the knowledge that people might need help, that some kinds of events or conditions are likely to help them, and that certain kinds of actions are likely to bring about the relevant events or conditions. It also involves the ability and desire to carry out such actions in specific cases. An altruistic act, then, is a complex cognitive achievement. When and how does the capacity for altruistic action emerge in the normal course of development? And how does it change during the course of childhood? In this section, the research evidence is examined for answers to these questions.

Developmental Trends

We begin by considering the following report from a longitudinal study conducted by Radke-Yarrow and Zahn-Waxler (see Radke-Yarrow, Zahn-Waxler & Chapman, 1983):

> . . . a child at 12 months, when confronted with a peer's cries, responds with a primitive distress cry of her own and turns to her mother to be nestled and stroked. A few weeks later, when her mother has scalded her hand, the child cries, nestles into her mother but also hugs her mother—now giving some comfort as well as getting comfort. At 17 months, in the presence of a crying baby, her expression is concerned and tearful, but she strokes the baby's head, hugs and pats him, offers toys, and finally tries to bring her mother to the rescue (p. 32).

This account of one child's development over a period of only a few months is interesting in a number of different ways (compare, also, a similar incident described by Hoffman, 1975, page 612). Radke-Yarrow and her colleagues do not provide us with this little girl's name, but let us call her Jessica. At 12 months, Jessica cries in response to the cries of a peer. She does not seem to differentiate herself from the other, and perhaps is therefore unable to offer comfort to the other child. Within a few weeks, however, she manages to combine her own desire for comfort upon noticing her mother's distress, with the possibility of offering her mother a hug as well. By the age of 17 months, Jessica is able to differentiate her own concern from that of the baby, and manages both to conceive and to carry out at least four different strategies to calm the baby's distress.

Of course, no brief excerpt can offer us all of the information that we might like, and the interpretation of this one is certainly open to question. Even granting that Jessica's behavior at 17 months appears intentional, we may still remain uncertain about her motives. Was her main aim to reduce the baby's distress? Or was her principal concern rather to eliminate unpleasant auditory stimulation from her own environment? Answers to these questions are by no means clear. On the basis of the information contained in this excerpt, however, many of us would probably be inclined to label 17-month-old Jessica's actions toward the baby as altruistic.

How is it possible that a child as young as 17 months could manage the complex cognitive tasks, upon the mastery of which we have said that altruistic action depends? The achievement is enormous, and nothing should detract from our amazement that such a young child should prove able to make it. This being said, however, it is also worth noting several factors which combine to make Jessica's situation seem particularly favorable. First, her mother (who made the observation) was present; Jessica's own level of psychological comfort or security was therefore probably relatively high when the baby began to cry (cf.

Lamb, in this volume). Second, it seems likely, given what we know of toddlers' lives, that the crying baby was a familiar person, perhaps even a sibling. Third, the other's distress was very clearly signaled by the baby's apparently loud and persistent crying. Finally, the kinds of actions needed in order to implement an altruistic intention (e.g., making physical contact, offering toys) were familiar and well-practiced elements of Jessica's pre-existing behavioral repertoire.

Although all four of these factors are probably relevant to the 17-month-old's ability to undertake altruistic action, I focus here on research which bears on the last two only. The available evidence clearly suggests developmental trends in both children's ability to identify cues of distress in other people, and in the size and complexity of the behavioral repertoires available to them for responding to any perceived needs for altruistic action. I first describe some of the research findings on infants and very young children, and then turn to the evidence relevant to preschool and elementary school children.

Negative responding to certain very clear signs of another's distress seems to be present essentially from birth. Simner (1971), as well as Sagi and Hoffman (1976) have reported that the vocal properties of another baby's cries seem to promote crying in newborn infants. In the Simner (1971) study, for example, infants were more likely to cry when they heard a tape recording of another newborn's cry than when they heard white noise, or no noise, or indeed, a computer simulation of a newborn's cry. We are, of course, not likely on this basis to credit the newborn with a capacity for altruistic action. Reports such as these do, however, provide evidence of a particular sensitivity to signs of distress in others very early in life.

Similar accounts of older infants' and toddlers' distress in response to crying in peers also exist. Hay, Nash, and Pederson (1981) failed to find moment-to-moment correspondence between the crying patterns of 6-month-old playmates, but did report evidence that one infant's crying had cumulative effects on a peer of the same age. Especially when there were no potentially distracting toys available in the infants' environment, the conditional probability of one infant's crying, given that the other had been crying, increased dramatically over intervals of time as short as 30 seconds. Crying in response to the distress of a peer has also been reported among 1- and 2-year-olds (Radke-Yarrow et al., 1983).

There is also evidence that infants can discriminate among a variety of different facial expressions (see Bornstein, in this volume). For example, Buhler and Hetzer (1928; cited in Radke-Yarrow et al., 1983) found that infants are able to discriminate angry and smiling faces by the age of about six or seven months. These reports have been confirmed by La Barbera, Izard, Vietze and Parisi (1976), as well as by Wilcox and Clayton (1968). Cohn and Tronick (1983) have recently reported that 3-month-olds respond differently when their mothers show depressed, as opposed to normal affect. Studies of early language use offer convergent evidence on this point; soon after children learn to speak, their utterances seem to reflect comprehension of the meanings of various facial expressions such as those associated with sadness (Bretherton, McNew & Beeghly-Smith, 1981; Bretherton & Beeghly, 1982).

By the age of two, then, most children must be capable of discriminating and responding to a variety of relatively clear expressions of distress in the people around them. A marked tendency to react with distress to the cries of others appears much earlier. To the extent that this kind of responsiveness can be taken as evidence for the existence of an empathic predisposition, the available evidence suggests that such a predisposition is either present very early in life, or develops quite rapidly during the first several months.

A limited repertoire of cooperative and other prosocial behaviors also seems to be well-established by the end of infancy. For example, Hay (1979) studied early forms of cooperation and sharing among 12-, 18-, and 24-month-olds as they played in the presence of their parents. At 12 months, almost every child was observed to show objects to others, and half also gave objects to parents during play. At 18 months, all the children both showed and gave toys. Rheingold, Hay, and West (1976) studied 15- to 18-month-olds in similar situations; they reported that all babies demonstrated forms of prosocial behavior, such as the giving and showing of objects, and that most shared not only with their parents, but also with unfamiliar adults. Similar observations of early sharing and cooperative behavior have also been made by others (Eckerman, Whatley & Kutz, 1975; Lamb, 1978; Ross & Goldman, 1977).

A particularly interesting study in this vein was reported by Rheingold (1982). Children at 18, 24, and 30 months were observed while their parents or other adults carried out a number of common household chores (e.g., folding laundry, sweeping, setting a table). In spite of the fact that the adults did not ask for assistance, all of the children did in fact offer help. Sixty-five percent of the 18-month-olds, 95% of the 24-month-olds, and all of the 30-month-olds helped on more than half of the tasks their parents performed. Thus, not only did the majority of children participate in their parents' work, most offered assistance on the majority of tasks. Almost all of the children also participated in the work performed by unfamiliar adults. While the children sometimes imitated their parents' behavior, they also went beyond simple imitation in their efforts to complete tasks (e.g., by placing bits of paper onto a dustpan by hand when they were not able to do this using a broom).

One intriguing aspect of Rheingold's (1982) findings was that the children's efforts were sometimes accompanied by their utterance of intention statements (e.g., "fold clothes"; "I'm going to pick up these books") and/or by their signaling verbally when a task had been completed (e.g., "all clean"; "I'm all through with my little broom"). The frequency of these utterances increased with the age of the child, but even the 18-month-olds offered some remarks of this sort. As Rheingold (1982) notes, verbalizations like these do not prove that the children intended to be helpful. They are interesting, however, because they seem to provide evidence of the children's awareness of their contributions to the completion of joint tasks, and because they therefore raise at least the possibility that these children's activities may not have been merely prosocial, but altruistic as well.

In a longitudinal study, Radke-Yarrow and Zahn-Waxler (in press) trained mothers to record instances of their children's prosocial behavior over a period of 9 months. On the basis of the mothers' observations, Radke-Yarrow and Zahn-Waxler reported that, even by 10 to 12 months, children responded with some regularity to evidence of distress in others. The most frequent response at this age was "a frown, a sad face, cries, and/or visual checking with the caregiver" (Radke-Yarrow et al., 1983, page 30). By 18 to 24 months, children's responses often included physical contact and positive initiations to the distressed person. By the age of two, children began to bring objects to the individual in distress, verbalize sympathy, make suggestions, and bring somebody else to help. They also began to try alternative strategies if an initial attempt at providing comfort failed. Not all of the children's responses were positive or prosocial in nature; in a small minority of instances, children attempted to avoid, escape, or even attack a person in distress. Overall, although the results do not permit unambiguous interpretation in terms of altruism, they are at least consistent with the idea that there is a substantial expansion during the second year in children's repertoires for prosocial behavior.

By the age of three, then, most children seem able to discriminate and comprehend some of the major expressions of negative emotion in others and to respond to them in a variety of appropriate ways. They also seem, at least sometimes, to be motivated to share, to reduce the distress, and to participate in the activities of the people around them. Further, they are often capable of doing these things. We turn now to the further developments that take place as children grow older.

One such area of development involves children's ability to recognize relatively subtle cues of another person's distress. In a study by Pearl (1979), 4- and 8-year-olds were exposed to videotaped scenes in which a child had difficulty in performing a task. When cues to the actor's distress were highly salient and explicit, younger children were as likely to recognize distress as older children. When the cues were more subtle, however, young children were less likely to infer sadness or frustration, whereas older children continued to do so. In their longitudinal study of children from 2 to 7 years of age, Radke-Yarrow and Zahn-Waxler (in press) also found that older children seemed responsive to a wider range of cues to distress. When one considers the variety of subtle and often indirect ways in which both children and adults may signal distress, it seems likely that we still have much to learn about the development of the ability to recognize these signals.

It has often been suggested that, throughout the preschool and elementary school years, the frequency of prosocial behavior increases with age (see, for example, Bryan, 1975, pages 163–165). As Radke-Yarrow and her colleagues

(1983) have suggested, however, this proposition is in need of close scrutiny. Although, as we have already seen, there is evidence for increases in the frequency of prosocial behavior during early childhood, no such simple trend seems to characterize changes during the middle or later years of childhood. After reviewing the results of over 75 different studies, Radke-Yarrow and her colleagues concluded that "the data from existing research do not support a simple unidirectional trend" (1983, page 42). As these authors have pointed out, when one considers the enormous array of diverse activities that might be included under the rubric of prosocial behavior, particularly for older children, this conclusion should perhaps not seem surprising.

Although the actual frequency of prosocial behavior probably does not increase during middle and later childhood, there is some evidence that the size and adequacy of children's repertoires of skills for prosocial action does expand. A fascinating glimpse of the possibilities here is provided in a study by Burleson (1982). In this study, first- through twelfth-graders were asked to respond to hypothetical situations in which a same-sex peer was experiencing distress; each child was asked to describe all of the ways in which he or she might be able to offer comfort in each of four different situations. The main findings were that the size and diversity of children's repertoires of comforting strategies grew with age, and that the rated quality of the strategies they suggested improved with age also. For instance, first graders were more likely to suggest strategies that involved denial of the feelings of the distressed other, whereas older children more often sought to acknowledge and to legitimize the peer's perspective. Thus, Burleson's results suggest that, at least in the domain of verbal comforting skills, children's repertoires for altruistic action do increase with age.

In summary, the evidence reviewed suggests that the predisposition to react negatively to clear signs of others' distress exists very early in life, that the ability to conceive and carry out altruistic actions may emerge at some time during the second year, and that the frequency and variety of prosocial behavior increases after that time up until the age of about 3 or 4 years. Although prosocial behavior does not seem to increase in frequency after the age of about 4 years, there is some evidence suggesting that the ability to recognize cues of distress improves and that the repertoire of behavioral strategies for accomplishing altruistic aims expands during the course of middle and later childhood. What factors might explain these trends?

Underlying Factors

A number of hypotheses about possible factors underlying the observed trends have been advanced. These include explanations based on concepts as diverse as guilt, intelligence, perspective-taking skill, and empathy. Although there has been little systematic research on the first two topics, a considerable body of data has accumulated with respect to the latter two concepts (see, for example, detailed reviews by Kurdek, 1978; Radke-Yarrow et al., 1983). A substantial amount of research has also been directed to the relationship between children's reasoning about and actual performance of prosocial behavior (see Eisenberg, 1982, for a detailed review).

Although no investigator has suggested that any unidimensional explanation can account for the full range of developmental phenomena in this area, empirical studies often tend to focus on the relationships between children's prosocial behavior and one or two measures of an explanatory concept of interest. The specific measures of both prosocial behavior itself and the constructs entertained as possible mediators of this behavior vary widely among studies. It is perhaps for this reason that research findings are often disparate and difficult to evaluate.

As an example, consider the research on relationships between perspective-taking skill and prosocial behavior. The principal prediction here is that improvements in the ability to appreciate others' perspectives should be associated with increased tendencies to act in a prosocial manner. Measures of perspective-taking have included social, affective, cognitive, and perceptual tasks; measures of prosocial behavior have typically assessed either sharing or helping, but these have, of course, been defined differently in different studies. Some investigators have found the expected positive relationships (e.g., Krebs & Sturrup, 1974; Rubin & Schneider, 1973); others have not (e.g., Eisenberg-Berg & Lennon, 1980; Emler & Rushton, 1974). Some findings have been mixed (Iannotti, 1978; Rothenberg, 1970). The situation with regard to research on empathy and children's prosocial behavior is very similar (see Radke-Yarrow et al., 1983). On the basis of the existing evidence, definitive conclusions on these issues do not seem warranted.

Although research on the role of perspective taking and empathy has not yet proven conclusive, studies of children's conceptions of and reasoning about prosocial behavior have been illuminating. In particular, studies have examined children's reasoning about their own prosocial behavior, as well as their conceptions about the behavior of their peers. We briefly consider some of the results of this research.

A number of investigators (e.g., Dreman & Greenbaum, 1973; Eisenberg-Berg & Neal, 1979; Ugurel-Semin, 1952) have asked children to explain the reasons for their own prosocial behavior. The general finding has been that when children are questioned about their motives for particular prosocial behaviors, such as instances of sharing or helping, they are most likely to explain them by referring to what might be called sociocentric intentions. Although young children also give reasons based on pragmatic considerations (e.g., their own qualifications as helpers), even among preschoolers explanations that focus on the needs of other people are among the most common responses. Reasoning that focuses on altruistic motives for prosocial behavior increases in frequency with age (Eisenberg, 1982; Ugurel-Semin, 1952).

Notably absent from the reasoning of even the youngest children tested in this research (viz., 4-year-olds) are explanations of their own prosocial behavior by reference to the demands of authority figures or to the desire to avoid punishment. This latter finding is particularly interesting in light of the prevalence of authority- and punishment-oriented reasoning in young children's responses to questions about moral transgressions (see Hoffman, in this volume). When young children are asked their reasons for avoiding transgressions, they often focus on manifestly selfish motives (e.g., the desire to avoid punishment); when they are asked their reasons for performing prosocial behavior such as sharing, on the other hand, they often focus on apparently altruistic intentions (e.g., the desire to satisfy another's needs). In short, the interpretations of their own prosocial behavior offered even by preschool children are often made in terms of what seem to be altruistic motives.

Eisenberg-Berg and her colleagues have also investigated the development of reasoning about prosocial behavior in the context of hypothetical dilemmas (e.g., Eisenberg-Berg, 1979; Eisenberg-Berg & Hand, 1979; Eisenberg-Berg & Roth, 1980). For example, Eisenberg-Berg and Hand (1979) found that preschoolers used principally hedonistic (i.e., selfish) and needs-oriented (i.e., altruistic) reasoning when explaining their choices in hypothetical prosocial moral conflicts. When the same children were re-tested 18 months later, they demonstrated more needs-oriented and less hedonistic reasoning (Eisenberg-Berg & Roth, 1980). Older children show continuing decreases in immature forms of reasoning, such as hedonistic reasoning, and increases in more mature (e.g., abstract and/or internalized) forms (Eisenberg, 1982; Eisenberg-Berg, 1979).

The relationships between prosocial moral reasoning on hypothetical dilemmas and prosocial behavior among young children have also been studied. Eisenberg-Berg and Hand (1979) found that 4-year-olds' frequency of sharing with other children in their nursery school was positively related to the incidence of needs-oriented reasoning, and negatively related to the incidence of hedonistic reasoning that they demonstrated in response to prosocial moral dilemmas. Examining this general relationship in more detail, the authors discovered that it was attributable to the correlations between children's reasoning and their spontaneous sharing in the nursery school environment; children's sharing in response to requests from their peers was unrelated to their reasoning on the prosocial dilemmas. As Eisenberg-Berg and Hand (1979, page 361) have noted, these findings "are consistent with the conclusion that sharing in response to a request may be motivated by less altruistic considerations than is spontaneous sharing." Thus, as these authors suggested, the results of this research serve to emphasize that it is "important to consider the motivations underlying behaviors that superficially appear to involve altruism."

Finally, there has also been some research on the development of children's attributions of kindness in the behavior of others (see Eisenberg, 1982, for a review). The most interesting finding here has been that, when judging the kindness of another person's actions, young children (e.g., kindergartners) do not seem to discriminate between intentional and unintentional behavior. By second grade, however, this distinction is crucial to children's attributions of kindness (Baldwin & Baldwin, 1970). When these results are considered along with Smith's (1978) finding that young children regard a much wider array of behaviors as intentional than do older children or adults, they again serve to underscore the way in which children's understanding of intentionality can affect their interpretations of prosocial behavior.

The overall yield of research on factors underlying developmental trends in children's prosocial behavior, and in children's interpretation of the prosocial behavior of others, has been uneven. Although there has been a great deal of research in some areas, and much less in others, the strength of the conclusions that seem to be warranted in any particular area bears little relation to the amount of research. The clearest findings show that even young children frequently offer interpretations of their own prosocial behavior in terms of motives that might be considered altruistic, that there are reliable developmental trends in reasoning about prosocial behavior, and that these trends appear to be related to children's actual behavior. It also seems to be true that, in comparison with older children and adults, young children may often over-attribute altruistic intentions in the prosocial behavior of others.

Summary

The results of research on the emergence and development of altruistic action suggest a number of interrelated conclusions (cf., Hoffman, 1975). First, the predisposition to react negatively to clear signs of another's distress appears to exist very early in infancy. It seems reasonable to assume that such a predisposition might give rise to altruistic aims quite early in life, and the available data, although still very scanty, are consistent with this view; the earliest manifestations of truly altruistic actions seem to emerge at some point during the second year. At this time, children's ability to separate their own from another's distress become sufficient to allow them to generate responses that might be expected to reduce the other's distress. As one might expect, however, the 2-year-old's repertoire for altruistic action remains quite limited.

The frequency and variety of prosocial behavior seem to increase up until the age of about 3 or 4 years. After that time, significant developments take place both in the ability to recognize relatively subtle cues of distress in others, and in the size of children's behavioral repertoires for responding to such distress, but not, apparently, in the actual frequency with which children exhibit prosocial behavior. Whether the frequency of altruistic action per se changes during this period cannot be determined on the basis of available evidence. The data do, however, suggest that there are significant changes in children's reasoning about prosocial episodes with age and that these are related to children's actual performance of prosocial behavior.

AGGRESSION, ALTRUISM, AND SELF-REGULATION IN CHILDHOOD

Having reviewed some of the research evidence on the development of aggression and altruism in childhood, we return to the consideration of both aggressive and altruistic action in the context of children's efforts to achieve self-regulation. As has already been said, self-regulation entails the successful achievement of personally selected aims or goals. As such, efforts to achieve self-regulation presuppose the existence of at least one goal or intention to be realized through action, and they involve the selection, from an available repertoire, of those actions which are expected to result in achievement of that goal. Thus, both the emergence of the aims themselves and the creation of a repertoire of strategies for achieving these aims are important aspects of the development of self-regulation. Let us consider the development of aggression and altruism in these terms.

In developmental terms, the emergence of truly aggressive or altruistic aims is an important milestone. Although these intentions seem to appear very early in childhood, they nevertheless depend upon a number of cognitive achievements. Some of the cognitive prerequisites for the emergence of aggressive or altruistic action seem to be knowledge that the self can be differentiated from others, that other people can be hurt or helped, that particular kinds of conditions or events are particularly likely to hurt or help them, and that one's own behavior can bring about these conditions or events. Thus, the first appearance of a truly aggressive or altruistic action presupposes the accomplishment of a number of sophisticated cognitive tasks; hence, it is an event of real developmental significance.

Having conceived an aggressive or an altruistic intention, a child immediately faces the problem of translating it into action. We have seen evidence of the growth of children's repertoires in this regard, both in the area of aggression (e.g., the increasing use of verbal skills in aggressive encounters among older children) and in the area of altruism (e.g., the development of the skills involved in comforting another person who is distressed). Growth in the size and accessibility of children's repertoires for aggressive and altruistic action is a major accomplishment of the childhood period.

Thus, both the emergence of aggressive and altruistic intentions and the creation of a repertoire of strategies for the implementation of these intentions in action are important aspects of the development of aggression and altruism during the childhood years. It is perhaps tempting to imagine that this is all that is involved in the development of aggressive and altruistic action in childhood. To do so, however, would be a mistake, for if we stop here, we may overlook one of the most interesting aspects of the topic—the role of self-control. Before examining the contribution of self-control to changes in children's aggression and altruism with age, however, we need to pause briefly in order to consider, from a more general perspective, the relationship between self-control and self-regulation.

It has been suggested that self-regulation involves the successful achievement of personally selected aims and goals, and that this means that the domain of self-regulation is essentially coterminous with the realm of effective, intentional action. What is perhaps most surprising about this realm is how many of our day-to-day activities it encompasses. In our normal, everyday lives as adults, for example, we go to bed at the hours of our own choosing at night, and arise at the times we deem appropriate in the morning; we dress ourselves, feed ourselves, and prepare ourselves for the anticipated events of the day. All of these activities, and countless others like them, however conventional or habitual they may have become, are done to realize personal intentions, and most often they are done successfully. What is first of all remarkable, then, is how effective our attempts at self-regulation normally seem to be, and how little effort they normally seem to require. Self-regulation is so ordinary that most of the time we scarcely even notice that it is taking place.

There are times, however, when something seems to go wrong. I find that I do not feel sleepy at the hour I have chosen as my bedtime, or that I am not ready to arise when my alarm rings in the morning. The clothes I had planned to wear turn out to be wrinkled or spotted; my favorite breakfast foods are missing from the refrigerator. At times such as these, the achievement of a goal is blocked, or the realization of one goal interferes with the achievement of another; effective self-regulation is challenged. A problem emerges and the need for ''self-control'' becomes evident. It is a breakdown, or the threat of a breakdown, in the normal stream of self-regulated behavior that makes what we call self-control seem necessary. Perhaps it is the very infrequency with which such problems arise that makes them seem so noticeable, so extraordinary, when they do.

Thus, one might think of self-control as the ''figure'' and self-regulation as the ''ground'' of voluntary activity. The need for self-control emerges only against a background of voluntary activity because it is only out of attempts to achieve personal goals that the possibility of failure in doing so could arise. It is only in the context of the belief that I normally, or at least sometimes, am in control of my actions that the possibility that I am not could seem problematic or threatening, or indeed have any meaning at all. It is only my normal ability to fit my actions easily to self-articulated intentions or rules that makes it seem remarkable when special efforts become necessary. Hence, the emergence of self-control as an issue—the very possibility of taking ''extraordinary'' measures to make my actions fit with pre-established intentions or rules—depends on the ''ordinary'' ability to do so almost without thinking. One might say, then, that the problem of self-control rests on the assumption of self-regulation.

How, then, do problems of self-control arise in the context of children's aggressive and altruistic actions? One sort of threat to self-regulation occurs when a child wants to achieve a particular goal but does not know how to go about it. For instance, as has already been mentioned, a young child who wants to comfort a distressed adult may not have a repertoire of comforting skills that is adequate to the task. Threats to self-regulation can also stem from a situation in which the achievement of one aim is seen as interfering with the accomplishment of another. A child may want to achieve certain instrumental goals, such as the possession of desirable toys, may have available only physically violent methods with which to achieve these goals, and yet want also to maintain harmonious relations with peers. As other children tend to dislike peers who are considered aggressive (Dodge, 1980; Dodge & Frame, 1982), the child in this position may experience a conflict between attempts to achieve instrumental goals on the one hand, and efforts to accomplish social goals on the other. Let us examine this possibility more closely.

As Maccoby (1980, page 149) has emphasized, physical violence "carries a high cost; it is painful to the aggressor, and it jeopardizes continued social contact." Thus, children who use violence to achieve their instrumental (e.g., non-hostile) aims do so at the risk of being disliked and so avoided by their victims. To the extent that these victims are part of the fabric of everyday life, the price of aggression for these children is ultimately the risk of severing social connections with the people around them. Since this is, of course, a very high price to pay, the recognition of a conflict between the use of violence to accomplish one's instrumental goals and the possibility of simultaneously achieving highly valued social goals might be expected to trigger a search for alternatives to violence. The recognition of a problem in self-regulation, in other words, might be expected to result in efforts at self-control. The developmental trends that characterize the period of early childhood, as we have seen, are consistent with the idea that most children arrive at something very much like this kind of recognition during this period.

What is important to notice here is that recognition of conflicts can pave the way for discovery of solutions. Until children become aware of a problem, they are not likely to make efforts to solve it. It is the recognition of a threat to self-regulation that gives rise to efforts at self-control; it is the recognition of the difficulty in coordinating the simultaneous pursuit of more than one goal that gives rise to problem-solving attempts, and ultimately to the discovery of non-violent methods of achieving instrumental aims. Thus, beginning to recognize conflicts of this kind is an important developmental step.

The recognition of conflicts between various goals requires that more than one goal be kept in mind at the same time, and this may be very difficult for the young child. As long as a child focuses attention on any one goal to the exclusion of others, conflicts arising in the coordination of goals will not be recognized. As we know from studies of cognitive development (see Kuhn, in this volume), there is enormous improvement during the early and middle childhood years in the ability to keep more than one concept in mind simultaneously. Thus, it is perhaps no coincidence that children's ability to limit their use of violence to the pursuit of aggressive aims expands dramatically during these years.

For a young child to notice and respond appropriately to conflicts among his or her various social and instrumental aims is a difficult cognitive achievement.

Because the task is so demanding, it is reasonable to assume that it might not be undertaken at all—much less, successfully—unless the conditions are relatively favorable. What circumstances might be expected to make this kind of task more or less accessible to a child?

As physical violence is a readily available aspect of the young child's behavioral repertoire (Shure, 1982), and as overlearned responses are more likely than novel ones to be produced under stressful conditions, we might expect that in stressful circumstances, violent strategies would be the first to come to a child's mind. Certainly, the available evidence suggests this is the case throughout early childhood (Shure, 1982; Spivack, Platt & Shure, 1976). Under conditions of lower stress, however, a child might well be able to delve deeper into his or her repertoire of behavioral strategies, and to find more adaptive solutions to interpersonal problems. Thus, we might expect that, other things being equal, young children in particular would exhibit more violent, antisocial behavior under conditions that are highly stressful, and that they might exhibit more prosocial behavior in circumstances of greater psychological comfort or security.

Evidence from a variety of sources would seem to be consistent with this view. During the toddler period, one factor that contributes to a child's feelings of psychological comfort is the quality or security of that child's relationship with the mother or other principal caregiver (Ainsworth, Blehar, Waters & Wall, 1978; Bowlby, 1969). Thus, it is not surprising that toddlers who have secure relationships with their mothers are found to be more cooperative with their peers (Easterbrooks & Lamb, 1979; Matas, Arend & Sroufe, 1978), and are more likely to initiate positive interaction with unfamiliar adults (Main & Weston, 1981). A child's emotional state or mood is also an important indicator of psychological comfort, and so it makes sense that children who are rated as happier overall seem to exhibit more prosocial behavior than those who are not (Strayer, 1980). Similarly, children who are momentarily induced into a positive or happy frame of mind are more likely to behave in prosocial ways than those who are put into negative or sad frames of mind (Moore, Underwood & Rosenhan, 1973; Underwood, Froming & Moore, 1977). We can summarize these findings by saying that, as one might expect, conditions of psychological comfort or security seem to facilitate children's production of prosocial behavior.

In childhood, then, we learn that antisocial behavior carries a high price, and that, when our capacity for self-regulation is threatened, violence should be our instrument of last resort. The result should be that for older children, as for adults, aggression arises mainly out of insecurity—when our capacity for self-regulation is threatened most severely—and that altruism arises out of security—when our capacity for self-regulation seems most assured. There is, of course, little doubt that, in this case, as in so many others, the external conditions of our lives exert substantial influence over our psychological states.

It is important, however, to realize that it is not just external events or conditions in themselves that create psychological states of security or insecurity in us, but also our *interpretations* of these events or conditions. Most of us, for example, will not donate our last dollar to a charitable cause, because we fear that if we do, we may then be unable to satisfy our own basic needs. Some people, however, will—and do—give their last dollar to charity (see, for example, Kumin, 1983). On the other hand, there are also relatively wealthy people who nevertheless remain concerned about their financial security, and do not donate to charities at all. It is not only the objective conditions of wealth or poverty, then, that determine or cause altruistic actions in these cases, or in others like them. It is also the interpretations that we make, which result in the rules that we follow, which in turn generate what prediction of our actions is possible. Thus, in seeking to understand the development of aggression and altruism, we need to concern ourselves not only with a search for objective causes of behavior, but also with a study of subjective rules of interpretation, and of their applications in action.

REFERENCES

Ainsworth, M. D. S., Blehar, M., Waters, E., & Wall, S. *Patterns of attachment*. Hillsdale, N.J.: Lawrence Erlbaum Associates, 1978.

Anscombe, G. E. M. *Intention*. Ithaca, NY: Cornell University Press, 1957.

Baldwin, A., & Baldwin, C. Children's judgments of kindness. *Child Development*, 1970, *41*, 29–47.

Bandura, A. *Aggression: A social learning analysis*. New York: Holt, Rinehart & Winston, 1973.

Bandura, A. *Social learning theory*. Englewood Cliffs, N.J.: Prentice-Hall, 1977.

Baron, R. A. *Human aggression*. New York: Plenum Press, 1977.

Berkowitz, L. *Aggression: A social-psychological analysis*. New York: McGraw-Hill, 1962.

Bowlby, J. *Attachment and loss, Volume 1: Attachment*. New York: Basic Books, 1969.

Bretherton, I., & Beeghly, M. Talking about internal states: The acquisition of an explicit theory of mind. *Developmental Psychology*, 1982, *18*, 906–921.

Bretherton, I., McNew, S., & Beeghly-Smith, M. Early person knowledge as expressed in gestural and verbal communications: When do infants acquire a 'theory of mind'? In M. E. Lamb & L. R. Sherrod, Eds., *Infant social cognition*. Hillsdale, N.J.: Lawrence Erlbaum Associates, 1981.

Bronson, W. C. Developments in behavior with age mates during the second year of life. In M. Lewis & L. A. Rosenblum (Eds.), *The origins of behavior: Friendship and peer relations*. New York: Wiley, 1975.

Bryan, J. H. Children's cooperation and helping behaviors. In E. M. Hetherington (Ed.), *Review of child development research* (Vol. 5). Chicago: University of Chicago Press, 1975.

Burleson, B. R. The development of comforting communication skills in childhood and adolescence. *Child Development*, 1982, *53*, 1578–1588.

Camras, L. A. Facial expressions used by children in a conflict situation. *Child Development*, 1977, *48*, 1431–1435.

Camras, L. A. Children's understanding of facial expressions used during conflict encounters. *Child Development*, 1980, *51*, 879–885.

Cavell, S. *Must we mean what we say?* Cambridge, England: Cambridge University Press, 1976.

Cavell, S. *The claim of reason: Wittgenstein, skepticism, morality, and tragedy*. New York: Oxford University Press, 1979.

Cohn, J. F., & Tronick, E. Z. Three-month-old infants' reaction to simulated maternal depression. *Child Development*, 1983, *54*, 185–193.

Dawe, H. C. An analysis of two hundred quarrels of preschool children. *Child Development*, 1934, *5*, 139–157.

Dodge, K. A. Social cognition and children's aggressive behavior. *Child Development*, 1980, *51*, 162–170.

Dodge, K. A., & Frame, C. L. Social cognitive biases and deficits in aggressive boys. *Child Development*, 1982, *53*, 620–635.

Dodge, K. A., & Newman, J. P. Biased decision-making processes in aggressive boys. *Journal of Abnormal Psychology*, 1981, *90*, 375–379.

Dreman, S. B., & Greenbaum, C. W. Altruism or reciprocity: Sharing behavior in Israeli kindergarten children. *Child Development*, 1973, *44*, 61–68.

Easterbrooks, M. A., & Lamb, M. E. The relationship between quality of infant–mother attachment and infant competence in initial encounters with peers. *Child Development*, 1979, *50*, 380–387.

Eckerman, C. O., Whatley, J. L., & Kutz, S. L. Growth of social play with peers during the second year of life. *Developmental Psychology*, 1975, *11*, 42–49.

Eisenberg, N. The development of reasoning regarding prosocial behavior. In N. Eisenberg (Ed.), *The development of prosocial behavior*. New York: Academic Press, 1982.

Eisenberg-Berg, N. Development of children's prosocial moral judgment. *Developmental Psychology*, 1979, *15*, 128–137.

Eisenberg-Berg, N., & Hand, M. The relationship of preschoolers' reasoning about prosocial moral conflicts to prosocial behavior. *Child Development*, 1979, *50* 356–363.

Eisenberg-Berg, N., & Lennon, R. Altruism and the assessment of empathy in the preschool years. *Child Development*, 1980, *51*, 552–557.

Eisenberg-Berg, N., & Neal, C. Children's moral reasoning about their own spontaneous prosocial behavior. *Developmental Psychology*, 1979, *15*, 228–229.

Eisenberg-Berg, N., & Roth, K. Development of young children's prosocial moral judgment: A longitudinal follow-up. *Developmental Psychology*, 1980, *16*, 375–376.

Emler, N. P., & Rushton, J. P. Cognitive-developmental factors in children's generosity. *British Journal of Sociology and Clinical Psychology*, 1974, *13*, 277–281.

Ferguson, T. J., & Rule, B. G. Effects of inferential set, outcome severity, and basis of responsibility on children's evaluations of aggressive acts. *Developmental Psychology*, 1980, *16*, 141–146.

Goodenough, F. L. *Anger in young children*. Minneapolis: University of Minnesota Press, 1931.

Hartup, W. W. Aggression in childhood: Developmental perspectives. *American Psychologist*, 1974, *29*, 336–341.

Hartup, W. W., & DeWit, J. *Determinants and origins of aggressive behavior*. The Hague: Mouton, 1974.

Hay, D. F. Cooperative interactions and sharing between very young children and their parents. *Developmental Psychology*, 1979, *15*, 647–653.

Hay, D. F., Nash, A., & Pederson, J. Responses of six-month-olds to the distress of their peers. *Child Development*, 1981, *52*, 1071–1075.

Hay, D. F., & Ross, H. S. The social nature of early conflict. *Child Development*, 1982, *53*, 105–113.

Hoffman, M. L. Developmental synthesis of affect and cognition and its implications for altruistic motivation. *Developmental Psychology*, 1975, *11*, 607–622.

Iannotti, R. J. Effect of role-taking experiences on role-taking, empathy, altruism, and aggression. *Developmental Psychology*, 1978, *14*, 119–124.

Krebs, D., & Sturrup, B. Role-taking ability and altruistic behavior in elementary school children. *Personality and Social Psychology Bulletin*, 1974, *1*, 407–409.

Kumin, M. Carla: "It's very hard to say I'm poor." *The Nation*, May 7, 1983, 559, 575–577.

Kurdek, L. A. Perspective-taking as the cognitive basis of children's moral development. *Merrill-Palmer Quarterly*, 1978, *24*, 3–28.

La Barbera, J. D., Izard, C. E., Vietze, P., & Parisi, S. A. Four- and six-month-old infants' visual responses to joy, anger, and neutral expressions. *Child Development,* 1976, *47,* 535–538.

Lamb, M. E. The development of sibling relationships in infancy: A short-term longitudinal study. *Child Development,* 1978, *49,* 1189–1196.

Levine, L. E. Mine: Self-definition in 2-year-old boys. *Developmental Psychology,* 1983, *19,* 544–549.

Maccoby, E. E. *Social development: Psychological growth and the parent-child relationship.* New York: Harcourt Brace Jovanovich 1980.

MacIntyre, A. *A short history of ethics.* New York: Macmillan, 1966.

Main, M., & Weston, D. R. The quality of the toddler's relationship to mother and to father: Related to conflict behavior and the readiness to establish new relationships. *Child Development,* 1981, *52,* 932–940.

Matas, L., Arend, R. A., & Sroufe, L. A. Continuity of adaptation in the second year: The relationship between quality of attachment and later competence. *Child Development,* 1978, *49,* 547–556.

Maudry, M., & Nekula, M. Social relations between children of the same age during the first two years of life. *Journal of Genetic Psychology,* 1939, *54,* 193–215.

Moore, B. S., Underwood, B., & Rosenhan, D. L. Affect and altruism. *Developmental Psychology,* 1973, *8,* 99–104.

Mussen, P., & Eisenberg-Berg, N. *Roots of caring, sharing, and helping: The development of prosocial behavior in children.* San Francisco: W. H. Freeman and Company, 1977.

Nasby, W., Hayden, B., & DePaulo, B. M. Attributional bias among aggressive boys to interpret unambiguous social stimuli as displays of hostility. *Journal of Abnormal Psychology,* 1980, *89,* 459–468.

Parke, R. D., & Slaby, R. G. The development of aggression. In E. M. Hetherington (Ed.), *Carmichael's manual of child psychology, Volume IV.* New York: Wiley, 1983.

Patterson, C. J. Self-control and self-regulation in childhood. In T. M. Field, A. Huston, H. C. Quay, L. Troll, & G. E. Finley (Eds.), *Review of human development.* New York: Wiley, 1982.

Patterson, G. R., Littman, R. A., & Bricker, W. Assertive behavior in children: A step toward a theory of aggression. *Monographs of the Society for Research in Child Development,* 1967, *32* (Serial No. 113).

Pearl, R. A. *Developmental and situational influences on children's understanding of prosocial behavior.* Paper given at the biennial meetings of the Society for Research in Child Development, San Francisco, 1979.

Piaget, J. *The origins of intelligence in children.* New York: International Universities Press, 1952.

Radke-Yarrow, M., & Zahn-Waxler, C. Roots, motives, and patterns in children's prosocial behavior. In J. Reykowski, J. Karylowski, D. Bar-Tal, & E. Staub, (Eds.), *Origins and maintenance of prosocial behaviors.* New York: Plenum Press, in press.

Radke-Yarrow, M., Zahn-Waxler, C., & Chapman, M. Children's prosocial dispositions and behavior. In P. H. Mussen (Ed.), *Carmichael's manual of child psychology* (Vol. IV, 4th ed.). New York: Wiley, 1983.

Rheingold, H. L. Little children's participation in the work of adults, a nascent prosocial behavior. *Child Development,* 1982, *53,* 114–125.

Rheingold, H. L., Hay, D. F., & West, M. J. Sharing in the second year of life. *Child Development,* 1976, *47,* 1148–1158.

Ross, H. S., & Goldman, B. D. Establishing new social relations in infancy. In T. Alloway, L. Kramer, & P. Pliner (Eds.), *Advances in the study of communication and affect (Vol. 3): Attachment behavior.* New York: Plenum Press, 1977.

Rothenberg, B. B. Children's social sensitivity and the relationship to interpersonal competence, intrapersonal comfort, and intellectual level. *Developmental Psychology,* 1970, *2,* 335–350.

Rubin, K. H., & Schneider, F. W. The relationship between moral judgment, egocentrism, and altruistic behavior. *Child Development,* 1973, *44,* 661–665.

Rule, B. G., Nesdale, A. R., & McAra, M. J. Children's reactions to information about the intentions underlying an aggressive act. *Child Development*, 1974, *45*, 794–798.

Rushton, J. P., & Sorrentino, R. M.(Eds.) *Altruism and helping behavior: Social, personality, and developmental perspectives.* Hillsdale, N.J.: Lawrence Erlbaum Associates, 1981.

Sagi, A., & Hoffman, M. L. Empathic distress in the newborn. *Developmental Psychology*, 1976, *12*, 175–176.

Savin-Williams, R. C. Dominance hierarchies in groups of early adolescents. *Child Development* 1979, *50*, 142–151.

Shantz, D. W., & Voydanoff, D. A. Situational effects on retaliatory aggression at three age levels. *Child Development*, 1973, *44*, 149–153.

Shure, M. B. Interpersonal problem solving: A cog in the wheel of social cognition. In F. Serafica (Ed.), *Social cognitive development in context*. New York: The Guilford Press, 1982.

Simner, M. L. Newborn's response to the cry of another infant. *Developmental Psychology*, 1971, *5*, 136–150.

Smith, M. C. Cognizing the behavior stream: The recognition of intentional action. *Child Development*, 1978, *49*, 736–743.

Spivack, G., Platt, J., & Shure, M. B. *The problem solving approach to adjustment*. San Francisco: Jossey-Bass, 1976.

Staub, E. *Positive Social Behavior and Morality: Social and Personal Influences* (Vol. 1). New York: Academic Press, 1978.

Staub, E. *Positive social behavior and morality: Social and personal influences* (Vol. 1). New York: Academic Press, 1978.

Strayer, J. A naturalistic study of empathic behaviors and their relation to affective states and perspective-taking skills in preschool children. *Child Development*, 1980, *51*, 815–822.

Ugurel-Semin, R. Moral behavior and moral judgment of children. *Journal of Abnormal and Social Psychology*, 1952, *47*, 463–474.

Underwood, B., Froming, W. J., & Moore, B. S. Mood, attention, and altruism: A search for mediating variables. *Developmental Psychology*, 1977, *13*, 541–542.

Wilcox, B. M., & Clayton, F. L. Infant visual fixation on motion pictures of the human face. *Journal of Experimental Child Psychology*, 1968, *6*, 22–32.

10 Developmental Psychopathology

Thomas M. Achenbach
University of Vermont

INTRODUCTION

Unlike most of the topics addressed in this book, the developmental study of psychopathology is not an established subspeciality of developmental psychology. Rather, it is a vast no-man's land, explored by emissaries from a variety of disciplines but not firmly dominated by any. This chapter, therefore, deals with developmental issues from diverse perspectives.

For those who are attracted by the challenge of shaping new paradigms, this is an exciting period when a few committed researchers can have a major impact on how troubled children are helped. Yet, it will require patience and a tolerance of ambiguity to fashion the disparate pieces into a coherent whole. It will also demand a readiness to span academic developmental psychology, the study of psychopathology, and clinical applications.

Prehistorical Background

The history of developmental psychopathology per se is too brief to warrant being treated separately as "history." Instead, as we sift through the raw materials of a developmental psychopathology, we will allude to the historical development of the relevant ideas where necessary. Early views of adult psychopathology, however, form a *prehistory* out of which the elements of a developmental psychopathology have evolved. A brief examination of this prehistory can alert us to the recurrent cycles that characterize attitudes toward psychopathology.

Adult mental disorders have been of interest since at least the time of the ancient Greeks. Greek and Roman medical theories ascribed behavioral abnormalities to humoral imbalances and malfunctioning organs. Hysteria, for example, was thought to be caused by wanderings of the womb (Greek *hystera* = womb), although psychological factors were also invoked.

During the Middle Ages, medical theories vied with theological theories of abnormal behavior. Whether a mental disorder was blamed on organic dysfunction or demons, however, "treatment" often consisted of rejection, incarceration, or punishment, although more humane attitudes were also evident at times (Neugebauer, 1979).

Toward the end of the eighteenth century, the reforming spirit of the Enlightenment spread to the care of the insane. The discovery that simply unchaining mental patients could lead to improvement helped instigate a therapeutic approach known as *moral treatment*. In the United States, moral treatment was centered in a network of small private "retreats." These retreats were intended to provide a family environment, employment, exercise, and kindly but firm "persistence in impressing on patients that a change to more acceptable behavior was expected" (Bockoven, 1963, p. 76).

The apparent success of moral treatment spurred efforts to cure the insane poor by modeling new state hospitals after the retreats. By the 1860s, however, disappointing results led to renewed pessimism about mental disorders. The state hospitals, originally inspired by moral treatment, became grimly custodial.

Why had moral treatment failed? There were three main reasons: One was that the early cure rates had been inflated by statistical fallacies, such as counting every release from a retreat as a cure, even though the same patient was soon readmitted. A second reason was that the big state hospitals were never funded well enough to provide the family-like environment that might have accounted for any success the retreats did have. A third was that the impoverished clientele of the state hospitals lacked the requisite skills and secure homes to facilitate adaptation to the outside world, should they improve while hospitalized.

The disillusionment with moral treatment is therefore not surprising. Yet, cycles of unjustified faith in a promising new paradigm, followed by bitter disappointment and hostile reactions against it, have been repeated again and again in modern attitudes toward maladaptive behavior. As will be evident, most approaches to the psychopathology of childhood and adolescence are offshoots of approaches to adult psychopathology. As such, they have been afflicted with the same cyclical symptoms. Before considering each of the important approaches, however, let us ponder an overarching conception of developmental psychopathology within which to integrate whatever is worth preserving from each approach.

A Conceptual Framework for Developmental Psychopathology

A developmental approach to psychopathology is not easily encapsulated in a brief, dictionary-like definition. Instead, it represents a way of looking at maladaptive behavior that is characterized by the following key features:

1. To judge whether an individual's behavior is "deviant," we need to know *what is typical for comparable individuals* at the same level of development. This requires normative data on large representative samples of individuals stratified by important demographic variables, and using assessment methods that are geared to each developmental level.

2. To judge whether an individual's behavior is "pathological," we need to know the *likely outcome* of this behavior in subsequent developmental periods. This requires longitudinal or follow-up studies of individuals showing particular behavior patterns in order to determine which patterns have especially unsatisfactory outcomes.

3. To understand maladaptive behavior, we must view it in relation to the individual's previous developmental history, the developmental tasks the individual faces, and the progress of important adaptive competencies. This requires a knowledge of normal development in such areas as biological maturation, cognition, emotional functioning, social competencies, and academic skills.

4. To design appropriate interventions, we need to know how to *facilitate development* rather than merely to reduce discomforts, remove "symptoms," or restore a previous level of functioning. This requires a knowledge of developmental processes and the mechanisms of behavioral change.

5. To evaluate the effects of interventions, we need *long-term comparisons of outcomes* following specific interventions and no-treatment control conditions. Evaluations of the outcomes must assess developmental progress as well as alleviation of the problems that initially prompted the interventions.

All of the above are relevant to the study of psychopathology at all stages of the life-cycle. They could well provide guidelines for a life-span developmental psychopathology. It is in the period from birth to maturity, however, that the need for a developmental approach is most compelling for the following reasons:

1. Conspicuous developmental changes occur much more rapidly in so many more areas during this period than during adulthood. For example, 6-month-olds, 4-year-olds, 8-year-olds, and 16-year-olds differ far more dramatically from each other in physical, cognitive, social, emotional, and educational development than do adults who are separated by almost any span of years.

2. The period from birth to maturity is marked by a host of conspicuous developmental milestones, such as walking, talking, bowel control, the onset of schooling, learning to read, involvement in peer groups, puberty, and school graduation. Although there are also adult developmental milestones, they are less explicit and more variable in their nature and timing, depending heavily on differences in occupation, marriage, parenting, etc.

3. Children's problems, competencies, and needs must be judged in light of their requirements for further development, whereas most adults have reached plateaus in their physical, cognitive, social, and educational development.

4. The judgment that a child needs help is typically made by others, such as parents and teachers, whereas adults often seek help for themselves, formulate their own referral complaints, and spontaneously assume the role of patient.

5. Because children are so dependent on their families, family functioning has a more decisive impact on children's problems and what is done about them than is true for most adults, who are freer to alter their family circumstances.

6. There are marked differences between children's disorders, which typically involve exaggerations of normal behavior or failures to develop important behaviors, and adult disorders, which more often involve marked declines from attained levels or the emergence of behavior that is clearly *pathognomonic* (i.e., indicative of pathology).

Many approaches to child psychopathology rest on assumptions derived from adult psychopathology. These assumptions can unduly bias the study of psychopathology during the period of rapid development. We must therefore distinguish those aspects of each approach that may facilitate the developmental study of psychopathology from those aspects that may hinder it. After considering the major approaches, we address current problems and issues for the developmental study of psychopathology.

NOSOLOGICAL APPROACHES

Efforts to categorize abnormal behaviors as specific disease entities evolved during the nineteenth century as a result of two related factors. One was the movement to provide large-scale institutional care. This necessitated arrangements for different types of management problems, such as violent versus depressed behavior. A second factor was the growth of research on the organic causes of disease and the extension of organic disease models to mental disorders. This became enshrined in the dogma that "mental diseases are brain diseases," as it was expressed in Wilhelm Griesinger's influential psychiatric textbook of 1845 (trans., Robertson & Rutherford, 1867).

Both the institutional management needs and the growing commitment to the organic disease model stimulated efforts to distinguish among types of disorders.

It was hoped that descriptions of symptom syndromes would ultimately distinguish between disease entities, which would then be found to have different organic causes.

The most successful prototype of the organic disease model was *general paralysis* (later called *paresis,* i.e., "incomplete paralysis"). Progressively more precise descriptions between 1798 and the 1840s converged on a syndrome that was defined mainly by mental symptoms, such as memory loss and irrationality, combined with physical symptoms of motor impairment, and usually ending in death. From the 1840s through the 1870s, research revealed inflamed brain tissue in most patients who died of paresis. Syphilitic infection was confirmed as the cause of paresis by the end of the nineteenth century.

Organic abnormalities also helped to define certain syndromes of mental retardation. *Down syndrome,* for example, was first described in 1866 by Langdon Down, an Englishman who thought its characteristic "mongoloid" facial features reflected an evolutionary throwback to the "mongol race." In this case, however, it took nearly a hundred years to discover that an extra chromosome was responsible (Lejeune, Gautier, & Turpin, 1959/1963).

Kraepelin's Nosology

Aside from a few clear-cut syndromes characterized by fairly obvious physical abnormalities, early efforts to distinguish among types of mental disorders yielded a hodgepodge of conflicting descriptions, based on diverse assumptions and conceptual principles. As it became clear that most disorders did not automatically present self-evident syndromes, efforts were made to integrate the descriptions within more general classification systems, or *taxonomies.*

The most influential taxonomy was published by Emil Kraepelin in 1883 and was progressively revised and expanded over the next 40 years (Kraepelin 1883/1915). Kraepelin's taxonomy provided a framework for psychiatry that is still evident today. His first edition was based on the assumption that all mental disorders, like paresis, are caused by brain pathology. The purpose of the taxonomy was to provide descriptive categories for discriminating among disease entities, whose different organic etiologies could then be sought. It was a *nosology* (classification of diseases) in the sense that each category was assumed to represent a distinctive disease entity.

In later editions, Kraepelin added psychological processes and the course of the disorder to descriptions of symptoms as defining criteria. For example, *dementia praecox* ("insanity of the young," renamed "schizophrenia" by Eugen Bleuler in 1911) was distinguished from manic-depressive psychosis on the basis of psychological differences and the more favorable outcomes observed in manic-depressive conditions.

By 1915, Kraepelin had also added disorders that were assumed to have psychological rather than organic causes, as well as a category of personality disorders bordering between illness and ordinary eccentricity. Despite this broadening to include disorders not assumed to have organic causes and other deviations from the disease model, Kraepelin's nineteenth century nosological paradigm continues to have a major impact on views of psychopathology. In the following sections, we consider contemporary variations on the nosological theme.

The Diagnostic and Statistical Manual of Mental Disorders

The American Psychiatric Association's *Diagnostic and Statistical Manual* (the "DSM") is widely used to classify mental disorders for purposes of medical records and third party payments. The DSM is in the form of a nosology in which each disorder is presented as a separate diagnostic entity. In the first edition of the DSM ("DSM-I," 1952), there were only two main categories of child and adolescent disorders: Adjustment Reaction and Schizophrenic Reaction, Childhood Type. "Adjustment reaction" referred to problems interpreted as relatively transient responses to stress; "schizophrenic reaction" referred to severe psychopathology that was not likely to be transient. Although adult diagnoses could also be applied to children, 70% of children seen in mental health clinics were either undiagnosed or were diagnosed as having adjustment reactions (Achenbach, 1966; Rosen, Bahn, & Kramer, 1964).

The second edition of the DSM ("DSM-II," 1968) added several behavior disorders of childhood (e.g., Hyperkinetic Reaction; Withdrawing Reaction), but many children were still diagnosed as having adjustment reactions (Cerreto & Tuma, 1977).

The third edition of the DSM ("DSM-III," 1980) departs in several ways from the earlier editions, as well as adding many new disorders of infancy, childhood, and adolescence. One major departure is the listing of criteria that have to be met for each diagnosis. These criteria involve yes-or-no judgments as to the presence of each characteristic required for each diagnosis, plus rules giving certain diagnoses precedence over others. For example, the diagnosis of Schizoid Disorder of Childhood or Adolescence requires that the disturbance not be "due to" Pervasive Developmental Disorder, Conduct Disorder, or any psychotic disorder, such as Schizophrenia.

Besides specifying criteria for each disorder, DSM-III provides the following five dimensions or "axes":

Axis I: (a) Clinical syndromes (e.g., Schizoid Disorder)
          (b) Conditions that are not attributable to a mental disorder but are a focus of attention or treatment (e.g., "parent–child problem," such as child abuse)

Axis II: (a) Personality disorders (e.g., Compulsive Personality)
          (b) Specific developmental disorders (e.g., Developmental Reading Disorder)
Axis III: Physical disorders and conditions
Axis IV: A 7-point rating scale for severity of psychosocial stressors
Axis V: A 5-point rating scale for highest level of adaptive functioning during the past year.

DSM-III represents a major effort to make diagnostic criteria more explicit and reliable, and to broaden diagnosis by taking medical conditions, life stresses, and adaptive functioning into account. It reflects efforts to free diagnostic classification from unsubstantiated theoretical inferences, such as psychoanalytic interpretations of neurotic behavior. In effect, DSM-III constitutes a return to the ideals of early Kraepelinian nosology in striving for noninferential descriptions of disorders of unknown etiology.

DSM-III also constitutes a return to another aspect of nineteenth-century nosological thinking: the medical disease model for psychopathology. Early drafts of DSM-III held that all mental disorders are medical disorders. This claim was moderated in the final version, but DSM-III repeatedly refers to disorders as "illnesses." Based on the nosological concept of categorical disease entities, the architects of DSM-III formulated each category by starting from

> . . . a clinical concept for which there is some degree of face validity. Face validity is the extent to which the description of a particular category seems on the face of it to describe accurately the characteristic features of persons with a particular disorder. It is the result of clinicians agreeing on the identification of a particular syndrome or pattern of clinical features as a mental disorder. Initial criteria are generally developed by asking the clinicians to describe what they consider to be the most characteristic features of the disorder (Spitzer & Cantwell, 1980, p. 369).

The clinical concepts of most DSM-III adult disorders, such as schizophrenia, date from Kraepelin's nosology. In defining their categories, the DSM-III committee was able to draw on existing research diagnostic criteria (RDC) for the major categories of adult disorders. Unlike the adult disorders, however, many of the child and adolescent disorders had *no* counterparts in previous nosologies or research diagnostic criteria. Spitzer and Cantwell's (1980) reference to "face validity" therefore concerns the diagnostic concepts held by those who formulated DSM-III's categories of childhood and adolescent disorders. Their formulations of these disorders were not validated in any other way.

Current research on the DSM-III childhood and adolescent categories shows that some may, in fact, correspond to empirically derived taxonomic distinctions (e.g., Edelbrock, Costello, & Kessler, 1984). However, the reliability of the

DSM-III childhood and adolescent diagnoses appears too low to inspire much confidence. Two studies have shown that DSM-III diagnoses made from standardized case histories were less reliable than DSM-II diagnoses, which were themselves not very reliable (Mattison, Cantwell, Russell, & Will, 1979; Mezzich & Mezzich, 1979). Furthermore, Appendix F of the DSM-III *Manual* shows lower reliability for the diagnoses of children than for the diagnoses of adults on Axes I, II, IV, and V (Axis III was not reported).

The reliability of childhood diagnoses actually *declined* from an early draft to a later draft of the DSM on all four axes that were assessed, in contrast to the increasing reliability of adult diagnoses on all four axes. Any benefits of the rejuvenated nosological approach for adult disorders have thus not been evident for children's disorders. Nevertheless, DSM-III offers a clear example of the classical nosological model as applied to disorders of childhood and adolescence. We return later to this model for purposes of comparison with other approaches.

The GAP Nosology

The neglect of children in DSM-I prompted the Committee on Child Psychiatry of the Group for the Advancement of Psychiatry (GAP) to propose an alternative classification of childhood and adolescent disorders (GAP, 1966). As with other nosological approaches, the GAP committee followed the traditional procedure of starting with clinical concepts of disorders, but they tried to incorporate more developmental considerations than did the DSM. For example, they proposed a category of *healthy responses* to encompass those behavior problems typical of most children at certain developmental periods. These included the separation anxiety 6-month-old babies show when their parents leave; preschool children's phobias; the compulsive behavior of middle childhood; adolescent identity crises; and grief reactions to the death of loved ones.

Although the GAP committee held that its definitions were as "operational" as possible and involved a minimum of inference, no assessment operations were specified for determining whether a child manifested a particular disorder. Some definitions relied heavily on psychoanalytic inferences, as exemplified by the GAP (1966) definition of psychoneurotic disorders:

> . . . disorders based on unconscious conflicts over the handling of sexual and aggressive impulses which, though removed from awareness by the mechanism of repression, remain active and unresolved. . . . The anxiety, acting as a danger signal to the ego, ordinarily sets into operation certain defense mechanisms, in addition to repression, and leads to the formation of psychological symptoms which symbolically deal with conflict, thus achieving a partial thought unhealthy solution (pp. 229–230).

Considering the degree of inference required for GAP diagnoses, it is not surprising that the reliability was poor. An Australian study in which diagnosticians read a standard set of case histories (including some contributed by each participant) yielded 59% agreement for very broad diagnostic categories, such as Psychoneurotic Disorders versus Psychotic Disorders (Freeman, 1971). An American study obtained 40% agreement for broad diagnostic categories and 23% for more specific diagnoses (Beitchman, Dielman, Landis, Benson, & Kemp, 1978). Correcting for chance agreements would have further reduced the reliability estimates in both studies.

In short, although the GAP sought to rectify the DSM's neglect of developmental considerations and lack of differentiation among childhood disorders, its nosological categories were also derived from the clinical concepts of a committee of psychiatrists. As with the DSM of the same era, the result was a mixture of narrative description and theoretical inference that specified no operations for assessing the putative disorders. The poor agreement among diagnosticians working from identical data suggested that merely cloaking a nosology in developmental language did not ensure a reliable fit to the disorders of childhood.

Clinically Identified Syndromes

Aside from their effects on formal taxonomies, nosological assumptions have affected views of individual syndromes. The following three disorders illustrate contemporary disease entity concepts of child psychopathology.

Early Infantile Autism.   This syndrome was first proposed by Leo Kanner in 1943 after he had seen eleven children who shared certain striking peculiarities. Kanner summarized their peculiarities in terms of two cardinal symptoms:

1. Extreme self-isolation, evident from the first years of life.
2. Obsessive insistence on the preservation of sameness (Eisenberg & Kanner, 1956).

The children Kanner diagnosed as autistic also avoided eye contact with others ("gaze aversion") and showed intriguing speech abnormalities, ranging from a complete lack of speech or delayed onset, through echolalia (exact repetition or "echoing" of others' speech), reversal of personal pronouns (substitution of "you" for "I"), and metaphorical speech, apparently lacking communicative intent. Long-term follow-ups of 96 of Kanner's cases showed that, despite signs of high intelligence in many, only 11 achieved adequate adjustments. Even these 11 remained severely limited in interpersonal relationships (Eisenberg & Kanner, 1956; Kanner, 1971; Kanner, Rodrigues, & Ashenden, 1972). Other follow-up studies agree with Kanner's finding that very few autistic children achieve even marginal social adjustments in later life (Lotter, 1978).

Kanner's (1943) initial hypothesis was that autistic children have an "innate inability to form the usual, biologically provided affective contact with people" (p. 250). Despite Kanner's careful descriptions and his hypothesis of an organic etiology, however, others quickly extended the concept of autism to children having few of the abnormalities he described. Furthermore, psychoanalytic theorists blamed autism on parental behavior and unconscious attitudes, singling out mothers who were said to be immature, narcissistic, overintellectual, and incapable of mature emotional relationships (Despert, 1947; Rank, 1949). Indictments were also leveled at mothers who "wish that [their] child should not exist" (Bettelheim, 1967, p. 125) and "parents [who] inadvertently hated one another and used the child emotionally" (Wolman, 1970, p. vii).

There has recently been a marked return to organic hypotheses about autism. Yet, even when autism was interpreted in psychoanalytic terms, it was conceived as a generic entity that the sensitive clinician could detect lurking beneath diverse phenotypes. The striking behavior of autistic children, autism's very early onset, and its seeming resistance to a variety of environmental regimes certainly argue for a disease-like condition. Nevertheless, varied interpretations of the putative underlying disease and varied criteria for diagnosing it have continued to limit agreement among diagnosticians (Cohen, Caparulo, Gold, Waldo, Shaywitz, Ruttenberg, & Rimland, 1978).

Hyperactivity. Like autism, hyperactivity has become a popular nosological construct. In contrast to the extreme deviance and rarity of autism, however, hyperactivity involves behaviors that nearly all children show occasionally. Furthermore, hyperactivity typically becomes a cause for clinical concern during the elementary school years, rather than during the very early years. And, once hyperactivity is evident, it seldom remains such a devastating lifetime affliction as autism. Why, then, has hyperactivity been viewed as a disease-like condition?

Two early findings helped make hyperactivity an especially tempting candidate for nosological categorization. One was Bradley's (1937) finding that the amphetamine *Benzedrine* seemed to reduce overactivity in disturbed children. This suggested a specific organic defect underlying hyperactivity.

The other finding grew out of efforts by Strauss, Lehtinen, and Werner to develop methods for diagnosing and educating brain-damaged children (Strauss & Lehtinen, 1947). Normal children, retarded children with brain damage, and retarded children without known brain damage were compared on a battery of perceptual and cognitive tasks. Behavioral differences between the brain-damaged and other children were then interpreted as signs of brain damage.

Largely from this research, a picture of the "brain damaged child" emerged that included the following features: Hyperactivity, impulsivity, distractibility, short attention span, emotional lability, perceptual-motor deficits, and clumsiness. Children who had these problems but no direct evidence of brain damage were assumed to have subtle brain damage, designated as: *Strauss syndrome, diffuse brain damage, minimal brain damage, minimal brain dysfunction,* or *minimal cerebral dysfunction.* "MBD" (minimal brain damage or dysfunction) soon became a synonym for "hyperactivity." Some workers not only equated

MBD with hyperactivity, but with the terms LD (learning disability) and SLD (specific learning disability; e.g., Ochroch, 1981).

As with autism, the nosological constructs of MBD and hyperactivity seemed to expand far beyond the observations on which they were based. The absence of operational criteria allowed the diagnosis to be made in idiosyncratic ways. An analysis of clinicians' use of a standardized set of case materials, for example, showed differences in the cues the clinicians used, their weighting of the cues, and their awareness of the diagnostic "policies" guiding their judgments (Ullman, Egan, Fiedler, Jurenec, Pliske, Thompson, & Doherty, 1981).

When psychiatric nosology first became differentiated with respect to childhood disorders (DSM-II, 1968), hyperactivity was designated as "hyperkinetic reaction of childhood (or adolescence)," characterized by "overactivity, restlessness, distractibility, and short attention span" (p. 50). DSM-II made a distinction between the behavioral phenotype and organic brain damage: "If this behavior is caused by organic brain damage, it should be diagnosed under the appropriate non-psychotic *organic brain syndrome*" (DSM-II, 1968, p. 50).

Furthermore, research during the 1970s and early 1980s showed that most "hyperactive" children are probably not brain damaged and that brain damage does not necessarily result in hyperactivity (e.g., Brown, Chadwick, Shaffer, Rutter, & Traub, 1981; Shaffer, McNamara, & Pincus, 1974).

As brain damage became a less viable explanation of hyperactivity, other organic causes were sought. These have included neurotransmitter abnormalities, abnormalities of arousal in the central nervous system, food sensitivities, food allergies, developmental delays, and constitutional patterns of temperament (see Achenbach, 1982, Chapter 11, for a review of these).

In formulating its child categories, the DSM-III committee decided that attention deficits were more primary than overactivity in what DSM-II had called the Hyperkinetic Reaction. DSM-III therefore replaced the Hyperkinetic Reaction with the category of Attention Deficit Disorders (ADD), divided into two subtypes: (1) ADD *with* Hyperactivity, and (2) ADD *without* Hyperactivity.

To be diagnosed ADD, a child must manifest at least three out of a list of five items considered to represent inattention, and three out of a list of six items considered to represent impulsivity. For ADD *with* Hyperactivity, two out of a list of five items representing hyperactivity are also required. The wording of each item implies a quantitative dimension; for example, "*easily* distracted," "*often* acts before thinking," "runs about or climbs on things *excessively*." Yet each item must be judged in a yes-or-no fashion and the overall criterion for inattention, for impulsivity, and for hyperactivity must be met in a yes-or-no fashion.

Thus, even though the wording of the items and the requirement of a certain number of items from each list imply quantification, the decision rules impose a categorical nosological construct on the diagnostic process: Each child is diagnosed as either having the disorder or not having it, with no provision for gradations in intensity, nor in the certainty of the diagnosis. Later sections deal with the implications of this categorical model for common behaviors that vary in degrees such as those used to diagnose ADD.

Childhood Depression.   Interest in childhood depression has taken a course quite different from interest in autism and hyperactivity. Despite early reports of manic-depressive disorders in children (Kasanin & Kaufman, 1929), the psychoanalytic theory that was dominant from the 1930s through the 1960s held that true depressive disorders were impossible before the superego was fully internalized during adolescence (see Kashani, Husain, Shekim, Hodges, Cytryn, & McKnew, 1981). Following the spread of drug therapies and growing enthusiasm for biological explanations of adult depression in the 1960s, however, the quest for childhood depression began again.

Since neither DSM-I nor DSM-II included childhood depression, and children do not spontaneously complain of depression, one approach was to infer depression from a variety of other problems. In arguing for the use of antidepressant drugs with children, Frommer (1967), for example, inferred depression in:

> children who complain of non-specific recurrent abdominal pain, headache, sleep difficulties, and irrational fears or mood disturbances such as irritability, unaccountable tearfulness, and associated outbursts of temper. Such children often develop sudden difficulty in social adjustments, which previously were normal; they may either withdraw themselves from the family circle and former friends or display outright aggressive and antisocial behavior (p. 729).

Other advocates of antidepressant medication diagnosed children as depressed if they showed dysphoric (unhappy, irritable, hypersensitive, or negative) mood and self-deprecatory thoughts, plus at least two of the following: aggression, sleep disturbance, a change in school performance, diminished socialization, a change in attitude toward school, the loss of usual energy, or an unusual change in appetite and/or weight (Weinberg, Rutman, Sullivan, Penick, & Dietz, 1973). Based on the assessment of these symptoms by a pediatric neurologist who informally interviewed children and their parents, Weinberg et al. diagnosed 63% of children referred to an educational clinic as suffering from a "depressive illness."

Childhood depression was further broadened by the concept of *masked depression*—depression that is inferred from aggressive, hyperactive, and other troublesome behavior used defensively "to ward off the unbearable feelings of despair" (Cytryn & McKnew, 1979, p. 327). Psychophysiological reactions, truancy, running away, sexual promiscuity, and fire setting were also added as signs of masked depression (see Kovacs & Beck, 1977). The zealous quest for depression underlying so many different behaviors and the resulting reports of epidemics of previously undiagnosed depressive illness prompted one observer to dub childhood depression "the MBD of the 1980s."

Although the concept of masked depression has since been retracted by its authors (Cytryn, McKnew, & Bunney, 1980), the search for even "unmasked" depression as a generic entity among children is still plagued by a lack of agreement among various categorical criteria. One reason for these disagreements is that broad, inferential criteria classify a much larger proportion of children as depressed than do more stringent criteria. Carlson and Cantwell (1982), for example, found that the Weinberg et al. (1973) criteria produced considerably more diagnoses of depression than did the DSM-III criteria for a major depressive disorder in the same children. (The DSM-III criteria were written for adult disorders but include some extrapolations downward to children.) However, as neither set of criteria is quantified, the more stringent criteria cannot be calibrated to the less stringent criteria in any systematic way: Not all children diagnosed by the more stringent criteria are included in the group diagnosed by the less stringent criteria, and the two sets of criteria cannot be made more congruent by adjusting cutoff points on quantitative dimensions, because they do not employ any.

Conclusion

In the nineteenth century, it was assumed that a descriptive nosology would identify diseases whose different organic etiologies could then be found. Current nosological approaches imply that disorders exist as categorical entities, each of which has a specific etiology. Although this view need not employ exclusively organic etiologies, as the GAP nosology and the psychoanalytic interpretations of autism did not, it is currently associated with an implicit assumption in favor of organic etiologies.

In considering three popular candidates for the status of nosological entities, we saw that early infantile autism seems most like a disease entity, featuring very early onset and enduring abnormalities that do not appear to be situational or quantitative variations of normal behavior. Nevertheless, different conceptions of this disorder continue to produce diagnostic disagreements.

The second candidate considered, hyperactivity (now called Attention Deficit Disorder with Hyperactivity), has been blamed on a variety of organic abnormalities, but involves situational and quantitative variations of behavior that most children occasionally show. The overt problem behavior is relatively easy to identify, but the imposition of unvalidated categorical constructs on quantitative variations in the behavior provokes continuing diagnostic disagreements.

The third candidate considered, childhood depression, has been summarily cast into the nosological mold without prior refinement of the phenotypic picture. Whereas the application of the nosological paradigm to hyperactivity raises problems in categorizing quantitative variations of behavior, current nosological constructs of childhood depression still face problems of *which* phenomena to include as criteria.

MULTIVARIATE APPROACHES

Faced with a lack of well-defined disorders on which to focus their efforts, researchers have turned to statistical methods for empirically identifying syndromes of behavior problems that tend to co-occur in children. After some rudimentary efforts in the 1940s and 1950s, the advent of electronic computers spawned a host of multivariate studies in the 1960s and 1970s. In most of these studies, ratings obtained on behavior checklists were factor analyzed to identify syndromes of covarying behavior problems. Despite differences in the rating instruments, raters, samples of children, and methods of analysis, there was considerable convergence on certain syndromes (see Achenbach & Edelbrock, 1978, and Quay, 1979, for detailed reviews). High correlations have also been obtained between syndromes scored from different checklists (Achenbach & Edelbrock, 1983). Some of the empirically identified syndromes resemble those that are evident in the nosological approaches, although there is no clear correspondence between other syndromes identified by the two approaches.

Contrasts Between Multivariate and Nosological Approaches

Even where there are similarities between the multivariate and the nosological syndromes, there are also some important differences:

1. As we have seen, existing nosologies represent negotiated formulations of clinicians' concepts of disorders. Multivariate syndromes, by contrast, are derived statistically from covariation among scores on items rated for samples of children.

2. The criterial attributes of the nosological categories must be assessed according to yes-or-no judgments, whereas the criterial attributes of multivariate syndromes are usually assessed in terms of quantitative gradations.

3. Based on yes-or-no judgments of each criterial attribute, a nosological diagnosis culminates in a yes-or-no decision about whether a child has a particular disorder. Multivariate syndromes, on the other hand, are scored in terms of the degree to which a child manifests the characteristics of a syndrome. This is because quantitative indices of each criterial attribute are combined into a summary index of how strongly the child manifests the syndrome. However, cutoff points can also be established on the distribution of scores for a syndrome, in order to discriminate among particular classes of children, if desired.

4. The criteria for nosological diagnoses imply comparisons with "normal" agemates, but they specify no operations for determining how a particular child compares with normal agemates. The quantification of multivariate syndromes, by contrast, provides a metric for comparing one child with other children, such as normal agemates.

5. Because nosological categories are defined in terms of discrete types of disorders, children who show characteristics of several types must either get multiple diagnoses or must be placed in a single category according to rules for preempting one diagnosis with another—often with no empirical basis for doing so. The multivariate approach, by contrast, lends itself to a profile format for describing a child in terms of his or her standing on multiple syndromes, without requiring forced choices as to which ones preempt the others.

6. Through cluster analyzing profiles, we can construct a taxonomy of the patterns of scores obtained on all the syndromes of the profile. We can also quantify the degree of a child's resemblance to each profile type, further reducing reliance on categorical forced choices (see Edelbrock & Achenbach, 1980, for detailed examples).

Syndromes Identified Through Multivariate Approaches

Multivariate methods may not contribute much to the initial discovery of rare and extreme abnormalities, such as autism. Once these abnormalities have been detected clinically, however, multivariate methods can sharpen the syndromal construct by assessing their discriminative power and covariation among children having the target disorder and other disorders that must be discriminated from it (cf., Prior, Perry, & Gajzago, 1975).

Few children display abnormalities as blatant as autism. Instead, most childhood disorders involve behaviors that most children show to some extent, further complicated by the variability of each child's behavior. Detection of patterns among these behaviors therefore poses a more challenging information processing task than the detection of blatant abnormalities. It is in this information processing task that multivariate methods can be especially helpful.

What have multivariate analyses of children's behavior problems found? Table 10.1 summarizes the main findings of multivariate studies of behavior problem ratings from case histories, mental health workers, teachers, and parents. The *narrow-band* syndromes listed in Table 10.1 are specific groupings of behavior problems that are roughly analogous to the syndromes comprising taxonomies such as the DSM. The *broad-band* syndromes in Table 10.1 are more global groupings of behavior that subsume many of the narrow-band syndromes. For example, the broad-band Undercontrolled syndrome includes behaviors such as fighting, destructiveness, disobedience, and impulsivity. Hierarchical analyses of relations between broad- and narrow-band syndromes show that the narrow-band Aggressive, Delinquent, and Hyperactive syndromes group together to form a broad-band Undercontrolled syndrome (e.g., Achenbach, 1978; Achenbach & Edelbrock, 1979). It is therefore possible to score children on syndromes at both the narrow- and broad-band levels of the hierarchy. The child's standing on the broad-band syndromes may be useful for general management purposes, whereas the differentiated picture provided by scores on the narrow-band syndromes may facilitate more precise assessment, treatment, and research.

Most multivariate studies have not separated boys and girls of different ages. However, when separate analyses have been done, they have shown age and sex similarities in some syndromes, but important age and sex differences in others. Achenbach and Edelbrock (1979), for example, found a syndrome among disturbed girls that is characterized mainly by cruelty toward animals and people, but no clear counterpart of this syndrome was found among boys. Important age differences were manifest in a syndrome dubbed "Depressed" that was found for 6- to 11-year-olds of both sexes but not for adolescents.

The detection of the Cruel syndrome for girls and the Depressed syndrome for elementary school-aged children does not mean that the behaviors of these syndromes were absent from other groups. Cruelty to animals and people was actually reported more often for boys than for girls (Achenbach & Edelbrock, 1981). But the different forms of cruelty did not occur together consistently

TABLE 10.1
Number of Studies in which Syndromes Have Been Identified
through Multivariate Analyses of Data from Various Sources. (From
Achenbach, 1982, p. 556)

Syndrome	Case Histories	Mental Health Workers	Teachers	Parents	Total
Broad Band					
Overcontrolled	2	1	5	6	14
Undercontrolled	3	3	5	7	18
Pathological Detachment	3	—	1	—	4
Learning problems	—	—	1	1	2
Narrow Band					
Academic Disability	—	1	—	3	4
Aggressive	3	4	1	8	16
Anxious	1	2	1	2	6
Delinquent	3	1	—	7	11
Depressed	2	1	—	5	8
Hyperactive	3	2	1	7	13
Immature	—	1	—	3	4
Obsessive-Compulsive	1	—	—	2	3
Schizoid	3	4	—	5	12
Sexual Problems	1	2	—	3	6
Sleep Problems	—	—	—	3	3
Social Withdrawal	1	1	1	5	8
Somatic Complaints	1	—	—	7	8
Uncommunicative	—	1	—	2	3

enough among boys to form a separate syndrome, as they did for girls. Similarly, the depressive behaviors comprising the Depressed syndrome were reported at least as often for adolescents as for younger children. Yet, for adolescents, they occurred in conjunction with a much greater variety of other behaviors, rather than forming a clear-cut syndrome, as they did for younger children.

Profiles of Multivariate Syndromes

Syndromes of covarying behaviors identified through multivariate analyses can be cast into a profile that represents a child's standing on all syndromes simultaneously. To provide a common metric across the syndromes, scores on each syndrome are converted to standard scores based on normative samples or other reference samples.

Whereas syndromes reflect covariation among reported behaviors across samples of children, profiles provide a more comprehensive picture of each child's overall behavior pattern. Cluster analyses of profiles for clinically referred children have revealed some profile types that are elevated only on one syndrome (Edelbrock & Achenbach, 1980). In Figure 10.1 for example, profile type D for 12- to 16-year-old boys is elevated mainly on the Hyperactive syndrome. This pattern is what would be expected for boys diagnosed as having ADD with Hyperactivity. (The Z scores to the left of the profiles indicate standard deviation units from the mean of *clinically referred* boys. Thus, the mean score for the Hyperactive syndrome in profile type D is one standard deviation above the mean for *clinically referred* boys; it would be still more deviant from the mean of normal 12- to 16-year-old boys.)

Note that the Hyperactive syndrome is nearly as elevated in profile type C as it is in type D. If we were to consider the behaviors of the Hyperactive syndrome in isolation, we might lump type C and type D boys together, as a categorical nosology would. However, if we were to consider the entire profile pattern, we would see that, although they have high scores on the Hyperactivity syndrome, type C boys are still more deviant on the Immature and Aggressive syndromes of the profile. They also differ from type D boys in that they are more deviant on the Hostile Withdrawal syndrome, but less deviant on the Obsessive–Compulsive syndrome. Profiles E and F in Figure 10.1 illustrate a similar contrast between two patterns that each have high scores on the Delinquent syndrome.

A nosology such as the DSM takes account of differences in patterns by adding each diagnosis a boy qualifies for or by preemptively excluding certain diagnoses. This makes sense if each diagnosis has a proven etiology that explains why one diagnosis precludes another. However, in the absence of known etiologies or a litmus test for positively diagnosing each disorder, the multivariate profile approach preserves a more comprehensive basis for a taxonomy of phenotypes than does the categorical nosological approach.

Boys Aged 12-16

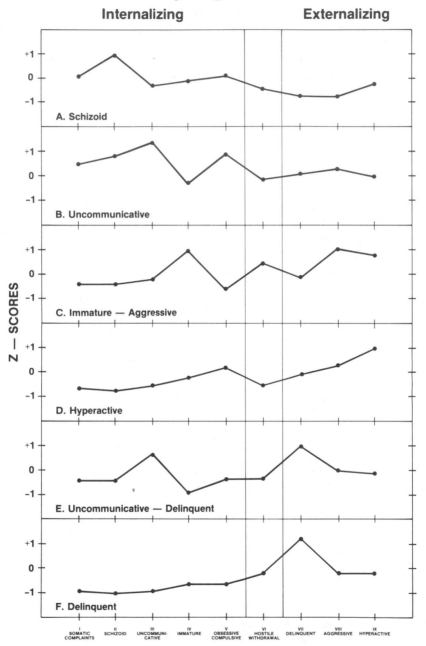

FIG. 10.1. Behavior profile types identified through cluster analyses. (From Achenbach & Edelbrock, 1983, p. 79.)

Conclusion

Lacking a differentiated nosology of childhood disorders, researchers have employed multivariate analyses to identify syndromes of covarying behaviors. Despite differences in rating instruments, raters, subject samples, and analytic methods, these analyses show considerable convergence on a few broad-band syndromes and more numerous narrow-band syndromes. Multivariate syndromes utilize quantitative variations in criterial attributes and in aggregates of attributes, rather than yes-or-no judgments of each attribute and of the syndromes themselves.

Aside from preserving quantitative variations, multivariate syndromes lend themselves to profile formats that reveal children's *patterns* across all syndromes. These patterns provide a more comprehensive basis for phenotypic taxonomies than do categorical nosologies. By viewing a child's scores across a profile in relation to those of his/her peers, we can assess the child's deviance for each syndrome, rather than making categorical judgments of each syndrome in isolation, without an operational basis for comparison with peers.

GENERAL THEORETICAL APPROACHES TO PSYCHOPATHOLOGY

As we saw in preceding sections, the nosological and the multivariate approaches identify types of disorders without explaining them according to a single theory. The approaches considered in this section attempt to *explain* psychopathology on the basis of general theories of psychological functioning. We consider here only the two global theoretical approaches that have had the most impact on views of child psychopathology—psychoanalytic theory and learning theory. Because space limits preclude comprehensive treatment of these theories, the emphasis is on those aspects that have the most relevance to developmental psychopathology; other aspects of these theories are discussed in later sections.

Psychoanalytic Theory

Sigmund Freud's psychoanalytic theory grew out of his attempts to treat hysterical neuroses in the 1880s and 1890s. His patients displayed dramatic physical symptoms, such as paralyses, that violated the known principles of anatomy. Freud hypothesized that the symptoms were caused by conflicts between forbidden impulses seeking expression and psychological defenses against these impulses. His concept of conflicting psychological forces is the cornerstone of *psychodynamic* theory.

Libido Theory and Psychosexual Development.   In investigating his patients' psychological conflicts, Freud concluded that the forbidden impulses were usually of a sexual nature. By urging patients to relax and say whatever came to mind—a process he called *free association*—Freud found that the patients' thoughts usually led back to childhood sexual experiences, especially seductions by adults. At first, Freud thought that the repression of these memories was the basis for adult neurosis. However, he later concluded that many of the seductions could not actually have occurred.

Why did so many patients "recall" sexual experiences that did not happen? Freud (1905/1953) inferred that the experiences were childhood fantasies that had been triggered by sexual desires directed toward adults, especially the parent of the opposite sex. These desires, he hypothesized, originated in the biologically determined sex drive, which was the source of the affective excitation he termed *libido*. From patients' free associations, Freud inferred that the libido was at first centered in the *oral* area, then the *anal* area, and then, between the ages of about 3 and 5, in the *phallic* area—the penis of the boy and the clitoris of the girl.

It was during the *phallic phase* that sexual desires toward the opposite-sex parent became intense. As a result, the child became hostile toward the same-sex parent, who was seen as a competitor. The typical outcome of this Oedipal situation was that the same-sex parent responded with punitive threats, which caused the child to repress the offending sexual impulses. Repression was enforced by a process of *identification* with the same-sex parent—in becoming as much as possible like the same-sex parent, the child symbolically won the opposite-sex parent while at the same time reducing threats from the same sex-parent.

Internalized prohibitions associated with the same-sex parent helped hold sexual impulses in check during the *latency period,* until puberty intensified genital sexual urges, reawakened Oedipal conflicts, and provoked the *Sturm und Drang* of adolescence. Freud's portrayal of the sequence of these libidinal phases from birth through adolescence is known as his *theory of psychosexual development.*

Personality Structure and Development.   Freud's theory of personality structure and development is also relevant to developmental psychopathology. As Freud's concepts of conflicting psychological forces grew more complex, he organized them in terms of three different aspects of personality structure: the *id,* encompassing those impulses that stem from biological drives; the *ego,* encompassing the executive functions of personality that mediate between id impulses and external reality; and the *superego,* consisting of the ideals and prohibitions that are internalized via identification with the same-sex parent as a resolution of the Oedipal conflict. These three constructs have retained key roles in modern psychoanalytic views of development and psychopathology. The ego, in particular, became the centerpiece of later theory, as it was assigned ever wider functions in construing reality, detecting threats, experiencing anxiety, and activating defenses against anxiety. Anxiety came to be viewed as the *bete noire* of psychopathology, with different disorders interpreted as reflecting different psychodynamic responses to it.

Implications of Psychoanalytic Theory for Developmental Psychopathology. Whereas Kraepelin provided the nosology, Freud provided the most popular explanations for psychopathology. Like Kraepelin, Freud focused on adult disorders, but his theory dealt with their developmental origins, inferred largely from adult recollections of childhood. Although Anna Freud and others psychoanalyzed children, their early reports dealt mainly with elaborations of analytic theory, illustrated with anecdotal observations. Miss Freud's (1965) "Developmental Profile" for assessing children psychoanalytically has been illustrated in several case histories, but no reliability or validity data have been published (see Achenbach, 1982, for details).

The nature of psychoanalytic theory makes decisive tests difficult. However, a longitudinal study of the development of children's behavior disorders suggests that many of Freud's developmental inferences may have mistakenly imputed a causal role to certain intrapsychic variables that were actually *effects* of other problems:

> "in the young child, anxiety has not been evident as an initial factor preceding and determining symptom development. . . . However, intrapsychic conflict and psychodynamic defenses . . . have been evident in older children as later developments in the child's response to the unfavorable and sometimes threatening consequences of an initial maladaptation. . . . It is, therefore, not surprising that in retrospective studies that begin when the child already presents with an elaborated psychological disturbance, the prominent phenomena of anxiety and psychodynamic defenses dominate clinical thinking, and come to be labeled as primary, rather than as secondary, influences on the genesis of behavior disturbance" (Thomas, Chess, & Birch, 1968, pp. 188–189).

Learning Theories

Theories of learning are diverse, but the following common features distinguish the learning theory approach from the psychoanalytic approach:

1. Learning theories originated with laboratory studies of learning, primarily in animals, rather than with clinical studies of psychopathology.
2. Learning theories focus mainly on observable environmental stimuli and observable responses by the organism, rather than inferred mental events.
3. Learning theories attempt to explain most behavioral change at most ages with a single set of principles, rather than invoking a theory of development per se.
4. Learning theories emphasize environmental rather than biological and intrapsychic causes of psychopathology.

Origins of Learning Theories. Systematic learning theories arose at about the same time as psychoanalytic theory, with laboratory studies by Pavlov, Bekhterev, and Thorndike suggesting general principles that were then extrapolated to a variety of human behavior. John B. Watson (1913, 1919), the "father of behaviorism," became the leading proponent of learning theory explanations for personality and psychopathology. He argued that most fears and other behavior problems stem from faulty conditioning. Although initially sympathetic to the psychoanalytic advocacy of freer attitudes toward sex and the discussion of personal problems, Watson eventually contended that behaviorist studies of children would replace psychoanalysis, which he said was "based largely upon religion, introspective psychology, and Voodooism" (1924, p. 18).

Whereas psychoanalysis began as a therapy for adults and was later extended to children, therapies based on learning theory were applied mainly to children. In a classic case, for example, Mary Cover Jones (1924) applied various conditioning principles to the treatment of a 2-year-old boy's phobia of rabbits. Holmes (1936) reinforced children for coping with their fear of the dark, while Mowrer and Mowrer (1938) used an alarm triggered by urine on a bed pad to cure children of bedwetting. However, it was not until the 1960s that therapies based on learning theories became widespread.

Subsequent Development of Learning Theories. What happened between the burst of enthusiasm for learning based therapies in the 1920s and their revival in the 1960s? A great deal of laboratory research and refinement of learning theory was carried out by Clark Hull, B. F. Skinner, Neal Miller, and others. By the 1950s, efforts to apply more sophisticated learning theories to psychopathology became widespread. Rather than attempting to change problem behavior, however, these efforts mainly translated the clinical theory and lore of psychoanalysis into the language of learning theory.

The most ambitious of these translations was *Personality and Psychotherapy,* by John Dollard and Neal Miller (1950). Dedicating their book to "Freud and Pavlov and their students," Dollard and Miller sought "to combine the vitality of psychoanalysis, the rigor of the natural-science laboratory, and the facts of culture" (p. 3). They called psychotherapy a "window to higher mental life" and "the process by which *normality is created*" (pp. 3, 5). Accepting psychoanalytic views of psychopathology and its treatment, Dollard and Miller mainly sought to state these views in more rigorous terms derived from laboratory research on learning. Despite the basic contrasts listed earlier, psychoanalytic and learning theories converged in several ways:

1. Both explained mental processes largely in terms of principles of *association*, whereby sequences of thoughts are governed by previous contiguities among ideas, similarity of content, and other shared features. This associationistic view of mental processes was the basis for the psychoanalytic technique of free association, as well as the psychoanalytic theory of mental symbols.

2. Psychoanalytic theories and most learning theories postulated that reduction of organically based drives promoted the learning of important responses, attitudes, and emotions.

3. Psychoanalytic theory and learning theories made anxiety a central explanatory construct for psychopathology.

4. Psychoanalytic theory and learning theories blamed childhood experiences for most adult psychopathology but did not actually test the relationships that were assumed.

Conclusion

As of the 1950s, laboratory-based learning theories and clinical psychoanalytic theory seemed likely to merge in a sophisticated general theory of psychopathology, its development, and its treatment. This did not happen, however. Instead, the late 1950s and 1960s saw both a flowering of new therapies and an upsurge of developmental theory that took very different directions. In the following sections, we first consider these therapies, and then the developmental theory. It should be noted here, however, that learning and psychoanalytic theories both implied developmental etiologies for psychopathology. Yet, neither the theories nor their synthesis were based on the direct study of human development, nor did they generate therapies whose efficacy had been empirically demonstrated. Rather, they were rich heuristic systems whose appeal lay in their apparent capacity for explaining a wide variety of phenomena.

THERAPEUTIC APPROACHES EMERGING IN THE 1950s AND 1960s

Behavioral, pharmacological, nondirective, and family therapies emerged as new approaches to treatment in the 1950s and 1960s. Rather than being dictated by a general theory, these therapies were developed largely as specific techniques.

Behavior Therapies

Despite the efforts of Dollard, Miller, and others to promote a synthesis of learning theory and psychoanalysis, most behavior therapies of the late 1950s and 1960s reflected reactions against psychoanalysis. For example, in *Psychotherapy by Reciprocal Inhibition,* which heralded the renaissance of behavior therapies, Joseph Wolpe (1958) described himself as originally ''a staunch follower of Freud.'' But Wolpe grew skeptical of the universality of the Oedipus complex and the efficacy of psychoanalysis beyond the production of comforting insights. Drawing concepts from Pavlov and Hull, Wolpe defined neurotic behavior as ''. . . any persistent habit of unadaptive behavior acquired by learning in a physiologically normal organism. Anxiety is usually the central constituent of this behavior, being invariably present in the causal situation. . . . By anxiety is meant the autonomic response pattern or patterns that are characteristically part of the organism's response to noxious stimulation'' (1958, pp. 32–34).

Unlike other extrapolations of learning concepts to psychopathology at that time, Wolpe applied his directly to the removal of neurotic symptoms. He did this by training more favorable responses that would "reciprocally inhibit" anxiety responses to particular stimuli. In Wolpe's main method, known as *systematic desensitization,* patients construct anxiety hierarchies ranging from the things that make them most anxious down to the things that make them minimally anxious. The patient is then taught relaxation responses that Wolpe believes are antagonistic to anxiety. Thereafter, the patient is induced to imagine the anxiety stimuli one-by-one, beginning with the least threatening in the hierarchy. As each stimulus is imagined, the patient is to inhibit anxiety by making relaxation responses. Although young children may not be able to do everything required for this procedure, the same principles have been applied to *in vivo desensitization* of children by presenting the actual feared stimuli in a graded sequence while the child is engaged in pleasurable activities (cf., Lazarus, Davison, & Polefka, 1965).

Other behavioral methods are derived from Skinner's operant-conditioning paradigm. Rather than attempting to extinguish anxiety by pairing threatening stimuli with nonfearful responses, operant methods change the reinforcement contingencies of the target behavior. For example, positive-reinforcing consequences are made contingent on responses that are to be strengthened, whereas negative consequences are made contingent on responses that are to be weakened.

At first, behavior therapists implied that their techniques were rigorously derived from "modern learning theory." However, paradoxes arose from the apparent success of methods that were theoretically contradictory. A method known as *implosive therapy* or *flooding,* for example, is exactly opposite to Wolpe's systematic desensitization: It presents massive doses of the feared stimuli under the assumption that anxiety responses will quickly extinguish when no harm results from facing the feared stimuli. And there is evidence that implosive therapy can work with very fearful children (e.g., Ollendick & Gruen, 1972). Many other behavioral techniques likewise have ambiguous ties to general learning theories (see Achenbach, 1982, for further details).

In an article entitled "The End of Ideology in Behavior Modification," London (1972) argued that the ideology of learning theory had been a useful source of metaphors, paradigms, analogies, and a sense of theoretical identity, but that a technological orientation had become more appropriate than an ideological orientation. By this he meant that the mechanical gadgetry and therapeutic techniques of behavior modification were developing faster than any integrative theory. Proving that each innovation was derived from learning theory was therefore less important than finding useful guides wherever possible. As this view has spread, behavioral techniques have been increasingly combined with other approaches, such as biofeedback, residential treatment, family therapy, group therapy, drug therapy, cognitive approaches, psychodynamic approaches, and educational approaches (see Achenbach, 1982). The result is that behavioral technology is evident in diverse mental health services to children and adults, but that it is not a direct derivative of any one learning theory. Instead, the technology has a life of its own that generates ad hoc miniature theories and trial-and-error applications to many specific problems.

Pharmacotherapies

During the 1950s, it was discovered that certain drugs initially developed for other purposes seemed to reduce florid psychotic symptoms in seriously disturbed adults. Further refinement of these drugs led to a revolution in the care of adult mental patients: Major tranquilizers—such as chlorpromazine (Thorazine)—made it possible to reduce physical restraints and to release violent and excited patients from hospitals; antidepressants—such as imipramine (Tofranil)—stimulated the functioning of severely depressed patients. Milder versions of these drugs, such as Valium, became widely prescribed by physicians of diverse specialities and popular in heavily advertised nonprescription forms. Although the biological mechanisms were not well understood, the apparent benefits of pharmacotherapy turned psychiatry toward psychopharmacology and away from psychoanalysis.

As discussed earlier, Bradley's (1937) report that amphetamines reduce hyperactivity contributed to the nosological conception of hyperactivity. However, few children manifest the florid psychotic or depressive symptoms for which major tranquilizers and antidepressants are prescribed. Despite the occasional use of adult drugs with children, there was little evidence for the efficacy of drugs other than stimulants with childhood disorders (Campbell & Small, 1978).

Even the efficacy of stimulant drugs in reducing overactive behavior was not followed by long-term improvements in the social and academic functioning of hyperactive children (e.g., Gittelman, 1982). Nevertheless, as we saw earlier in this chapter, enthusiasm for the psychopharmacological models spawned by adult drug therapies has inspired a hunt for childhood versions of pharmacologically treatable depressive disorders. Whether these disorders exist remains to be seen, but it seems clear that pharmacotherapies, like behavior therapies, now have a life of their own that cannot be credited to any one particular theory.

Nondirective Play Therapy

In nearly all nonorganic therapies in which a therapist meets with children on a one-to-one basis, the therapist provides play materials and the opportunity to play. The assumption is that children feel more comfortable and can express themselves better in play than in purely verbal interviews. Psychoanalytically oriented therapists view play as symbolically reflecting unconscious thoughts and conflicts, just as the free associations of adult patients do. Behavior therapists also use play to get at problems the child is not willing, or able, to discuss.

They may then try to ameliorate behavior problems through play, as by reinforcing the child for approaching feared stimuli in play. In neither the psychoanalytic nor the behavioral approach, however, is the play per se viewed as *therapy*. In nondirective play therapy, by contrast, the child's play is the essential instrument of therapy.

Nondirective play therapy extends Carl Rogers's (1951) nondirective client-centered therapy to children. Just as the client-centered therapist nondirectively encourages adult patients to verbalize their feelings, face them, and learn to control or abandon them, so the play therapist encourages the child to do the same things through play. According to Virginia Axline (1969), a leader in nondirective play therapy, maladjustment occurs when the inner "drive for complete self-realization" is blocked; the function of therapy is to help overcome this maladjustment by enabling children to achieve a sense of power as individuals in their own right. They can then develop new ways of coping with their problems.

During the early years of play therapy, some efforts were made to document its effects and perfect its technique (e.g., Seeman, Barry, & Ellingwood, 1964). However, as nondirective play therapy has been greatly outpaced by the development of behavior therapies, the term "play therapy" has become a synonym for most forms of child psychotherapy in which play materials are used. In effect, nondirective play therapy has merged with psychodynamic concepts to form a common approach to psychotherapy in which children are encouraged to express themselves through play and talk, while the therapist offers support, interpretations, and occasional guidance or advice.

Conjoint Family Therapy

Most therapies for children include work with the child's family, although this usually means that the therapist meets separately with the parents and child. In the 1950s, however, *conjoint family therapy* emerged in which all members of the family meet together with one or two therapists. In one of the first published illustrations, Bell (1961) portrayed conjoint family therapy as a way of dealing more quickly and effectively with problems imputed to a child (the "identified patient"). Bell outlined four phases of the therapy:

1. The *child centered phase,* in which the therapist builds a relationship with the children of a family by being especially attentive to them, supporting their requests for changes in parental behavior, and tending to ignore parental criticism.
2. The *parent-child interaction phase,* in which parents' complaints about the child are prominent and the parents and child tend to talk *about* each other rather than *to* each other.
3. The *father–mother interaction phase,* in which parents express conflicts with each other that are assumed to cause the child's problems.

4. The *termination phase,* in which emphasis on parental interaction and the "identified patient" gives way to an emphasis on the interactions among all family members.

Family therapists view the family as a social system in which each member's behavior is a function of pressures existing in the system as a whole (Goldenberg & Goldenberg, 1980). The problems of the identified patient are viewed as symptoms of family stress. Because these symptoms serve a definite function in the family, removing them without other changes in the family is expected to produce symptoms in other family members, or the dissolution of the family system itself.

Despite agreement on the family as a system, family therapists vary widely in their therapeutic philosophies and techniques. Some see the parents alone for a couple of sessions and obtain a family history, whereas others see the parents and identified patient together from the beginning. Still others insist on seeing all family members together at all times.

Although family therapy has generated a large literature and many schools of thought, controlled research is meager. In one of the few adequately controlled studies, Wellisch, Vincent, and Ro-Trock (1976) found a significantly lower rate of rehospitalization for adolescents who had received family therapy during psychiatric hospitalization than for a control group receiving individual psychotherapy. Yet a comparison of outcomes for adolescent delinquents receiving three types of family therapy or a no-treatment control condition showed that not all forms of family therapy produce the same results (Klein, Barton, & Alexander, 1980). The conditions were:

1. *Behavioral family therapy* (family members were prompted and reinforced for clearly communicating their thoughts and for negotiating contractual compromises);
2. *Client-centered family therapy;*
3. *Psychodynamic family therapy;*
4. *No-treatment control.*

Follow-ups showed a recidivism rate of 26% for delinquents receiving behavioral family therapy, which was significantly better than for the client-centered therapy (47%), the psychodynamic therapy (73%), and the no-treatment control condition (50%). Furthermore, significantly fewer siblings of adolescents in the behavioral therapy group later had court contacts (20%) than in the no-treatment (40%), client-centered (59%), or psychodynamic (63%) groups. This suggested that family systems were favorably altered by behavioral methods, but not by the other approaches to family therapy. Within the groups receiving the behavioral approach, however, those having therapists with the best skills in interpersonal relations had the best outcomes of all (Alexander, Barton, Schiavo, & Parsons, 1976). Not only the method of therapy, but the therapists' skills thus played an important role.

Conclusion

After being dominated by psychodynamic approaches, mental health services of the 1950s and 1960s were augmented with a variety of new therapeutic techniques. Although behavior therapies were nominally rooted in learning theory, they rapidly assumed diverse forms that were not dictated by any particular learning theory and could not be integrated within a single theory. The serendipitous discovery of the effects of certain drugs on adult psychotic symptoms helped to stimulate biological research, but the initial discoveries did not result from theories of psychopathology. Nondirective play therapy and conjoint family therapy were likewise sources of miniature theories more than they were derivatives of theories.

Aside from being relatively independent of grand theories, the new therapies shared another important feature: They were almost totally nondevelopmental, in that they focused neither on the developmental history of disorders, nor on differences in the developmental levels of the children treated, nor on their subsequent developmental needs. Instead, they focused on the current status of each disorder and sought to change it by ameliorating environmental contingencies, biochemical variables, constraints on the inner drive for self-realization, or family systems. We turn now to developmental approaches that are relevant to the study of psychopathology.

DEVELOPMENTAL APPROACHES

Most of what has been considered so far concerns psychopathology rather than development. When developmental considerations arose, they were secondary to other concerns. For example, the psychoanalytic theory of psychosocial development was constructed from adult recollections in order to explain the origins of neurosis. Likewise, learning theories blamed most adult psychopathology on childhood learning experiences. Learning principles were assumed to be the same for children and adults, although certain variables, such as verbal labels, were assumed to acquire new roles at certain ages (Dollard & Miller, 1950; Kendler & Kendler, 1970).

Whereas the major therapeutic approaches have not dealt much with development, the major developmental theories have not dealt much with the treatment of psychopathology. We turn now to three developmental theories that are potentially relevant to psychopathology (see Kuhn, this volume, for more on these theories).

Piaget's Theory

Without recounting all of the important aspects of Jean Piaget's theory, let us consider those features that are most relevant to the developmental study of psychopathology.

Cognitive Developmental Periods.   The best known feature of Piaget's theory is its sequence of cognitive developmental periods: The *sensorimotor* period, the *preoperational* period, the *concrete operational* period, and the *formal operational* period. The hypothesized characteristics of these periods are familiar to most students of developmental psychology. Whether or not these periods embody precisely the cognitive systems claimed by Piaget, they certainly reflect important differences in the ways children process information. Yet none of the major nosological, theoretical, or therapeutic approaches to psychopathology take these differences into account. Although all approaches implicitly recognize differences between infancy and later childhood, they do not take systematic account of the differences in the level of language, reasoning powers, logical assumptions, and use of information that distinguish, for example, 4-year-olds, 8-year-olds, and adolescents.

Figurative versus Operative Aspects of Cognition.   Another feature of Piaget's (1977) theory that is relevant to the developmental study of psychopathology first becomes crucial around the age of 18 months. At this age, Piaget hypothesized, the sensorimotor period is brought to a close by the child's increasing ability to form mental representations. According to Piaget, the process of mental representation has two aspects. The *figurative* aspect encompasses mental signifiers, such as images, symbols, and words, that stand for particular stimuli. These signifiers are roughly analogous to the contents of mental life hypothesized by other theories, such as the mental symbols of psychoanalytic theory and the covert mediating responses of learning theories. Piaget called these mental signifiers *schemas*. Prior to about 18 months of age, Piaget hypothesized that the only schemas are percepts evoked by sensory stimulation. After about 18 months, however, mental schemas can be generated with increasing independence of perceptual input. It is this capacity for purposely representing stimuli via mental schemas that marks the transition from sensorimotor to preoperational thought.

Piaget called the second aspect of mental representation the *operative* aspect. In contrast to the mental signifiers of the figurative aspect, the operative aspect refers to organized mental activities that are analogous to the behavioral schemes evident during the sensorimotor period; in early infancy, for example, the sucking scheme, is an organized series of actions encompassing the recognition, grasp, and sucking of suckable objects. Sensorimotor schemes are physical activities, but mental schemes are cognitive activities through which the contents (schemas) of thought are manipulated. (Translations of Piaget's work often use the terms *schema* and *scheme* interchangeably, but, in the 1960s, Piaget clarified that *schemas* are mental signifiers belonging to the figurative aspect of thought, whereas *schemes* are organized mental activities belonging to the operative aspect.)

Piaget's distinction between the operative and figurative aspects of thought has no clear counterpart in other developmental theories. Yet, according to

Piaget, cognitive development consists mainly of changes in the operative aspect of thought. Even during the sensorimotor period—from birth to about 18 months—Piaget noted big enough changes in overt schemes to warrant dividing the period into six stages. More pervasive changes in operative functioning are marked by the transition to the concrete operational period between ages 5 and 7, and the transition to the formal operational period at about age 11.

Aside from the advent of mental signifiers at the end of the sensorimotor period, Piaget did not ascribe major developmental changes to the figurative aspect of thought. Nevertheless, the progressive acquisition of new signifiers, such as words, and the growth of operative powers to use signifiers in new ways continue to contribute to the development of mental functioning.

The distinction between the figurative and operative aspects of thought enabled Piaget to provide a far more differentiated picture of mental development than did psychoanalytic or learning theorists, whose preoccupation with the *contents* of thought left little room for changes in the *operations* and *structure* of thought. However, despite applications of Piagetian concepts to social thinking under the banner of *social cognition* (e.g., Flavell & Ross, 1981), a large gap remains to be bridged between the differentiated Piagetian picture of cognition and the developmental study of psychopathology.

Causes of Development.   Piaget hypothesized four major sources of development:

1. *Organic maturation;*
2. *Experience* gained through interactions with the physical world, whereby the child observes phenomena and actively experiments to find out how things happen;
3. *Transmission of information* from other people by language, modeling, and teaching;
4. *Equilibration.*

The first three contributors to development—maturation, experience, and social transmission—have counterparts in most theories. But Piaget believed that these three were not enough to explain cognitive development. Instead, cognitive development involves the construction of new mental representations when a child's existing concepts prove inadequate. The process of *equilibration* is especially crucial in the major transitions from one period of cognitive development to the next. It brings the other contributors to development together in the construction of higher-order cognitive structures from lower-order structures that have reached their limits. To use a computer analogy, cognitive structures resemble computer programs, whereas schemes are similar to subroutines of these programs, and schemas resemble the encoded data that these programs manipulate and transform. Unlike computers, however, living organisms can create for themselves new cognitive challenges to which they respond through the process of equilibration by constructing new representations and operations.

Although Piaget never fully clarified the equilibration process, it represents a crucial aspect of cognition and adaptive activity in general. The essence of this activity is the struggle to overcome gaps and contradictions in our comprehension of the world and ourselves. This kind of activity is an essential part of healthy development and needs far more attention in the developmental study of psychopathology.

Werner's Theory

Heinz Werner's theory is considerably less detailed and has generated less research on development than Piaget's theory. Yet, Werner was far more ambitious about the scope of developmental theory. His conception of developmental psychology was not restricted "either to ontogenesis or phylogenesis, but seeks to coordinate within a single framework forms of behavior observed in comparative animal psychology, in child psychology, in psychopathology, in ethnopsychology, and in the general and differential psychology of man in our own culture" (Werner, 1957, p. 125).

The Orthogenetic Principle.   According to Werner's *orthogenetic principle,* developmental changes entail a progression from undifferentiated functioning to functioning that is *differentiated, specialized,* and *hierarchically integrated.* By hierarchic integration, Werner meant that specific functions become coordinated within higher levels of organization. One-word utterances, for example, give way to multi-word utterances in which individual words function as components of higher-order grammatical structures, such as subjects and predicates. Subjects and predicates, in turn, are integrated within sentences, which are still higher in the hierarchy of grammatical organization.

Rather than generating specific hypotheses subject to test, Werner's strategy was to illustrate his orthogenetic principle with examples from organic development, psychopathology, anthropology, and the behavior of brain damaged people. Perhaps the most relevant to developmental psychopathology was research designed to demonstrate developmental parallels between ontogenesis, microgenesis, and pathogenesis. *Microgenesis* refers to the short-term development of concepts, percepts, and behavior, whereas *pathogenesis* refers to the development of psychopathology.

As an example, Werner (1957) compared the Rorschach responses of normal adults who saw ink blots presented tachistoscopically at progressively longer exposures, with the responses of normal children and disturbed adults who saw the blots at normal exposure times. Werner found that the percentage of Rorschach responses that were based more on details than on global, undifferentiated percepts increased with exposure time. This illustrated the *microgenesis* of more differentiated percepts as exposure lengthened. *Ontogenesis* was illustrated by more detailed percepts among older children than younger children. *Pathogenesis* was illustrated by similar contrasts between responses by diagnostic groups hypothesized to be developmentally primitive (hebephrenic and catatonic schizophrenics), developmentally intermediate (paranoids), and developmentally advanced (normal adults).

Field Independence versus Dependence.   The best known research emerging from Werner's approach has concerned the cognitive style of *field independence versus dependence*. Field independence refers to independence from distracting cues in a perceptual context, or "field", surrounding a target stimulus. Field dependence, by contrast, involves reliance on contextual cues. Field independence has been found to increase between the ages of 8 and 17, but the rank of each individual's scores within a sample remains fairly stable from year to year (Witkin, Dyk, Faterson, Goodenough, & Karp, 1962). This suggests stable individual differences that endure despite developmental changes. Although much of the variance in field independence–dependence can be accounted for by measures of cognitive level, such as mental age on an IQ test (Weisz, O'Neill, & O'Neill, 1975), personality differences also correlate with this cognitive style. Field-dependent people, for example, seem especially sensitive to social cues, whereas field-independent people are better at cognitive analysis (Witkin & Goodenough, 1980).

Although Werner viewed developmental theory as a way to link our understanding of normal development, psychopathology, and individual differences at all ages, his plausible generalizations about developmental increases in "differentiation" might be of more value if they generated operational measures of specific variables that presumably become differentiated. Without more specific hypotheses about why children become less field-dependent with age and why catatonics give less differentiated Rorschach responses than do paranoids, there are too many possible explanations for these findings to be very informative. People who are diagnosed as catatonic, for example, are likely to be less motivated, more withdrawn, and more heavily medicated than people who are diagnosed as paranoid. All of these differences could reduce catatonics' verbal responsiveness, which would, in turn, reduce the percentage of their Rorschach responses based on perceptual details.

Erikson's Theory

Erik H. Erikson's (1963, 1980) theory of *psychosocial development* is an outgrowth of Freud's theory of psychosexual development. Erikson, however, stresses the social aspects of development rather than the distribution of libido or the origins of adult neurosis. The interface between society and the developing individual is highlighted in his basic assumptions:

(1) that the human personality in principle develops according to steps predetermined in the growing person's readiness to be driven toward, to be aware of, and to interact with, a widening social radius; and (2) that society, in principle, tends to be so constituted as to meet and invite this succession of potentialities for interaction and attempts to safeguard and to encourage the proper rate and the proper sequence of their unfolding (Erikson, 1963, p. 270).

Stages of Psychosocial Development.   Although Erikson divides childhood development into stages approximating Freud's phases of libidinal development, his stages are defined not only in terms of ascendant erogenous zones, but also in terms of *modes of action* employed by the child and the *modalities of social interaction* that characterize interpersonal exchanges at each stage. The initial stage, for example, is dominated by a general incorporative mode that includes incorporation of stimuli through the sense organs, as well as through the mouth. Erikson therefore calls this stage the *oral-sensory stage,* rather than just the oral stage, as Freud called it. The dominant mode of action at this stage is the *incorporation* of input from the outside world. Because the infant's social interactions center on getting others to provide for its needs and receiving what they give, the social modality is called *getting.* The four subsequent psychosocial stages are a *second oral-sensory stage* in which more active incorporation is the child's dominant mode and *taking* is the social modality; the *anal-urethral-muscular stage;* the *locomotor and infantile genital stage;* and the *rudimentary genital stage.*

Erikson does not specify why development progresses from one stage to the next, but he maintains that the failure of the appropriate mode to dominate a stage can disrupt subsequent stages. If a baby repeatedly vomits, for example, this premature dominance of the *eliminative mode* (which normally dominates the anal-urethral-muscular stage) may hinder the learning of the social modality of getting. These disruptions can affect later personality development.

Nuclear Conflicts.   Erikson is probably best known for the *developmental crises* or *nuclear conflicts* he ascribes to particular stages. The two oral-sensory stages, for example, raise conflicts over the development of *basic trust versus distrust.* A resolution in favor of basic trust depends on the mother's success in satisfying the child's needs, thereby instilling in the child a sense of trust in the mother and the world she represents. Erikson's conceptions of later conflicts, especially the adolescent conflict over *identity versus role confusion,* have received abundant attention in the developmental and psychodynamic literature and have influenced psychotherapy for both children and adolescents.

Although Erikson's theory has not produced a distinctive therapeutic method or testable explanations for psychopathology, several studies have found evidence for sequences of conflictual concerns like those that Erikson hypothesizes (e.g., Ciaccio, 1971; Constantinople, 1969; Waterman, Geary, & Waterman,

1974). Even though the hypothesized conflicts do seem to exist, these studies have suggested that most people continue to experience certain conflicts even as others rise and fall.

Conclusion

Developmental theories provide a rich picture of various aspects of development. An interweaving of Piaget's theory and Erikson's theory, in particular, offers an understanding of normal development and its problems. Table 10.2 summarizes relations between these theories and Freud's theory of psychosexual development, as well as the normal achievements, common behavior problems, and clinical disorders characterizing each period.

Despite the value of comprehensive overviews of development, the sense of understanding bestowed by global theories has not revealed the causes nor provided efficacious methods for the treatment or prevention of most childhood disorders. We therefore turn now to some major problems facing developmental research on psychopathology.

CURRENT PROBLEMS AND ISSUES

As we have seen, there is great diversity among the approaches that touch on the developmental study of psychopathology, but no single approach deals comprehensively with it. Instead, there are nosological approaches to psychopathology in general that are based largely on medical models for severe adult disorders, but are not of much demonstrated value for children's disorders. As an alternative to nosological approaches, there are multivariate approaches for extracting syndromes from the quantitative covariation among reported behaviors. In the absence of known etiologies, multivariate approaches can make more efficient use of phenotypic data than do the arbitrary decision rules imposed by categorical nosologies. Multivariate approaches also lend themselves to comprehensive descriptive profiles that can serve as a basis for taxonomies of behavior patterns. So far, multivariate behavioral descriptions have been cross-sectional, although comparisons of the syndromes found at different ages suggest developmental differences that are worth testing in longitudinal studies, as discussed later.

Aside from the nosological and multivariate approaches to the identification of disorders, two general theoretical approaches to the understanding of psychopathology were considered: Psychoanalytic theory and learning theory, both of which implied developmental origins for psychopathology, but were not based on the study of children's development. Although both had major impacts on views of psychopathology, and efforts were made to join them in a grand synthesis, they gave way in the 1950s and 1960s to a variety of new therapeutic approaches that were not dictated by any general theory.

TABLE 10.2

Relations Between Developmental Theories, Achievements, Behavior Problems, and Clinical Disorders. (From Achenbach, 1982, p. 67.)

Approximate Age	Cognitive Period	Psychosexual Phase	Psychosocial Conflict	Normal Achievements	Common Behavior Problems[a]	Clinical Disorders
0–2	Sensory-Motor	Oral	Basic Trust vs. Mistrust	Eating, digestion, sleeping, social responsiveness, attachment, motility, sensory-motor organization	Stubbornness, temper, toileting	Organically based dysfunctions, anaclitic depression, autism, failure to thrive
2–5	Pre-Operational	Anal	Autonomy vs. Shame and Doubt	Language, toileting, self-care skills, safety rules, self-control, peer relationships	Argues, brags, demands attention, disobedient, jealous, fears,[c] prefers older children, overactive, resists bedtime, shows off, shy,[c] stubborn, talks too much, temper, whines	Speech and hearing problems, phobias, unsocialized behavior
		Phallic-Oedipal	Initiative vs. Guilt			
6–11	Concrete Operational	Latency	Industry vs. Inferiority	Academic skills, school rule-governed games, hobbies, monetary exchange, simple responsibilities	Argues, brags,[b] can't concentrate,[b] self-conscious, shows off, talks too much[c]	Hyperactivity, learning problems, school phobia, aggression, withdrawal
12–20	Formal Operational	Genital	Identity vs. Role Confusion	Relations with opposite sex, vocational preparation, personal identity, separation from family, adult responsibilities	Argues, brags[b]	Anorexia, delinquency, suicide attempts, drug and alcohol abuse, schizophrenia, depression

[a]Problems reported for at least 45% of children in nonclinical samples.
[b]Indicates problem reported for ≥45% of boys only.
[c]Indicates ≥45% of girls only.

439

Just as the major approaches to psychopathology have not been based on developmental research, so the major approaches to development have not involved much research on child psychopathology. In the case of Piaget's theory, this is understandable, because Piaget sought to construct a genetic epistemology rather than to explain psychopathology. However, Piaget's picture of developmental sequences and processes, and his distinction between the operative and the figurative aspects of thought, are important for all aspects of development, maladaptive as well as adaptive. Whether we try to determine what has gone wrong when we see a disturbed child or try to help the child, it is always important to know the child's level of cognitive functioning, the limits and misconceptions entailed, and the potential for further growth.

Werner and Erikson were interested in applying their developmental theories to psychopathology, but mainly so as to illustrate their general developmental principles. Unlike Piaget, they did not provide extensive methodologies for testing their concepts empirically.

In light of where we've been, where should we be going? Although several different literatures relate to the development of psychopathology, they do not share a coherent program of research. Instead, each literature is preoccupied with a particular approach, to the neglect of cross-cutting issues. Because no single approach really takes the developmental study of psychopathology as its central objective, it is important to lay out central issues that require study in their own right. The following sections highlight some of these issues.

Operationally Defining Disorders

The lack of accepted operational definitions for disorders of childhood and adolescence has prevented differing approaches from converging on a common set of target phenomena. When applied to childhood disorders, the traditional nosological approach has been handicapped by the lack of a taxonomic data base on which to build its categories, and by a precommitment to diagnostic constructs that must be judged as present or absent. Although DSM-III provides explicit decision rules for each diagnostic category, these rules are arbitrary rather than being derived from data on differences among disorders. Furthermore, these decision rules do not constitute operational definitions, because no measurement operations are specified for determining whether a child's behavior meets the specified criteria.

In contrast, multivariate approaches are designed to derive target disorders from empirical data and to quantify criterial attributes. Because the disorders are defined in terms of scores on particular instruments, multivariate approaches also provide operational definitions. However, as with any taxonomic effort, multivariate approaches require decisions about what data to use in formulating taxa, what taxa are useful for what purposes, and what cutting points should be used to discriminate between the normal and the "pathological" range, as well as between one taxon and another. These are questions that should be answered through programmatic research. In the absence of known etiologies or clear-cut organic markers, this type of research is a form of psychometric bootstrapping— i.e., trial-and-error revision of measures in order to strengthen their relations to each other and to admittedly imperfect validity criteria.

In some disorders, such as autism, the age of onset and clear-cut pathognomonic behavior argue for a taxon of the classical nosological type, while multivariate approaches can help to sharpen distinctions among children who meet the categorical criteria of the taxon. In other disorders, multivariate findings may provide the initial basis for the taxa, but other types of data may then be needed to refine the taxa and to search for etiologies. Whatever approach is taken, however, it should be recognized that clarifying the central phenomena is a prerequisite for effective research on most aspects of developmental psychopathology.

Differential Clinical Assessment

Related to the problem of operationally defining disorders is the problem of differential clinical assessment. Although operational definitions specify procedures for determining which taxonomic criteria a child meets, clinical assessments must provide a more comprehensive picture than does a taxonomy of disorders. It is always important to know the child's family situation, developmental history, medical condition, level of cognitive functioning, school record, peer relations, special competencies, and important life stresses. Some of these may contribute to taxonomic decisions, but no taxonomy will ever be comprehensive enough to take detailed account of all of them. Instead, taxonomies overlook many individual characteristics in order to highlight those few that can define a class of individuals.

When assessing a child, decisions may be needed in relation to several different taxonomies. For example, a boy's behavior may be deviant in a way that meets the criteria for a particular behavior disorder. The boy's IQ may be low enough to classify him as "mildly retarded." This, in turn, may classify him as eligible for special education. He might also have organic problems that classify him as having a perceptual-motor handicap. These multiple classifications serve different purposes and are not mutually contradictory. However, they do not add up to a very clear picture of the boy and his specific needs.

In trying to help individual children, we need a comprehensive, idiographic picture of each child that cannot be derived from all the relevant taxonomic criteria. In practice, clinicians have relied much more on idiographic assessment than on linking children to overarching taxonomies. Clinical interviews with children and their parents, a developmental history taken from the parents, comments by teachers, and projective tests are commonly used in deciding what is wrong and what to do about it. Even behaviorally oriented clinicians rely much more on these procedures than on the direct observations in natural environments that the behavioral literature espouses (Wade, Baker, & Hartmann, 1979). One weakness of all of these methods is that the data are obtained in ways that vary from case to case, are of unknown reliability and validity, and cannot be compared with normative baselines for a child's age.

Not only for taxonomic purposes, then, but also for purposes of formulating an idiographic picture of the child that distinguishes that child from other children, we need assessment procedures of proven reliability and validity, based on normative data. Procedures such as interviews, ratings by parents and teachers, self-reports, behavior samples, and tests may all contribute valid assessment data, but research is required to determine what unique contribution each procedure can make, and to standardize the best of these procedures for use across diverse settings.

Longitudinal Course of Adaptive and Maladaptive Behavior

The previous two sections dealt with research that is largely cross-sectional—operationally defining disorders and making differential assessments of children at a particular point in time. Although children's past histories are always relevant to the definitions of disorders and to broader clinical assessment, the main value of both of these enterprises lies in their relation to the children's future development. In short, the ultimate purpose of operational definitions and differential assessment is to facilitate children's development. But this requires knowledge of the typical outcomes of each disorder. This knowledge, in turn, requires longitudinal research that compares the developmental course of children grouped according to type of disorder and other variables, subject to differential assessment. Although etiological research is also important, the multi-determined nature of most childhood behavior disorders means that longitudinal follow-up studies may yield quicker and surer benefits for troubled children than will etiological research.

For example, suppose we start with 6- to 11-year-old children for whom parents and teachers have filled out standardized rating forms at intake into several mental health settings. Forms of this sort for obtaining data on children's problems and competencies are coming into widespread use. They have been subjected to multivariate analyses to produce empirically derived scales for scoring behavioral problems and competencies. The scales have been normed and cast in profile formats. As illustrated in Figure 10.1, cluster analyses have identified profile patterns shared by substantial subgroups of clinically referred children (see Achenbach & Edelbrock, 1983, for details).

Profiles from parent and teacher ratings of large samples of children provide a good picture of the range of problems for which children are typically referred. The standardization of ratings and the classification of children by profile types give us a starting point from which to compare outcomes for children who differ in their initial problems and competencies, as seen by important adults in their natural environments.

If we have parents and teachers fill out the same rating forms again at certain intervals, such as every 6 months for 2 years, we can track the course of the child's problems and competencies as judged by these important adults. We can then determine whether the patterns of problems and competencies manifested at intake can predict outcomes over the 2 years. In particular, we can determine whether any patterns have much worse or better outcomes than others. Even if the clinical services are heterogeneous (as they are in most settings), findings of especially poor outcomes for a particular profile pattern would indicate that this was a group in need of close study to determine why their outcomes are so poor and what can be done to help them. Conversely, a group with exceptionally good outcomes could be examined to identify the factors responsible. For example, were they especially well suited to the services offered? Or might they be especially competent and able to improve regardless of the services? Or might their problems have been specific to a particular developmental period?

Further variables can be readily added to a study of this type. For example, demographic and family data routinely obtained at intake (e.g., socioeconomic status, race, rural versus suburban versus urban residence, marital status of parents, number of siblings) may augment the predictive power of profile patterns. Other data, such as IQ and medical conditions, may also be important. However, the more variables that are included, the larger the samples needed and the greater the risk of chance findings that must be controlled by adjusting significance levels. Furthermore, such studies should also incorporate cross-validation, either in new samples or by splitting samples in half and testing the findings from one half in the other half of the sample.

Studies of this sort can also address interesting developmental questions by analyzing changes in reported behavior patterns occurring as children grow older. For example, as shown in Figure 10.1 cross-sectional research has yielded a profile characterized by exceptional elevations on Uncommunicative and Delinquent syndromes for 12- to 16-year-old boys. Although the Uncommunicative and Delinquent syndromes have also been found among 6- to 11-year-old boys, cluster analyses revealed no profile type characterized by peaks on both these syndromes for 6- to 11-year-old boys. If we follow disturbed 10-year-old boys for three years, would a distinct group show the Uncommunicative-Delinquent profile by the time they are adolescents? If so, what profile patterns did they show before the Uncommunicative-Delinquent pattern emerged?

Or, if we begin with 10-year-old boys whose profiles are elevated on Somatic Complaints, will they continue to show a particular pattern in adolescence, when cross-sectional analyses have not revealed a Somatic Complaints profile? Or do they have such good outcomes that the Somatic Complaints profile can be considered a transitory developmental phenomenon that disappears by the time the boys reach adolescence?

In summary, it seems clear that even short-term longitudinal studies of the problems and competencies of children already identified as disturbed can be of great value for understanding childhood psychopathology and development.

Moreover, these studies can improve services to children by pinpointing groups in need of help not yet provided, as well as by laying the groundwork for devising new ways to help these children. By first identifying those currently having the worst outcomes, we can also concentrate etiological research where it is most needed, rather than initiating etiological studies without knowing the usual outcomes of the disorders we are studying.

Experimental Intervention and Prevention

The most powerful strategy for testing causal relations is the experimental manipulation of the hypothesized causal variable to see whether it affects the dependent variable of interest. Drug therapies are tested in experimental studies that employ as a control condition inactive placebo drugs identical in appearance to the drug under test. Because the patients and evaluators do not know which is the placebo and which is the active drug, this is known as a "double-blind placebo-controlled" procedure. Experimental studies of this sort have shown that hyperactivity can be reduced with stimulant drugs (e.g., Henker, Whalen, & Collins, 1979).

The double-blind placebo-controlled experiment is viewed as an ideal to be emulated in the evaluation of all therapies. Approximations to experimental evaluations of drug therapies have been carried out with behavior therapies (see Achenbach, 1982), but most nondrug therapies cannot approximate the double-blind placebo-controlled study for several reasons:

1. Placebo conditions cannot be created that are both ethical and convincing alternatives to the active treatment.
2. The differences between experimental and control conditions are too obvious to enable patients and evaluators to remain blind.
3. The onset and offset of the hypothesized therapeutic effects cannot be precisely controlled.
4. Treatments such as psychotherapy, nondirective play therapy, and family therapy aim to bring about general changes in functioning that are not assessable via short-term measures of specific behaviors.

Efforts at prevention face even greater obstacles, because the target disorders are not yet evident when the intervention takes place. This means that experimental manipulations must be made with subjects who are not motivated by current distress and may never develop the target disorders. Furthermore, because the target disorders have not emerged when the preventive efforts are made, the evaluation of the interventions must last until well into the period at which the disorders would ordinarily emerge.

In light of the foregoing obstacles, it should not be surprising that there are few well controlled experimental evaluations of interventions for child psychopathology other than drug and behavior therapies. Nevertheless, it is incumbent on advocates of particular therapeutic or preventive methods to demonstrate that they are effective and not harmful. How can this be done?

Because experimental studies are so costly, time-consuming, and methodologically difficult, they are likely to be worthwhile only after the tasks outlined in the preceding sections have been accomplished. That is, we should have reliable and valid operational definitions of the disorders, standardized procedures for differential clinical assessment, and longitudinal data on outcomes. If we have a good operational definition of a disorder, can reliably differentiate it from other disorders, and know that it usually has a poor outcome, then experimental studies of interventions for treating or preventing that disorder may be worthwhile.

The difficulty of creating appropriate placebo-control conditions argues for the comparison of two different treatments on similar groups of children who have the target disorder, rather than a treatment versus a no-treatment group. One treatment might be the therapy that these children ordinarily receive, whereas the second could be a new treatment based on close study of children having a behavioral pattern found to have poor outcomes in longitudinal follow-ups.

Suppose, for example, that a behavior profile pattern having peaks on depression, social withdrawal, and aggression has especially poor outcomes among 6- to 11-year-old boys. Close study of boys manifesting this pattern indicates that they lack skill in making friends, are often rejected by others, cannot communicate their feelings verbally, and react to frustration with extreme aggression. A possible intervention might be to train them in the skills required to make friends, to avoid doing things that precipitate rejection, to communicate their feelings verbally, and to react more constructively to frustration.

After pilot research to perfect a social skills training program, an experimental study can be designed to compare it with one or more treatments ordinarily administered to these boys. For example, it may be possible to compare the new treatment with two commonly used treatments, such as individual psychotherapy and family therapy. The candidates would be boys who at intake into a mental health service manifest behavior profiles with peaks on depression, social withdrawal, and aggression. Extensive differential assessment would be used to exclude boys who might be poor subjects due to major problems beyond the reach of the therapies to be tested, such as organic dysfunctions, very low cognitive ability, extreme family instability, or uncooperativeness.

If a boy met the criteria for the study and he and his family agreed to participate, a random procedure could be used to assign him to one of the three treatment conditions. Prior to the treatment, and again at six-month intervals thereafter, behavior ratings by the boys' parents and teachers, self-reports by the boys, and standardized clinical interviews would be used to assess behavioral change. Boys receiving the three treatments would ultimately be compared on these variables, plus others such as achievement test performance, friendships, and trouble with the law. Some of the evaluators, such as teachers and clinical interviewers, could be kept blind as to the treatment conditions, whereas other outcome variables, such as test performance and police records, would not be susceptible to influence through knowledge of the treatment conditions.

A single-factor design of this sort could be expanded by comparing two groups who have different initial behavioral patterns across two types of intervention in a two-by-two design. The very few studies reporting adequate subject-by-treatment analyses have revealed unexpected interaction effects that greatly outweighed the main effects of treatment (e.g., Love & Kaswan, 1974; Miller, Barrett, Hampe, & Noble, 1972). Thus, certain treatments may be helpful to some kinds of children but harmful to others. Unless the interactions between child characteristics and treatment effects are assessed, however, we will not know what treatments are optimal for which children.

Conclusion

In summarizing the approaches to development and psychopathology, it seems clear that no single approach really takes the developmental study of psychopathology as its central objective. We therefore considered several key tasks requiring programmatic research to foster a developmental understanding of psychopathology.

The first task was to construct reliable and valid operational definitions of disorders from empirical data. The second was to establish standardized assessment procedures that reliably and validly compare each child with other children. The third was to conduct longitudinal follow-ups aimed at determining the characteristic outcomes of particular patterns of adaptive and maladaptive behavior.

Once we have reliable and valid operational definitions of disorders, standardized procedures for differential clinical assessment, and longitudinal data on outcomes, it may then be worth mounting experimental studies of interventions for preventing or treating those disorders found to have poor outcomes. These tasks by no means exhaust the possibilities for significant developmental research on psychopathology, but they are of critical importance to almost all theories, disorders, and approaches to treatment.

REFERENCES

Achenbach, T. M. The classification of children's psychiatric symptoms: A factor-analytic study. *Psychological Monographs*, 1966, *80* (Whole No. 615).

Achenbach, T. M. The Child Behavior Profile: I. Boys aged 6-11. *Journal of Consulting and Clinical Psychology*, 1978, *46*, 478–488.

Achenbach, T. M. *Developmental psychopatholopy (2nd Edition)*. New York: Wiley, 1982.

Achenbach, T. M., & Edelbrock, C. S. The classification of child psychopathology: A review and analysis of empirical efforts. *Psychological Bulletin*, 1978, *85*, 1275–1301.

Achenbach, T. M., & Edelbrock, C. S. The Child Behavior Profile: II. Boys aged 12–16 and girls aged 6–11 and 12–16. *Journal of Consulting and Clinical Psychology,* 1979, *47,* 223–233.

Achenbach, T. M., & Edelbrock, C. S. Behavioral problems and competencies reported by parents of normal and disturbed children aged four through sixteen. *Monographs of the Society for Research in Child Development,* 1981, *46,* Serial No. 188.

Achenbach, T. M., & Edelbrock, C. *Manual for the Child Behavior Checklist and Revised Child Behavior Profile.* Burlington, VT: Dept. of Psychiatry, University of Vermont, 1983.

Alexander, J. F., Barton, C., Schiavo, R. S., & Parsons, B. V. Systems-behavioral intervention with families of delinquents: Therapist charcteristics, family behavior, and outcome. *Journal of Consulting and Clinical Psychology,* 1976, *44,* 656–644.

American Psychiatric Association. *Diagnostic and statistical manual of mental disorders.* Washington, D.C.: Author, First edition, 1952; Second edition, 1968; Third edition, 1980.

Axline, V. M. *Play therapy* (rev. ed.), New York: Ballantine Books, 1969.

Beitchman, J. H., Dielman, T. E., Landis, J. R., Benson, R. M., & Kemp, P. L. Reliability of the Group for the Advancement of Psychiatry diagnostic categories in child psychiatry. *Archives of General Psychiatry,* 1978, *35,* 1461–66.

Bell, J. E. Family group therapy. *Public Health Monograph, No. 64.* Washington, D.C.: United States Department of Health, Education, and Welfare, 1961.

Bettelheim, B. *The empty fortress.* New York: Free Press, 1967.

Bockoven, J. S. *Moral treatment in American psychiatry.* New York: Springer, 1963.

Bradley, C. The behavior of children receiving benzedrine. *American Journal of Psychiatry,* 1937, *94,* 577–585.

Brown, G., Chadwick, O., Shaffer, D., Rutter, M., & Traub, M. A prospective study of children with head injuries. III. Psychiatric sequelae. *Psychological Medicine,* 1981, *11,* 63–78.

Campbell, M., & Small, A. M. Chemotherapy. In B. B. Wolman, J. Egan, & A. O. Ross (Eds.), *Handbook of treatment of mental disorders in childhood and adolescence.* Englewood Cliffs, NJ: Prentice-Hall, 1978.

Carlson, G. A., & Cantwell, D. P. Diagnosis of childhood depression: A comparison of the Weinberg and DSM-III criteria. *Journal of the American Academy of Child Psychiatry,* 1982, *21,* 247–250.

Cerreto, M. C., & Tuma, J. M. Distribution of DSM-II diagnoses in a child setting. *Journal of Abnormal Child Psychology,* 1977, *5,* 147–155.

Ciaccio, N. V. A test of Erikson's theory of ego epigenesis. *Developmental Psychology,* 1971, *4,* 306–311.

Cohen, D. J., Caparulo, B. K., Gold, J. R., Waldo, M. C., Shaywitz, B. A., Ruttenberg, B. A., & Rimland, B. Agreement in diagnosis: Clinical assessment and behavior rating scales for pervasively disturbed children. *Journal of the American Academy of Child Psychiatry,* 1978, *17,* 589–603.

Constantinople, A. An Eriksonian measure of personality development in college students. *Developmental Psychology,* 1969, *1,* 357–372.

Cytryn, L., & McKnew, D. H. Affective disorders. In J. Noshpitz (Ed.), *Basic handbook of child psychiatry (Vol. 2).* New York: Basic Books, 1979.

Cytryn, L., McKnew, D. H., & Bunney, W. Diagnosis of depression in children: reassessment. *American Journal of Psychiatry,* 1980, *137,* 22–25.

Despert, L. Psychotherapy in childhood schizophrenia. *American Journal of Psychiatry,* 1947, *104,* 36–43.

Dollard, J., & Miller, N. *Personality and psychotherapy.* New York: McGraw-Hill, 1950.

Edelbrock, C., & Achenbach, T. M. A typology of Child Behavior Profile patterns: Distribution and correlates in disturbed children aged 6 to 16. *Journal of Abnormal Child Psychology,* 1980, *8,* 441–470.

Edelbrock, C., Costello, A. J., & Kessler, M. D. Empirical corroboration of the Attention Deficit Disorder. *Journal of the American Academy of Child Psychiatry,* 1984, in press.

Eisenberg, L., & Kanner, L. Early infantile autism, 1943–1955. *American Journal of Ortho-psychiatry,* 1956, *26,* 556–566.

Erikson, E. H. *Childhood in society* (2nd ed.). New York: Norton, 1963.

Erikson, E. H. Elements of a psychoanalytic theory of psychosocial development. In S. I. Green-span & G. H. Pollock (Eds.), *The course of life: Psychoanalytic contributions toward under-standing personality development (Vol. 1).* Adelphi, Md: NIMH Mental Health Study Center, 1980.

Flavell, J. H., & Ross, L. (Eds.) *Social cognitive development: Frontiers and possible futures.* New York: Cambridge University Press, 1981.

Freeman, M. A reliability study of psychiatric diagnosis in childhood and adolescence. *Journal of Child Psychology and Psychiatry,* 1971, *12,* 43–54.

Freud, A. *Normality and pathology in childhood.* New York: International Universities Press, 1965.

Freud, S. Three essays on the theory of sexuality (1905). In *Standard edition of the complete psychological works of Sigmund Freud (Vol. 7).* London: The Hogarth Press, 1953.

Frommer, E. A. Treatment of childhood depression with antidepressant drugs. *British Medical Journal,* 1967, *1,* 729–732.

Gittelman, R. *Prospective follow-up study of hyperactive children.* Presented at the American Acad-emy of Child Psychiatry, Washington, D.C., October, 1982.

Goldenberg, I., & Goldenberg, H. *Family Therapy: An overview.* Monterey, Cal.: Brooks/Cole, 1980.

Griesinger, W. *Die Pathologie und Therapie der psychischen Krankheiten* (1845). Translated as *Mental pathology and therapeutics* by C. L. Robertson & J. Rutherford. London: New Sydenham Society, 1867.

Group for the Advancement of Psychiatry. *Psychopathological disorders in childhood: Theoretical considerations and a proposed classification. GAP Report No. 62,* 1966.

Henker, B., Whalen, C. K., & Collins, B. E. Double-blind and triple-blind assessments of medica-tion and placebo responses in hyperactive children. *Journal of Abnormal Child Psychology,* 1979, *7,* 1–13.

Holmes, F. B. An experimental investigation of a method of overcoming children's fears. *Child Development,* 1936, *7,* 6–30.

Jones, M. C. A laboratory study of fear: The case of Peter. *Pedagogical Seminary,* 1924, *31,* 308–315.

Kanner, L. Autistic disturbances of affective contact. *Nervous Child,* 1943, *2,* 217–250.

Kanner, L. Childhood psychosis: A historical overview. *Journal of Autism and Childhood Schizo-phrenia,* 1971, *1,* 14–19.

Kanner, L., Rodrigues, A., & Ashenden, B. How far can autistic children go in matters of social adaptation? *Journal of Autism and Childhood Schizophrenia,* 1972, *2,* 9–33.

Kasanin, J., & Kaufman, M. R. A study of the functional psychoses in childhood. *American Journal of Psychiatry,* 1929, *9,* 307–384.

Kashani, J. M., Husain, A., Shekim, W. O., Hodges, K. K. Cytryn, L., & McKnew, D. H. Current perspectives on childhood depression: An overview. *American Journal of Psychiatry,* 1981, *138,* 143–153.

Kendler, T. S., & Kendler, H. H. An ontogeny of optional shift behavior. *Child Development,* 1970, *41,* 1–27.

Klein, N. C., Barton, C., & Alexander, J. F. Intervention and evaluation in family settings. In R. H. Price & P. E. Polister (Eds.), *Evaluation and action in the social environment.* New York: Academic Press, 1980.

Kovacs, M., & Beck, A. T. An empirical-clinical approach toward a definition of childhood depres-sion. In J. G. Schulterbrandt & A. Raskin (Eds.), *Depression in childhood: Diagnosis, treat-ment, and conceptual models.* New York: Raven Press, 1977.

Kraepelin, E. *Compendium der Psychiatrie.* Leipzig: Abel, 1st ed. 1883; 8th ed. 1915.

Lazarus, A. A., Davison, G. C., & Polefka, D. A. Classical and operant factors in the treatment of a school phobia. *Journal of Abnormal Psychology,* 1965, *70,* 225–229.

Lejeune, J., Gautier, M., & Turpin, R. Study of the somatic chromosomes of nine mongoloid idiot children, 1959. In S. H. Boyer (Ed.), *Papers on human genetics.* Englewood Cliffs, NJ: Prentice-Hall, 1963.

London, P. The end of ideology in behavior modification. *American Psychologist,* 1972, *27,* 913–920.

Lotter, V. Follow-up studies. In M. Rutter & E. Schopler (Eds.), *Autism: A reappraisal of concepts and treatment.* New York: Plenum, 1978.

Love, L. R., & Kaswan, J. W. *Troubled children: Their families, schools and treatments.* New York: Wiley, 1974.

Mattison, R., Cantwell, D. P., Russell, A. T., & Will, L. A comparison of DSM-II and DSM-III in the diagnosis of childhood psychiatric disorders. *Archives of General Psychiatry,* 1979, *36,* 1217–1222.

Mezzich, A. C., & Mezzich, J. E. *Diagnostic reliability of childhood and adolescent behavior disorders.* Presented at American Psychological Association, New York, September, 1979.

Miller, L. C., Barrett, C. L., Hampe, E., & Noble, H. Comparison of reciprocal inhibition, psychotherapy, and waiting list control for phobic children. *Journal of Abnormal Psychology,* 1972, *79,* 269–279.

Mowrer, O. H., & Mowrer, W. M. Enuresis: A method for its study and treatment. *American Journal of Orthopsychiatry,* 1938, *8,* 436–459.

Neugebauer, R. Medieval and early modern theories of mental illness. *Archives of General Psychiatry,* 1979, *36,* 477–483.

Ochroch, R. *The diagnosis and treatment of minimal brain dysfunction in children. A clinical approach.* New York: Human Sciences Press, 1981.

Ollendick, T., & Gruen, G. E. Treatment of a bodily injury phobia with implosive therapy. *Journal of Consulting and Clinical Psychology,* 1972, *38,* 389–393.

Piaget, J. The role of action in the development of thinking. In W. F. Overton & J. M. Gallagher (Eds.), *Knowledge and development. Vol. 1.* New York: Plenum, 1977.

Prior, M., Perry, D., & Gajzago, C. Kanner's syndrome of early-onset psychosis; A taxonomic analysis of 142 cases. *Journal of Autism and Childhood Schizophrenia,* 1975, *5,* 71–80.

Quay, H. C. Classification. In H. C. Quay & J. Werry (Eds.), *Psychopathological disorders of childhood (2nd ed.).* New York: Wiley, 1979.

Rank, B. Adaptation of the psychoanalytic technique for the treatment of young children with atypical development. *American Journal of Orthopsychiatry,* 1949, *19,* 130–139.

Rogers, C. R. *Client-centered therapy: Its current practice, implications, and theory.* Boston: Houghton-Mifflin, 1951.

Rosen, B. M., Bahn, A. K., & Kramer, M. Demographic and diagnostic characteristics of psychiatric clinic outpatients in the U.S.A., 1961. *American Journal of Orthopsychiatry,* 1964, *34,* 455–468.

Seeman, J., Barry, E., & Ellingwood, C. Interpersonal assessment of play therapy outcome. *Psychotherapy: Theory, Research, and Practice,* 1964, *1,* 64–66.

Shaffer, D., McNamara, N., & Pincus, J. H. Controlled observations on patterns of activity, attention, and impulsivity in brain-damaged and psychiatrically disturbed boys. *Journal of Psychological Medicine,* 1974, *4,* 4–18.

Spitzer, R. L., & Cantwell, D. P. The DSM-III classification of the psychiatric disorders of infancy, childhood, and adolescence. *Journal of the American Academy of Child Psychiatry,* 1980, *19,* 356–370.

Strauss, A. A., & Lehtinen, L. E. *Psychopathology and education of the brain-injured child.* New York: Grune & Stratton, 1947.

Thomas, A., Chess, S., & Birch, H. G. *Temperament and behavior disorders in children.* New York: New York University Press, 1968.

Ullman, D. G., Egan, D., Fiedler, N., Jurenec, G., Pliske, R., Thompson, P., & Doherty, M. E. The many faces of hyperactivity: Similarities and differences in diagnostic policies. *Journal of Consulting and Clinical Psychology,* 1981, *49,* 694–704.

Wade, T. C., Baker, T. B., & Hartmann, D. P. Behavior therapists' self-reported views and practices. *The Behavior Therapist,* 1979, *2,* 3–6.

Waterman, A. S., Geary, P. S., & Waterman, C. K. Longitudinal study of changes in ego identity status from the freshman to the senior year at college. *Developmental Psychology,* 1974, *10,* 387–392.

Watson, J. B. Psychology as the behaviorist views it. *Psychological Review,* 1913, *20,* 158–177.

Watson, J. B. *Psychology from the standpoint of a behaviorist.* Philadelphia: J. B. Lippincott, 1919.

Watson, J. B. *Behaviorism.* New York: People's Publishing Co., 1924.

Weinberg, W. A., Rutman, J., Sullivan, L. Penick, E. C., & Dietz, S. G. Depression in children referred to an educational diagnostic center: Diagnosis and treatment. *Journal of Pediatrics,* 1973, *83,* 1065–1072.

Weisz, J. R., O'Neill, P., & O'Neill, P. C. Field dependence–independence on the Children's Embedded Figures Test: Cognitive style or cognitive level? *Developmental Psychology,* 1975, *11,* 539–540.

Wellisch, D. K., Vincent, J., & Ro-Trock, G. K. Family therapy versus individual therapy: A study of adolescents and their parents. In D. H. L. Olson (Ed.), *Treating relationships.* Lake Mills, IO: Graphic Publications, 1976.

Werner, H. The concept of development from a comparative and organismic point of view. In D. B. Harris (Ed.), *The concept of development.* Minneapolis, MN: University of Minnesota Press, 1957.

Witkin, H. A., Dyk, R. B., Faterson, H. F., Goodenough, D. R., & Karp, S. A. *Psychological differentiation.* New York: Wiley, 1962.

Witkin, H. A., & Goodenough, D. R. Cognitive styles: Essence and origins. *Psychological Issues,* 1980, *No. 51.*

Wolman, B. B. *Children without childhood.* New York: Grune & Stratton, 1970.

Wolpe, J. *Psychotherapy by reciprocal inhibition.* Stanford, CA: Stanford University Press, 1958.

11 Applied Developmental Psychology

Edward Zigler
Matia Finn
Yale University

INTRODUCTION

The view that social science should be directed toward the solution of contemporary social problems and the amelioration of society's ills is increasingly accepted among researchers. This is especially true among developmental psychologists because developmental psychology, which is concerned with the study of children and families, has by its very nature practical applications and relevance.

During the past two decades our society has undergone vast technological, economic, and demographic changes. These changes have virtually transformed social conditions and have given rise to a rapid and continuous expansion of unresolved problems faced by children in every socioeconomic sector. Examples of these problems are high infant mortality rates, poor health care for pregnant women and children, teenage pregnancy, and depression and suicide among youth. Other problems are escalating divorce rates and the trends toward single-parent families and the care and socialization of infants and young children for a large portion of time by caregivers who are nonrelatives. All of these contribute to stresses on family life.

The problems faced by children are pervasive and national in scope; their solution requires that action be taken at every level of government. Federal support for social programs for children and families has grown, especially in the 1960s and 1970s, but we are now also aware of some of the limitations of government action and of the importance of incorporating scientific methods and principles into the social policy decision-making process, in order to ensure the effectiveness of social services. Although applied developmental psychologists and other social scientists increasingly recognize the critical role of social science research in the formulation of public policies and programs that can change the adverse conditions under which children are growing up, for researchers, the involvement in public policy making is a major transition from their traditional role as academics confined to the university setting. Inasmuch as the knowledge and expertise of social scientists are needed in the policy arena, researchers are discovering that they not only can contribute to the welfare of children, but their work benefits from the contact and stimulus of direct experience.

In this chapter, we discuss applied developmental psychology in the context of new roles for scientists that have evolved during the past two decades and that continue to evolve. We begin our discussion with the definition of the terms *applied* and *basic research,* and provide examples of the existence and importance of the reciprocity between these two investigative strategies. It is our contention that scientists who conduct research in applied settings often formulate hypotheses and explanations of their findings on the basis of principles drawn from basic research studies. In the same vein, applied settings offer opportunities for new learning and are, in effect, "natural laboratories" that have been proven important in the development of theoretical principles, as well as in the refinement of research methodologies. Included in our discussion of these opportunities are examples of applied research work that is stimulated by the changes in social conditions and an illustration of how government programs can give impetus to scientific inquiry.

The policy implications of research in child development are discussed throughout the chapter. We examine in particular the link between research and government action; the process of the acquisition and application of knowledge in the policy arena, as well as the possible uses and misuses of research data in this regard; and the various roles scientists can have in the policy process, along with the dilemmas that these roles pose. Finally, projecting our vision beyond the public sector, we focus on the need—now and in the future—for using scientific methodologies and research data in the appraisal of those alternatives to government action that can be taken by the private sector.

RESEARCH IN APPLIED DEVELOPMENTAL PSYCHOLOGY

Definition of Terms

We begin with the definition of the terms *applied research* and *basic research* and the clarification of the distinctions and relationships between these two approaches. We define applied research as any research designed to meet society's perceived needs. Basic research, then, is all other research that is motivated by the desire to expand human knowledge and our understanding of ourselves and our environment.

We do not believe that there is any real chasm between applied and basic research, as we demonstrate in the course of this chapter. However, researchers have the tendency to identify themselves and their work with either one form or the other. Thus, there are two camps, and the infighting that goes on between them is illustrated by the distinctions made when defining these two types of research. For example, "pure research" is a term often used synonymously with basic research. The use of the word "pure" carries with it a connotation of objectivity and high-mindedness, at the same time implying that what is not pure—in other words, applied research—must be sloppy. Applied researchers, on the other hand, refer to their work as "goal-oriented" or "mission-oriented" research. Here the implication is that basic researchers have no goals or purposes and must therefore be conducting aimless studies.

Aside from the pure versus mission-oriented distinction, Garner (1972) identifies four other common sets of attributes on which the distinction between basic and applied research is based: It is basic research that generates general knowledge and applied research that generates specific knowledge; experiment as a method is used in basic research only and observation is the method used in applied research; research conducted in a laboratory is by definition basic research and research carried out in a field setting automatically falls into the category of applied research; and finally, an analytic approach characterizes basic research and a holistic approach characterizes applied research.

Although these characterizations are correlated to some degree in practice, the dichotomy between basic and applied research is not so great as is suggested by these commonly made distinctions. Garner (1972) and Bryant (1972) provide several examples that provide evidence for a reciprocal relationship between basic and applied research in that these two methods of study actually overlap and contribute to one another for the benefit of both. This reciprocity between basic and applied research is especially evident in developmental psychology. Studies on child abuse, for example, draw upon basic research to form a foundation and better understanding of what is clearly applied work. Child abuse is a most visible and pressing problem confronting applied psychologists today (Parke & Collmer, 1975). Research seeking explanations of inappropriate interaction patterns between abusive parents and their children has great social relevance. Studies are being conducted in response to the problem of widespread and increasing child abuse in the United States (Gerbner, Ross, & Zigler, 1980; Gil, 1970). Despite the applied nature of child abuse research, Ainsworth (1973), studying the development of attachment in families where abuse occurs, has drawn upon the basic research work of Harlow, who provided evidence that infant rhesus monkeys will cling to surrogate (terrycloth) mothers that emit frightening blasts (Harlow, 1961) and to their natural mothers who physically abuse them (1963). Harlow's findings have important implications for the detection and prevention of child abuse. They support the clinical evidence that abused children seek to be with their abusive parents (Ainsworth, 1980).

Harlow's studies also contribute to Ainsworth's theories that abuse occurs in instances where insecure attachment develops between the parent and child, that identifiable characteristics of the parent and/or child foster "anxious attachment," and that these parents and children harbor more frustrations and anger than do other parents and children. On the basis of her formulations, Ainsworth suggests the construction of instruments that measure parent–child attachment, and that can be used to help identify families who run the risk of abuse. She also suggests that programs aimed at promoting secure parent–child bonds may help to alleviate the child abuse problem.

In the same way that applied research is enhanced by contributions from basic studies, the work of applied researchers adds to the store of basic knowledge and aids in the construction of theories that are needed to guide that research. This is best illustrated in studies conducted on kibbutz life in Israel. Psychologists, as well as researchers from other disciplines, have taken advantage of a national experiment in socialization practices to study the kibbutz as a social experiment and childrearing laboratory. The information gained from the many kibbutz studies conducted since about 1950 has clear implications, not only for the development and socialization of Israeli children reared in a kibbutz, but also for children in this country: The increase in the number of working mothers is here associated with major changes in family life, and the trend toward the socialization of children by caregivers who are nonrelatives (Zigler & Finn, 1982). Researchers are studying the relationship between kibbutz childrearing practices and the kibbutz-raised children's personality development (Kaffman, 1965), sex-role development (Rabin, 1970), and moral attitudes (Retting, 1966). These studies are examples of applied research in that they are motivated by the need to know whether kibbutzim produce healthy, useful members of society. However, as Beit-Hallahmi and Rabin (1977) point out in a review of the kibbutz literature, kibbutzim offer a natural experimental design for studies in developmental psychology, and, although kibbutz studies provide valuable knowledge that is of great social significance, they also add to our basic knowledge of the development of the self-concept (Handel, 1961), the development of mental and motor faculties (Kohen-Raz, 1968), and of children's relationships with parents and peers (Rabin & Goldman, 1966; Sharabany, 1974) under different childrearing practices.

The importance of the reciprocity between basic and applied research is further illustrated by the fact that scientists often refine their understanding of a problem through the use of different research designs and methodologies. This point is made by Garner (1972) and Bryant (1972) in relation to research in the general area of psychology. Bronfenbrenner (1977a,b) makes the same point in relation to developmental psychology by saying that experimental, laboratory based research has not produced sufficient gains in the understanding of the determinants of human behavior. He goes on to suggest an ecological approach to the study of child development whereby scientists can examine an individual in the context (or system) in which he or she is embedded. It is Bronfenbrenner's contention that this is a broader approach to research in human development, focusing on the progressive accommodation, throughout the life-span, between the growing organism and the changing environments in which it lives and grows. These environments include not only the immediate settings containing the developing person, but also the larger social contexts, both formal and informal, in which the settings are embedded. Bronfenbrenner (1977a,b) emphasizes that, in terms of method, the ecological approach entails the use of rigorously designed experiments, both naturalistic and contrived, beginning in the early stages of the research.

Weisz (1978), in a review of recent critiques of the generalizability of developmental principles, raises an important question: Can we expect the psychological study of human development to yield durable principles that are valid across changes in time, culture, and cohort? He proposes that although the answer is probably yes, this answer must be qualified by an analysis of the form that enduring principles are likely to take and the process by which they are likely to be discovered. In unearthing and validating durable developmental principles, Weisz notes the need for the complementarity of diverse methodologies, including laboratory based and ecological approaches of varying complexity. Zigler (1963) also argues for the use of diverse methodologies and suggests that developmental psychologists should include both natural observation and experimental methods in their research, as both these methods have an important role to play in theory construction.

Building on our discussion of the reciprocity that exists between applied and basic research, we show by discussion and examples throughout the remainder of this chapter: (1) how applied settings offer opportunities for research that is essential for the further development of knowledge and theory on the process of human development; and (2) the practical implications of this research for the development of policies that affect children and families.

New Developments in Applied Developmental Psychology

We have named some of the acute problems facing children and families today. An elaboration of each of the needs of children and families is beyond the scope of this chapter; in-depth discussions of these appear in other contexts (Advisory Committee on Child Development, 1976; Keniston, 1977; Zigler & Finn, 1982). It suffices to say that these problems stem in part from the changes in social conditions that are taking place in our society. These societal changes offer unique and important opportunities for learning and the conduct of research. Take, for example, the study of infant behavior—in particular, research on the consequences of placing infants in day care (Frye, 1982). This research is being conducted because a large number of women, many of whom have infants and children under the age of three (Hofferth, 1979; Hoffman & Nye, 1974), are working and have to rely on the use of day care. Research on fatherhood (Lamb, 1976) is another example. Although fathers have played an important role in children's lives through the centuries, it was not until recently that scientists began to focus on the role of fathers in child development. Again, this interest on the part of scientists is triggered by changes in the traditional roles assumed by men and women. Both of these areas of research provide additional dimensions to our understanding of human development and behavior.

In order to highlight the opportunities for research that applied settings offer, let us look at family life in the context of some demographic changes and focus on two areas—day care and divorce—that have great implications, not only for what we as psychologists can learn about children, but also for the social responsibilities of psychologists who can, through research and the application of knowledge, provide guidelines for programs and actions that would better the lot of children.

The American family has undergone rapid and radical changes. In the 1980s, it is significantly different from what it was thirty years ago. In documenting the changes the American family has undergone, there have been some who have noted its demise. Let us state at the outset that we believe that the family is and will remain not only viable but also the first and most important institution in determining child growth and development. It is imperative, however, that we acknowledge the multiple forms that families may now take. The traditional nuclear family in which the husband is the breadwinner, the mother the housewife, and in which there are two or more children living at home, represents fewer than 7 percent of all families in the United States (U.S. Bureau of the Census, 1979). Other arrangements include both parents as wage-earners with one or more children living at home; married couples with no children or none living at home; single-parent families; unrelated persons living together; and what have come to be termed "blended" families (also known as "reconstituted," or "new extended" families), which occur in cases of divorce and the remarriage of one or both parents.

There has also been progressive fragmentation and isolation for the family in its childrearing role. First, we have seen the loss of the extended family, which occurred because of the need for people to move frequently in search of jobs (Packard, 1972). As a result, many families do not have the immediate access to the experience and counsel of their elders, nor the support system for child care they could once count on. Second, and even more pronounced in its effects on children, has been a shrinkage in the so-called "nuclear" family consisting of mother, father, and children. Today, many more children than ever before are living in single-parent families. The number of single-parent families grew by nearly 2 million between 1970 and 1978 (Norton, 1979). Currently, one fifth of all children in the United States are being raised in single-parent families. The majority of single-parent households are headed by women with low income and are likely to include children below the age of five (Comptroller General, 1979). Divorce, which we focus on in more detail later in the chapter, is one reason cited for the increase in single-parent families. After divorce, the most rapidly growing category of single parenthood involves unmarried women (Advisory Committee on Child Development, 1976). Living in a home without a father and experiencing the divorce of their parents represent for children new conditions and stresses that bear investigation by researchers. What are the consequences for growth and development of growing up in a single-parent family? What is the impact of divorce on children? These are some of the questions research psychologists are likely to ask.

The increase in the number of working mothers (Hoffman & Nye, 1974) is another change that significantly affects the development of children. What is especially significant about the increase in the number of working mothers is the nature of their participation in the labor force. Whereas in the past women, and mothers in particular, tended to work part-time and to move in and out of the labor force depending on the ages of their children, mothers today have a commitment, or a need, to work full-time even while their children are very young. What is more, a significant proportion of women are found not only to work full-time but to hold more than one full-time job (Brozan, 1980). The potential impact of this trend on children is enormous in that families have to rely on out-of-home care for children and to delegate childrearing to others who are nonrelatives.

Child Day Care

Several political and social science issues are associated with the growth in the number of working mothers and the reliance among an increasing number of families on out-of-home care for their children.

First, there are not enough day care facilities in this country to accommodate all the children who need day care. Over 10 years ago, at the 1970 White House Conference on Children, this fact was recognized and the conclusion drawn that making more day care services of good quality available was the number one priority for our nation in the effort to alleviate the problems faced by children and families (White House Conference on Children, 1970). Despite this national proclamation, the years have passed and the need for more day care services not only continues, it has been exacerbated. This is a serious problem. Families are experiencing a great deal of stress trying to accommodate parents' work schedules to a variety of different day care arrangements. When they cannot, children are left alone at home, often in the care only of siblings not much older than they are. This is an especially acute problem with school-age children. Approximately two million children between the ages of 7 and 13 come home from school to an empty house (Congressional Record, 1979). These ''latchkey'' children, so called because they carry their house keys on strings around their necks, are left to their own resources during critical hours of the day. Reports of children encountering burglars or being victimized by molesters are not uncommon. In a recent study in Detroit, an investigator discovered that one sixth of the fires in that city involved an unattended child (Smock, 1977). Aside from the safety aspect of leaving children unattended at home, the phenomenon of latchkey children in our society is an empirical issue that calls out for investigation because of possible repercussions for the social and emotional development of these children whose contacts with adults over the course of a day are minimal.

Second, there is the issue of quality child care and the cost of this care. While research indicates that the quality of care a young child receives makes a difference in terms of developmental outcome and psychological growth and development, most parents cannot afford to stay home to care for their own children, nor do they earn enough to afford quality care if they work. According to the findings of the National Child Care Consumer Study (Rodes & Moore, 1975), 54% of the infants (ages 0–2 years) who require out-of-home care are in family day care homes and 27% of them are in infant day care centers. Among the 3- to 5-year-old group, 57% are in day care centers, whereas 32% are in family day care homes. In terms of the quality of care either in family day care homes or in day care centers, not much is known beyond studies that indicate that among family day care homes the quality of care appears to be homogeneous (Jones & Prescott, 1982). Among day care centers, however, a large proportion have been found to be of poor or fair quality (Keyserling, 1972).

A key problem to our understanding of the quality day care issue is the fact that the statistics presented above are compiled from information made available from licensed homes and centers. However, many children who require day care are placed in unlicensed settings that are not accountable to public authority, and not much is known about the kind of care children receive in these places. Yet unlicensed settings are not the only settings that are not monitored. Even among licensed centers, standards are often lax or unenforced. Some states, such as New York and Connecticut, have reasonable day care standards that are enforced. But there are other states, for example Florida and New Mexico, where it is permissible for one adult to care for up to ten infants. This staff-to-child ratio is not only not conducive to optimal development, it is clearly dangerous. In the case of fire, how could one caregiver bring ten infants to safety?

Child advocates have been fighting to guarantee quality child care in centers across the nation and to enforce uniform standards for the regulation of these centers for over a decade (Cohen & Zigler, 1977; Nelson, 1982). The proposed regulations would impose minimum requirements on day care centers in order to ensure that children are protected from fires, have nutritious meals, and are cared for by adults who are trained in child development principles. Lengthy moratoriums on such regulations were imposed due to a so-called lack of data from the research that would document the need for uniform standards. When more data became available (Abt National Day Care Study, 1979), however, other obstacles were imposed. For example, when, in the face of considerable opposition, Health and Human Services Secretary Patricia Harris had the courage to approve the Federal Interagency Day Care Requirements (FIDCR; Federal Register, March 19, 1980), their implementation was deferred due to budgetary restraints. The decision to defer the requirements was upheld despite a proposal by Senator Alan Cranston (California) that made the budgetary impact of FIDCR negligible (Zigler & Goodman, 1980).

The enactment and enforcement of federal day care standards are important in several respects, especially with regard to the training of caregivers of infants and young children. The long-term consequences of day care, especially infant day care, are not yet known. However, from the research of the past few decades we know that an important factor in a child's development is the quality of the child's interaction with the adults in his or her life. Children need to be reared not only in a safe environment, but in an environment that is nurturant as well. In the same vein, parents must be assured that their children are taken care of by adults who are trained and competent. In 1972 the U.S. Office of Child Development, with the support of national organizations concerned with children's development and welfare, established a consortium, the sole focus of which was to upgrade the quality of care children receive in day care centers. Then known as the Child Development Associate Consortium (CDAC: now known as the CDA National Credential Program), this nonprofit organization, with the help of the nation's leading psychologists and early childhood educators, developed an assessment and credentialing system for child care workers (Ward, 1976). Because of it, we can now determine what qualities are essential for effective child care in group situations. For example, providing quality care for young children not only means making appropriate meals available; it also involves an understanding on the part of the caregiver of the basic principles of children's growth and development as well as the importance and function of play in a young child's life.

The CDA project exemplifies the interface between social policy and child development research. Providing adequate and appropriate training for child caregivers in an effort to ensure quality care for children is a major task facing policymakers today. As researchers, we have made progress in delineating the skills and competencies that are necessary for the care of preschool children in groups, and in our ability to formally recognize the workers who possess such skills. However, we need to expand the CDA project to include appropriate child care training and assessment of workers in infant day care centers, family day care homes, and school-age day care programs (Zigler & Kagan, 1981). In addition, we must evaluate the CDA project and document its merits: For example, do children who are cared for by CDA's receive better quality care than children who are cared for by noncredentialed child care workers?

It is evident that policy decisions regarding child day care should be made on the basis of research findings. These findings can help clarify policy options and provide directions for the operation of programs. For example, although child advocates have assumed for many years that an appropriate staff-to-child ratio is a key ingredient in quality care, researchers are finding out that providing care to small rather than large groups of children is more important than having more caregivers (Roupp et al., 1979).

Beyond the need for a sound empirical base upon which we can make day care policy decisions, research is also needed to ascertain the impact of day care attendance on the children's development. Recent reviews of the day care literature (Belsky & Steinberg, 1978; Rutter, 1981; Zigler & Gordon, 1982) point out that although many gains have been made in the research on day care, the available research is limited primarily to studies of the impact of attendance at high-quality centers on measures of children's interactions with their mothers (e.g., Kagan, Kearsley, & Zelazo, 1978; Farran & Ramey, 1977; Caldwell, Wright, Honing & Tannenbaum, 1970). Our understanding of the impact of day care attendance on child development is further limited due to several methodological problems encountered in the designs of studies related to day care (Seitz, 1982), as well as our inability and lack of commitment thus far to conducting longitudinal studies involving children in day care. These limitations are reflected in the inconclusive and controversial nature of the research. Some researchers, for example, contend on the basis of their data that there are no harmful effects associated with placing children in day care (Rutter, 1982). Others also on the basis of their data, do find that day care can be harmful to children (Fraiberg, 1977). Part of the reason why research findings are inconclusive is that the widespread use of out-of-home care for young children is a relatively recent phenomenon; we will have to wait several more years before we can ascertain any long-term effects of day care.

In addition to the need for longitudinal studies on the impact of day care, we also need to broaden the scope of the research and look more closely at those variables that can affect the impact of day care attendance on children's development. In a study on day care children's responsiveness to adults (Robertson, 1982), it was found that the type of preschool care (home care or day care center), interacting with other factors, significantly influenced children's behavior in three ways: (1) it influenced the children's responsiveness to adults, with specific effect depending on the children's socioeconomic status and sex; (2) it influenced the cooperativeness and obedience of boys in school, but not of girls; and (3) it affected the academic achievement ratings for middle-class subjects but not for lower-class subjects. These findings point to the fact that the impact of day care on children's development is likely to be different given the type of care as well as the individual children involved. Our task as researchers, then, is not simply to find out whether or not day care is harmful to children, but what facets of the day care experience can mediate or enhance these effects, and for which individual children.

Research on parent involvement in day care is a case in point. Parents whose children are in day care still have the primary responsibility for the care and nurturing of their children, but they now carry out this responsibility in concert with caregivers. As the care and socialization of children has become, in effect, a joint effort between parents and caregivers, we contend that it is in the child's best interest for parents to form a close relationship with the caregivers in order to create a partnership in the rearing of the child. Any discontinuities that exist between the home and day care program operate to the child's detriment. Lippit (1968), for example, suggests that a lack of collaboration between the two major socializing agencies—the family and the day care program—could cause a child to experience problems of competitive demands for time, incompatible models of appropriate behaviors, or inconsistent styles of adult regulation of child behavior.

Substantial evidence points out that the more parents are involved in the out-of-home experiences of their children, the more the children will benefit from those experiences (Bronfenbrenner, 1975; Valentine & Stark, 1979). Much of this evidence is derived from studies related to early intervention that are discussed in the next section of this chapter. We know very little about parent involvement in day care. In the few studies that have been done on the subject (Powell, 1977, 1978; Zigler & Turner, 1982), it was found that parents tend to spend a minimal amount of time in the day care center and to interact with caregivers only occasionally, usually at the point of their arrival at or departure from the day care center. In the matter of parent involvement in day care, developmental psychologists can make important contributions. The parent–caregiver relationship needs to be facilitated, but before we can make any recommendations in this regard and perhaps develop a model for this facilitation, we need to advance our knowledge of this area.

Children of Divorce

Another area in which research carries widespread social implications are studies involving children of divorce. Close to 1.2 million divorces, involving 3.5 million people, including children, were reported in 1980 (National Center for Health Statistics, 1980). Children under the age of 18 are involved in approximately 65 percent of the divorces taking place in this country (Carter & Glick, 1976), and it has been estimated that between 32 and 46 percent of the children who have grown up in the 1970s (Bane, 1976) will experience either the separation or the divorce of their parents. Despite these facts, there have been relatively few studies that examine the impact of divorce on children. As a result, too little is known about the child's experience during divorce; the extent to which children of divorced parents risk developing emotional and psychological problems; and whether there are effects of divorce that are not immediately noticeable in children but are likely to appear at a later age.

However, several researchers have made strides toward the resolution of some of these questions. The two most influential research projects on the impact of divorce on children began in the early 1970s. One of these is headed by Mavis Hetherington and her colleagues Martha Cox and Roger Cox, who employ quasi-experimental studies. The other is headed by Judith Wallerstein and Joan Kelly from the Marin County (California) Mental Health Center, whose research methods are based on their clinical experience with children of divorce and those from nondivorced families. Both of these projects provide what social scientists regard as classic studies in the area of children of divorce. Others who have contributed to our knowledge of the impact of divorce on children include Joseph Goldstein, Anna Freud, and Albert Solnit, whose work is a vivid example of the synthesis of theoretical principles organized and presented in such a way as to be coherent and relevant to specific practical situations. In their books *Beyond the Best Interests of the Child* (1973) and *Before the Best Interests of the Child* (1979) the authors have drawn from their experiences in law and psychiatry to write about the possible repercussions of divorce on children and to suggest guidelines for decisions on custody issues.

To summarize the research findings to date, it appears that for children the divorce of their parents is not a single event but a sequence of experiences, each one representing a transition and each requiring adjustments (Wallerstein & Kelly, 1979). The transitions center around the shift from the family life prior to the divorce; the disequilibrium and disorganization immediately following the divorce; the experimentation with a variety of coping mechanisms, living arrangements, and relationships; and the eventual reorganization and attainment of equilibrium. The households in which divorce has occurred are characterized by greatly increased disorganization as well as by marked changes in the management of children, including inconsistency of discipline, diminished communication and nurturance, and the holding of fewer expectations of mature behavior from the children (Hetherington, Cox, & Cox, 1978).

Almost all children experience divorce and the transition periods that follow it as painful experiences (Kelly & Wallerstein, 1976; Levitin, 1979). Even those children who eventually recognize the divorce of their parents as constructive initially undergo considerable stress with the breakup of the family. The facts that so many other children in this nation are involved in divorce and that divorce has become socially acceptable have not been found to alleviate the pain, as documented by a recent book by and for the children of divorce (Rofes, 1980).

Research evidence suggests that the most critical period for the entire family, including the children, is the first year after divorce. The evidence also points to the fact that children can and do rally to cope with the crisis. Their ability to cope, however, as well as the intensity of their distress, have been found to be related to:

1. Their age: the preschool child has been found to be more vulnerable and susceptible to the emotional and psychological problems associated with the divorce and the period of a few years after the divorce;

2. Their sex and birth order: boys have been found to suffer for longer periods than girls and to exhibit more behavioral problems and difficulties in

their relationships with their mothers and other adults and peers; children without siblings experience more distress and psychological problems during the early stages of post-divorce than do children who have siblings (Hetherington, 1979).

Parents also undergo emotional, psychological, and economic stresses following divorce. Often, the parents' distress is so acute that they neglect to provide their children with sufficient attention, to prepare the children for the marital breakup, and to recognize their children's painful experiences with divorce. Researchers note that the intensity and duration of a child's emotional and psychological distress are related to the psychological status of the custodial parent and the subsequent availability and involvement of the noncustodial parent.

The most tragic and vulnerable children of divorce are those who are involved in legal battles on custody issues and visitation rights. These legal battles can continue indefinitely because any decision on any of the issues is modifiable by the courts. A parent's rage against an ex-spouse can also continue for many years and is often expressed in continued litigation over the children. Clinicians note that the fight for the children serves a psychological need in a parent and often wards off a severe depression (Bodenheimer, 1974–75; Watson, 1969; Westman et al., 1970).

The courts attempt to make custody decisions on the basis of the "best interests of the child." In practice, however, the explication of this principle is far from easy. Judges and lawyers are often unable to determine what the best interests of the child may be, and they have little help in this regard, as few psychologists or other mental health professionals look on the court as an arena of their interest. When the courts do have psychological services attached to them, these are often understaffed or staffed by people who are not trained to work with children (Wallerstein & Kelly, 1979). Goldstein, Freud, and Solnit's books (1973, 1979) provide some guidance for decisions on custody issues. Based on the principles of developmental psychology the authors recommend, for example, that decisions regarding child custody be resolved in accelerated proceedings rather than long, drawn-out procedures; that they have final effect and not be reversible; and that they award full custody to the one "psychological parent." There is controversy surrounding these recommendations (e.g., Benedek & Benedek, 1977), but the efforts of these authors have resulted in the availability of at least some criteria on which legal professionals can base their decisions. Referring back to the earlier discussion of the reciprocity that exists between applied and basic research, one can see here the value inherent in the knowledge and theoretical principles that are put to use in practical situations.

What we have described is admittedly only a brief summary of some of the research literature on the impact of divorce on children. Other issues, notably visitation rights (Jacobson, 1978; Wallerstein & Kelly, 1980), the long-term effects of divorce (Anderson, 1968; Hetherington, 1972; Landis, 1963) on both parents and children, and the effects of different lifestyles associated with divorce—for example, living in single-parent households (Hetherington, Cox, & Cox, 1979; Herzog & Sudia, 1973) or living in blended families due to the remarriage of one or both parents (Price-Bonham & Blaswick, 1980)—are also discussed to some extent in the research literature. However, the information presented should be sufficient for the reader to realize that the research on divorce has widespread implications.

Understanding how and when divorce affects children, as well as some of the behavioral manifestations of the impact of divorce on children is important not only to research and clinical psychologists but also to others who come in contact with children and families. Teachers, for instance, need to be alerted to these findings so that they can be sensitive to any changes in children's behavior during school and offer children and parents appropriate advice and guidelines about possible ways they can cope with the changes going on in their lives. Pediatricians should also be alerted to these findings, for the same reasons. Most significantly, lawyers and judges who have primary and extensive involvement in divorce cases should be made aware of the research and its implications. Ideally, psychological support for parents and children should be offered when divorce proceedings begin. Some important developments in divorce cases are the use of mediators rather than lawyers and settling cases outside the confines of the courtroom whenever possible (Bahr, 1981). The increasing use of mediators, who are often psychologists or social workers with access to legal advice, is admittedly due to the high legal costs of divorce. Families who have used divorce mediation, however, consider the psychological support for the parents as well as the children associated with the method as one of its major benefits.

THE INTERPLAY BETWEEN PSYCHOLOGICAL
RESEARCH AND SOCIAL PROGRAMS FOR CHILDREN

The opportunities for research and learning that applied settings offer are also evident in the development of social programs and policies for children and families. In this regard, a reciprocal relationship exists between research and policy. DeLone (1982) notes that any policy approach designed to facilitate human development must be based on good theory and an understanding of what development is and how it occurs, and that it must be a theory that can be translated into action, which he defines as a set of resource allocations and decisions that will lead to the desired outcomes provided by the theory. It is his contention that, in relation to public policy, a theory is no better than its application, and vice versa. Acknowledging the axiom that social policy should be based on science, Bronfenbrenner (1974) proposes that, particularly in the field of developmental psychology, science also needs social policy, not only as a guide for organizational activities but also to provide what he regards as two essential elements in any scientific endeavor—vitality and validity.

Design and Evaluation of Social Programs

During the past two decades, a wide range of social programs have been implemented, many of them aimed at improving children's lives. The participation of developmental psychologists in the design and evaluation of these programs illustrates the link and reciprocity between psychological research and government action. Although describing many of the programs that have been developed (for a historical perspective on the field of early intervention, see Zigler & Berman, in press; Salkind, in press) is beyond the scope of this chapter, we focus much of our discussion on one such program, Project Head Start. Head Start's wide scope, as well as its commitment to evaluation and change, have permitted an evolutionary approach to the task of designing effective interventions for children and families and have allowed it to serve as a stable base from which to experiment with a number of early intervention service models and methods (for an annotated history of Project Head Start, see Zigler & Valentine, 1979).

Project Head Start began in the summer of 1965 as part of the "War on Poverty," a massive effort to eradicate social class inequities in the United States. One facet of this effort was preschool intervention, which, it was hoped, would provide young children with an inoculation against the ills resulting from poverty. Project Head Start differed from other intervention efforts of the early sixties in that its planners were careful to avoid using a deficit model based on the notion of "cultural deprivation" or "cultural disadvantage" (Zigler & Berman, in press). The focus of the deficit model is to provide poor children with learning experiences supposedly lacking in their impoverished environment. In contrast, Project Head Start focused on a cultural relativistic approach that respected the children's many cultures. One way this was achieved was through parent participation (Valentine & Stark, 1979). This included parents' work in the daily activities of the program and their involvement in the planning and administration of Head Start centers in the community. Parent participation has by now become an important and often required aspect of programs for children. In the early years of Head Start, however, it was regarded as a significant break from past practices, in which paid professionals dictated the operation of poverty programs. Several incidental benefits of parent involvement have been realized (A Review of Head Start Research, 1982). One such benefit is suggested by a finding of the Coleman report (Coleman et al., 1966); namely, that children's school performance improved when they felt more control over their lives. Children's locus of control was associated first with family background and second with variance in school performance. Because parents' attitudes are likely to influence those of their children, parental participation in decision making could promote both parents' and children's feeling of control and lead to increased effort, performance, and self-satisfaction on the part of the children.

Project Head Start has always been regarded by the public, by Congress, and by many of its participants as a demonstration project. It has been a source of learning for developmental psychologists and scientists from other disciplines, and to this day it holds a unique position as a national laboratory for the design of effective intervention for children and adults (Zigler & Seitz, 1982b). Continued experimentation in Head Start has led to a number of innovative approaches to early intervention that are exemplified by the changes that have taken place in the program since its inception. These changes are reflected in many other early intervention programs and in our general understanding of them. There has been, for instance, disillusionment over the years with the notion that early childhood is a critical period for intervention (cf., Clarke & Clarke, 1976). By extending the provision of Head Start services to include earlier as well as later stages of development, which was made possible by Head Start's Home Start and Follow Through efforts (Rhine, 1981), we have come to appreciate the importance of continuous intervention from one stage of life to the next (Seitz, 1982). Another example is the Child and Family Resource Program (CFRP), which is a Head Start demonstration that has been praised by the Comptroller General (1979) for being cost effective and comprehensive. The underlying concepts of the CFRP are that children need to be served at different developmental stages, and that effective early intervention lies not in a single program designed to aid children alone, or to remediate any one particular problem, but in a host of family support services. Thus, CFRPs serve families with children from the prenatal period through age eight via the utilization of existing community services. Other Head Start innovations that have made significant contributions to services and programs for children include the Head Start Handicapped Children's Effort, an attempt to deal sensitively with mainstreaming handicapped children even before they reach school age; and the Child Development Associate (CDA) program, which focuses on the training and assessment of child care workers.

The CDA program is based on the assumptions that the elements of quality care can be specified and evaluated, and that competency in caring for young children can be formally recognized through a credentialing process (Zigler & Kagan, 1981). The CDA program is now widely used not only as a basis for training of Head Start staff but also in the assessment and credentialing of child care and early education workers throughout the country. Finally, one major contribution of Project Head Start can be seen in the use of social competence rather than IQ score changes as the criteria by which to evaluate the success of early intervention programs.

Evaluation of Head Start and Other Social Programs

Federal support of Head Start and other programs has been substantial. Although the early seventies witnessed the beginning of a decline in public funds allocated for social services in general, annual expenditures for early intervention programs were nearly $3 billion in 1979 (Federal Programs Related to Children, 1979). The expansion in the number of programs for young children and in the amount of money spent on these programs has been accompanied by a sizeable evaluation enterprise in order to justify the usefulness of early intervention programs.

For many years, the argument for the need for early intervention programs for certain populations, and the question of how effective these programs are have been focused in academic journals of developmental psychology and other disciplines and have constituted primarily a scientific interest (Salkind, in press) in the effects of programs on children's growth and development. Over the years we have learned that this perspective alone is not sufficient and that we should also include in any evaluation effort a policy perspective; that is, we should address the concerns of taxpayers and policymakers about the costs and benefits of programs.

The recognition on the part of researchers of the need to address both the scientific and policy issues inherent in social program evaluation has greatly increased our understanding of the ways in which programs affect children as well as our ability to document these programs through a variety of evaluation methodologies. Several methods have thus emerged that have been applied to evaluation research, and some problems have been encountered in that area. These problems are important. They have resulted not only in the search for, and application of, more valid evaluation methodologies and more realistic expectations of what evaluations can and cannot tell us, but they have also resulted in changes in theoretical issues related to intellectual development.

Methods in Evaluation Research.   Given the different perspectives associated with the evaluation of social programs, a useful definition of evaluation, incorporating both the scientific and policy perspectives, is that offered by Travers and Light (1982), who define evaluation as the systematic inquiry into the operations of a program, the services it delivers, the process by which these services are provided, the costs involved, the characteristics of the population served, and the outcome or the impact of the program on its participants. There are two types of evaluation associated with social services. The first is called *process evaluation.* One example of this is the monitoring effort in Head Start programs to guarantee that each Head Start center delivers the services mandated by the program. Process evaluation, then, ascertains those types of services that are available to the recipients.

The second type of evaluation is *outcome evaluation.* This involves the assessment of the verifiable impact of the program or service. This type of evaluation is important as a source of knowledge and direction. It provides us with information about which programs work and which do not. This is especially relevant to policymakers who are faced with the many unmet needs of America's children and limited public funds and must decide whether to continue programs or to allocate funds to new programs that hold the promise of achieving a specific end. Since outcome evaluation involves the investigation of the consequences of programs that attempt to alter key variables in people's lives, it also has the potential of adding to our store of basic knowledge and may lead to discoveries about human behavior.

The classic design for outcome evaluation studies has been, at least in attempt, the experimental model. In this model, an experimental and a control group are chosen at random from the target population of those who receive a specific program and those who do not. Measures are taken of the relevant criterion variable (for example, IQ score) both before the program starts and after it ends. Any differences between the two groups at the end of the program are used to determine the success or failure of the program. The experimental model presents some restrictions in that social programs are not always developed or implemented in such a way as to allow its use in evaluation (Abt, 1974). What is more, the exclusive use of this model may fail to yield other important or useful information: What are the needs of the participants? Has the program secured community acceptance? The need for answers to these and other questions has led to the use of a variety of quasi-experimental and non-experimental designs in the evaluation of programs (Campbell & Erlebacher, 1970).

Aside from the changes in the design of evaluation studies, the validity and utility of evaluation studies have also been improved through the use of different methods of analysis. One of these is known as secondary analysis (Cook, 1974), the reanalysis of data for purposes of answering the original research question with better statistical techniques or answering new questions with old data (primary analysis, on the other hand, is the original analysis of data in a research study). Another method is meta-analysis (Glass, McGraw, & Smith, 1981), the statistical analysis of the summary of findings of many empirical studies. An example is the study by the System Development Corporation (Coulson et al., 1972) of data collected by regional Head Start Evaluation and Research Centers between 1966 and 1968. The data used in the study came from nine quasi-experimental programs that were part of a systematic planned variation study originally designed to assess the effects of different approaches in Head Start programs on children of different characteristics. Both these methods of analyzing provide an added dimension to evaluation research.

Several other evaluation methodologies have been developed because of the increased recognition of the need to address the concerns of taxpayers and policymakers regarding programs. In the world of policy, budget considerations receive priority, so evaluations from this perspective are usually related to costs and effectiveness.

Examples of evaluations that have policy perspectives are cost-benefit analysis and cost-effectiveness analysis. Both methodologies focus on fiscal concerns, but they are different. Cost-benefit analysis looks at both the costs of the program and the benefits associated with the program in terms of dollars, usually expressed as the "amount of money invested" and the "amount of money returned." Cost-effectiveness analysis is used when the outcomes or benefits of a program, or policy, cannot be measured in dollars. Karnes, Teska, Hodgins, and

Badger (1970), for example, have reported a positive change in parents' ratings of a child's school performance as a function of participation in an early childhood program. This change is considered a beneficial outcome because it indicates greater parent involvement in the child's education and a greater understanding of the child's school performance, but effectiveness in this case can be measured only in units other than dollars.

In response to the economic realities and the pressure to demonstrate to taxpayers and policymakers the return to society of public investments, social scientists have become involved in the development of cost-benefit analyses that have proven meaningful to both psychologists and legislators. One of these is the Economic Analysis of the Ypsilanti Perry Preschool Project (Weber, Foster, & Weikart, 1978). In this study, the benefits and costs for the experimental group were compared with those of the control group, using the human capital approach of economics. The economic benefits of the preschool program were quantified; then, by comparing the costs of the program with these economic benefits, the rate of return on the investment was calculated. The study was based on a small sample, and, the researchers note, the computations required the making of some broad assumptions about the applicability of census data to the studied cohorts. Nonetheless, the results showed that the benefits to society outweighed the costs of the program. The economic benefits to society were derived from: (1) less costly education (that is, fewer children of the experimental group repeated a grade and/or were placed in special education programs); (2) higher projected lifetime earnings for this group; and (3) time release from child care responsibilities for the mothers of the children in the experimental group.

Similar findings on other intervention programs were obtained by the Consortium for Longitudinal Studies (1981), which pooled the information from several of the older and more complete early childhood education studies and, using the Economic Analysis described above, demonstrated the cost-effectiveness of such programs in the long run. In another compilation of program findings, longitudinal data, and cost measures of selected early intervention programs, Antley (1982) also demonstrates the cost-effectiveness of several early intervention models.

What We Have Learned from Program Evaluation.   In our discussion of some of what psychologists have learned through their involvement in program evaluation, let us look at the evaluation of Project Head Start, which in many ways became the test of whether early intervention efforts could be successful. The most noted Head Start evaluation was the Westinghouse report (1969), the first large-scale study to examine the impact of Head Start on later school achievement. There were shortcomings to this evaluation. First, the evaluation criteria did not reflect the fundamental goals of Head Start, and, second, as we have now come to appreciate, its reliance on the IQ as a measure of success presented problems.

The children who were evaluated in the Westinghouse study were enrolled in summer Head Start programs in 1965, 1966, 1967, and 1968. Much has been written about the Westinghouse study and its impact (e.g., Cicirelli, 1974; Datta, 1974, 1979). Briefly summarized, the findings of the study indicated that the IQ improvements associated with children's participation in Head Start programs tend to "fade out." Although the study had numerous methodological problems (see Campbell & Erlebacher, 1970; Smith & Bissell, 1970; White, 1970), many were quick to use it as ammunition in their efforts to eliminate or decrease public spending for early intervention. So strong was the negative feeling about preschool programs generated by the Westinghouse study that additional evidence about Head Start's positive outcomes rarely, if ever, came to light. An example is the Kirschner report (1970), which assessed the effects of the presence of Head Start programs on overall community responsiveness to the poor and made it abundantly clear that Head Start served as a catalyst for communities to improve their educational, health, and social services to the poor.

Since the Westinghouse report, an extensive amount of literature discussing and even refuting its findings has accumulated (e.g., Campbell & Erlebacher, 1970; Ryan, 1974). The problems associated with the study, however, have led to our greater understanding of evaluation research in general and the refinement of the methodologies involved. We have come to appreciate that our ability to perform outcome evaluation depends on the degree to which the goals of the program are well presented and held constant throughout the life of the program (Zigler & Trickett, 1978). The programs included in the cost-benefit analyses mentioned earlier had stated at the outset the explicit educational goals to be attained by the children involved. However, in the case of Project Head Start, the goals were originally presented vaguely, were later changed, and various of its most promising components were not highlighted. The same is true of the Women, Infants, and Children (WIC) Program, in which $200 million per year is spent on the provision of dairy products to pregnant mothers and young children. Although the benefits of this program are potentially enormous, given what we know from the research on the relationship between prenatal nutrition and intellectual (Winick, 1976), emotional (Pollit & Thompson, 1977), and physical development, the WIC program cannot be evaluated (Solkoff, 1977) because no one enunciated at the outset what its circumscribed and measurable goals might be; that is, whether its goals are to improve the nutritional status of women and children or to eliminate poverty.

Another problem that has emerged in relation to evaluation is the selection of outcome measures. The most often utilized outcome measure during the past 20 years of early childhood intervention programs has been the IQ score, or the magnitude of change in a child's IQ score. Using the IQ score as a measure in the evaluation of programs afforded the opportunity to avoid the rigors of goal-sensitive outcome evaluation by concluding that a children's program was a success if it resulted in higher IQs and was a failure if it did not (Zigler &

Trickett, 1978). Various theoretical and methodological problems are associated with the use of the IQ score in this way (Cronbach, 1971; McClelland, 1973). Despite the reservations that have been voiced regarding the use of the IQ score as an outcome measure, it is still widely used in evaluation efforts. There are several reasons for the initial popularity of the IQ score and for its continued use. One is historic—early intervention efforts in many cases were initiated in order to examine the degree to which IQ scores can be influenced by life experiences (cf., Garber & Heber, 1977; Gordon, 1973; Gray & Klaus, 1965; Karnes et al., 1970; Levenstein & Sunley, 1968; Skeels, 1966).

Another reason for the popularity of the IQ score as an outcome measure is that standard IQ tests are well-developed instruments. Their psychometric properties are well documented, a factor that allows a user to avoid difficult measurement problems. IQ tests are also readily available and easy to administer. This attractiveness is further enhanced if other tests are employed (e.g., the Peabody Picture Vocabulary Test, the Otis–Lennon Mental Ability Test) because high correlation is found between these 10-minute tests and the longer Stanford–Binet Intelligence Scale or the Wechsler Intelligence Scale for Children.

Also, no other test has been found to be related to so many behaviors of theoretical and practical significance (Kohlberg & Zigler, 1967; Mischel, 1968). As early childhood intervention programs are popularly regarded as efforts to prepare children for school, the fact that the IQ is the best available predictor of school performance is a compelling rationale for its use as an assessment criterion. Beyond the school issue, if compensatory education programs are directed at correcting deficiencies across a broad array of cognitive abilities, the best single measure of the success of these programs is improvement on the IQ test, which reflects a broad spectrum of these abilities.

Finally, once it became obvious that the most common outcome of any intervention program, including a hastily mounted eight-week summer effort, was a 10-point increase in IQ (Eisenberg & Connors, 1966), the IQ test became an instant success as a tool for demonstrating the effectiveness of early intervention. Over the years, we have acquired more insight into the cause of the IQ changes resulting from participation in early childhood intervention programs such as Head Start. Considerable empirical evidence has shown that these changes in IQ reflect motivational changes that influence test performance rather than a change in the actual nature of formal cognitive functioning (Seitz, Abelson, Levine, & Zigler, 1975; Zigler, Abelson, & Seitz, 1973; Zigler, Abelson, Trickett, & Seitz, 1980; Zigler & Butterfield, 1968).

Given some of the advantages associated with the use of the IQ score as an outcome measure, it is useful at this point to reflect on what the IQ test actually measures, as well as on some of its limitations. As is elaborated in other contexts (see Zigler & Trickett, 1978), the IQ test should not be viewed as a pure measure of formal cognition, but as a polyglot sample of behavior that is influenced by three empirically related, but conceptually distinct, collections of variables.

First, it does measure a collection of formal cognitive processes such as abstracting ability, reasoning, speed of visual information processing, and all those other formal cognitive processes that appear and reappear with regularity in factor analytic studies of human intelligence test performance. Second, the standard intelligence test is also an achievement test that is highly influenced by the child's particular experiences. This is an important point in that it represents a major disadvantage in some situations. If we ask children what a "gown" is and they reply that they do not know, it is easy to assume that there is something inadequate about the memory storage or retrieval systems that are aspects of their formal cognitive systems. However, if the children have never in their experience encountered a gown, they will fail the item even though there may be nothing wrong with their memory storage and retrieval systems.

Finally, intelligence test performance is greatly influenced by a variety of motivational and/or personality variables that have little to do with either formal cognition or achievement variables. Among economically disadvantaged children there is a tendency to answer questions with the standard reply "I don't know." This reply does not necessarily reflect a lack of ability, nor a lack of knowledge, but it could reflect the children's desire to terminate or minimize their interaction with the examiner. Why this is so is not exactly clear, but it could be because the children dislike the examiner, or because they dislike the testing situation, or both. Clearly, given the demands of our society, children who have adopted the 'I don't know' strategy are not likely to utilize their cognitive systems optimally. If they continue with this strategy, they are unlikely to obtain those rewards, such as high grades in school or attractive jobs after school, that society dispenses for behaving in the manner it prefers.

It is this tripartite conception of IQ test performance that explains why IQ performance successfully predicts a wide variety of behaviors and, if conceptualized and used properly, may be useful in the evaluation of programs. However, along with some of the disadvantages associated with the use of the IQ test that we have highlighted, there is a controversy surrounding its use in the evaluation and prediction of children's performance (e.g., Jensen, 1979). Although it is difficult to avoid the use of standardized assessment procedures (Travers & Light, 1982), alternative assessment instruments have been considered and to some extent developed. The "generative tests" developed to assess the value and impact of the High/Scope Cognitively Oriented Curriculum (Weikart, 1982) are examples of these. In generative tests—created to avoid some of the testing problems associated with the use of IQ tests with disadvantaged children—students provide both questions and answers, and have full control over the sophistication of their responses. Another example is the Learning Potential Assessment Device (Feuerstein, Krasilowsky, & Rand, 1974), which is an approach to the assessment of the cognitive modifiability of the child.

It has also been proposed (Zigler, 1970, 1973) that social competence rather than IQ should be employed as the major measure of the success of early intervention efforts. The relationship between IQ and social competence has been made explicit in other contexts (e.g., Zigler & Trickett, 1978) and is implied in the preceding discussion of what the IQ tests measure. There are problems associated with the use of social competence measures, not the least of which is the lack of agreement among psychologists as to what social competence is (Anderson & Messick, 1974) and therefore of what a social competence index should consist. Nonetheless, psychologists have sufficient knowledge of human development to warrant, at the very least, an arbitrary definition of social competence. It has been suggested (Zigler & Seitz, 1982a; Zigler & Trickett, 1978) that a social competence index should include the following: First, measures of physical health and well-being, including appropriate weight for age, inoculation history, etc; second, a measure of formal cognitive ability; third, achievement measures such as the Caldwell Preschool Inventory or the Peabody Individual Achievement Test and/or a variety of school-age achievement tests; and finally, the measurement of motivational and emotional variables, which may include the measurement of effectance motivation, including indicators of preference for challenging tasks, curiosity, variation-seeking, and mastery motivation; outerdirectedness and degree of imitation in problem solving; positive responsiveness to social reinforcement; locus of control measured for both parents and children; expectancy of success; aspects of self-image; measures of learned helplessness; and the child's attitude toward school.

Principles of Evaluation Research.   Psychologists have learned a great deal about how to conduct program evaluation and have significantly refined their evaluation methodologies. The evolution of the design of intervention programs, as well as of our understanding and ability to evaluate them are proof of psychologists' increased maturity in this regard. A number of evaluation specialists have documented what we now know to be the essentials of adequate evaluation research (see Guttentag & Streuning, 1975; Streuning & Guttentag, 1974). In summing up our discussion on the valuation of social programs we briefly highlight several of the major principles that have emerged over the past 20 years of evaluations of early intervention efforts.

The first principle is that programs must be evaluated broadly rather than by laboratory measures only. As Travers and Light (1982) note, the choice of measures and/or research designs should be based on an assessment of the full range of possibilities in light of the goals and circumstances of the particular program under evaluation. To this end, evaluators are urged to give careful consideration to several types of information that may illuminate the working of the programs. Some examples of these types of information are the characteristics of the quality of life of children in programs in which the children spend a large portion of their day; descriptions of the social environment of the children—for example the adults with whom they come in contact—as these have the greatest potential for enhancing or thwarting the children's development; and the relationships between program clients and staff. This information can not only yield important data on the actual operation of the program, it can also enhance our understanding of the variations in effectiveness within and across programs.

A second, related principle is that both process and outcome evaluation are necessary for complete program evaluation. As defined earlier, process evaluation is a check to determine whether services are actually delivered and how they are delivered. Outcome evaluation is an assessment of the impact of programs. Neither a process nor an outcome evaluation is sufficient by itself. For example, despite the fact that Head Start centers vary enormously from one locale to another, researchers in early studies compared graduates of Head Start on a national basis with children who had not attended Head Start (Cicirelli, 1969). There was undoubtedly as much variation within the groups as there was between them, but the studies failed to document this. Over the years, it has become common practice to monitor the activities that actually occur in intervention programs and to compare differences within programs (e.g., Huston-Stein, Friedrich-Cofer & Susman, 1977). Thus, the use of both types of evaluation can yield valuable lessons about the intervention program.

The third principle is that because the effects of early intervention are complex, oversimplification in their assessment must be avoided. In the early years of intervention programs, scientists, using what has since come to be regarded as a narrow interpretation of the results, may have been able to declare compensatory education programs as failures (Jensen, 1969). But we now know that program evaluation is not a simple matter. Indeed, in their quest to find out not only if a program is a success or failure, but why it is a success or failure, researchers are learning to specify particular populations, particular ages, and particular modes of service delivery systems, and what the particular intervention means in relation to these mediating factors, rather than expecting to find that the program is merely a "success" or a "failure."

Uses of Research in Social Policy

Although many opportunities for social scientists to direct their attention to research that has social utility exist today, the application of psychological findings and thought to the improvement of social conditions and human welfare is not a simple task; there are doubts, uncertainties, and problems associated with the increased participation of researchers in the social policy decision-making process. It is useful, therefore, to mention some of the uses of research in the policy arena and to examine the relationship between social science research and social policy.

Weiss (1978) points out that there are many possible ways in which psychological research can be put to use in the construction of social policy. An ideal use of the research, and the most common understanding of the relationship between research and policy, is in problem solving. This approach assumes that a concrete and well-defined problem needs to be solved, and that empirical evidence is available, or can become available, to be used to generate a solution or to choose among several alternative solutions. Underlying this approach is the assumption that there is consensus among decision makers on the goals they wish to achieve. This, however, may not always be the case, as we have shown earlier with the Women, Infants, and Children (WIC) program.

Research can also create its own use. Weiss (1977, 1978) refers to this model of social science utilization as the knowledge-driven model. In this model, the assumption is that due to the compelling nature of the research findings, applications are bound to follow. However, unless there are active public education efforts on behalf of researchers that include dissemination of the research findings, this type of use of research is unlikely to occur.

Research may often be used as political ammunition. Even after policymakers have reached decisions and are committed to a particular policy direction, they may use social science research to bolster their arguments. This use of the research is acceptable, as long as the information is not distorted and all aspects of the research are presented. However, the research is sometimes used simply to advance self-interest. Examples of such misuses include those politicians who cite research results supporting their views but neglect to cite those results which do not, and policymakers who delay taking an action, arguing that the needed research evidence is not available. This is clearly documented in the case, discussed earlier, of the moratorium on the Federal Interagencies Day Care Requirements. Other examples of unacceptable use of the research involve social scientists who, in serving their own interests, attempt to gain fame by influencing policy, securing government funds, and widely advocating their own views. The book *School Can Wait* (Moore, Moore, Willey, Moore & Kordenbrock, 1979), is an example of ideology parading as social science and is a blatant misuse of the research. In the book, the authors advocate that children refrain from attending school until late childhood, even though there is no research evidence to substantiate this view. The authors in this case do not cite research findings to substantiate specific examples in their writing; rather, they note that their views stem from the influence of noted social scientists, which they acknowledge, thereby implying that there is empirical evidence for their claims.

The last use of social science research to be discussed, "research as conceptualization," is the most amorphous and perhaps the most important (Weiss, 1977). This definition of the use of the research involves sensitizing policymakers to new issues, turning research problems into policy issues, clarifying alternatives, and supplying a common language. Although this is a "softer" use of the research than is commonly desired, it can have far-reaching effects. Generalizations from the accumulation of research in a specific area can, over time, change the climate of ideas, becoming part of the social consciousness and eventually the basis of social policies. This was clearly illustrated by Caplan and his colleagues (Caplan, 1975; Caplan & Rich, 1977; Rich & Caplan, 1976), who interviewed 204 policymakers in the executive branch of the federal government and asked them if, on the basis of their experience, they could think of instances where a new program, a major program alternative, or a social or administrative policy, legislative proposal, or technical innovation could be traced to the social sciences. Although 82 percent of the respondents replied ''Yes'' to this question, the examples they gave were not of empirical studies. Rather, they cited general ideas and principles garnered from social science knowledge. One can see, of course, that there is a negative aspect to this use of research in policy—myths and social fads are quite likely to become part of the knowledge that is accessible to, and utilized by, the public. Unfortunately, these myths often go unchallenged and become the basis for new policy. One example of this problem is the belief that ''fade-out'' is the inevitable fate of any positive effects of preschool intervention programs. However, there is a positive side to the use of generalities derived from social science research. Consider the case of Project Head Start, which began at the time when the prevailing social science theories on the role of the environment in human development, and the War on Poverty on the political front, converged to produce this educational program for disadvantaged children. Thus, the principles drawn from social science knowledge can and do have a positive impact on the formulation and implementation of social policies.

Problems in the Utilization of Social Science Research.   Despite the potential inherent in the utilization of social science knowledge in the policy arena, there are several problems that impede the application of that knowledge. One commonly cited problem is the conflict in values between researchers and policymakers (Mayntz, 1977; Weiss, 1977, 1978; Weiss & Bucavalas, 1977), which results in the failure to use social science knowledge as the basis for policy decisions. The general assumption is that social science knowledge is value-free while policies are made in a value-laden context. This differing characterization of research and policy is misleading. Research in the social sciences is not value-free; even the most basic research takes on the values of the investigators. This is evident in the questions the researchers ask, the methodologies used, the presentation of the results, and the interpretation of the data. An example may be drawn from research that clearly demonstrates the influence of the values of the investigators on the way in which problems are studied. In this example, we briefly describe three approaches to the study of child abuse (for a more detailed analysis of each of the approaches, see Parke & Collmer, 1975).

In the first approach, the psychiatric analysis of child abuse, investigators assume that the causes of abuse lie within the parent who is ill or abnormal. The research, therefore, focuses on identifying those traits or characteristics that are common to abusive parents. The solution to the child abuse problem advocated by researchers using this approach is usually individual or group therapy for abusive parents. In the second approach, the sociological model, researchers view child abuse as a response to stress and the frustrations of everyday life, as well as to the social values of one's culture. Conditions such as cultural attitudes toward violence, family size, social isolation, economic status, and environmental stress, rather than inherent individual traits, are considered to be the primary factors in abuse cases. From the point of view of this approach, the control of abuse results from changes in societal values and conditions; thus, the elimination of poverty or the provision of family support systems would be considered potential solutions to the child abuse problem. Finally, researchers using the social-situational approach to the study of child abuse focus on the patterns of interaction between abusive parents and their children, and the conditions under which the abuse occurs. Factors such as the use of discipline, the child's role in abuse, and interferences in the mother–child attachment process are considered important contributors to child abuse. Because the cause of abuse is not considered to be inherent in the individual but in the context in which abuse occurs, intervention efforts in this approach emphasize the modification of maladaptive behaviors by both parents and children. The close relationship between the values of the scientist and the direction the research takes can be seen from this description. Thus, depending on the values guiding the research, the understanding of the problem as well as the solutions proposed will differ.

A second problem is the perceived conflict between social science research and policy making, which stems in part from the fact that research is generally viewed as basic, not applied, and therefore irrelevant to social problems. This position is clearly inaccurate. Not only do developmental psychologists draw on applied settings for new opportunities for learning about human development, the American government is clearly looking to social scientists for answers to many questions of social relevance. Within the past decade, the federal government has spent nearly $2 billion on the production and application of social science knowledge, a majority of which went to research (Study Project on Social Research and Development, 1978). In addition, the evaluation requirements written into many federally funded social programs have resulted in the use of research methodologies in applied settings. The applied nature of much social science research, as well as the attitudinal and societal changes that have resulted from it, are documented in a recently completed study conducted by the National Academy of Sciences (1982). Among the benefits to society of social science research in general, the report includes the reformulation of lay understanding in areas such as racial and sex differences, and the invention of information gathering techniques, such as survey research, which enable politicians to keep abreast of public opinion on a variety of topics.

Despite these developments, there are many scholars who adhere to the notion of a conflict between social science research and policy making. Lindblom and Cohen (1979), for example, contend that policymakers encounter frustration when working with social scientists. Lindblom and Cohen suggest that the problem is one of researchers who need to clarify their own professional practices and confusions they have about what they actually do and what scientific conventions persuade them they must or ought to be doing, before they can expect optimal use of their research in the policy arena.

Perhaps the major problem in the utilization of social science research in policy settings relates to the fact that social scientists are perceived as unable to provide clear answers to policy questions, or, looked at from another perspective, that policymakers are not asking questions that lead to valid and reliable research. This problem arises because of unrealistic expectations about the kinds of questions that social science can answer and the number of studies necessary for appropriate answers. Those who expect single studies to have an impact on policy are likely to be disappointed, for the effects of these studies are usually small or nonexistent (Cohen & Garet, 1975; Cohen & Weiss, 1977; Rich & Caplan, 1976). If single studies do not have an impact on policy, what is the effect of the research accumulated in any one area? At times, studies on a particular topic can illuminate a policy direction. For example, the studies conducted by the Children's Defense Fund on foster care, provided a clear policy option—namely, the provision of financial subsidies to encourage the adoption of children in foster care—that was eventually enacted into law (Child Welfare Act of 1980). However, the proliferation of research studies on a particular topic sometimes results, not in a more adequate or definitive answer to a policy question, but in additional confusion (Cohen & Garet, 1975; Cohen & Weiss, 1977) because the research can be both contradictory and complex, and may not provide a consensus from which to draw undisputed solutions. However, even in these cases, the use of research studies can be advantageous, in that it can lead to a clarification of differences and perspectives, as well as improved research methodologies. For instance, after the primarily negative findings of the Westinghouse evaluation of Head Start in 1969 were published, questions about proper assumptions, subject selection biases, methodologies, and program goals arose. The results of this questioning included improved methodological and statistical techniques for the evaluation of programs, the use of a wider range of methodologies, and an interest in outcome variables other than school achievement in evaluation efforts.

Encouraging the Use of Research in the Policy Arena: The Role of Developmental Psychologists

One of the most perplexing issues facing applied developmental psychologists is the extent of their participation in the social policy process. There are those who contend that although scientists need to be aware of the policy process, they should limit their participation to the production and provision of sound empirical evidence that can be used as the basis for conceptualizing policies (Tallman, 1976, 1979). Others, however, view the role of social scientists as including social activism and advocacy in behalf of social causes.

In order to encourage more extensive use of broad principles from child development research as the basis for social policies, Lynn (1978) suggests that developmental psychologists should know the dynamics entailed in the policy process. It is also suggested that social scientists should participate in a broad-based lobby in behalf of children, and that they identify appropriate leverage points within government and work through these to develop and implement policies for children (Zigler & Finn, 1981). These suggestions are made in light of the fact that although federal efforts in behalf of children and their families are extensive and varied, it is difficult to identify any overarching and consistent goals for the support of children in America. Programs have been enacted piece-meal over an extended period of time with little apparent attention paid to their collective impact or their interrelationships. As Steiner (1976) notes, "public involvement in [this] field is federal agency-by-federal agency, congressional committee-by-congressional committee" (p. vii). This state of affairs exists as well in state and local level policies and services for children and their families. The lack of coordinated effort is only one problem, however. Other problems include the inadequate allocation of funds for child and family services, and policies and programs that are contradictory to what we know about children from the research on child development. One such contradiction is exemplified in this nation's foster care system. We know from many years of accumulated research that a child suffers without a sense of continuity and consistency in the environment. When children need out-of-home placements, therefore, it is important that their lives be stabilized and that a permanent and supportive home for them be found. Beneficial programs for children at risk within their own family situation would include preventive family support services. If children must be removed from their families, they should be placed in the least restrictive environments, preferably with relatives and near their families. Reviews of children in the foster care system should be made periodically, and, if the children are not returned to their families, termination of parental rights should be hastened and the adoption of those children encouraged (Cranston, 1979). Despite these possible solutions, and the fact that they are cost-effective (Zigler & Finn, 1982), some 500,000 children remain adrift in the foster care system in this country (Edelman, 1979), where they are moved from one home to another for indefinite periods. In some states, the average time spent in foster care is nearly five years (Keniston, 1977). There are reports that 62 percent of children placed in foster care remain out of their homes for their entire childhood. Only 15 to 25 percent of them return home, and the number of children who are eventually adopted is even lower—less than 15 percent (Keniston, 1977). As a result of research on the effects of foster care on children, the documentation of the status of the foster care system, *and* continued advocacy for changes that should be made, researchers as well as child advocates have been instrumental in facilitating the enactment of the Child Welfare Act of 1980, which ensures modifications in the way foster children are treated (Children's Defense Fund, 1978). Although this is an encouraging development, foster care represents only one of many childhood problems that need to be resolved.

Our ability to address those problems rests on the efforts of social scientists to inform not only policymakers, but, even more importantly, the general public of the needs of children (Zigler & Finn, 1981). No society acts until it has a sense of the immediacy of a particular problem. This has been illustrated in the founding of the Great Society in the mid-sixties. During that time, social issues were written up on the front pages of newspapers and were in the forefront of national attention. There were daily stories on welfare mothers, reports on poverty, and expositions on hunger in the United States. Hence, there was sympathy for the poor and support for the War on Poverty and its associated social programs. Today, no top national newspaper or television network covers social services on a regular basis (Lyn, 1980). Worse, there are indications that journalists interested in covering these issues are discouraged from doing so (Lyn, 1980). The problems that received such attention in the 1960s—for example, poverty and inadequate health care—are still with us and have worsened. However, the news media are inundated with stories on foreign affairs, the consequences of inflation, the national budget, and so on, with the result that public recognition of the needs of children is limited.

There are indications, however, that developmental psychologists are becoming aware of the need for public education on issues related to children. For many years it has been our pattern as researchers to function in isolation and to discuss human problems, as well as possible solutions for them, with each other either at professional conferences or in professional journals. Most researchers' assumptions about the audience they reached and influenced were probably fairly modest. That is, they hoped their colleagues would notice their work, appreciate its implications, and carry the ideas one step further. Now, this approach is changing. Researchers in the field of developmental psychology are acknowledging the need to disseminate their knowledge in the context of the popular media, not only by presenting research findings to policymakers but also indirectly, by addressing more general changes in viewpoint toward a topic or an issue. An example of this type of activity by researchers is the creation of a committee chaired by Robert McCall on the role of research and the media within the Society for Research in Child Development. In a recent article, McCall and his colleagues summarize some of the procedural elements in the knowledge dissemination process and illuminate the skills researchers need in order to communicate research findings to the public or other interested parties (McCall, Lonnberg, Gregory, Murray, & Leavitt, 1981).

Finally, in delineating the role of applied researchers in the area of social science and social policy, Ballard, Brosz, and Parker (1981) note that there are several requirements for the successful application of knowledge to social problems. Among these are the need for early and continued collaboration between researchers and policymakers in order to establish and maintain trust, and the need for scientific credibility on the part of researchers. This latter requirement cannot be overemphasized. Applied researchers, while they must pay attention to approaches for the utilization of their research, must also maintain credibility in the scientific research community. Academic credibility facilitates the application of social science knowledge—including theories, methods, and data bases—to social problems. In an effort to ensure the use of our research in practical ways that can help children and families, we must always ensure that we maintain a disciplinary and professional identity as scientists.

INTEGRATION OF CHILD DEVELOPMENT RESEARCH AND SOCIAL POLICY: BEYOND THE PUBLIC SECTOR

In this chapter, the link between child development research and government has been described. During the past two decades of social action, much of the activity was in the hands of the federal government. There are trends, however, that indicate that the role of the federal government will diminish in the coming years, not only in terms of the amount of money to be allocated for social services, but also in terms of the direction these services will take (Hayes, 1982). These trends include the climbing deficits in the national budget, the political temper of the times to allocate increasingly smaller amounts of money for social services, and public support in favor of less government intervention.

Although these developments are associated with a certain amount of optimism regarding the potential for increased activity at the state and local levels (Finn, 1981), the reality of dwindling government funds means that we must look beyond the public sector for the support of children and families in need. There are possibilities in the private sector's support of family life. In this respect, researchers can form an alliance with executives in industry who have the ability to institute changes that will have a positive effect on children and families.

One way in which the private sector can exert its influence to benefit children and families is in the area of work and family life. With the two-paycheck family now the norm rather than the exception, and with the increase in single-parent households, the impact of the workplace on family life has become a relevant issue. The relationship between these two institutions has been the subject of several recent studies that emphasize an important point: Work and family life are not, as has been assumed, separate worlds, but are interdependent and overlapping, with functions and behavioral rules within each system influencing processes within the other (Brim & Abeles, 1975; Kanter, 1977). This interplay between work and family life, and its effect on children are very much within the concern of developmental psychologists.

To the extent that there are children present, life for the dual-career family is stressful. Day care arrangements must be made for the infant and preschool child; before- and after-school facilities have to be found for the older child;

school vacations and those days when a child is sick carry with them the need for still other solutions. As worker satisfaction and productivity have been found to be functions of family stability and other processes within the family system (Kanter, 1977), it behooves industry to offer services and benefits that help families.

In a recent national survey on families at work (Yankelovich, Skelly, White, Inc., 1981), the strains on the family in which both parents work are documented. The greatest concern for the parents interviewed in this study is the quality and amount of guidance, discipline, and attention their children receive while the parents are at work. In their attempts to balance work and family life, the respondents noted that of the benefits employers might offer that would help them in this regard, benefits for child care would rank the most important. Among these child care benefits, the respondents included paid personal days specifically for child-related responsibilities; paid pregnancy, maternity and paternity leaves; and child day care facilities.

Although the role of industry in this regard has been slow to develop, several attempts have been made to accommodate the needs of families. These include changes in the work structure to allow flexible working arrangements (Kuhne & Blair, 1978), part-time work opportunities (Schwartz, 1974), and job sharing (Olmsted, 1979). Companies are required by law to offer maternity leaves (Bureau of Business Practice, 1979). At best, these are for three months, although school teachers, for example, are able to take up to a year's leave of absence without pay in order to stay with their newborn infants. As a nation, however, we lag far behind other countries in our pronatal policies. According to Kamerman and Kahn (1976), European nations make provisions for 6 to 12 months maternity *or* paternity leave with pay in order to facilitate childrearing, and facilities for child care are available in cases in which both parents choose to work. The research questions that need to be addressed in these changes in work schedules and employee benefits include the impact of the changes, not only on productivity, but on children and families as well. Do parents who take advantage of flexible working arrangements actually spend time with their children? Do these **working arrangements facilitate the reduction of stress in parents? Given the option for maternity and paternity leaves, do parents use them? For** the past several years, corporations' responsibilities for the provision of day care services to their employees have been discussed. Several major corporations in the United States have instituted a variety of child day care programs. Stride Rite Corporation in Boston has a company-based day care center as one of its employee benefits packages. Employees pay for day care at a rate ranging from 10 percent of their salary to a maximum of $25 a week (McIntyre, 1978). Levi Strauss & Company in San Francisco, after seven years of research and experimentation, concluded that day care services should be closer to where people live rather than to where they work (McIntyre, 1978). As a result of these findings, Levi Strauss's policy is to "advocate the concept" of family day care homes.

However, although the company does support research on the matter, it does not have a reimbursement program for those employees who use family day care homes.

Company-based day care may not be entirely satisfactory, and subsidizing these centers is expensive. Therefore, several businesses—for example, a hospital, a telephone company, and a factory—could together support a day care program that is central to where their employees work. This would prove convenient for the employees, as well as inexpensive, because several businesses would be contributing to the cost of the center and part of the costs could be paid by the employees themselves.

Several other suggestions on the role of industry in facilitating family life are elaborated in other contexts (Zigler & Finn, 1982; Zigler & Finn, in press). These include helping to promote interdependence among families within neighborhoods, as well as the provision of referral centers or networks of family support systems, all of which, in view of the information presented in our earlier discussion on the status of family life, are important resources for the support of the family. However, unless executives in the private sector are apprised of the needs of the families in their employ, as well as of some of the ways in which these needs can be met, it is unlikely that much progress will be made in this area. The role of developmental psychologists would include, therefore, not only continued research on aspects of work and family life but also the dissemination of the findings to those in the private sector who have the power to make policy changes.

SUMMARY AND CONCLUSION

In our discussion of applied developmental psychology we have shown the reciprocity that exists between applied and basic research, and we have highlighted the opportunities for new learning that applied settings offer, as well as the contributions that developmental psychologists can make in the policy arena. Our discussion has centered on the possibilities for research on children's development in view of the economic and demographic changes our society is experiencing, as well as on research related to the design and evaluation of social programs.

It is clear from this discussion that developmental psychologists have opportunities to learn from research in social settings and to contribute to the improvement of human life. In addition, if they are to be effective, applied developmental psychologists cannot work entirely within their own discipline. This is true in relation to both the acquisition and the implementation of knowledge wherein principles drawn from basic research and collaboration with policymakers can significantly influence applied developmental psychology and its inherent potential to meet the needs of children.

It is also evident that tensions and uncertainties underlie efforts to integrate child development research and social policy. Although these are not insurmountable (Masters, 1983), they nevertheless influence researchers' decisions to address policy issues in their work or to consider the social relevance of their research. Fortunately, there is considerable encouragement and support today for developmental psychologists to engage in research that has social utility and to focus on the practical implications of their studies. This is evidenced, for example, by the growing number of child development and social policy centers in several universities, as well as the inclusion of policy courses in numerous graduate programs in developmental psychology. The purpose in both these cases is to provide comprehensive training for psychologists in issues that are related to policy (Masters, 1983). The effort to train researchers at the intersect of child development research and social policy is still in its infancy and is subject to considerable variance among programs. But it should lead to more widespread efforts among researchers to resolve the needs of children and families through participation in the policy process. As to the direction these efforts would take, our suggestions include the collaboration of developmental psychologists with public and private sector policymakers in the development of programs and policies that are based on principles taken from child development research, and recognizing that our role as psychologists includes the sharing of knowledge from this research with the general public. Only through these activities can we anticipate, over time, changes in awareness of the needs of children and families, and, eventually, public demand for the solution to these needs.

REFERENCES

Abt, C. C. Social programs evaluation: Research allocation strategies for maximizing policy payoffs. In C. C. Abt (Ed.), *The evaluation of social programs*. Beverly Hills, CA: Sage Publications, 1974.

Abt National Day Care Study *Day care centers in the United States: A national profile, 1976–1977*. Cambridge, MA.: Abt Associates, 1979.

Advisory Committee on Child Development. *Toward a national policy for children and families*. Washington, DC: National Academy of Sciences, 1976.

Ainsworth, M. D. S. The development of infant–mother attachment. In B. M. Caldwell & H. N. Riccuiti (Eds.), *Review of child development research*. Vol. 3. Chicago: University of Chicago Press, 1973.

Ainsworth, M. D. S. Attachment and child abuse. In G. Gerbner, C. Ross, & E. Zigler (Eds.), *Child abuse: An agenda for action*. New York: Oxford University Press, 1980.

Anderson, R. E. Paternal deprivation and delinquency. *Archives of General Psychiatry*, June 1968, *18*, 641–649.

Anderson, S., & Messick, S. Social competency in young children. *Developmental Psychology*, 1974, *10*, 282–293.

Antley, T. R. et al. *A case for early intervention: Summary of program findings, longitudinal data, and cost-effectiveness.* Seattle, WA: Model Preschool Center Outreach Program, Experimental Education Unit, 1982.

Bahr, S. J. Divorce mediation: An evaluation of an alternative divorce policy. *Networker,* Winter 1981, *2*(2), 1.

Ballard, S. C., Brosz, A. R., & Parker, L. B. Social science and social policy: Roles of the applied researcher. In J. Grum & S. Wasby (Eds.), *Tha analysis of policy impact.* Lexington, Mass.: Lexington Books, 1981.

Bane, M. J. Marital disruption and the lives of children. *Journal of Social Issues,* 1976, *32,* 103–117.

Beit-Hallahmi, B., & Rabin, A. I. The kibbutz as a social experiment and child-rearing laboratory. *American Psychologist,* 1977, *32,* 532–541.

Belsky, J., & Steinberg, L. The effects of day care: A critical review. *Child Development,* 1978, *49,* 929–949.

Benedek, R. S., & Benedek, E. P. Post-divorce visitation: A child's right. *Journal of the American Academy of Child Psychiatry,* 1977, *16,* 256–271.

Bodenheimer, B. M. The rights of children and the crises in custody litigation in and out of state. *University of Colorado Law Review,* 1974–75, *46,* 495–508.

Brim, O. G. Jr., & Abeles, R. P. Work and personality in the middle years. *Social Science Research Council Items,* 1975, *29,* 29–33.

Bronfenbrenner, U. Developmental research, public policy, and the ecology of childhood. *Child Development,* 1974, *45,* 1–5.

Bronfenbrenner, U. Is early intervention effective? In H. J. Leichter (Ed.), *The family as educator.* New York: Teachers College Press, 1975.

Bronfenbrenner, U. *The experimental ecology of human development.* Cambridge, MA: Harvard University Press, 1977. (a)

Bronfenbrenner, U. Toward an experimental ecology of human development. *American Psychologist,* July 1977, *32,* 513–531. (b)

Brozan, N. Women now hold 30 percent of 2nd jobs. *The New York Times,* June 24, 1980, p. B6.

Bryant, G. Evaluation of basic research in the content of mission orientation. *American Psychologist,* Oct. 1972, *27*(10), 947–950.

Bureau of Business Practice. *Fair Employment Practice Guidelines, 1979. 170*(9).

Caldwell, B. M., Wright, C. M., Honing, A. S., & Tannenbaum, J. Infant day care attachment. *American Journal of Orthopsychiatry,* 1970, *40,* 397–412.

Campbell, D. T., & Erlebacher, A. How regression artifacts in quasi-experimental evaluations can mistakenly make compensatory education look harmful. In J. Hellmuth (Ed.), *The disadvantaged child,* Vol. 3: *Compensatory education: A national debate.* New York: Brunner/Mazel, 1970.

Caplan, N. S. The use of social science information by federal executives. In G. Lyon (Ed.), *Social research and public policies.* Hanover, N.H.: Dartmouth College, 1975.

Caplan, N. S., & Rich, R. F. *Open and closed knowledge inquiry systems: The process and consequences of bureaucratization of information policy at the national level.* Unpublished manuscript, University of Michigan, 1977.

Carter, H. J., & Glick, P. *Marriage, divorce and economic study.* Cambridge, Mass.: Harvard University Press, 1976.

Children's Defense Fund. *Children without homes.* Washington, D.C., 1978.

Cicirelli, V. G. *The impact of Head Start: An evaluation of the effects of Head Start on children's cognitive and affective development.* Washington, D.C.: National Bureau of Standards, Institute for Applied Technology, 1969.

Cicirelli, V. G. Westinghouse summary—The impact of Head Start. In C. C. Abt (Ed.), *The evaluation of social programs.* Beverly Hills, CA: Sage Publications, 1974.

Clarke, A. M., & Clarke, A. O. B. *Early experience: Myth and evidence.* London: Open Books, 1976.

Cohen, D. K., & Garet, M. S. Reforming education policy with applied social research. *Harvard Educational Review*, 1975, *45*, 17–43.

Cohen, D. K., & Weiss, J. A. Social science and social policy: Schools and race. In C. H. Weiss (Ed.), *Using social research in public policy making*. Lexington, MA: Lexington Books, 1977.

Cohen, D., & Zigler, E. Federal day care standards: Rationale and recommendations. *American Journal of Orthopsychiatry*, July 1977, *47*(3).

Coleman, J. S., Campbell, E., Hobson, C., McPartland, J., Mood, A., Weinfeld, F., & York, R. *Equality of educational opportunity*. Washington, DC: U.S. Government Printing Office, 1966.

Comptroller General of the United States. *Report to the Congress: Early childhood and family development programs improve the quality of life for low income families*. (Document No. [HRD] 79–40). Washington, D.C.: U.S. Government Accounting Office, Feb. 6, 1979.

Congressional Record, January 15, 1979, S76–77.

Consortium for Longitudinal Studies. Lasting effects of early education. *Monographs of the Society for Research in Child Development*, 1981.

Cook, T. D. The potential and limitations of secondary evaluations. In M. W. Apple et al. (Eds.), *Educational evaluation: Analysis and responsibility*. Berkeley, CA: McCutchan, 1974.

Coulson, J. M. et al. *Effects of different Head Start program approaches on children of different characteristics: A report on analyses of data from 1966–67 and 1967–68 national evaluations*. Technical Memorandum TM-4862–001/00 (EDO-70859). Santa Monica, CA: Systems Development Corp., 1972.

Cranston, A. (Testimony). U.S. Congress, Senate Committee on Finance, Subcommittee on Public Assistance, *Proposals Related to Social and Child Welfare Services, Adoption Assistance and Foster Care*. Ninety-sixth Congress, September 24, 1979.

Cronbach, L. I. Five decades of public controversy over mental testing. *American Psychologist*, 1971, *30*, 1–14.

Datta, L. The impact of the Westinghouse/Ohio evaluation of Project Head Start: An examination of the immediate and longer term effects and how they came about. In C. C. Abt (Ed.), *The evaluation of social programs*. Beverly Hills, CA: Sage Publications, 1974.

Datta, L. Another spring and other hopes: Some findings from national evaluations of Project Head Start. In E. Zigler & J. Valentine (Eds.), *Project Head Start: A legacy of the war on poverty*. New York: Free Press, 1979.

DeLone, R. H. Early childhood development as a policy goal: An overview of choices. In L. Bond & J. Joffe (Eds.), *Facilitating infant and early childhood development*. Hanover, NH: University Press of New England, 1982.

Edelman, M. W. Children instead of ships. *The New York Times*, May 14, 1979, p. A19.

Eisenberg, L., & Connors, C. K. *The effect of Head Start on developmental process*. Paper presented at the 1966 Joseph P. Kennedy, Jr. Foundation in Scientific Symposium on Mental Retardation, Boston, April 11, 1966.

Farran, D. C., & Ramey, C. T. Infant day care and attachment behaviors toward mothers and teachers. *Child Development*, 1977, *48*, 1112–1116.

Federal Register, March 19, 1980.

Federal programs related to children (Pub. No. [OHDS] 80-30180). Washington, D.C.: U.S. Department of Health, Education, and Welfare, Aug. 1979.

Feuerstein, R., Krasilowsky, D., & Rand, Y. Innovative educational strategies for the integration of high-risk adolescents in Israel. *Phi Delta Kappa*, 1974, *55*, 1–6.

Finn, M. Surviving the budget cuts: A public policy report. *Young Children*, September 1981.

Fraiberg, S. Every child's birthright: In defense of mothering. New York: Basic Books, 1977.

Frye, D. The problem of infant day care. In E. Zigler & E. Gordon (Eds.), *Day care: Scientific and social policy issues*. Boston: Auburn House, 1982.

Garber, H., & Heber, R. The Milwaukee project. In P. Mittler (Ed.), *Research to practice in mental retardation*. Baltimore, MD: University Park Press, 1977.

Garner, R. The acquisition and application of knowledge: A symbiotic relation. *American Psychologist,* Oct. 1972, *27*(10), 941–946.

Gerbner, G., Ross, C. J., & Zigler, E. *Child abuse: An agenda for action.* New York: Oxford University Press, 1980.

Gil, D. G. *Violence against children: Physical abuse in the United States.* Cambridge, MA: Harvard University Press, 1970.

Glass, G. V., McGraw, B., & Smith, M. *Meta-analysis in social research.* Beverly Hills, CA: Sage Publications, 1981.

Goldstein, J., Freud, A., & Solnit, A. *Beyond the best interests of the child.* New York: Free Press, 1973.

Goldstein, J., Freud, A., & Solnit, A. *Before the best interests of the child.* New York: Free Press, 1979.

Gordon, I. J. *An early intervention project: A longitudinal look.* Gainesville, FL: University of Florida, Institute for Development of Human Resources, 1973.

Gray, S. W., & Klaus, R. A. An experimental preschool program for culturally deprived children. *Child Development,* 1965, *36,* 887–898.

Guttentag, M., & Struening, E. L. *Handbook of evaluation research, Vol. 2.* Beverly Hills, CA: Sage Publications, 1975.

Handel, A. Self-concept of the kibbutz adolescent. *Megamot,* 1961, *11,* 142–159.

Harlow, H. F. The development of affectional patterns in infant monkeys. In B. M. Foss (Ed.), *Determinants of infant behavior.* Vol. 1. New York: Wiley, 1961.

Harlow, H. F. The maternal affectional system. In B. M. Foss (Ed.), *Determinants of infant behavior.* Vol. 3. New York: Wiley, 1963.

Hayes, D. *Making policies for children: A study of the federal process.* Washington, DC: National Academy Press, 1982.

Herzog, E., & Sudia, C. E. *Boys in fatherless families* (DHEW Pub. No. [OCD] 72–33). Office of Child Development, U.S. Department of Health, Education & Welfare. Washington, DC: U.S. Government Printing Office, 1973.

Hetherington, E. Effects of father absence on personality development in adolescent daughters. *Developmental Psychology,* 1972, *7,* 313–326.

Hetherington, E. M. Divorce: A child's perspective. *American Psychologist,* 1979, *34*(10), 851–858.

Hetherington, E. M., Cox, M., & Cox, R. The aftermath of divorce. In J. Stevens & M. Mathews (Eds.), *Mother-child/father-child relationships.* Washington, DC: National Association for the Education of Young Children, 1978.

Hetherington, E. M., Cox, M., & Cox, R. The development of children in mother-headed families. In H. Hoffman & D. Reiss (Eds.), *The American family: Dying or developing.* New York: Plenum, 1979.

Hofferth, S. C. Day care in the next decade: 1980–1990. *Journal of Marriage and the Family,* 1979, *41,* 649–657.

Hoffman, L., & Nye, F. I. *Working mothers.* San Francisco: Jossey-Bass, 1974.

Huston-Stein, A., Friedrich-Cofer, L., & Susman, E. J. The relation of classroom structure to social behavior, imaginative play and self-regulation of economically disadvantaged children. *Child Development,* 1977, *48,* 908–916.

Jacobson, D. The impact of marital separation/divorce on child: Parent–child separation and child adjustment. *Journal of Divorce,* 1978, *4,* 341.

Jensen, A. R. How much can we boost IQ and scholastic achievement? *Harvard Educational Review,* 1969, *39,* 1–123.

Jensen, A. R. *Educational differences.* London: Methuen, 1979.

Jones, E., & Prescott, E. A. Day care: Short- or long-term solutions? *Annals/AAPSS,* 461, May 1982.

Kaffman, M. A comparison of psychopathology: Israeli children from kibbutz and from urban surroundings. *American Journal of Orthopsychiatry,* 1965, *35,* 509–520.

Kagan, J., Kearsley, R., & Zelazo, P. *Infancy: Its place in human development.* Cambridge, MA: Harvard University Press, 1978.

Kamerman, S.B., & Kahn, A. J. *European family policy currents: The question of families with very young children.* Unpublished manuscript, Columbia University, School of Social Work, 1976.

Kanter, R. M. *Work and family in the United States: A critical review and agenda for research and policy.* New York: Russell Sage Foundation, 1977.

Karnes, M. B., Teska, J. A., Hodgins, A., & Badger, E. Educational intervention at home of mothers of disadvantaged infants. *Child Development,* 1970, *41,* 925–935.

Kelly, J. B., & Wallerstein, J. S. The effects of parental divorce: Experience of the child in early latency. *American Journal of Orthopsychiatry,* 1976, *46,* 20–32.

Keniston, K. *All our children.* New York: Harcourt Brace Jovanovich, 1977.

Keyserling, M. D. *Windows on day care.* New York: National Council of Jewish Women, 1972.

Kirschner Associates, Albuquerque, New Mexico. *A national survey of the impacts of Head Start centers on community institutions.* (ED045195). Washington, D.C.: Office of Economic Opportunity, May 1970.

Kohen-Raz, R. Mental and motor development of kibbutz, institutionalized, and home-reared infants in Israel. *Child Development,* 1968, *39,* 489–504.

Kohlberg, L., & Zigler, E. The impact of cognitive maturity on the development of sex-role attitudes in the years four to eight. *Genetic Psychology Monographs,* 1967, *75,* 89–165.

Kuhne, R., & Blair, C. Changing the workweek. *Business Horizons,* April 1978, *21*(2).

Lamb, M. E. The role of the father: An overview. In M. E. Lamb (Ed.), *The role of the father in child development.* New York: Wiley, 1976.

Landis, J. T. Social correlates of divorce or nondivorce among the unhappily married. *Marriage and Family Living,* May 1963, *25,* 178–180.

Levenstein, P., & Sunley, R. Stimulation of verbal interaction between disadvantaged mothers and children. *American Journal of Orthopsychiatry,* 1968, *38,* 116–121.

Levitin, T. E. Children of divorce: An introduction. *Journal of Social Issues,* 1979, *35*(4).

Lindblom, C. E., & Cohen, D. K. *Usable knowledge.* New Haven, CT: Yale University Press, 1979.

Lippit, R. Improving the socialization process. In J. A. Clausen (Ed.), *Socialization and society.* Boston: Little, Brown & Co., 1968.

Lyn, J. Filed and forgotten: Why the press has taken up new issues. *Washington Journalism Review,* May 1980, *2*(4), 32–37.

Lynn, L. E. (Ed.), *Knowledge and policy: The uncertain connection.* Washington, DC: National Academy of Sciences, 1978.

Masters, J. C. Models for training and research in child development and social policy. In G. Whitehurst (Ed.), *Annals of Child Development. Vol. 1.* Greenwich, CT: JAI Press, 1983.

Mayntz, R. Sociology, value freedom, and the problems of political counseling. In C. H. Weiss (Ed.), *Using social research in public policy making.* Lexington, MA: Lexington Books, 1977.

McCall, R. B., Lonnborg, B., Gregory, T. G., Murray, J. P., & Leavitt, S. Communicating developmental research to the public: The Boys Town experience. *Newsletter.* Society for Research in Child Development, Fall 1981, pp. 1–3.

McClelland, D. C. Testing for competence rather than for intelligence. *American Psychologist,* 1973, *28,* 1–14.

McIntyre, K. J. Day care: An employer benefit, too. *Business Insurance,* December 11, 1978, 11–36.

Mischel, W. *Personality and assessment*. New York: Wiley, 1968.

Moore, R. S., Moore, D. N., Willey, T. J., Moore, D. R., & Kordenbrock, D. K. *School can wait—The natural child: The first eight years*. Provo, UT: Brigham Young University Press, 1979.

National Academy of Sciences. *Research in behavioral and social sciences: A national resource*. Washington, DC: National Research Council, 1982.

National Center for Health Statistics. *Mortality Advance Report*. PHS/DHHS, September 17, 1980.

Nelson, J. R. The politics of federal day care regulation. In E. Zigler & E. Gordon (Eds.), *Day care: Scientific and social policy issues*. Boston: Auburn House, 1982.

Norton, A. Portrait of the one-parent family. *The National Elementary Principal*, 1979, *59*, 32–35.

Olmsted, B. Job sharing: An emerging work-style. *International Labour Review*, May-June 1979, *118*(3).

Packard, V. *A nation of strangers*. New York: Simon & Schuster, 1972.

Parke, R., & Collmer, C. Child abuse: Interdisciplinary review. In E. M. Hetherington (Ed.), *Review of child development research. Vol. 5*. Chicago: University of Chicago Press, 1975.

Pollitt, E., & Thompson, C. Protein-calorie malnutrition and behavior: A view from psychology. In R. J. Wurtman & J. J. Wurtman (Eds.), *Nutrition and the brain. Vol. 2*. New York: Raven Press, 1977.

Powell, D. *The coordination of preschool socialization: Parent and caregiver relationships in day care settings*. Presented to the Society for Research in Child Development, New Orleans, March 1977.

Powell, D. The interpersonal relationship between parents and caregivers in day care settings. *American Journal of Orthopsychiatry*, 1978, *48*(4).

Price-Bonham, S., & Blaswick, J. The noninstitutions: Divorce, desertion and remarriage. *Journal of Marriage and the Family*, Nov. 1980, pp. 959–972.

Rabin, A. I. The sexes: Ideology and reality in the Israeli kibbutz. In B. M. Edward & L. C. Williamson (Eds.), *Sex roles in a changing society*. New York: Random House, 1970.

Rabin, A., & Goldman, H. The relationship of severity of guilt to intensity of identification in kibbutz and non-kibbutz children. *Journal of Social Psychology*, 1966, *69*, 159–163.

Retting, K. S. Relation of social systems to intergenerational changes in moral attitudes. *Journal of Personality and Social Psychology*, 1966, *4*, 400–414.

Review of Head Start Research Since 1970, A. Prepared by C.S.R. Inc. for the Administration for Children, Youth, and Families, Department of Health and Human Services, Contract #185–81–C–026, 1982. Draft Copy.

Rhine, W. R. (Ed.). *Making schools more effective: New directions from follow through*. New York: Academic Press, 1981.

Rich, R. F., & Caplan, N. *Instrumental and conceptual uses of social science knowledge in policy-making at the national level: Means/ends matching versus understanding*. Unpublished manuscript, University of Michigan, 1976.

Robertson, A. Day care and children's responsiveness to adults. In E. Zigler & E. Gordon (Eds.), *Day care: Scientific and social policy issues*. Boston: Auburn House, 1982.

Rodes, T., & Moore, J. National child care consumer study (USHHS). Washington, D.C.: Administration for Children, Youth, and Families, 1975.

Rofes, E. (Ed.). *The kids book of divorce: By, for and about kids*. New York: Vintage Books, 1980.

Roupp, R. et al. *Children at the center: Final Report of the National Day Care Study. Vol. 1*. Cambridge, MA: Abt Books, 1979.

Rutter, M. Socio-emotional consequences for day care for preschool children. *American Journal of Orthopsychiatry*, 1981, *51*, 4–28.

Rutter, M. Social-emotional sequelae of day care. In E. Zigler & E. Gordon (Eds.), *Day care: Scientific and social policy issues*. Boston: Auburn House, 1982.

Ryan, S. (Ed.). *A report on longitudinal evaluations of preschool programs. Vol. 1. Longitudinal evaluation* (Pub. No. [OTTO] 72–54). Washington, DC: U.S. Department of Health, Education, and Welfare, 1974.

Salkind, N. J. The effectiveness of early intervention. In E. Allen & E. Goetz, *Early childhood education: Special environmental and legal considerations*, in press.

Schwartz, F. N. New work patterns for better use of womanpower. *Management Review*, May 1974, 4–12.

Seitz, V. A methodological comment on "the problem of infant day care." In E. Zigler & E. Gordon (Eds.), *Day care: Scientific and social policy issues*. Boston: Auburn House, 1982.

Seitz, V., Abelson, W. D., Levine, E., & Zigler, E. Effects of place of testing on the Peabody Picture Vocabulary Test scores of disadvantaged Head Start and non-Head Start children. *Child Development*, 1975, *46*, 481–486.

Sharabany, R. Intimate friendship among kibbutz and city children and its measurement. Unpublished doctoral dissertation, Cornell University, 1974.

Skeels, H. M. Adult status of children with contrasting early life experiences: A follow-up study. *Monographs of the Society for Research in Child Development*, 1966, *31* (3, Serial No. 105).

Smith, M. S., & Bissell, J. S. Report analysis: The impact of Head Start. *Harvard Educational Review*, 1970, *40*, 51–104.

Smock, S. M. *The children: The shape of child care in Detroit*. Detroit: Wayne State University Press, 1977.

Solkoff, J. Strictly from hunger. *New Republic*, June 11, 1977, 13–15.

Steiner, G. *The children's cause*. Washington, DC: Brookings Institute, 1976.

Struening, E. L., & Guttentag, M. (Eds.) *Handbook of evaluation research. Vol. 1*. Beverly Hills, CA: Sage Publications, 1974.

Study Project on Social Research and Development. *The federal investment in knowledge of social problems. Vol. 1*. Washington, DC: National Academy of Sciences, 1978.

Tallman, I. *Passion, action, and politics*. San Francisco: W. H. Freeman, 1976.

Tallman, I. Implementation of a national family policy: The role of the social scientist. *Journal of Marriage and the Family, 41*(3), 1979.

Travers, J. R., & Light, R. J. (Eds.) *Learning from experience: Evaluating early childhood demonstration programs*. Washington, DC: National Academy Press, 1982.

U.S. Bureau of the Census. *Current population reports* (Series P-23, No. 84). Washington, DC: U.S. Department of Commerce, 1979.

Valentine, J., & Stark, E. The social context of parent involvement in Head Start. In E. Zigler & J. Valentine (Eds.), *Project Head Start: A legacy of the war on poverty*. New York: Free Press, 1979.

Wallerstein, J. S., & Kelly, J. B. Children and divorce: A review. *Social Work*, 1979, *24*, 468–475.

Wallerstein, J. S., & Kelly, J. B. *Surviving the breakup: How children and parents cope with divorce*. New York: Basic Books, 1980.

Ward, E. H. CDA: Credentialing for day care. *Voice for Children*, 1976, *9*(5), 15.

Watson, A. The children of Armageddon: Problems of children following divorce. *Syracuse Law Review*, 1969, *21*, 231–239.

Weber, C. U., Foster, P. S., & Weikart, D. P. An economic analysis of the Ypsilanti Perry Preschool Project. *Monographs of the High/Scope Educational Research Foundation* (Series No. 5), 1978.

Weikart, D. Preschool education for disadvantaged children. In J. Travers & R. Light (Eds.), *Learning from experience: Evaluating early childhood demonstration programs*. Washington, D.C.: National Academy Press, 1982.

Weiss, C. H. (Ed.) *Using social science research in public policy making*. Lexington, MA: Lexington Books, 1977.

Weiss, C. H. Improving the linkage between social science research and public policy. In L. E.

Lynn, Jr. (Ed.), *Knowledge and policy: The uncertain connection.* Vol. 5. Study Project on Social Research and Development. Washington, DC: National Academy of Sciences, 1978.

Weiss, C. H., & Bucuvalas, M. J. The challenge of social research to decision making. In C. H. Weiss (Ed.), *Using social research in public policy making.* Lexington, MA: Lexington Books, 1977.

Weisz, J. R. Transcontextual validity in developmental research. *Child Development,* 1978, *49,* 1–12.

Westinghouse Learning Corp. *The impact of Head Start: An evaluation of the effects of Head Start on children's cognitive and affective development.* Executive Summary (EDO 36321). Washington, D.C.: Clearinghouse for Federal Scientific and Technical Information, June 1969.

Westman, J. C. et al. The role of child psychiatry in divorce. *Archives of General Psychiatry,* Nov. 1970, 416–421.

White, S. The national impact study of Head Start. In J. Hellmuth (Ed.), *The disadvantaged child.* Vol. 3. *Compensatory education: A national debate.* New York: Brunner/Mazel, 1970.

White House Conference on Children. *Report to the President.* Washington, DC: U.S. Government Printing Office, 1970.

Winick, M. *Malnutrition and brain development.* New York: Oxford University Press, 1976.

Yankelovich, Skelly, White, Inc. *The General Mills American Family Report 1980–81.* Minneapolis: General Mills, 1981.

Zigler, E. Metatheoretical issues in developmental psychology. In M. Marx (Ed.), *Theories in contemporary psychology.* New York: Macmillan, 1963.

Zigler, E. The environmental mystique: Training the intellect versus development of the child. *Childhood Education,* 1970, *46,* 402–412.

Zigler, E. Project Head Start: Success of failure? *Learning,* 1973, *1,* 43–47.

Zigler, E., Abelson, W. D., & Seitz, V. Motivational factors in the performance of economically disadvantaged children on the Peabody Picture Vocabulary Test. *Child Development,* 1973, *44,* 294–303.

Zigler, E., Abelson, W. D., Trickett, P. E., & Seitz, V. *Is intervention really necessary to raise disadvantaged children's IQ scores?* Unpublished manuscript, Yale University, New Haven, CT 1980.

Zigler, E., & Berman, W. Discerning the future of early childhood intervention. *American Psychologist,* in press.

Zigler, E., & Butterfield, E. C. Motivational aspects of changes in IQ test performance of culturally deprived nursery school children. *Child Development,* 1968, *39,* 1–14.

Zigler, E., & Finn, M. From problem to solution: Changing public policy as it affects children and families. *Young Children,* May, 1981.

Zigler, E., & Finn, M. A vision of childcare in the 1980's. In L. Bond & J. Joffe (Eds.), *Facilitating infant and early childhood development.* Hanover, NH: University Press of New England, 1982.

Zigler, E., & Finn, M. The future policy of prevention in child psychiatry. In S. de Schill (Ed.), *The search for the future: Psychotherapy, psychoanalysis, mental health,* in press.

Zigler, E., & Goodman, J. On day care standards—again! *Networker,* Fall 1980, 2(1), 1.

Zigler, E., & Gordon, E. (Eds.) *Day care: Scientific and social policy issues.* Boston: Auburn House, 1982.

Zigler, E., & Kagan, S. L. The child development associate: A challenge for the 1980's. *Young Children,* July 1981.

Zigler, E., & Seitz, V. Future research on socialization and personality development. In E. Zigler, M. Lamb, & I. Child (Eds.), *Socialization and personality development* (2nd ed.). New York: Oxford University Press, 1982. (a)

Zigler, E., & Seitz, V. Head Start as a national laboratory. *Annals,* AAPSS, 461, May 1982. (b)

Zigler, E., & Trickett, P. E. IQ, social competence, and evaluation of early childhood intervention programs. *American Psychologist,* 1978, *33,* 789–798.

Zigler, E., & Turner, P. Parents and day care workers: A failed partnership? In E. Zigler & E. Gordon (Eds.), *Day care: Scientific and social policy issues*. Boston: Auburn House, 1982.

Zigler, E., & Valentine, J. (Eds.). *Project Head Start: A legacy of the war on poverty*. New York: Free Press, 1979.

12

The Life-Span Perspective in Developmental Psychology

Paul B. Baltes
Max Planck Institute for Human Development and Education

Hayne W. Reese
West Virginia University

INTRODUCTION

We define the goals of developmental psychology as the description, explanation, and modification of intraindividual change in behavior across the life span, as well as the interindividual differences in such change (Baltes, Reese, & Nesselroade, 1977). The basic assumption is that life-long changes in the behavior of individuals are not random and that many of these changes can be understood in terms of principles of development. This definition also emphasizes that the life-span development of different individuals is similar in some respects and different in others. Thus, we need to understand not only how individuals develop alike, but also how differences in life-span development come about, and how and why individuality occurs in development.

What Is the Life-Span Perspective?

This chapter presents a life-span perspective on psychological development. A life-span perspective is one based on the belief that the changes (growth, development, aging) shown by people from the time of their conception, throughout their lives, and until the time of their death are usefully conceptualized as developmental. Life-span developmental psychologists take one or both of the following two approaches to their subject matter: They focus on a category of behavior (e.g., memory, intelligence, or personality) and study it in terms of the life-long processes of constancy and change, or, they work on the holistic delineation of age periods (e.g., infancy, childhood, adolescence, adulthood, or old age), and the interconnections among these periods. These two approaches, particularly when considered together, make life-span developmental psychology an umbrella over the subject of developmental psychology itself.[1]

The history of developmental psychology (Baltes, 1979, 1983; Groffmann, 1970; Reinert, 1979) shows that a life-span conception of human development was already inherent in the first major works on developmental psychology written at the turn of the 18th–19th century (e.g., Carus, 1808; Tetens, 1777). Historical considerations of developmental psychology also reveal marked cultural differences in topical emphasis and approach. For example, in Anglo-American circles a life-span conception of psychological development is a rather recent phenomenon and developmental psychology has been identified primarily with child development. In contrast, German developmental psychology exhibits a long historical tradition of viewing development as a life-long process (e.g., Baltes, 1979; Groffmann, 1970; Lehr, 1980: Reinert, 1979; Thomae, 1959, 1979).

An important point to note is that, on the whole, the life-span perspective in psychology is more theoretical than empirical, although empirical work is increasing. A series of conferences at West Virginia University on conceptual and empirical issues in life-span developmental psychology has continued since 1969 (Baltes & Schaie, 1973; Callahan & McCluskey, 1983; Datan & Ginsberg, 1975; Datan & Reese, 1977; Goulet & Baltes, 1970; McCluskey & Reese, in press; Nesselroade & Reese, 1973; Turner & Reese, 1980); an annual research series, *Life-Span Development and Behavior,* began publication in 1978 (Baltes, 1978; Baltes & Brim, 1979, 1980, 1982, 1983); several research journals (e.g., *Human Development, International Journal of Behavioral Development*) focus explicitly on life-span developmental work. Life-span perspectives are evident in other disciplines concerned with human development as well, such as anthropology (Kertzer & Keith, 1983), biology (Finch & Hayflick, 1977), and sociology (Brim & Wheeler, 1966; Elder, 1975; Featherman, 1983; Kohli, 1978; Riley, Johnson, & Foner, 1972; Rosenmayr, 1978). Within sociology, the field of life-course sociology has gained a status comparable to that held by life-span developmental psychology.

The term "perspective" has been chosen to make clear that life-span developmental psychology is not a single, coherent theory nor a collection of theories. Rather, it is an orientation to the study of psychological development (Baltes, Reese, & Lipsitt, 1980; Labouvie, 1982).

What is meant by the terms perspective or orientation? A perspective is not a precisely defined metatheoretical paradigm (Overton & Reese, 1973; Reese & Overton, 1970). Rather, it is something akin to a set of prototypical beliefs

---

[1]In psychology, "life-span" is the most preferred term to denote the study of life-long development. In sociology and anthropology, the term "life-course" is often used (for a comparable use of that term in psychology, see Bühler, 1933).

(Cantor & Mischel, 1979) about a phenomenon. Prototypical beliefs are initial assumptions, or orientation principles, that are formulated more as guidelines than as firmly held assumptions or empirical generalizations. As such, they are easily modifiable in the face of contradictory research findings. For example, the life-span perspective holds that development continues throughout life, but evidence that the development of a particular characteristic is limited to some particular segment of the life-span would not cause one to abandon the life-span perspective. Rather, one might first search for evidence that this characteristic exhibits changes in other segments of the life-span, or simply modify the belief in life-long development by limiting its supposed generality in the following manner: For most (rather than all) characteristics, development continues throughout life.

Thus, in science, a perspective is an emerging theoretical view or research strategy by which a given phenomenon is defined, studied, and interpreted. How a perspective is translated into a specific theory and its associated method can vary widely. After a given phenomenon is initially delineated, there is a great variation (pluralism) in the way psychologists define, describe, and explain properties of the phenomenon under investigation. The same is true for the ways research and theory in life-span developmental psychology have evolved.

Prototypical Beliefs in Life-Span Psychology

The life-span perspective is an orientation to the study of development, and as such it should include a set of prototypical beliefs about development. Because a certain amount of pluralism exists when a perspective is implemented, one is tempted to argue that the specification of many additional definitional features of the life-span perspective is undesirable. Yet, some recurrent features are found in much of the work on life-span development. These features are seen by many as a pattern of beliefs. In the long run, therefore, it may be possible to speak of something like a "family" of life-span developmental models and theories (Reese & Overton, 1970).

In our view, a working definition of the life-span perspective contains the following set of prototypical beliefs (Baltes, Reese, & Lipsitt, 1980; Featherman, 1983; Lerner & Busch-Rossnagel, 1981; Riley, 1983):

1. Ontogenetic development is a *life-long process*. No age period holds primacy in regulating the nature of development. Moreover, during development and at all stages of the life span, both continuous (cumulative) and discontinuous (innovative) processes are at work.

2. Considerable *plurality* is found in the patterns of change that constitute development, as evinced, for example, in interbehavior variability. The course of development varies markedly for different classes or domains of behavior.

3. Also, a lot of *intraindividual plasticity* (modifiability within the individual) is found in psychological development. Depending on the life conditions experienced by an individual, his or her developmental course may take many forms.

4. Ontogenetic development can also vary substantially by *historical-cultural conditions*. How ontogenetic (age-related) development proceeds is markedly influenced by the kind of sociocultural conditions existing in a given historical period and the way these evolve over time.

5. Any particular ontogeny (individual development) can be understood as the outcome of the interactions (dialectics) among three systems of developmental influences: *age-graded, history-graded,* and *nonnormative*. The developing person reacts to and acts within this set of systems.

6. Psychological development needs to be viewed within the *interdisciplinary context* provided by other disciplines (e.g., anthropology, biology, sociology) that are concerned with human development. The life-span perspective's openness to interdisciplinary connections goes beyond mere acknowledgment. Its interdisciplinary posture implies that a "purist" psychological view offers but a partial representation of behavioral development from conception to death in a changing society.

None of the six principles delineating the life-span perspective is in itself novel. In fact, many developmental psychologists argue that these principles express the focus of any developmental approach. This argument has some merit. If the life-span perspective is unique in any way, it is in its substantive focus on life-long development and the extent to which these six principles are seen in coordination, thereby representing an integrative pattern of prototypical beliefs.

One of the major goals of this chapter is to illustrate the coordinated features defining the life-span perspective with concrete examples to convey the uniqueness of a life-span perspective in the study of psychological development. At the same time, we need to be careful not to convey the notion that the life-span perspective demands this particular set of beliefs (and no other) about human development. However, whether one associates this or some other set of beliefs with the life-span perspective, the set will include the basic assumption of life-span development: Development is a life-long process. This assumption needs to be considered as such, irrespective of one's conceptual framework in the sense of a coordinated perspective. Indeed, much important work on life-span development (e.g., Horn's [1970, 1982] model of the development of fluid/crystallized intelligence, or Labouvie-Vief's [1980, 1982] reformulation of Piaget's theory of cognitive development to encompass aspects of adult development) is guided less by the kind of life-span perspective presented above than by a domain-specific focus and analysis in the face of the life-span developmental processes of constancy and change.

3. An Overview of the Chapter

In the following sections, the particular set of beliefs representing the life-span perspective is described in more detail. This description is also used as a framework for a selective review of research and theory in life-span developmental psychology. We emphasize issues pertaining to developmental method and theory as well.

Why should a chapter on the life-span perspective in developmental psychology include an additional focus on developmental method and theory? On the one hand, this approach reflects the tradition leading to life-span developmental psychology in the United States. Much work in the field was spurred by methodological advances, for example, dealing with longitudinal design and the need to separate components of historical change from those of ontogenetic change when examining psychological development (see Baltes, 1968; Nesselroade & Baltes, 1979; Nesselroade & von Eye, 1984; Neugarten & Datan, 1973; Riegel, 1976; Schaie, 1965).

On the other hand, the additional focus on method and theory also reflects an issue more fundamental than the mere acknowledgment of a particular historical origin. Since the inception of the life-span view, beginning with its origins in the 18th and 19th centuries, life-span scholars (e.g., Tetens, Quetelet) have consistently emphasized the need to articulate the methodological and theoretical underpinnings of developmental psychology (Baltes, 1983). In our view, this perhaps self-conscious concern with method and theory has arisen because life-span research represents an "extreme," amplified case of developmental scholarship. It deals, for example, with long-term change and extended causal and temporal linkages. Consequently, life-span researchers are forced to make the methodological and theoretical characteristics and imperatives—and limitations—of a developmental approach as explicit as possible. Similar efforts also exist, of course, in other areas of developmental scholarship (e.g., McCall, 1977; Montada, 1979; Wohlwill, 1973).

MAJOR PERSPECTIVES OF LIFE-SPAN DEVELOPMENTAL PSYCHOLOGY

We now describe the meaning of each of the prototypical beliefs chosen to delineate the life-span perspective. In doing so, we also point out that the course of development depends largely on what happens *throughout* the life of the organism, not only on what happens in early life (see Brim & Kagan, 1980, for a comprehensive treatment of this topic). Moreover, we show that the nature of ontogenetic development not only has significance for individuals themselves, it is also important for their social environment and for the future of society.

Development as a Life-Long Process

Examples. If humans were born as "mature" adults in terms of perception, cognition, personality, and so on, and if they remained that way for their entire lives, then developmental psychology would not be necessary. A general psychology describing a set of invariant laws and principles governing behavior and interindividual differences would do just as well. Our intuitive knowledge about apparent age changes—in physique and language behavior, for example—tells us that a general assumption of ontogenetic fixity is not true. But, although organisms do show ontogenetic changes, are these changes restricted to any one period of the life-span?

The first principle of life-span developmental psychology is that those behavior-change processes that fall under the general rubric of development can occur at any point in the life span, from conception to death. Figures 12.1A and 12.1B illustrate the principle of life-long development with two examples. At this point, it is less important to discuss the validity of the models presented than to understand the principle underlying them.

Figure 12.1A summarizes life-span findings in the area of psychometric intelligence as proposed by Horn (1970, 1978, 1982) on the basis of his and Cattell's (1971) theory of fluid and crystallized intelligence. Cattell and Horn have identified two major types of intellectual performances in intelligence tests: fluid intelligence and crystallized intelligence. This theory is derived in part from a factor analytic study of intercorrelations among primary mental abilities. Fluid intelligence refers to basic processes of information processing and problem solving, such as perceiving relationships, educing correlates, maintaining awareness in reasoning, and forming abstract concepts. Crystallized intelligence involves similar cognitive activities as they are applied to content domains (language, knowledge) that are typical of a given culture. In a sense, crystallized intelligence is the outcome of long-term learning processes (cultural experience, education, professional specialization, etc.).

One important feature of the fluid/crystallized theory of intelligence is that it reflects a life-span perspective. Fluid and crystallized intelligence emerge with development; when measured quantitatively, both types of intelligence exhibit life-long, yet distinct features of change. For example, the course of life-span change in these two categories of intelligence differs in its trajectory. The initial part of the trajectory is similar: Both fluid and crystallized intelligence increase with chronological age into adulthood. This picture is similar to the incremental curve familiar from most work in child development. Subsequently, however, the average trends differ. Crystallized intelligence continues to increase through most of adulthood and old age, although more slowly than in childhood and perhaps reaching a plateau. Fluid intelligence, on the contrary, shows signs of a decline beginning in middle adulthood. (The onset of this decline, however, varies markedly among individuals: see Baltes, Dittmann-Kohli, & Dixon, 1984; Schaie, 1979; Willis & Baltes, 1980.)

A. Different Forms of Intelligence

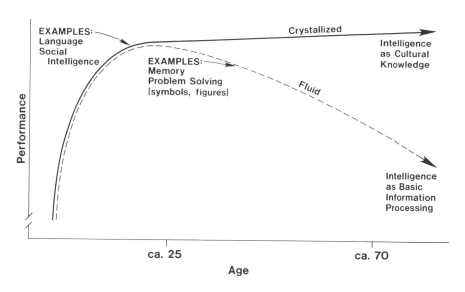

B. Personality

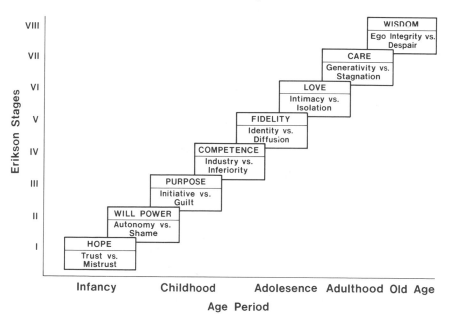

FIGS. 12.1A and 12.1B. Two examples of life-long development: Cattell and Horn's (Cattell, 1971; Horn, 1970, 1978) model of psychometric intelligence and Erikson's (1959, 1968) model of personality development.

Figure 12.1B gives another illustration of life-long developmental change, this time in personality. The model depicted was developed by Erikson (1959, 1968). His model of personality development posits eight interconnected stages and associated sets of psychosocial crises that are assumed to dominate the development of the individual at different stages of life, for example trust vs. mistrust in infancy, and ego integrity vs. despair in old age. Each stage and its associated psychosocial crisis define a central disposition or theme of personality such as ''hope'' for the first stage, and ''wisdom'' for the last stage. These stage-specific dispositions are shown in the top part of each box in Figure 12.1B.

These two models illustrate the notion of life-long development. They show that developmental change can occur at any point in the life course. In general, life-span developmentalists believe that no developmental stage, age, period, or state is by itself more interesting than any other. The major restriction to this posture may be that because causation is temporally ordered, only earlier events can influence later ones. Because of their temporal location in the life span, then, conditions happening earlier in life may have broader subsequent influence than events that occur at a later time, for example, shortly before death.

Distal vs. Proximal Models of Developmental Connectedness.   So far, we have said little about the type of connectedness that is implied between points in the life span. The notion of life-long development permits several conceptions of the ways later behavioral changes relate to earlier behavioral changes. There is little agreement among life-span researchers as to which conception is the most apt, perhaps because so many different conceptions are possible. (For lengthier presentations on the topic of models of change, see Meacham, 1980; Riegel, 1972; Singer & Spilerman, 1979; van den Daele, 1974.)

The possible conceptions of developmental connectedness differ on at least four dimensions:

1. Development may be *continuous* or *discontinuous*. Continuous means that the nature of a behavior after change can be predicted from the nature of the behavior before change. Discontinuous means that this kind of prediction is impossible. For example, in Piaget's theory the ''concrete operational'' mode of thinking cannot be predicted from the prior, ''preoperational'' mode of thinking. This development is therefore discontinuous.

2. Development may also be *continuous* or *discontinuous* in the sense that the same causal processes operate or do not operate throughout development. For example, Piaget's theory is continuous in this sense because the processes of assimilation, accommodation, and equilibration are assumed to operate throughout development.

3. Development may be *cumulative* or *innovative*. Cumulative means that prior behaviors are incorporated in later ones; innovative means that novel behaviors emerge. For example, Piaget's theory is cumulative with respect to

specific mental operations that are carried over from one stage to the next, but it is innovative in the way these operations are organized as a structured whole.

4. Development is *proximal* if it can be explained without referring to the individual's earlier history, that is, if all the causes referred to in the explanation occur concurrently with the behavioral change. Development is *distal* if events that occurred earlier in the individual's lifetime must also be included in the explanation. For example, Piaget's theory involves distal explanation in that performance on a formal operations task requires knowing the present (concurrent) cognitive stage of the individual as well as his or her educational and/or occupational background (see Piaget, 1972).

Life-span researchers believe that considering facets of each of the dimensions mentioned is useful in arriving at a comprehensive model of developmental connectedness, although they disagree on their specific importance—with one exception. They agree that both proximal and distal causes are important for many developmental changes. Later development is not always a continuation of earlier processes; therefore, the explanation of later development is in many cases more proximal than distal. Thus, later development can be seen as involving innovative (novel) features that have little direct connection to earlier processes. These innovative–discontinuous developments can occur because new conditions arise during ontogenesis. The sources of these new conditions are: (1) the processes of historical change, (2) idiosyncratic life events (Baltes, Reese, & Lipsitt, 1980), and also (3), with growing resources, individuals coming to function as "producers of their own development" (Lerner & Busch-Rossnagel, 1981).

Development as a Pluralistic (Multifaceted) System of Change Patterns

The preceding observations on distinct forms of life-long development and models of developmental connectedness foreshadow a certain plurality or multiplicity in defining the nature of development. How can one represent this plurality, graphically and conceptually?

Examples. Figure 12.2 is a symbolic illustration of the fact that life-span development can take many forms. As a whole, life-long development is a system of diverse change patterns. These change patterns differ, for example, in terms of time extension (onset, duration, termination), direction, and order. The figure shows that developmental functions have different times of onset across the life span, differing in their temporal location, and that some developmental functions are irreversible, while others reverse or decline after varying intervals of time.

As early as 1927, Hollingworth made this basic point in the following manner:

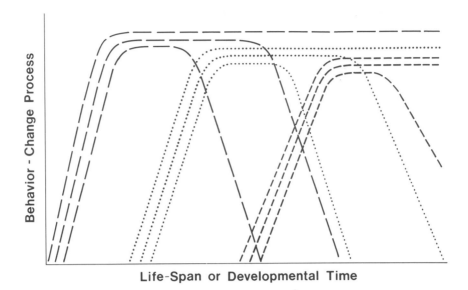

Life-Span or Developmental Time

FIG. 12.2.   Hypothetical examples of life-span developmental processes: Developmental processes differ in onset, duration, termination, and direction when charted in the framework of the life span. However, developmental change is both quantitative and qualitative, not all developmental change is related to chronological age, and the initial direction is not always incremental (after Baltes, Reese, & Lipsitt, 1980, Figure 1, p. 73).

If we try to represent the course of human life by a curve of growth or a curve of development, we find at once that no single curve is adequate to portray the actual complexity of the individual's history. Different features begin to appear at different times; mature at different rates; begin to decline, if decline they do, at different times, and proceed here also at different rates . . . a very complex set of curves would result if we had actual measurements of the way in which each feature develops (p. 324).

One way to give substance to the life-span trajectories presented in Figure 12.2 is to think of the kinds of demands and opportunities that individuals face as they move through life. Havighurst (1948/1972, 1973), for example, has formulated the concept of *developmental tasks*. Developmental tasks involve a series of problems, challenges, or life adjustment situations that come from biological development, social expectations, and personal action. These problems "change through life and give direction, force, and substance to . . . development . . ." (Havighurst, 1973, p. 11). Thus, in Figure 12.2 the different life-span curves can be interpreted to reflect different developmental tasks.

Developmental tasks are associated with: (1) age periods such as infancy, childhood, adolescence, adulthood, and old age; (2) settings such as the family, school, and the job world; (3) personal decisions about education, career, marriage, and retirement; and (4) adjustment tasks related to the occurrence of historical or nonnormative life events (see Section B.5.). However, developmental tasks differ in their degree of developmental connectedness. Some imply the continuation of past processes; others have a strong focus on innovative features of the age period involved with its unique "pushes and pulls."

The terms *multidimensionality* and *multidirectionality* are among the key concepts used by life-span scholars to describe facets of plurality in the course of development, and to promote a concept of development that is not bound by a single criterion of growth in terms of a general increase in size or functional efficacy. Interbehavior variability is one example of plurality in development. Interbehavior variability means that different classes or domains of behavior (e.g., components of memory or dimensions of intelligence) reveal distinct courses of ontogenetic change.

One may wonder why interbehavior variability in development is important, when different domains of behavior obviously do not develop equally. The primary reason is that up to early adulthood the dominant pattern of behavioral change is one of general growth; that is, an increase in whatever indices one uses to measure structure and function. This view of development as a collection of incremental functions (growth) is the central posture of child developmental theory and research. Once one moves beyond early adulthood, however, the picture is much more complex. Moreover, once one considers the aspects of decline as salient features of change (as is suggested by research on aging), one begins to realize that both growth and decline may be characteristic of all developmental processes, including those that take place in childhood (Labouvie-Vief, 1982; Ross, 1981). Examples of behavioral growth and decline in childhood include, on the one hand, cooperativeness and various aspects of language comprehension and production (growth), and, on the other, incontinence, thumb sucking, and the relative loss of certain cognitive heuristics such as maximization strategies (decline).

One concrete example that further illustrates the concepts of multidimensionality and multidirectionality in development, is intelligence. Intelligence is a multidimensional construct. It consists of several subcomponents, for example, fluid vs. crystallized intelligence. Furthermore, these components differ in the direction of their development. This is an example of the multidirectionality of development. Consider again the distinct trajectories in Figure 12.1A for fluid vs. crystallized intelligence. Fluid intelligence shows a turning point in adulthood (toward decline); crystallized intelligence exhibits the continuation of an incremental function.

Fluid and crystallized intelligence, then, exhibit both multidimensionality and multidirectionality, and provide a good example of a pluralistic conception of development. Memory is another good example. Memory can be represented as a multidimensional process involving several components (e.g., "primary" vs.

"secondary" memory). Memory also exhibits multidirectionality, as sensory and primary memory exhibit little, if any, age-related decline, while the organizational and retrieval components of memory exhibit much age-related decline. Thus, the organizational and retrieval components of memory exhibit a life-span function that is somewhat similar to that of fluid intelligence (Craik, 1977; Hultsch & Dixon, 1984; Reese, 1976a).

Other illustrations of multidimensionality and multidirectionality in developmental change come from the study of achievement motivation and attachment behavior. In achievement motivation, for example, the first part of life is generally a time of acquisition of standards and motives for accomplishment in a variety of domains, including academic success in education and success in occupational life. Multidimensionality in this instance refers to the possibility of domain-specific classes of achievement behavior. What about multidirectionality? Although we do not yet know for sure, for many individuals the last third of life appears to require a reorientation of achievement motivation (Brim, 1974; Heckhausen, in press). In old age, a generalized and fairly large amount of extinction or transformation of achievement motivation may take place for many individuals.

A similar view can be taken of attachment behavior and other aspects of interpersonal systems. Here, life-long changes consist not only of aspects of acquisition but of subsequent transformations in and losses of interpersonal relationships as well (Antonucci, 1976; Hagestad, 1982; Kahn & Antonucci, 1980; Lerner & Ryff, 1978). The formation of interpersonal relationships is a central theme of early life in areas such as parent–infant bonding. The rest of the life span includes further modification of this one type of strong and salient interpersonal attachment. In addition, new interpersonal relationships are acquired, maintained, transformed, and extinguished. These additional relationships and losses involve the domains of marriage, family formation, kinship networks, and a variety of friendship systems in rather distinct life settings (school, work, senior citizen homes, etc.). The development of attachment behavior, like achievement motivation and intelligence, may therefore include not only changes in one homogeneous class of behavior and in one direction, but multidimensional and multidirectional changes as well.

Actually, the pattern is even more complex than Figure 12.2 has shown. First, not all developmental change is of the simple, quantitative kind. Therefore, we need to consider qualitative changes in development, which require the charting of different *classes* of behavior rather than simple, quantitative functions. A good illustration of qualitative change during ontogeny comes from biology. In biology, the term metamorphosis is used to denote the dramatic change in form seen, for example, in insects as they evolve from egg to larva to pupa, and finally to the adult form of the insect. In developmental psychology, concerns about stages of cognitive development (Piaget) or about age-linked transformations in the system of intellectual abilities (Reinert, 1970) exemplify a similar view.

Second, a system with fixed multidimensionality may change in its level or rate of functioning, as it develops, but the dimensionality of a system may undergo change as well.

Intraindividual Plasticity (Modifiability)

A third principle in the life-span perspective refers to the degree to which the same individuals might develop differently if conditions were different. This issue and its associated knowledge base fall under the heading of intraindividual plasticity or modifiability (Baltes & Baltes, 1980; Baltes & Schaie, 1976; Gollin, 1981; Lerner, 1984).

The usual way to introduce the question of variability in development is to focus on interindividual (between-person) differences in development and to show how different life conditions (genetic differences, social class factors, historical changes, dimensions of childrearing, etc.) regulate the rate and level of psychological ontogeny. This general interindividual differences approach is shared by life-span researchers. In fact, they often argue that interindividual variability is a hallmark of life-span changes, especially in adulthood and old age. Such a view is occasionally counterposed to some models of child development (such as Piaget's cognitive structuralism), in which homogeneity and universality of change are the cornerstones of the developmental edifice (Thomae, 1979).

The life-span perspective has taken the issue of variability beyond interindividual differences to the level of intraindividual analysis. This posture is similar to that taken in some other areas of developmental scholarship, for instance, in single-subject research and in learning research—especially of the social learning and operant type (Baer, 1973; M. Baltes & Lerner, 1980; Bandura, 1977). The search is for the range of plasticity on the individual level, for knowledge about the degree to which individuals could develop differently if the conditions of their lives were different.

Note that the issue is not whether fairly fixed interindividual differences exist (for instance, those associated with genetic and social-class factors); they do. Whether the question of intraindividual plasticity has been ignored in other developmental specialities is also not at issue here. In fact, as is illustrated by such longstanding research areas as the role of sensory deprivation in the development of perception (Hebb) or the effects of compensatory education on cognitive development, it has not. What is different in life-span research is a much greater emphasis on intraindividual plasticity (Lerner, 1984).

Research on intellectual and cognitive development during adulthood and old age can be used to illustrate the salience of intraindividual plasticity in life-span research (Baltes & Schaie, 1976; Baltes & Willis, 1982; Denney, 1982; Featherman, 1983; Horn, 1982; Labouvie-Vief, 1977, 1984; Schaie, 1979; Willis & Baltes, 1980). An extensive body of data showing substantial interindividual differences in development (e.g., by social class, education, level of IQ, cohort membership), and a substantial amount of interability variation (e.g., fluid vs. crystallized intelligence) set the scene. The ensuing picture was one of a complex system of abilities evincing differential life-span trajectories, especially for adulthood and old age. Furthermore, the obtained variability suggested interpretations that included the operation of performance factors (practice, motivation) as a major source of the change and variability observed.

One of the subsequent recent research efforts focused on the extent to which the observed interindividual variability in level of intellectual performance during adulthood could be accounted for by performance variation (plasticity) *within* individuals. For example, elderly people were given practice in solving the type of intelligence problems used to measure fluid intelligence (Baltes & Willis, 1982). The key research hypothesis was that older persons, on the average, have relatively little test experience and everyday practice in fluid intelligence but that they possess the reserve—the "latent" competence—to raise their level of performance on fluid intelligence tasks to that of younger adults. The research outcome—illustrated in Figure 12.3—supported this view. After a fairly brief program of cognitive practice, many older adults (age range 60–80) exhibited levels of performance comparable to those observed in many younger adults.

The point here is not to discuss the significance of the findings of Baltes and Willis (1982) and others on plasticity, or inferences about aging decline in fluid

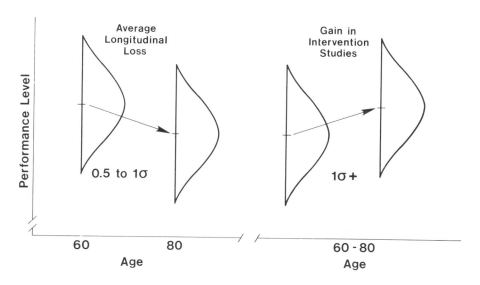

FIG. 12.3. Amount of age decline in fluid intelligence (average longitudinal loss) and its modifiability due to practice and training (after Baltes, Dittmann-Kohli, & Dixon, 1984).

intelligence (see Baltes & Schaie, 1976; Donaldson, 1981; Horn & Donaldson, 1976, 1977; Schaie & Baltes, 1977; Willis & Baltes, 1981). Rather, the point is to show that knowledge about *intra*individual plasticity is as important as knowledge about *inter*individual variability.

In order to achieve a comprehensive understanding of a given developmental process such as intellectual development, one must attend equally to notions of interindividual variability and intraindividual plasticity. This joint concern for variability and plasticity has come to the forefront in life-span research because the available evidence suggests that the life-span course of development is more malleable than has been assumed (Brim & Kagan, 1980). Regarding intelligence during adulthood and old age (up to age 70), for instance, any change could be modified fairly easily within the range usually observed for the existing population of adults. As a consequence, the interpretation advanced is that whatever one observes in aging is but one of many possible outcomes. Knowing the range and limits of intraindividual functioning, therefore, is a cornerstone of life-span theory (Baltes, Dittmann-Kohli, & Dixon, 1984).

Life-Span Development: Ontogenesis and Evolution (Biocultural Change)

The fourth and fifth principles of the life-span perspective deal with the relationship between individual development (ontogenesis) and evolutionary development (Baltes, 1983; Brent, 1978; Lerner, 1984; Lerner & Busch-Rossnagel, 1981; Skinner, 1966). Evolutionary development, or phylogenesis, refers to the long-term processes associated with the formation and growth (and extinction) of species, including the origins of humankind. Together, ontogenesis and phylogenesis constitute the two major systems of change.

Evolution and cultural change are relevant to individual life-span development in three ways. First, both are involved in the ongoing processes of individual development. The processes of individual development are governed on the one hand by principles of ontogenesis, but also by factors associated with the concurrent process of biocultural change on the other. Second, evolution is one of the major antecedents of ontogenesis: Evolution has resulted in and is associated with a program of genetics (heredity) and cultural transmission (socialization). Note that evolution is not only a matter of genetics, but also of sociocultural transmission, which is the reason why we often choose the term *"biocultural."* The third reason is the reverse relationship between evolution and ontogenesis: This is the role played by life-span development in the maintenance and continual evolution of the human species and society. In this respect, what individuals do and how they change throughout their lifetime function as the major antecedents of future human evolution. Sexual coupling, procreative behavior, and parenting, for example, are obviously important in determining not only the gene pool of the future, but also the kind of sociocultural transmissions operating during future socialization endeavors.

Let us illustrate further the reasons for considering the interplay between ontogenetic and evolutionary processes in life-span developmental psychology.

Individual Development in a Changing Society.   The first link between ontogenetic and evolutionary processes concerns the ongoing process of biocultural change and its relationship to individual ontogeny. This link has attracted much attention in life-span research, initially because of methodological concerns (Baltes, 1968; Schaie, 1965); later, because of theoretical issues such as dialectics (Riegel, 1976).

The life-span development of individuals covers a substantial period of time, say from 1900 until 1980 for people who were born in 1900 and who reached 80 years of age. During such a long period of time many changes occur, not only in the ontogenetic status of individuals, but also in the biocultural ecology in which they develop. Thus, two systems are developing: individuals and societies. Individuals develop in a changing world (Riegel, 1976). From this perspective it follows that the "causes" or determinants of individual development are not located only in the individual or a stable, historically invariant process of socialization. Determining factors are also associated with the nature of the constancy and change of the bioculture that surrounds the individual as a macro-ecological environment (Bronfenbrenner, 1979).

The role of a changing society came to the forefront in life-span research on cohort differences (Baltes, Cornelius, & Nesselroade, 1979; Riley et al., 1972; Schaie, 1965). In this kind of research, the age-development of several birth cohorts is studied in a comparative manner. Figure 12.4 illustrates the basic designs known as cross-sectional and longitudinal sequences.

What are some of the outcomes obtained by the application of sequential methodology? Figure 12.5 shows the outcome of one study in which sequential methodology has been applied to study personality development in adolescence (Nesselroade & Baltes, 1974). The result is shown for two traits of personality: achievement motivation and independence. The primary finding is that the age-development of these traits is not the same for adolescents in different cohorts (i.e., born at different points in time). For example, in 1970 14-year-olds were fairly high in achievement motivation; but two years later, in 1972, 14-year-olds were the lowest of all groups on this variable. Another way of looking at the data is to note that the two younger cohorts (those born in 1957 and 1958) exhibited large declines in achievement motivation as they grew older, and the two older cohorts remained fairly constant in this trait. Thus, the study reveals differences between birth cohorts born as little as one year apart. The outcome on independence does not show such dramatic cohort differences. The cohorts differ in the

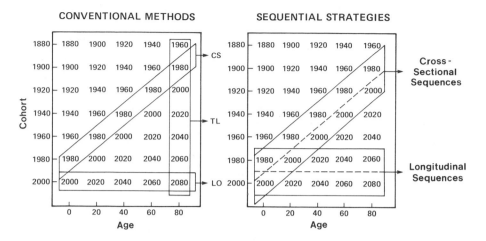

FIG. 12.4. Conventional (CS: cross-sectional, TL: time-lag, LO: longitudinal) and sequential strategies in developmental psychology (after Baltes, 1968; Schaie, 1965).

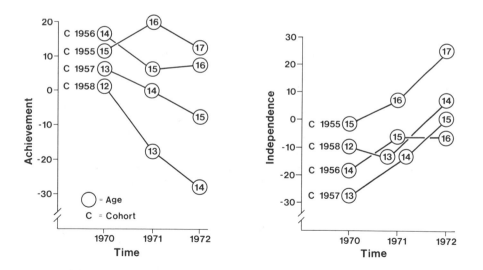

FIG. 12.5. Longitudinal development of adolescents from several birth cohorts (1955, 1956, 1957, 1958) over a two-year period (1970 to 1972). Data from Nesselroade and Baltes (1974).

rate of change and in the levels of independence attained, but all exhibit increases in independence with increasing age.

The marked differences in the achievement motivation of adjacent birth cohorts indicate that personality development during adolescence does not always follow a fixed course, such as a linear increase with age toward greater achievement motivation. On the contrary, the way adolescents develop is determined in part by the nature of the cultural context—the historical moment—during which the adolescent personality develops. In the Nesselroade and Baltes (1974) study, the cultural context was such that, especially with the younger adolescents, a trend toward less achievement motivation emerged. Two developing systems (individual, society) need to be considered together in order to understand the nature of human development.

Life-span research with sequential methods exists with other age groups, cohorts, and measurement systems (see Baltes, Cornelius, & Nesselroade, 1978, for review). Schaie's (1979, 1983; Schaie & Hertzog, 1983) 21-year cohort-sequential study on adult intelligence is particularly relevant. It shows much cohort variation in adult intellectual development. In fact, up to the ages of 60–70, cohort variation in intellectual abilities is as large as the age variation. Only after age 70 does there appear to be an increasingly consistent pattern of age decline, especially in fluid intelligence.

Here, however, the central purpose is not to summarize extant cohort-sequential research. Rather, the focus is on the role of biocultural change in the study of behavioral development. Note also that cohort effects are not fixed. Because of their association with historical change, cohort effects can vary markedly, for example, by historical epoch and behavior domain. This age by cohort interaction is the basis for psychologists' interest in articulating new paradigms such as dialectics (Reese, 1977a; Riegel, 1976) and contextualism (Lerner, 1984; Reese, 1976b, 1977b), and searching for interdisciplinary dialogue, especially with sociologists and social historians (Elder, 1981; Featherman, 1983; McCluskey & Reese, in press).

Are cohort differences and biocultural change always relevant for the study of psychological development? Most likely they are not. Cohort differences are more likely to be a concern for those aspects of development that are not stabilized in the process of genetic and cultural evolution. Thus, cohort variation in cognitive development during childhood is relatively small and primarily involves issues of rate (Kendler, 1979; Reese, 1974). For the cognitive domain and that period of the life span, evolutionary and societal conditions provide a fairly stable system of influences.

In adulthood and old age, however, the biological and social systems are much more likely to undergo changes, as these periods of the life span are not (yet) part of a stabilized system of genetic and societal controls. Because cohort differences can have rather different empirical and theoretical significance, Baltes, Cornelius, and Nesselroade (1979) have distinguished among several ways which cohort variation can be treated in developmental psychology (e.g., as error, historical disturbance, quantitative variation in frequency and rate, or as a theoretical/dialectical process).

Individual Development as Antecedent to Evolution. The third manner in which individual development and evolution relate to each other is especially explicit when a life-span approach to development is taken. It involves the connection between individual development and the future of the human species and society.

Why does a life-span view make the importance of individual development for the future of the species and society so apparent? As we move beyond childhood, it becomes increasingly evident that significant components of behavior are directly related to the maintenance and further evolution of the human species. They include marriage, reproduction (fertility), parenting, grandparenting, and perhaps even death. These events and behaviors are surely important for the life of a single individual. However, they are also part of evolutionary and biocultural transmission. Note that without certain ontogenetic behaviors, such as reproduction and parenting, biocultural continuity would cease. The nature of individuals' life-span development has direct consequences for subsequent generations.

Among developmental psychologists, Erikson has perhaps been the most explicit spokesman regarding the role of life-span development for the future of the human species and society. Figure 12.1 includes his eight-stage model of the life-span development of personality. The last two stages (generativity: care; ego integrity: wisdom) of Erikson's model are very much concerned with generational transmissions and the role a given "aging" individual has played and is playing in this process.

Similar perspectives are reflected, for example, in research on the parent–child relationship in infancy and childhood. Life-span views of human development amplify this position, however. We study ontogenetic development not only for its meaning in the individual's life span, but also for its ramifications for societal functioning and species survival. This explicit concern for the role of human development in the shaping of the future of mankind assigns new significance to extant research areas. Research topics such as the study of intergenerational relations (Bengtson & Black, 1973; Hagestad, 1982), generational transmission of personality (Featherman, 1980; Scarr & Weinberg, 1978), and the perceived meaning of life (Butler, 1963) are examples of a central concern for understanding the relationship between ontogenesis and evolution. Imagine for a moment what would happen if: (1) adults became reluctant to conceive and rear children; or, (2) the living conditions of children became so deficient that their development into effective adults was seriously threatened. Such a situation would endanger the generational flow. Ontogeny and evolution are indeed intrinsically related and codetermined. A focus on the important role of behavior in evolution is easily overlooked if a narrow age-limited approach to developmental psychology is taken.

Diverse and Multiple Influences on Development

The preceding discussions imply that development through the life span is co-determined by a large number of factors and that development is based on a complex system of antecedents and processes. Some of these factors are common to most people. Other determinants of development are less common, less a part of "universal" biosocial and environmental ontogenesis, and show much variation. Apparently, then, pluralism in the form of development is paralleled by a certain pluralism in the causal–analytic explanation of life-span change (Baltes, 1983). How should one conceptualize such explanatory pluralism? The following life history of a fictitious person illustrates this point before we proceed to a more formal discussion.

A Life History.   Alice is conceived and born with a set of biological properties (genes) that carry with them a program (life plan) for biological growth. She enters a world consisting, for her, primarily of family and home environment. That world also contains something akin to a "life plan" for Alice—a series of environmental controls, opportunities, and supports (nutrition, parenting, etc.) that are "delivered" to our developing Alice in a certain sequence. The series reflects Alice's behavioral and biological characteristics, but also society's (and her parents') understanding of what children need and in which direction they should change. The life plan of these biological and environmental factors involves a fairly general sequence of organism–environment interchanges and events dealing with physical growth and the promotion of intellectual and social behavior in a variety of settings: at home, in school, at work, during leisure, and in other settings as Alice reaches adulthood and old age. Because of genetic similarity among all members of the human species and the existence of a set of age-related expectations and controls, Alice's life development has much in common with that of other individuals.

In addition, Alice is exposed to (seeks out, or interacts with) other determinants that are less a part of an "average" ontogenetic life plan. She experiences physical and cultural events that are not as common for most people. For example, Alice's life develops in particular settings related to social class, ethnicity, and regionality. These settings require adaptive behavior in their own right; therefore, the behavior of our sample individual, Alice, will undergo certain changes. The course of Alice's life-span development is codefined by a fairly general ontogenetic (biological and environmental) plan of influences and by "interindividual differences" factors. These interindividual differences factors reflect both genetic and environmental conditions.

Our developing Alice also faces demands and situations that are unique to her (Bandura, 1982). For example, Alice's hair color (e.g., red) may elicit particular behaviors from her peers, or she may be susceptible to allergies. She may also participate in the geographical and cultural relocation of her family, perhaps by moving from a rural to a city environment, or from the United States to France. Alice may also have the exciting opportunity to participate in a special program for the gifted or, by happenstance, meet a teacher who encourages her interests in drama and acting. Other equally unique (idiosyncratic) but less enticing life events may also occur. Alice may have to live without her father because of divorce, his military service, or his death. Thus, she may become part of a somewhat less common family constellation; as a young adult, she may have trouble finding employment and the satisfaction of her desires for a successful occupational career. Later in life, Alice may undergo the stress of having an accident, or cancer, or losing her spouse or a significant friend because of premature death.

These and other personal life events shape the course of Alice's development. They do not do so independently, but are part of a complex set of interacting, codetermining factors. Clearly, Alice's life history is complex. In order to emphasize Alice's active role, one should also mention the individual's own contribution to the course of his or her development (Lerner & Busch-Rossnagel, 1981; Neugarten, 1969). Although Alice's life-span development is not like the trajectory of a cannon ball, largely regulated by the thrust and direction of its take off, we nevertheless assume that it has regularities and can be described and explained.

A Taxonomy of Influences.   The system of factors that regulate life-long development can be organized in many ways. Figure 12.6 summarizes one formal approach to putting some order into Alice's life history and, more generally, into the complexity of development across the life span. The intent of this display, then, goes beyond organizing Alice's individual development. Rather, it organizes the types of influences or causes—similarities as well as differences—that regulate the nature of life-span development for many individuals. The model presented in Figure 12.6 is not a theory of life-span development. It is only a heuristic device, akin to a model, that we hope is helpful in the search for a preliminary understanding of behavioral development, both regarding its order and regarding its many variations (Baltes, Reese, & Lipsitt, 1980).

The figure identifies three categories of influences that developing individuals such as Alice need to deal with (process, react to, act on) as their lives progress: *age-graded* influences, *history-graded* influences, and *nonnormative* influences. These three influences operate, their effects accumulate with time, and, as a package, they are responsible for how lives develop.

Before we define the three categories of influences further, consider Table

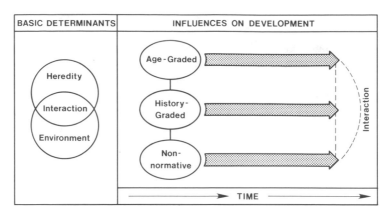

FIG. 12.6   Representation of three major influence systems in life-span development: age-graded, history-graded, and nonnormative life events. The developing individual reacts to and acts within these influence systems. (After Baltes, Cornelius, & Nesselroade, 1979.)

12.1. This table presents some concrete examples and shows that the three categories can be characterized by other properties, such as prevalence of occurrence and temporal predictability (Brim & Ryff, 1980; Reese & McCluskey, in press; Reese & Smyer, 1983). Prevalence of occurrence refers to the generality of the influence, that is, the proportion of individuals affected by a specific influence in a given population. Temporal predictability is the age relatedness of the influence. The table shows the average prevalence of occurrence and temporal predictability for the three categories of influences. For specific influences in all three categories, prevalence of occurrence ranges from low to high. For example, people with Huntington's chorea begin to exhibit the symptoms in middle age, therefore the influence of the symptoms is age-graded. However, the prevalence of this disorder in the population is low. Nevertheless, most age-graded influences seem to be high in prevalence, leading to the characterization of prevalence as high, on the average, for this category of influences. Temporal predictability (age-relatedness) is by definition high for age-graded influences and low for nonnormative influences; but it ranges from low to high for history-graded influences. For example, the bombings of Berlin and of London in World War II probably affected all age groups (low temporal predictability of the influence), but social change toward modernity may affect the young more than the old (high temporal predictability of the influence).

Age-graded influences are identical to what most child psychologists and gerontologists have considered the major source of influence on development (see Datan & Ginsberg, 1975). They are defined as those biological and environmental determinants that: (1) have a fairly strong relationship with chronological age and are therefore fairly predictable in their temporal sequence (onset, duration); and (2) are, for the most part, similar among individuals. Biological

514

TABLE 12.1
Categories of Influence on Development: Examples and Characteristics[a]

Category of Influence	Example	Other Characteristics[a]	
		Prevalence of Occurrence	Temporal Predictability
Age-graded	Biological variables (e.g., length of gestation, time of pubescence) Socialization goals and developmental tasks Family life cycle Educational and occupational life	High	High
History-graded	Social change toward modernity Economic changes and events (e.g., Great Depression) War, epidemic, famine Changes in the labor market Changes in family composition	Moderate	Moderate
Nonnormative	Award or lottery win Cultural migration (relocation) Death of sibling Accident, illness, birth defect Period of employment	Moderate	Low

[a]Statements about characteristics are suggestive of averages only. For a similar taxonomy of the properties of life events see Brim and Ryff (1980). For evaluation and modification, see Reese and Smyer (1983).

515

maturation and age-graded socialization events are examples of age-graded influences.

History-graded influences also involve both biological and environmental determinants. These influences, however, are associated with historical time (McCluskey & Reese, in press; Neugarten & Datan, 1973) and define the larger context in which individuals develop. We judge history-graded influences to have moderate generality and moderate temporal predictability, on the average.

Some examples of history-graded influences are those physical-environmental and social change events that are associated with a long-term movement toward modernity or industrialization (Inkeles & Smith, 1974; Luria, 1976); so-called cohort effects (Baltes, Cornelius, & Nesselroade, 1979: Reese, 1974); and major historical events, such as wars and economic depressions (Elder, 1979; Elder, Liker, & Jaworski, in press). Historical changes in childrearing (see Lipsitt & Reese, 1979, pp. 114–115), or in the demographic characteristics of a given society such as age distribution, the composition of social classes, family structure, and the occupational world are also history-graded influences on development (Riley, 1979).

Nonnormative influences also include both biological and environmental determinants (Callahan & McCluskey, 1983; Filipp, 1981). Their major characteristic is that their occurrence, patterning, and sequencing are not clearly tied to a dimension of developmental time, whether ontogenetic or historical. Of course, nonnormative influences do occur in time, but they do not follow a general and predictable course. Although the temporal predictability of nonnormative influences is low, their occurrence varies considerably in prevalence. Some nonnormative influences happen to most people (though at different points in time); others are rare. At the same time, nonnormative influences can have a major impact on the course of development (Bandura, 1982; Filipp, 1981).

Some examples of nonnormative influences are the antecedents and patterns of antecedents that are associated with unique family constellations; special opportunities such as awards; career changes; relocation; physical traumata; birth defects; special talents; accidents; temporary unemployment; divorce; institutionalization; or, the death of a loved one or some other significant person. Belonging to a given subpopulation (ethnic, social, race) can also be seen as a nonnormative influence as long as this event provides the individual with fairly unique experiences. In such a case, however, the prevalence (interindividual similarity) and temporal predictability would be higher than is true for the other nonnormative events listed.

The impact of particular nonnormative life events is not generally the same for all people. It depends on specific conditions of timing, patterning, duration, and the resources available to individuals. Following earlier work by the Dohrenwends, as well as that by Holmes and Rahe, a number of life-span developmental psychologists (e.g., Brim & Ryff, 1980; Filipp, 1981; Hultsch & Plemons, 1979; Reese & McCluskey, in press; Reese & Smyer, 1983) have recently discussed the role of such "significant" nonnormative life events (both positive and negative ones) in the explanation of life-span development.

In summary: Figure 12.6 shows how life-span researchers focus on complex and pluralistic explanations of behavioral development. Some of the influences, particularly the age-graded, result in interindividual similarity in development. They are the salient "stuff" of those classic ontogenetic theories that have been associated with physical maturation and age-graded socialization, such as Piaget's theory of cognitive development or Freud's theory of psychosexual development. These age-graded influences vary, of course, in timing and intensity, for example as a function of gender, social class, genetic background, and other features of ecology (Bertram, 1981; Bronfenbrenner, 1979; Featherman, 1983). The second category of influences, history-graded, compounds this variability through the impact of historical changes on the course of life-span development. The third category of influences, the nonnormative, renders the individuality or idiosyncracy of behavioral development most apparent. As a group, nonnormative influences are probably the most powerful sources of individual uniqueness in development, after genetic differences (Scarr & Weinberg, 1983). Together, the three kinds of influences explain why the life-span development of individuals exhibits both similarities and differences: We all develop similarly in some ways but differently in others.

Life-Span Profile of Influences.   Knowing how the three categories of influence evolve with age and how, on the average, they look as a package for different individuals and different behaviors is a major objective of life-span work. Unfortunately, we do not have much information on this question of packaging and average profile. Thus, from a scientific point of view, the following observations are somewhat speculative.

In an earlier article (Baltes, Reese, & Lipsitt, 1980), we organized our thinking on the role of the three influences (age-graded, history-graded, nonnormative) through the life span by speculating about their probability of occurrence and their impact on behavioral development at successive age levels. Conceptually, this could be done either by quantifying the cumulative effect of the influences with age, or by estimating how much change and interindividual variability in change each influence is responsible for at any stage of the life span.

We speculate that, when measured in terms of the relative strength of their effect on development, age-graded influences exhibit a primary peak in childhood and a second, lesser peak in old age. This average life-course profile for age-graded influences is based on a number of considerations. Regarding the peak in childhood, many areas of child development exhibit a fairly high degree of universality in behavioral change. These areas include childhood ontogeny of physical growth, language, and cognition. During childhood, these areas exhibit quite a bit of regularity in their direction and sequentiality, and are fairly robust across environmental and genetic variation except, perhaps, for extreme cases of biological abnormality and environmental deprivation. We believe, then, that the regularity in childhood trends such as these can be explained by the predominant role of age-graded influences that are associated with developmental biology, and the age-graded structure of society. In childhood, these age-graded systems are fairly stabilized.

As a child grows older, however, the dominant role of age-graded influences declines. Two processes contribute to the decline in the role of age-gradation. First, most genetically controlled processes of maturation may have run their course by the end of childhood—indeed, a significant proportion are completed in infancy. Second, during the same period, individuals generally become more autonomous with respect to external controls; hence, they are relatively less constrained by society's age-graded program of expectations and sanctions (e.g., Meyer, in press; Rosow, 1974).

The resurgent peak of age-graded influences in old age reflects in part the possibility that dying and death have biologically based programs (Fries & Crapo, 1981; Strehler, 1977). More and more people are now reaching the maximum length of life of the human species. Thus, more and more people of about the same age participate in the process of dying. This process of dying extends over time and may involve certain features of age-correlated regularity. Riegel and Riegel (1972), for example, have discussed a process called "terminal drop" in intelligence, which is a sharp decline in intelligence beginning about five years before death (when death occurs from natural causes). Moreover, as the population consists of a larger and larger proportion of older people, society may introduce programs for the elderly that have stronger characteristics of age-gradation than in the past, when growing old was more the exception than the rule (Meyer, in press).

The probable average life-course profile for history-graded influences is even less clear at this time. In the past, developmental psychologists did not concern themselves very much with biocultural change. Moreover, other disciplines that are more directly concerned with biocultural change (e.g., anthropology, sociology) have often not included stage of life as an important component in their work. Baltes, Reese, and Lipsitt (1980) have speculated that the role of history-graded influences is particularly strong in adolescence and early adulthood. Adolescence and early adulthood are periods in which individuals show a high consciousness about what society is and should be all about, and in the ways they can influence its future course. Moreover, much of one's foundation for adulthood (career, lifestyle, family life) is centered in these periods and mediated by the nature of the current socioenvironmental climate (Bengtson & Black, 1973; Buss, 1979). Therefore, we suspect that history-graded influences have their most prominent relative influence on development during the periods of adolescence and early adulthood.

The life-span role of nonnormative influences (nonnormative life events) is perhaps the least understood, again, in part, because it is of recent scientific vintage. The elevation of nonnormative influences to an important position in developmental research is a departure from past practice. Moreover, the conception of these influences is somewhat different from what developmental psychologists have become accustomed to, because many nonnormative life events are not immediately based on a conception of time, such as chronological age and history. In this respect, many nonnormative life events seem, on the surface, to be more nondevelopmental than developmental.

Actually, we do not know how frequent and intense nonnormative influences are as the life course progresses. However, we speculate that, with increasing age, nonnormative life events take on a more important role in determining the course of life-span development, particularly in later life. This speculation is based on a number of ideas, some of which were expressed earlier. First, for many behaviors evolutionary genetic control probably declines with age. Second, the empirical evidence shows that adults and older individuals are very different from one another. This finding of heterogeneity (dissimilarity) or lack of commonality correlates well with the notion that nonnormative influences become more salient influences. Third is the related idea of individualization. Several models of life-span development (e.g., those of Charlotte Bühler and C. G. Jung) contain the notion that individuals are constantly moving toward increased individual expression. This process of individualization, again, would fit well with the belief that nonnormative influences become very important in the second half of life. Finally, the *impact* of nonnormative life events may increase in later life, particularly in old age, whether or not these events are more frequent or intense. During aging, the biological and psychological reserves (resources) available to the individual probably decrease. As a consequence, older individuals are more likely to be affected by nonnormative events, especially those that are stressful (Baltes, Dittmann-Kohli, & Dixon, 1984).

Because of the preliminary nature of the life-span profiles discussed, we need to emphasize again that they are presented simply as didactic devices to illustrate how similarities and differences in life-span development can come about. Very likely, the pattern and profile of age-graded, history-graded, and nonnormative influences can differ drastically, for different individuals as well as for different behaviors.

If, on the average, the life-span profile presented is a reasonable approximation to past and future evidence about behavioral development, it would help us understand why different age-specialties in developmental psychology have emphasized one type of influence over the others. On the one hand, if age-graded influences play a pivotal role in childhood, child development researchers have been correct in emphasizing the age-graded factors of maturation and socialization. Adulthood development researchers, on the other hand, after exploring age-graded models and finding them wanting, have quite properly looked into alternative kinds of influences. History-graded, and particularly nonnormative, influences are likely candidates for these alternatives.

Life-Span Developmental Psychology and Neighboring Disciplines

The sixth prototypical principle of the life-span perspective is its interdisciplinary commitment. We illustrate this view first by describing the existence of a developmental approach in other scientific fields, and then by mentioning a few references and areas that may whet the appetite for further reading. Excellent summary discussions of the interdisciplinary linkages of the life-span perspective can be found in Abeles and Riley (1976), Featherman (1983), and Sorenson, Weinert, and Sherrod (in press).

Other Developmental Sciences.   In order to appreciate the role of interdisciplinary work, it is useful to begin by pointing to the fact that developmental psychology is not the only developmental emphasis. Many disciplines deal with the primary orientation of developmental psychology, that is, with the study of change (Baltes & Goulet, 1970).

These other developmental sciences differ from developmental psychology not only in *what* they study, but in *how* they explain their subject matter. The classic developmental science is perhaps history. It is concerned with the study of constancy and change in a large number of attributes (anthropological, economic, political, psychological, sociological, etc.) and usually concentrates on large aggregates of people as entities, such as countries or cultures. Other examples of developmental sciences are anthropology, archaeology, and astronomy. Each of these sciences is inherently concerned with change.

Even if a given scientific discipline is not, as is developmental psychology, devoted entirely to the study of constancy and change, it may nevertheless have a subspecialty that focuses on change or development.

Developmental psychologists should look to other "change-oriented" or developmental disciplines for ideas about research and for information that may help to describe and explain behavioral development in a comprehensive manner. Knowledge about evolution, biological growth, history, and social structure, for example, is useful if we are to understand cognitive or social development more fully.

Life-Span Orientation in Neighboring Disciplines.   What about life-span perspectives in other developmental sciences? Although a life-span orientation is rather new in neighboring disciplines, as it is in psychology, it does exist (Featherman, 1983).

Sociology, the study of the organization and functioning of human society, is perhaps the neighboring discipline that is most active in developing and promoting a life-span orientation (Brim & Wheeler, 1966; Cain, 1964; Clausen, 1972; Elder, 1975; Featherman, 1983; Kohli, 1978; Neugarten & Hagestad, 1976; Riley et al., 1972; Riley, 1983; Rosenmayr, 1978). A number of research approaches in sociology have a life-span perspective (although sociologists prefer to speak of the "life cycle" or of a "life-course" approach). For example, in the sociology of socialization, researchers have argued that individuals learn and unlearn roles throughout life, and that individuals pass through status systems that are age-graded. In the sociology of the family, researchers have emphasized the notion of the family life-cycle (Hill & Mattesich, 1979).

What about a life-span approach in other fields? One field that also has a growing interest in a life-span approach is *education* (Reinert, 1980; Schaie & Willis, 1978; Willis, in press). The evolving educational subspecialties of lifelong education and continuing education reflect this orientation. The major assumption of these educational emphases is that education should not be concentrated solely in the first part of life; rather, important educational needs and opportunities also occur in adulthood and old age. These educational needs are related to general life-long goals of individual development (Havighurst, 1948/1972), as well as to the processes of cultural change (Dubin, 1972) and needs that are associated with particular individual life experiences (e.g., educational rehabilitation following accidents or illness). Organizing life-span educational needs and opportunities around age-graded, history-graded, and nonnormative influences may be a useful approach.

In *anthropology,* the science that deals with the physical and cultural development (evolution) of humankind, the life span has been a typical scheme for ethnographic research since the early work of Franz Boas, a widely known American anthropologist. Thus, in many anthropology books on primitive cultures, one finds chapters on successive age periods (infancy, childhood, etc.) or an integrative chapter on the life cycle. In addition, the beginnings of systematic theoretical work on the role of age systems can be found in anthropology (Kertzer & Keith, 1983; Stewart, 1977).

A life-span orientation is also found in *economics,* the science dealing with the production, distribution, and consumption of goods and services. Some economists believe that viewing individuals in their life span is helpful in understanding the labor market, or the manner in which individuals make economic and consumption decisions (Engermann, 1978; Featherman, 1983; Ghez & Becker, 1975).

The *biological sciences* have also made use of a life-span approach (Finch & Hayflick, 1977; Fries & Crapo, 1981; Thorbecke, 1975; Timiras, 1972). Biologists, in fact, have extensively used the term ontogenesis, which refers to the development of an individual organism from conception to death. However, as is true in psychology, most of the developmental work in biology has not emphasized life-span coverage and integration. On the contrary, biologists have tended to distinguish between development (Lund, 1978) on the one hand, and aging (Strehler, 1977) on the other. In this view, biological development, occurring primarily during the first half of life, is primarily concerned with aspects of growth and differentiation. Biological aging, in contrast, is often seen by biologists as a process that is separate from growth. Aging refers not only to processes of growth and increased capacity, but also to processes of deterioration and increasing vulnerability. Developmental psychologists should keep abreast of this distinction in biology, in order to evaluate whether the separation of development and aging by biologists is an historical accident or a conceptually and empirically sound perspective.

It is beyond the scope of this chapter to articulate in depth the conceptual nature of interdisciplinary connections in the study of life-span development. Featherman's (1983) position paper is an excellent starting point. A minimum understanding of other disciplines is mandatory, however, for a number of reasons.

First, a multidisciplinary perspective helps one to understand the incompleteness of any discipline's theory of behavioral development. For example, as psychologists study vocational interests and career development, sociologists and economists are ready to point out that these phenomena are subject to factors of social stratification and conditions of the labor market. Similarly, as psychologists investigate parent–child relationships, family sociologists point to the important role of historical changes in defining family structure and functioning, including aspects of household structure and fertility patterns.

Second, interdisciplinary work is more than the mere recognition of the incompleteness of one's discipline and the strength of other disciplines. The quest is also for interdisciplinary efforts in the sense of knowledge integration rather than the separatist differentiation of disciplinary knowledge bases. The life-span perspective is used by some as a forum for these integrative efforts. Elder's (1981) work on the relationship between conditions of history (e.g., economic depression) and personality development is an example, as is Riley's (1983) work on the age-cohort stratification model. This line of interdisciplinary scholarship in human development, fostered (among other reasons) by life-span considerations, is a catalyst not only for dialogue between fields but also for the continued generation of interdisciplinary knowledge. One consequence of this interdisciplinary trend has been that many publication outlets created for life-span writing (e.g., *Human Development, Life-Span Development and Behavior*) and professional meetings frequented by life-span scholars (e.g., Gerontological Society, International Society for the Study of Behavioral Development) have an explicit commitment to multidisciplinary participation, much more so than is true for the field of child development. (An exception is the Society for Research in Child Development, which is explicitly multidisciplinary.)

SUMMARY

Life-span developmental psychology is presented in this chapter not as a theory but as a perspective. As a perspective, it coordinates a number of substantive, theoretical, and methodological principles about the nature of behavioral development. None of these principles is new. What is unique is the kind of emphasis and coordination advanced.

The first principle is that development is a life-long process. No single period in the life span can claim general primacy for the origin and occurrence of important and interesting developmental changes. A second principle of the life-span perspective is that the courses of developmental changes can vary markedly, both among individuals and among behaviors. Developmental changes are pluralistic and complex; they can take many different forms. This principle represents a clear departure from the traditional conceptions of development, which use biological growth as the major criterion for deciding what changes constitute development. A third principle refers to the role of variability at the individual level of analysis, i.e., intraindividual plasticity. Depending on the life conditions experienced by a given individual, his or her developmental course can take many forms.

A fourth principle of the life-span perspective is that evolution (phylogeny) and individual development (ontogeny) are intricately related. Although developmental psychology focuses primarily on ontogenesis and ontogenetic principles, it recognizes that individual development (1) is in part regulated by genetic and cultural evolution; (2) contributes to the future evolution of society; and (3) is affected at any given point in time by factors of biocultural change. The last point is important because it states that the causes influencing individual development are not always of the ontogenetic (age-graded) type.

The fifth principle of the life-span perspective is that various influences interact (and are mediated and transformed by the developing individual) in the production of life-span development. The three categories of these influences are age-graded, history-graded, and nonnormative. The different categories seem to have different temporally ordered profiles, explaining why life-span development may be (1) continual, (2) multidirectional, and (3) differential.

Finally, a sixth principle refers to the cross- and interdisciplinary context of knowledge about psychological development. As one attends to more broadly gauged phenomena of development, such as life-long processes, one must acknowledge that a purist psychological concept of development is inherently incomplete.

To illustrate interdisciplinary connections, the concluding section of the chapter dealt with life-span approaches in other disciplines. One example is sociology, in which a subspecialty of life-cycle or life-course sociology is emerging. Education, anthropology, and economics are other examples. An opposing trend is seen in biology, which appears to be less oriented toward a life-span developmental approach than toward a "separatist" movement. This separatist movement in biology considers development (growth) and aging to be two distinct subspecialties. This discrepancy between the social and biological sciences deserves attention.

What is the long-range impact of life-span developmental scholarship? We agree with Featherman's recent assessment:

> By challenging such long-standing premises as the universality of developmental changes, the determinant role of childhood for adult personality and behavior, and uniform and irreversible senescence, life-span perspectives provide new insights into human potential and humanistic agenda for both basic and applied research. In a fundamental sense, the real payoff of life-span research may emerge from revisions of our insights into ourselves—into our species potentials and our active role in their evolutionary past and future, at most if not all points in the life cycle (1983, p. 46).

The life-span perspective may eventually result in a new discipline that is likely to be interdisciplinary in scope. A belief in the possible realization of such a broadly based intellectual potential associated with the life-span perspective may indeed be one example of how the social sciences continue to experience a sense of scholarly vision that is focused on integrative knowledge rather than disciplinary specialization.

In addition to encouraging cross-disciplinary enterprises, the life-span perspective can play a double role in the future of developmental psychology itself. On the one hand, its goal is to provide a knowledge base that considers development a life-long process in a changing society. On the other hand, the resulting knowledge about the life-long processes of development will be helpful in linking age-specific knowledge into a larger, overarching framework. To accomplish this goal within psychology, we must not consider the primary strength of the life-span perspective to be its role in cross-disciplinary or interdisciplinary dialogue. Rather, the life-span perspective must be tested and advanced within the confines of developmental psychology. That task seems to us to be the major challenge facing the life-span perspective in the coming decade.

REFERENCES

Abeles, R. P., & Riley, M. W. *A life-course perspective on the later years of life: Some implications for research.* (Social Science Research Council Annual Report). New York: Social Science Research Council, 1976.

Antonucci, T. Attachment: A life-span concept. *Human Development,* 1976, *19,* 135–142.

Baer, D. M. The control of the developmental process: Why wait? In J. R. Nesselroade & H. W. Reese (Eds.), *Life-span developmental psychology: Methodological issues.* New York: Academic Press, 1973.

Baltes, M. M., & Lerner, R. M. Roles of the operant model and its methods in the life-span approach to human development. *Human Development*, 1980, *23*, 362–367.

Baltes, P. B. Longitudinal and cross-sectional sequences in the study of age and generation effects. *Human Development*, 1968, *11*, 145–171.

Baltes, P. B. (Ed.). *Life-span development and behavior* (Vol. 1). New York: Academic Press, 1978.

Baltes, P. B. Life-span developmental psychology: Some converging observations on history and theory. In P. B. Baltes & O. G. Brim, Jr. (Eds.), *Life-span development and behavior* (Vol. 2). New York: Academic Press, 1979.

Baltes, P. B. Life-span developmental psychology: Observations on history and theory revisited. In R. M. Lerner (Ed.), *Developmental psychology: Historical and philosophical perspectives*. Hillsdale, N.J.: Lawrence Erlbaum Associates, 1983.

Baltes, P. B., & Baltes, M. M. Plasticity and variability in psychological aging: Methodological and theoretical issues. In G. Gurski (Ed.), *Determining the effects of aging on the central nervous system*. Berlin: Schering, 1980.

Baltes, P. B., & Brim, O. G., Jr. (Eds.). *Life-span development and behavior* (Vol. 2–5). New York: Academic Press, 1979, 1980, 1982, 1983.

Baltes, P. B., Cornelius, S. W., & Nesselroade, J. R. Cohort effects in behavioral development: Theoretical and methodological perspectives. In W. A. Collins (Ed.), *Minnesota symposia on child psychology* (Vol. 11). Hillsdale, N.J.: Lawrence Erlbaum Associates, 1978.

Baltes, P. B., Cornelius, S. W., & Nesselroade, J. R. Cohort effects in developmental psychology. In J. R. Nesselroade & P. B. Baltes (Eds.), *Longitudinal research in the study of behavior and development*. New York: Academic Press, 1979.

Baltes, P. B., Dittmann-Kohli, F., & Dixon, R. A. New perspectives on the development of intelligence in adulthood: Toward a dual-process conception and a model of selective optimization with compensation. In P. B. Baltes & O. G. Brim, Jr. (Eds.), *Life-span development and behavior* (Vol. 6). New York: Academic Press, 1984.

Baltes, P. B., & Goulet, L. R. Status and issues of a life-span developmental psychology. In L. R. Goulet & P. B. Baltes (Eds.), *Life-span developmental psychology: Research and theory*. New York: Academic Press, 1970.

Baltes, P. B., Reese, H. W., & Lipsitt, L. P. Life-span developmental psychology. *Annual Review of Psychology*, 1980, *31*, 65–100.

Baltes, P. B., & Schaie, K. W. (Eds.). *Life-span developmental psychology: Personality and socialization*. New York: Academic Press, 1973.

Baltes, P. B., & Schaie, K. W. On the plasticity of intelligence in adulthood and old age: Where Horn and Donaldson fail. *American Psychologist*, 1976, *31*, 720–725.

Baltes, P. B., & Schaie, K. W. (Eds.) *Life-span developmental psychology: Personality and socialization*. New York: Academic Press, 1973.

Baltes, P. B., & Willis, S. L. Plasticity and enhancement of intellectual functioning in old age: Penn State's Adult Development and Enrichment Program (ADEPT). In F. I. M. Craik & S. E. Trehub (Eds.), *Aging and cognitive processes*. New York: Plenum Press, 1982.

Bandura, A. Self-efficacy: Toward a unifying theory of behavioral change. *Psychological Review*, 1977, *84*, 191–215.

Bandura, A. The psychology of chance encounters and life paths. *American Psychologist*, 1982, *37*, 747–755.

Bengtson, V. L., & Black, K. D. Intergenerational relations in socialization. In P. B. Baltes & K. W. Schaie (Eds.), *Life-span developmental psychology: Personality and socialization*. New York: Academic Press, 1973.

Bertram, H. *Sozialstruktur und Sozialisation: Zur mikrosoziologischen Analyse von Chancenungleichheit*. Darmstadt: Luchterhand, 1981.

Brent, S. B. Individual specialization, collective adaptation and rate of environmental change. *Human Development*, 1978, *21*, 21–33.

Brim, O. G., Jr. *The sense of personal control and life-span development*. Unpublished manuscript, Foundation for Child Development, New York, 1974.

Brim, O. G., Jr., & Kagan, J. Constancy and change: A view of the issues. In O. G. Brim, Jr. & J. Kagan (Eds.), *Constancy and change in human development*. Cambridge, MA: Harvard University Press, 1980.

Brim, O. G., Jr., & Ryff, C. D. On the properties of life events. In P. B. Baltes & O. G. Brim, Jr. (Eds.), *Life-span development and behavior* (Vol. 3). New York: Academic Press, 1980.

Brim, O. G., Jr., & Wheeler, S. *Socialization after childhood: Two essays*. New York: Wiley, 1966.

Bronfenbrenner, U. *The ecology of human development*. Cambridge, MA: Harvard University Press, 1979.

Bühler, C. *Der menschliche Lebenslauf als psychologisches Problem*. Leipzig: Hirzel, 1933.

Buss, A. R. Dialectics, history, and development: The historical roots of the individual–society dialectic. In P. B. Baltes & O. G. Brim, Jr. (Eds.), *Life-span development and behavior* (Vol. 2). New York: Academic Press, 1979.

Butler, R. N. The life-review: An interpretation of reminiscence in the aged. *Psychiatry*, 1963, *26*, 65–76.

Cain, L. D., Jr. Life-course and social structure. In R. E. L. Faris (Ed.), *Handbook of modern sociology*. Chicago: Rand McNally, 1964.

Callahan, E. C., & McCluskey, K. A. (Eds.). *Life-span developmental psychology: Nonnormative life events*. New York: Academic Press, 1983.

Cantor, N., & Mischel, W. Prototypes in person perception. In L. Berkowitz (Ed.), *Advances in experimental social psychology* (Vol. 5). New York: Academic Press, 1979.

Carus, F. A. *Psychologie. Zweiter Teil: Specialpsychologie*. Leipzig: Barth & Kummer, 1808.

Cattell, R. B. *Abilities: Their structure, growth, and action*. Boston: Houghton Mifflin, 1971.

Clausen, J. A. The life-course of individuals. In M. W. Riley, M. Johnson, & A. Foner (Eds.), *Aging and society* (Vol. 3). *A sociology of age stratification*. New York: Russell Sage Foundation, 1972.

Craik, F. I. M. Age differences in human memory. In J. E. Birren & K. W. Schaie (Eds.), *Handbook of the psychology of aging*. New York: Van Nostrand Reinhold, 1977.

Datan, N., & Ginsberg, L. H. (Eds.). *Life-span developmental psychology: Normative life crises*. New York: Academic Press, 1975.

Datan, N., & Reese, H. W. (Eds.). *Life-span developmental psychology: Dialectical perspectives on experimental research*. New York: Academic Press, 1977.

Denney, N. W. Aging and cognitive changes. In B. B. Wolman (Ed.), *Handbook of developmental psychology*. Englewood Cliffs, N.J.: Prentice-Hall, 1982.

Donaldson, G. Letters to the editor: On cognitive training research in aging. *Journal of Gerontology*, 1981, *36*, 634–638.

Dubin, S. Obsolescence or lifelong education: A choice for the professional. *American Psychologist*, 1972, *27*, 486–498.

Elder, G. H., Jr. Age-differentiation in life course perspective. *Annual Review of Sociology*, 1975, *1*, 165–190.

Elder, G. H., Jr. Historical change in life patterns and personality. In P. B. Baltes & O. G. Brim, Jr. (Eds.), *Life-span development and behavior* (Vol. 2). New York: Academic Press, 1979.

Elder, G. H., Jr. History and the family: The discovery of complexity. *Journal of Marriage and Family*, 1981, *43*, 489–519.

Elder, G. H., Jr., Liker, J. K., & Jaworski, B. J. Hardship in lives: Historical influences from the 1930s to old age in postwar America. In K. A. McCluskey & H. W. Reese (Eds.), *Life-span developmental psychology: Historical and cohort effects*. New York: Academic Press, in press.

Engermann, S. Economic perspectives on the life course. In T. K. Hareven (Ed.), *Transition: The family and the life course in historical perspective*. New York: Academic Press, 1978.

Erikson, E. H. Identity and the life cycle. *Psychological Issues Monograph I*. New York: International Universities Press, 1959.

Erikson, E. H. Life cycle. In *International encyclopedia of the social sciences*. New York: Macmillan & Free Press, 1968.

Featherman, D. L. Schooling and occupational careers: Constancy and change in worldly success. In O. G. Brim, Jr. & J. Kagan (Eds.), *Constancy and change in human development*. Cambridge, MA: Harvard University Press, 1980.

Featherman, D. L. The life-span perspective in social science research. In P. B. Baltes & O. G. Brim, Jr. (Eds.), *Life-span development and behavior* (Vol. 5). New York: Academic Press, 1983.

Filipp, S. H. (Ed.). *Kritische Lebensereignisse*. Munich: Urban & Schwarzenberg, 1981.

Finch, C. E., & Hayflick, L. (Eds.). *Handbook of the biology of aging*. New York: Van Nostrand Reinhold, 1977.

Fries, J. F., & Crapo, L. M. *Vitality and aging*. San Francisco: Freeman & Company, 1981.

Ghez, G. R., & Becker, G. S. *The allocation of time and goods over the life cycle*. New York: Columbia University Press, 1975.

Gollin, E. S. (Ed.). *Developmental plasticity: Behavioral and biological aspects of variations in development*. New York: Academic Press, 1981.

Goulet, L. R., & Baltes, P. B. (Eds.). *Life-span developmental psychology: Research and theory*. New York: Academic Press, 1970.

Groffmann, K. J. Life-span developmental psychology in Europe. In L. R. Goulet & P. B. Baltes (Eds.), *Life-span developmental psychology: Research and theory*. New York: Academic Press, 1970.

Hagestad, G. O. Parent and child: Generations in the family. In T. Field, A. Huston, H. C. Quay, L. Troll, & G. E. Finley (Eds.), *Review of human development*. New York: Wiley, 1982.

Havighurst, R. J. *Developmental tasks and education* (3rd ed.). New York: McKay, 1972. (Originally published, 1948.)

Havighurst, R. J. History of developmental psychology: Socialization and personality development through the life span. In P. B. Baltes & K. W. Schaie (Eds.), *Life-span developmental psychology: Personality and socialization*. New York: Academic Press, 1973.

Heckhausen, H. Achievement and motivation through the life span. In A. Sorenson, L. Sherrod, & F. Weinert (Eds.), *Life-span perspectives on human development,* in press.

Hill, R., & Mattessich, P. Family development theory and life-span development. In P. B. Baltes & O. G. Brim, Jr. (Eds.), *Life-span behavior and development* (Vol. 2). New York: Academic Press, 1979.

Hollingworth, H. L. *Mental growth and decline: A survey of developmental psychology*. New York: Appleton, 1927.

Horn, J. L. Organization of data on life-span development of human abilities. In L. R. Goulet & P. B. Baltes (Eds.), *Life-span developmental psychology: Research and theory*. New York: Academic Press, 1970.

Horn, J. L. Human ability systems. In P. B. Baltes (Ed.), *Life-span development and behavior* (Vol. 1). New York: Academic Press, 1978.

Horn, J. L. The aging of human abilities. In B. B. Wolman (Ed.), *Handbook of developmental psychology*. Englewood Cliffs, N.J.: Prentice-Hall, 1982.

Horn, J. L., & Donaldson, G. On the myth of intellectual decline in adulthood. *American Psychologist*, 1976, *31*, 701–719.

Horn, J. L., & Donaldson, G. Faith is not enough: A response to the Baltes-Schaie claim that intelligence does not wane. *American Psychologist*, 1977, *32*, 369–373.

Hultsch, D. F., & Dixon, R. A. Text processing in adulthood. In P. B. Baltes & O. G. Brim, Jr. (Eds.), *Life-span development and behavior* (Vol. 6). New York: Academic Press, 1984.

Hultsch, D. F., & Plemons, J. K. Life events and life-span development. In P. B. Baltes & O. G. Brim, Jr. (Eds.), *Life-span development and behavior* (Vol. 2). New York: Academic Press, 1979.

Inkeles, A., & Smith, D. H. *Becoming modern.* Cambridge, Mass.: Harvard University Press, 1974.

Kahn, R. L., & Antonucci, T. C. Convoys over the life-course: Attachment, roles, and social support. In P. B. Baltes & O. G. Brim, Jr. (Eds.), *Life-span development and behavior* (Vol. 3). New York: Academic Press, 1980.

Kendler, T. S. Cross-sectional research, longitudinal theory, and a discriminative transer ontogeny. *Human Development,* 1979, *22,* 235–254.

Kertzer, D. I., & Keith, J. (Eds.). *Age and anthropological theory.* Ithaca, NY: Cornell University Press, 1983.

Kohli, M. (Hrsg.). *Soziologie des Lebenslaufs.* Darmstadt: Luchterhand, 1978.

Labouvie, E. W. Issues in life-span development. In B. B. Wolman (Ed.), *Handbook of developmental psychology.* Englewood Cliffs, N.J.: Prentice-Hall, 1982.

Labouvie-Vief, G. Adult cognitive development: In search of alternative interpretations. *Merrill Palmer Quarterly,* 1977, *23,* 227–263.

Labouvie-Vief, G. Beyond formal operations: Uses and limits of pure logic in life-span development. *Human Development,* 1980, *23,* 141–161.

Labouvie-Vief, G. Dynamic development and mature autonomy: A theoretical prologue. *Human Development,* 1982, *25,* 161–191.

Labouvie-Vief, G. Intelligence and cognition. In J. E. Birren & K. W. Schaie (Eds.), *Handbook of the psychology of aging* (2nd ed.). New York: Van Nostrand, 1984.

Lehr, U. Die Bedeutung der Lebenslaufpsychologie für die Gerontologie. *Aktuelle Gerontologie,* 1980, *10,* 257–269.

Lerner, R. M. *On the nature of human plasticity.* New York: Cambridge University Press, 1984.

Lerner, R. M., & Busch-Rossnagel, N. (Eds.). *Individuals as producers of their development: A life-span perspective.* New York: Academic Press, 1981.

Lerner, R. M., & Ryff, C. D. Implementation of the life-span view of human development: The sample case of attachment. In P. B. Baltes (Ed.), *Life-span development and behavior* (Vol. 1). New York: Academic Press, 1978.

Lipsitt, L. P., & Reese, H. W. *Child development.* Glenview, Ill: Scott, Foresman, 1979.

Lund, R. D. *Development and plasticity of the brain.* New York: Oxford University Press, 1978.

Luria, A. R. *Cognitive development: Its cultural and social foundations,* (M. Cole, Ed.; M. Lopez-Morillas & L. Solataroff, Trans.). Cambridge, Mass.: Harvard University Press, 1976.

McCall, R. B. Challenges to a science of developmental psychology. *Child Development,* 1977, *48,* 333–344.

McCluskey, K. A., & Reese, H. W. (Eds.). *Life-span developmental psychology: Historical and cohort effects.* New York: Academic Press, in press.

Meacham, J. A. Formal aspects of theories of development. *Experimental Aging Research,* 1980, *6,* 475–487.

Meyer, J. The institutionalization of the life course. In A. Sorenson, L. Sherrod, & F. Weinert (Eds.), *Life-span perspectives on human development,* in press.

Montada, L. Entwicklungspsychologie auf der Suche nach einer Identität. In L. Montada (Hrsg.), *Brennpunkte der Entwicklungspsychologie.* Stuttgart: Kohlhammer, 1979.

Nesselroade, J. R., & Baltes P. B. Adolescent personality development and historical change: 1970–72. *Monographs of the Society for Research in Child Development,* 1974, *39* (1, Whole No. 154).

Nesselroade, J. R., & Baltes, P. B. (Eds.). *Longitudinal research in the study of behavior and development.* New York: Academic Press, 1979.

Nesselroade, J. R., & Reese, H. W. (Eds.). *Life-span developmental psychology: Methodological issues.* New York: Academic Press, 1973.

Nesselroade, J. R., & von Eye, A. (Eds.). *Individual development and social change: Explanatory analysis.* New York: Academic Press, 1984.

Neugarten, B. L. Continuities and discontinuities of psychological issues into adult life. *Human Development,* 1969, *12,* 121–130.

Neugarten, B. L., & Datan, N. Sociological perspectives on the life cycle. In P. B. Baltes & K. W. Schaie (Eds.), *Life-span developmental psychology: Personality and socialization.* New York: Academic Press, 1973.

Neugarten, B. L., & Hagestad, G. O. Age and the life-course. In R. H. Binstock & E. Shanas (Eds.), *Aging and the social sciences.* New York: Van Nostrand, 1976.

Overton, W. F., & Reese, H. W. Models of development: Methodological implications. In J. R. Nesselroade & H. W. Reese (Eds.), *Life-span developmental psychology: Methodological issues.* New York: Academic Press, 1973.

Piaget, J. Intellectual evolution from adolescence to adulthood. *Human Development,* 1972, *15,* 1–12.

Reese, H. W. Cohort, age, and imagery in children's paired-associate learning. *Child Development,* 1974, *45,* 1176–1178.

Reese, H. W. The development of memory: Life-span perspectives. In H. W. Reese (Ed.), *Advances in child development and behavior* (Vol. 11). New York: Academic Press, 1976. (a)

Reese, H. W. Models of memory development. *Human Development,* 1976, *19,* 291–303. (b)

Reese, H. W. Discriminative learning and transfer: Dialectical perspectives. In N. Datan & H. W. Reese (Eds.), *Life-span developmental psychology: Dialectical perspectives on experimental research.* New York: Academic Press, 1977. (a)

Reese, H. W. Toward a cognitive theory of mnemonic imagery. *Journal of Mental Imagery,* 1977, *2,* 229–244. (b)

Reese, H. W., & McCluskey, K. A. Dimensions of historical constancy and change. In K. A. McCluskey & H. W. Reese (Eds.), *Life-span developmental psychology: Historical and cohort effects.* New York: Academic Press, in press.

Reese, H. W., & Overton, W. F. Models of development and theories of development. In L. R. Goulet & P. B. Baltes (Eds.), *Life-span developmental psychology: Research and theory.* New York: Academic Press, 1970.

Reese, H. W., & Smyer, M. A. The dimensionalization of life events. In E. C. Callahan & K. A. McCluskey (Eds.), *Life-span developmental psychology: Nonnormative life events.* New York: Academic Press, 1983.

Reinert, G. Comparative factor analytic studies of intelligence throughout the human life span. In L. R. Goulet & P. B. Baltes (Eds.), *Life-span developmental psychology: Research and theory.* New York: Academic Press, 1970.

Reinert, G. Prolegomena to a history of life-span developmental psychology. In P. B. Baltes & O. G. Brim, Jr. (Eds.), *Life-span development and behavior* (Vol. 2). New York: Academic Press, 1979.

Reinert, G. Educational psychology in the context of the human life span. In P. B. Baltes & O. G. Brim, Jr. (Eds.), *Life-span development and behavior* (Vol. 3). New York: Academic Press, 1980.

Riegel, K. F. Time and change in the development of the individual and society. In H. W. Reese (Ed.), *Advances in child development and behavior* (Vol. 7). New York: Academic Press, 1972.

Riegel, K. F. The dialectics of human development. *American Psychologist,* 1976, *31,* 689–700.

Riegel, K. F., & Riegel, R. M. Development, drop, and death. *Developmental Psychology,* 1972, *6,* 306–319.

Riley, M. W. (Ed.). *Aging from birth to death: Interdisciplinary perspectives.* Boulder, CO: Westview Press, 1979.

Riley, M. W. Age strata in social systems. In R. H. Binstock & E. Shanas (Eds.), *Handbook of aging and the social sciences* (rev. ed.). New York: Van Nostrand, 1983.

Riley, M. W., Johnson, M., & Foner, A. (Eds.). *Aging and society* (Vol. 3): *A sociology of age stratification.* New York: Russell Sage, 1972.

Rosenmayr, L. (Ed.). *Die menschlichen Lebensalter.* München: Piper, 1978.

Rosow, I. *Socialization to old age.* Berkeley: University of California Press, 1974.

Ross, L. The "intuitive scientist" formulation and its developmental implications. In J. Flavell & L. Ross (Eds.), *Social cognitive development.* New York: Cambridge University Press, 1981.

Scarr, S., & Weinberg, R. A. The influence of "family background" on intellectual attainment. *American Sociological Review,* 1978, *43,* 674–692.

Scarr, S., & Weinberg, R. A. The Minnesota adoption studies: Genetic differences and malleability. *Child Development,* 1983, *54,* 260–267.

Schaie, K. W. A general model for the study of developmental problems. *Psychological Bulletin,* 1965, *64,* 92–107.

Schaie, K. W. The primary mental abilities in adulthood: An exploration in the development of psychometric intelligence. In P. B. Baltes & O. G. Brim, Jr. (Eds.), *Life-span development and behavior* (Vol. 2). New York: Academic Press, 1979.

Schaie, K. W. The Seattle Longitudinal Study: A twenty-one year exploration of psychometric intelligence in adulthood. In K. W. Schaie (Ed.), *Longitudinal studies of adult psychological development.* New York: Guilford Press, 1983.

Schaie, K. W., & Baltes, P. B. Some faith helps to see the forest: A final comment on the Horn and Donaldson myth of the Baltes-Schaie position on adult intelligence. *American Psychologist,* 1977, *32,* 1118–1120.

Schaie, K. W., & Hertzog, C. Fourteen-year cohort-sequential analyses of adult intellectual development. *Developmental Psychology,* 1983, *19,* 531–543.

Schaie, K. W., & Willis, S. L. Life-span development: Implications for education. *Review of Educational Research,* 1978, *6,* 120–156.

Singer, B., & Spilerman, S. Mathematical representations of developmental theories. In J. R. Nesselroade & P. B. Baltes (Eds.), *Longitudinal research in the study of behavior and development.* New York: Academic Press, 1979.

Skinner, B. F. The phylogeny and ontogeny of behavior. *Science,* 1966, *150,* 1205–1213.

Sorenson, A., Sherrod, L., & Weinert, F. (Eds.). *Life-span perspectives on human development,* in press.

Stewart, F. H. *Fundamentals of age-group systems.* New York: Academic Press, 1977.

Strehler, B. L. *Time, cells, and aging* (rev. ed.). New York: Academic Press, 1977.

Tetens, J. N. *Philosophische Versuche über die menschliche Natur und ihre Entwicklung.* Leipzig: Weidmanns Erben und Reich, 1777.

Thomae, H. (Ed.). *Entwicklungspsychologie.* Göttingen: Hogrefe, 1959.

Thomae, H. The concept of development and life-span developmental psychology. In P. B. Baltes & O. G. Brim, Jr. (Eds.), *Life-span development and behavior* (Vol. 2). New York: Academic Press, 1979.

Thorbecke, G. J. (Ed.). *Biology of aging and development.* New York: Plenum Press, 1975.

Timiras, P. S. *Developmental physiology and aging.* New York: Macmillan, 1972.

Turner, R. R., & Reese, H. W. (Eds.). *Life-span developmental psychology: Intervention.* New York: Academic Press, 1980.

Van den Daele, L. D. Infrastructure and transition in developmental analysis. *Human Development,* 1974, *17,* 1–23.

Willis, S. L. Towards an educational psychology of the adult learner. In J. E. Birren & K. W. Schaie (Eds.), *Handbook of the psychology of aging* (rev. ed.). New York: Van Nostrand, in press.

Willis, S. L., & Baltes, P. B. Intelligence in adulthood and aging: Contemporary issues. In L. W. Poon (Ed.), *Aging in the 1980's: Psychological issues.* Washington, DC: American Psychological Association, 1980.

Willis, S. L., & Baltes, P. B. Letters to the editor. On cognitive training research in aging: Reply to Donaldson. *Journal of Gerontology,* 1981, *36,* 636–638.

Wohlwill, J. F. *The study of behavioral development.* New York: Academic Press, 1973.

13

Development Viewed in its Cultural Context

Barbara Rogoff
Mary Gauvain
Shari Ellis
University of Utah

INTRODUCTION

Cross-cultural research permits psychologists a broader perspective on human development than is available when considering human behavior in a single cultural group. This expanded view holds important implications for a psychology that has grown out of Western thought and has been tested almost exclusively on Western societies.[1] By allowing psychologists to view variations on human behavior not normally found in mainstream U.S. or Western European society, cross-cultural observation aids in the understanding of human adaptation. Cross-cultural research may allow psychologists to disentangle variables highly associated in one culture but less so in another. In addition, cross-cultural investigations can make use of variations within a single society to examine naturally occurring cause–effect relationships that cannot be manipulated experimentally. Most importantly, cross-cultural research forces psychologists to look closely at the impact

---

[1]In cross-cultural psychology, the term 'Western' is used to refer to technological, industrialized, modern cultures such as the United States, Canada, Western Europe, or Russia. While it is not geographically appropriate, it is more satisfactory than its substitutes which generally carry unwarranted value judgments regarding degree of civilization, development, or cultural advancement.

Please note that our use of the term culture is intentionally broad. While we focus on comparisons of groups differing in their societal membership and examinations of the workings of culture within groups, we believe our arguments are appropriate for groups differing in other background experiences (e.g., age or gender). We also note that Western cultures and non-Western cultures are not homogeneous; societal and subcultural variation of all sorts provide valuable material for comparisons among groups or examination of patterns within groups.

of their own belief systems (folk psychology) on scientific theories. When subjects and researchers are from the same population, interpretations of development may be constrained by implicit cultural assumptions.

Some of the broad questions that have been consistently emphasized in cross-cultural work include whether certain mental abilities are universal or vary across cultures, and how individual personality may relate to cultural characteristics such as subsistence methods or value systems. These lines of research have yielded interesting results, which are reviewed in detail in a number of excellent sources: Bornstein (1980); Dasen (1977); Field, Sostek, Vietze, and Leiderman (1981); Laboratory of Comparative Human Cognition (1979, 1981); Leiderman, Tulkin, and Rosenfeld (1977); Munroe and Munroe (1975); Munroe, Munroe, and Whiting (1981); Serpell (1976); Triandis and Heron (1981); Wagner and Stevenson (1981); and Werner (1979). In this chapter we do not review the extensive research examining cultural universals and variations in human thinking, personality, and behavior. However, we do briefly describe some investigations of universality and variation that refine our understanding of human functioning.

The bulk of this chapter discusses the way in which research involving culture has led psychologists to conceptualize the relationship between culture and thought or behavior. In much cross-cultural research to date, this relationship has been examined using a model in which culture serves as an independent variable (or a set of independent variables) and behavior (or thought) is regarded as the dependent variable, or outcome, of variation in cultural variables. Culture and behavior are conceived as separate variables, rather than mutually embedded aspects of cultural and individual systems. The influence of culture on the individual is frequently studied by correlating an aspect of culture with an aspect of individual functioning. For example, the correlation between the complexity of social structure in the culture and the personality characteristics of its members may be examined. Then investigators may undertake a closer examination of the contexts in which behavior occurs or is taught in varying cultural settings, in the interest of understanding how a particular aspect of culture may influence a particular aspect of individual behavior. For example, how might participation in a technological society encourage children to be more or less nurturant, aggressive, or competitive. This kind of close examination focuses attention on *how* culture can channel development. Whiting (1976) urges that we attempt to "unpackage" independent variables such as culture, social class, schooling, and gender. Because developmental psychologists have similarly become concerned with the process of change rather than simply correlating broad categories of experience and behavioral outcomes (Brown, 1982), this chapter stresses the guidance provided for the field of developmental psychology by cross-cultural emphasis on the contexts in which culture meets individual.

Our primary theme is that human development is guided by the opportunities provided by culture to learn and practice particular skills and behavior. We stress the cultural and contextual basis of development, from the perspective that culture and context are meshed with development rather than separate from it. We argue that to understand children's actions (or to compare them with those of other children of a different age or culture), it is essential to place these actions in the context of the children's interpretation of the task to be accomplished, the goal in performing the activity, and the broader social context of such activities in the children's experience. Although many of our examples are taken from research on cognitive development, we include studies of the role of context in children's social skills wherever possible. In fact, the incorporation of contextual considerations in the study of development de-emphasizes the distinction between cognitive and social development, because thinking occurs in social settings, and socialization occurs in problem-solving situations.

In this chapter, we first refer to the usefulness of cross-cultural research for testing the universal applicability of existing theories and for examining and refining empirical relationships between sociocultural variables and human development. We then focus on concerns raised in cross-cultural research with how to conceptualize the role of the context of human activity. We review studies that suggest the impossibility of understanding human nature without considering the context in which people develop and use their skills. We contrast concepts of development and indicate recent theoretical directions and empirical studies that attempt to integrate aspects of context with conceptions of human activities and development.

CROSS-CULTURAL TESTING OF WESTERN THEORIES AND FINDINGS

This section briefly describes some ways that cross-cultural research can revise existing theories and refine our understanding of the relation between experience and human functioning.

Testing Existing Theories

Cross-cultural research has been useful in testing psychological theories based on observations in Western cultures for their applicability under other circumstances. Such research may provide crucial counterexamples demonstrating limitations or challenging the basic assumptions of a theory. For example, Malinowski's investigations with Trobriand Islanders (1927) calls into question the foundations of the Oedipal complex in Freud's theory. Freud's theory developed in a society in which the father played both the role of mother's lover and of child's disciplinarian. Among the Trobrianders, however, the roles are separated: The mother's lover is her husband, and the child's disciplinarian is his maternal uncle. Since the Trobriand boys' resentment is directed toward their uncle and not their mother's husband, it appears that the sexual relationship between mother and father may not be related to young boys' resentment toward their father as postulated in the Oedipal complex. This finding illustrates that cross-cultural research can raise questions not only about the universal applicability of a theory, but also about the postulates of the theory itself.

Another theoretical approach that has received considerable attention in cross-cultural tests of universality is Piaget's (1971) theory of cognitive development (see reviews by Dasen, 1977; Dasen & Heron, 1981; Greenfield, 1976; Price-Williams, 1980). This research has demonstrated great variation in the rate of Piagetian cognitive development and has examined the question of whether Piaget's stages appear in the same order in different cultures. Cross-cultural research demonstrating the rarity of formal operational performance among non-literate adults has led to widespread concern that this stage represents a culturally specific course of development, perhaps best represented by the 'Western scientist.'[2] Largely because of the cross-cultural evidence, Piaget revised his stance on the formal operational stage, stating in 1972 that this stage may be one that appears only in specific familiar domains rather than being a structured ensemble. Later research conducted in the U.S., investigating performance on formal operational tasks across domains, supports this reformulation (Kuhn & Brannock, 1977).

These examples illustrate the ways in which cross-cultural research may suggest refinements in a theory or raise questions to be addressed in further theoretical development. Findings such as these reaffirm the complexity of psychological phenomena and highlight the importance of the cultural context in which psychological phenomena occur and in which psychological theories develop.

Cross-cultural research may also discover impressive regularities across cultures in developmental phenomena. For instance, there is marked similarity across cultures in the sequence and timing of sensorimotor development as well as in the age of onset of smiling and separation distress (Gewirtz, 1965; Goldberg, 1972; Konner, 1972; Super, 1981); the order of stages in language acquisition is also constant across a large variety of cultural groups (Bowerman, 1981; Slobin, 1973). Through cross-cultural research, we may become aware of patterns of variation and similarity in human activity, advancing our understanding of human development and of the ways in which experience relates to behavior.

Refining Relationships Between Experience and Behavior

Cross-cultural research can be useful in calling attention to the assumptions regarding human "nature" which go unnoticed by researchers who share the cultural background of the people they study. Doing research in another culture can make one aware of aspects of human behavior which are not noticeable until

---

[2]It should be noted, however, that only 30% of U.S. undergraduates perform in a formal operational way (Ashton, 1975).

they are missing or differently arranged, as with the fish who reputedly is unaware of water until removed from it. The fact that human activities are often arranged differently in other cultures allows researchers to examine the pattern of particular variables when they fit differently with other variables in the cultural system.

Cross-cultural research helps to clarify the relationship between experience and behavior by extending the range of variation beyond that available for study in the researcher's own culture and by rearranging variables which may be highly correlated in one culture but not in another. For example, Sears and Wise (1950, reported in Whiting & Child, 1953) conclude that the older a baby is when weaned, the greater the associated emotional disturbance. However, their Kansas City sample was weaned very early: Only 5 out of 70 children had not been weaned by the age of 7 months. Using a worldwide sample of 52 societies, Whiting and Child (1953) found that the age at weaning ranged from 6 months to 5½ years with 2½ years the median. In only one culture were the children weaned as early as those of the Kansas City sample. What is particularly interesting is that with this worldwide variation in the age of weaning, it was possible to modify Sears and Wise's conclusion: Up to age 13–18 months, it appeared to be true that the older the baby was, the more it became disturbed. But after this peak, weaning became easier as children grew older, with older children frequently weaning themselves as their interests diversified. Given the narrow range of variation available in this U.S. sample, the developmental progression would have been predicted inaccurately.

Other investigations of the relationship between experience and behavior are available in studies of mother–infant contact and relationships on the Israeli kibbutz. In some kibbutzim, children live separately from their parents and are tended in a children's house from early infancy by a children's nurse. Research suggests that infants separated daily from their mothers nevertheless evidence greater interest in staying close to their mothers than to the caretakers with whom they spend great amounts of time (Fox, 1977). It is also interesting that the babies develop strong bonds with their infant roommates (Zaslow, 1980). This suggests that, with extensive contact, infants show a level of social involvement presumed beyond their maturational level in studies (Maudry & Nekula, 1939; Parten, 1933) using U.S. infants who tend to be relatively isolated from other infants (Zaslow & Rogoff, 1978).

Cross-cultural studies also allow investigators to vary factors that cannot be disentangled in one culture but that are less highly associated in other cultures, allowing a form of "natural experiment." For example, studies of mother–child households carried out in the U.S. have, in addition to the absence of the father in the household, a stigma of "broken household," which labels the family structure as aberrant and undesirable. In other cultures (e.g., in polygynous settings), however, mother–child residence patterns are the usual family structure and their effects could be studied without being confounded by a public attitude of undesirability. For example, low male salience in polygynous households has been related to boys' sex-role development and to societal practices such as masculine-oriented initiation rites and the institutionalization of male participation in pregnancy (the *couvade,* see Munroe & Munroe, 1975).

Another example of covarying factors that are difficult to disentangle in U.S. research is the relation between children's chronological age and the amount of schooling they have received. U.S. researchers commonly use age (Wohlwill, 1970) as a proxy for maturation or for some sort of general experience with the world. But, as the Laboratory of Comparative Human Cognition (1979) notes, "to some people it seems that cognitive developmental research in the United States has been measuring *years of schooling,* using *age* as its proxy variable" (p. 830). Developmental studies often find a discontinuity in various skills and knowledge structures about age 5–7 (White, 1965), which happens to be the age of the onset of schooling in the U.S. If we are to understand development without confounding maturation with amount of schooling, it is very useful to examine the development of skills in cultures in which schooling is not mandatory or where age and schooling are not so tightly related (see Rogoff, 1981).

A third example of the opportunity that cross-cultural research provides for disentangling intertwined variables is available in observations of children's companionship. It has been noted that Americans emphasize children's peer relations over sibling relations (Ruffy, 1981; Wolfenstein, 1955). Lack of companionship between siblings may not relate to their kinship but to other differences characterizing siblings vs. unrelated peers in Western societies. In Western cultures, sibling interaction implies cross-age relations, since children born of monogamous marriages are unlikely to be very close in age. But in polygynous families there are likely to be same-age siblings living within the same compound. In addition, Western children are separated from siblings through age-graded institutions such as school, while children in nonWestern cultures are less subject to the age-grading of schools and are highly involved in caring for younger siblings (Weisner & Gallimore, 1977). However, even in the U.S., sibling interaction may be common if families are isolated from other families, if children are responsible for tending siblings, or if children are not attending school (Ellis, Rogoff, & Cromer, 1981; Fitchen, 1981; Gump, Schoggen, & Redl, 1963; Hicks, 1976; Young, 1970). Cross-cultural observations of prevalence and preference for sibling interaction suggest that age differences between siblings, age grading, and availability of siblings and unrelated companions may be at least as important to consider as the relatedness variable in accounting for a child's choice of companions.

The preceding discussion illustrates how cross-cultural research has modified developmental theories and provided fresh perspectives on the relation between experience and human behavior and development. Through extensive work focusing on cultural variation in human development (reviewed in sources cited on p. 534), the attention of researchers has been drawn to the role of context in human activity. Next we discuss how cross-cultural research has focused the attention of developmentalists on the role of context in human development. By context we mean any physical or social feature of an activity that channels behavior.

THE ROLE OF CONTEXT IN DEVELOPMENT

Although most approaches in psychology have considered aspects of context to be relevant to the study of the person (e.g., in the need to specify the stimulus or describe the task), understanding the role of context has generally been secondary to examining characteristics of the person. This is true of developmental as well as cross-cultural psychology, in that the basic research strategy is to search for the influence of broad classes of experience (e.g., culture, SES, age, gender) that influence broad classes of individual outcome (e.g., IQ, personality, cognitive level). The focus generally has been on the individual as the basic unit of analysis, with human activity explained in terms of motives, personality, and social and cognitive traits and capacities. Characteristics of the person have been assumed to be relatively stable across situations.

Recently, however, psychologists have become increasingly concerned with the role of context (Bronfenbrenner, 1979; Cole, Hood, & McDermott, 1978; Gelman, 1978; Rogoff, 1982; Siegel, 1977). This concern was sparked to a significant extent by some early cross-cultural observations of the variability of people's performances in differing contexts. Cross-cultural researchers who supplemented their "experimental" measures of performance with ethnographic observations of people's everyday activities have been struck by the fact that people who have difficulty with a particular task in the laboratory may spontaneously use the skill of interest in their everyday activities (see discussion in Cole, Hood, & McDermott, 1978; Laboratory of Comparative Human Cognition, 1979; Rogoff, 1981). Gladwin (1970) reports that Micronesian navigators who show extraordinary skills in memory, inference, and calculation in sailing from island to island perform abominably on standard tests of intellectual functioning. Scribner (1976) points out that subjects who perform poorly on logical syllogisms in a test situation often can be observed using elegant reasoning in other situations, such as giving hypothetical arguments for avoiding answering logical reasoning problems. Cole (1975) and Labov (1970) similarly describe people who seem to lack communicative abilities in a testing situation but who exhibit very skillful and logical persuasive skills in everyday social interaction, such as talking the experimenter into buying a beer.

Contextual variation is increasingly noted in U.S. research indicating that children's behavior in their familiar environments and in the laboratory differs (DeLoache, 1980; Kessel, 1979; Laboratory of Comparative Human Cognition, 1979; Neisser, 1976; Todd & Perlmutter, 1980). For example, young children routinely have difficulty with egocentrism in referential communication tasks (Erickson, 1981; Glucksberg, Krauss, & Higgins, 1975), yet in everyday situations they adjust their communication to meet the needs of their listeners (Gleason, 1973; Shatz & Gelman, 1977). Similarly, toddlers have difficulty in laboratory memory tests but demonstrate impressive memory for locations of objects hidden in their own homes (DeLoache & Brown, 1979) and impressive recall and strategic capacities in other quasi-naturalistic tasks (Wellman & Somerville, 1980). Infants use an egocentric frame of reference in looking for an object in the laboratory, but use a nonegocentric frame of reference when tested at home (Acredolo, 1979). Babies are more likely to display separation protest when left by their mothers in a laboratory situation than in the home (Ross, Kagan, Zelazo, & Kotelchuck, 1975). Such findings indicate that children's behavior often differs in laboratory tasks compared to more familiar contexts.

A common reaction to the findings that laboratory skills appear different from behavior outside of the lab is to encourage the study of people's actions in their natural environments. It is assumed that valid measures of people's real psychological processes will be found only in natural environments (Charlesworth, 1976). While it is important to examine activities outside of the laboratory, the dichotomy of laboratory vs. "natural" behavior is an oversimplification. Focusing the issue on a field vs. laboratory distinction (McCall, 1977; Parke, 1979; Weisz, 1978; Wohlwill, 1981) overlooks the fact that there is no one situation in which people's *real* capabilities and processes can be uncovered. This view assumes that it is possible, under ideal circumstances, to attribute underlying capacities or processes to internal functioning of people without concern for the context of their activity.

Thinking as well as acting, however, are intricately interwoven with the context of the activity underway. For example, children's communication skills appear to vary depending on whether their listener is a peer or a teacher (Steinberg & Cazden, 1979) or whether they are at home or at school (Shultz, Florio, & Erickson, 1982). One parent's interactions with an infant decrease in the presence of the other parent (Lamb, 1978), and children's peer interactions are more negative when their mothers or teachers are present (Abramovitch, Pepler, & Corter, 1982; Cook-Gumperz & Corsaro, 1977; Field, 1979; Huston-Stein, Friedrich-Cofer, & Susman, 1977). Fifth graders are more likely to evidence altruism when they know they are observed by an experimenter (Zarbatany, Hartmann, Gelfand, & Ramsey, 1982). One must attend to the context in order to understand psychological processes. This is the case for any situation in which development is studied, including the laboratory context, which is not context-*free* as researchers frequently seem to assume. Context is a complex and structured feature of psychological events, one that is not separate from the activity of the person (Rogoff, 1982).

These concerns are crucial in cross-cultural comparisons (or any comparisons based on group membership, e.g., age or gender comparisons), because such comparisons assume that the factor compared is equivalent for the groups compared, and that other factors do not simultaneously vary. Cross-cultural psychologists distinguish degrees of sensitivity to the broad contexts of human functioning in discussions of *emic, imposed etic,* and *derived etic* research strategies (Berry, 1969). In an emic approach, an investigator attempts to maintain the rich interplay of all aspects of the cultural context in the description of a cultural group. Such research may make use of ethnographic observation and participation in the activities of the culture studied.

In an imposed etic approach, an investigator attempts to make general statements about human functioning across cultural groups, but with insufficient attention to the cultural contexts used to support the generalization. Thus, by definition the investigator carrying out an imposed etic study is too quick to impose a culturally inappropriate understanding of the phenomenon of interest, usually uncritically importing theory and measures from research done in Western settings. The ideas and procedures are not sufficiently adapted to the culture being studied, and although the researcher may "get data," the researcher is in jeopardy of misinterpreting the results. The imposed etic approach could involve applying questionnaires, behavioral coding systems, or experimental procedures without modifying them to fit the culture and without seeking evidence that the behavior observed means the same thing to the subjects as to the foreign experimenter.

In contrast, in the derived etic approach the researcher adapts general statements regarding human functioning to fit each cultural group studied. The resulting statements are informed by emic approaches in each culture and are sensitive to the cultural context and the varying meaning of the variables across cultures. Clearly, cross-cultural psychologists aspire to use the derived etic research strategy by coming to understand the cultural contexts studied, adapting procedures to fit the cultures studied, and adapting theories to fit the sensitive tests and observations made in a variety of cultures. Even when the variable of interest requires little inference to observe (e.g., touching, eye contact, carrying practices), some understanding of the cultural milieu is necessary to determine the contexts in which the data are to be gathered (e.g., place in daily routine, cast of characters present) and how the behavior is to be interpreted (e.g., in terms of stimulation or sensitivity).

In the following sections we summarize cross-cultural evidence suggesting that in order to understand behavior it is necessary to attend to the immediate physical and interactional context of the activity, to the person's goal and understanding of the activity, and to the appropriate means of reaching the goal. These goals and means are to a large extent socially defined as well as socially managed. The familiarity of the task materials, purpose of the activity, and features of the social situation are intertwined with culture in ways making it difficult to assume that comparisons of an individual's performance can be made without consideration of the complexity of the context of the performance. Cultural differences may reflect varying exposure to activities differing in their organization, purpose, and social function.

Task Materials and Meaningfulness of the Activity

The relative familiarity of task materials to different populations has obvious relevance to attempts to ensure cultural appropriateness of tasks (Price-Williams, 1962). Irwin and McLaughlin (1970) found that nonliterate Liberian adults were more successful in classifying bowls of rice than classifying geometric stimuli (both differing in color, shape, and number). A sequel to that study (Irwin, Schafer, & Feiden, 1974) reported that U.S. undergraduates responded to requests to sort bowls of rice with the same hesitance and bewilderment as shown by Liberian nonliterates when asked to sort cards decorated with squares and triangles. Both groups, when tested with unfamiliar materials, sorted in a manner considered less advanced than when tested with familiar materials.

But as Cole, Sharp, and Lave (1976), Greenfield (1974), and Lave (1977) have argued, it is not only familiarity of materials that must be considered in comparisons of groups. If the materials are familiar but the task to be performed on the materials is unfamiliar, or if both materials and task are familiar but performing that particular task with those particular materials is unfamiliar, the activity is likely to be perceived as foreign.

The importance of the familiar relation of materials and task is illustrated by several studies in which developmental or cross-cultural differences disappear when the task materials are related in a meaningful, familiar way. Memory research has traditionally tried to minimize the relationships between items (e.g., in free recall, memory span, or paired-associates tasks) in an attempt to equate the circumstances of memory tests given to different people because associations between items are differentially affected by prior experience. However, sophisticated subjects (especially those who have experienced formal schooling) invent connections between items, for example, by clustering by category or elaborating associations. Young children or people from non-Western cultures are usually less familiar with schooling and consequently with associational strategies developed in practice with the lists of decontextualized items associated with literacy (Goody, 1977). Hence, they experience difficulty remembering lists with little or no familiar or meaningful relations among items (Flavell, 1977; Rogoff, 1981).

List-memory tasks may be contrasted with everyday memory problems such as remembering the plot of a story or the location of a store downtown. The information in everyday memory problems is meaningfully interrelated. The familiar organization of the materials or contextual organization can be used by the subject as a structure for recall, rather than requiring organization to be imposed on unrelated items. Research involving contextually organized verbal or spatial information, such as recall of stories or of scenes, has found cross-cultural similarities rather than differences in performance by children and adults (Mandler, Scribner, Cole, & DeForest, 1980; Rogoff & Waddell, 1982). Cultural differences in memory performance may be limited to tasks which exclude reliance on contextual organization of materials for structuring memory performance.

The use of unfamiliar or meaningless materials and tasks may be an important feature accounting for some findings of developmental and cultural differences in laboratory tasks. Greenfield and Childs (1977) and Kelly (1977) have found impressive performance by non-Western children using an indigenous kinship system to explore relational thinking and an indigenous botanical classification system to test class inclusion concepts.

Familiarity of materials and tasks is intimately related to the activities that are usual for the subjects. Serpell (1979) contrasted Zambian and English children's ability to copy visual displays in four activities differing in familiarity for the two cultures. The Zambian children performed better when asked to copy two-dimensional figures formed of strips of wire (an activity that Serpell observed Zambian children engaging in frequently), whereas the English children surpassed the Zambians in copying two-dimensional figures with paper and pencil (a common activity of English but not Zambian children). No differences were found in activities to which the two groups had similar exposure: copying positions of adults' hands and modeling figures out of clay. The results support the conclusion that cultural differences reflect varying exposure to particular activities, rather than a general cognitive difference between groups.

Problems of representativeness of task do not disappear in research relying on naturalistic observations. Zaslow and Rogoff (1981) argue that the choice of context for observation and the interpretation of behavior observed provides a crucial problem for cross-cultural comparisons of early interaction:

> Although studies of early social interaction do not necessarily involve introducing unfamiliar materials, tasks, or contexts, the fact that these studies involve *sampling* behavior makes it necessary to consider comparability of the situation (social and otherwise) sampled, and of the behaviors selected for observation. Identical contexts (e.g., mother-infant interaction without others present) may not sample equally representative proportions of the infant's experience in different cultures. Behaviors chosen for observation on the grounds that they sample the range of social interactions in one culture may sample behaviors incompletely in another, providing a distorted view of interaction. Identical behaviors need not have the same connotations in different cultures (p. 249).

For example, in cultures in which it is rare for a caregiver and infant to be alone together, the imposition of dyadic interaction might yield data confounded by the reactions of both child and caregiver to being isolated from the usual social group (Sostek, Vietze, Zaslow, Kreiss, van der Waals, & Rubinstein, 1981). Bowerman (1981) similarly notes that the traditional technique of taping mother-child interaction to elicit children's speech is unsuited to cultures in which children are seldom conversational partners with adults. In cross-cultural comparisons of observed behavior it is essential to consider the equivalence of the segment of behavior sampled and the meaning of the activity and behaviors to the participants in each culture. Price-Williams (1975) notes that:

> Among Hausa mothers, the custom is not to show affection for their infants in public. Now those psychologists who are concerned with nurturance and dependency will go astray on their frequency counts if they do not realize this. A casual ethnographer is likely to witness only public interaction; only when much further inquiry is made is the absence of the event put into its proper perspective (p. 17).

Perhaps the most crucial aspect of a task that makes it or its components meaningful is the presence of a meaningful purpose for the activity. Brown (1975), Lave (1980), Leont'ev (1981), and Smirnov and Zinchenko (1969) point out that cognitive research has concentrated on memory or thinking as a goal in itself, rather than as the means to a practical goal, e.g., to remember something of importance or to solve a real problem. The arbitrariness of performance as a goal in itself may account for many developmental and cultural differences. Istomina (1977) found that preschool children's recall of a list of items was much better when the children were asked to remember items to bring back from a play store than in standard free recall tasks.

It is often difficult to ascertain the subject's idea of the purpose of an experimental task. People unfamiliar with experiments may invoke a purpose for the activity that is at odds with the experimenter's intent. The potential mismatch between the experimenter's and the naive subjects' approach to a task is illustrated by an anecdote provided by Glick (1975). He found that in a classification task Kpelle subjects sorted 20 objects into functional groups (e.g., knife with orange, potato with hoe) rather than categorical groups and would often volunteer, on being questioned further, that that was the way a wise man would do things. "When an exasperated experimenter asked finally, 'How would a fool do it', he was given back sorts of the type that were initially expected—four neat piles with food in one, tools in another, and so on" (p. 636). Super, Harkness, and Baldwin (1977) and Skeen, Rogoff, and Ellis (1983) suggest that the classification of real items in everyday life (e.g., in organizing a kitchen or dresser drawers) is not as exhaustive or taxonomic as laboratory researchers expect to find with mature classifiers. Categorization in real life, in contrast to that which occurs in the laboratory, is primarily functional and varies with the purpose of the activity. In the laboratory, the practical goal is typically removed and the subjects are left with their knowledge and inferences regarding what the experimenter is likely to consider an appropriate classification scheme.

The appropriate solutions, goals, tasks, and materials represented in traditional laboratory studies of cognition bear a marked resemblance to activities familiar in the school situation. Several authors have suggested that the difficulty met by young children and relatively traditional peoples in laboratory tests is due to their limited experience with formal schooling (Rogoff, 1981; Sharp, Cole, & Lave, 1979). People who have more schooling, such as older children and Western peoples, may do better on cognitive tests because tests are usually a sample of the activities specifically taught in school. As Cole, Sharp, and Lave (1976) and Charlesworth (1976) point out, versions of most traditional cognitive tasks can be found in Binet's early measures predicting school performance. In addition, familiarity with performing a task merely for the purpose of being evaluated may relate to experience with Western schooling, a particular social setting.

Social Situation

The social context of an activity organizes materials and tasks in meaningful ways. As emphasized by Vygotsky (1978), the social context affects development at both the institutional and material level, as well as at the interpersonal level. At the institutional level, cultural history provides organizations and tools useful to cognitive activity (through institutions such as school and inventions such as the calculator or literacy) and practices facilitating socially appropriate solutions to problems (e.g., norms for the arrangement of grocery shelves to aid shoppers in locating or remembering what they need; common mnemonic devices). The society provides organization for human activity in institutions such as schools and political systems, in which particular forms of behavior are encouraged.

Social Institutions.   An example of the role of societal institutions in psychological functioning comes from research on moral development, which may relate to the political system of an individual's society. Kohlberg (1969) takes the position that moral development stages are comparable across cultures, with "higher" performance on moral development interviews indicating "more adequate" morality. The first two stages in Kohlberg's hierarchy of moral development (see Hoffman, this volume) focus on avoiding punishment and getting reward, and the third emphasizes achieving the approval of others. The fourth stage is defined in terms of obedience to the laws set down by those in power, i.e., to be a good citizen and keep social order. The fifth and sixth stages emphasize moral principles established through mutual agreement or on the basis of universal ethical principles; if social rules conflict with moral principles, individuals may morally decide not to follow the rules of society.

Edwards (1981) contests this view, arguing that the bureaucratic systems' perspective of Stage Four is appropriate for people whose political frame of reference is a large industrialized society, but inappropriate for people in small traditional tribal societies: "The two types of social systems are very different (though of course both are valid working types of systems), and thus everyday social life in them calls forth different modes of moral problem solving whose adequacy must be judged relative to their particular contexts (p. 274).'' Stages Five and Six are rare in cross-cultural studies and Edwards proposes that these ''metaethical reflections on morality'' should be eliminated from the system, leaving a sequence of moral development with three universal stages and a fourth present for some adults in large industrialized societies with formal institutions. The political institutions of a society may channel individual moral reasoning by providing standards for the resolution of moral problems.

An important cultural institution is Western schooling, which similarly structures behavior by providing norms and strategies for performance that are considered advanced in cognitive tests. Schooling may provide students with a common view of what is ''clever'' (e.g., classification of objects by taxonomic category rather than by their function). An emphasis on fast performance, as in a timed test, may be unusual in many cultures. Goodnow (1976) suggests that differences between cultural groups may be ascribed largely to the interpretation of what problem is being solved in the task, and to different values regarding ''proper'' methods of solution (e.g., speed, reaching a solution with a minimum of moves or redundancy, physically handling materials versus ''mental shuffling'').

The cultural tools and techniques used in school involve certain conventions and genres, such as Western conventions for representing depth in two-dimensional pictures; the common format of test items (e.g., multiple choice); and the genre of the story problem (similar to the logical syllogism), in which one must rely only on information given in the problem to reach the answer. Luria (1976) found that Central Asian subjects did not treat verbal logical problems (syllogisms) as if the premises constituted a logical relation, but as if they were unrelated judgments requiring verification from direct experience. While Luria (and others) take the peasants' responses as indicative of logical shortcomings, it is clear from transcripts that the subjects did not conceive the problem in the same manner as the experimenter. The syllogism was handled by the subjects as a request for an opinion. Many nonliterate subjects refused to answer, not accepting the problem as a self-contained puzzle with the truth determinable from the stated premises. They protested that they ''could only judge what they had seen'' or ''didn't want to lie.'' Here is an example of the interaction between a peasant and the experimenter (Luria, 1976):

[Syllogism:] In the Far North, where there is snow, all bears are white. Novaya Zemlya is in the Far North and there is always snow there. What color are the bears there?
. . . ''We always speak only of what we see; we don't talk about what we haven't seen.''
[E:] But what do my words imply? [The syllogism is repeated.]
''Well, it's like this: our tsar isn't like yours, and yours isn't like ours. Your words can be answered only by someone who was there, and if a person wasn't there he can't say anything on the basis of your words.''
[E:]. . . But on the basis of my words—in the North, where there is always snow,

the bears are white, can you gather what kind of bears there are in Novaya Zemlya? "If a man was sixty or eighty and had seen a white bear and had told about it, he could be believed, but I've never seen one and hence I can't say. That's my last word. Those who saw can tell, and those who didn't see can't say anything!" (At this point a young Uzbek volunteered, "From your words it means that bears there are white.")
[E:] Well, which of you is right?
"What the cock knows how to do, he does. What I know, I say, and nothing beyond that!" (pp. 108–109)

The subject and the experimenter seem to disagree about what kind of evidence one should accept as truth. The subject insists that truth should be based on first-hand knowledge, or perhaps on the word of a reliable, experienced person. (He obviously does not include the experimenter in the latter category.) Given differing criteria for determining truth, the peasant's treatment of the syllogism cannot be taken as evidence of his logical functioning. Luria notes that the nonliterate subjects' reasoning and deduction were excellent when dealing with immediate practical experience. However, in a system of "theoretical thinking," they showed several differences from literate subjects. They refused to accept the premise as a point of departure for subsequent reasoning; they treated the premise as a message about some particular phenomenon rather than as "a priori"; and they treated the syllogism as a collection of independent statements rather than as a unified logical problem.

Cole, Gay, Glick, and Sharp (1971) found that when the problem format was changed to evaluating someone else's conclusion from the premises, rather than personally answering a question on the basis of the premises, nonschooled subjects had much less difficulty. This supports the argument that nonschooled subjects were uncomfortable having to answer a question for which they could not verify the premises. When the subjects did not need to assert that a conclusion was true, they were willing to consider whether that answer was a logical conclusion and examined the hypothetical premises and conclusion to see if they fit logically.

Scribner (1977) suggests that verbal syllogisms represent a specialized language genre that is recognizably different from other genres. Through practice with the genre, individuals become able to handle more complex versions of it and understand the form of the problem. In Western schooling, people may become familiar with the genre through experience with story problems and other verbal problems in which the answer must be derived from the relationships presented in the problem. Hence, it appears that logical reasoning practices cannot be separated from the formats developed for such thinking in cultural institutions such as schools. Other institutions such as courts, markets, and families may share these formats or have their own conventions in different cultures.

Social Interaction.   In addition to considering the influence of social institutions on development, Vygotsky (1978) also emphasizes the immediate social interactional context of activity. Social interaction structures individual activity, especially as information regarding tools and practices is transmitted through interaction with more experienced members of society during development. Particular patterns of interpersonal relations are organized by institutional conventions and the availability of cultural tools. Social aspects of experimental and observational situations are unfamiliar to some groups. For example, the relationship between Experimenter and Subject in an experiment may be rapidly grasped by Western children familiar with testing in school, but may be highly discrepant from familiar adult–child interactions for non-Western children and adults. In addition, schooling provides familiarity with having to answer questions on content material before it has been fully mastered. The practice of testing school children at an arbitrary point in the learning process may be unusual in cultures where learners begin to participate in an activity only when they feel competent at the skill being learned (Cazden & John, 1971).

Schooled children are likely to have had more practice figuring out what an adult is really asking when the adult does not reveal all aspects of performance that will be evaluated. Sharp, Cole, and Lave (1979) found that schooled subjects were more sensitive to the nuances of their experimental instructions. Pinard, Morin, and Lefebvre (1973) found that with minimal training in a conservation task, nonschooled children showed far more spontaneous switches to conserving responses than did nonconserving schooled children, supporting the idea that the nonschooled children were simply learning what it was that they were being asked, whereas the schooled children may have already understood the question even if they could not answer it correctly. Nonschooled children, having less experience with a testing situation, may be more concerned with showing respectful behavior to the tester and trying to figure out the tester, than with trying to figure out the problem. Kiminyo (1977) points out that the nonschooled child will be more likely to change an answer when asked ''why?'' by an adult, as this traditionally means the adult considers the child's answer incorrect rather than indicating that the child should explain his or her reasoning. Kiminyo argues that Western education in African settings teaches skills and rules for such performance in examinations, making schooled African children better prepared to justify their answers in Piagetian tests.

Schooled people are more familiar with an interview or testing situation in which a high-status adult, who already knows the answer to the question, requests information of a lower-status person, such as a child. It is not uncommon in traditional societies for the interaction between adults and children to be characterized in terms of commands by the adult and compliance by the child (Harkness & Super, 1977). Traditional adults seldom ask children's opinions (Blount, 1972). In a traditional society, a year of school dramatically increases a child's ability to finish an experiment—regardless of the correctness of the answers—and increases the number of words used in responding (Super, 1977).

An example of how conventions of social interaction influence cognitive test performance is provided by Rogoff and Mistry (in press), who note that it is culturally inappropriate for Mayan children to speak freely to an adult. When carrying messages to adults, they must politely add the word "cha" ("so I have been told"). In a recall task, when asked to tell a story to an adult, the Mayan children's excessively bashful utterances were frequently punctuated with the word "cha." Their performance also indicated that they were responding as if being grilled rather than narrating a story. Although the Mayan children usually mentioned a fact from each of the main episodes of the story, they did so in a disjointed fashion as if they were listing the answers to questions regarding the facts of the story. The experimenter found it continually necessary to ask "What happened next?" In contrast, the U.S. children's more fluent recalls were marked by much more narrative connections between pieces of information and less need for prompting questions, suggesting that they were more familiar with the social situation of the task.

Irvine (1978) notes that findings of Piagetian nonconservation by nonschooled Wolof adolescents and adults (Greenfield, 1966) might be due to the test-like social features of the experimental setting:

> Outside the schoolroom, it is rare for a Wolof adult to ask another adult, or even a child more than six or seven years old, a question to which he or she already knows the answer. Where this kind of questioning does occur it suggests an aggressive challenge, or a riddle with a trick answer. . . . [S]ubjects unaccustomed to school room interrogation would be in a poor position to understand the researcher's motives or to guess what sort of response was wanted of them (Irvine, 1978, p. 304).

The nonschooled children may simply be responding to a strange situation involving a powerful adult by trying to give an answer that the adult might be presumed to expect, since she had crossed the ocean to ask what, to her, must be an important question. This idea is supported by the fact that Greenfield's nonschooled Wolof subjects gave conservation responses essentially equal to those of the schooled subjects when they themselves poured the water in the conservation test.

Irvine (1978) informally investigated adults' conservation responses by modifying the setting of examination. Her subjects were informants who dropped in to visit her in the familiar setting of a village household. She presented the task in the context of questions about language (explaining to the ignorant language-learner words like "more" and "the same" using water and beakers for illustration), rather than as a test. Irvine paused and waited for elaborations of initial responses or indicated that she did not understand. Several of the informants' initial responses suggested nonconservation, with responses strikingly similar to the ones recorded by Greenfield. However each informant subsequently elaborated with a response clearly reflecting conservation (e.g., "The glasses are not the same, but the waters are the same.'' p. 306). Although discrepancies between Irvine's and Greenfield's observations are not resolved (see Greenfield, 1979), the work clearly illustrates that the cultural institutions which organize social interaction must be considered in order to interpret the skills displayed.

Even in naturalistic observations, the behavior of those observed is influenced by their interpretation of the social situation. Like the experimenter, the observer plays a social role which must be taken into account when considering the constraints on the interaction observed. The observer may be regarded as an intruder, a visitor, or a strange alien, but it is not likely that the observer's presence is ignored: ''It seems likely that one influence of the observer on parents is to produce a heightened frequency of behavior that the participants judge to be more socially desirable and inhibit behavior considered socially undesirable'' (Pedersen, 1980, p. 181). Field and Widmayer (1981) note that mothers' objectives for interaction vary across cultures, with Cuban American mothers interested in ''educating'' their children and Black American mothers concerned about not spoiling their children by giving them too much attention. Such agendas might be differentially exhibited in the presence of an observer from another culture, depending on the presumed similarity between the mothers' and the observer's cultures.

The reports of researchers observing early interaction in other cultures indicate that the presence of an observer leads to changes in behavior and that subjects interpret the observational context differently in diverse cultures. Among the Zinacantecos, a group of Mayan Indians living in Mexico, Brazelton (1977) describes fear of the observer in both adults and infants:

> We were automatically endowed with 'the evil eye' until I assured mothers that I was a 'curer' and could counteract it if I had it. However the effects of stranger anxiety in the baby were powerfully reinforced by his parents' constant anxiety about our presence. We were unable to relate to babies after nine months of age because the effect was so powerful (p. 174).

Brazelton expresses concern about the impact on the data of such an intense reaction to the observer.

On the other hand, the appearance of an observer may produce great interest rather than fear, which nevertheless disrupts the observation. Munroe and Munroe (1971) report that in Logoli (East African) households, as soon as the observer arrived, the infant was readied for display. It was picked up and brought to the observer for inspection. This cooperation on the part of the Logoli mothers made for difficulty observing the usual caretaking of the infants. Hence, the Munroes changed their observational procedure to data taken from a first glance (a ''snapshot'') of the infant and its surroundings, before the observer's presence was noticed and disrupted the ongoing activity.

A study by Graves and Glick (1978) suggests how American middle-class mothers interpret what is expected of them when being observed. Graves and

Glick contrasted behaviors of mothers with their 18- to 25-month-old children when the mothers thought they were being observed (video equipment was conspicuously running) and when they thought they were simply waiting in an observation room (repairs were "being made" on the video equipment; in fact, observations were made from behind a one-way mirror). The mothers' behavior when they thought they were being observed seemed to reflect their concept of "good mothering." Speech to the children doubled when the mothers thought they were being observed; mothers used more indirect directives, produced more test questions, engaged in more naming and action routines, made more evaluative comments, asked more questions, and spent more time in joint interactive focus with their children, than when they thought they were not being observed.

Clearly, there is a problem of comparability in studies contrasting the observed behavior of two groups whose responses to, or even tolerance for, the presence of an observer differ substantially. Researchers must be alert to the fact that being observed or interacting with an experimenter is not a context-free situation. It is a social context with meaning varying for different populations.

Familiarity of the activity and its goals, as well as the social context of behavior, influence the behavior of individuals. To compare the characteristics of individuals across cultures (or ages or gender), it is necessary to consider their behavior as embedded in a complex system of activities and social situations usual in their experience. To interpret differences, the context of the behavior observed must receive considerable attention. In the next section, we compare concepts of development that differ in how they handle the relation between an individual's previous experience and current behavior.

CONCEPTS OF DEVELOPMENT

The relation between cultural variables and individual functioning has often been cast in terms of the effects of broad aspects of culture on broad aspects of individual characteristics. Attempts to understand *how* the culture meets the individual (or how the individual develops in culture) suggest that the relation of culture and behavior resides in the particular learning experiences of individuals. While there should be nothing surprising in the idea that people learn what they know or develop skills through practice, there are differences in how general the learning experiences and the resulting performances are expected to be, and therefore in how cultural differences are explained.

The Laboratory of Comparative Human Cognition (1980) has drawn a distinction between two models of learning, the "Central Processor Model," which they suggest characterizes the assumptions of existing developmental theory and research, and the "Specific Learning Model," which they offer as a substitute. The two models are diagrammed in Fig. 13.1.

In the Central Processor Model, the person experiences a variety of events, each of which contributes some strength or power to a central processor, which is

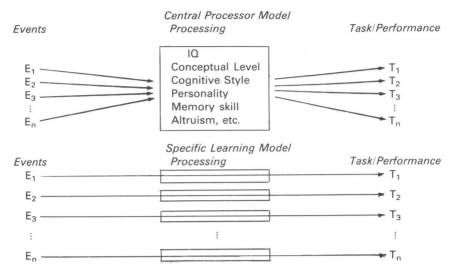

FIG. 13.1   Diagrams of Central Processor Model and Specific Learning Model of learning and performance. (Adapted from the Laboratory of Comparative Human Cognition, 1980.)

conceived as consisting of somewhat general abilities or skills. When a subject is faced with a particular task, he or she makes use of the general ability contained in the central processor to perform the task. The central processor is assumed to function similarly on a large variety of tasks. As an example we may take the construct "intelligence." The individual's "intelligence" is developed through a variety of experiences which strengthen it, and the person deploys intelligence in a similar way when solving a number of tasks that are presumed to require intelligence for successful performance. It is worth noting that the background experience that builds intelligence does not necessarily bear an obvious relation to the task the subject is asked to perform. Thus, researchers may ask whether maternal employment or number of siblings influence "intelligence," as evidenced on a task requiring people to remember a string of numbers backwards. A correlation may be found, and the researchers would then try to identify a mechanism by which the independent variable could conceivably influence task performance. For example, research based on Berry's (1976) ecocultural theory focuses on determining which ecological and childrearing variables (e.g., hunting and gathering for subsistence, nomadic vs. sedentary settlement pattern, level of sociopolitical stratification, restrictiveness in socialization) promote "psychological differentiation," which is assumed to be characteristic of an individual across a variety of social, perceptual, and cognitive tasks. The Central Processor Model represents views of development that assume that context plays little role in thinking or behavior and that personality, behavioral propensities, and skills are general.

The Specific Learning Model has grown out of cross-cultural attempts to understand developmental processes. Recognizing that behavior and skills are closely tied to the context of practice, researchers in cross-cultural human development are currently developing the Specific Learning Model as an alternative to the Central Processing Model. (See especially Laboratory of Comparative Human Cognition, 1980; Rogoff & Lave, 1984.) The Specific Learning Model has a much closer tie between the events experienced by individuals and the tasks on which their performance is observed.[3] In this model, the individual develops skills in particular tasks through experience in related activities. Skills are customized to the particular task. There is no assumption that experience in Event E_1 builds skills that generalize broadly to performance in Task T_3. Research focuses on specific relations between performance on tasks and previous experience in similar events. For example, an investigation may relate performance on a test requiring people to remember a string of words with experience memorizing strings of foreign words in Koranic schooling (Scribner & Cole, 1981; Wagner, 1978). The problem with this alternate model is that we are left with the question of how far and by what means generalization occurs.

Experience in a variety of similar events builds skills that, although specifically groomed in practiced activities, may be applied to related but novel tasks. Each task we perform is both somewhat novel and somewhat similar to previously experienced events, either in the form presented or in the way we reorganize it for solution. It would be a gross oversimplification to assume that because there is contextual variation in performance, the specificity of skill is infinitely narrow. The problem here is to determine to what extent there is transfer from one experience to performance on a somewhat novel task and how such transfer occurs. What prediction can be made from successful performance on, say, a logical syllogism? That the individual (a) will do well on the next syllogism? (b) will do well on other kinds of logic problems? (c) will be logical in many situations? or (d) is smart? The question of generality is an empirical one that has received little attention due to the predominance of the Central Processor Model in developmental psychology. This problem is not solved but instead posed by the alternate Specific Learning Model. We return to this question after a more complete discussion of the two models.

The Central Processor Model and Questions of Context

Psychologists have long debated the amount of transfer expected from specific activities to other activities (Vygotsky, 1962). Thorndike's (1914) discussion of "mental discipline" described the common view that:

> The words accuracy, quickness, discrimination, memory, observation, attention, concentration, judgment, reasoning, etc., stand for some real and elemental abili-

---

[3]The LCHC also refers to this model as the "Functional Practice" or "Cultural Practice" Model.

ties which are the same no matter what material they work upon; that . . . in a more or less mysterious way learning to do one thing well will make one do better things that in concrete appearance have absolutely no community with it (p. 272).

Most depictions of stages (e.g., Piaget's concrete operational stage), capacities (e.g., spatial skill, metamemory), or personality traits (e.g., competitiveness, altruism) assume that the stage, capacity, or trait characterizes the child's thinking and behavior across a large number of task situations (Ekehammer, 1974; Feldman, 1980; Fischer, 1980; Lewis, 1978; Mischel, 1979; Piaget, 1971). Usually the existence of the stage, capacity, or trait is evaluated through the use of a single task or a small sample of tasks assumed to be representative of the domain of problems that children meet. However, when multiple tasks are given, the assumption of widespread generality of stage, capacity, or trait is usually not upheld (Brainerd, 1978; Fischer, 1980; Fowler, 1980; Siegler, 1981). Skills that are logically similar appear at different ages or do not cluster together on similar tasks performed by the same individuals (Feldman, 1980; Reese, 1977).

Piaget's theory contends that task performances relate to each other in an interrelated structure (structure d'ensemble), but it requires the concept of décalage to account for time lags in tasks that are formally similar. Piaget (1971) considered it impossible to develop a general theory of time lags in, for example, class inclusion problems involving two different sets of objects. He claimed the time lags were due to variation in the "resistances" of the different types of object.

Cross-cultural research has borrowed tests, interpretations of performance, and the concept of developmental stages from Piaget. The research uses the tests Piaget developed to probe the thinking of Western European children. For example, the test for liquid conservation involves pouring equal amounts of liquid into identical containers, having the child verify that they contain the same amount, then pouring the contents of one of the containers into another of a different shape. A child who answers that they are still the same amount is considered a conserver, and one who maintains that there is more water in one container is considered a nonconserver. Piaget was most interested in understanding how the child reasoned, rather than in whether the child knew the right answer. He used a "clinical method" in which children's answers were probed and questions reworded in an individual fashion in order to understand *how* the children reached their answers. Cross-cultural research using Piaget's tests has generally not followed the clinical method, but has standardized the questions and sometimes not even asked the children to explain their answers. This facilitates comparison of populations, but uses Piaget's tasks as intelligence test items in which reasoning is not probed but explanations are simply assessed for correctness.

Researchers have also borrowed Piaget's interpretation of what Piagetian tests indicate: underlying development in logical thinking. There is reason to doubt that comparing quantities of water necessarily taps the same process in all cultures. Since the child's reasoning is seldom explored, all one can safely conclude from most studies is that the child has compared two glasses of water and answered "the same" or "not the same." Whether this tests the child's understanding of the world is another matter.

In addition to borrowing the specific tests and the interpretation of performance, cross-cultural researchers have made use of the theoretical concept of developmental progression. If nonschooled 9-year-olds do not conserve and nonschooled 13-year-olds do conserve, the researcher concludes that it is not until the age of 13 that nonschooled children enter the stage of concrete operations, which implies more than simply whether a child can conserve or not. It implies, in addition, a generalized structure of thought that is assumed to permeate much, if not all, of the child's intelligence. This is a far bigger inferential leap than simply concluding that it is not until the age of 13 that nonschooled children learn a particular skill or concept (e.g., to impose organization spontaneously on material to be remembered, to explain the dimensions used in classifying geometric stimuli). Borrowing the concept of generalized cognitive development along a time line, the researcher may claim that one population is retarded relative to another, or even that one population is stunted in cognitive development (if adults do not pass the test either). Such analyses result in unwarranted conclusions about the logical stage of people, on the basis of their performance on a few tests in which their opinions about the quantity of deformed materials is obtained.

Psychologists apparently assume that it is possible to examine psychological processes without concern for the content or context of what is being processed; that is, to neutralize the task so that performance reflects 'pure process' (see Cole & Scribner, 1975; Price-Williams, 1980; Rogoff, 1982). The research reviewed in previous sections of this chapter suggests that behavior does not involve abstract, context-free competences that may be used generally across widely diverse problem domains; rather, it involves skills tied to somewhat specific types of activity in particular contexts. Behavior in one situation may not generalize to another, even though we may be able to name some process (e.g., role-taking, sharing, competing, remembering, problem-solving) that both activities have in common. People with experience in one type of problem will be able to apply the skill to that kind of problem, but not necessarily to another problem with which they are less familiar.

The Specific Learning Model and Questions of Transfer

In order to make use of previously learned skills or information, people must be able to generalize some aspects of knowledge and skills to new situations which differ in at least some details from the problems they have previously experienced. People would be very limited if they could only apply what they learn to identical problems met repeatedly. Thus, while performance is somewhat specific to the context of practice, the notion of strict specificity of skills will not account for the flexibility of application of skills from one problem to another. Accounting for transfer in terms of a mechanical process of generalization from one problem to another on the basis of formal or physical similarities of the problems themselves does not take into account the systems nature of contexts, involving not only the form of the problem but also the purpose of solving it and the social context in which the activity is embedded.

People transform novel problems, making them resemble familiar situations by actively—but not necessarily consciously—seeking analogies across problems. A person's interpretation of a problem in any particular activity may be important in applying skills already developed in another context. The person uses the context of the problem to apply familiar information and skills to the novel problem, metaphorically transferring aspects of the familiar context to the new problem (Burstein, 1981; Petrie, 1979). Bartlett (1958) asserts that generalization "is not in the least likely to occur . . . unless there is active exploration of the situation that offers it an opportunity" (p. 95). Gick and Holyoak (1980) demonstrate that with story problems that differ but have the same structure and logically isomorphic solutions, subjects do not transfer relevant information from one problem to another unless they first notice the underlying similarity, even though the transfer is relatively simple once the similarity is suggested. And Duncker's (1945) experiments on functional fixedness demonstrate that the ease with which subjects employ materials in unconventional uses in problem solving depends on the relation of the problem to the familiar context of use of the materials.

Even more important than the active role of the individual in bridging contexts is the part played by other individuals and cultural scripts for problem solution in guiding the individual's application of information and skills to a new situation. We discuss this process in some detail in the next section, in which we summarize some theoretical frameworks that provide an appealing solution to the problem of context's role in development and in the application of knowledge and skills to new situations.

FUNCTIONAL APPROACHES TO DEVELOPMENT

Theoretical Formulations

In this section we review some theories that emphasize that ways of thinking and behaving are not characteristics of the person separate from the context in which the person functions. We focus on Soviet work influenced by Vygotsky (1962, 1978; Wertsch, 1979a,b) and work by the Laboratory of Comparative Human Cognition (1979, 1980). Some similar ideas are contained in Gibson's (1979) ecological theory but without the focus on culture contained in the Vygotsky and LCHC frameworks. While several other theories (Feldman, 1980; Fischer, 1980) have attempted to involve context in explanations of cognitive development, their consideration of context has been limited to the structure or features of the task or to the domain of knowledge. They have not incorporated the purpose of the activity or the interpersonal and cultural context in which an activity is embedded. The functional approaches we discuss in this section emphasize that behavior is directed toward accomplishing goals and that these goals are socially defined and mediated by other members of the culture.

Vygotsky's theory stresses the adaptation of behavior to fit the context and the structuring of context to support behavior. This perspective focuses on the social adaptation of humans to their environments through cultural history. As such, the study of development and the cultural context are both central to the examination of the processes of human functioning. To understand how culture relates to individual psychological functioning, the process of development or adaptation is examined rather than simply studying outcomes or static states. Development is not assumed to take a fixed, unidimensional course toward a unique or ideal end point; rather, the individual is expected to differentiate to fit the niche or cultural setting.

Rather than focusing on individual responses to environmental stimuli as the unit of analysis, the Vygotskian approach focuses on the concept of *activity*. Leont'ev (1981) has elaborated the Vygotskian concept of activity, a molar unit of analysis involving goals, means, and conditions that mediates between the individual and the context. The cultural practice theory of the LCHC (1980) also focuses on activity by identifying "socially assembled situations" as the unit of analysis rather than working from characteristics of individual persons or cultures. "Socially assembled situations" are cultural contexts for action and problem solving that are constructed by people as they interact with one another. Cultural practices employed in socially assembled situations are learned systems of activity in which knowledge consists of standing rules for thought and action appropriate to a particular situation, embodied in the cooperation of individual members of a culture. The Laboratory of Comparative Human Cognition argues that descriptions of what people "know-to-do" are distorted if they do not consider the social circumstances in which that knowledge is displayed and interpreted. In such an approach, the distinction between social and cognitive functioning fades.

Both the Laboratory of Comparative Human Cognition and Vygotskian approaches emphasize the *practice* of socially constructed modes of thinking, where cognition involves *doing* goal-directed action. In related work, Scribner and Cole (1981) define practice as "a recurrent, goal-directed sequence of activities using a particular technology and particular systems of knowledge" (p. 236).

In a functional approach, thought and action are integrated. Both mental and physical processes are means by which an organism achieves practical results that are relevant in particular contexts. The purpose of cognition is not to produce thoughts but to guide intelligent action. Leont'ev (1981) objects strongly to the dualism of mental and physical processes, on the basis that mental activity develops from processes that put the agent in "practical contact with objective reality." Similarly, ecological psychologists (see Gibson, 1979; Michaels & Carello, 1981) emphasize the confluence of perception and action, integrating perceptual learning and the acquisition of motor skills. Perception tailors the animal's actions to its environment. The point of perception is appropriate action: to act adaptively, the person needs to perceive the environment accurately; to perceive effectively requires putting oneself in a position to obtain information (Gibson, 1982).

In the Vygotskian approach, thought develops from experience in socially structured activity through the internalization of the processes and practices provided by society and its members. As discussed earlier, the social context influences the individual's patterns of behavior through cultural institutional tools of action and thought (and norms for the use of those tools), such as arithmetic systems and electronic calculators, and mnemonic strategies, writing systems, and paper. Such tools—indeed all objects—are socially developed and defined. Social and nonsocial objects are not distinguished, because even with "natural" objects, their significance for people is socially determined.

The Vygotskian view of cognition emphasizes that the social unit in which the child is embedded channels development, and suggests that, rather than deriving explanations of activity from the individual plus secondary social influences, we should focus on the social unit of activity and regard individual functioning as its product. This stance makes it of foremost importance to consider the role of the formal institutions of society and the informal interactions of its members as central to the process of development. In order to understand development, we must attend to the role played by such influences as formal schooling, television, the characteristics of children's toys, and the formal and informal instructional roles played by adults and other individuals expert in the activity and by peers as they coordinate joint activities.

The cultural institutional context reaches the individual largely through interaction with other members of the society. The social interaction of children with people who are proficient with the skills and tools of society is essential to development. Indeed, the child's individual social and cognitive activity derives from his or her interactions with other people. Vygotsky (1962, 1978) emphasizes that development occurs in situations where the child's problem solving is guided by an adult who structures and models the appropriate solution to the problem (in the "zone of proximal development"—the region of sensitivity to instruction where the child is not quite able to manage the problem independently and can benefit most from guidance). Cole (1981) argues that the zone of proximal development is "where culture and cognition create each other." Through experience in the zone of proximal development, the child's individual mental functioning develops. Adults are instrumental in arranging the occurrence of cognitive tasks for children, and they facilitate learning by regulating the difficulty of the task and providing a model of mature performance. Formal instruction and informal social interaction embed the child in the application of appropriate background information for a new problem, thereby providing experience in generalizing knowledge to new problems.

The process of interaction requires the creation of a common framework for the coordination of action and the exchange of information. Communication relies on the establishment of an intelligible context of interaction; this coordination facilitates generalization, in that new information has to be made compatible with the newcomer's (novice's, child's) existing knowledge. In the process, the child is led toward an understanding of this new information or situation. For example, in observations of mothers teaching their children how to perform classification tasks, Rogoff, Gauvain, and Gardner (in preparation) observe that 84% of the mothers guided the child in transferring relevant concepts from more familiar settings to a relatively novel laboratory task with statements such as "we're going to organize things by categories. You know, just like we don't put the spoons in the pan drawer and all that stuff." The language used in communication removes some of the complex alternative interpretations of an event by coding it in a particular way. In this way, cultural expectations are transmitted by linguistic labels in which events regarded as similar are coded similarly by a cultural group. The structuring provided in communication serves as a "scaffold" (Wood, 1980) for the novice, providing bridges between the old knowledge and the new. In making new information compatible with the child's current knowledge and skills, an adult guides the child in generalization to the new problem.

The answer offered, then, by a functional approach to the problem of how generalization from specific contexts occurs, is that individuals actively seek bridges from one situation to another and are greatly assisted by others who have more or different experience and make the analogy intelligible to the newcomer. Development and learning are not spontaneous but guided and channeled by other people experienced in the culturally developed modes of handling situations.

In the next section, we review some cross-cultural research that is consistent with the functional approaches we have described. Although some of these investigations of the relation between cultural experience and individual functioning have been influenced by Vygotsky's theories, others have not. Nevertheless, they have in common an emphasis on examination of the process of adaptation of people in their wider social/cultural milieux.

Research on the Functional Fit of Cultural Experience and Individual Development

Several recent lines of investigation illustrate the functional relation between learning experiences and the cognitive skills developed. In the following sections, we review some examples of the development of particular skills in domains of practice encouraged or structured by the cultural milieu. Along with the many studies previously reviewed in this chapter, they form the empirical basis of the sociocultural, functional theories of development we have described.

Cognitive Skills.   Lave (1977) examined arithmetic skills used by Liberian tailors varying in amount of schooling and in amount of tailoring experience. She designed the problems to involve identical arithmetic skills, but to vary in resemblance to arithmetic problems met in school and in tailoring. The results showed a specific relation between the type of math experience obtained and skill in the different types of math problems. Neither arithmetic skills learned in school nor those learned in the practical problems of tailors generalized to arithmetic problems different from either type.

Scribner (1984) investigated arithmetic calculation by U.S. dairy workers whose day-to-day experiences provide them with practice in calculations involving numbers of single cartons and cases (full of cartons) of milk products. The workers' responsibilities varied, either manipulating numbers of cartons and cases to fill orders, accounting for deliveries using numbers on computer forms, or billing for the product using entirely symbolic numerical representations. Scribner gave calculation problems in these different formats, and found that calculation skill and strategies corresponded to the daily use to which the individual habitually applied such calculation. Scribner argues that skilled practical thinking is goal-directed and adapted to the changing properties of problems and task conditions.

Rogoff and Gauvain (1983) tested Navajo women with varying amounts of experience in weaving and in formal school. They gave tests of pattern continuation that varied in resemblance to weaving processes (continuing yarn patterns on small looms) and school procedures (continuing paper-and-pencil patterns in workbooks). The results showed a specific relationship between experience and pattern continuation skill: Experience as a weaver related to performance on patterns resembling the process of weaving, and experience in school related only slightly to performance on any patterns.

Serpell (1979) found that Zambian and English children's skills in copying patterns were tied to the activities they had practiced. Each group was most skilled in copying patterns using media and processes with which they were familiar. Zambian children excelled in copying figures formed of wire strips, and English children excelled in copying figures drawn on paper. There were no cultural differences in skill at copying patterns in activities of equal familiarity to both groups.

Literacy Effects.   Scribner and Cole (1981) expected a specific functional relation between the practice of literacy and consequent cognitive skills. To test this, they studied ''general'' and ''specific'' cognitive skills used by the Vai people of Liberia, who varied in use of several types of literacy. The Vai people independently developed a phonetic writing system, widely available throughout the society, consisting of a syllabary of 200 characters with a common core of 20–40. Vai individuals may also be literate in Arabic or in English or not literate in any script. English is the official national language and is learned in Western-style schools; Arabic is the religious script and is learned in traditional Qur'anic schools emphasizing the rote memorization of religious passages usually without understanding; Vai script is used for the majority of personal and public needs and is transmitted outside of any institutional setting, with a nonprofessional literate teaching a friend or relative over a period of two weeks to two months.

Scribner and Cole predicted that literacy in the Vai script would not have the general intellectual consequences that have been suggested to be the result of high levels of school-based literacy, as Vai literacy does not involve new knowledge or the examination of ideas. To test for general cognitive consequences of literacy, Scribner and Cole studied performance on logic and classification tasks and found little difference between nonschooled Vai literates and Vai people not literate in any script.

To test for specific effects of learning and using the various scripts, they examined the component skills involved in Vai people's literacy in Vai script, Arabic, and English, compared with nonliteracy. (Note that English literacy is confounded with Western-style schooling.) In describing a board game in its absence, Vai literates (who frequently write letters requiring communication carried in the text and not supported by context) were more successful than Arabic literates and people not literate in any script. The English literates (high school students) were highly successful in this task as well.

Since Vai script is written without word division, the authors suspected that Vai literates might be skilled in the integration of syllables into meaningful linguistic units. Vai literates were better at comprehending and repeating sentences broken into slowed syllables than were Arabic literates and nonliterates. When the sentences were presented word by word instead of syllable by syllable, the Vai literates had no advantage over the other literates.

The authors demonstrated specific consequences of Qur'anic schooling with a memory task resembling learning of the Qur'an (learning a string of words in order, adding one word to the list on each trial). On this task, English students ranked first, but here the Arabic literates showed better performance than either the Vai literates or the nonliterates. On other memory tests (Scribner & Cole, 1981; Wagner, 1978), Arabic literates showed no superiority in performance over the Vai literates and the nonliterates, suggesting a very specific transfer of learning rather than general transfer.

Also consistent with the conclusion that literacy promotes specific skills is Olson's (1976, 1977) statement that human intellect cannot be separated from the technologies (e.g., writing, speech, numerical systems) invented to extend cognitive processes. He argues that the conception of a general quality of mind (underlying ability) is useless, as it is only in the interaction with the technology (writing, navigational system, and so on) that cognitive processes operate:

All tasks or performances that we require from children in intelligence tests reflect competence with our technologies. They assess the level of competence of a child or an adult in using some artifact that we find important in our culture. . . . If it is agreed that our measures of intelligence reflect different kinds of symbolic competencies, it is perfectly legitimate to measure this level of competence to determine, for example, if a child requires more practice, but it is illegitimate to draw any inferences about so-called underlying abilities (Olson, 1976, p. 195).

Infant Development.   Super (1981) and Kilbride (1980) argue that the controversy over "precocious" sensorimotor development in African infants is best resolved by considering the practices of the cultural system in which the babies develop. They present evidence that the items on tests of infant development do not function uniformly, and that the variation from item to item is meaningful. African infants routinely surpass U.S. infants in their rate of learning to sit and to walk, but not in learning to crawl or to climb stairs. They report that African parents provide experiences for their babies that are intended to teach sitting and walking. Sitting skills are encouraged by propping very young infants in a sitting position supported by rolled blankets in a hole in the ground. Walking skills are encouraged by exercising the newborn's walking reflex and by bouncing babies on their feet. But crawling is discouraged, and stair-climbing skills may be limited by the absence of access to stairs. Infant sensorimotor tests assess an aggregate of skills varying in rate of development according to opportunity or encouragement to practice them, rather than involving a general skill or a uniform set of skills.

Super (1981) also suggests that infant sleep patterns vary as a function of culturally determined sleeping arrangements. In the U.S., the common developmental milestone of sleeping for eight uninterrupted hours by four to five months of age is regarded as a sign of neurological maturity. In other cultures, however, the infant often sleeps with the mother and is allowed to nurse on demand with minimal disturbance of adult sleep. In this arrangement, there is less parental motivation to enforce "sleeping through the night," and Super reports that in this arrangement, the developmental course of sleeping is at variance with that observed in the U.S. Babies continue to wake about every four hours during the night to feed, which is about the frequency of feeding during the day. Thus, it appears that this developmental milestone, in addition to its biological basis, is culturally mediated; that is, it is adapted to the context in which it develops.

Personality and Sex Role Development.   Whiting and Whiting (1975) observe that the social behaviors displayed by children in six cultures varied according to the age and gender of the people with whom they were interacting. Children displayed nurturance in the company of infants, aggression with peers, and dependence with adults. Analyses of sex differences in these behaviors revealed worldwide trends in which older girls (age seven to eleven years) were more nurturant than boys of their age; younger girls (age three to seven years) were more responsible than their male counterparts; and boys were more aggressive than girls (Whiting & Edwards, 1973). Whiting and Edwards discuss these sex differences in terms of the tasks usually assigned girls and boys in the six cultures. The nurturant behavior of the older girls was probably related to the fact that they were far more likely to be assigned infant care than were boys. Girls of all ages were assigned chores near or inside the home, requiring compliance to mother, while boys were allowed to play or work (e.g., herd animals) farther from home and in the company of peers. In addition, girls were assigned chores at a younger age than were boys.

The impact of task assignment on social behavior is examined by Ember (1973) in a study of sex differences among children in a Luo community in Kenya. While Luo mothers attempted to assign girls and boys chores that were culturally defined as feminine and masculine, respectively, the absence of an elder sister in some homes required boys to undertake some of the feminine chores. Ember found that Luo boys who were assigned feminine work in the home, especially infant care, were less aggressive and more prosocial than boys who did not have these task assignments. The importance of Ember's finding is that the nurturance exhibited by Luo boys with experience in tending infants generalized to their interactions with other individuals. Hollos (1980) similarly reports that Hungarian 6- to 8-year-olds who began school later and spent more time after school at home tending siblings were less competitive than children who spent their time with same-age peers in a collective educational setting beginning at about age two.

Whiting's (1980) model for the development of patterns of social behavior stresses the importance of setting variables, especially the characteristics of individuals and activities that occupy a setting. Children are assigned to different settings on the basis of their sex, age, kinship, and relative status. In turn, different settings are marked by varying activities and amounts of time spent with infants, peers, adults, siblings, teachers, etc. Whiting hypothesizes that the patterns of social behavior learned and practiced in the most frequented settings may transfer to new settings or to individuals of different status. Certainly one task of childhood is to learn which patterns of social behavior are appropriate to transfer to novel settings.

Summary of Functional Approaches to Development

In this section we discussed theoretical approaches and empirical studies that focus on the functional relation of cultural experience and individual development. To understand the process of children's development in their cultural context, functional approaches emphasize examining the adaptations to particular contexts made by children and those around them. It is assumed that since development is adapted to the cultural context, the course of development is multidirectional; there is no unique end point or developmental trajectory for children in general. Children's skills in thinking and acting are regarded as developing for the purpose of solving practical problems, which vary according to the cultural context. This development involves children's adapting and adopting the tools and skills of their culture, aided by other people.

CONCLUSION

We have argued that research and theory focusing on how culture channels development provides important perspectives on variation and universal patterns of human development. One of the most important lessons of the cross-cultural perspective is that the development of personality, cognitive skills, and behavioral patterns is intimately related to the immediate social and physical contexts and the broader cultural contexts in which children are embedded.

We have suggested that the particular contexts forming culture be examined in order to understand the process of child development. This contrasts with the treatment of culture simply as an unexamined independent variable, or child development as the general progression of the child's skills without regard for the contexts in which these skills are developed and employed. It is necessary to "unpackage" culture and the skills children practice in order to place their actions in the context of their interpretation of the tasks to be accomplished, the goals in performing the activities, and the broader sociocultural contexts of children's activities.

We discussed functional approaches to development which are presently being developed, influenced by cross-cultural perspectives and by Vygotsky's theory. These approaches emphasize that in development, children adapt their cognitive and social skills to the particular demands of their culture through practice in particular activities. Children learn to use physical and conceptual tools provided by the culture to handle the problems of importance in routine activities, and they rely on more experienced members of their culture to guide their development.

A major contribution that cross-cultural research and theorizing have made to developmental psychology is the notion that the meaningfulness of the materials, demands, goals, and social situation of an activity channels an individual's performance on a task. Sociocultural experience and individual functioning are fundamentally tied to one another and are, thus, companions in human behavior and development.

ACKNOWLEDGMENTS

We are grateful for the comments of Marc Bornstein, Michael Lamb, Kathy Lewkowicz, and Barbara Radziszewski.

REFERENCES

Abramovitch, R., Pepler, D., & Corter, C. Patterns of sibling interaction among preschool children. In M. E. Lamb & B. Sutton-Smith (Eds.), *Sibling relationships: Their nature and significance across the lifespan.* Hillsdale, NJ: Lawrence Erlbaum Associates, 1982.

Acredolo, L. P. Laboratory versus home: The effect of environment on the nine-month-old infant's choice of spatial reference system. *Developmental Psychology,* 1979, *15,* 666–667.

Ashton, P. T. Cross-cultural Piagetian research: An experimental perspective. *Harvard Educational Review,* 1975, *45,* 475–506.

Bartlett, F. C. *Thinking: An experimental and social study.* New York: Basic Books, 1958.

Berry, J. W. On cross-cultural comparability. *International Journal of Psychology,* 1969, *4,* 119–128.

Berry, J. W. *Human ecology and cognitive style.* New York: Wiley, 1976.

Blount, B. G. Parental speech and language acquisition: Some Luo and Samoan examples. *Anthropological Linguistics,* 1972, *14,* 119–130.

Bornstein, M. H. Cross-cultural developmental psychology. In M. H. Bornstein (Ed.), *Comparative methods in psychology.* Hillsdale, NJ: Lawrence Erlbaum Associates, 1980.

Bowerman, M. Language development. In H. C. Triandis & A. Heron (Eds.), *Handbook of cross-cultural psychology* (Vol. 4). Boston: Allyn & Bacon, 1981.

Brainerd, C. J. The stage question in cognitive-development theory. *Behavioral and Brain Sciences,* 1978, *1,* 173–181.

Brazelton, T. B. Implications of infant development among the Mayan Indians of Mexico. In P. H. Leiderman, S. R. Tulkin, & A. Rosenfeld (Eds.), *Culture and infancy.* New York: Academic Press, 1977.

Bronfenbrenner, U. *The ecology of human development.* Cambridge, MA: Harvard University Press, 1979.

Brown, A. L. The development of memory: Knowing, knowing about knowing and knowing how to know. In H. W. Reese (Ed.), *Advances in child development and behavior* (Vol. 10). New York: Academic Press, 1975.

Brown, A. L. Learning and development: The problem of compatibility, access, and induction, *Human Development,* 1982, *25,* 89–115.

Burstein, M. H. Concept formation through the interaction of multiple models. *Proceedings of the third annual conference of the Cognitive Science Society.* Berkeley, CA: August, 1981.

Cazden, C. B., & John, V. P. Learning in American Indian children. In M. L. Wax, S. Diamond, & F. O. Gearing (Eds.), *Anthropological perspectives in education.* New York: Basic Books, 1971.

Charlesworth, W. R. Human intelligence as adaptation: An ethological approach. In L. B. Resnick (Ed.), *The nature of intelligence.* Hillsdale, NJ: Lawrence Erlbaum Associates, 1976.

Cole, M. An ethnographic psychology of cognition. In R. W. Brislin, S. Bochner, & W. J. Lonner (Eds.), *Cross-cultural perspectives on learning.* New York: Wiley, 1975.

Cole, M. *The zone of proximal development: Where culture and cognition create each other.* University of California San Diego, Center for Human Information Processing report #106, September 1981.

Cole, M., Gay, J., Glick, J. A., & Sharp, D. W. *The cultural context of learning and thinking.* New York: Basic Books, 1971.

Cole, M., Hood, L., & McDermott, R. P. Concepts of ecological validity: Their differing implications for comparative cognitive research. *The Quarterly Newsletter of the Institute for Comparative Human Development,* 1978, *2,* 34–37.

Cole, M., & Scribner, S. Theorizing about socialization of cognition. *Ethos,* 1975, *3,* 250–268.

Cole, M., Sharp, D. W., & Lave, C. The cognitive consequences of education. *Urban Review,* 1976, *9,* 218–233.

Cook-Gumperz, J., & Corsaro, W. Social-ecological constraints on children's communicative strategies. *Sociology,* 1977, *11,* 411–433.

Dasen, P. R. (Ed.). *Piagetian psychology: Cross-cultural contributions.* New York: Gardner Press, 1977.

Dasen, P. R., & Heron, A. Cross-cultural tests of Piaget's theory. In H. C. Triandis & A. Heron (Eds.), *Handbook of cross-cultural psychology* (Vol. 4), Boston: Allyn & Bacon, 1981.

DeLoache, J. S. Naturalistic studies of memory for object location in very young children. *New Directions for Child Development,* 1980, *10,* 17–32.

DeLoache, J. S., & Brown, A. L. Looking for big bird: Studies of memory in very young children. *The Quarterly Newsletter of the Laboratory of Comparative Human Cognition,* 1979, *1,* 53–57.

Duncker, K. On problem solving. *Psychological Monographs,* 1945, *58,* 85–93.

Edwards, C. P. The comparative study of the development of moral judgment and reasoning. In R. H. Munroe, R. L. Munroe, & B. B. Whiting (Eds.), *Handbook of cross-cultural human development.* New York: Garland, 1981.

Ekehammar, B. Interactionism in personality from a historical perspective. *Psychological Bulletin,* 1974, *81,* 1026–1048.

Ellis, S., Rogoff, B., & Cromer, C. C. Age segregation in children's social interactions. *Developmental Psychology,* 1981, *17,* 399–407.

Ember, C. R. Feminine task assignment and the social behavior of boys. *Ethos,* 1973, *1,* 424–439.

Erickson, F. Timing and context in everyday discourse: Implications for the study of referential and social meaning. In W. P. Dickson (Ed.), *Children's oral communication skills.* New York: Academic Press, 1981.

Feldman, D. H. *Beyond universals in cognitive development.* Norwood, NJ: Ablex, 1980.

Field, T. Infant behaviors directed toward peers and adults in the presence and absence of mother. *Infant Behavior and Development,* 1979, *2,* 47–54.

Field, T. M., Sostek, A. M., Vietze, P., & Leiderman, P. H. (Eds.). *Culture and early interactions.* Hillsdale, NJ: Lawrence Erlbaum Associates, 1981.

Field, T. M., & Widmayer, S. M. Mother–infant interactions among lower SES Black, Cuban, Puerto Rican and South American immigrants. In T. M. Field, A. M. Sostek, P. Vietze, & P. H. Leiderman (Eds.), *Culture and early interactions.* Hillsdale, NJ: Lawrence Erlbaum Associates, 1981.

Fischer, K. W. A theory of cognitive development: The control and construction of hierarchies of skills. *Psychological Review,* 1980, *87,* 477–531.

Fitchen, J. M. *Poverty in rural America: A case study.* Boulder, CO: Westview Press, Inc., 1981.

Flavell, J. H. *Cognitive development.* Englewood Cliffs, NJ: Prentice-Hall, 1977.

Fowler, W. Cognitive differentiation and developmental learning. In H. W. Reese & L. P. Lipsitt (Eds.), *Advances in child development and behavior* (Vol. 15). New York: Academic Press, 1980.

Fox, N. A. Attachment of Kibbutz infants to mother and metapelet. *Child Development,* 1977, *48,* 1228–1239.

Gelman, R. Cognitive development. *Annual Review of Psychology,* 1978, *29,* 297–332.

Gewirtz, J. L. The course of infant smiling in four child-rearing environments in Israel. In B. M. Foss (Ed.), *Determinants of infant behavior* (Vol. 3). London: Methuen, 1965.

Gibson, E. J. The concept of affordances in development: The renascence of functionalism. In W. A. Collins (Ed.), *Minnesota symposium on child psychology* (Vol. 15). Hillsdale, NJ: Lawrence Erlbaum Associates, 1982.

Gibson, J. J. *The ecological approach to visual perception.* Boston: Houghton Mifflin, 1979.

Gick, M. L., & Holyoak, K. J. Analogical problem solving. *Cognitive Psychology,* 1980, *12,* 306–355.

Gladwin, T. *East is a big bird.* Cambridge, MA: Belknap Press, 1970.

Gleason, J. B. Code switching in children's language. In T. E. Moore (Ed.), *Cognitive development and the acquisition of language.* New York: Academic Press, 1973.

Glick, J. Cognitive development in cross-cultural perspective. In F. Horowitz et al. (Eds.), *Review of child development research* (Vol. 4). Chicago: University of Chicago Press, 1975.

Glucksberg, S., Krauss, R. M., & Higgins, E. T. The development of referential communication skills. In F. D. Horowitz (Ed.), *Review of child development research* (Vol. 4). Chicago: University of Chicago Press, 1975.

Goldberg, S. Infant care and growth in urban Zambia. *Human Development,* 1972, *15,* 77–89.

Goodnow, J. J. The nature of intelligent behavior: Questions raised by cross-cultural studies. In L. B. Resnick (Ed.), *The nature of intelligence.* Hillsdale, NJ: Lawrence Erlbaum Associates, 1976.

Goody, J. *The domestication of the savage mind.* Cambridge: Cambridge University Press, 1977.

Graves, Z. R., & Glick, J. The effect of context on mother–child interaction. *The Quarterly Newsletter of the Institute for Comparative Human Development,* 1978, *2,* 41–46.

Greenfield, P. M. On culture and conservation. In J. S. Bruner, R. R. Olver, & P. M. Greenfield (Eds.), *Studies in cognitive growth.* New York: Wiley, 1966.

Greenfield, P. M. Comparing dimensional categorization in natural and artificial contexts: A developmental study among the Zinacantecos of Mexico. *Journal of Social Psychology,* 1974, *93,* 157–171.

Greenfield, P. M. Cross-cultural research and Piagetian theory: Paradox and progress. In K. F. Riegel & J. A. Meacham (Eds.), *The developing individual in a changing world* (Vol. 1). Chicago: Aldine, 1976.

Greenfield, P. M. Response to "Wolof 'magical thinking': Culture and conservation revisited" by Judith T. Irvine. *Journal of Cross-Cultural Psychology,* 1979, *10,* 251–256.

Greenfield, P. M., & Childs, C. P. Understanding sibling concepts: A developmental study of kin terms in Zinacantan. In P. R. Dasen (Ed.), *Piagetian psychology: Cross-cultural contributions.* New York: Gardner Press, 1977.

Gump, P., Schoggen, P., & Redl, F. The behavior of the same child in different milieus. In R. C. Barker (Ed.), *The stream of behavior.* New York: Appleton-Century-Crofts, 1963.

Harkness, S., & Super, C. M. Why African children are so hard to test. In L. L. Adler (Ed.), *Issues in cross-cultural research. Annals of the New York Academy of Sciences,* 1977, *285,* 326–331.

Hicks, G. *Appalachian valley.* New York: Holt, Rinehart & Winston, 1976.

Hollos, M. Collective education in Hungary: The development of competitive, cooperative and role-taking behaviors. *Ethos,* 1980, *8,* 3–23.

Huston-Stein, A., Friedrich-Cofer, L., & Susman, E. J. The relation of classroom structure to social behavior, imaginative play and self-regulation of economically disadvantaged children. *Child Development,* 1977, *48,* 908–916.

Irvine, J. T. Wolof 'magical thinking': Culture and conservation revisited. *Journal of Cross-Cultural Psychology,* 1978, *9,* 300–310.

Irwin, M. H., & McLaughlin, D. H. Ability and preference in category sorting by Mano school-children and adults. *Journal of Social Psychology,* 1970, *82,* 15–24.

Irwin, M. H., Schafer, G. N., & Feiden, C. P. Emic and unfamiliar category sorting of Mano farmers and U.S. undergraduates. *Journal of Cross-Cultural Psychology,* 1974, *5,* 407–423.

Istomina, Z. M. The development of voluntary memory in preschool-age children. In M. Cole (Ed.), *Soviet developmental psychology.* White Plains, NY: Sharpe, 1977.

Kelly, M. Papua New Guinea and Piaget—An eight-year study. In P. R. Dasen (Ed.), *Piagetian psychology: Cross-cultural contributions.* New York: Gardner Press, 1977.

Kessel, F. S. Research in action settings: A sketch of emerging perspectives. *International Journal of Behavioral Development,* 1979, *2,* 185–205.

Kilbride, P. L. Sensorimotor behavior of Baganda and Samia infants. *Journal of Cross-Cultural Psychology,* 1980, *11,* 131–152.

Kiminyo, D. M. A cross-cultural study of the development of conservation of mass, weight, and volume among Kamba children. In P. R. Dasen (Ed.), *Piagetian psychology: Cross-cultural contributions.* New York: Gardner Press, 1977.

Kohlberg, L. Stage and sequence: The cognitive-developmental approach to socialization. In D. Goslin (Ed.), *Handbook of Socialization.* New York: Rand McNally, 1969.

Konner, M. Aspects of the developmental ethology of a foraging people. In N. Blurton-Jones (Ed.), *Ethological studies of child behavior*. Cambridge: Cambridge University Press, 1972.

Kuhn, D., & Brannock, J. Development of the isolation of variables scheme in experimental and 'natural experiment' contexts. *Developmental Psychology, 1977, 13*, 9–14.

Laboratory of Comparative Human Cognition. Cross-cultural psychology's challenges to our ideas of children and development. *American Psychologist, 1979, 34*, 827–833.

Laboratory of Comparative Human Cognition. *Culture and cognitive development*. Unpublished manuscript, University of California, San Diego, 1980.

Labov, W. The logic of non-standard English. In F. Williams (Ed.), *Language and poverty*. Chicago: Markham, 1970.

Lamb, M. E. The effects of social context on dyadic social interaction. In M. E. Lamb, S. J. Suomi, & G. R. Stephenson (Eds.), *Social interaction analysis: Methodological issues*. Madison, WI: University of Wisconsin Press, 1978.

Lave, J. Tailor-made experiments and evaluating the intellectual consequences of apprenticeship training. *The Quarterly Newsletter of the Institute for Comparative Human Development, 1977, 1*, 1–3.

Lave, J. What's special about experiments as contexts for thinking. *Quarterly Newsletter of the Laboratory of Comparative Human Cognition, 1980, 4*, 86–91.

Leiderman, P. H., Tulkin, S. R., & Rosenfeld, A. (Eds.). *Culture and infancy*. New York: Academic Press, 1977.

Leont'ev, A. N. The problem of activity in psychology. In J. V. Wertsch (Ed.), *The concept of activity in Soviet psychology*. Armonk, NY: Sharpe, 1981.

Lewis, M. Situational analysis and the study of behavioral development. In L. A. Pervin & M. Lewis (Eds.), *Perspectives in interactional psychology*. New York: Plenum, 1978.

Luria, A. R. *Cognitive development: Its cultural and social foundations*. Cambridge, MA: Harvard University Press, 1976.

Malinowski, B. *The father in primitive psychology*. New York: Norton, 1927.

Mandler, J. M., Scribner, S., Cole, M., & DeForest, M. Cross-cultural invariance in story recall. *Child Development, 1980, 51*, 19–26.

Maudry, M., & Nekula, M. Social relations between children of the same age during the first two years of life. *Journal of Genetic Psychology, 1939, 54*, 193–215.

McCall, R. B. Challenges to a science of developmental psychology. *Child Development, 1977, 48*, 333–344.

Michaels, C. F., & Carello, C. *Direct perception*. Englewood Cliffs, NJ: Prentice-Hall, 1981.

Mischel, W. On the interface of cognition and personality: Beyond the person–situation debate. *American Psychologist, 1979, 34*, 740–754.

Munroe, R. H., & Munroe, R. L. Household density and infant care in an East African society. *Journal of Social Psychology, 1971, 83*, 3–13.

Munroe, R. H., Munroe, R. L., & Whiting, B. B. (Eds.). *Handbook of cross-cultural human development*. New York: Garland, 1981.

Munroe, R. L., & Munroe, R. H. *Cross-cultural human development*. Monterey, CA: Brooks/Cole, 1975.

Neisser, U. General, academic, and artificial intelligence. In L. B. Resnick (Ed.), *The nature of intelligence*. Hillsdale, NJ: Lawrence Erlbaum Associates, 1976.

Olson, D. R. Culture, technology, and intellect. In L. B. Resnick (Ed.), *The nature of intelligence*. Hillsdale, NJ: Lawrence Erlbaum Associates, 1976.

Olson, D. R. The languages of instruction: The literate bias of schooling. In R. C. Anderson, R. J. Spiro, W. E. Montague (Eds.), *Schooling and the acquisition of knowledge*. Hillsdale, NJ: Lawrence Erlbaum Associates, 1977.

Parke, R. D. Interactional designs. In R. B. Cairns (Ed.), *The analysis of social interactions*. Hillsdale, NJ: Lawrence Erlbaum Associates, 1979.

Parten, M. B. Social play among preschool children. *Journal of Abnormal and Social Psychology,* 1933, *28,* 136–147.

Pedersen, F. A. *The father–infant relationship: Observational studies in the family setting.* New York: Praeger, 1980.

Petrie, H. G. Metaphor and learning. In A. Ortony (Ed.), *Metaphor and thought.* Cambridge: Cambridge University Press, 1979.

Piaget, J. The theory of stages in cognitive development. In D. R. Green, M. P. Ford, & G. P. Flamer (Eds.), *Measurement and Piaget.* New York: McGraw-Hill, 1971.

Piaget, J. Intellectual evolution from adolescence to adulthood. *Human Development,* 1972, *15,* 1–12.

Pinard, A., Morin, C., & Lefebvre, M. Apprentissage de la conservation des quantités liquides chez des enfants rwandais et canadiens-français. *International Journal of Psychology,* 1973, *8,* 15–23.

Price-Williams, D. R. Abstract and concrete modes of classification in a primitive society. *British Journal of Educational Psychology,* 1962, *32,* 50–61.

Price-Williams, D. R. *Explorations in cross-cultural psychology.* San Francisco: Chandler & Sharp, 1975.

Price-Williams, D. R. Anthropological approaches to cognition and their relevance to psychology. In H. C. Triandis & W. Lonner (Eds.), *Handbook of cross-cultural psychology* (Vol. 3). Boston: Allyn & Bacon, 1980.

Reese, H. W. Discriminative learning and transfer: Dialectical perspectives. In N. Datan & H. W. Reese (Eds.), *Life-span developmental psychology: Dialectical perspectives on experimental research.* New York: Academic Press, 1977.

Rogoff, B. Schooling and the development of cognitive skills. In H. C. Triandis & A. Heron (Eds.), *Handbook of cross-cultural psychology* (Vol. 4). Boston: Allyn & Bacon, 1981.

Rogoff, B. Integrating context and cognitive development. In M. E. Lamb & A. L. Brown (Eds.), *Advances in developmental psychology* (Vol. 2), Hillsdale, NJ: Lawrence Erlbaum Associates, 1982.

Rogoff, B., & Gauvain, M. The cognitive consequences of specific experiences: Weaving versus schooling among the Navajo. Unpublished manuscript, University of Utah, 1983.

Rogoff, B., Gauvain, M., & Gardner, W. Guidance in cognitive development: Structural analyses. To appear in J. Valsiner (Ed.), *Individual subjects in scientific psychology,* New York: Plenum, in press.

Rogoff, B., & Lave, J. *Everyday cognition: Its development in social context.* Cambridge, MA: Harvard University Press, 1984.

Rogoff, B., & Mistry, J. Memory development in cultural context. In M. Pressley & C. Brainerd (Eds.), *Progress in cognitive development.* Springer-Verlag, in press.

Rogoff, B., & Waddell, K. J. Memory for information organized in a scene by children from two cultures. *Child Development,* 1982, *53,* 1224–1228.

Ross, G., Kagan, J., Zelazo, P., & Kotelchuck, M. Separation protest in infants in home and laboratory. *Developmental Psychology,* 1975, *11,* 256–257.

Ruffy, M. Influence of social factors in the development of the young child's moral judgments. *European Journal of Social Psychology.* 1981, *11,* 61–75.

Scribner, S. Situating the experiment in cross-cultural research. In K. F. Riegel & J. A. Meacham (Eds.), *The developing individual in a changing world* (Vol. 1). Chicago: Aldine, 1976.

Scribner, S. Modes of thinking and ways of speaking: Culture and logic reconsidered. In P. N. Johnson-Laird & P. C. Wason (Eds.), *Thinking.* Cambridge: Cambridge University Press, 1977.

Scribner, S. Studying working intelligence. In B. Rogoff & J. Lave (Eds.), *Everyday cognition: Its development in social context.* Cambridge, MA: Harvard University Press, 1984.

Scribner, S., & Cole, M. *The psychology of literacy.* Cambridge, MA: Harvard University Press, 1981.

Serpell, R. *Culture's influence on behavior.* London: Methuen, 1976.

Serpell, R. How specific are perceptual skills? A cross-cultural study of pattern reproduction. *British Journal of Psychology*, 1979, *70*, 365–380.

Sharp, D., Cole, M., & Lave, C. Education and cognitive development: The evidence from experimental research. *Monographs of the Society for Research in Child Development*, 1979, *44*, (1–2, Serial No. 178).

Shatz, M., & Gelman, R. Beyond syntax: The influence of conversational constraints on speech modifications. In C. E. Snow & C. A. Ferguson (Eds.), *Talking to children*. Cambridge: Cambridge University Press, 1977.

Shultz, J. J., Florio, S., & Erickson, F. Where's the floor? Aspects of the cultural organization of social relationships in communication at home and in school. In P. Gilmore & A. A. Glatthorn (Eds.), *Children in and out of school*. Washington, DC: Center for Applied Linguistics, 1982.

Siegel, A. W. "Remembering" is alive and well (and even thriving) in empiricism. In N. Datan & H. W. Reese (Eds.), *Life-span developmental psychology: Dialectical perspectives on experimental research*. New York: Academic Press, 1977.

Siegler, R. S. Developmental sequences within and between concepts. *Monographs of the Society for Research in Child Development*, 1981, *46*, (2, Serial No. 189).

Skeen, J., Rogoff, B., & Ellis, S. Categorization by children and adults in communication contexts. *International Journal of Behavioral Development*, 1983, *6*, 213–220.

Slobin, D. I. Cognitive prerequisites for the development of grammar. In C. A. Ferguson & D. I. Slobin (Eds.), *Studies of child language development*. New York: Holt, Rinehart, & Winston, 1973.

Smirnov, A. A., & Zinchenko, P. I. Problems in the psychology of memory. In M. Cole & I. Maltzman (Eds.), *A handbook of contemporary Soviet psychology*. New York: Basic Books, 1969.

Sostek, A. M., Vietze, P., Zaslow, M., Kriess, L., van der Waals, F., & Rubinstein, D. Social context in caregiver–infant interaction: A film study of Fais and the United States. In T. M. Field, A. M. Sostek, P. Vietze, & P. H. Leiderman (Eds.), *Culture and early interactions*. Hillsdale, NJ: Lawrence Erlbaum Associates, 1981.

Steinberg, Z. D., & Cazden, C. B. Children as teachers—of peers and ourselves. *Theory into Practice*, 1979.

Super, C. M. *Who goes to school and what do they learn?* Paper presented at the meeting of the Society for Research in Child Development, New Orleans, 1977.

Super, C. M. Behavioral development in infancy. In R. H. Munroe, R. L. Munroe, & B. B. Whiting (Eds.), *Handbook of cross-cultural human development*. New York: Garland, 1981.

Super, C. M., Harkness, S., & Baldwin, L. M. Category behavior in natural ecologies and in cognitive tests. *The Quarterly Newsletter of the Institute for Comparative Human Development*, 1977, *1*, 4–7.

Thorndike, E. L. *Educational psychology*. New York: Teachers College, 1914.

Todd, C. M., & Perlmutter, M. Reality recalled by preschool children. *New Directions for Child Development*, 1980, *10*, 69–85.

Triandis, H. C., & Heron, A. (Eds.) *Handbook of cross-cultural psychology*. (Vol. 4). Boston: Allyn & Bacon, 1981.

Vygotsky, L. S. *Thought and language*. Cambridge, MA: MIT Press, 1962.

Vygotsky, L. S. *Mind in society*. Cambridge, MA: Harvard University Press, 1978.

Wagner, D. A. Memories of Morocco: The influence of age, schooling, and environment on memory. *Cognitive Psychology*, 1978, *10*, 1–28.

Wagner, D. A., & Stevenson, H. W. *Cultural perspectives on child development*. San Francisco: Freeman, 1982.

Weisner, T. S., & Gallimore, R. My brother's keeper: Child and sibling caretaking. *Current Anthropology*, 1977, *18*, 169–190.

Weisz, J. R. Transcontextual validity in developmental research. *Child Development*, 1978, *49*, 1–12.

Wellman, H. M., & Somerville, S. C. Quasi-naturalistic tasks in the study of cognition: The memory-related skills of toddlers. *New Directions for Child Development*, 1980, *10*, 33–48.

Werner, E. E. *Cross-cultural child development*. Monterey, CA: Brooks/Cole, 1979.

Wertsch, J. V. *A state of the art review of Soviet research in cognitive psychology*. Unpublished manuscript, Northwestern University, 1979. (a)

Wertsch, J. From social interaction to higher psychological processes: a classification and application of Vygotsky's theory. *Human Development*, 1979, *22*, 1–22. (b)

White, S. H. Evidence for a hierarchical arrangement of learning processes. In L. P. Lipsitt & C. C. Spiker (Eds.), *Advances in child development and behavior* (Vol. 2). New York: Academic, 1965.

Whiting, B. B. The problem of the packaged variable. In K. F. Riegel & J. A. Meacham (Eds.), *The developing individual in a changing world*. Chicago: Aldine, 1976.

Whiting, B. B. Culture and social behavior: A model for the development of social behavior. *Ethos*, 1980, *8*, 95–116.

Whiting, B. B., & Edwards, C. A cross-cultural analysis of sex differences in the behavior of children aged 3 to 11. *Journal of Social Psychology*, 1973, *91*, 171–188.

Whiting, B. B., & Whiting, J. W. M. *Children of six cultures*. Cambridge, MA: Harvard University Press, 1975.

Whiting, J. W. M., & Child, I. L. *Child training and personality*. New Haven: Yale University Press, 1953.

Wohlwill, J. F. The age variable in psychological research. *Psychological Review*, 1970, *77*, 49–64.

Wohlwill, J. F. *Ecological representativeness in developmental research: A critical view*. Paper presented at the meetings of the Society for Research in Child Development, Boston, April, 1981.

Wolfenstein, M. French parents take their children to the park. In M. Mead & M. Wolfenstein (Eds.), *Childhood in contemporary cultures*. Chicago: University of Chicago Press, 1955.

Wood, D. J. Teaching the young child: Some relationships between social interaction, language, and thought. In D. R. Olson (Ed.), *The social foundations of language and thought*. New York: Norton, 1980.

Young, V. H. Family and childhood in a Southern Negro community. *American Anthropology*, 1970, *72*, 269–288.

Zarbatany, L., Hartmann, D. P., Gelfand, D. M., & Ramsey, C. *The ecological validity of experiments on children's charitable behavior*. Presented at the meeting of the American Psychological Association, Washington, D.C., August, 1982.

Zaslow, M. Relationships among peers in kibbutz toddler groups. *Child Psychiatry and Human Development*, 1980, *10*, 178–189.

Zaslow, M., & Rogoff, B. *A framework for considering cross-cultural differences in children's peer interactions*. Paper presented at the meetings of the Society for Cross-Cultural Research, New Haven, February, 1978.

Zaslow, M. J., & Rogoff, B. The cross-cultural study of early interaction: Implications from research in culture and cognition. In T. Field, A. Sostek, P. Vietze, & H. Leiderman (Eds.), *Culture and early interactions*. Hillsdale, NJ: Lawrence Erlbaum Associates, 1981.

Author Index

Numbers in *italics* denote pages with bibliographic information.

A

Abeles, R. P., 481, *485,* 521, *524*
Abelson, W. D., 49, *79,* 461, *490, 491*
Abramov, I., 99, *126*
Abramovitch, R., 540, *565*
Abt, C. C., 468 *484*
Achenbach, T. M., 410, 415, 418, 419, 420, 421, 422, 425, 428, 439, 442, 444, *446, 447*
Acredolo, C., 169, *177*
Acredolo, L. P., 540, *565*
Adamson, L., 255, *276*
Adelson, J., 315, *320*
Ahrens, R., 248, *271*
Ainsworth, M.D.S., 247, 249, 265, 266, 267, *271, 272,* 399, *400,* 453, *484*
Alexander, J. F., 431, *447, 448*
Allport, G. W., 123, *126*
Als, H., 255, *276*
Alston, W. P., 288, *319*
Ambron, S. R., 282, *319*
Ambrose, J., 251, *271*
Amsel, E., 169, *179*
Anderson, E. P., 265, *272*
Anderson, N., 169, *177*
Anderson, R. E., 463, *484*
Anderson, S., 473, *484*
Angell, J. R., 12, *28*
Anscombe, G. E. M., 375, *400*
Antley, T. R., 469, *484*

Antonucci, T. C., 504, *524, 528*
Apfel, N. H., 65 *78*
Appelbaum, M. I., 68, *78*
Arend, R. A., 268, *271, 275,* 360, *367,* 399, *402*
Arlman-Rupp, A., 198, *240*
Armor, D. J., 313, *319*
Armstrong, S. L., 191, *234*
Aronfreed, J., 291, 299, 314, *319*
Ashbrook, E. F., 195, 206, *238*
Ashenden, B., 413 *448*
Ashmore, R. D., 333, *363*
Ashton, P. T., 536, *565*
Aslin, R. N., 89, 90, 95, *126, 127, 128,* 250, *273*
Atkin, C., 312, *319*
Auroux, M., 99, *131*
Axline, V. M., 430, *447*

B

Bachen, C. M., 311, 312, *323*
Bacon, M. K., 338, *363*
Badger, E., 468, 471, *488*
Baer, D. M., 6, 22, *28, 29,* 138, 152, *177,* 260, *271, 272,* 505, *524*
Bahn, A. K., 410, *449*
Bahr, S. J., 464, *485*
Baier, K., 288, *319*
Baker, C. L., 227, *234*

573

Subject Index